MATTHIAS ERZBERGER

AND THE DILEMMA OF GERMAN
DEMOCRACY

Matthias Erzberger

and the Dilemma of German Democracy

By Klaus Epstein

Princeton University Press

Princeton, New Jersey

1959

Publication of this book has been aided by
the Ford Foundation program to support
publication, through university presses,
of works in the humanities and social sciences.

Printed in the United States of America
by Vail-Ballou Press, Inc., Binghamton, N.Y.

To my parents
Fritz and Herta Epstein

PREFACE

Matthias Erzberger, the subject of this biography, played a conspicuous role in German politics before and during the First World War and in the formative years of the Weimar Republic. After entering the *Reichstag* in 1903 he made his reputation by exposing the scandals that marred Germany's colonial record. Erzberger soon achieved power in the Catholic Zentrum, the pivotal party of Imperial politics, as leader of its democratic left wing. The World War brought him an opportunity to achieve a prominence that knew no precedent in German parliamentary life. He was placed in charge of Germany's foreign propaganda, ran an intelligence network, and was sent on many important diplomatic missions. His opposition to the disastrous policy of submarine warfare gave him the reputation of a prophet. He was the key actor in the crisis of July 1917 that brought the fall of Chancellor Bethmann-Hollweg and the creation of a new *Reichstag* majority dedicated to a peace without annexations. The new majority, composed of Zentrum, Left Liberals, and Right Socialists, foreshadowed the Weimar coalition that was to replace the Imperial regime in 1918.

Erzberger took a prominent part in the establishment of parliamentary government under Prince Max of Baden, and was delegated to sign the armistice which ended the First World War on November 11, 1918. He continued to serve as armistice commissioner for the all-Socialist Government which emerged from the November Revolution. He strengthened the right-wing Socialist Friedrich Ebert in his policy of smashing the Communists in the winter of 1918–1919. Erzberger reorganized his own Zentrum party and made it a powerful force in the Weimar Assembly. When the Allies handed Germany the Treaty of Versailles, Erzberger took the leading role in inducing Germany to ratify it. Though his policy prevented an Allied military occupation of most of Germany, it also tainted the Weimar Republic with responsibility for a deep national humiliation. Erzberger became Finance Minister in 1919. He gave the country an entirely new tax system during a tenure of only nine months. His progressive policies made him the most prominent champion of German democracy, and aroused the fury of nationalists, militarists, and conservatives alike. He was driven out of office after a celebrated political trial in 1920, and was assassinated by nationalist fanatics a short time afterwards.

No man in Germany in the last hundred years had been more bitterly hated. He had come to symbolize the Weimar Republic, and his enemies hoped to discredit the new democratic state by discrediting him. But why had he become such a symbol? Partly, no doubt, it was his character. He loved responsibility, and never shirked unpleasant tasks. It took a very courageous man to sign the humiliating armistice, and to antagonize all men of property by assuming the Finance Ministry when huge new taxes had to be raised. Erzberger's humble birth and lack of formal education—he was the son of a tailor in a remote Württemberg village—provoked the disdain that always meets a parvenu. His religion—he was a devout Catholic who never hesitated to champion Catholic claims—encountered much hostility among the Protestant upper class of the Empire. But his worst crime in the eyes of German nationalists and Conservatives was his championship of international conciliation in foreign policy and democratic development in domestic policy. Erzberger was hated because he swung his party, the Zentrum, from opposition to advocacy of these two policies. He thereby created grave embarrassment for the Wilhelmine ruling class during the First World War and assumed a major role in the formation of the Weimar Republic.

Erzberger was vulnerable to attack because his personality did not conform to the public's image of a proper *Reichstag* deputy. His extraordinary energy, intelligence, and capacity for hard work aroused both envy and irritation. His ruthlessness, combined with flexibility and superb political instincts, made him a dangerous man to tangle with in party controversy. His rapidity, impulsiveness, and willingness to learn from his own mistakes gave him a reputation for opportunism. His grand carelessness about appearances, especially in matters involving possible connections between his public career and his private monetary affairs, convinced millions of Germans that he was corrupt. His character had many strong sides but was not cast to secure popularity.

His career throws much light upon the internal history of Germany in the first two decades of this century. The preoccupation of historians with foreign and military policy, with special reference to the problem of responsibility for the First World War, has led to a relative neglect of Germany's internal problems. The working of the Imperial constitution, the role of parties in the *Reichstag,* the cleavages within the Zentrum Party, the breakthrough of the democratic principle in the rise of new leaders like Erzberger, and the general problem of the introduction of parliamentary government have all received less attention than they deserve. The fact that a major figure like Erzberger, who was one of the three or four most influential deputies before 1914 quite apart from his later importance, has never been treated in a scholarly biography is in itself significant.

ACKNOWLEDGMENTS

It is a pleasure to acknowledge the help and kindness I have received from many people in the completion of this book. I owe a particular debt of gratitude to Stephen Graubard, Hanna and Charles Gray, Ernest May, and George Nadel. Not only have they read and criticized large portions of the manuscript, but they have stimulated and guided my development as a historian over the last few years.

The following people kindly read and commented upon individual chapters: William Emerson, Franklin Ford, Raymond Grew, Stuart Hughes, Michael Karpovich, Arno Mayer, and Donald Rohr.

I am deeply grateful to Mrs. Paula Erzberger and Dr. Josef Hammer for giving me access to the Erzberger papers. Archivdirektor Dr. Georg Winter and Archivrat Dr. Wilhelm Mommsen were most helpful in extending the facilities of the Bundesarchiv, where the Erzberger papers are deposited.

The Fulbright Commission gave me a fellowship to Germany in 1955–1956 which allowed me to complete the research on this book. The Harvard Foundation provided a grant for the typing of the final draft. My editor, Miss Miriam Brokaw, made innumerable improvements in the manuscript.

My father helped me at every stage of composition, and was a never-failing source of bibliographical information. My mother typed part of an early draft. My wife, finally, has shared the labor all the way from our joint researches in the Bundesarchiv to the final reading of the proofs, while the onerous job of typing up my illegible scrawl was all her own.

K.E.

CONTENTS

CONTENTS

CONTENTS

MATTHIAS ERZBERGER:

AND THE DILEMMA OF GERMAN
DEMOCRACY

MATTHIAS ERZBERGER

CHAPTER I

EARLY LIFE (1875–1903)

MATTHIAS ERZBERGER was born in the little Württemberg village of Buttenhausen on September 20, 1875. Buttenhausen lies in the center of the Swabian Alps that stretch from the Black Forest to the ancient city of Ulm near the Bavarian border. The Danube runs along the southern edge of the mountains. Some thirty miles west of Ulm, on an elevation overlooking the river, stands the fine baroque monastery of Obermarchtal, where Marie Antoinette was entertained on her journey to Paris some hundred years before Erzberger was born; she later presented her wedding gown to her Benedictine hosts, who placed it in their treasure chamber where it can still be seen today. The Lauter River, a little stream twelve feet wide, enters the Danube not far from the monastery. It waters a valley that is rarely broader than a quarter of a mile, with steep rocks bearing the ruins of picturesque castles on both sides. Bichishausen, a village containing the little Catholic church where Erzberger was baptized, lies some fifteen miles upstream. The two-room schoolhouse where he learned his letters can still be seen near the church.

Buttenhausen, his birthplace, lies three miles farther north. It consists only of a main street and several side alleys. The movement of the very few cars that penetrate this remote country is impeded by ox-drawn carts and long files of ducks and chickens. The population, then as now, is about 2,000. In Erzberger's time it was a surprising mixture, half Protestant and half Jewish, with the Jews carrying on a flourishing cattle trade going back to the Middle Ages. The Erzbergers were one of the few Catholic families residing there, and Matthias' Catholicism may have owed some of its militancy to this minority condition. The house in which he was born still stands on a small elevation above the Lauter River. It is built of stone and consists of two stories, connected by a narrow and steep stairway. The first floor contains a living room, a master bedroom, and a primitive kitchen and bathroom, all very tiny; the second floor has three small bedrooms. The living room alone is heated by a wooden stove, and here Matthias must have spent the long winter evenings with his three brothers and two sisters. The winters are long and severe in the Swabian Alps.

Very little is known about Erzberger's family background. His father, Josef Erzberger, was a master tailor who supplemented his income by serving as postman; in his latter capacity he won a local repu-

3

tation for adventurousness by being the first man to ride a bicycle in the Lauter Valley. His neighbors must have thought well of his character and abilities, for they elected him *Gemeindepfleger* (a village official), a great honor for a Catholic in a village peopled by Protestants and Jews. Erzberger's mother, Katherina Flad, came from a Protestant family in nearby Fladhof, but became a Catholic after her marriage in 1873.[1] Matthias was the eldest of her six children. Of his brothers one became a postman and another a typesetter, while one sister married a tailor in a nearby village. It has proved impossible to learn details about the two others, whose life also remained humble.

The contrast between the brilliant career of Matthias and the obscurity of his brothers and sisters was later exploited by his political enemies to question his paternity. They went to great pains both before and after his death to attempt to prove an illegitimate Jewish origin—to them an easy key for explaining his nefarious character. The most detailed story claims that his mother, described as a Jewish Buttenhausen village girl, served as a maid in the Munich house of the Jewish antique dealer Bernheimer in 1877, became pregnant, and was sent home with a considerable gift of money which allegedly induced Josef Erzberger to marry her quickly and accept Matthias as his son.[2] Not a shred of conclusive evidence was ever adduced to prove this tale, yet the claim that he was Jewish is frequently made in hostile pamphlets, usually accompanied by caustic remarks about the Buttenhausen Jewish cattle-dealers' milieu, the probability of his real name being Herzberger, Schmerzberger, or some other Judaized version of Erzberger, along with much innuendo of a similar tendency.

A great deal of Erzberger's personality and politics must be explained by the three factors of humble origin, Catholicism, and Swabian temperament. The ruling class of the Wilhelmine Empire was quite unwilling to accept the son of a Buttenhausen tailor—the log-cabin myth had no potency in Germany. Erzberger began life without money or family connections and was therefore forced to rely upon industry, ability, and aggressiveness. These qualities do not make a man popular, and it is difficult for a social climber to renounce the methods of his ascent after his arrival at the top. His family circumstances did not allow university study and he therefore entered public life with no more formal education than that of a grade-school teacher.

When such a man became an authority in many fields, including the

---

[1] Ernst Bauer, *Erzberger. Bilder aus seinem Leben und Wirken, Kämpfen und Leiden* (Munich, 2nd ed., 1925), p. 14. Henceforth cited as Bauer, *Erzberger*.

[2] F. C. Holtz, "Matthias Erzberger, ein Jude und Verräter," *Fridericus*, Vol. XVII, No. 5, Sept. 1934.

most abstruse questions of finance, his fellow-politicians looked upon him with a mixture of exasperation, incredulity, and envy. Erzberger's failure to secure higher education also meant that he lacked in later life the personal contacts that were usually established during one's university years—not only the corps brotherhoods of the sons of the ruling class, but also the important Catholic corporations which counted for much in Catholic political life and also in securing bureaucratic jobs. When Erzberger was to enter parliamentary life, he was disdained as an outsider, and later he was feared when he threatened to use his parliamentary power to advance the claims of men outside the charmed circle.

Erzberger never served in the army because his Württemberg home district had a surplus of eligible draftees; the mustering officers preferred obedient peasant boys to incipient intellectuals.[3] This deprived him of the chance to become a reserve officer, another handicap in the militarized society of Imperial Germany. He thus lacked family background, university connections, and a reserve officer's patent; as a Catholic he belonged to a religion that was despised by most members of the ruling class. The East German Junkers, the top-level bureaucrats, most industrialists, and almost all General Staff officers were Protestants and looked upon Catholicism as a regrettable anachronism.

Erzberger was raised, and he lived and died, a fervid Catholic. His religious opinions have no history. Dr. Josef Hammer, the priest who was probably his closest personal friend, states that Erzberger never had a crisis of faith.[4] His mind was essentially of a utilitarian cast, an instrument serving practical aims. He never thought of using it to question the validity of his religious view of life. This is remarkable for an intellectual of the late 19th century, when science stood at the zenith of its prestige and claimed to have established criteria for judging ultimate questions. Erzberger's education was purely Catholic and it insulated him from much of modern secular culture; but despite this sheltered childhood he always showed great sensitivity to new social, political, and cultural currents. His mind had the robust self-confidence of the man who has risen out of a humble milieu; such minds, as can best be seen by the case of Erzberger's contemporary H. G. Wells, usually succumb easily to a facile rationalism, intolerant of tradition. Erzberger never fell into this error. He was always free of the superficiality of the dogmatic liberal, while also avoiding the paralyzing

[3] Karl Bachem, *Vorgeschichte, Geschichte, und Politik der Zentrumspartei* (Cologne, 9 vols., 1926–1932), IX, 406. Henceforth cited as Bachem, *Zentrumspartei.*
[4] Josef Hammer, *Erzberger. Erinnerungsblätter eines persönlichen Freundes* (type-written manuscript in *Bundesarchiv*), p. 10. Henceforth cited as Hammer, *Erzberger.*

skepticism of the intelligent liberal. His instinctive, unrationalized Catholicism was the source of the deep internal self-assurance that characterized his political conduct.

Erzberger felt throughout his career that his specific policies were rooted in the unshakable foundations of Catholic social and political thinking. His Catholicism also explains his political party affiliation. Socialist and Liberal ideology was based upon materialism, rationalism, and denial of the supernatural—all condemned by the Church. Both movements were proud of their anti-clericalism. The Conservative Party was North German, Protestant, and upper class in its outlook; a lower-class Catholic South German could not make it his political home. Erzberger was, therefore, both by tradition and a process of elimination, born into the Zentrum Party. His political loyalties were predetermined by the circumstances of his heredity and environment, and could not possibly become a matter of deliberate choice.

His Swabian origin further determined that he should stand on the left wing of the Zentrum. This party, as we shall see later, was very heterogeneous, but its Württemberg section had deep roots in the democratic traditions of the German southwest. A dislike of aristocracy, of privilege, and of Prussian militarism was common ground among his fellow Württembergers. It was accompanied by the provincial pride that characterizes Swabians, which they justify in the light of Swabia's disproportionate contribution to German culture (Hegel, Schiller, Hölderlin), but which hostile critics ascribe to sterile envy of the greater political achievements of Prussia and Austria. Erzberger shared these views and also had many traits that are popularly attached to Swabians. They are known as the Scotsmen of Germany for their industriousness. Erzberger usually worked sixteen hours a day and rarely took a vacation. Many Swabians possess "schwäbische Gutmütichkeit," a combination of kindness and gullibility that is easily exploited by others. He had a fair share of this lovable fault which led to great political vulnerability. "Schwabenstreiche" (literally, blows struck by Swabians) are performed by men who combine courage and imagination with naïveté; many of Erzberger's projects failed because he refused to see obstacles that were obvious to men much less able. His hatred of bureaucratic routine and copy-book maxims of administration was certainly non-Prussian.

Many of his worst enemies in later life were North Germans who were not accustomed to Swabian ways. His foes saw calculation and racketeering where there was only impulsiveness and carelessness, while some friends falsely conceded that he was devoid of principle.

The following description of his impulsive personality, written by a good friend immediately after his death, gives a good impression of the man:

> Matthias the Cheerful was not constituted to save the world. He had no desire, like Landauer and Liebknecht, to stand at the dawn of a new era, or die a martyr's death, not even a beautiful death. His life was not constructed like a Gothic building but rather as a colorful, wide stretching peasant dwelling, not elevating, but warm and comfortable. The plan of his life had a beautiful simplicity. He believed in God, he was a child of the people, he knew his arithmetic. His worst vice was a passion for work that could not leave matters alone. He was accustomed to confer, to study, to counsel, to talk and to write, from early dawn to late at night. The large, broadshouldered, obese man believed in himself. . . . He loved life, any observer could see that; he loved his activities, loved politics, loved power, loved to advance his friends, loved wine and steak, and had a good Catholic love of God.[5]

Little is known of Erzberger's childhood. He was sent to the Catholic school at Bichishausen three miles down the valley, living during the week with his paternal grandfather at nearby Gundelfingen. One of the teachers recognized Matthias' unusual abilities and persuaded the father to prepare him for a teaching career. This offered the opportunity for some social advancement at a cost the family could afford. He was sent in succession to the *Präparandenanstalt* (preparatory school) at Gmünd where he completed a three-year course in two years (1889–1891) by skipping a class, and to the *Lehreranstaet* (teachers' seminary) at Saulgau (1891–1894). A schoolfellow at the latter institution, Wilhelm Schussen, who later attained a minor literary reputation, recalled after Erzberger's death his youthful impressions.[6] He said that the future statesman had always been at the top of his class. Erzberger's phenomenal memory, which enabled him to repeat whole pages after a single reading, amazed his schoolmates. Everyone, he himself included, felt that a great future lay before him, while the direction of his ambition was indicated by his being the only subscriber in the entire seminary to a metropolitan newspaper.

Another schoolmate, Oskar Jacob, has also written down his recollections:

> Who cannot remember the young man with the lively face that was always cheerful, and the intelligent eyes which peered through thick glasses? Our Matthias was always good company, but he never expressed his zest

[5] Stefan Grossman, "Erzberger," in *Das Tage-Buch*, ii (Sept. 3, 1921), 1047–48.
[6] Wilhelm Schussen's preface to Bauer, *Erzberger*, pp. 2–6.

for living in song—for this would inevitably have been disharmonious—but rather in practical jokes. And he was always courteous and ready to help. His popularity with the headmaster was frequently exploited to get permission for outside passes. The headmaster's dictum was: "One cannot say 'No' when Matthias asks for something." Everybody admired in Erzberger his clear, sharp intellect and excellent memory. He was, moreover, a model of industry, recognizing that effort lies at the root of all great achievement.[7]

Erzberger's report cards for the years 1891–1893 survive, and show that he was always the first in a class of twenty-five.[8] He excelled in religion, pedagogy, German literature, mathematics, history, geography, science, and French, and was always commended for talent, industry, and moral conduct. He was weak only in minor subjects: music (consisting of singing, piano, organ, violin, and musical theory), drawing, athletics, and handwriting. The list of subjects shows the practical purpose of the teachers' training college and incidentally reveals how elementary its curriculum was compared with that of a university. It also refutes the story given currency at the time of the 1918 armistice negotiations that he was completely ignorant of French.[9]

We must picture young Erzberger as a student whose qualities were felt to be spectacular by teachers and fellow-students alike. It is more difficult to get a clear view of his personality at this time. His vitality and good nature are undisputed, but the account, cited above, also contains some hostile observations.[10] His industry, ambition, and consciousness of superior powers made him arrogant and egocentric; his robust physical and psychological composition made him blind to the personal problems of others; one feels the emergence of a man who has many acquaintances but few intimates. He formed no lifelong friendships at Saulgau, though after his elevation he was never condescending towards his former college mates. He sent an affectionate telegram to the 25th class reunion at Ravensburg in 1919, when he stood at the height of his political career.[11]

Erzberger entered the Württemberg school service in 1894, serving successively as apprentice teacher at Marbach and Goeppingen. He was also *Amtsverweser* (teacher performing the duties, but not yet having

[7] Oskar Jacob in an obituary in the "Magazin für Pädagogik," quoted by Hammer, *Erzberger*, p. 4.

[8] *Erzberger Papers*, File 38.

[9] Prince Bülow loved to harp on this. See his *Denkwürdigkeiten* (Berlin, 1931), IV, 22.

[10] Schussen in Bauer, *Erzberger*, p. 4.

[11] Letter from Friedrich Albers to Dr. Hammer, Nov. 22, 1928, in *Erzberger Papers*, File 38.

the rank, of a regular appointee) at Feuerbach near Stuttgart. No material survives concerning his teaching career; one must assume that it never absorbed his complete attention. He read widely on political questions and never missed a public meeting. In Germany political rallies often allow for considerable audience participation, with people being invited to enter their names in a regular speakers' list and being given the floor for a few minutes during the discussion period. This device is often successful in securing the attendance of men whose views are hostile to the sponsors. Erzberger often went to Socialist and Liberal meetings to show his fighting mettle. He won a local reputation by once crossing swords with Konrad Haussmann, the great leader of Swabian democracy, who was about twice Erzberger's age. The older man at first treated the young schoolteacher in a patronizing manner, but was soon forced upon the defensive by Erzberger's superb mastery of the subject matter.[12] They were to sit together in the Prince Max of Baden Cabinet a quarter of a century later, with Erzberger replacing Haussmann at the last moment as the Chancellor's choice for the job of Armistice Commissioner.

At a public discussion in 1895 Erzberger's entire life was changed by meeting Joseph Eckard, one of the leaders of the young Württemberg Zentrum Party. Eckard (1865–1906),[13] a priest turned politician, was the man Erzberger admired most during his Württemberg years. The son of a vintner, Eckard studied theology at Tübingen and became vicar in the industrial town of Ludwigsburg. He was soon appalled by the inroads which Marxist Socialism was making upon his parishioners, and he resolved upon a vigorous counter-program to save their Catholic faith while working to remedy their social grievances. His first step was to become an editor of the *Deutsches Volksblatt,* the Stuttgart Catholic newspaper, in 1890. His main effort was put into public lectures aimed at spreading Catholic social doctrine, as recently elaborated by the great encyclicals of Leo XIII. The topic of the 1895 meeting which Erzberger attended was "The Danger of the Development of International Capitalism," and he participated vigorously in the discussion. To substantiate his arguments he quoted from memory whole sentences from Eckard's speech, and followed this by a lucid dissection of all weak points. This feat caused Eckard to exclaim "I have discovered a political genius," and immediately to offer him an editorial

[12] Hammer, *Erzberger,* p. 6.
[13] For a sketch of his career, see M. Gasteiger, *Die Christliche Arbeiterbewegung in Süddeutschland* (Munich, 1908), pp. 385–87.

job on the *Deutsches Volksblatt*. Erzberger accepted without hesitation. He had found his natural calling as a journalist and agitator.[14]

The next seven years of his life (1896–1903) were devoted to the Catholic social movement in Württemberg. Adolf Gröber (1854–1919), who was to play a great role in Erzberger's life, had founded the Württemberg branch of the Zentrum in 1895, a full quarter century after the party had become well-established in North Germany.[15] The *Kulturkampf* had ended and economic questions were becoming paramount. The non-renewal of the Anti-Socialist Law in 1890 had revealed the compact strength of the rising Marxist movement. To meet these problems, the *Volksverein für das Katholische Deutschland* (People's League for German Catholics) was founded in 1890 as a parent organization for many Catholic leagues of workers, peasants, and artisans.[16] These aimed at promoting the economic and cultural interests of their members, while simultaneously immunizing them against Socialist agitation. Gröber and Eckard took the lead in founding the Stuttgart central office of the *Volksverein,* the latter specializing in organizing workers' leagues. Erzberger became Eckard's chief assistant in this work, while formally assuming charge of artisans' organization.[17]

He was sent to study economics at the Catholic University in Freiburg, Switzerland, in the summer of 1896, as preparation for his new tasks. This was his first trip to the country which was to become the center of his propaganda operations in World War One twenty years later. Upon his return he became a regular Sunday lecturer throughout Württemberg, spreading Catholic social doctrine to groups of peasants, artisans, and workers. The young agitator never spared himself. One of his meetings for Stuttgart masons was attended by exactly five persons, who were startled to hear themselves harangued for an hour and a half. One of Erzberger's friends reproached him for this excessive effort, but was silenced by the answer: "No, I have won these five men; they will become five propagandists for our cause, and for this reason I was compelled to give them a comprehensive picture." [18]

Erzberger's initial efforts were devoted to founding workers' educa-

---

[14] Josef André, "Wie Erzberger Politiker wurde: Der Arbeitersekretär," in Erzberger Heft, *Deutsche Republik,* edited by Josef Wirth, I, 690 (Aug. 26, 1927). Henceforth cited as *Erzberger Heft.*

[15] Bachem, *Zentrumspartei,* Vol. VIII, Ch. II.

[16] See the great history by Emil Ritter, *Die Katholisch-Soziale Bewegung Deutschlands im neunzehnten Jahrhundert und der Volksverein* (Cologne, 1954).

[17] Ritter, *op.cit.,* p. 177. On the *Arbeitervereine,* see J. Joos, *Die Katholischen Arbeitervereine* (M. Gladbach, 1913).

[18] André, *Erzberger Heft,* p. 691.

tional leagues (*Arbeitervereine*), and he became known as an *Arbeitersekretär* (literally, secretary of the workers' movement). The role of these organizations was to discuss problems affecting the workers' social and economic status and to spread information about the workers' rights under existing social legislation. This soon became Erzberger's specialty; the result was not only general lecturing but also a vast correspondence of replies to individual inquiries concerning employers' accident liability laws, protecting tenants against landlords, rights acquired by sickness insurance, and many other matters. His successor as *Arbeitersekretär,* Josef André, states that Erzberger answered some 3,100 inquiries of this nature in the course of the single year 1902–1903. Erzberger had the encyclopedic knowledge, sureness of judgment, and capacity for rapid work required for this task. Of the spirit that animated him, the following letter to André gives, despite its pompous verbiage, a sincere expression:

> You are taking over an important task. To be an *Arbeitersekretär* means to be an advocate (*Anwalt*) of the people, especially of the poor, means to help those who are oppressed, troubled, or discouraged. . . . I have encountered in my years as part-time *Arbeitersekretär* so much undeserved suffering, I could write an entire book about it. Our bureaucrats have no idea of all this suffering. . . . What you need in your new position is active, helping, creative love towards our poor Catholic people and to all that approach you, wherever they may stand politically. To serve the people is to serve God and also the state. Always seek to reconcile the working class to the state and utilize religious-moral factors to elevate the economic condition of our working people.[19]

Erzberger attended his first international conference as the delegate of the Württemberg *Katholische Arbeitervereine* at Zurich in August 1897. A Swiss workers' league had issued invitations for this congress on labor legislation to socialists and non-socialist organizations alike. Erzberger and the other Christian (non-socialist) delegates were impressed by the centralized discipline and cohesion of their socialist rivals, and they resolved to develop a nationwide Christian trade-union movement that could compete with them on equal terms.[20] The primarily educational workers' leagues, while fulfilling a genuine cultural need, could not do much to put pressure on the employer for the improvement of working conditions; but their transformation into independent trade unions necessarily aroused the fury of Catholic Conservatives and Socialist competitors alike. Erzberger worked hard in

[19] *ibid.,* pp. 691–92.
[20] Gasteiger, *op.cit.,* pp. 246–49.

the next few years, both as publicist and as organizer, to start a
national Christian system of unions.

Erzberger began his career as one of Germany's most indefatigable
pamphleteers with a brochure on *Christian or Socialist Trade Unions?*
in 1898.[21] One can find in it all the qualities of his later pamphlets:
directness of approach to the problem at hand; simplicity of statement
that avoids all ornamental rhetoric; a comprehensive thoroughness that
analyzes all aspects of a question; an honest attempt to meet all reasonable objections to his point of view; unshakeable conviction in his own
position; and an effortless facility of composition. A paraphrase of
Erzberger's argument can be found in Appendix 1, which gives the
detailed story of his leading role in the development of Germany's
Christian Trade Union movement.

Plans for a founding congress were laid in the Düsseldorf meeting
of the *Katholikentag* (the annual Catholic Congress) in 1898. Erzberger was one of a seven-man committee that planned two regional
conferences, one for South Germany and one for North, preliminary
to a national congress. He was the main speaker both at the southern
conference held at Ulm, and the ensuing national congress held at
Mainz on May 21, 1899. The most controversial question was whether
the new unions should be purely Catholic or whether Protestants
should be admitted on an interconfessional basis. Erzberger successfully championed the latter position on common-sense grounds: the
primarily economic work of the unions made sectarianism impracticable. Erzberger became the Stuttgart representative on the twelve-
member national executive board of the Christian Trade Unions.

While Erzberger took this leading part in founding trade unions
for the proletariat, he was also busy promoting the *Schwäbischer Handwerkerbund* (Swabian Artisans' League). Catholic social thinkers
attached great importance to the preservation of the artisan class now
threatened by the advance of industrialism. They called for a revival of
the spirit and organization of the medieval guild and its adaptation
to modern conditions. Erzberger organized an artisans' conference at
Ulm on April 13, 1899, attended by fifteen priests and twenty-eight
delegates from already existing craft organizations. The purpose was
to establish a Württemberg-wide organization. The protocols of this
meeting were later printed by Erzberger.[22] They show that he master-
minded the proceedings, but carefully selected Schall, a baker from

---

[21] Erzberger, *Christliche oder Sozialdemokratische Gewerkschaften?* (Stuttgart, 1898).
[22] Erzberger, *Material zur Handwerkerfrage. Aus den Verhandlungen der Handwerkerkonferenz in Ulm am 13. April 1899* (Stuttgart, 1899).

Gmünd, Schadler, a carpenter from Wachthausen, and Mayer, a pastry cook from Spaichingen, to do most of the talking. He did not hesitate to expand, and sometimes to correct by tactful interpretation, the remarks of his puppets. His draft for the statutes of the new league was accepted after perfunctory discussion. Schall then defined the tasks of the new league as consisting of education on craftsmen's rights under existing legislation, the formation of new guilds (despite the preposterous Socialist charge that this fostered medieval obscurantism), the establishment of cooperatives to secure cheap credit, and the promotion of better relations between masters and apprentices. He warned against allowing the intrusion of political or religious questions into the practical work of the league.

Erzberger, while agreeing with Schall's remarks, found them too general and he expanded upon them with some very homely suggestions. He was anxious to have guild members come together regularly, but he recognized the impossibility of getting suitable speakers for formal meetings. He therefore proposed instruction in drawing twice a week during the winter months. This was to be supplemented by a regular weekly night of discussion upon technical problems and social legislation. He called this a more profitable way of spending an evening than aimless political discussion over beer and tobacco. Artisans must cooperate to secure public contracts upon a non-competitive basis and to put pressure on municipalities to subsidize crafts in view of their semi-governmental function of regulating production. In all these practical activities he sought to raise the occupational pride of artisans, while always emphasizing the great task of defeating the atheistic and subversive agitation of the Socialists. The *Handwerkerbund* formed in accordance with Erzberger's suggestions proved a great success under his leadership. Membership rose to 4,000 by the end of 1899. Erzberger showed his energy by addressing 62 craft meetings in the course of a single year. He answered 1,100 written inquiries on specific questions of artisan law within the same period—and this was only one of his many activities.[23]

Erzberger's main effort until his election to the *Reichstag* (1903) went into journalism, and here his constant theme is hostility to Marxism. The enmity is based upon his strong religious convictions and not any attachment to the socio-economic *status quo*. He began to write a series of pamphlets under the general title of *Material for Counteracting Socialist Agitation,* with the purpose of refuting Socialist views on militarism, religion, female labor, the stock exchange, and other

[23] Ritter, *op.cit.,* p. 182.

subjects. In the pamphlet on militarism [24] he acknowledges the justice of Socialist opposition to many features of Prussian militarism but asserts that the Socialists have no monopoly in the field of criticism. The Zentrum has led the fight against the quixotic practice of duelling, the extravagant pensions paid to prematurely retired officers, the horrors of military courts sitting *in camera,* the arrogance of the military caste towards civilians, the pervasive influence of the reserve officers' spirit in civil life, and the waste of the taxpayers' money on showy parades. The Zentrum, in contrast to the Socialists, has not confined its criticism to empty demagogic declamation but has made specific reform proposals of a nature to win serious consideration by the military administration. It has secured an Imperial order restricting duelling (January 1, 1897), has used its parliamentary power to induce Chancellor Hohenlohe to promote a reform of military court procedure (1898), and has shown its constant solicitude for the body and soul of the conscript by securing him a warm meal every evening and adequate time for religious services on Sundays. The Socialists have very properly criticized the international arms race, with its constant military increases, but so has the Zentrum. The latter opposed the military bills of 1874, 1889, and 1893, while its abstention from the 1887 vote was out of deference to the Holy Father. But the Zentrum, as a responsible party which rejects demagogic competition with the Socialists, recognizes that the precarious position of Germany in the center of Europe necessitates a large army and one in a maximum state of technological advance. It has supported the artillery increases of 1890 and 1897, and it endorses the structure of an army based upon a professional core and an annual supply of conscripts. The Socialist proposal for a Swiss-type militia is wildly impractical in Germany. Such a militia would be no less expensive than the existing army, and militarily much less efficient, while Germany would be utterly defenseless in the difficult transition from one kind of army to another. This remained one of Erzberger's strongest convictions in later years.[25] The whole pamphlet is acute in simultaneously agreeing with many specific Socialist views while exposing the fundamental Socialist error of ignoring the realities of the existing international situation.

In the pamphlet on *Social Democracy and Religion* [26] Erzberger denounces the hypocrisy of the Socialist plank, adopted at the 1891 Erfurt congress, that religion is to be considered a private matter. The left

---

[24] Erzberger and Josef Eckard, *Sozialdemokratie und Militär* (Stuttgart, 1898).

[25] See, for example, *Reichstag Debates,* Vol. CCLXXXIV, April 24, 1912, pp. 1368–89.

[26] Erzberger, *Sozialdemokratie und Religion* (Stuttgart, 1899).

wing of the party frankly avows its hostility to this part of the program at every party congress, while the right wing defends it solely for opportunist reasons to avoid embarrassment in rural agitation. The Socialists do not dare to assault religion directly, but their indirect attacks are just as insidious and in the long run as effective. They wish to establish compulsory secular schools without religious instruction, and to deprive churches of all financial support. The latter would be fatal in a Socialist state monopolizing all the means of production. They proclaim Marxism as a substitute religion, and champion modern science, with its superficial criticism of alleged religious superstition. For these reasons the gulf between Socialism and Christianity is unbridgeable, a conviction to which Erzberger subscribed to the end of his life. He recognized, however, after 1917 that political cooperation with the Socialists was necessary, and that it had become safe because of the decline of doctrinaire atheism among the Marxist leaders.

It is unnecessary to follow Erzberger in his polemic against the Marxist position on other questions.[27] In every case he rakes through Socialist congress protocols and comes up with damaging quotations, which he sometimes quotes out of context or invests with a distorted meaning. He capitalizes upon the Socialists' skepticism of the possibility of securing improvements for the worker within the existing social order. This makes them lukewarm, and sometimes even hostile, towards many Zentrum reform proposals, and they frequently kill possible reforms by advocating impracticable amendments. At other times they oppose desirable bills for purely doctrinaire reasons: their advocacy of equality for women, for example, makes them hostile to some legislation specifically protecting women's interests. They voted against the 1896 stock-exchange law because stock regulation, especially as demanded by agrarian pressures and paternalistic principles, did not square with their historical dogma of the full working out of laissez-faire prior to the advent of socialism. Such a vote placed the fundamental anti-capitalism of the party in a curious light.[28]

Erzberger's polemic against the Socialists is always characterized by a real attempt to meet Socialist arguments; he accepts the Socialists as genuine opponents to be refuted, not as utopian anarchists that must be put under lock and key. This places him in a rare category indeed among the pamphleteers of the time.[29] He recognizes the tragedy of the

[27] Erzberger, *Sozialdemokratie und Frauenarbeit, Börse, Zentrum, Anarchie* (Stuttgart, 1899).
[28] *ibid.*, pp. 3–11.
[29] In this he can share Theodor Heuss's eulogy of Naumann. See Heuss, *Friedrich Naumann, Der Mann, das Werk, die Zeit* (Stuttgart, 2nd ed., 1949), p. 78.

polarization of German political life into irreconcilable Conservative and Socialist extremes, but does not yet know how to bridge the dangerous gulf. His aim is to prevent the Christian part of the working class from yielding to the Socialist contagion, thus allowing it to play a mediating role in the future.

Erzberger did not confine himself to writing ephemeral pamphlets on problems of the hour. He used his leisure—it is surprising that he found leisure amidst his many activities—to write a full-scale history of the secularization of Church property in Württemberg during the Napoleonic period.[30] His thorough work of four hundred and forty pages was based upon wide research in state and ecclesiastical archives. It places the specific Württemberg developments in the general framework of German and European history. Erzberger analyzes in successive chapters the 18th century background, the notorious Regensburg Diet which decided on the secularizations under French pressure, the territorial acquisitions of Württemberg, the means by which the secularizations were carried out, and the deplorable religious consequences. This analysis is followed by a detailed account of the specific steps leading to the secularization of each monastery. The book shows that Erzberger had the qualities of an excellent historian: a passion for detail, a love of archival work, a lucid power of generalization that never lost the forest for the trees, and an imagination that could breathe life into dusty records. His purpose was undoubtedly political, to register Catholic claims for compensation rather than to discover truth for its own sake, but ulterior motives have more often than not been the inspiration of significant historical work.

Erzberger undertook all these tasks—agitation, organization, pamphleteering, and historical research—while holding a regular job as a member of the staff of the *Deutsches Volksblatt.* He secured a perfect command of parliamentary business by reporting regularly on the sessions of the Württemberg *Landtag.*[31] The Zentrum Party leaders Gröber and Eckard appreciated his polemical skill and asked him to write several pamphlets on local Württemberg questions, especially on those of a fiscal nature.[32] Erzberger's expertise in all financial questions, which was later to facilitate his political rise and lead to his great achievements as Finance Minister, dates from this period. His work for

---

[30] Erzberger, *Die Säkularisation in Württemberg von 1802–10. Ihr Verlauf und ihre Nachwirkungen* (Stuttgart, 1902).

[31] Wilhelm Keil, a prominent Socialist journalist and politician, describes their joint journalistic work in "Der Journalist und Parlamentarier," in *Erzberger Heft,* pp. 692–93.

[32] See Erzberger, *Die Steuerreform in Württemberg* (Stuttgart, 1899). I have been unable to locate a copy of this pamphlet.

the Christian Trade Unionists and artisans was supplemented by the organization of a Peasants' League. This must have further enlarged his knowledge of the concerns of the humble people of his native region.[33]

All of Erzberger's work, except in journalism, was unpaid, but the latter gave him a sufficient income to think of founding his own household. A betrothal while still a schoolteacher in Feuerbach was terminated for unknown reasons in 1894; the girl married an engineer and migrated to America.[34] He was too busy in the next five years to contemplate marriage, but he became engaged in 1899 to Paula Eberhard, the daughter of a prosperous merchant in the old episcopal town of Rottenburg. They were married on February 13, 1900. The marriage proved an unusually happy one. His wife gave him domestic refuge from the ferocious antagonism of political life, a refuge that was soon to be sorely needed.

Erzberger was elected to the *Reichstag* in the election held on June 16, 1903, at the unusually young age of twenty-eight, becoming the youngest member of that body. Gröber had secured his nomination for an absolutely safe Zentrum seat. The 16th *Reichstag* district was located in the southeastern part of Württemberg around the town of Biberach. It was primarily a Catholic and agrarian area, with towns that were still in the craft stage of economic development and as such quite untouched by Socialist agitation. Thus Erzberger found a constituency that shared his democratic, religious, and progressive but anti-Socialist views.

His electioneering in 1903 aimed at frightening the pious peasant voters with the red bogey, and easily exposed the folly of the Socialist agrarian program.[35] The Socialists admitted the plight of the small peasant but were unwilling to do much about it. They disliked what they called the reactionary property instinct and religious superstition of the countryside, and did not wish to perpetuate these by saving smallholds from what they believed to be inevitable extinction. They carefully concealed their ultimate program—namely, the elimination of private productive property—from the rural voters; they were interested in fanning rather than alleviating peasant discontent. Their demagogic campaign against food tariffs, while effective in urban areas, placed them in a hopeless position in the countryside.

[33] André, *Erzberger Heft,* p. 690. Erzberger's chief assistant in this work was Kailbach, a priest. See Ritter, *op.cit.,* p. 177. I was unable to ascertain details about the Peasants' League.

[34] Letter of Josef Jaisle to Dr. Hammer, March 9, 1948. *Erzberger Papers,* File 38.

[35] See Erzberger, *Die Sozialdemokratie in früheren Tagen* (Stuttgart, 1903). Pages 22–32 deal with the Socialist agrarian program.

Erzberger supported the official Zentrum Party manifesto which gives a good statement of the issues that agitated German party politics in the first years of the 20th century. The main items were the defense of universal franchise (perennially threatened by the Conservatives since 1867) and of the secret ballot (recently achieved) in *Reichstag* elections. The manifesto called for legal reform, especially for the total abolition of the still privileged status of duelling; support of the army, navy, and colonies, but without impairing fiscal stability; the repeal of the special law exiling the Jesuits, the last relic of the *Kulturkampf;* support of all *Mittelstand* (shopkeepers, artisans and some white-collar workers) interests threatened by big capital and big labor; state control of cartels and monopolies; extension of factory legislation and social insurance; the establishment of *Arbeitskammern* (elective bodies including representatives of both labor and capital) with the aim of promoting class harmony;[36] and support of the 1902 tariff against both selfish agrarians on the Right and free trade doctrinaires on the Left.[37]

Erzberger went to Berlin to his first *Reichstag* session in order to support this program. He brought with him a superb knowledge of Württemberg affairs, great organizational experience, and his journalistic skill, but he had as yet little familiarity with the great problems confronting Germany at home and abroad. The 1903 Zentrum platform had, like most other party manifestoes at the time, avoided these; its items had all dealt with unexceptionable generalities or with appeals to pressure group interests. The problems of foreign policy were completely ignored, though Germany would in a few years be at war against most of the world. The unresolved constitutional problems of the Empire—which amounted to a permanent constitutional crisis because a large part of the population was fundamentally opposed to the existing state—were likewise unmentioned. These problems concerning foreign and constitutional affairs were to be decisive in shaping Erzberger's parliamentary career. They must be analyzed before we can continue the biographical narrative.

[36] See Erzberger, *Die Industrie-(Arbeits) Kammern im Reichstage* (Jena, 1905).
[37] For full text of the 1903 election manifesto, see Erzberger, *Das deutsche Zentrum* (Amsterdam, 2nd ed., 1912), pp. 136–41.

CHAPTER II

POLITICAL CONDITIONS IN GERMANY

T HE most important European development in the years when Erzberger began his political career was the deterioration of Germany's international position, leading to her so-called encirclement. This was more the result of apprehensions arising from her rising strength than of any especially aggressive actions on her part, though it was promoted by mistakes in both foreign policy and in blustering diplomatic manners. A united, dynamic Germany, rising in population and industry, disturbed the European equilibrium by her very existence, and was bound to provoke the cooperation of Russia, France, and England against what was felt to be a common danger. The Franco-Russian alliance had been an established fact for a decade; but it did not present a real menace to Germany until the Russian army and railroad system became modernized and the French Republic became consolidated after passing through the Dreyfuss crisis. Great Britain had experienced the dangers of "splendid isolation" during the Boer War, and had sought to escape them at first by a close rapprochement with Germany. The German Emperor had met the British proposals in a procrastinating and blackmailing spirit, thus setting the stage for the Anglo-French Entente of 1904. The isolation of Germany and Austria became complete when Italy became hesitant about her obligations under the Triple Alliance.

Many of the diplomatic moves of the period, such as the British offers to Germany 1898–1901 and the Italian agreements with France, remained unknown to the general public in all the affected countries. In Germany, especially, foreign affairs were rarely discussed in the *Reichstag*. Successive Chancellors took the attitude that such weighty matters exceeded the understanding of mere parliamentarians. Party leaders were not expected to possess a profound knowledge of foreign countries or to develop coherent conceptions of foreign policy, and Erzberger was to prove no exception to this rule. *Reichstag* debates on diplomatic questions tended to be perfunctory, and did little to educate the German public about international realities. The ruling class, spoiled by the great achievements of Bismarck, was characterized by a spirit of parvenu arrogance in its view of other countries. Complacency was the prevalent note despite occasional feelings of insecurity. Few foresaw the looming military catastrophe, fewer still the necessity of reforming the German constitution in order to prepare the nation to survive a prolonged crisis. The latter was not even contemplated because of the nearly universal expectation that a modern war would be short and decisive and therefore would not bring any great social strains regardless of whether it ended in victory or defeat.

The main reason why the German constitution required reform was that millions of Germans were deeply alienated from the existing structure of government. Germany had not yet made the transition from a bureaucratic monarchy, ruling by its inherent traditional right (*Obrigkeitsstaat*), to a parliamentary democracy where the people exercise popular sovereignty in choosing their rulers (*Volksstaat*).[1] The structure of German constitutional life retained the dualism characteristic of the Middle Ages, with a monarchical executive cooperating or quarrelling with representative institutions without any organic relationship existing between the two. The course of German political development during the 19th century had differed sharply from that of the Western democracies.[2] Both England and France had evolved a parliamentary system based upon broad franchise. The political leaders in both countries were considered the executors of the popular will. The people felt that the government was in fact their government, and in times of crisis this identification between the people and the state was the source of enormous physical and moral energies. This was to be shown during the First World War, when there was near unanimity about war aims in the Western democracies, whereas in Germany there was bitter contention, with millions of people believing that the government was needlessly prolonging the war in order to serve upperclass interests that meant nothing to the masses. Germany lacked a close relationship between governors and governed. In ordinary times this did not matter much. The Imperial regime had many virtues. Its administration was the most efficient and least corrupt on the Continent. Its social legislation was the most advanced in Europe. Economic gains were made at a dizzying pace. German scholarship was the envy of the world. Above all, there was a pride in the attainment of national unity under Bismarck's leadership—the realization of a dream that had preoccupied a whole generation of Germans. The nation was proud to carry her proper weight in Europe after centuries of weakness.

But the roots of Germany's internal problems lay in the manner of

[1] The German terminology in stating the problem is that popularized by Hugo Preuss, *Das Deutsche Volk und die Politik* (Jena, 1915). The chapter owes much to Johannes Ziekursch, *Politische Geschichte des Neuen Deutschen Kaiserreiches* (Frankfurt, 1925), I, 206ff; Arthur Rosenberg, *Entstehung der Deutschen Republik* (Berlin, 1928), Ch. 1; and Hans Delbrück, *Regierung und Volkswille* (Berlin, 1914).

[2] This is the main theme of the great book of Heinrich Heffter, *Die Deutsche Selbstverwaltung im 19. Jahrhundert* (Stuttgart, 1950).

its national unification. It had not been achieved through a popular revolution sweeping aside the obstacle of the existence of thirty-eight individual states. The Frankfurt parliament of 1848 had failed in this task, and had been dissolved as soon as the old powers of Prussia and Austria had reestablished the order which had been shaken by temporary panic. What liberal votes and parliamentary resolutions could not accomplish, Prussian blood and iron could, as Bismarck told his critics in 1862. He moulded the framework of national unity after defeating Austria and making Prussia the leading German power. He relied on Prussia's military might, not the force of national opinion—though the latter rallied to him as soon as his success had become apparent. The result was a political structure in which Prussia inevitably assumed the leading role—an unreformed Prussia whose anachronistic political and social system aroused deep hostility among the masses. The predominance of Prussia was only barely concealed by the surface concessions made to the demands of modern liberal and democratic sentiment.

Imperial Germany had a *Reichstag* (national parliament) with full budgetary powers. It was elected by a completely democratic manhood suffrage, which Bismarck had introduced on the mistaken assumption that the masses were much more conservative than his Liberal opponents elected on the basis of a plutocratic franchise. The Iron Chancellor realized in later life that his calculation had failed, but he never found a chance of reversing his handiwork. The *Reichstag* developed into a fairly accurate mirror of German political opinion, despite the antiquated boundaries of the constituencies (with no redistricting after 1867) and the absence of proportional representation (a serious fault in a country with a multi-party system). Several parties had developed for the representation of different interests: the Conservatives represented agriculture and a part of the lower middle class; the National Liberals, heavy industry and the complacent part of the professional intelligentsia; the *Freisinn* Liberals, commerce and the discontented but non-Socialist part of the intelligentsia; the Socialists, the urban proletariat; and the Zentrum, the Catholic population in all its social diversity.

The function of the *Reichstag* was to champion the interests of these various groups in legislation, and to ventilate the grievances of the German people. Leaders like Erzberger could win prominence through their oratorical power or their skill in influencing legislation. *Reichstag* discussions of new laws was very thorough, and the government was forced to negotiate with the parties as independent powers. The power of the purse could be used to influence the policies of the Imperial government, but it could not be used for the further purpose of determining the person of the Chancellor and his various Secretaries of State. Erzberger and his fellow-parliamentarians knew when they entered the *Reichstag* that they could never achieve executive positions. The appointment of the Chancellor was an Imperial prerogative, and the withholding of supplies in order to coerce the Emperor to appoint a *Reichstag* Cabinet would have been a revolutionary act. It would have constituted the decisive transition from a bureaucratic monarchy to a parliamentary democracy, and this was certain to be fought by the Emperor, the princes, and the ruling class.

Sovereignty in Imperial Germany resided not in the people but in the collective body of princes and free cities who sent delegates from their governments to the *Bundesrat* (Federal Council). This body had the right to pass on legislation before it went to the *Reichstag*. The *Bundesrat* embodied the federal principle of the Empire. The constituent states—such as Prussia, Bavaria, Saxony, and Württemberg—all had distinct historical personalities, and all strove to exercise their share of influence upon Imperial policy. The *Bundesrat* was more a conference of ambassadors than a First Chamber of parliament, though binding decisions could be made by majority vote. In practice, *Bundesrat* decisions were usually the product of delicate negotiations among the governments of the leading states. Many excellent legislative proposals were never submitted to the *Reichstag* because the *Bundesrat* vetoed their introduction, while pleading difficulties with the *Bundesrat* became a favorite device of Chancellors who nominally supported popular demands but felt no urge to translate them into legislation. The votes in the *Bundesrat* were roughly proportional to the size and population of the various states, with Prussia holding the lion's share of 17 out of 43 votes. It also controlled at least 5 more from small adjoining states which were incapable of resisting her wishes. This gave the Prussian delegates—appointed by the Prussian government—a regular working majority and constituted one of the institutions guaranteeing Prussian domination of the Empire.

The second guarantee lay in the personal union of the Prussian with the Imperial Crown. The King of Prussia was *ipso facto* German Emperor, and his two prerogatives constantly reenforced each other. The Prussian Crown was heir to a great tradition. The House of Hohenzollern had raised a sandy province of Eastern Germany to the position of the leading German power—a great family achievement that guaranteed

22

it a secure position in the affections of many Prussians. The Hohenzollern tradition was one of the enlightened absolutism striving consciously for the general welfare as the monarch understood it. In practice, royal policy had been closely identified with the position of the ascendant Junker class within Prussia; yet this fact had done little to impair its prestige among the masses until the rise of Socialism in the 1880's. The absolute monarchy had made some concessions to the parliamentary spirit after 1848 by consenting to the establishment of a Prussian-wide parliament—yet this body could not claim to control the government. It had been sharply defeated in the constitutional conflict of 1862–1866 when it had attempted to dictate military policy to the Crown. The defeat of parliament in that conflict meant that the monarch remained the strongest force in the Prussian state.

The office of Emperor had its roots in quite different traditions. Its introduction in 1871 had served the purpose of symbolizing national unity as opposed to Prussian or any other kind of particularism. It was intended to revive the glorious memories of the Medieval Empire of Barbarossa. The leading Prussian class, the Junkers, had no connections with this medieval tradition, but it was cherished by the bourgeois nationalist groups whose support Bismarck needed to broaden the foundations of his essentially Prussian-Junker Empire. The prerogatives of the Emperor, *qua* Emperor, were narrowly defined but very important: they included the conduct of foreign and military policy and the appointment of the Imperial Chancellor. They excluded, for example, the right of vetoing *Reichstag* legislation. Yet the limitations did little to diminish Imperial influence, for the Emperor possessed veto rights by virtue of his other position, that of King of Prussia. The intertwining of the residual absolutism of the King of Prussia with the important constitutional powers of the Emperor of Germany, institutionalized by the personal union of both offices, as well as by the Prussian hegemony in the *Bundesrat,* made the Hohenzollerns the strongest monarchs in Europe. The King-Emperor must, by the nature of his position and the absolutist traditions of the dynasty, resist all attempts of increasing the powers of the *Reichstag.* He must also resist all attempts that aimed at breaking the Prussian hegemony of the Empire, since his Prussian prerogatives were essential for his domination of Imperial politics. These tendencies were brought into especially sharp focus by the personality of William II, who loudly proclaimed his pride in the Prussian absolutist traditions while often going further and deriving his powers from God himself. His openly expressed contempt

of Parliament, and the constitutional structure which made the proclamation of his contempt possible gave a note of impotent futility to
German parliamentary life.

The two chief subordinates of the King-Emperor were the Prussian
Prime Minister and Imperial Chancellor. Experience showed that
union of the two offices in the same person was necessary to avoid
endless friction, thus further guaranteeing the Prussian hegemony of
the Empire—though the relationship naturally worked both ways, with
Imperial considerations also influencing internal Prussian matters (as
Prussian particularists never ceased to complain). The Chancellor–
Prime Minister was forced to work with both the Imperial *Reichstag,*
based upon democratic franchise, and the Prussian *Landtag,* which
was composed of two chambers: the *Herrenhaus* (upper) and
Abgeordnetenhaus (lower), neither of which was based upon democratic foundations. The *Herrenhaus* was a completely aristocratic preserve, with its composition made to suit the diseased romanticist-
medievalist imagination of Frederick William IV. The majority of its
members were irreconcilably hostile to the modern democratic spirit,
and its legislative record made the English House of Lords look like a
progressive institution. The royal prerogative of creating new members prevented the *Herrenhaus* from becoming a total obstacle to modern reforms. But this prerogative was exercised for political purposes
only once—in 1872—and William II was always reluctant to contemplate it. We shall see later that the Prussian *Herrenhaus* managed to
oppose the introduction of the democratic franchise in Prussian elections as late as the summer of 1918.

For the *Abgeordnetenhaus* was, and until 1918 remained, based upon
a suffrage system which was one of the curiosities of modern political
practice. This was the famous three-class voting system whereby
voting power was proportionate to a man's tax load. The total revenue
of a given constituency was divided into three equal parts, and the
taxpayers were correspondingly divided into three classes—upper,
medium, and lower—with each class paying an equal total sum. The
upper class might include two or three millionaires paying heavy
taxes; the medium class a hundred or two hundred moderately affluent
people—doctors, lawyers, and small businessmen; while the lower
class might number thousands of factory workers or farm hands, whose
combined small taxes would equal the taxes paid by three rich men or
two hundred middle-class people. The voting power of each of the
three classes was exactly equal in the primary elections that chose the
electoral college, which in turn selected the members of the Prussian

parliament. This system guaranteed a Conservative composition of the Prussian *Abgeordnetenhaus,* and one which was bound to diverge increasingly from that of the *Reichstag* elected on a one-man, one-vote basis. The latter contained, as of 1903, 125 Right-wing members (Conservatives and National Liberals), who were opposed by 115 deputies of the Left (*Freisinn Liberals and Socialists*), with 103 Zentrum members holding the balance of power in a House of 397 members. The Prussian *Abgeordnetenhaus,* on the other hand, contained 281 members of the Right (including 202 Conservatives), while the Left held only 32 *Freisinn* seats, with all Socialists being rigorously excluded by the operation of the three-class franchise system. The 97 Zentrum votes did not weigh decisively in a House numbering 434, as the Right did not need them and a Left coalition could never secure a majority.

The decisive fact governing Prussian politics was that the Conservatives held 46 percent of the seats of the lower House of the *Landtag* and that therefore a Prussian Premier wishing parliamentary support (a desirable though not necessary condition) must be in substantial accord with Conservative views. Yet in his other capacity, as Imperial Chancellor, he had to work with a *Reichstag* where the Conservatives held only 19 percent of the seats and where a Left coalition hostile to the Conservative Party was at all times possible. It required superb skill to antagonize neither *Landtag* nor *Reichstag,* and the tendency was to avoid friction by avoiding controversial legislation in both Prussia and Germany—but this was increasingly difficult in a dynamic society with new problems constantly coming to the fore.

The figures show that the Conservative Party could secure, under the three-class voting system, something close to an independent parliamentary majority in Prussia. This Conservative Party based itself primarily upon the East Elbian Junkers. The Junkers have assumed an almost legendary role in German history, and one must cut through a good deal of myth to understand their real condition. They were not ogres devoting their leisure to plotting world wars, as is sometimes supposed in the West; nor were they parasitic exploiters of the rural proletariat, as is officially maintained in the East. They were a vigorous class of medium-sized estate owners, personally supervising their agricultural operations and proud of their Conservative political principles. They had nothing of the self-conscious decadence of the French nobility of 1789 which had lost the conviction that its privileged position was justifiable. The Junkers saw themselves as the foundation of the Prussian state, and thus sincerely believed that an assault upon their privileges was treason. They differed from the English gentry by being relatively poor, by their lack of intermarriage with the moneyed class, and above all by the provincialism of their cultural horizons. They deeply feared all *Reichstag* politicians like Erzberger who displayed any democratic tendency. Their economic position was seriously threatened by the development of a world grain market in the late 19th century. The sandy East German soil, especially as worked by ignorant farm laborers, could not compete with the American Middle West. The Junker clamor for high protective tariffs and other legislative benefits arose as much from necessity as greed. As a class, the Junkers successfully used their entrenched political power to buttress their failing economic position; this was made possible by the curious intertwining of Prussian with Imperial affairs. They controlled the Prussian *Landtag* through the three-class voting system; the Prussian *Landtag* influenced the composition of the Prussian government; the Prussian government controlled the majority of the *Bundesrat;* and the *Bundesrat* was the dominant institution in national legislation. Hence the Prussian franchise system became the main topic of German political controversy. The parties of the Left demanded its reform, with the ultimate goal of assimilating it to the completely democratic *Reichstag* system; while the Conservatives looked upon it as the Ark of the Covenant that must be protected against tampering by sacrilegious hands. A democratic franchise would make the Socialist instead of the Conservative element dominant in Prussia, and this prospect was utterly intolerable to the Imperial ruling class.

The Conservative control of Prussia and Germany could not have remained unshaken until 1918 had it depended merely upon an electoral device—indeed, the democratic franchise of the Weimar Republic was to give Prussia a predominantly Socialist government without destroying Junker influence in the state. This influence was solidly entrenched in the army and bureaucracy. The officer corps had not maintained its original Junker monopoly, but it was nonetheless deeply permeated by Junker Conservative prejudices. These included deep contempt for Liberals, Jews, and Democrats; pathological aversion to Socialists; pride in loyalty to the person of the King rather than to parliamentary institutions; hostility to Catholics whose religion forbade duelling, and to Zentrum politicians like Erzberger, who agitated against duelling; and a firm belief that war was a necessary and even beautiful part of the divine order, and that pacifism and regard for international law were the product of cowardice and weakness. These views were combined with a high sense of personal honor and great professional skill. The experience of World War One was to show that this skill was limited to technical and organizational questions, and did not suffice for mastering the higher problems of strategic planning, where technical problems must be viewed in a political context, and where narrow political prejudices easily lead to a faulty assessment of moral and political imponderables.

The defects of the officer corps would not have mattered much if the General Staff had been subordinated to civilian authority. But such subordination would have been contrary to the traditions of both Prussia and the Empire. The General Staff was directly responsible to the Emperor and was in no way under the control of the Chancellor. A very strong Chancellor, like Bismarck, might prevail over the military in foreign policy questions even in wartime, but even Bismarck encountered difficulties in 1866 and 1870. A Chancellor of more ordinary capacities, like Bethmann-Hollweg, could not veto military decisions made by the General Staff even though they should involve large political implications. During World War One the soldiers were responsible for such policies as the violation of Belgian neutrality and the submarine campaign which provoked America's entry into the war. The officer corps, because of its narrow social recruitment, also became increasingly divorced from that large section of the German people which believed in a liberal, democratic, and anti-militarist way of life. The result was severe friction both before and during the war and an impairment of the moral unity of the nation.

The bureaucracy shared many of the views of the officer corps, though often in an attenuated form due to the infiltration of some bourgeois and liberal elements. Professional advance came more readily if one possessed a title, though exceptional ability would do as a substitute. Both university corps membership and a reserve officer's patent were practically essential to make one's way. The bureaucracy felt itself the administrative arm of the monarchy, and stood for no nonsense about being the people's servants except in a very paternalist sense. Its personal incorruptibility and high administrative competence gave it an excellent *esprit de corps*. It often showed considerable concern for the problem of the little man, but it resented any pressure by public opinion or by parliamentarians. Its behavior towards individuals was arrogant and towards the *Reichstag* patronizing. It feared any advance of parliamentary government as a challenge to its prerogatives and a threat to the upper classes from which it was primarily recruited. It hated a man like Erzberger who frequently intervened in bureaucratic affairs without consulting copybooks of sound administration.

The Lutheran Church was a further pillar of the monarchical state.

Many livings were controlled by Junker proprietors, who naturally appointed clergymen of their own political persuasion. The prominent Orthodox wing of the Church—the Liberals played little role outside university circles—identified itself completely with the monarchist-conservative *status quo*. Clergymen had their salaries paid by the state, and were often in the position of civil servants whose specialty was religious affairs. They usually supported the Conservative Party at election time. Their hatred of Socialist atheism colored their entire political outlook. The few pastors with more conciliatory ideas, like Friedrich Naumann, ran into trouble with their consistories and were branded as mavericks. The Lutheran clergy was naturally anti-Catholic, and disliked Catholic politicans like Erzberger who aggressively championed Catholic claims.

This, then, was the domestic condition of Germany: a lack of agreement on fundamentals, with a broad democratic-liberal-socialist movement, dominant in the national *Reichstag,* being confronted by a conservative-bureaucratic-monarchist state in Prussia, which was based upon *Herrenhaus,* three-class franchise, Junkers, Army, bureaucracy, and Lutheranism; while the interlacing of Prussian and Reich affairs required a Chancellor who was *persona grata* to Prussian Conservatism and *Reichstag* majority alike. The position of the Chancellor-Premier was far from enviable, since all the strains of the complicated political system focused especially upon him.

The position of the Chancellor had originally, like the entire Imperial constitution, been tailored to fit the gigantic stature of a Bismarck. The creation of that constitution had been a great achievement in 1867—so great that it was bound to invite idolization and thereby prevent its adaptation to new conditions. Bismarck had made a correct assessment of the real strength of different institutions and social forces as of that date, and of his ability to manipulate those forces into a tolerable degree of harmony. Junker Conservatism was the strongest force in Prussia after the defeat of the Liberals in the constitutional struggle; hence it must receive a paramount position. The traditional Prussian state had shown its vitality by defeating the aspirations of 1848 and by humbling the pretentions of Austria; therefore it must necessarily be dominant in any federal structure. The federal principle was deeply rooted in the tenacious allegiance of most Germans to their own region and dynasty, and its supersession by a unitary parliamentary state was impossible. The semi-autocracy of the Hohenzollerns had yielded great national results when administered by Bismarck; it could not be expected to capitulate before Liberal demands.

The hollowness of German Liberalism had been exposed by the facility with which most Liberals accepted the Empire; Bismarck could not be expected to yield to men that were hypnotized by his own success.

An unfavorable verdict on the Bismarckian impact upon German political life cannot be based upon the view that he miscalculated the real forces in Germany during the period of his prime—though he was seriously to misunderstand both Socialism and Political Catholicism in later life. It must rather be directed against certain fundamental limitations in his personal outlook and political principles which became enshrined in the constitution he created. He perpetuated the power of the Junker class and the Hohenzollern autocracy by entrenching both in a political structure that proved impossible to reform—but it must be remembered that he was a Junker himself and that his great achievements, especially in foreign policy, would have been inconceivable if he had been responsible to a parliamentary majority rather than a pliable old king. A statesman cannot jump over his own shadow. Germany's domestic difficulties in the early 20th century were not so much due to the Bismarckian constitution as the failure of a new generation to adapt that constitution to the needs of a new age. Bismarck is responsible to the extent that he failed to train a ruling group that could perpetuate his own work and successfully operate his very complex governmental machinery.

The complexity of that constitution was, however, deeply enmeshed in German realities, and was not the mere product of Bismarck's ingenuity. The Iron Chancellor had manipulated those realities successfully to suit his purposes; while his manipulative approach was determined by a sincere belief that domestic, like foreign policy, was fundamentally governed by the law of the jungle. He believed, as the last great European statesman in the Machiavellian tradition, that international relations were based purely upon power, with restraints arising not from law or a moral consensus but only from a rational calculation of opposing forces. He applied this same conception to the domestic scene, failing to see the need or the possibility of a moral consensus in the internal composition of the state. He had established his own power in Prussia by riding roughshod over the law and the constitution. His power had remained unshaken by Liberal speeches in Parliament or Liberal election victories in the country or Liberal fulmination in the newspapers. Why should he take public opinion, or parliaments, or constitutional barriers seriously? His position was based upon the support of individuals and groups that held material instruments of power: the Crown, the army, the bureaucracy, and the Junker class. He did not propose to yield that position to opponents armed only with high principles and moral convictions. His power at home, or his successes abroad, were not shaken by their hostility. Why then, should he conciliate them on any terms but his own? Instead of conciliation he relied upon manipulation, and applied a "divide and rule" policy that was unique in modern history. The Liberals were checked by his Conservative support, and when they recognized the hopelessness of their position they became torn by internal dissension. The Conservatives were made subservient to his wishes by his indispensability for checking the Liberal, and later the Socialist, tide. One institution could be played off against the other. When the democratic *Reichstag* proved refractory he could rely upon the plutocratic Prussian *Landtag,* and vice versa. When the federal states made difficulties in the *Bundesrat,* he could rely upon the unitary *Reichstag,* and vice versa. The internal policies of Bismarck constituted a fascinating game of manipulating parties and institutions, with the Chancellor changing his political allies repeatedly in his career. A moral consensus, a sense of common responsibility for the national welfare, could not develop in such a political climate. A manipulative Machiavellism, compounded by a cynical pursuit of material self-interest, was Bismarck's worst domestic legacy.

Several of Bismarck's successors recognized the need for constitutional reform, but none of them possessed the strength that could overcome the formidable obstacles in the way. Their task could have been facilitated by having a very wise or very weak Emperor, the former promoting, the latter acquiescing, in fundamental reforms. But William II was not cast for either role. He lacked any deep understanding of Germany's internal problems and he did not have the personality required for soothing antagonisms or minimizing constitutional friction. His unhappy talent for extremist speeches evoked hostility and ridicule both at home and abroad, and added to the burden carried by his advisors. His mania for travel and incapacity for steady work led to considerable confusion in the formulation of government policies. His exalted notions of divine-right monarchy made him inaccessible to parliamentarians, even those of an extreme Conservative hue; while a Left-wing Zentrum man like Erzberger did not dream of requesting, much less receiving, an audience before 1915. The Emperor's fundamental inadequacy for filling his great office is proved by his inability to develop a reform program that would bring Germany's institutions abreast of the requirements of an age of world crisis.

The imperative need confronting Germany was to transform the bureaucratic monarchy into a parliamentary democracy. This alone could reconcile the broad masses to the state and create a moral consensus that could transcend the Bismarckian "law of the jungle" in domestic politics. The existing state structure, based upon a divine-right monarch whose Prussian position required close cooperation with the anachronistic Junker class, must inevitably arouse the animosity of millions of Germans. Its clumsy institutional mechanism—especially the intertwining of Prussian with Imperial affairs, and the unenviable position of the Chancellor-Premier—could not provide the framework for efficient government. Its alienation from the parliamentary type of government prevalent in Western Europe was a major source of weakness in foreign policy by provoking hostility. The remedy for these evils lay in the introduction of the democratic franchise in Prussia and parliamentary institutions in the Empire. The achievement of these two objectives would constitute a political revolution; and this revolution could not possibly secure permanence unless buttressed by fundamental reforms in the structure of economic life, the bureaucracy, the army, and the Protestant Church. Such reforms would transform the traditional contours of the historic Prussian state beyond recognition, and assimilate Prussia into a democratic Germany in place of the present Prussian conservative hegemony over Germany.

Was such a comprehensive reform program possible? The existing constellation of forces practically forbade it. A summary enumeration of these historical forces may best explain why it was that Germany was unable to achieve parliamentary government before 1918, and why Erzberger, though a very prominent *Reichstag* member, could play only a limited political role until the war:

1. The strength of the monarchist-bureaucratic tradition in Prussia, combined with the stranglehold which Prussia exercised over Imperial institutions, as analyzed above. To establish parliamentary government meant to break the Prussian hegemony first, and this could be accomplished only after a social revolution in Prussia itself. The dominant Junker class was resolved to resist to the bitter end any tampering with its privileges. By controlling the bureaucracy and the army the Junkers possessed physical instruments of power to smash any attempts at violent change. No one doubted that the army, though a quarter of its recruits were sons of Socialists, would shoot at Socialist insurrectionaries if ordered to do so. There was indeed not much danger of matters coming to such a pass. The working class, while sullenly hostile to the Empire, hated it with something less than revolutionary intensity. Germany completely lacked a revolutionary tradition, and the manifest

hopelessness of revolutionary effort was not calculated to encourage new departures. The defeat of the army in the First World War was in fact to prove the prerequisite for the democratization of Prussia and the establishment of parliamentary government.

2. It must not be thought that the Prussianized Empire rested primarily upon army bayonets. These constituted an ultimate sanction that could be kept well in the background. The governmental structure possessed great prestige since it was associated with Bismarck's achievement of national unification. Conservatives could ask critics of the Empire, Where is administration more honest or efficient than in Germany? Where is economic progress faster? Could unification have been achieved by parliamentary means?—and many other questions pointing up the external splendor of Germany. Moreover, the prestige of the Empire became identified with nationalism, the strongest passion of the age. Conservatives charged that their liberal opponents wanted to replace the established "German constitution" by the "un-German" parliamentary system prevalent in Western Europe.

3. The socio-economic strength of the classes which had much to fear from an advance to democratic parliamentary government. The Junkers feared the break-up of their estates and the abolition of their privileged position in all the institutions they dominated. The manufacturing class feared drastic "soak the rich" taxes and the specter of socialization. Many middle-class elements, hypnotized by the successes of Bismarck, had accepted the values of the Junker class and abandoned their traditional Liberalism. Their interests were well protected by the Empire despite the fact that they possessed little direct political power. The Emperor, who prided himself on his modernity, was proud of associating with captains of industry, and proved accessible to their demands. They valued the protection from Leftist experiments provided by bureaucratic monarchy, and the National Liberal demand for parliamentary government shrank with every Socialist electoral gain.

4. The federal structure of the Empire was, even apart from the Prussian hegemony which it thinly concealed, a powerful barrier against parliamentary progress. Parliamentary government is essentially single-chamber government and has everywhere led to the atrophy of second chambers. An effective cabinet can be responsible to only a single house of the legislature, and this must necessarily be the lower house elected by the people. The establishment of parliamentary government in the Empire must thus enhance the power of the *Reichstag* and virtually eliminate the power of the *Bundesrat*, thereby reversing their positions in the Bismarckian scheme of things. This

would have been a great step towards the unitary state (*Einheitsstaat*) which was anathema not only to Prussian particularists but also to South German federalists. It would deprive the Bavarian and Württemberg governments of their direct influence upon national legislation, and reduce these proud semi-sovereign states to the role of provinces. Their dynasties resisted this as a matter of life and death; but even their peoples were to show great resistance to centralization as late as 1919 when the Weimar constitution was constructed.

5. The *Reichstag* power of the purse was limited by the practice of long-term military appropriations and the prevalent constitutional theory that Imperial finance should rely upon indirect taxes in order to leave direct taxes to the individual Länder (states)—a theory that was, incidentally, to have disastrous fiscal results before it was abandoned by Erzberger's great 1919 reforms. In a different general political context even the limited powers over the purse would have constituted a strong lever for attaining parliamentary government. But in Germany the precedent of the Prussian constitutional conflict of 1862–1866 stood in the way. In those early Bismarckian years the Prussian *Landtag* had refused to vote taxes until its will should prevail in military legislation. Bismarck had collected the previous year's taxes despite the lack of new appropriations and had dared the Liberals to do their worst. They had answered by speeches and constitutional declarations. The army and bureaucracy had remained reliable instruments of the monarchist government wielded by Bismarck. Everyone recognized that revolutionary outbreaks would be suicidal. It was a fatal turning point in German constitutional history, made more fatal when Bismarck used his period of unconstitutional tyranny to win great successes in foreign policy. The reference to a sterile parliament hampering the great statesman in his work of unification because of some constitutional proprieties became a stereotype of Conservative oratory. No one doubted that the Crown would be willing to fight another constitutional conflict, whether in Prussia or the Empire, and would win another victory if the *Reichstag* should press its claims.

6. The actual danger of such a conflict was minimal even apart from the fact that the Liberal-democratic forces could not expect victory. The *Reichstag* expressed much dissatisfaction with the government, but the opposition parties could never form a cohesive majority. *Freisinn* Liberals, Zentrum, and Socialists were all dissatisfied in one way or another. The Right-wing Liberals, organized in the National Liberal Party, had made their peace with the Empire, while still hoping for greater influence for Liberals in the administrative apparatus. The Left-

wing Liberals continued to champion parliamentary government, but they were only the insignificant remnant of the once great German Liberalism that Bismarck had first divided and then emasculated. They were split into three different factions that differed seriously on questions of social and military policy. The staunchness of their principles could no longer conceal the futility of their political conduct. Yet they were the only groups for whom the achievement of parliamentary government was the primary goal of German politics.

7. Erzberger's own Zentrum Party never assumed a clear-cut attitude on the question of constitutional reform; its heterogeneous social and geographical composition, which will be analyzed in the next chapter, made a common party attitude impossible. The Right wing of the party, concentrated in North Germany and led by Silesian magnates and Rhenish lawyers, differed from Conservative and National Liberal views in little except its Catholicism. It did not pretend enthusiasm for the official party plank that called for the introduction of the democratic franchise in Prussia. The Prussian Zentrum leaders allied themselves with the Conservatives in opposing the very mild suffrage reform proposals advanced by Bethmann-Hollweg in 1910. Why should they oppose the three-class system which protected them against Socialist competition at election time, and gave them most Rhenish constituencies without serious contest? A democratic voting system for Prussia would only lead to gains for Marxist atheism. The Left wing of the party, in which Erzberger would soon play the leading role, generally favored the democratization of German political life; but its leaders, coming primarily from South Germany, had little influence upon Prussian affairs. In the question of promoting parliamentary government—a natural corollary of their democratic outlook—they were paralyzed by the tenacious federalism of the Bavarian Zentrum voters, who on most other questions constituted the core of the party Left wing. These shared the provincial pride in Bavaria's special destiny that was common ground throughout the state, and feared all government coming from Berlin, whether such government be bureaucratic or parliamentary. The development of parliamentary government must inevitably increase the centralization emanating from Berlin, which the Bavarians already believed much too far advanced. The result of their views was a paradoxical outlook. The Bavarian Zentrum deputies were democrats at home, proud of the liberal institutions which they loved to contrast with Prussian barbarism; while in Berlin they were conservative defenders of the federalist constitution that thinly screened a Prussian hegemony that they sincerely loathed. Their position made

it impossible for the Left wing of the Zentrum Party to develop clear views on constitutional reform.

The Zentrum Party had many good reasons, apart from the federalist outlook of its Bavarian wing, for opposing parliamentary government. It enjoyed influence without responsibility under the existing system. The fundamental opposition of the Socialists and *Freisinn* Liberals to the established order made it imperative for successive Chancellors to woo Zentrum support. The Zentrum held the balance of power that could create either a governmental or an oppositionist *Reichstag* majority. The development of parliamentary government would strengthen anti-clericalism by giving greater power to Socialists and Liberals—the Imperial regime, whatever its faults, was an ostentatious champion of "Christian civilization." The events of the war were to show that the Zentrum could, under Erzberger's leadership, become the ally of the forces working for a parliamentary regime; but this was made possible only by conditions so desperate as to force a fundamental political realignment. In the complacent years before 1914 the Zentrum accepted the constitutional *status quo*.

8. The Socialists had among their objectives the achievement of parliamentary government. But it was for many Socialists a secondary consideration compared to the attainment of socio-economic changes. The theorists of a stateless millennium could not be expected to attach great value to one particular type of state organization over another; moreover, the Marxist ideology had classified parliaments as instruments for serving bourgeois, not proletarian, interests. What advocacy the Socialists gave the cause of parliamentary government was close to the kiss of death, since they compromised it by association with their extreme views on religious, economic, and international questions. The Conservatives could plausibly argue that Marxist doctrinaires could not be entrusted with even a share of political power in a parliamentary coalition, and their argument was convincing because the Socialists, after excommunicating their Revisionists, talked far more extremely than most of them really felt.

9. What sense there was of looming international crisis also militated against precipitating a constitutional conflict. Many moderates in the middle parties believed that constitutional changes were overdue, but they feared to promote them in a political climate where the intransigence of both Right and Left flourished. The Right would resist parliamentary government to the point of military despotism, while the Socialists were unfit to assume power because of their unrealistic conceptions of foreign policy. The precarious geographical position of

Germany, surrounded on three sides by hostile powers, did not allow experiments involving either Junker despotism or Socialist folly.

10. The spirit of the Wilhelmine *Reichstag,* based upon its possession of pseudo-parliamentary powers only, was a further obstacle in the way of the successful working of full-blown parliamentary institutions. The parties enjoyed considerable influence without being forced to act in a responsible manner. In a parliamentary coalition, ruling a multi-party state, the various parties are compelled to compromise with one another in order to agree upon a common program. They learn that the interests of others must be accommodated to one's own, and the rough edges tend to be taken out of controversies. This is especially true in the representation of pressure-group interests. It was far otherwise in the German *Reichstag.* Parties got into the habit of representing particular interests—agrarian, industrialist, *Mittelstand,* or labor—with carefree irresponsibility. The polarization of the German people, resulting in the first place from the absence of any agreement on fundamentals such as is presupposed by successful parliamentary institutions, was further promoted by irresponsible party politics. It was not the business of party leaders to find a common line through compromise—that was the function of the government contemplating national problems from its unparliamentary elevation. Parliamentary leaders became spokesmen for narrow interests, not practitioners of the art of compromise, while leaders of national stature, enjoying prestige outside their own parties, could hardly emerge at all. We shall see later that when the establishment of parliamentary government came in 1918, the *Reichstag* majority was unable to nominate a suitable Chancellor from its own ranks, and was forced to accept a Baden prince as head of the ministry.

11. The final factor that worked against the attainment of parliamentary government was the deep-seated complacency of the German population. This was partly rooted in the fact that there was no breakdown of the Imperial system that could be detected by the ordinary citizens; quite the contrary, Germany had not known war for a generation, economic progress was splendid, and law and order were guarded by a clean and efficient administration. These achievements had all come without the active political participation of the masses, and these understandably got into the habit of looking towards the government for assuming the political initiative. Only a self-governing people can develop self-governing capacity. The political education of the German people had been neglected. But, worse still, the governing groups had little understanding of the problems confronting Germany. The Emperor mistook histrionics for policy; the bureaucracy could

produce only competent officials like Bethmann-Hollweg, not statesmen with political flair; the army officers' outlook was clouded by
anachronistic values; the Junkers cared only for the protection of their
narrow privileges; while the capitalists were too busy making money
to concern themselves with political problems. All of these groups were
dazzled by the splendid external glitter of the Empire. A sober, capable
ruling class in an authoritarian regime presents many advantages, especially in foreign policy, over a parliamentary government responsive
to mass public opinion. But Germany did not have this kind of governing class; its leaders had little idea that Germany was facing an international catastrophe which would find her handicapped by deep, unresolved domestic problems. With complacency in the ruling class and
political immaturity in all classes, the problems of the future were
rarely properly diagnosed, and remedies were completely neglected.

Erzberger participated in the complacency prevalent in political circles at the beginning of his political career. He shared the pride of his
generation in German achievements, and believed they rested on secure
foundations. His insight into foreign dangers was to come only in the
last years before the First World War. His understanding of Germany's
domestic crisis was to make him a champion of the establishment of
parliamentary government by 1909, though his hostility to the Socialists prevented an active alliance with them—the prerequisite of constitutional progress—until 1917. Erzberger stood in his age rather than
above it, but he had the great gift of always remaining a learner. By the
time he reached decisive influence he understood the German problem
in approximately the terms sketched above; but this was at the end of
a long parliamentary apprenticeship extending from 1903 until the outbreak of war in 1914.

CHAPTER III

RISE TO PARLIAMENTARY PROMINENCE
(1903–1907)

The Zentrum Party and Its Leaders

E RZBERGER moved from Stuttgart to Berlin in late 1903 to be at hand for his first *Reichstag* session. He withdrew from all of his Württemberg activities in order to concentrate his entire attention upon the national scene. We have seen, on the basis of the 1903 Zentrum election manifesto, that this was not a period of stirring political passions or of great parliamentary issues. The Chancellor, Count Bülow, rather prided himself upon his capacity for avoiding "internal crises." The outlook for the next few years was one for detailed but uncontroversial legislation, especially in social and economic questions. This situation was favorable for a person of Erzberger's ambitions and talents. Great dramatic issues were bound to be monopolized by the established Zentrum Party leadership; while dry and complex legislative proposals gave him a perfect opportunity for making his parliamentary reputation by speaking frequently on the basis of his encyclopedic knowledge of social and economic issues developed in his Württemberg years.

Erzberger eagerly desired to make a name for himself, and he wanted as a first step to secure influence in the parliamentary Zentrum Party. The latter proved far more difficult than the former. The leading figures of the party disliked young politicians who threatened their own positions, and they especially disliked Erzberger because his personality did not fit into the normal parliamentary type. They were critical of his lack of university study, professional experience, and drawing-room manners. His recommendations were unflagging energy, unconcealed ambition, and great ability, and these have never made for popularity.

Erzberger's technique for securing influence in the party was essentially simple. He must force his entry by capitalizing upon his aggressive activity, and not hesitate to appear impertinent in rejecting all advice calculated to curb him. His conduct was made possible by the fact that Zentrum Party leadership resided in a weak committee in 1904. A strong leader would never have tolerated Erzberger's independent course; he would either have smashed Erzberger politically or have utilized his skills in a disciplined way. The Zentrum had become a great party under the strong leadership of Ludwig Windthorst (1812–

1891), the man who had successfully defied Bismarck in the *Kultur-kampf*. Windthorst had lived long enough to preside over the evolution of the party from an opposition position to a generally pro-government role. He was succeeded in the leadership by Ernst Lieber (1838–1902), a strong figure though he could not stand comparison with his great predecessor. He never found an adequate successor.[1]

When Erzberger came to Berlin the party was guided by a committee of which Adolf Gröber, Peter Spahn, Count Georg Hertling, and Karl Trimborn were the leading members. All four were to remain prominent until near the end of Erzberger's career, and their names will constantly reappear in our story. A brief characterization of each will show the difficulties in the way of Erzberger's rise, but also the fact that Erzberger was never blocked by a man of Windthorstian capacity. Adolf Gröber (1854–1919) was the only one of the four to whom Erzberger originally owed something in his elevation—Gröber had selected him to run for the safe Biberach constituency, and was to help him get a seat on the important Budget committee in 1904. They were often compared in the public mind as two contrasting types of Catholic Swabian democrats. They shared a deep religious piety and leadership of the Left wing of the Zentrum Party, but otherwise differed markedly in qualities and career. Erzberger was at first known as Gröber's protégé. Gröber was essentially an able second-rater whose rather limited achievements secured luster through his saint-like personality. Erzberger, on the other hand, was destined to rise into the front rank of Germany's statesmen, but his great achievements were to be tarnished by a reputation for inappropriate if not dishonorable personal conduct. A contrast between their careers reveals much about both men.

Gröber, who was twenty-one years Erzberger's senior, entered the *Reichstag* in 1887 after completing an excellent legal education and running through the junior stages of a judicial career. Windthorst admired his legal knowledge and introduced him immediately into the inner councils of the party. His rise thereafter was continuous but never spectacular. Erzberger, by contrast, entered the *Reichstag* in 1903 with no preparation other than journalism and political agitation. His desire for a prominent role was resisted by the existing party leadership, and his rise was that of a party rebel. Gröber entered the Württemberg *Landtag* in 1889 and divided his time between Stuttgart and Berlin; Erzberger avoided this mistake by concentrating completely upon

[1] See H. Cardauns, *Ernst Lieber. Der Werdegang eines Politikers bis zu seinem Eintritt in das Parlament* (Wiesbaden, 1927); M. Spahn, *Ernst Lieber als Parlamentarier* (Gotha, 1906), and Bachem, *Zentrumspartei*, VI, 134–44.

national affairs and staying out of local Württemberg politics. Gröber remained in some other ways a regional figure with a provincial outlook that Erzberger quickly transcended. Thus Gröber once stated in a military debate that it was the duty of Prussians, not Württembergers, to pay for the representative expenses of the King-Emperor. "The Emperor is not my Monarch, he is only my federal commander-in-chief (*Bundesfeldherr*). My Monarch sits in Stuttgart." [2] This was an accurate constitutional statement; but Erzberger, as a member of the younger generation for whom the Empire was a glorious national reality rather than a constitutional formula, could never have dreamed of making it. There were other factors that prevented Gröber's rise to national leadership. His industry nearly equalled Erzberger's, but it tended to concentrate monomaniacally upon one subject at a time. He lacked Erzberger's happy faculty for delegating work to able assistants and of viewing every subject matter within the general political context. Gröber sometimes suffered from a poor sense of proportion that amounted to lack of political instinct; this quality was best revealed during the war, when he practically retired for several months to his *Reichstag* study in order to draft a perfect code of parliamentary procedure.[3] His health was sapped by diabetes after middle life and this strengthened his predilection for the life of a scholarly recluse.[4] His social contacts were limited to the narrow body of his Zentrum colleagues. He never married, deciding early in life that the claims of a political career and home life could not be reconciled. Erzberger, in contrast, never knew the feeling of being tired; he loved the stimulation and fresh ideas coming from contact with new people, and he would have found it difficult to live without the refuge of a happy domestic life.

Gröber, especially as he grew older, possessed other eccentricities that made people feel uncomfortable in his presence. His patriarchal bearded countenance was awe-inspiring, and his mode of life gave him the reputation of a saint. People were startled by his utter indifference to money, promotion, and women. He always took rooms in a monastery, whether living in Berlin, Stuttgart, or on vacation, hearing mass every day and confessing once a week. His friends knew that he contemplated joining the Capuchin order, and that he regularly participated in spiritual exercises at a Jesuit institute.[5] For Erzberger, though

[2] H. Cardauns, *Adolf Gröber* (M. Gladbach, 1921), p. 52.
[3] *ibid.*, p. 126.
[4] *ibid.*, p. 116.
[5] *ibid.*, pp. 152–54.

a devoted son of the Church, such fanaticism was quite inconceivable; he was too much absorbed in manipulating mundane affairs to feel the inclination to engage in mystical flights.

Gröber's political achievements were remarkable for a man with such qualities. The creation of the Swabian Zentrum Party was his work. His prepared orations in the *Reichstag*—he lacked Erzberger's flair for impromptu debate—made ministers tremble. For twenty years he was one of the half-dozen leading Zentrum deputies and he rose to be party leader in 1917–1919. Prince Max of Baden selected Gröber to steer the constitutional changes through the *Reichstag* in October 1918. With all this, it must yet be remembered that the man was greater than his work. He presented to his countrymen an inspiring example of integrity, moral zeal, and devotion to duty—something which Erzberger, whose name looms much larger in history, could not do.[6]

Peter Spahn (1846–1925), a Rhenish judge with a narrow and legalistic mind, had sat in the *Reichstag* since 1884 and had also played a great role in the Prussian *Landtag* from 1882–1909. In his later controversies with Erzberger he often resented the arrogance of the younger man in questioning a judgment based upon legislative experience extending back to the time when Erzberger was still a village lad in Buttenhausen. Spahn was oblivious to enthusiasm and new ideas throughout his entire life, and was complacently satisfied with the Empire and Prussia as he knew them. His career in the Prussian judicial service had been brilliant despite his Catholicism and Zentrum Party leadership—ordinarily severe obstacles to official preferment. In the years of Erzberger's political ascent he was a prominent judge (*Oberlandesgerichtspräsident*) in Kiel (1905–1910) and Frankfurt (1910–1917), and he later advanced to the position of Prussian Minister of Justice (August 1917 to November 1918). He always combined his judicial duties with his parliamentary work, even after becoming official party leader (1912–1917); though this professional work took him away from the *Reichstag* for at least half the week. His strength was overtaxed by endless railroad commuting between Berlin and Kiel and Frankfurt. Erzberger had difficulty understanding a man who combined politics with another calling, and he always disliked Spahn's stuffy and legalistic approach to political questions. Spahn was conventional, traditional, and over-cautious, while Erzberger was open-minded, impulsive,

[6] The only existing biography of Gröber is the slim volume by his friend Cardauns, from which most of the above details are taken. See also Bachem, *Zentrumspartei*, vii, 64–75.

41

careless of precedent, and often reckless of consequences. They were made to be sharp personal enemies.[7]

Count Hertling (1843–1919) was a man of far greater stature. He was a Catholic *grand seigneur* of the type that had predominated in the Zentrum in Windthorst's days. A touch of anachronism explains the sterility of his outwardly distinguished career. The scion of an old Hessen-Darmstadt family with strong Austrian connections, he had been horrified by the Bismarckian foundation of a Prussianized Empire. His early ambition was to become a professor of philosophy, but his academic advance was impeded both by his political views and by his adherence to Neo-Thomism when Neo-Kantianism remained the fashionable philosophy. A transfer from the Prussian University of Bonn to the Bavarian Munich was necessary before he could secure a full professorship. Windthorst had persuaded him to enter the *Reichstag* in 1875 on the ground that a Catholic must bear testimony to his Church in evil days of persecution. Hertling placed himself under a severe strain by attempting to do justice to both his *Reichstag* work and his Munich professorship. Windthorst, an eminently practical man, was sometimes impatient of Hertling's metaphysical preoccupations and shrewdly brought him down to earth by appointing him Zentrum expert on social questions. The philosopher worked himself into the unfamiliar subject matter with his customary thoroughness and began his never-finished rapprochement with the industrial-democratic age. In most ways he remained deeply conservative. He always considered Social Democrats to be beyond the pale of respectable people. He had an instinctive attachment to the monarchist-bureaucratic state, and always looked with contempt upon parliamentary business. The diffuse oratory of the *Reichstag* that held him away from his Munich professorship was bound to irritate his erudite and precise mind. His loyalty to his new Bavarian home merged with the anti-Prussian ideals of his youth to make him a confirmed federalist. With his background one might expect deep hostility to Erzberger's ways; in fact, Hertling took a comparatively lenient attitude towards the escapades of the younger man. He recognized Erzberger's tremendous ability and by 1908 predicted for him the future leadership of the party.[8] He saw the futility of resisting an apparently inevitable event, and preferred to use his influence to domesticate Erzberger while this could still be done. The two were to remain on relatively good, at times even intimate, terms until

[7] On Spahn, see Bachem, *Zentrumspartei*, vi, 146–47.
[8] *ibid.*, vii, 100.

they publicly quarrelled after Hertling's elevation to the Chancellorship in 1918.[9]

Karl Trimborn's (1854–1921) career presents an instructive parallel to Erzberger's. He was the son of a prosperous Cologne lawyer, working in his father's office until he decided to enter the *Reichstag* and Prussian *Landtag* in 1895. Windthorst had picked him to become chief organizer of the *Volksverein für das katholische Deutschland* five years earlier, and organization rather than policy remained his specialty until the end of his life. He rose to be president of the *Volksverein* after the death of the founder Franz Brandts [10] in 1914, and was chairman of the Rhenish Zentrum Party from 1894 to 1921. His outlook remained in many ways Rhenish and provincial, to the point of his actively participating in the pseudo-separatist 1918 movement that aimed at making the Rhineland independent of the Prussian State. He never took up permanent residence in Berlin, and devoted much time to his duties as a Cologne municipal councilman. The contrast with Erzberger's national outlook and preoccupation with large policy questions is striking.

Their parliamentary careers were also very different. When Trimborn entered the *Reichstag* in 1896 he specialized in social questions as a junior colleague of Hertling's. The party elders considered him a radical big-city democrat, and for years tried to muzzle the expression of his views. Trimborn was not the man to defy the admonition of more experienced men; he lacked Erzberger's arrogant confidence in his own powers. Trimborn's distrust of himself was strengthened by a speech defect that made the delivery of long orations a torture, and he lacked the ambition that can conquer such handicaps. His letters to his wife show frequent querulousness, complaints about bad health, and a sense of martyrdom for embarking upon the rigors of parliamentary life. The Erzberger *élan* and joy in political combat is lacking. Trimborn was never really at home in great political questions. He almost never spoke on foreign, military, or financial topics. His rise in the Zentrum Party to the top leadership (1919–1921) following Gröber's death was due to his industry, organizational skill, and inability to make enemies.[11]

[9] On Hertling, see his autobiography, *Erinnerungen aus meinem Leben* (2 vols., Munich, 1919–1920); Karl Graf von Hertling, *Ein Jahr in der Reichskanzlei* (Freiburg, 1919); Hans Eisele, "Hertling," in *Hochland,* x (Sept. 1913), 750–55; V. Naumann, *Profile* (Munich, 1925), pp. 13–33; and K. Bachem, "Hertling," in *Deutsches Biographisches Jahrbuch 1917–20* (Stuttgart, 1928), pp. 416–25.

[10] W. Hohn, *Franz Brandts* (M. Gladbach, 1914).

[11] The only biography of Trimborn is the slim memoir by H. Cardauns, *Karl Trimborn* (M. Gladbach, 1922), the value of which is enhanced by the printing of

Each of these four leaders—Gröber, Spahn, Hertling, and Trimborn —had difficulty in exercising a steady influence upon the Zentrum Party because of other preoccupations and of failure to take up permanent Berlin residence, as Erzberger had done. Erzberger's complete absorption in political life made him an essentially new political type in the Zentrum Party: the professional, full-time politician. The emergence of this type—already known for some decades in the Socialist party, where paid editorships were available—reflected the rising democratic movement of the country. The masses were no longer contented to be served by their betters who dedicated part of their busy lives to politics out of *noblesse oblige.* The payment of salaries to deputies since 1902 had further encouraged full absorption in politics. For Erzberger this was in any case a dictate of his temperament. It was to give him great political advantages. In his quarrels with his superiors he was to have the advantage of the man on the spot who was always available for conferences to mobilize his supporters. His regular attendance at all *Reichstag* sessions—while Spahn was in Kiel, Hertling in Munich, Gröber in Stuttgart, and Trimborn in Cologne—gave him a superior mastery of current parliamentary business, and allowed him to speak frequently for the party while his seniors were away and could not be consulted. This lack of consultation between Erzberger and the official leaders, combined with his youthful aggressiveness that cared little for consequences, was to create great difficulties for the party.[12]

The absence of firm party leadership was especially serious at a time when party unity was threatened by the rising importance of social and economic questions. The Zentrum Party, composed of variegated socio-economic groups, was held together by common Christian principles and the memory of the *Kulturkampf.* All the other parties had, as we have seen, a clear-cut class basis. The Socialists championed the proletariat; the *Freisinn,* the commercial classes; the National Liberals, the industrialists; and the Conservatives, the agrarians. The Zentrum, on the other hand, prided itself upon its appeal to all Catholic groups, irrespective of class. It was compelled to develop social policies that could win the endorsement of Silesian landlords, Ruhr trade unionists, Rhenish industrialists, Swabian artisans, and Bavarian peasants alike. Considerable tension between a Right and a Left wing was inevitable, and this was accentuated by regional differences. The Zentrum strength

---

several family letters. See also K. Bachem, "Trimborn," in *Deutsches Biographisches Jahrbuch,* Vol. III, 1921 (Stuttgart, 1927), pp. 263–65.

[12] Julius Bachem, a prominent writer for the *Kölnische Volkszeitung,* emphasized the bad consequences of the frequent absence of Zentrum leaders from Berlin, in an article on March 17, 1906, reprinted in Bachem, *Zentrumspartei,* VI, 345–46.

in the 1903 *Reichstag* was 103 members. Twelve of the 103 came from Silesia and constituted the core of an extreme Right wing that was separated from Prussian Conservatism only by its Catholic religion. Twenty-eight were elected in the Rhineland. A minority of these came from the Catholic trade union movement, but most represented the view of the Catholic professional bourgeoisie; its outlook, best symbolized by Peter Spahn, was a liberal conservatism which accepted the *status quo* while admitting the need for minor improvements. Westfalia sent nine Zentrum members to the *Reichstag,* mostly paternalistic aristocrats.

The core of the Left wing of the party came from Southern Germany. Baden and Württemberg together sent 11 Zentrum men to Berlin, all imbued with the democratic egalitarian spirit of the southwest. The Zentrum voters in this region were peasants and artisans of the type that dominated Erzberger's own Biberach constituency. Bavaria sent nearly one-third—30 out of 103—of the party strength to Berlin. Many of these were priests whose outlook mirrored that of their urban and rural lower-class parishioners. Most of the delegates represented constituencies dominated by the small peasantry. These peasants concentrated their political attention upon hatred of Prussia and love of agrarian tariffs; their economic interests led to a frequent community of views with the Prussian Junkers whom they anathemized upon every other ground. We have seen above how their federalism prevented them from opposing the existing authoritarian structure of government, while being fervidly opposed to Prussian militarism, bureaucracy, and industrialism.

The peasant demagogue Claus Heim was the best example of all these attitudes. When Erzberger began to expose the colonial iniquities perpetrated primarily by Prussian officials and North German merchants, Heim cheered him on. When the conservative North German Zentrum leader Peter Spahn came to the defense of Erzberger's targets in the bureaucracy, Heim organized a Bavarian rally behind Erzberger. But when Erzberger in 1919 turned his hand to promoting parliamentary government and nationalizing Germany's railroads—two great steps towards centralization—Heim became one of his most bitter opponents, and he led the postwar Bavarian secession from the Zentrum Party.[13] Until the war Heim and his Bavarians had been nearly instinctive supporters of whatever Erzberger did. The established leaders knew that to discipline Erzberger meant more than dealing with a

---

[13] For a good personality sketch of Heim, see Karl Schwend, *Bayern zwischen Monarchie und Diktatur* (Munich, 1954), pp. 61–64.

single individual. It meant antagonizing the entire South German democratic Left wing of the party, of which Erzberger was the most prominent member. This they hesitated to do in view of the ever-precarious unity of the heterogeneous party. Erzberger's audacity in defying his seniors came partly from his temperament but was also rooted in the inherent strength of his position.

Erzberger's Early Reichstag Work

In this party situation Erzberger began his spectacular political rise. He exploited his capacity for impromptu debate by intervening in the *Reichstag* whenever a topic came up for discussion where his Württemberg experiences were relevant. A list of some of his speech topics during his first session (December 1903 to June 1904) reveals the range of his interests. He spoke on the condition of the coinage, Sunday rest for postal and railroad workers, a commission to study artisan problems, compensation to areas burdened by military garrisons, protecting cobblers against military competition, inspecting meat in households, improving the pay of army civilian employees, and protecting vintners against the losses caused by phylloxera vastatrix—to mention only a few of his speeches.[14] He realized the advertising value of irritating opponents and goading them into personal reply; his first two major orations (January 26 and February 5, 1904) were sharp retorts to Socialist criticism of Zentrum social policies. They provoked angry counter-retorts from Fischer and Wurm, the two Socialist specialists in exposing the alleged hollowness of Zentrum social views. The clash established Erzberger's reputation as a relentless foe of Marxism, a reputation which lasted well into the war.[15]

The established Zentrum leaders were irritated by so much speech-making from so young a parliamentarian. They were accustomed to distributing speech topics among themselves, and expected freshmen members to be seen rather than heard. The least a young man was supposed to do was to consult the leaders about his activities, and to yield to advice and reprimand. But Erzberger proved, now as later, completely impervious to remonstrance from party hierarchs. He compounded the sin of speaking out of turn by the great effectiveness of his speeches. The benches usually filled up whenever he spoke: his fluency, wit, and knowledge were admired by friend and foe alike. His marvelous memory, combined with his industry, soon gave him a reputation

---

[14] Erzberger, *Die Zentrumspolitik im Reichstage* (Koblenz, 1904), Vol. I, *passim.* Henceforth cited as Erzberger, *Zentrumspolitik.*
[15] *Reichstag Debates,* Vol. CIIIC, Jan. 26, 1904, pp. 510–16 and Feb. 5, 1904, pp. 714–20.

for omniscience, especially in matters of parliamentary precedent. He used the years 1903–1905 to work systematically through the stenographic protocols of the *Reichstag* sessions for the last thirty years, taking copious notes for his filing cabinet.[16] He generously shared this knowledge with members of all parties, with even Socialists coming to consult him to gather historical material for their speeches. He could easily flatter the collective pride of the *Reichstag* some years later by drawing upon his files to publish an anthology of parliamentary humor —a collection that promoted an *esprit de corps* in a body that was usually bitterly divided upon partisan lines.[17]

Erzberger's omniscience did not separate him, as frequently happens with studious parliamentarians, from the broad currents of public opinion. He was placed on the Committee on Petitions during his first *Reichstag* session, which was a converging point for the pressure-group politicking of Imperial Germany. His cool and unsentimental attitude towards politics must have been reenforced by his Committee experience. He began at this time the practice of indiscriminate helpfulness—not only to his constituents, but to anyone with any kind of introduction to him—which was to arouse so much ridicule and hostility in later years. Erzberger became the most accessible deputy in Berlin, and he found time to see an amazing number of people. He counselled them about whatever problems they were encountering with government officials. He readily gave them introductions to any officials who might be helpful in dealing with their particular cases. The latter often resented what they considered undue pressure, and were irritated by Erzberger's view that any citizen was entitled to a hearing by nearly any official whom he wanted to see. Erzberger's kindheartedness was often better than his judgment of men, and as his power grew he occasionally allowed his name to be used by dubious characters for dubious ends.

Gröber helped Erzberger to secure appointment to the powerful Budget Committee in 1904—a most unusual assignment for a man lacking seniority, but one for which Erzberger was well-prepared by mastery of financial questions won in his Württemberg pamphleteering days.[18] He immediately became the hardest worker on the Committee, volunteering whenever there was a dull job to be accomplished. He was

[16] Hugo Baur, "Erzbergers Werdegang," in *Allgemeine Rundschau,* April 18, 1931, p. 245.
[17] Erzberger, *Der Humor im Reichstage. Eine systematische geordnete Sammlung von Parlamentsscherzen* (Berlin, 1910).
[18] Bachem, *Zentrumspartei,* VI, 343, emphasizes Gröber's role and states that the Zentrum *Fraktionsvorstand* never discussed the selection.

placed, for example, in charge of a bill reforming the system of military pensions. This involved the treatment of minute legal and financial questions such as the differential claims of enlistees and draftees, the method of determining the percentage of disability for injuries suffered in the military service, the scaling of payments, the opportunity for appealing rejected claims to a higher tribunal, and the question of the best method of financing the whole scheme. His report won universal praise for its lucid and lively analysis of a complex subject matter. The Prussian Minister of War, General Karl von Einem, was enthusiastic, exclaiming: "If a new motion is made in the Committee and I do not immediately understand its significance, I ask Erzberger. He always gives me a prompt answer, and understands the subject matter much better than all of my officers combined." Erzberger received an official expression of gratitude from the military administration for his work.[19] He popularized the terms of the new law in two pamphlets that became standard reading throughout the military establishment, and his name became a household word among millions.[20] The broad class of military pensioners henceforth admired him as their vigorous champion.[21]

Erzberger also used his pen to focus attention upon the grievances of other groups. He won special popularity among the Catholic clergy by tackling the controversial question of raising their salaries to equal those of Protestant clergymen. In Germany both the Protestant and Catholic Churches are established by law, and priests and pastors receive their salaries from the state, as do other civil servants. Erzberger set out to prove by careful statistical calculation that Catholic priests were everywhere, except in Bavaria, paid less than their Protestant colleagues. He ridiculed the Protestant view that this difference was justified by the Catholic doctrine of celibacy. The state, when paying its other officials, did not discriminate against bachelors; salaries were everywhere set proportionate to the complexity of the work and the skill required to perform it, not to the personal circumstances of the recipient. Erzberger playfully argued that this principle really required that Catholic priests should be paid more than Protestant pastors, since their obligations to administer sacraments were more extensive— though he virtuously asserted that the Catholic Church would never

[19] ibid., 351. General von Einem, who was generally contemptuous of parliamentarians, gives a favorable sketch of Erzberger in his Erinnerungen eines Soldaten (Berlin, 1933), pp. 69–70.
[20] Erzberger, Das neue Militärpensionsgesetz für Mannschaften und Militäranwärter (Berlin, 1906) and Was man von dem neuen Militärpensionsgesetz wissen muss (Berlin, 1906).
[21] Bülow, in his Denkwürdigkeiten, II, 217, claims credit for the pension law, while ungenerously failing to mention Erzberger.

press such a claim. It would never ask for any favors, but it must insist upon its rights. The German states prided themselves upon their religious impartiality, yet their discrimination against Catholic priests belied their pretensions. Moreover, most of the states had legal and moral obligations to the Church under the provisions of the 1802 acts of secularization. Erzberger referred back to his 1902 book on the Württemberg spoliations in which he had proved that the state received more income from the *interest* of the confiscated property than it spent annually upon the Church. He argued that this intolerable situation must be terminated as being contrary to common sense, justice, historic rights, and the principle of religious equality.[22]

Another Erzberger pamphlet championed a Zentrum proposal—the so-called *Toleranzantrag* (motion for tolerance)—which aimed at eliminating remaining discriminations against Catholics.[23] Erzberger admitted that the general position of the Church was satisfactory in most parts of Germany, but he emphasized the irritating restrictions that remained in the Protestant states of Saxony, Brunswick, and Mecklenburg. Here the state required specific permission before any Catholic Church service could be held, priests were not allowed to take up permanent residence, the erection of monasteries was prohibited, and Catholic religious instruction in the schools was officially discouraged. There was little chance that the governments of these states would voluntarily end such administrative harassments, since the Catholic minority was small and the Protestant majority approved the existing system of discrimination. The Zentrum therefore proposed that the Imperial government pass a national law to compel the individual states to adhere to certain general principles of tolerance. Such a law would mean a great centralizing advance violating the federalist principles of the Zentrum; but the party championed it, nonetheless, since its allegiance to the principle of religious freedom was stronger than to federalist decentralization. The *Reichstag* majority approved the *Toleranzantrag* on several occasions, but the government always pleaded *Bundesrat* difficulties and thereby killed the matter. The liberation of the Church from its remaining fetters had to wait until the Weimar constitution.

Erzberger's pamphlet was a vigorous refutation of the arguments of the opponents of the *Toleranzantrag*. The Liberals loved to ridicule the

[22] Erzberger, *Beiträge zur Parität in Württemberg* (Stuttgart, 1903); a more general statement came in Erzberger, *Klerus und Gehaltsfrage. Beiträge zur Parität in den deutschen Bundesstaaten* (Cologne, 1908).

[23] Erzberger, *Der Toleranzantrag der Zentrumsfraktion des Reichstages* (Osnabrück, 1906).

49

Catholic Church, which they always denounced as the most intolerant of Churches, for appearing as a wolf in sheep's clothing when championing tolerance. Erzberger distinguished sharply between *dogmatic* tolerance (that is, granting error the same standing as truth, which no self-respecting Church could admit) and *political* tolerance (that is, the grant of complete religious liberty to all confessions, which was imperative in the modern inter-confessional state). Erzberger claimed that the Catholic Church had, in modern times at least, been a frequent champion of religious freedom in the political sense; his favorite historical examples were the founding of Maryland in 1634, the Declaration of Indulgence of James II in 1687, and the basic Papal Encyclical *Immortale Dei* of November 1, 1885. He gladly accepted the challenge of Protestants who liked to exhibit a "chamber of horrors" filled with proofs of intolerant Catholic doctrine; he loved nothing better than to engage in historical polemics. He argued that the 1302 bull *Unam Sanctam* had relevance only in the medieval context; that the 1864 Syllabus of Errors was a series of *ad hoc* assertions which were capable of a variety of interpretations (showing incidentally the broad freedom existing within the Church); while Pius IX's famous June 22, 1868 allocution on the proper state-Church relationship (to whose extreme language the Liberals attached great importance) was primarily directed against the unilateral Austrian breach of the 1855 Concordat which had just preceded. Erzberger's technique of argument was always to refute the very worst allegations that his opponents could make and then to proceed with a vigorous counterattack. In this pamphlet he asked German Protestants to search for the beam in their own eye. He presented a highly provocative analysis of the rise of religious liberty in modern Germany. The Protestants were accused of inventing the "horrible principle of *cuius regio eius religio*" and of glorifying the omnipotent state with its right to interfere in religious affairs. Religious freedom based upon the skepticism of the ruler had existed in Frederician Prussia, but institutionally it first emerged in the states of the 1806 Confederation of the Rhine, dominated by Catholic France; it was made part of the Federal Constitution by the 1815 Treaty of Vienna, negotiated under the paramount influence of Catholic Austria. This argument was calculated to irritate some of the most cherished prejudices of Protestant German nationalists.

An important factor in Erzberger's rise to power was his management of an article distribution service for Zentrum Party newspapers (*Zentrumskorrespondenz*).[24] He purchased a near-bankrupt service

24 Bachem, *Zentrumspartei*, VI, 343.

when moving to Berlin in 1903, and showed his journalistic flair by making the articles more informative and more sprightly—while simultaneously earning a good deal of money for himself. His articles quickly became the daily food of hungry editors of small Zentrum papers, thus giving Erzberger an enormous influence on much of Catholic opinion in the provinces. In this way he avoided the isolation from grass-roots sentiment that frequently afflicted national leaders. Erzberger specialized in sensational stories and prided himself on beating competing services to the news. His haste resulted in frequent inaccuracies that necessitated recantations damaging to his reputation. His friend Josef Hammer urged him in 1907 to abandon the entire enterprise; but Erzberger refused on grounds of financial necessity. He argued that he must build up a sufficient fortune so that his family could live from the interest without cutting into capital in case of his early death, and that this could not be done without his journalistic income.[25] The argument revealed the anxieties of a man of humble origins who had married above his social station, and for that reason felt exaggerated financial responsibilities to his family. He kept on with his article service until the war.

A quite different type of publication did much to increase his political reputation. This was an annual volume describing the work of the Zentrum Party in the *Reichstag,* patterned upon two publications which performed the same service for two state legislatures. Erzberger's mentor Joseph Eckard wrote an annual survey on the work of the Zentrum Party in Württemberg. Karl von Savigny, a minor Prussian Zentrum leader, chronicled the work of the Prussian *Landtag.*[26] Erzberger's volumes were always compact, well-written, and filled with useful quotations. They became indispensable reference books for politicians and editors, with their value depending upon their unimpeachable accuracy despite their speedy publication within a week of the end of each *Reichstag* session. Erzberger not only described, he also lauded, the work of the Zentrum Party; the same can be said of his account of the various party leaders, above all himself. He used the annual volumes for self-advertisement by describing his own speeches and motions far more frequently and at greater length than his objective standing in the party warranted.[27]

25 Hammer, *Erzberger*, p. 8.
26 Bachem, *Zentrumspartei*, VI, 343.
27 This is best shown by the indexes of the first two volumes of Erzberger's *Zentrumspolitik*. The June 1904 volume mentioned Gröber, the South German leader, 44 times; Spahn and Trimborn, the two Rhenish leaders, 26 and 25 times respectively; while the efforts of Matthias Erzberger, freshman from Biberach, were noted upon 35 oc-

These multifarious activities brought Erzberger prominence, but he still needed identification with a big issue in order to become a well-known public figure outside parliament. He showed his uncanny political instinct by beginning to specialize in colonial questions in 1905 just before they became the center of political interest. Previously he had spoken exclusively on the social and economic problems that were familiar to him from his Württemberg work. But in his third session (1905–1906) his attention shifted to African affairs, a field where the Zentrum lacked a spokesman who could develop the party position with authority. To most Zentrum leaders and voters, especially in South Germany, colonial enterprises appeared as a Hanseatic hobby to be tolerated but never encouraged; to dignify them by serious study was considered a questionable preoccupation. Erzberger rose above such prejudices and immersed himself in colonial pamphlets and official reports, and soon became the main Zentrum orator on all colonial problems.[28]

Erzberger's Campaign against Colonial Scandals

Erzberger was horrified by the number of scandals that he uncovered throughout the German colonial administration. He found, as Socialist critics had done before him, a total absence of a single policy-making body responsible for determining the principles of the treatment of natives, economic development, or the organization of a colonial civil service. The *Reichstag* lacked any effective voice in colonial affairs, except insofar as these involved its budgetary powers. The government had frequently made these powers nugatory by spending as it saw fit and then demanding supplementary appropriations which could not be rejected. Erzberger advocated an enlargement of *Reichstag* control and its natural corollary, the education of an alert public opinion, as the best way of bringing order into colonial administration.[29]

The lack of system was only one part of what Erzberger called the "colonial fiasco." He found many instances of gross incompetence and, worse still, brutality on the part of individual officials—cases of pecula-

---

casions—including a long transcript of one of his anti-Socialist speeches that took up 20 pages in a slender volume of 174. In the June 1905 volume Erzberger has advanced to first place in the number of references: the score is Erzberger 40, Spahn 38, Gröber 32, Trimborn 14.

[28] The best surveys of Zentrum colonial policy are Hans Pehl, *Die deutsche Kolonialpolitik und das Zentrum 1884–1914* (Limburg, 1934), and Bachem, *Zentrumspartei*, v, 50–60.

[29] Erzberger, *Die Kolonial-Bilanz* (Berlin, 1906), pp. 22–27. *Reichstag Debates,* ccxvi (March 19, 1906), 21, 29–36.

tion, torture, and even murder. The mistreatment of natives was partly the result of crude views of Negro inferiority held by the German bureaucrats, partly due to their failure to secure specific training for their difficult jobs. Colonial officials were expected, like all German civil servants, to hold law degrees from German universities, though the relevance of knowing the German civil code for the effective government of Negroes was far from self-evident. Bureaucratic helplessness in the face of the unfamiliar was often the cause of callous brutality. Erzberger suggested as a remedy the exemplary punishment of some notorious offenders—whereas the Berlin colonial office had previously done its best to screen culprits—and the establishment of a new school specializing in the training of overseas administrators. He demanded that colonial officials must implement the Christian ethic in their relationship with the natives, recognizing that Negroes had immortal souls exactly as did Germans—an unfashionable doctrine that caused a *Reichstag* tumult when baldly expressed by Erzberger. His religious principles made him immune to any kind of racial chauvinism.[30]

The third target in Erzberger's campaign was the privileges granted to colonial companies by a negligent government. A firm named Tippelskirch possessed a monopoly for supplying goods to German troops stationed in Southwest Africa; Erzberger, using information provided by some of Tippelskirch's jealous competitors, showed that the government was being charged fantastic prices. The ensuing publicity forced a cancellation of the contract. The Hamburg shipping firm of Woermann held a monopoly of shipping rights to the same colony, and used it to charge rates far above what other companies charged for comparable hauls. Erzberger forced a cancellation of this contract also. The German Colonial Society for South West Africa owned 32 percent of the land of that colony. Its stockholders made considerable profits while the colony received heavy administrative subsidies from the Imperial exchequer. Erzberger called for ending this anomaly by curtailing the privileges of the company. His zeal in detecting injustice and his hatred of any form of privilege made Erzberger the *bête noir* of all who held a vested interest in colonial abuses.[31]

---

[30] Erzberger, *Kolonial-Bilanz*, pp. 73–85; Erzberger, *Kolonial-Berufe* (Berlin, 1912), *passim*. The *Reichstag* tumult occurred on March 19, 1908, Vol. ccxxxii, pp. 4092–4103, especially p. 4098. See also Erzberger, *Zentrumspolitik*, vi (1908), 11–12, 73–85.

[31] For the Tippelskirch contract, see Erzberger, *Zentrumspolitik* ii (1905), 71–78; Erzberger, *Kolonial-Bilanz*, pp. 69–71; Erzberger, *Die Wahrheit über die deutschen Kolonien* (Berlin, 1908), pp. 30–32; *Reichstag Debates*, ccxvi (March 23, 1906), 2235–38. For the Woermann contract, Erzberger, *Kolonial-Bilanz*, pp. 71–73; *Reichstag Debates*, Vol. ccxvi, March 24, 1906, pp. 2257–58 and April 4, 1906, pp. 2605–07. For the South West African Company, Erzberger, *Die Wahrheit*, pp. 34–35; Erzberger, *Millionen-*

Chancellor Bülow, yielding to pressure from the Emperor himself, appointed Prince Ernst zu Hohenlohe director of the colonial administration in the spring of 1906, with a mandate to reform the abuses which Erzberger and others had uncovered. The prince possessed few qualifications for his new office except his princely status and unemployed condition. Erzberger was not alone in thinking him unsuited for a job that required a zealous reformer. His prejudices were also aroused by Hohenlohe's prominent position in the anti-Catholic Evangelical League. At any rate Erzberger gave the new official no mercy, and continued his exposure of colonial abuses. Hohenlohe proved helpless in the face of these attacks, and even his exceptionally able assistant, the young economist Karl Helfferich, was forced to retreat step by step in the face of Erzberger's relentless revelations. The bitter personal hostility between these two brilliant men, which was to have such fateful consequences for both of their careers, dated from this period.[32]

Erzberger's crusade against colonial scandals did not meet with much approval on the part of the elders of the Zentrum Party, who did not share his moral zeal and wanted to avoid trouble with the government. When Erzberger extended his campaign to include the personal grievances of individual officials who had complained to him about their mistreatment, Peter Spahn was outraged by a procedure that tended to undermine bureaucratic discipline, though Erzberger argued that bad administration and mistreatment of lower by higher officials tended to go together. When Erzberger made a specific mistake in discussing the injustice done to a court clerk named Koch (who had been a valuable informant on some East African atrocities), Spahn saw an opportunity of teaching his aggressive Zentrum colleague a lesson. He openly repudiated Erzberger's campaign against colonial scandals in the name of the party and told the *Reichstag* that the young Swabian deputy spoke only for himself. Almost any other man would have been silenced by this kind of rebuke from his party leader, but Erzberger took the floor with perfect nonchalance at a later stage of the debate:

> I have spoken my view, which I have never concealed from anybody. Then Dr. Spahn expressed his own view (*Privatansicht*) which happens to diverge from mine. One should not be surprised that differences of view

geschenke (Berlin, 1910), *passim;* Erzberger, *Zentrumspolitik*, VIII (1910), 44–48, and IX (1911), 47–48.

[32] For a hostile view of Hohenlohe, see Bachem, *Zentrumspartei*, VI, 334–36; a more favorable view, Joachim Haferkorn, *Bülows Kampf um das Reichskanzleramt im Jahre 1906* (Würzburg, 1939), pp. 46–48. The main clashes between Erzberger and Hohenlohe and Helfferich can be found in *Reichstag Debates*, Vol. CCXIV, Dec. 14, 1905, pp. 320–38, and Jan. 18, 1906, pp. 632–37.

sometimes exist in a big parliamentary party of more than a hundred members. I do not bear grudges if I am attacked by a member of my own party. This cannot always be prevented, and of course everyone has the right to express his own opinion: this is exactly what I claim for myself.[33]

Erzberger implicitly asserted a complete equality of status with the distinguished Zentrum leader who was twice his own age.

The party elders resented both Erzberger's independence and his patronizing airs. Karl Bachem, a prominent Rhenish deputy, demanded that the party recall Erzberger from the Budget Committee. The proposal was, however, resented by the democratic South German elements in the party, especially the Bavarians under Heim. They were delighted by Erzberger's defiance of the North German leaders, and were strong enough to prevent any disciplinary action. Bachem then petulantly withdrew from the Budget Committee himself, thereby enhancing Erzberger's real power by leaving him as the main party spokesman there. Erzberger, now wearing the aura of a successful rebel, continued his campaign against the hapless Hohenlohe.[34]

The latter, recognizing his own inadequacy, resigned in September 1906, with Erzberger being generally credited with his scalp. Hohenlohe was succeeded by Bernhard Dernburg, a man with the reputation of a ruthless businessman. He made a good start by cancelling the Tippelskirch and Woermann contracts. Erzberger sought to help him by handing over most of the material which he had collected concerning abuses. This cooperation soon came to a violent end. Dernburg resented, as Spahn had done earlier, the interest taken by Erzberger and a fellow Zentrum deputy, Hermann Roeren, in disciplinary cases pending against two subordinate colonial officials, Wistuba and Pöplau, who had leaked official information to the deputies. When Roeren made an attack upon the mistreatment of some missionaries in Togo during the *Reichstag* session of December 3, 1906, Dernburg retaliated by asserting that Roeren and Erzberger had improperly sought to apply political pressure in order to influence pending judicial decisions. He denounced this kind of *Nebenregierung* (roughly, backstairs government) as destructive of executive responsibility and political morals. Roeren replied by a sharp attack upon Dernburg's stock-jobbing past, while Erzberger proclaimed his solidarity with Roeren (who had been the primary target of Dernburg's assault). They both denied his

---

[33] *Reichstag Debates,* Vol. ccxvi, March 15, 1906, p. 2049. The Koch case is discussed by Erzberger in *ibid.,* March 13, 1906, pp. 1979–80, and March 15, 1906, pp. 2048–49, and in *Kolonial-Bilanz,* pp. 85–89.

[34] Bachem, *Zentrumspartei,* vi, 346–48.

charges.[35] The controversial facts can be found in Appendix II insofar as they concern Erzberger.

The quarrel was patched up on the following day, but it had revealed a dangerous degree of tension between the government and one wing of the Zentrum Party. This tension was made more dangerous by the fact that Bülow was probably looking for a quarrel with the Zentrum at this time. His prestige had been undermined recently by the failure of his Moroccan policy; his position at court was threatened by, among other things, Protestant intriguers who emphasized his alleged friendliness towards Catholics. His opponents exploited the fact that his wife was a Catholic and that he had discriminated less against Catholics than any previous Chancellor. Bülow probably thought that he could best buttress his tottering personal position by breaking with the Zentrum Party and winning an election by fanning the always latent anti-Catholic passions. He believed that he could win the *Freisinn* for his policies and construct a political "block" extending from the *Freisinn* to the Conservatives.[36]

His opportunity came on December 13, 1906. The Zentrum, with Spahn taking the lead, cut a governmental request for a supplementary military appropriation to suppress a native insurrection in Southwest Africa by nine million marks on the second reading. The reduction was accompanied by specific recommendations for economies, and was in any case subject to reconsideration on the third reading. Bülow easily could have secured a compromise with the Zentrum, but he deliberately threw down the gage of battle. He dissolved the *Reichstag* because he saw the opportunity of denouncing the Zentrum as an anti-colonial, hence anti-national party. Bülow wanted to give the German voter the impression that the Southwest African vote was but the culmination of a long line of "anti-colonial sins." The fact that it had been preceded by Erzberger's prolonged campaign against colonial abuses, and by the dramatic explosion between Dernburg, Roeren, and Erzberger ten days earlier, gave some plausibility to this charge.[37]

[35] *Reichstag Debates,* Vol. ccxviii, Dec. 3, 1906, pp. 4084-4118. Dernburg felt in a strong position because he knew that the regular Zentrum leadership would not come to the defense of their colleagues. Bülow describes a meeting with Spahn and Gröber in which the two deputies were critical of Erzberger, and even quotes Gröber as regretting having brought Erzberger to the *Reichstag* in the first place. *Denkwürdigkeiten,* I, 268-69.

[36] For an unfavorable view of Bülow's motives, see Bachem, *Zentrumspartei,* VI, 390-93; a favorable view, Theodor Eschenburg, *Das Kaiserreich am Scheideweg* (Berlin, 1929), *passim;* a neutral view, George D. Crothers, *The German Elections of 1907* (New York, 1941), pp. 95-103.

[37] On Spahn's essentially friendly attitude towards the government in December 1906, see the article by his son, Martin Spahn, "Das Jahr 1906," in *Das Deutsche Volk,*

The government, supported by the Conservative and Liberal parties, portrayed the Zentrum as composed of selfish politicians who placed parliamentary advantage above the needs of the heroic German soldiers fighting in the African desert. A famous cartoon presented Erzberger and Roeren smirking while looking at a dead German soldier in Southwest Africa. The caption read "We place the interests of the party above his welfare." [38] Right-wing organizations found in Erzberger their most inviting target, thereby making him for the first time a figure of national prominence. The *Flottenverein* (Navy League), a supposedly non-partisan organization, financed the distribution of pamphlets written by the press section of the colonial department under the titles of *Lies of Mr. Erzberger* and the *Manufacturing of Colonial Lies*.[39] Erzberger was embarrassed because many Zentrum people blamed him for provoking the dissolution by his unauthorized campaign against colonial scandals. They forgot that the breach with the government had actually come on a motion sponsored by Erzberger's enemy Spahn, and that Bülow would never have used an unimportant colonial vote for a dissolution if he had not been searching for a pretext to dissolve in any case. Erzberger, blamed by friend and foe alike, put in some very strenuous campaigning to prove his value to the party. He attempted to assume the offensive by accusing Bülow of absolutist designs, emphasizing that the Chancellor had repeatedly disregarded the budgetary rights of the *Reichstag*. He also accused him of dividing the German nation by exacerbating existing religious hostilities.[40]

The election involved Erzberger in an unpleasant incident that was to plague him until the end of his life. He published two anonymous articles in the *Bayrischer Kurier,* a prominent Zentrum daily, on February 4 and 5, 1907, the last two days of the campaign. These exposed *The Agitation of the Navy League* during the preceding weeks, showing how that supposedly non-partisan organization, which included both Protestant and Catholic members, had engaged in blatantly pro-government and anti-Zentrum agitation. Erzberger's proof was conclusive: he printed letters which the League's business manager, General August Keim, had written to several branch chairmen, advising them on how to proceed in agitation against Erzberger and the Zentrum. Keim did not challenge the authenticity of the letters, but

---

Vol. III (Berlin, July 15, 1908), *passim.* The view of Arthur Rosenberg, in *Entstehung der deutschen Republik,* p. 52, that Spahn wanted to retaliate against Dernburg's assault on Erzberger and Roeren, is refuted by Bachem in *Zentrumspartei,* VI, 365.

[38] Erzberger, *Bilder aus dem Reichstagswahlkampf 1907* (Berlin, 1907), p. 26.

[39] Erzberger, *ibid.,* p. 48. A. Keim, *Erlebtes und Erstrebtes* (Hannover, 1925), p. 125.

[40] These were the main themes of Erzberger's election pamphlet, *Warum ist der Reichstag aufgelöst worden?* (Berlin, 1906).

he charged that they had been stolen from his office. He brought suit against the editor of the *Bayrischer Kurier,* Paul Siebertz. The official investigation soon centered around a filing clerk named Oscar Janke, whom the public prosecutor's office sought to arrest on March 16, 1907. It was soon learned that he had disappeared into a Belgian Benedictine monastery and was unavailable for questioning. The letters had been returned to the League's files after having been copied, but this did not really diminish the nature of the crime. The court was interested in Erzberger as the presumed author of the articles. He was summoned to appear at the Siebertz trial and was asked two specific questions by the judge: (1) did he know how the articles had gotten into the *Bayrischer Kurier?* and (2) did he know whether Janke had provided the materials for the articles? Erzberger refused to answer both questions upon the ground of possible self-incrimination. It was clear that he had received the letters from Janke and had used them in order to attack the Navy League. His enemies charged that he had instigated the theft, and said this method of obtaining information was characteristic of the man. This version was never proved. Erzberger later asserted that his self-incrimination referred not to the theft but only to the violation of the copyright (*Urheberschaft*) of the letters, a far less serious offense. Janke had brought him the letters of his own accord, because he resented the scurrilously anti-Catholic campaign of the Navy League. Erzberger in effect admitted both the authorship of the articles and the acceptance of materials improperly extracted from the League files. His moral repute certainly suffers on account of this conduct. Yet it must be remembered that he acted under great provocation. He was striking a blow in self-defense: the Navy League was engaged in a systematic campaign of character assassination directed against himself, and against Catholics generally; it was breaking its own statutes that dictated political non-partisanship, and was abusing the trust placed in it by thousands of Catholic navy enthusiasts who had contributed to its funds. One regrets the methods and materials used by Erzberger in his sensationally effective counter-attack; but politics is a rough game, and in the bitter campaign of 1907 neither side was willing to give quarter.[41]

[41] On the entire Janke case, see Grotthuss, "Erzberger, ein Kalauer der Weltgeschichte," in *Der Türmer,* Heft 9 (Feb. 1918), pp. 517–18, a latter-day summary. General Keim gives his account in *op.cit.,* pp. 118–25, printing some pertinent documents, including the declaration of the Berlin *Landgericht I Strafkammer,* p. 119, and Siebertz' Oct. 1, 1907, apology, pp. 122–23. The matter was gone over thoroughly during the 1920 Erzberger-Helfferich trial. See *Der Erzberger-Prozess* (Berlin, 1920), pp. 751–56, 855–56, 878, 901–02, 1051–53. Henceforth cited as *Prozess.* For a defense of Erzberger's conduct see S. Löwenstein, *Der Prozess Erzberger-Helfferich,* pp. 88–91.

Bülow won a hollow victory in the election. His so-called Block of Conservatives, National Liberals, and *Freisinn* won 216 out of 397 seats, though it represented only 43 percent of the votes (with the result being influenced by the anachronistic apportionment of electoral districts). The Zentrum, which succeeded in increasing its seats from 100 to 105, came close to being a moral victor, though it was now thrown into an opposition position by the side of the Social Democrats. Yet it would stay in this position only as long as the Block held together; and since Conservatives and *Freisinn* disagreed on most of the issues confronting Germany (including the crucial issue of the three-class voting system), Bülow was whistling in the dark when he hopefully spoke of "the marriage between the Conservative and the Liberal spirit." The Zentrum leaders confidently looked forward to a time when the Conservatives, harassed by their Liberal allies, would wish to resume cooperation with the Zentrum.[42]

Erzberger's colonial campaign succeeded in stimulating an enlightened public opinion on colonial questions. Dernburg, despite his personal quarrel with the Zentrum deputies, saw the essential justice of their charges, and implemented their proposals both before and after the election. He thereby aroused the hostility of the very interests that had opposed Erzberger's reformist attempts, as Erzberger pointed out early in 1908 in a pamphlet with the subtitle *Brilliant Justification of the Colonial Policy of the Zentrum by Staatssekretär Dernburg*.[43] Erzberger hailed the substitution of the "Christian principle of humanity, justice, and charity" for "the materialist principle that looks upon the natives as objects for exploitation by whites."[44] Dernburg instituted "Negro-preserving policies," gave over-all direction to the colonial administration, improved the education of colonial civil servants, and revoked many of the unjustifiable privileges granted to private firms. When he proved insufficiently firm towards the South West African Company in the question of diamond regulations in 1910, Erzberger —who had been his friendly champion after 1907, forgetting personal antipathies—turned against him and helped drive him out of office.[45] But by that time Germany's colonial administration could stand comparison with that of any other power.

Erzberger deserves much of the credit for the vast improvement in Germany's colonial record after 1906. His role as a parliamentarian re-

[42] The election results are ably analyzed by G. Crothers, *op.cit.,* pp. 166–84.
[43] Erzberger, *Die Wahrheit über die deutschen Kolonien. Glänzende Rechtfertigung der Kolonialpolitik des Zentrums durch Staatssekretär Dernburg* (Berlin, 1908).
[44] *ibid.,* pp. 6–15.
[45] Bachem, *Zentrumspartei,* VII, 131.

stricted him to the function of critic and gadfly, but his courageous exposures in the critical years 1905–1906 nonetheless marked the turning point in Germany's colonial policy. His criticisms were unfortunately to be used by the victorious powers at Versailles in 1919 in order to secure a moral basis for depriving Germany of her colonies. This was to lead Erzberger's nationalist critics to charge him with unpatriotically supplying ammunition to the enemy.[46] But Erzberger's criticisms, by leading to necessary reforms, had in fact deprived the Entente of a real moral case to justify their annexationist policies. Erzberger's ultra-patriotic critics never understood that real patriotism does not consist of indiscriminate pride in one's country, but rather of actively making one's country something to be proud of. This kind of patriotism had sustained Erzberger's courage in his great task of calling for colonial justice and efficiency. In his specific methods he had sometimes erred, and some of his criticisms had shot beyond the mark. These deficiencies were the result of his restless activity and zeal; without these qualities he never would have dared to take on the entire colonial administration almost singlehandedly. He had his reward in the initiation of important reforms, and in the achievement of a great public position for himself in Germany's parliamentary life.

[46] Allied Reply to German Counter-proposals, June 16, 1919, Part IV, section 1. Printed in Alma Luckau, *The German Delegation at the Paris Peace Conference* (New York, 1941), p. 434.

Note: A detailed analysis of Erzberger's colonial campaign is contained in an article by the present author, "Erzberger and the German Colonial Scandals 1905–1910," to be published by the *English Historical Review* in 1959.

CHAPTER IV

THE PREWAR YEARS (1907–1914)

Introduction

ERZBERGER had become one of the most prominent figures of the Zentrum by 1907, but his weight in the inner councils of the party was as yet negligible. His authority as colonial expert was unchallengeable, but his use of this position had earned him the enmity of the entire conservative wing of the party. It ascribed the undesirable election results of 1907 to Erzberger's recklessness, and forced him for about two years into a temporary eclipse. He recaptured the limelight only at the time of the finance reform of 1909. His formal admission to the *Fraktionsvorstand* (party executive committee) was delayed until February 7, 1912, but he played a very influential role, both inside and outside the party, long before that date.

Erzberger took a prominent part in the discussion of all major political questions in the last five years before the war—in the *Reichstag*, at public meetings, and in an endless stream of pamphlets and newspaper articles. He developed a comprehensive social and economic policy on which the party could unite despite its heterogeneous composition. He took a mediating position when ideological cleavages threatened party solidarity in the so-called *Zentrumsstreit*, which dealt with the question: should the Zentrum be a narrow Catholic or a broad interconfessional party? Erzberger remained a vigorous champion of Catholic grievances, excoriating the harassment of monastic orders, the discrimination against Catholics in the bureaucracy, and the continued prevalence of duelling in the German army. He took a prominent role in denouncing the oppression of the Polish population of the Prussian East, condemning the chauvinism and ruthlessness that gave Germany such a bad reputation abroad.

The prewar international tensions forced Erzberger to pay some attention to foreign affairs, and his conceptions of foreign policy date from these years. He took a leading role in promoting Germany's military and naval armaments. Political controversy centered largely around methods of raising sufficient taxes to cover the ever-increasing cost of national security. Erzberger acted, from his vantage seat in the Budget Committee, as party spokesman on all financial legislation. The 1909 finance reform had major political implications by leading to Bülow's fall from power. The Emperor used it as a good occasion for firing his

Chancellor, believing that he had been betrayed the previous year in the famous *Daily Telegraph* Incident. Erzberger played a significant role in fanning William's suspicions against Bülow. The immovability of German politics was revealed, however, when the Incident had no constitutional consequences, though it convinced some people—including Erzberger—that Germany must advance in the direction of giving the *Reichstag* enlarged powers. Erzberger believed on the eve of the World War One that the introduction of the parliamentary system had become inevitable, while simultaneously holding completely false notions concerning the future structure of German politics. He expected a governing coalition of Zentrum and Conservatives to win a majority in the *Reichstag,* and was unmeasured in his abuse of Liberals and Socialists. It was ironical that he himself was to become the main architect of the Weimar coalition—composed of Zentrum, Liberals, and Socialists—only three years later.

Family Life

Erzberger's temporary eclipse after 1907 arose not only from dissatisfaction with his part in provoking the Chancellor into dissolving the *Reichstag.* The Zentrum hoped to break up the "Bülow Block" by wooing the Conservatives, who were uneasy about Bülow's concessions to their Liberal Block partners. The Zentrum strategy required a shift to the Right within the party and the neutralization of the Left around Erzberger. The older leaders—Spahn, Hertling, Gröber, and Trimborn—now seized a firmer grip upon the leadership, and were resolved to suppress future instances of indiscipline. Their task was facilitated by the fact that Erzberger's reputation was clouded by the Pöplau and Janke affairs (both up for trial in 1907). Erzberger was forced to lie low until making his comeback at the time of the finance reform of 1909, when the party found his expert knowledge indispensable in the Budget Committee.

The political fallowness of the years after 1907 enabled Erzberger to devote more time to his family and friends than he was able to at any other period of his life. His close friendship with Dr. Josef Hammer, who was to administer his papers and financial affairs after his assassination, dates from 1906. Hammer, a fellow Württemberger five years Erzberger's junior, was an ordained priest. His bishop had sent him to the University of Berlin to get a doctorate in classics. He met Erzberger while serving as priest at the famous St. Hedwig's Hospital, which was located close to Erzberger's apartment. They took many walks together until Hammer left Berlin in 1908, and saw each other at frequent intervals until Erzberger's death.[1] He has remained deeply devoted to the memory of his famous friend, and has written a memoir that contains valuable information about Erzberger's private life.

Hammer describes Erzberger's marriage with Paula Eberhard as follows:

> It united two apparently opposite natures: he was full of virile energy and combative audacity; she was of frail health and of dignified, almost shy reserve. And yet they supplemented one another so as to be united in an unusually happy and harmonious marriage. He was extremely considerate of her delicate health, she rewarded him by an unselfish love and by running a model household.[2]

Hammer was responsible for saving Mrs. Erzberger's life in 1908. She had tuberculosis and was convinced that there was no chance of recovery; four of her brothers and sisters had already died of the same disease. She resisted Erzberger's urging that she go to Italy for a cure, wishing to die by the side of her husband rather than in some distant land. It turned out to be fortunate that Hammer came down with a serious case of pleurisy at this time, requiring prolonged convalescence in Italy. He persuaded Mrs. Erzberger to go to Lake Garda with him for several months, where she was completely restored to health.[3] She has lived to ripe old age; when I visited her in Stuttgart in 1956 she was still deeply grateful for Dr. Hammer's help. She then lived with her only surviving daughter in a Catholic nursing home, with her apartment showing many signs of the simple piety which all of Erzberger's friends hailed as the mainspring of her character.

Erzberger's mother took care of the grandchildren while Mrs. Erzberger was recovering in Italy. The oldest child and only boy, Oskar, was born in Stuttgart on December 18, 1900, and early showed qualities akin to his father. He entered the humanist Bismarck Gymnasium in Berlin-Wilmersdorf in 1907, and showed special aptitude in history and mathematics. His first sister, Maria, was born in Stuttgart on October 13, 1902.[4] Hammer gives the following description of the Erzberger household:

> It was dominated by a spirit of piety, regularity, and punctuality, with both parents devoting much time to the religious education of their children. Erzberger was most delighted when Oskar and Maria showed an interest in religious questions, and he demanded a written résumé of the main points covered by the Church sermon every Sunday. The first

[1] The information about Dr. Hammer comes from personal talks with him.
[2] Hammer, *Erzberger,* p. 97.
[3] Personal information from Dr. Hammer and Mrs. Erzberger.
[4] Hammer, *Erzberger,* p. 98.

communion service in which the children participated was a great family event. Erzberger wrote this dedication in the prayer book that he presented to Maria that day.

"Dear Maria! The most beautiful day of your life is this April 14, 1912, on which the Saviour first entered into your innocent heart. May you be ready throughout your entire life to receive him at all times—be it as dispenser of grace or as judge! This is the only wish of your father." [5]

The children were devoted to their father, sometimes complaining that they saw so little of him. His *Zentrumskorrespondenz* kept him in Berlin all summer while his family was vacationing in the country. As the children grew older he sometimes took them on some of his political trips, and Maria loved to remember later how he frequently broke off political conversations with his colleagues in order to answer her questions. The family rather stood in awe of his work, though there was never any stuffy adulation. Erzberger loved to bring home political caricatures directed against himself, and these delighted the entire family circle.[6] A second daughter, Gabriele, was born in Berlin on March 20, 1914, twelve years after the next oldest child. When I visited her in 1956 she was working as a translator in a Stuttgart insurance firm. She scarcely remembered her father, having been only seven when he was assassinated, and those seven years had seen Erzberger preoccupied with the war and the postwar chaos. So she had even less of her father than her brother and sister, and even they had seen little of him during the relatively tranquil years from 1907 to 1914. Erzberger's métier was politics, and he subordinated all personal considerations to his political career.

Social and Economic Policy

One of Erzberger's main preoccupations in the prewar years was to develop a comprehensive social and economic policy that could keep the conflicting social elements within the Zentrum in a tolerable degree of harmony. He felt that to compromise internal Zentrum differences was performing a service not only to the party but also to the nation. Zentrum cleavages represented a microcosm of the cleavages of the nation as a whole, and their resolution provided a formula for national unity. Erzberger liked to boast about the role of his party in promoting stability and compromise, and claimed that if it did not exist it would have to be invented for the good of the Fatherland:

> The main value of the Zentrum lies in the fact that it protects our Fatherland against sudden political crises based upon party maneuvers,

[5] *ibid.*, p. 99.
[6] *ibid.*, p. 100.

that it insists upon a certain continuity in our internal policies and that it always seeks a compromise between the extremes of Right and Left; this makes it a strong bulwark against Social Democracy. The German Empire cannot do without the Zentrum without running into trouble; this judgment is justified by a look both at the past and the present as well as the composition of the party. The Zentrum, alone among German parties, mirrors most clearly the Imperial idea (*Deutschen Reichsgedanken*) because it comprehends all the geographical and economic groups (*Stämme und Stände*) of the Empire.[7]

Erzberger thought that the Zentrum Party was especially well qualified to reconcile social antagonisms because its Christian principles were equally hostile to the opposite theoretical extremes of *laissez faire,* which ignored the basic dictates of justice, and meddling state socialism, which destroyed the spirit of industry, economy, and self-help. His own social policy consisted of championing protection, social insurance, state-supervised cartels, and an independent trade-union movement. He was a strong protectionist all his life, for common-sense rather than nationalist reasons.[8] He saw that German agriculture could not compete with the American Middlewest. He argued that industrial tariffs had not impeded German economic development; the rate of progress had, indeed, been more rapid in the protectionist states of Germany and America than in free-trade England. He believed that Germany's advanced social legislation required the protection of high tariff walls. Erzberger was especially proud of the German social insurance system, and liked to emphasize the role of the Zentrum in its creation.[9] It not only mitigated avoidable human suffering but also promoted self-respect by replacing charity with legal claims. He was impatient with those conservative critics who blamed it for not achieving Bismarck's aim of breaking the Socialist grip over the working class. A progressive social policy must be understood as a Christian mandate rather than as an opportunist political device.[10]

Erzberger's attitude towards cartels showed a ready acceptance of what he recognized to be an inescapable fact of modern industrialism. He never shared the Liberal worship of competition, and had the common sense to see that monopolists do not necessarily behave in the manner described by *laissez-faire* economists. He relied upon a strong state to restrain monopolist abuses—preferably a democratic state, but

[7] Erzberger, *Zentrumspolitik*, x (1912), 104.
[8] A good statement of his protectionist views can be found in his anti-Socialist pamphlet, *Sozialdemokratie und Zollpolitik* (M. Gladbach, 1908).
[9] Erzberger gave a full account of the comprehensive 1911 insurance code in his *Zentrumspolitik*, ix (1911), 126–60. He was evidently not clear in his mind about the feasibility of unemployment insurance. *ibid.,* xii (1914), 49–50.
[10] Erzberger, *Politik und Völkerleben*, pp. 54–57.

even a Junker-dominated state was unlikely to become a narrow tool of capitalist interests. He was not impressed by the American record of trust-busting, and in any case thought this policy unsuitable under the very different conditions in Germany.[11] Erzberger saw in strong trade unions a valuable corrective to the power of cartels, though it would be too much to say that he developed an explicit concept of "countervailing power." He valued unions not only for their material achievements but also for their educational function of giving the working class experience in organization and discussion. His attitude towards Socialist unions became more mellow as he was personally removed from the organizational struggle, but he continued to taunt the Socialist unions for their subservience to the impracticable aims of the Socialist Party.[12] All these views on protection, insurance, cartels, and unions emerged from Erzberger's practical grasp of German realities, not from adherence to any general theory; they were not much more than an expression of Zentrum policy as it had developed over the prior forty years. His reformism was purely pragmatic at this time. Erzberger's acceptance of a general theory of social reconstruction—the doctrine of Christian Solidarism developed by the Jesuit Heinrich Pesch—came only after the war; by that time he had lost much of his optimism about the German social structure, and saw the need for fundamental changes in the *status quo* in accordance with a general plan.

The Zentrumsstreit and Catholic Grievances

The unity of the party was endangered not only by social conflicts. It seemed for a while that ideological cleavages might prove even more dangerous. The years from 1909 to 1913 saw the so-called *Zentrumsstreit,* or conflict concerning the nature of the party, flare up into bitterness. A group centered around Berlin, and therefore known as the *Berliner Richtung,* wanted to make specifically Catholic principles the guideposts for all party activity in every field. A larger group, centered around Cologne and therefore known as the *Kölnische Richtung* wanted, on the contrary, a party dedicated to general Christian rather than to specifically Catholic principles. It feared that a confessional Catholic party must inevitably arouse Protestant bigotry. The Cologne leaders desired a maximum of cooperation with like-minded Protestant elements, foreshadowing in this the post-1945 Christian Democratic Union. Both sides believed with passionate intensity that their view,

---

[11] *ibid.,* pp. 52–53. Erzberger, *Zentrumspolitik,* VI (1908), 141–42.
[12] Erzberger, *Politik und Völkerleben,* pp. 53–54.

and theirs alone, could safeguard the interests of Catholicism in the somewhat alien climate of Wilhelmine Germany. The Cologners believed that the Berliners were narrow doctrinaires. The Berliners retorted by accusing the Cologners of being lukewarm in their Catholic faith; they even denounced some Cologne leaders to the Vatican as fit candidates for excommunication. The ensuing bitterness of both sides led to a lapse in the good manners and broadminded charity that had characterized the Zentrum Party since Windthorst's days.[13]

Erzberger was at first identified in the popular mind with the *Berliner Richtung*. His colleague in the colonial campaign, Hermann Roeren, was the main leader of the Berliners. Count von Oppersdorff, a Silesian magnate with whom Erzberger was on intimate terms, edited *Klarheit und Wahrheit,* the main organ of the Berlin group. Erzberger ghost-wrote a pamphlet in 1910 against Martin Spahn, the son of his old Zentrum enemy Peter Spahn.[14] The son had carried the Cologne position to the point where he was disavowed by the leaders of this group. He wanted the Zentrum Party to practically accept the principles of Prussian Conservatism to make it lose its "alien" character. Spahn was already on the political road that led him to join the Nationalist Party in the early years of the Weimar Republic.[15]

The popular identification of Erzberger with the Berlin position was based upon his personal associations and his prominent role in the campaign against Spahn. Erzberger had, in fact, too much good sense to take a sectarian view of the Zentrum Party. His practical mind was bound to be repelled by the Berlin attempt to secure a correct ideological definition of the party. He saw the folly of referring all party decisions to the arbitrament of specifically Catholic principles. What were Catholic principles in the field of financial, military, and foreign

[13] The best account of the *Zentrumsstreit* is Bachem, *Zentrumspartei*, Vol. VII, Ch. III, though it reads like a pamphleteering attack on the *Berliner Richtung*. Ludwig Bergsträsser, "Der Riss im Zentrumsturm," in *Akademische Blätter*, Vol. XXV, Nr. 16 (Berlin, Nov. 16, 1910), pp. 241–46, is a dispassionate account by a Liberal Protestant. The main documents are printed in Ludwig Bergsträsser, *Der Politische Katholizismus* (Munich, 1923), II, 332–87. The best statement of the Berlin position is H. Roeren, *Zentrum und Kölner Richtung* (Trier, 1913).
[14] Count von Oppersdorff, *Eine Gewissensfrage. Ist Martin Spahn ein Zentrumsmann?* (Berlin, 1910). Erzberger's authorship was known to the Spahn family. Letter of Richard Müller to K. Bachem, Oct. 12, 1928, in *Bachem Papers*.
[15] Erzberger gives an account of the Spahn matter in *Zentrumspolitik*, IX (1911), 6–8. Spahn has a revealing autobiographical sketch in the collection of conservative biographies edited by Hans von Arnim and Georg von Below, *Deutscher Aufstieg* (Berlin, 1925), pp. 479–88. The best expression of Spahn's political views is in his *Deutsche Lebensfragen* (Munich, 1914), which was answered by Joseph Hess in his *Deutsche Lebensfragen? Eine Auseinandersetzung mit Martin Spahn* (Düsseldorf, 1914).

policy? They simply did not exist. Erzberger deplored the tactic of the Berliners of questioning the religious faith of their opponents. He was skeptical about the chances of securing wide Protestant support for the Zentrum, but he supported all steps in this direction. He thought that the whole controversy had led to unnecessary party divisions, and had distracted attention from the major task of seeing that Catholics secured justice within the existing framework of German society.[16]

Erzberger saw in the championing of Catholic grievances not only a dictate of justice but also a valuable cement of party unity. Some Zentrum leaders advocated a cautious attitude in the face of Protestant prejudices, but this was not Erzberger's view. He was never one to suffer in silence for fear of provoking retaliation. His attitude is revealed in this truculent statement, which explains his relationship to the bureaucracy in a nutshell:

> To achieve this end [i.e. termination of discrimination against Catholics] the Catholic population must fight all down the line and secure remedies through the weapon of public exposure. One can understand the reasons for Catholic silence in the past, but one cannot approve them. One frequently encounters the view—for heaven's sake, do not bring up this matter in parliament or the press, it would only lead to renewed chicanery. This attitude reveals a total lack of understanding of bureaucracy. Bureaucrats fear only one thing: publicity. Those who kow-tow before bureaucrats are lost; they will only find bureaucrats increasingly arrogant and brutal. Silence and patience are the most fruitful soil for bureaucratic cruelty; while bureaucrats give way to, and indeed fear, those who know how to use their elbows.[17]

Erzberger drew up a bill of particulars against the bureaucrats who administered anti-Catholic laws with bigoted severity. The anti-Jesuit law of 1872 was a relic of the *Kulturkampf;* its worst clause, the total banishment of Jesuits from Germany, had been recently repealed. But the paragraphs banning Jesuit associations and prohibiting Jesuits from carrying out the work of the Order remained. The Prussian bureaucracy defined a Jesuit association as existing whenever two Jesuits lived in the same house; they defined the prohibited activities to include the individual celebration of the mass. Erzberger vainly demanded a more tolerant interpretation of the law. He also denounced

---

[16] Erzberger made strong attacks upon the *Berliner Richtung* in his *Der Stille Kulturkampf* (Hamm, 1912), pp. 52–53, *Das Deutsche Zentrum* (Amsterdam, 2nd ed., 1912), Ch. II, and *Politik und Völkerleben* (Würzburg, n.d. [1914]), p. 18. A bitter Berlin reply is Montanus (pseud.), "Opus 117," in *Klarheit und Wahrheit*, Vol. 1, No. 44 (Nov. 3, 1912), pp. 354–56, a review of Erzberger's *Der Stille Kulturkampf*.

[17] Erzberger, *Der Stille Kulturkampf*, pp. 5–6.

the chicanery employed in harassing several other Catholic orders. Permission to establish new settlements was usually refused, or granted only after an endless bureaucratic run-around. Officials insisted upon frequent visitations to check alleged immoral practices. Many German orders—excluded from Germany by prohibition or harassment—had established schools in neighboring countries, and Catholic parents had long sent their children to these institutions. This was virtually prohibited by a decree in May 1912 that condemned the allegedly un-German education offered. Great obstacles were placed in the path of those wishing to establish Catholic schools in those parts of Northern Germany to which Catholics had recently migrated. Several small North German states continued their legal discrimination against Catholics, because the *Toleranzantrag*—which Erzberger had championed so eloquently in 1905—had never been enacted into law. Erzberger saw in all these practices a "silent *Kulturkampf*" that self-respecting Catholics could no longer tolerate.[18]

Another major grievance was the discrimination practiced against Catholics in both the Imperial and the Prussian bureaucracy. Erzberger assembled statistics that showed that both Germany and Prussia were approximately 62 percent Protestant and 36 percent Catholic; yet the bureaucracy was 71 percent Protestant and only 27 percent Catholic. These figures did not tell the whole story, for the worst discrimination was the virtual exclusion of Catholics from the really important administrative posts; only Catholics who repudiated the Zentrum Party had a reasonable chance of promotion. In the officer corps the religious ratio was 83 percent Protestant and 16 percent Catholic, due to the Protestant-Junker predominance but also due to the dilemma presented to Catholic officers by the prevalent code of honor that required duelling despite the fact that this was absolutely prohibited by the Church.[19]

Erzberger had clashed with General von Heeringen, the War Minister, in a military debate on April 24, 1912, on Heeringen's defense of the expulsion of non-duellers from the officer corps. Erzberger decided to develop his views on this question in a special pamphlet. He analyzed the concept of honor, traced the history of duelling, marshalled the arguments against it, described present malpractices, and suggested remedies. Erzberger defined honor as a personal attribute, which in

---

[18] *ibid.,* pp. 21–30.

[19] *ibid.,* pp. 17–21. Erzberger also defended the Catholic position when some Protestants got excited about the imposing, by Pope Pius X, of an anti-Modernist oath upon Catholics, and wanted to remove jurors from public positions. See his *Der Modernisteneid* (Berlin, 1911), a reply to such Protestant attacks as Hermann Mulert, *Antimoderisteneid, freie Forschung, und theologische Fakultäten* (Halle, 1911).

the Christian (as opposed to the Aristotelian) conception was independent of the opinion of others—indeed a Christian's worth was measured by his defiance of community standards if these were contrary to the law of God. His honor could not be injured by the action of other parties, hence it could not be defended by shooting down those parties. Duelling did not fit into the Christian conception of values, and it was condemned by all of the Christian churches and by Christian secular rulers. Yet the practice continued at the present time, and indeed remained semi-mandatory in the German army whenever a challenge was issued. Duelling and fencing were part of the way of life of the student corps at the university. There were stringent laws against duelling, but the public prosecutor refused to enforce those laws. Erzberger thought that this privileged status for duelling was a public scandal, a view that was calculated to provoke upper-class animosities since almost all leading Protestant Germans were proud of their happy university years, and identified themselves with the army.[20]

Erzberger was never satisfied merely to denounce an abuse; he always made specific remedial suggestions. He demanded a new cabinet order that would prohibit duelling in the army on pain of dismissal from the service. He advocated the establishment of special honor courts to give an alternative method of protection to those who persisted in taking a non-Christian view of their personal honor. Erzberger hoped that the Anti-Duelling League, founded by Father Raimundus, OP (formerly Prince Löwenstein), to whom his book was dedicated, would have an educational effect upon public opinion. Erzberger was hopeful that this Catholic grievance and national scandal would soon be eliminated. He simply could not believe that a practice so contrary to reason, religion, and social order could continue to prevail.[21]

Championing Polish Grievances

Erzberger's Catholic zeal also made him an opponent of the Prussian mistreatment of the predominantly Catholic Polish population of the eastern provinces.[22] A gift for understanding or governing alien populations was not one of the virtues of Imperial Germany. The record in Alsace-Lorraine, North Schleswig, and Posen included some administrative achievements, but failed completely to secure the affection of the alien populations. The case of Prussian Poland was especially notorious. The Poles were making rapid progress in population and

[20] Erzberger, *Duell und Ehre* (Würzburg, 1912). Also his *Zentrumspolitik*, x (1912), 69–73.
[21] Erzberger, *Duell und Ehre*, pp. 37–52.
[22] Erzberger, *Der Kampf gegen den Katholizismus in der Ostmark. Material zur Beurteilung der Polenfrage durch die deutschen Katholiken* (Berlin, 1908).

educational achievement, thereby arousing the fear and anger of German nationalists. The Prussian state had sought to meet this challenge by founding a Settlement Commission in 1886 charged with establishing German settlers in the east. Bülow, by way of proving his strident nationalism, had supplemented this policy by such measures as the compulsory expropriation of Polish-owned land for purely ethnic reasons which, in Erzberger's words, "one would not have believed possible in a civilized nation."[23] The anti-Polish policy culminated in a law in 1908 that prohibited the use of the Polish language at public meetings. Erzberger thought that any attack on the use of the mother tongue was a clear violation of natural law. He was horrified by the entire concept of Germanization which lay at the root of these policies, all the more since Germanization also meant Protestant discrimination against Catholics.[24]

Erzberger showed that the Settlement Commission was discriminating systematically against the settlement of Catholics, presumably on the grounds that Catholics were poor Germans. He noted that of some 100,000 Germans settled since 1887 only 3½ percent were Catholics, and called upon his fellow Catholics to protest against this discriminatory situation. His aim, of course, was not to increase the proportion of Catholics helped by the Commission, but rather to blacken its character in the eyes of Zentrum voters.[25]

Erzberger was completely incapable of moderating this anti-Polish policy, but he found consolation in demonstrating that it was a grotesque failure. The land farmed by Germans had actually decreased by a considerable area since 1886. The 100,000 Germans settled since 1887 were a drop in the bucket compared to the 4,000,000 Poles who were multiplying rapidly. The atmosphere of national struggle in the province of Posen had become intolerable. Espionage and denunciation of allegedly un-national behavior flourished among Poles and Germans alike. Economic and social boycotts were frequent. The Poles took vigorous counter-measures against their German oppressors by founding cooperatives, banks, fellowships for gifted Polish students, and cultural associations. Erzberger rejoiced at this Polish resistance, and opposed the increased repression which it provoked:

> It is not surprising that the Poles resist the measures of the [Prussian] state; for they are being treated worse than the natives in our colonies. The question whether or not the Poles were the initial aggressors [in

[23] *ibid.*, p. 5.
[24] *ibid.*, pp. 34–51. Also Erzberger, *Zentrumspolitik*, VI (1908), 28–57 for the entire *Vereinsgesetz*, of which the language prohibition was one section.
[25] Erzberger, *Der Stille Kulturkampf*, p. 14.

boycott measures, cultural associations etc.] is of no practical importance; a wise government rejoices when its citizens take measures to improve their cultural welfare; but with the Poles this natural striving is treated as a crime that has to be repressed by the most stringent laws. The Pole must fight against this system if he retains a spark of national pride, exactly as does the German wherever his native tongue and national customs are threatened (in Russia, Hungary etc.). But when the Poles offer resistance one speaks of insubordination and disloyalty. . . ."[26]

Erzberger's campaign against the Polish policy of his government attained the moral grandeur of his exposure of colonial abuses. He placed the dictates of justice above a narrowly chauvinist view of national self-interest, thereby provoking the wrath of professional patriots. Yet his broad conception of national interest was far more profound than the crude views of his critics. Erzberger knew that the barbarous anti-Polish policies were doing irreparable injury to Germany's reputation abroad. He recognized that they put a severe strain upon the Austro-German alliance, the keystone of German foreign policy, because the Poles were an influential group in the Hapsburg monarchy.

Erzberger's Conceptions of Foreign Policy

Erzberger's belief in the Austrian alliance reflected the Catholic Great German views current in South Germany. He looked upon the 1879 alliance as Bismarck's partial repentance for the civil war of 1866. Erzberger was deeply interested in the fate of the last great Catholic monarchy in Europe. He took an optimistic view of future Hapsburg prospects, probably because he overestimated the strength of a unifying clericalism as a check upon centrifugal nationalism. Hence he never took the view that Germany had tied herself to a corpse and ought to look for more viable allies. He rejoiced at all signs of Austrian diplomatic vigor. He criticized Bülow during the Bosnian crisis of 1908–1909 for faltering initially in his duty towards Germany's ally, and approved of the German semi-ultimatum to Russia in March 1909 that allowed Austria her great prestige victory. His Hapsburg sympathies made him blind to the claims of Serb nationalism, which he distrusted as a cat's paw for Russian imperialism.[27]

Erzberger's democratic, clerical, and pro-Hapsburg views all combined to make him a sharp foe of Tsarist Russia. His democratic principles made him abhor the bureaucratic absolutism that had survived the 1905 revolution. His anti-Prussian background made him in-

[26] Erzberger, *Kampf gegen den Katholizismus,* pp. 60–61.
[27] Erzberger, *Zentrumspolitik,* VII (1909), 48–50.

different to the traditional dynastic ties between the Hohenzollerns and Romanovs, and he disliked the Russian ruling class for its affinity to Prussian Junkerism. His Catholicism was hostile to the aggressive Greek Orthodoxy propagated by Moscow. His sympathy for the Poles made him sensitive to the oppression of Russian Poland. Erzberger saw in Pan-Slavism a danger not only to the Hapsburg Empire but to Europe as a whole. He saw that the establishment of Russian power in Prague would be a mortal blow to Germany's security. He never criticized Caprivi's failure to renew the Reinsurance Treaty in 1890, and evidently looked upon Russian hostility as an inescapable fact of life. These views formed the natural background for his enthusiastic support of the policy of liberating the border nationalities of the Russian Empire during the First World War.[28]

Erzberger hoped for a genuine rapprochement with France while at the same time fearing that the Franco-Russian alliance placed an insuperable obstacle in its way. He criticized Bülow's handling of the First Morocco Crisis because the German Chancellor had not accepted Rouvier's proffered hand after the fall of Delcassé. The 1909 Franco-German rapprochement over Morocco was a case of too little and too late, though Erzberger gave it his full approval. He was distressed by the rise of Poincarist revanchism in the years before 1914, and thought that France was the main culprit in the arms race which was placing intolerable burdens upon Germany and France alike. Erzberger supported Franco-German reconciliation and attended the Basel meeting of the international parliamentary union in 1913. He avoided the extreme Francophobia which was prevalent among German Catholics after the anti-clerical measures of 1904. For Erzberger, France was not only the country of Masonry, atheism, and epicurean materialism, but also the center of modern Catholic social thought from Lamennais to Marc Sangnier.[29]

Erzberger's attitude toward England was marked by prejudice and ignorance, though at times these were overcome by his common sense. He never visited England and had little direct contact with English people, and his temperament was completely alien to the entire Puritan tradition. He shared the common Continental attitude that the frequent British identification of self-interest and high moral principle reveals a special national talent for hypocrisy. He accepted the interpretation of English foreign policy that ascribed English greatness to

[28] For Erzberger's attitude towards Russia, see his *Erlebnisse,* p. 11, quoting a 1914 memorandum.
[29] Erzberger, *Zentrumspolitik,* VII (1909), 50, and *Die Rüstungsausgaben des deutschen Reichs* (Stuttgart, 1914), Ch. III.

the exploitation of Continental dissensions in the name of the balance of power. Erzberger shared the common German view that English opposition to German naval expansion was a characteristic act of national impertinence. He was especially aroused by one of Churchill's speeches in which the English statesman called the British navy a necessity while Germany's was only a luxury, and threw out the following retort:

> I must say a word against the assertion that the navy is an unnecessary luxury for Germany. One can consider the navy a luxury only from the point of view of the arsonist; he believes that a fire department is a luxury [*laughter*] but other people do not. We will not allow ourselves to be pressured by such speeches, no matter how highly placed the orator, into abandoning the view that Germany, now that it is a great power with world-wide obligations, requires a big Navy.[30]

Erzberger was insufficiently aware of the supreme importance for Germany of reaching a political understanding with England. He was too much a son of the late Wilhelmine Empire to recognize that the precarious geographical position of Germany dictated a special caution in foreign policy. With Russian hostility inevitable and rapprochement with France problematical, the minimum aim of German policy should have been to prevent English hostility. Erzberger recognized this fact only during occasional moments of insight. He then rejected the pessimistic theory that English hostility was inevitable in the light of either Germany's commercial expansion or her achievement of a strong Continental position (the view of Tirpitz and his school). While recognizing the strength of English Germanophobia he was well aware that there were counter-forces at work, especially in the Liberal Party that governed after 1905. He could be critical of the irresponsible attitude of much of the German press in its comments on English affairs, stating that it antagonized broad strata of English opinion gratuitously.[31]

The great flaw of Erzberger's outlook on English affairs was that he never understood the fundamental fact that the development of the German navy could be interpreted by England only as a mortal threat against her very existence as a great power. This view was common ground for Tories and Liberals alike. They thought that a naval agreement safeguarding England's supremacy was the only alternative to a naval race that must inevitably poison political relations between the two countries. Germany did not aim at building a navy equal to Brit-

[30] *Reichstag Debates,* Vol. CCLXXXIII, April 24, 1912, p. 1377.
[31] Erzberger, *Zentrumspolitik,* II (1905), 67–68.

ain's; but the avowed plan of a "risk fleet," the term for a navy which would present England with the risk of such severe losses in combat that she would hesitate to enter into a war with Germany, was almost as intolerable for Britain. Erzberger fully accepted the concept of the risk fleet, and thereby assumed his share of responsibility for the disastrous deterioration of Anglo-German relations. He accepted the foolish notion that the "risk fleet" was the bulwark of peace because it served to prevent a frivolous English attack.[32] He categorically rejected a naval limitation treaty:

> We cannot accept an understanding with England at the price of our naval defense (*Seewehr*). National reasons preclude such an understanding. To renounce a navy appropriate to our power position would make the German people an English satellite—and this we do not want. A voluntary renunciation of the building of a navy according to our own judgment would be the end of Germany's world policy (*Weltmachtspolitik*). Such a renunciation would amount to admitting the bankruptcy of that naval policy which my friends have successfully supported for the last seventeen years.[33]

One may say, in summary, that Erzberger's views on foreign policy were no wiser than those of most of his contemporaries, and that they were quite inadequate to cope with the real dangers confronting Germany. He accepted the European system of competing sovereign states as he found it, and wished only to protect Germany's security within it. His assessment of the states that composed that system was often arbitrary and subjective. He did not subordinate his personal inclinations to the austere and objective doctrine of Reason of State. Hence he failed to advise sound policies which might have given Germany a maximum degree of security. His hopeful judgment about the future of Austria and his uncritical acceptance of the Big Navy policy were his main mistakes.

Many Europeans living before 1914 condemned the entire European state system, with its inevitable alliances leading to inevitable wars. They thought to overcome it by the call for a higher type of international order symbolized by the aspirations of Cobden and Gladstone. Erzberger was not one of these, though the universalist tradition of his Church might have provided him with a basis for transcending the individual sovereign state as the ultimate political value. His conversion to League of Nations and disarmament principles was to come only after the experiences of the First World War. In the prewar era Erz-

---

[32] *ibid.*, IX (1911), 66–71. Also Erzberger, *Rüstungsausgaben*, p. 28.
[33] *Reichstag Debates*, Vol. ccxciii, Feb. 19, 1914, p. 7506.

berger opposed any general system of disarmament and exercised his intellectual acuteness in pointing out the difficulties inherent in such a system. Sovereign nations could not readily agree upon the ratio of their respective forces without one or both sides experiencing insecurity and loss of prestige. They could never agree upon an adequate inspection system. They could not agree upon compulsory arbitration in cases where their vital interests were involved. Even seemingly technical matters, like the codification of maritime law, were impossible to achieve in the light of divergent national interests when contemplating the contingency of war.[34]

Erzberger deplored the strain which was put upon international confidence and domestic social progress by the wasteful accumulation of armaments, and he especially deplored the prevalence of a militarist spirit generated by feelings of national insecurity. But he saw no possibility of overcoming this international anarchy and only hoped that the fear of the magnitude of a modern war might put the spirit of peace into the hearts of statesmen. He foresaw the horrors of a total war between peoples inflamed by nationalism, and the vast economic dislocation that would be caused by the breakdown of interdependent industrial economies. His prophetic anticipations were for once not matched by constructive proposals to avoid disaster. He was caught in the shackles of a historically established international system that was stronger than the good will and insights of the men of the age. The international system based upon competing states ruled by rational statesmen with limited aims had been made anachronistic by the development of democracy, nationalism, and the industrial revolution; Erzberger, like most of his contemporaries, approached these new factors in a too optimistic spirit, and did not fully recognize that they demanded a complete revision of thought about war and diplomacy. His partial perception of the implications of democracy and industrialism did not make him a crusader for a better international system. Such a crusade would, in any case, have been hopeless in Welhelmine Germany.

Military and Financial Policy

Erzberger clearly saw what the Socialists obstinately refused to see, that unilateral disarmament would be suicidal for a country in Germany's precarious position. His realism was based upon expert knowl-

---

[34] Erzberger, *Politik und Völkerleben*, pp. 32–35. Erzberger had approved of Hertling's April 30, 1907 ridicule of disarmament proposals in *Zentrumspolitik*, v (1907), 32. He endorsed Bethmann's opposition to disarmament in his *Rüstungsausgaben*, Ch. IV.

edge of military affairs. He had become the regular reporter on military bills for the Budget Committee of the *Reichstag* after his successful championing of the 1906 military pensions law. Successive War Ministers praised his work for the army despite the fact that he had quarrelled with them over the duelling question and various other reforms primarily aimed at helping the common soldier.[35] Erzberger was a prominent champion of the great military increases of 1911, 1912, and 1913—a fact which always embarrassed his Nationalist critics because it did not fit into their image of a man utterly devoid of patriotism. The government relied heavily upon Erzberger in all military debates, and this was especially true at the time of the great 1913 Army Expansion bill. Erzberger urged the proposed increase by pointing to the danger of an ever-worsening international situation: Russia recovering from the Russo-Japanese war, the explosive situation in the Balkans, the heavy armament increases in Russia and France, the Italian preoccupation with Africa, and the hostility of England.[36] He ridiculed the Socialist opposition by exposing its sterile adherence to doctrinaire principles in defiance of common sense. Socialist newspapers admitted, indeed advertised, the imminence of international dangers; yet Socialist leaders would not abandon their doctrinaire habit of voting against all military bills regardless of the dangers confronting Germany. He vainly pleaded with them to abandon an attitude which, if successful, would leave Germany open to attack by the Tsarist autocracy.

Erzberger was always convinced, and proved to his own satisfaction in a pamphlet published in June 1914, that Germany was the relatively innocent victim of an arms race started by her potential enemies.[37] Both Russia and France spent more annually on armaments per head of population than did Germany and Austria, although they were poorer countries and were not in a precarious geographical position in the center of Europe. He deplored the incessant advances of arms expenditure since 1900, blaming this upon the increasing rate of technological innovation but especially upon the "encirclement policy" (*Einkreisungspolitik*) of England, France, and Russia against Germany. He claimed that Bismarck's policy during the period of German diplomatic ascendancy had, in contrast, aimed so obviously at peace that it had not provoked an arms race of similar intensity. Erz-

---

[35] Such as free railroad tickets home once a year, convenient training periods for reservists, limitation of the military punishment of *Dunkelarrest* (confinement in a darkened room), etc. Erzberger, *Zentrumspolitik*, XI (1913), 44-47 and XII (1914), 35-39.
[36] Erzberger, *Zentrumspolitik*, XI (1913), 21-35.
[37] Erzberger, *Rüstungsausgaben*, Ch. III.

berger proved that Germany had not led the pace in quantitative expansion or technological innovation. Germany had been slow in the development of the self-loading rifle, the machine gun, heavy artillery, bicycle companies, and military aviation. Her naval authorities had proved laggards in the development of dreadnoughts and submarines. Erzberger vainly pressed for the rapid development of military aviation in the summer of 1912.[38] Germany's army was lagging not only in equipment but also in sheer numbers. Fiscal considerations prevented military service from being truly universal. Some 100,000 eligible young men—Erzberger had been one of these—did not receive the annual call to the colors. Germany introduced a permanent two-year term of service in 1893, while France returned to a three-year term in 1913. The great German army expansion in 1913 had been a belated response to French and Russian military preparations. The Russians had received vast French credits to build strategic railroads in Poland that would speed up Russian mobilization. The French had planned the lengthening of their term of service and a big armament loan before Germany had announced the provisions of her 1913 military bill. Germany could, in view of these facts, defy the common accusation of being the prime mover in the armament race; the question was rather whether she had done enough to prepare herself for all future contingencies.[39]

Erzberger was appalled by the costs of armaments, but took comfort in the fact that these were far less than those of either victory or defeat in war. He sincerely believed that a strong Germany was the best guarantee of European peace.

> A weak Germany has historically increased the danger of war, besides making her the European cockpit. Our strong Empire has in contrast become a pillar of peace, though this peace is purchased by ever-increasing military expenditures. The price has been heavy, but certainly not too heavy, as is proved by the continuous increase of our national wealth. Forty years of high military expenditures cost less than half a year of victorious war, not to speak of the price of military defeat. One of the casualties of defeat would be the unity of the Empire.[40]

Erzberger defended military expenses as an insurance premium carried by the Empire; his statistical mind delighted in putting this in specific numerical terms. He figured that military expenses in 1914

[38] See his correspondence with Tirpitz, then vacationing in Switzerland, in Alfred von Tirpitz, *Erinnerungen* (Leipzig, 1920), pp. 119–21.

[39] The view that the War Ministry and *Reichstag* ought to have made more strenuous armament efforts is the main thesis of Hans Herzfeld, *Die deutsche Rüstungspolitik vor dem Weltkriege* (Bonn, 1923).

[40] Erzberger, *Rüstungsausgaben*, p. 7.

amounted to 2.2 billion marks, which constituted only 5.6 percent of the national income (40 billions) and .67 percent of the estimated national wealth (320 billions). This was an insurance policy that Germany was easily able to carry.[41]

The government secured the passage of successive military bills with relatively little difficulty in the prewar era, thanks largely to the support of the Zentrum Party and its military expert, Erzberger. The raising of the necessary taxes proved a far more contentious matter, and was to lead to the major parliamentary struggles of the period. We have already seen the difficult fiscal problem which was raised by the federal structure of the Empire. The Bismarckian principle of confining Imperial finance to indirect taxes and leaving the direct taxes to the individual states was increasingly obsolete in the light of Germany's modern needs. The financial experts of parties that were strongly federalist in outlook—like Erzberger's Zentrum Party—were naturally slow to recognize this fact. They preferred tinkering with the existing inadequate system to embarking upon a fundamental tax reform program. The consequences had become little short of disastrous during the last years of Bülow's Chancellorship.

Bülow had been a great spendthrift who more than doubled the national debt in his nine years of power (from 2.2 to 4.75 billions). Much of the increased expenditure was inevitable in view of Germany's military needs and advanced social legislation, but this increased expenditure ought to have been accompanied by new sources of revenue. Bülow, an aristocratic dilettante, though his mother came from a prominent Hamburg family, did not pretend to be much interested in financial questions. His dislike of throwing contentious issues into the *Reichstag*—unless as part of a grand political design as in 1906—made him a proponent of "muddling through." A looming deficit of 500 millions in the 1909 budget forced the government to abandon its drifting policy and to work out a comprehensive reform program. The specific proposals were for some 380 millions in new excise taxes on articles of general consumption and 117 millions in what were called *Besitzsteuern* (taxes on wealth) divided between 25 millions in increased matricular contributions (payments by the individual Länder into the Imperial treasury) and 92 millions to be collected from inher-

[41] *ibid.*, p. 62. Erzberger was a vigorous champion of military economies. See his clash with Tirpitz over dining allowances for naval officers. Herzfeld, *op.cit.*, p. 90, and Erzberger, *Zentrumspolitik*, x (1912), 73–75. He attacked Krupp's monopoly contract for supplying steel to the navy. *Ibid.*, VIII (1910), 58–68. This did not mean any opposition to the private manufacture of arms. He opposed the nationalization of armament factories, but also defended the existing state arsenals against accusations levied by private industry. Erzberger, *Rüstungsausgaben,* Chs. V and VII.

itances, including landed estates. The system of matricular contributions was especially dear to federalist hearts. Its sole advantage arose from the fact that Länder taxes were primarily direct taxes upon wealth, thereby making the total German tax structure more equitable than it could be if exclusive reliance were placed upon indirect Imperial taxes. The entire system of matricular contributions was to be finally abolished by Erzberger in 1919. His introduction of a national income tax ended the equity argument for financial federalism, and made the old clumsy system completely indefensible.

The major controversy in 1909 dealt with the proposed 92 millions to be raised by taxing landed and other inheritances, with Erzberger acting as spokesman for his party in opposing the government proposal. The Zentrum Party saw an excellent opportunity of breaking up the Bülow Block by exploiting its internal dissension on the proposed land tax. The Liberal wing of the Block—both National Liberals and *Freisinn*—favored the inheritance tax as a progressive measure and a symbol of their opposition to narrow Junker interests. The Conservatives, on the other hand, feared the tax—however infinitesimal its incidence—as an entering wedge for further taxation of their land by a *Reichstag* under increasingly Leftist control. They looked upon the entire question as primarily one of prestige; their power in the state was symbolized by their virtual immunity from Imperial taxation. They had never been enthusiastic about either Bülow or the Block, and were becoming still less so as the *Freisinn* began to demand concessions in Prussian questions—especially the reform of the franchise—as the price of continued support of the Block. The Conservatives were in a receptive mood when the Zentrum proposed the replacement of the Bülow Block by a new Conservative-Zentrum voting alliance.

Erzberger's opposition to the inheritance taxes must be judged in the light of this political consideration. His primary objective was to break the Block, appease the Conservatives, and promote Bülow's fall from power by depriving him of his parliamentary majority—the only remaining basis of his power, since he had recently lost the favor of the Emperor. Erzberger's arguments against the tax on landed inheritances were ideally tailored to fit many Zentrum and Conservative prejudices. He thought that the intervention of the cold hand of the state at the very moment of family bereavement was contrary to the German family sense. He thought that the tax discriminated unfairly against agricultural property, whose tangibility made evasion far more difficult than was the case with mobile capital—an argument appealing to the standing Zentrum hostility to stock-jobbers and mere moneyed

wealth. He thought that the tax was inequitable since inheritance circumstances differ very much from family to family according to the
number and previous wealth of the affected heirs.[42] These arguments
were not of such weight as to deter Erzberger from becoming the main
architect of the comprehensive inheritance tax of 1919.

There was talk in 1909 of introducing an Imperial income tax as an
alternative to the controversial land succession taxes. This would have
broken the Bismarckian principle of excluding the Empire from the
field of direct taxes. Erzberger was among the strongest opponents of
such a change in fiscal policy. He saw—what was undoubtedly true—
that such a tax could not simply be added to the state income taxes of
Prussia, Württemberg, or the thirty odd other states, because the methods of assessing and collecting income taxes differed from state to state.
The addition of an Imperial income tax to the prevailing rates would
penalize those states with an efficient and progressive system. The alternative was to set up an Imperial tax-collecting machinery that would
replace the existing heterogeneous Länder systems. This is exactly what
Erzberger himself created in 1919. But in 1909 he was still bitterly opposed to such a fiscal and constitutional revolution. He argued that
centralized tax collecting machinery would represent a great advance
towards the unitary state and a sharp blow against the federalist system.
He said that the Zentrum, as a federalist party dedicated to preserving
the historical diversity of the German people, could never support such
a centralizing advance.[43] He forgot Disraeli's advice: "I tell my young
men, in politics never say 'never.'" Erzberger's extreme statements in
1909 caused him considerable embarrassment in later years.

The specific fiscal problem of 1909—the elimination of the anticipated deficit of 500 millions—led to the collapse of the Bülow Block
and the creation of a Zentrum-Conservative voting coalition. The excises proposed by the government were essentially granted, with the
Reichstag appropriating 365 million out of 380. Erzberger made much
of this 15-million cut in taxes that fell primarily on the consumption of
the poor. The increase in the matricular contributions of 25 millions
was accepted, but the inheritance tax was rejected by the votes of the
Zentrum and Conservatives. There remained the problem of finding
fiscal substitutes for the 92 millions which it would have raised. These
would have to be taxes on wealth in order to minimize the political
danger incurred by defeating the popular inheritance duties. Erzberger
was among those who proposed alternative taxes that hit real-estate

[42] Erzberger, *Zentrumspolitik*, VII (1909), 83–88.
[43] *ibid.*, 92–95.

speculators, bankers, stockjobbers, capitalists, and dividend clippers, all groups that tended to vote Liberal. The specific proposals that were enacted placed 40 millions in new taxes upon the transfer and unearned increment of land (to be collected only at the time of sale, hence hitting almost exclusively urban landowners since rural property rarely changed hands); 70 millions in taxes upon stock issues, stamps on dividend coupons, cheques, and long-term bills of exchange. The combined yield of these taxes on wealth was estimated at 110 millions, compared to the government proposal of only 92 millions. The surplus of 18 millions more than balanced the 15-million cut in the government requests for indirect taxes. It was hailed by Erzberger as proof that the Zentrum-Conservative proposals were more progressive—that is, more severe upon the wealth of the rich rather than the consumption of the poor—than the original plans of the government. The 1909 finance reform was successful in eliminating the Imperial deficit, and Erzberger —whatever one may think of his political motives in rejecting the land inheritance tax—deserves a full share of the credit for this. The Imperial budget was to show surpluses until 1912.[44]

A new deficit in the Imperial budget was threatened by the 1912 military bill. The *Reichstag* felt that it ought to vote some new taxes on property, but could not agree upon a specific implementation of this laudable intention. The result was a motion proposed jointly by Erzberger for the Zentrum and Ernst Bassermann for the National Liberals inviting the government to introduce proposals for new taxes on wealth by April 30, 1913. There was no indication of the specific taxes which the *Reichstag* majority desired, which was a singular admission of the inability of the *Reichstag* to develop a constructive financial policy of its own—an evil omen for the cause of parliamentary government in Germany.[45]

Germany's financial situation was complicated still further by the passage of the great 1913 military bill. The government accompanied it by the audacious proposal of a capital levy (the so-called *Wehrbei-*

---

[44] *ibid.*, Ch. III. Erzberger, *Müssen wir Zentrum wählen? Die Zentrumspolitik im Lichte der Wahrheit* (Berlin, n.d. [1911]), Ch. IV. Erzberger took a special interest in the implementation of the 1909 tax on the unearned increment of land. He deferred to the Conservatives in supporting the exemption of dynastic lands from the tax. Erzberger, *Zentrumspolitik,* IX (1911), 95–109.

[45] *ibid.*, 90–94. The budget as a whole is discussed in *ibid.,* 76–109. The Conservative leader Count Kuno Westarp, in his *Konservative Politik im letzten Jahrzehnt des Kaiserreichs* (Berlin, 1935), I, 247–49, uses his account of the Erzberger-Bassermann motion to make a general attack on Erzberger's character. This should be compared with the very laudatory view of Erzberger's financial statesmanship expressed by Adolf Wermuth, former Finance Minister, in *Ein Beamtenleben* (Berlin, 1922), p. 304.

trag) calculated to raise 1,200 million marks, to pay for what was advertised as a unique effort to enhance Germany's security. This kind of tax had never been tried anywhere previously, and it naturally led to much political and scholarly controversy. Erzberger eagerly threw himself into both. He published a comprehensive pamphlet on the problem of defining and collecting a capital levy.[46] Erzberger's expert advocacy smoothed the passage of the *Wehrbeitrag* through the *Reichstag*. His knowledge of capital levies was to prove of great value when he became Finance Minister in 1919. He then carried through a second capital levy (the *Reichsnotopfer*) to pay for the defeat in the war which the 1913 *Wehrbeitrag* had been unable to prevent.

The Dismissal of Bülow

Erzberger's prominence in political work was not confined to military and financial questions. He took an outspoken line in opposition to Bülow at the time of the *Daily Telegraph* interview in November 1908. The Emperor's prestige was severely shaken by the publication of one of his conversations with an English friend. His remarks showed an utter lack of understanding of both the English and the German mentality. The Emperor had described himself as an Anglophil in an Anglophobe country, had claimed authorship for the military plans that had defeated the Boers in 1900, and had stated that the German navy was being built against Japan rather than England. These were only the worst blunders of a generally incredible interview.

The content of the interview was properly blamed upon the Emperor, but the publication was due to a series of administrative blunders on the part of Bülow and the Foreign Office. The Emperor had observed all the proprieties of requesting the Chancellor's consent before permitting publication, and Bülow had bungled the matter badly while he was on vacation. The Chancellor, in the ensuing *Reichstag* debate, could not deny his formal responsibility; but he claimed—probably truthfully—that he had not read the article personally and that he certainly would have vetoed publication if he had. He thus threw the substantive onus upon the Emperor, and he even compelled William to make a public statement promising greater reticence in the future (November 17, 1908): a humiliation which William could neither forgive nor forget. Bülow won a temporary parliamentary triumph, but his conduct was stupid nonetheless, for he had mortally antagonized the Emperor, who resolved to fire him upon the first opportunity.

[46] Erzberger, *Der Wehrbeitrag* (Stuttgart, 1913).

The opportunity came six months later when Bülow's inheritance tax was defeated by the Zentrum-Conservative coalition.[47]

Erzberger championed a theory about Bülow's conduct which won the approval of the Emperor and fanned his anger against the Chancellor. It claimed, in an extreme form, that Bülow had deliberately concocted the publication of the explosive interview in order to ruin the public standing of the Emperor and throw him into dependence upon himself. Even if he had not planned the publication he had certainly read the interview and allowed it to pass. The proof of this surprising theory was found in alleged earlier official attempts to drag the Emperor into newspaper controversy, thus giving the appearance that the *Daily Telegraph* interview was the successful culmination of a long-range plan to discredit William. But these earlier articles were all of a rather ambiguous nature, and proof of Bülow's complicity in promoting their publication has never been found. The milder form of the theory, which was far more plausible, claimed that Bülow had not acted properly after the unfortunate publication. He ought to have minimized the importance of the interview (even if its authenticity could not be denied altogether) and to have monopolized responsibility himself and kept the Emperor out of controversy. Erzberger said that he ought to have acted as a screen absorbing criticism directed against the Emperor; but Bülow refused to make an unequivocal defense in the *Reichstag* and did nothing to counteract the storm of newspaper abuse that descended upon William.[48]

Bülow states in his *Memoirs* that this Erzberger theory was first brought to the Emperor's attention by the Court Master of Ceremonies (*Zeremonienmeister*) Eugen Röder, an Erzberger intimate. The former Chancellor suggests that Erzberger advanced it in some newspaper articles in order to curry Imperial favor for the Zentrum Party and establish a new Conservative-Zentrum "Blue-Black Block" to replace the "Bülow Block." Bülow was quite wrong about Erzberger's motives in the winter of 1908–1909. The party hierarchs did, indeed, desire cooperation with the Conservatives, but Erzberger resisted this policy until the early summer of 1909. He distrusted the Conservatives because

---

[47] The last word on the *Daily Telegraph* interview, clearing up all doubtful points while advancing no new theories, is Wilhelm Schüssler, *Die Daily Telegraph Affaire. Fürst Bülow, Kaiser Wilhelm und die Krise des Zweiten Reiches* (Göttingen, 1952).

[48] The theory is developed by Erzberger in his *Zentrumspolitik*, VII (1909), 14–33. The fullest statement is in Rudolf Martin, *Fürst Bülow und Kaiser Wilhelm II* (Leipzig, 1909). Schoen, the former Foreign Secretary, calls Erzberger the author of the theory in F. Thimme, ed., *Front wider Bülow*, p. 79. Schüssler, in *op.cit.*, p. 83, quotes William's marginal comment on Erzberger's newspaper statement of the theory: "The facts are absolutely correct."

of their participation in the anti-Catholic campaign of 1907 and their support of the anti-Polish policies in the Prussian East. Erzberger rather preferred *ad hoc* cooperation with shifting legislative partners for the future. He expected at this time that cultural and economic questions would recede into the background and that constitutional questions would become paramount. He looked forward to an enlargement of the powers of the *Reichstag* and expected the eventual introduction of the parliamentary system. For this purpose the Liberals and Socialists would become the natural allies of the Zentrum. He expected that the anti-clericalism of the Liberals would lose its virulence. Erzberger's hopes were not to be realized, and he soon supported the official party policy of breaking the Bülow Block by wooing the Conservatives.[49]

Erzberger's theory about the *Daily Telegraph* incident was undoubtedly false. Not only did it assume an excessive degree of cunning on Bülow's part, but a far simpler explanation of the facts was available. Bülow, whatever his faults, certainly knew the constitutional realities of German life. To antagonize the Emperor was suicidal for a Chancellor. His sole hope for retaining power after alienating William lay in diminishing the Imperial influence by establishing the full parliamentary system, or at least by building up a reliable parliamentary majority. The former was impossible and the latter was prevented by the internal friction within the Bülow Block. Thus Bülow had much to lose and nothing to gain from making himself responsible for the humiliation of William. Why, then, did he take the line that he had not read the article before publication, thereby throwing the onus upon William while assuming only a purely formal responsibility? The easiest, and partly correct explanation, is that this was probably the truth. But truthfulness would never be a paramount consideration with Bülow unless reinforced by other considerations. Here vanity and cowardice played a supplementary role. For Bülow to state that he, an experienced diplomat, had read the article and failed to foresee its explosive repercussions, would have made him the laughing-stock of Germany. A streak of cowardice reinforced this consideration. The publication of the interview had led to a spontaneous outburst of hostility against the Emperor, in quarters ranging from the Conservatives to the Socialists, which showed that a cumulative grievance had at last broken into the open. Bülow would have incurred great temporary unpopularity by

[49] Bülow, *Denkwürdigkeiten*, ii, 494, and iii, 61–62. Article by Erzberger, "Neuer Block oder alte Abwehrmehrheit," in *Der Tag*, Dec. 12, 1908. Erzberger explicitly wanted to adapt the German constitution to the model of Western Europe. This evoked a sharp reply from Martin Spahn in *Der Tag*, Jan. 6, 1909.

directing this wrath against himself in the manner which Erzberger suggested. These considerations make Erzberger's theory about Bülow's conduct implausible, but it must be emphasized that the theory probably had some influence upon William's decision to dismiss Bülow as soon as he dared.

The most remarkable fact about the entire *Daily Telegraph* incident is that it had no serious constitutional consequences whatsoever. While discrediting the Emperor and exposing the negligence of his Chancellor it did nothing to promote the obvious cure for both, an advance towards the parliamentary system. The Conservatives, while criticizing William and thus showing their manly lack of Byzantinism, were satisfied with the *status quo*. The Zentrum was more interested in breaking the Bülow Block and currying favor with the Conservatives than in promoting constitutional changes. The National Liberals believed Bülow could do no wrong, and considered him irreplaceable in the conduct of foreign policy. The *Freisinn* was impotent while the Socialists were beyond the pale of respectability. All parties took comfort in William's pledge of reticence for the future. A much greater shock than the publication of a disastrous interview was necessary in order to reform the frozen constitutional structure of Germany.

Political Problems, 1909–1914

Erzberger, elated by the collapse of the Bülow Block and the dismissal of his personal enemy Bülow in 1909, shared the prevalent satisfaction with the *status quo* for some years. He refused to get excited about the sabotage of Bethmann's very moderate proposals for the reform of the Prussian franchise in 1910 by the Zentrum-Conservative coalition of the *Landtag,* although he did criticize Bethmann for his remarkable February 10, 1910 attack upon democratic franchise systems. He took a complacent attitude towards the famous Oldenburg incident in the *Reichstag* (January 29, 1910). Oldenburg-Januschau, an East Prussian Junker whose nefarious career was to be consummated twenty-three years later by his participation in the intrigues which placed Hitler in power, intervened in a military debate to give the *Reichstag* his view of the proper relationship between monarch, army, and parliament: "The King of Prussia and Emperor of Germany must always be in position to tell any army lieutenant 'Go, take ten men and close up the *Reichstag!*'" Haussmann (Erzberger's old Württemberg rival) and the Socialist Noske (later a Cabinet colleague of Erzberger's) protested this insult to the *Reichstag*'s dignity, and Erzberger might have been expected to rally to their side. Yet in his survey of the incident he took a conspicuously neutral attitude, and obviously placed solidarity with the anti-parliamentary Conservatives above striking a blow in defense of the rights of the *Reichstag*.[50]

Erzberger's progressive attitudes reappeared, however, in the discussion of the Alsatian constitution in 1911, when he supported the introduction of a completely democratic franchise and adequate guarantees for the fiscal powers of the Second Chamber. He favored the grant of extensive self-government to the Alsatians as the sole remedy for the clumsiness of Prussian bureaucratic administration.[51] His hopes that the grant of self-government would be a major step towards Franco-German reconciliation was, however, doomed to be disappointed. It came exactly forty years too late.

Erzberger's pamphlet for the election which was held in January 1912 shows that he expected the Zentrum-Conservative voting alliance to continue in the new *Reichstag*. He feared the triumph of the "great coalition" (*Grossblock*) from Bebel (Socialists) to Bassermann (National Liberals) of which Friedrich Naumann was the most prominent champion, and which governed successfully in Baden against Zentrum and Conservatives. Its effective slogan "Against Knights and Saints" (*Ritter und Heilige*) met the democratic and secularist instincts of the age. Erzberger avoided all attack against the Conservatives and concentrated his fire exclusively upon the Liberals and Socialists. He accused the Liberals of wishing to unleash a new *Kulturkampf*. He repeated his chronic attacks against the Socialists as the party of irresponsible demagogy. Erzberger defended the 1909 finance reform—which the opposition parties made the main election issue—as a work of constructive legislation that had courageously solved the pressing problem of the national deficit. He refuted Liberal-Socialist criticism in detail, but was in the unfortunate position of never getting out of the defensive. His praise of the socio-economic legislation of the last few years—an able chronicle of many minor achievements consolidated by the great 1911 national insurance code—fell rather flat, as did his cry of "Protection in Danger." His pamphlet failed to buttress the sagging fortunes of the Zentrum.[52]

This last election of Imperial Germany was devoid of dramatic incident. Bethmann showed none of Bülow's flair for inflaming and manip-

[50] *Zentrumspolitik*, VIII (1910), 24–29. His criticism of Bethmann, in the form of endorsing Gröber's attack, is in *ibid.*, pp. 19–20. For Oldenburg's defiant account of his speech, see Elard von Oldenburg-Januschau, *Erinnerungen* (Leipzig, 1936), pp. 109–12.
[51] Erzberger, *Zentrumspolitik,* IX (1911), 11–23.
[52] Erzberger, *Müssen wir Zentrum wählen? Die Zentrumspolitik im Lichte der Wahrheit* (Berlin, n.d. [1911]).

ulating mass opinion. The result was a disaster for the government. The Socialist seats rose from 53 to 110, while all other parties suffered a decline. The Left Liberals fell from 49 to 42, the National Liberals from 50 to 43. The Conservatives fell from 90 to 62, despite the fact that many Zentrum supporters voted Conservative even on the first ballot in order to minimize Socialist gains. The Zentrum declined from 103 to 92 seats while its popular vote was reduced from 2.2 to 2 millions —the first considerable loss since the founding of the party. There were many explanations in the midst of considerable internal party recrimination. The easiest explanation was that at least 200,000 followers had obeyed party instructions and voted Conservative, though this could not be proved statistically. There were a variety of other explanations. Some of Roeren's followers of the *Berliner Richtung* had neglected to go to the polls. The opponents of the Zentrum-Conservative Block had exercised better voting discipline than their rivals. The Zentrum record was vulnerable because of the unpopular 1909 finance reform and the opposition to franchise reform in Prussia. The last two themes had been especially effective among the big city masses, where even the Catholics were losing some of their immunity to Marxism. All these reasons showed that the Zentrum could not rest upon its oars but must seek to stay abreast of the Leftist currents in German politics.

The new *Reichstag,* which was to remain until 1918 since no elections could be held in wartime, continued to give the Zentrum a balance-of-power position between the alternative of a Right and Left coalition. The Right parties—Conservatives, National Liberals, and some minor parties—held 147 seats out of 397. The Left parties—Socialists and Left Liberals—held 152 seats out of 397. The 92 Zentrum seats could be thrown either way. The party cooperated primarily with the Right in the five years after 1912, until Erzberger brought about the great shift in party alignments at the time of the Peace Resolution in 1917.[53]

The 1913 session saw the anti-militarist explosion of the *Reichstag* majority in the matter of the Zabern affair. Some Alsatian civilians in the little town of Zabern, northwest of Strassbourg, had been mistreated by some Prussian officers. The Minister of War, Falkenhayn, had immediately rallied to the side of the officers, completely oblivious to the merits of the case. Bethmann-Hollweg, despite his civilized instincts, felt himself compelled to defend the conduct of Falkenhayn.

[53] The best book on the background and results of the 1912 election is Walter Koch, *Volk und Staatsführung vor dem Weltkrieg* (Stuttgart, 1935). On the Zentrum swing to the left, see Erzberger, *Zentrumspolitik,* x (1912), 18.

The *Reichstag* then condemned Bethmann's attitude by a vote of 293–254, a notable index of the opposition to unbridled militarism felt by the vast majority of the German people. This vote also revealed the tragic isolation of Bethmann-Hollweg. Erzberger shared the deep indignation felt by the German masses and was contemptuous of Bethmann's failure to keep the soldiers under control. It anticipated his similar failure during the war, and it strengthened Erzberger's conviction of the indispensability of introducing the parliamentary system in order to make popular views prevail against autocratic whims and military influences. Yet he specifically rejected Scheidemann's view that the *Reichstag* should deliberately provoke a constitutional crisis by rejecting all appropriation bills.[54]

Erzberger's Political Views in 1914

Erzberger gave a systematic exposition of his political views in a pamphlet published just before the war.[55] He expected that the parliamentary system, as already existing in the Western democracies, would inevitably prevail in every modern community, with Germany proving no exception. Indeed he claimed that it was gradually being introduced in Germany, as witness the fall of Bülow when he could no longer rely upon parliamentary support. Monarchical autocracy was an anachronism in an age of broad political consciousness. The so-called German system of "constitutionalism," praised by Conservative theorists as a distinctive Germanic counterpart to foreign "parliamentary autocracy," was a nice word that vainly tried to conceal the rule of a caste-conscious, arrogant, inbreeding bureaucracy that ruled frequently in flagrant violation of public opinion (as in the Zabern affair). Erzberger readily admitted that the parliamentary system, especially as practiced in France and Italy, belied the hopes of Liberals by its nepotism, corruption, frivolous legislation, and the demoralization of the administrative apparatus. But he thought that these evils were even more prevalent in autocracies such as Turkey and Russia, and were unhappily not completely unknown under "German constitutionalism."

Erzberger expected certain favorable results from the introduction of the parliamentary system which make melancholy reading in the light of subsequent Weimar experience; though it must be emphasized that Weimar was inaugurated under exceptionally unfortunate circumstances which Erzberger could not possibly foresee.

1. He expected the full parliamentary system would develop a sense

[54] Erzberger, *Zentrumspolitik*, XII (1914), 11–22.
[55] Erzberger, *Politik und Völkerleben* (Würzburg, n.d. [1914]).

of responsibility in opposition parties, since they would constantly be confronted by the possibility of becoming the government. This prediction was accurate so far as the bulk of the Socialists was concerned; but Erzberger did not foresee that Socialist sobriety must lead to the break-away of an intransigent Left wing, and that the displacement of the Conservatives from their quasi-monopoly of power would lead to a reckless Rightist extremism that merged easily into the barbarism of Nazism.

2. Erzberger thought that parliamentary government would strengthen the real prestige of the monarchy by divorcing it from political controversy; he forgot that no Hohenzollern, raised in the divine-right traditions of that house, could possibly acquiesce in the reduction of monarchical power; certainly the Emperor and Crown Prince (the latter lived until 1951) would never do so. Erzberger was precluded by his Zentrum principles from recognizing the necessity of republicanism in Germany.

3. Erzberger expected that parliamentary government would close the chasm between the nation and the state by making the government the servant and not the master of the people. This union between state and people would, indeed, have occurred with all its blessings if parliamentary government had come as the result of gradual evolution rather than the shock of military defeat. When it came in 1919 it led only to the replacement of an intransigent Leftist opposition by an equally intransigent Right that identified itself no more with the Weimar Republic than the prewar Socialists had identified themselves with the Empire. A moral consensus of the nation, which is always the prerequisite, and sometimes the result of, successful parliamentary government, remained unachieved.

4. Erzberger further believed that the introduction of parliamentary government would lead to the fruition of political talents whose opportunities had been choked by the bureaucratic state. He no doubt thought of his own case. Under the Empire he could never be more than a great parliamentary critic, whereas under the new regime he was to become Finance Minister with no limit to his further rise. Yet the Weimar Republic, apart from a few exceptional cases such as Erzberger, Rathenau, and Stresemann, did not become a nursery of statesmen. Its Chancellors were generally less distinguished than their Imperial predecessors, and the average caliber of its ministers was rather lower than that of the Empire—if only because continuity became rare except in a few key offices. It must also be noted that the Republic allowed flourishing careers to Nazis who would have gotten nowhere

under the Empire. The disappointing results of Weimar cannot, of
course, be ascribed to the parliamentary system as such, but only to
the way in which it developed under the peculiar conditions of Germany. They do not prove that Erzberger was an exceptionally poor
prophet, but only the fascinating unpredictability of German developments.[56]

Erzberger recognized the "revolt of the masses" as the main theme
of 20th century history. He foresaw the inevitability, and despite occasional tactical hesitations approved, of the democratization of modern
life.

> The politicization of the masses cannot be stopped; it is the natural
> result of modern conditions. It is not in itself an evil, indeed is desirable
> for both the people and the state. Stupid citizens and politically indiffer-
> ent nations cannot meet the challenges of the present; an active political
> life produces participation in public events, gives a nation power and
> courage (*Lebensmut*), strengthens the sense of responsibility in rulers
> and other holders of power, and provides an indispensable control over
> their actions and omissions. Universal liability for military service and uni-
> versal payment of taxes forces the citizen in town and country to concern
> himself with politics. That this, if done in excess, has its disadvantages
> goes without saying.[57]

Erzberger saw and feared the danger of radicalization, under which
he understood the forward march of secularist ideas, whether in their
liberal or socialist form. He expected the future cleavage of political
life to run between those who adhered to "liberal" and those who adhered to "authoritarian" principles. He defined the difference between the two groups as being that the former made their own will the
ultimate source of their desires while the latter subordinated themselves
to the divine law.

> The *liberal system* is built upon one fundamental error, that the state
> is the source of all laws and rights (*Quelle allen Rechtes*); that the omnipo-
> tent state may regulate everything in accordance with its arbitrary will
> and is not bound by any higher norm; that the majority may decide
> whatever it pleases; that religion has nothing to say in the market-place
> of public affairs (one praises her all the more for her role in private affairs,
> but as a rule does not abide by her there either); that freedom is the
> great need of the people (*Parole des Volkes*) and the source of all prog-
> ress. The Liberal parties of all countries conform to this pattern, but so
> do the Social Democrats: the latter differ from Liberals only in economic

[56] Erzberger's views on the parliamentary system are in *ibid.*, Ch. III.
[57] *ibid.*, p. 6.

questions. The wealthy Liberal calls himself Liberal in one of its many forms, the poor Liberal is a Social Democrat.[58]

The opposition to this "liberal" principle was carried on by "authoritarian parties":

> The *authoritarian parties (Autoritätsparteien)* are governed in all their activities by the source of all authority, the personal God who has revealed Himself to man; they recognize and respect His laws and ordinances, never place themselves in opposition to them, but rather apply them for the welfare of nations. Their highest call is not freedom, the legislation of the state is not the source of all rights, they recognize rather the natural and the divine law. They derive their own authority and that of laws from the highest authority. The respect for the highest and irremovable Law-Giver gives their principles their peculiar internal strength (*ihrer Politik eine ganz andere innere Kraft und Stärke*).[59]

This attitude is characteristic of Erzberger's prewar thought and is remarkable for a man who was soon to lead the Zentrum into coalition with the Socialists and Liberals. It was rather inconsistent with his championing of parliamentary government, since it envisaged a degree of polarization of political life and an absence of moral consensus that would make an orderly transfer of power from government to opposition inconceivable. Erzberger evidently expected the "authoritarian parties" to secure a permanent majority. He believed that economic and social questions were well on the road to solution in the light of his Christian principles. The questions of the future would be primarily in the cultural and religious sphere, with a renewal of the *Kulturkampf* an ever-present danger. Erzberger was convinced that religion often lies at the root of seemingly secular problems, or at least provides the spirit for finding solutions to them. He cited as an example the problem of the declining birthrate of the German population, with its economic and military consequences. Erzberger, as a Catholic, naturally opposed birth control, and advocated giving the *Bundesrat* the power to ban trade in contraceptives. "The ethical level of a people shows itself very clearly in the frequency of child birth; at any rate degenerate peoples always show a rapid artificial decline in births, while youthful peoples with a consciousness of enhanced power are characterized by a rapid increase in numbers." [60] He saw in the strengthening of religious convictions the obvious answer to the population problem as well as to many other problems.

[58] *ibid.*, p. 8.
[59] *ibid.*, p. 11.
[60] Erzberger, *Zentrumspolitik*, XII (1914), 75.

His ideal was that of a God-fearing country where a religious spirit dominated in political life:

The crux of public controversies is usually religious even when on the surface these appear to be purely political in motive or mere economic power struggles. Religion is the queen of politics and national life; she is at the same time pole star, source of warmth and power, and primary goal (*Leitstern, Wärmequelle, Kraftstrom, und Ziel in gleicher Weise*). A policy hostile to religion leads a nation to misery and destruction; one friendly to religion brings strength, welfare, and growth in the sunny days of peace as well as the painful nights of national misfortune. Religion elevates and purifies (*edelt und adelt*) politics, which without religion degenerates into a struggle for the best place at the trough. For this reason victory in the political struggle must fall, despite all difficulties, to a Christian policy (*Christliche Staatspolitik*).[61]

The great blight upon Germany's future lay, in Erzberger's view, in the strength of Social Democracy, with its irreconcilable hostility to Christian ideals. Erzberger recognized the extreme difficulty of dealing with what he rightly diagnosed as an "illness of the heart":

Germany has the strongest Social Democracy among nations though it stands in the vanguard of social reforms. The causes of this remarkable phenomenon lie almost exclusively in the religious field; for even the most comprehensive social reform program cannot dry up the springs of Social Democracy. This is an illness of the heart and a case of the will gone astray (*eine Verirrung des Willens*); state and private efforts at enlightenment and active help may have a preventive or moderating effect; but only religion can bring real healing. Without the help of religion and the Church no way can be found out of this confusion (*Wirrsal*). For this reason we must consider the entire state effort to elevate the condition of the working class not so much from the point of view of the need of combatting Social Democracy, but rather from that of our elementary duty towards Christ and man.[62]

Only religion could provide a real cure, though social reforms, undertaken in the proper Christian spirit, could also help. A temporary solution lay in the cooperation of all non-Socialist parties against the Socialist danger.

The greatest task confronting the Reich at home is the smashing of the enormous strength of the Socialists; all other domestic questions must be subordinated to this crucial problem. . . . The Right, Zentrum, and National Liberals must take up this struggle [against the Socialists] with

[61] Erzberger, *Politik und Völkerleben*, p. 75.
[62] *ibid.*, pp. 54–55.

unity and resolution regardless of consequences—in the interest of the whole state (*Staatsganzen*). There is no more pressing problem in the present than this, and if these three parties fail future generations would rightly hold us guilty of party egotism, short-sightedness, and incapacity.[63]

Erzberger saw in religion, social reform, and bourgeois solidarity the main instruments for combatting Socialism. But he did not wish to neglect police measures either whenever these appeared appropriate. He was especially angered by the Socialist attitude towards international dangers. There was much Socialist talk about resisting mobilization, organizing a general strike, and taking other unpatriotic measures if war should break out. Erzberger advocated the strongest possible steps, including the jailing of all Socialist leaders during a war emergency, in order to protect the national safety.[64] He never forgot, and never allowed the Socialists to forget, that they had hesitated about supporting the government during the Second Moroccan Crisis (1911) at the risk of allowing the Cossacks to occupy Berlin.

The treasonable (*landesverräterische*) conduct of the Social Democrats during the [1911] Moroccan question requires special mention. While all the bourgeois parties stood behind the government, the German Social Democrats (but not their French and English party colleagues) organized so-called peace demonstrations that were calculated to foster the impression abroad that Germany wanted war [There follow several examples of Socialist statements, including a hint that Socialists would not obey their mobilization orders]. . . . We should never forget how the Socialists have sinned against the Fatherland during the last few months. They would cold-bloodedly surrender our Fatherland to foreign hordes, in the hope that this will create a situation where they can achieve their aims through revolution.[65]

It was fortunate for Germany that Bethmann-Hollweg took a calmer view of the Socialist danger in 1914, and recognized that the froth of Marxist phrases went only skin-deep. The vast majority of German Socialists were to prove their patriotism during the war.

Erzberger remained during the prewar years what he had become in 1906: one of the half-dozen most prominent *Reichstag* politicians. He became an accepted member of the Zentrum leadership who no longer needed to act as a maverick in order to achieve his purposes. His energy and aggressiveness were accepted by his colleagues as the peculiar hallmark of the man. He acted as the main spokesman of the

[63] Erzberger in a newspaper article in *Der Tag*, May 13, 1914, quoted by Max Taube, *Erzberger—Der Totengräber des Deutschen Reiches* (Berlin, 1919), p. 11.

[64] Erzberger in *Der Tag*, July 28, 1914, quoted in ibid., p. 10.

[65] Erzberger, *Müssen wir Zentrum wählen?*, p. 22.

Zentrum in financial and military questions, the two major fields for legislative combat. He also took a considerable share in debate on religious, political, and social questions. The leadership of the Left wing of the party was unchallengeably his, while the Right wing increasingly admitted that he was the predestined man to lead the entire party in the future. His unswerving hostility to Socialism partly blurred his democratic progressive views and made his gradual acceptance by the Right a comparatively easy matter. There was also a widespread conviction that some party shift to the Left was inevitable in order to stay abreast of the main current of German politics. If the war had not come, and a normal span of life had been granted him, Erzberger probably would have become another Windthorst or Lieber in the annals of German history: men who attained great parliamentary influence in a political context where parliament lacked a decisive voice in affairs. His stormy rise would have been forgotten in the glow of thirty-five years of constructive and respectable parliamentary life. The First World War and his restless craving for activity prevented the realization of this pleasing but unexciting idyll. They were to lead him ever more deeply into the cockpit of ferocious political controversy, and finally to a martyr's grave by the hand of assassins whose deed was openly hailed by millions of Erzberger's fellow-countrymen.

Note: For a more detailed account of Erzberger's role in the *Zentrumsstreit* mentioned on pp. 66–68, see my article, "Erzberger's position in the *Zentrumsstreit* before World War I," in *Catholic Historical Review*, XLIV (1958), 1–16.

CHAPTER V

PROPAGANDA AND WAR AIMS

Erzberger and Bethmann

THE outbreak of World War One saw Germany temporarily united by an outburst of patriotic solidarity that bridged the cleavages inherent in the Wilhelmine structure of society. The whole nation believed that it was fighting a defensive war, and even the Socialists voted for the war credits. But the national unanimity could not be long maintained. Germany soon divided into hostile groups on the two pressing issues of war aims and internal reforms. The Conservatives and National Liberals desired large annexations, both to enhance military security in future wars and to maintain the internal *status quo,* which could not survive an unsuccessful war. They feared above all that their control of Germany would be shaken by demands, such as the reform of the Prussian franchise and the introduction of the parliamentary system, which were advanced in the name of uniting the nation and rewarding the lower classes for their patriotic wartime service. The Socialists, on the other hand, demanded both internal reforms and a peace without annexations, and at times went so far as to accuse the ruling class of needlessly prolonging the war for their own selfish ends. The Zentrum and *Freisinn* Liberals took an essentially opportunist line, favoring annexations so long as the military outlook looked good while being willing to acquiesce in considerable domestic changes.[1]

Their position was shared by Chancellor Bethmann, an enlightened but somewhat colorless bureaucrat. He attempted to foster unity by vague and ambiguous speeches that could be interpreted as favoring either an annexationist or a *status quo* peace; he favored internal reforms but wished to postpone them until after the war. He was hated by the Conservatives because they realized that he was a moderate in war aims and a reformer in domestic affairs, distrusted by the Socialists because he lacked the personal force to make his views prevail. The Emperor faded into the background with the outbreak of war, and

---

[1] On German wartime politics generally, see the excellent books by V. Bredt, *Der deutsche Reichstag im Weltkriege* (Berlin, 1926), which is Vol. VIII of the work published by the Parliamentary Investigating Committee, under the title *Das Werk des Untersuchungsausschusses,* 4. Reihe, "Die Ursachen des deutschen Zusammenbruchs" (12 vols., Berlin, 1925–1929). Henceforth cited as *U.A.;* H. Gatzke, *Germany's Drive to the West* (Baltimore, 1950); A Rosenberg, *Entstehung der deutschen Republik* (Berlin, 1928); and E. O. Volkmann, *Die Annexionsfragen des Weltkriegs* (Berlin, 1926).

could give little support to his Chancellor. The General Staff was dominated by Conservatives who disliked Bethmann's conciliation of the Socialists. His position depended upon the support of the *Reichstag* and the absence of any obvious successor.[2]

Bethmann's cold and professorial personality made contact with *Reichstag* deputies difficult, but Erzberger was to prove an exception to this rule. The Chancellor found him a useful instrument for performing a great variety of wartime tasks. The two men complemented each other perfectly, and their relationship was based upon the attraction of opposites. Bethmann was slow, ponderous, and profound; Erzberger, quick, gay, and often superficial. Bethmann was weighted down by problems, groped gradually to solutions, procrastinated, and was doubtful about any conclusions even after he had reached them. Erzberger handled problems with a light touch, was never at a loss in imagining a great number of possible expedients, worked with phenomenal rapidity, and was arrogantly certain of whatever conclusion he had reached—though this did not prevent him from often coming to a quite different conclusion a few weeks later.

The harmonious cooperation between two such different men aroused considerable curiosity in the political community. Bülow once asked Erzberger outright how he explained his hold over Bethmann, and received the following answer (paraphrased in his *Memoirs*): "He did not know himself why the Chancellor was so fond of him. He was invited to dine with Bethmann at least once a week. Recently the Chancellor told him 'How do you manage to have so many bright ideas (*gute Einfälle*) all the time? I never have any!' Erzberger related this without any irony." [3]

Maximilian Harden, the famous publicist, quotes Bethmann as saying on the same point: "This man Erzberger! I wonder where he gets one new brain wave after another!" [4] Bethmann valued Erzberger's resourcefulness and gay love of responsibility. He admired Erzberger's political instinct and grasp of grass-roots sentiment, two qualities that were completely alien to his own character. Erzberger's power in the Zentrum Party made him well worth cultivating, and it was safer to have him for a friend than an enemy. For all these reasons Bethmann admitted Erzberger to his intimate circle, made him privy to Foreign

[2] There is no adequate biography of Bethmann. His incompleted memoirs, *Betrachtungen zum Weltkriege* (2 vols, Berlin, 1919–1921) are very important. A comprehensive Right-wing criticism is Hans von Liebig, *Die Politik von Bethmann-Hollweg* (Munich, 1919).

[3] Bülow, *Denkwürdigkeiten*, III, 210.

[4] Maximilian Harden in an obituary article in the Berlin *Nationalzeitung*, Aug. 28, 1921.

Office secrets, and used him on many important diplomatic missions. Erzberger's personal position in the *Reichstag* and his intimacy with the Chancellor enhanced his wartime power. His *Reichstag* colleagues were awed by his official responsibilities and access to top-secret knowledge. A Zentrum leader once complained to Wallraff, the Lord Mayor of Cologne: "When I tell a party meeting that the Chancellor told me something yesterday, Erzberger almost invariably cuts in: 'The facts are quite different. I had a conference with Bethmann just fifteen minutes ago—.' " [5] Bethmann, in turn, placed special confidence in Erzberger's judgment because of his influence with his *Reichstag* colleagues. In this way Erzberger attained a position that was unique in the parliamentary history of Germany.

Erzberger's Propaganda Work

The original basis of Erzberger's intimacy with Bethmann, and of his wartime power, was his assumption of responsibility for propaganda towards neutral countries. He was not called to the colors upon the outbreak of war because he had never served as a conscript and was therefore not subject to immediate mobilization. His political opponents later made fun of the healthy man of 38 who sat out the war in his Berlin armchair rather than in the trenches, but this was not the result of either cowardice or lack of patriotism upon Erzberger's part. As soon as war broke out, he offered his services to the Foreign, War, and Navy ministries in any capacity that they would consider appropriate. It must be remembered that he had served as *Reichstag* reporter on military questions for ten years and was probably the best-informed civilian on these matters in Germany. The government thought him too valuable to serve as a private in the army. The Admiralty and Foreign Office wanted him to serve as German propaganda chief toward neutral countries.[6]

An interesting light is thrown upon governmental conditions in Imperial Germany by the fact that Erzberger was initially approached to do propaganda work by two naval captains, Löhlein and Dänhardt, in the third week of August. They had courteously checked with Bethmann's deputy, Clemens von Delbrück, before visiting Erzberger, and Delbrück approved of their plans.[7] The captains wanted to set up a propaganda office under the auspices of the Navy Ministry but work-

[5] Max Wallraff, *Aus einem rheinischen Leben* (Berlin, 1926), p. 126.
[6] Bachem, *Zentrumspartei,* IX, 406.
[7] Erzberger, *Erlebnisse,* p. 4.

ing in close cooperation with the Foreign Office. Erzberger at first modestly refused their suggestion that he head the new office, stating frankly that he knew little about foreign countries and offering to serve in domestic press work instead; but he yielded to a strong appeal to his sense of patriotic duty, reinforced by the plea that no one better prepared than he was available. His main handicap in doing the work was inadequate personal familiarity with foreign nations. His chief assets were boundless energy, resourcefulness, and imagination in whatever activity he undertook. These more than compensated for the shortcomings inherent in his background, especially since Erzberger was good at choosing capable subordinates who could make up for his own deficiencies.

Erzberger recognized the extreme difficulty of the task before him. By the third week of August, world opinion had already crystallized against Germany on account of the unprovoked invasion of Belgium. This invasion was seen not only as the act of a bully assaulting a weak neighbor but also as the triumph of military expediency over all considerations of justice. Any German propagandist taking over Erzberger's task was confronted from the beginning by deep prejudices that made sales resistance to his efforts nearly insurmountable.

A further obstacle in Erzberger's path was Germany's complete lack of prewar preparation for foreign propaganda. The Imperial regime had cared little for the kind of impression it was making abroad. The Foreign Office had made a perfunctory attempt in 1910 to enlarge its press funds, with a view to influencing foreign opinion; but a coalition of Socialists, Liberals, and Zentrum, including Erzberger, had rejected the appropriation. It feared that the funds would be diverted to influence domestic opinion, since some of the personnel of the press section was not to the *Reichstag's* liking.[8] Erzberger recognized the inherent reasonableness of the Foreign Office demand, and he introduced a motion for the creation of a 300,000 marks fund "for the distribution of German news abroad" which the *Reichstag* accepted in 1911.[9] The Foreign Office failed, however, to develop a network of foreign propaganda contacts, or even to assemble a catalogue of potential pro-German sympathizers, as Erzberger learned to his dismay when he as-

[8] W. E. Schoen, *Erlebtes* (Berlin, 1921), p. 117. W. Nicolai, *Nachrichtendienst, Presse und Volksstimmung im Weltkrieg* (Berlin, 1920), p. 53.
[9] Erzberger, *Erlebnisse*, p. 3; Walter Vogel, "Die Organisation der Presse und amtlichen Nachrichtenstellen von Bismarck bis 1933," in *Die Zeitungswissenschaft*, ed. W. Heide and K. D'Ester, Vol. XVI, Nr. 7–8 (Berlin, 1941), p. 34. Cited henceforth as Vogel, *Organisation*. Erzberger urged the creation of a centralized press bureau in *Reichstag Debates*, Vol. CCLXXXIV, Apr. 24, 1912, p. 1378.

sumed his work. His first task was to collect a mailing list of several thousand foreign addresses, and he did this in the space of a few days.[10]

Erzberger rented permanent quarters for his propaganda office at Budapesterstrasse 14, in the heart of Berlin opposite the famous zoo. He found an efficient office manager in Fräulein Bretschneider, who had long run the business end of the *Zentrumskorrespondenz*.[11] He rapidly built up a staff of efficient translators, many of whom were foreigners, a fact to which some soldiers took exception. Erzberger's propaganda work was financed by Foreign Office funds, for which, by the nature of the case, he could never give a full accounting. Many legends arose later about the sums which were involved in his operations, but his own statement that they totalled "less than a dozen million marks" was never successfully challenged. The frequent charge that he enriched himself personally, or that he transferred personal funds abroad under the guise of his propaganda work, also remained unsubstantiated.[12]

The Chancellor gave instructions that Erzberger should be allowed to attend all secret conferences at the Foreign, War, and Admiralty ministries, on the sound principle that a successful propagandist must have inside knowledge of his country's policies. Erzberger was given complete freedom about using all information which he acquired in any way he saw fit. He was soon to make dramatic use of this authority in order to establish a reputation in neutral countries for speed, honesty, and accuracy—an aim perhaps suggested by his own unhappy experiences with his *Zentrumskorrespondenz* in earlier years. Bachem tells the following story, which he heard from Erzberger the day it happened.

The German small cruiser *Magdeburg* ran into some rocks off the Finnish Coast on August 27, 1914, and her commander blew up the ship in order to avoid capture by the Russians. When news of this reached an Admiralty conference the officers present urged all participants to maintain absolute silence about the unhappy event. Erzberger declared that such secrecy was useless, because he would immediately wire the news to 3,000 addresses abroad. Everyone urged him to desist from this purpose. But

---

[10] *ibid.*, p. 5. P. Eltzbacher, *Die Presse als Werkzeug der auswärtigen Politik* (Jena, 1918), p. 48ff. Georg Schreiber, *Zwischen Demokratie und Diktatur* (Münster, 1949), p. 90.

[11] He sold the *Korrespondenz* to Franz Fortmann at this time. Bachem, *Zentrumspartei*, IX, 406.

[12] Erzberger, *Erlebnisse*, p. 21. The question of the financing of the foreign propaganda was discussed in *Prozess*, pp. 645–54, 824–25, 930–31, 954–55, 1030–33. Erzberger frequently interceded for the grant of export and import licenses by way of payment for propaganda services abroad. *ibid.*, pp. 823–24, 896, and 593–97.

Erzberger observed: "The Russians know about the matter anyhow, and will wire it to Stockholm, whence it will be passed on to London, Paris, and all neutral countries; I shall stand discredited if neutrals receive this news only from the Entente countries but not from me; if, however, they hear it first from me they will recognize the objectivity of all my reports, and will believe me in the future when I report victories!" Erzberger ended by stating that he had full authority to act as he proposed.[13]

Erzberger encountered a severe obstacle in his propaganda work in the rigidity of the German military mind. The one-sided communiques of the High Command early became a laughing-stock in neutral countries. The military conception of manliness led to a veto of all propaganda methods appealing to pity—Erzberger wanted to win foreign sympathies by emphasizing the sufferings inflicted by Britain's blockade upon innocent women and children.[14] Worst of all was the utter indifference shown to what influential people in neutral countries thought about Germany. Erzberger had the idea of inviting former President Theodore Roosevelt to visit German military headquarters in September 1914 and had learned through American contacts that Roosevelt would accept such an invitation. This was during the very first weeks of the war when the Rough Rider, with his primitive admiration of action for action's sake, had come close to defending the German invasion of Belgium. The suggestion was vetoed by the High Command.[15]

Erzberger's propaganda efforts were primarily directed towards Catholics in neutral countries. When prominent French clergymen under the leadership of the rector of the Paris Catholic University, Alfred Baudrillart, published a famous attack on German Catholicism as the alleged ally of militarist Pan-Germanism, Erzberger organized a Committee of German Catholics to prepare a reply. He selected Professor Rosenberg of Paderborn to write a detailed refutation, after yielding to the plea of Pope Benedict to keep the German episcopate out of the controversy. The Pope naturally wanted to avoid direct polemics between high ecclesiastics of the warring countries, and Erzberger shared this view both as a faithful Catholic and as an advocate of the Church as an instrument of reconciliation standing above nationalist strife.[16]

[13] Bachem, *Zentrumspartei*, IX, 407.
[14] Erzberger, *Erlebnisse*, pp. 7–8.
[15] *ibid.*, p. 10. Roosevelt's initial pro-Germanism, with special reference to the question of Belgium, is documented by Henry F. Pringle in his *Theodore Roosevelt* (New York, 1931), pp. 578–81.
[16] Erzberger, *Erlebnisse*, pp. 11–12; Alfred Baudrillart, *La Guerre allemande et le Catholicisme* (Paris, 1915); A. J. Rosenberg, *Der deutsche Krieg und der Katholizismus* (Berlin, 1915).

Erzberger was the guiding spirit of the Committee to Defend German and Catholic Interests formed in July 1915. This committee sponsored many publications, both of a scholarly and a periodical nature. Georg Pfeilschifter's book on *German Culture, Catholicism, and the World War* was published in 15,000 German, 30,000 English, 10,000 French, 6,000 Italian, 10,000 Spanish, 15,000 Portuguese, and 6,000 Dutch copies.[17] Pfeilschifter also edited a collection of letters written by German Catholic soldiers to document the religious spirit prevailing in the German army.[18] Dr. Schnitzer composed regular *Catholic Weekly Letters* that were mailed to monasteries and congregations abroad. Professor Krebs of Freiburg University wrote *Catholic Monthly Letters* aimed at refuting the charges of barbarism and immorality levied against Germany in the neutral world. They were published in 30,000 copies in 7 languages. Meinertz and Sacher published a standard work on *Germany and Catholicism* under Erzberger's auspices.[19] These propaganda efforts were sufficiently successful to provoke the flattery of imitation in England, where the British Catholic Information Society under the Jesuit Martindale began a series of similar publications.[20]

Erzberger's main effort at influencing Catholic opinion consisted of collecting money for the Vatican. The fact is revealed in an important memorandum written by Karl Bachem, which is printed in Appendix III. The saintly Pius X had been a poor business administrator, and his successor found the coffers completely empty. When Erzberger learned of this fact he immediately organized a collection of money in Germany, approaching Catholics and Protestants alike. In his zeal he offered Prussian titles and decorations in return for big contributions, after having been told that serious consideration would be given to his recommendations. He supplemented the private fund by drawing upon the money which the Foreign Office had given him for his propaganda work abroad. The Pope, who was extricated from a difficult situation by Erzberger's efforts, was deeply grateful. He gave several gifts and decorations to Erzberger, including his own cardinal's hat, a precious ring, and the Grand Cross of the Order of Sylvester. Erzberger was proud of his work in serving both Catholic and German interests. The Vatican retained its independence of the increasingly pro-Entente feeling of Italy and was to act as the main force opposing Italy's entry into

[17] Georg Pfeilschifter, *Deutsche Kultur, Katholizismus, und Weltkrieg* (Freiburg, 1915–1916).
[18] Georg Pfeilschifter, *Sammlung katholischer Soldatenbriefe* (Freiburg, 1915).
[19] M. Meinertz and H. Sacher, *Deutschland und der Katholizismus* (Freiburg, 1918), 2 vols.
[20] For all these activities, see Erzberger's *Erlebnisse*, pp. 11–17.

the war. Erzberger maintained close contact with the Pope during his three missions to Rome in the spring of 1915.[21]

Erzberger's propaganda efforts were not exclusively directed at Catholics. He secured the services of the Berlin Lutheran Professor Deissmann for writing a *Weekly Letter* to prominent Lutherans in America. The executive secretary of the Federal Council of the Churches of Christ in America helped in the distribution of this publication. More important was a monthly *War Chronicle* which Erzberger financed in 100,000 copies. It was soon imitated by the British propaganda service.[22] Erzberger was happy when he secured the services of an Alsatian-French journalist, G. Loretz, in 1915, to edit a bi-weekly review for him. Loretz had had a fascinating career. Born in Alsace in 1860, he had fled to France in 1876 because of his French sympathies and to escape German military service. Here he had moved in revanchist circles and had even become private secretary to General Boulanger at the height of that demagogue's power. He had then become a well-known journalist while he gradually abandoned his anti-German views. By 1914 he was sufficiently suspect to the French authorities to be interned for a year, and after his release he was eager to work for Germany. Erzberger made him editor of the *Correspondence politique del' Europe centrale,* which was printed on a government press in Berlin, then sent by the Foreign Office to the Zurich embassy, and from there distributed to English, French, Italian, and Spanish newspapers in a manner calculated to conceal its official German origin. Loretz also edited a weekly *La Paix* in 50,000 copies for distribution among French and Italian prisoners of war.[23]

Erzberger's agents made various attempts in the course of the war to purchase foreign newspapers for Germany in Rome, Bucharest, and Paris—his denial in his *Erlebnisse* cannot be taken too literally.[24] Some of his contact men gave 10,000,000 francs to Bolo Pasha, the notorious organizer of defeatism in France, to purchase a leading Parisian newspaper, though Erzberger claims that he opposed this as a hopeless venture.[25] Erzberger had more obvious success with certain publications

[21] Memorandum by Karl Bachem, dated May 21, 1918, in *Bachem Papers,* File 89. Erzberger mentions his use of Foreign Office funds to help the Vatican in a letter to Hertling, Feb. 12, 1915, in *Erzberger Papers,* File 32. Bachem stated in a letter to F. von Buhl, May 16, 1918, that Erzberger collected the money with the explicit approval of Bethmann and Jagow. *Bachem Papers,* File 89.

[22] Erzberger, *Erlebnisse,* pp. 18–19.

[23] Erzberger, *Erlebnisse,* p. 20, does not mention Loretz by name. H. P. Hannsen, *Diary of a Dying Empire* (Bloomington, 1955), pp. 261–62.

[24] Erzberger, *Erlebnisse,* p. 10.

[25] Hannsen, *op.cit.,* p. 263. Erzberger established personal contact with the ex-Khedive of Egypt at the St. Gotthard Hotel in Zurich on March 16, 1915, who praised

which he sponsored in Switzerland. Two French Left-wing journalists, Henri Guilbeaux and Charles Hartmann, founded the newspapers *Demain* and *Paris Geneve* in 1917. The aim of both papers was to serve the German cause in France and above all in French Switzerland. Their sharp anti-Entente tone made them run foul of laws safeguarding Swiss neutrality, and they were suppressed by the Swiss government in late 1917. Both authors went to Soviet Russia shortly thereafter and thus avoided prosecution in the French courts after 1918. They were condemned to death *in contumaciam* by a military tribunal in February 1919 for the crimes of defeatist propaganda and receiving funds from the enemy.[26]

Erzberger's propaganda efforts were much embarrassed by his lack of exclusive authority in the field. His office was by no means the only one which attempted to influence public opinion abroad. The foolish absence of prewar preparations was followed by an equally foolish proliferation of official, semi-official, and unofficial propaganda agencies after the outbreak of war. Erzberger counted twenty-seven such agencies in October 1914, and he was instrumental in setting up a central coordinating body, the *Zentralstelle für Auslandsdienst,* under the direction of the former ambassador to Tokyo, Baron von Mumm. Erzberger, Paul Rohrbach, the well-known publicist, and Ernst Jäckh, the main champion of German-Turkish friendship, sat on the board of directors. Otto Hammann, the Foreign Office press chief, Wilhelm Solf, the Colonial Secretary, Arnold Wahnschaffe, Bethmann's Chancellery chief, August Stein, the Berlin correspondent of the *Frankfurter Zeitung,* Erzberger, and some others met daily at the Foreign Office to discuss the general war situation and work out propaganda directives. Hammann, in his account of these meetings, is full of praise for Erzberger's achievements, and emphasizes that Erzberger's national outlook was never distorted by any narrow confessional considerations.[27]

Bolo Pasha as a reliable man who had good French contacts and who desired peace. Gallieni's threat to shoot without trial anyone found negotiating with the enemy deterred Bolo from seeing Erzberger personally. Erzberger's report to Bethmann on a journey to Switzerland dated March 18, 1915, *Hertling Papers. Geheimes Staatsarchiv, Munich.* Henceforth referred to as *Hertling Papers.*

[26] *Petit Parisien,* Feb. 22, 1919; *Gazette de Lausanne,* Feb. 25, 1919. On the press laws safeguarding Swiss neutrality, see J. Ruchti, *Geschichte der Schweiz während des Weltkrieges 1914-19* (2 vols., Bern, 1928), I, 141–46.

[27] Erzberger, *Erlebnisse,* p. 5. Otto Hammann, *Bilder aus der letzten Kaiserzeit* (Berlin, 1922), pp. 113–26. Hammann was originally skeptical of Erzberger's propaganda efforts. H. Stegemann, *Erinnerungen aus meinem Leben und aus meiner Zeit* (Stuttgart, 1930), p. 274. On the overall organization of German propaganda, see H. D. Lasswell, *Propaganda Technique in the World War* (New York, 1927), pp. 22–24, and above all Vogel, *Organisation,* pp. 26–34. The main organizations competing in a chaotic bureaucratic tangle were the News Section (IIIb) of the Supreme Command under Nicolai,

It is difficult to arrive at a final judgment of Erzberger's propaganda activities. He did not prevent the majority of neutral opinion from being sharply anti-German, but it had been so from the very beginning of the war. He failed to build up sufficient public opinion in Italy and Rumania to prevent those two countries from entering the war against the Central Powers—but the self-interest of both countries stood to gain from hostility to the Central Powers, and propaganda can rarely triumph over self-interest. His success in influencing Catholic opinion in neutral countries is generally acknowledged (the next chapter will show how friendly Catholic opinion in Italy remained to the Central Powers until the entry into the war). Erzberger's efforts cannot be compared with the brilliant achievements of Lord Northcliffe in England and George Creel in America. He never held a clear-cut position of exclusive authority. He was always hampered by the military throughout the war, whereas Northcliffe and Creel served governments where civilian supremacy was unchallenged. His greatest drawback was that his country lacked the liberal-democratic principles, so vigorously enunciated by President Wilson, which gave Entente propaganda its universal appeal in enemy and neutral countries alike. To serve as propagandist for a nationalist, militarist, and semi-autocratic country, whose war effort was challenging the liberties and equilibrium of Europe, was to assume a task where great successes could not be expected. Erzberger did his best under very trying conditions.[28]

Erzberger's Extreme Annexationism in 1914

The militarist and chauvinist follies which embarrassed Erzberger's propaganda efforts were fully shared by himself in the early stages of

the Military Liaison Office to the Foreign Office under Haeften, the News Section of the Foreign Office under Hammann, the Censorship Office under the Military District Commanders, and Erzberger's Office. A joint letter from Erzberger, Rohrbach, and Jäckh to Bethmann on October 1, 1914, had produced the rudimentary coordination of the *Zentralstelle*. A further step towards centralization through the creation of the *Kriegspresseamt* in October 1915 did little to reduce the chaos. *ibid.*, p. 35.

[28] Erzberger's propaganda services, like all his other activities, were bitterly attacked by Right-wing politicians after the 1917 Peace Resolution. Count Westarp, the Conservative leader, asked the government some very pointed questions about Erzberger at the beginning of the June 7, 1918 *Reichstag* session. Deutelmoser, the Foreign Office representative, answered in a manner very friendly to Erzberger, while noting that most of Erzberger's propaganda activities and office personnel had, by friendly agreement, been gradually taken over by the Foreign Office itself during the previous year. Erzberger had been eager to lay down his responsibilities after the fall of Bethmann in July 1917, since he could not establish friendly contact with the succeeding Chancellors. See *Reichstag Debates*, Vol. cccxii, June 7, 1918, pp. 5261–62. Some of Erzberger's friends thought the Deutelmoser statement was insufficiently generous towards him, but Erzberger was satisfied, having drawn up the text with Deutelmoser himself. Erzberger to Dr. Paul Styger, one of his Swiss contacts, June 15, 1918. *Erzberger Papers*, File 37.

the war. He wrote an extremist memorandum in early September 1914, just before the German advance was stopped at the Marne, which caused him great embarrassment in later years. Erzberger demanded in the intoxication of victory:

1. Annexation of all of Belgium plus the French Channel coast up to Boulogne.

2. From France, the acquisition of Belfort for strategic reasons, the iron ore of Briey-Longwy for economic reasons, as well as the Channel coast mentioned above.

3. In the east, the dissolution of the Russian Empire into its component national parts: Poland and the Baltic countries to become German satellites, thus removing Russia from the Baltic; the Ukraine to become an Austrian satellite, thus removing Russia from the Black Sea. All territories annexed by Germany were to be incorporated in a loose form that granted internal autonomy but avoided representation of the new populations in the *Reichstag*.

4. The creation of a German Central African Empire incorporating the French and Belgian Congos.

5. A huge reparations bill to cover the following items: direct war costs, 10 billion marks; the rebuilding of East Prussia which the Russians devastated before Tannenberg; the repayment of the entire national debt, which might justly be imposed upon the enemy since 80 percent of it was incurred because of military expenses (henceforth saving the taxpayer 250 million marks in annual interest charges); the creation of a well-endowed veterans' fund to provide for the wounded and disabled; the rebuilding of cable and wireless stations which had been destroyed by the British; gifts to statesmen and generals on the precedent established in 1871; and a far-reaching housing program so that Germany's warriors would no longer live under slum conditions.[29]

This fantastic program, which, apart from all moral objections, completely failed to see that Europe would never tolerate a German hegemony, placed Erzberger by the side of the most extreme Conservatives in war aims. The only thing that can be said in Erzberger's excuse is the early date of the memorandum, before the difficulties of Germany's position had become apparent; and that Erzberger had the wisdom, unlike most of his annexationist colleagues, to abandon such foolish aims in the further course of the war.

Erzberger made several other extravagant statements early in the

[29] Tirpitz, *Politische Dokumente* (Berlin, 1924–1926), II, 69ff. Erzberger made excuses for his annexationism in *Reichstag Debates* Vol. cccxxviii, July 25, 1919, p. 1927.

war. A good example is his narrowly chauvinist plea for the annexation of all of Belgium in October 1914:

> England has wanted the present war and is guilty of instigating it. Its power and its imperial rule based upon the brutal exercise of power must be broken at any price. Two considerations of a purely military nature can alone be decisive in determining the future fate of Belgium, and no ominous croaking (*Unkenruf*) or arguments advanced by professional or amateur diplomats should carry any weight in such crucial matters. The first consideration is, that we cannot tolerate in the future upon our Western frontier an allegedly neutral state that is in reality a tool of powers hostile to us. The second consideration is: How can we guarantee for ourselves free passage through the English Channel in the face of English maritime supremacy? . . . All I wish to say is that the future fate of Belgium must be decided in the light of the military security of the German people. . . . The decisive consideration is: How can the Belgium which we now occupy be developed into the sharpest possible offensive and defensive weapon against England? The sword has been drawn, and the sword alone must decide about the future fate of Belgium. . . . The Emperor has never said that Germany does not wish to change her frontiers. He has never said that the position of the European powers will be unchanged by this bloody war. One can say still more: All Germans would be indignant if the present heavy sacrifices would not be followed by the rewards of victory, and the German people look at the future fate of Belgium exclusively from this point of view.[30]

Erzberger did his best to mobilize influential support for his Belgian and other war aims. On a visit to Munich in late 1914 he attempted to square a program of Prussian annexation of Belgium with Wittelsbach dynastic interests by suggesting Bavarian compensation in Alsace. Erzberger wrote to the Foreign Office that Hertling, the Bavarian Premier, agreed to Belgium's being attached to the Prussian Crown, provided that Alsace-Lorraine were partitioned at the same time and Alsace incorporated into Bavaria. The Bavarian King agreed with this program at a conference with Erzberger:

> The King emphatically approves this new solution of the Alsatian question as I have discussed it with the Premier. Belgium must become German regardless of difficulties. If Prussia should prove unwilling to absorb it he [the Bavarian King] would be willing to take it over himself, provided a Bavarian corridor could be established from the Bavarian Palatinate

[30] Erzberger in *Allgemeine Rundschau*, Oct. 1914, quoted by F. Hussong, *Erzbergers Wege*, pp. 39–40. Some repetitions have been deleted.

to Belgium. The German people cannot possibly renounce the aim of securing a stranglehold over Belgium.[31]

Bethmann thought this program ridiculous, and was annoyed that Erzberger, whose official responsibility was propaganda, was negotiating with Hertling and the Bavarian King about Belgium and Alsace. He instructed the Foreign Office to show Erzberger's report to Count Lerchenfeld, the Bavarian envoy to Berlin, with a statement emphasizing "the undesirable and dangerous consequences of private persons concerning themselves with such questions." [32] Lerchenfeld then wrote to Hertling protesting the royal views as reported by Erzberger, and urged Hertling to take steps to prevent Erzberger from further spreading the contents of his interview with the King.[33] Nothing further was heard from Erzberger's first diplomatic intervention with royalty.

Erzberger's annexationist views were supported by the advocacy of ruthless practices of warfare that ill became a future champion of League of Nations principles. His worst statements were made in a newspaper article titled "No Sentimentality." It was published in February 1915 at a time when naval circles were accusing Bethmann and his entourage of tenderness towards the British enemy. Erzberger, angered by such charges, reacted by advocating extreme measures, including the bombing of civilian targets in England as retaliation for British blockade practices. He went so far as to state the case in the following general way:

> The greatest ruthlessness in the conduct of war, provided it is applied rationally, actually constitutes the greatest humanity. It would be more humane, if one had the chance, to destroy all of London with one blow, than to allow a single fellow-German to bleed to death on the battlefield; the application of drastic measures is the quickest road to peace.[34]

The entire article is translated in Appendix IV.

The Evolution of Erzberger's War Aims to 1917

Erzberger's abandonment of extreme annexationist aims was very gradual. No one particular event or moment can be assigned as signalling a fundamental change of view. He wrote the following letter to August Thyssen, the great steel magnate, in June 1915:

[31] Erzberger to the Foreign Office, Dec. 29, 1914. *Erzberger Papers*, File 32.

[32] Bethmann to the Foreign Office, Jan. 2, 1915. *German Foreign Office Documents*, National Archives, File 1498. Henceforth cited as *F.O.*

[33] Lerchenfeld to Hertling, Jan. 8, 1915. *Hertling Papers.*

[34] Erzberger in *Anklamer Zeitung*, Feb. 18, 1915. Reprinted, with a salty commentary ridiculing Erzberger's change of view, in a leaflet published by the Saxony *Landespartei der Vaterlandspartei* in the autumn of 1917. Copy in *Bachem Papers*, File 90.

All influential people are convinced that peace should only be made upon a basis which provides real guarantees for the peaceful further development of the German nation. The following terms must be included among the list of real guarantees:

1. Belgium must become a military, political, and economic satellite of Germany, so that the power of this country can never again be used against us.

2. The acquisition of the French mining area of Briey and Longwy in order to eliminate our shortage of iron ore.

3. A considerable improvement of our Vosges frontier, so that German blood must never again water the crest of the mountain.

4. The acquisition of Belfort if possible, or at least the razing of its fortifications.

5. A considerable improvement of our strategic frontier in the east, while we must also remember that the acquisition of new areas for peasant settlement is one of the most important demands of our nation.

6. Payment of adequate reparations, in view of the fact that an annual additional tax load of 3 billion marks will be inevitable if the war continues for any length of time. Our people could scarcely carry such an additional burden, and it would certainly hamper Germany's future economic development, thereby guaranteeing a great economic victory for her two chief competitors, England and the United States.[35]

Erzberger's close association with the industrialist August Thyssen did much to give him the reputation of an extreme annexationist. He joined the board of directors of the Thyssens in May 1915.[36] This Catholic-owned firm had encountered—in Thyssen's view for confessional reasons—considerable difficulty with the Protestant bureaucrats of Prussia, who administered the elaborate network of wartime regulations. Thyssen needed an influential Berlin champion who would look out for his interests. He naturally turned to the Zentrum for help, since the National Liberal Party—ordinarily the party of heavy industry —was too Protestant to sympathize with his grievances. Thyssen had known Erzberger since about 1908, and had supplied him with ammunition for an attack upon the preferential position in government con-

[35] Erzberger to Thyssen, June 24, 1915. *Erzberger Papers,* File 27. This letter, and many other documents discussed in the course of this chapter, show that Erzberger was inaccurate in his testimony at the 1920 trial when he dismissed his September 2, 1914 memorandum as a brief aberration due to the flush of victory, and implied that he began to favor a peace of conciliation soon after the Marne debacle. *Prozess,* pp. 68–69, 82–83. See also his letter to Bethmann, June 28, 1915, quoted in Westarp, *Konservative Politik,* II, 53–54. His continued annexationism is all the more remarkable since Erzberger quotes Falkenhayn as telling him in the autumn of 1914 that the war was really lost after the Marne Battle. *Erlebnisse,* p. 314.

[36] The best sketch of Thyssen is in F. Pinner, *Deutsche Wirtschaftsführer* (Charlottenburg, 15th ed., 1925), pp. 66–74.

PROPAGANDA AND WAR AIMS

tracts given to Krupp and Stumm, two of his competitors. He admired Erzberger's energy and knowledge and conferred with him with increasing frequency about his business problems in the spring of 1915.

Thyssen soon became embarrassed because he took a great deal of Erzberger's time without remuneration, and he therefore invited him to join the board of directors of the firm at an annual salary of 40,000 marks. Erzberger, now deprived of the income from his *Zentrumskorrespondenz* and still concerned about the financial future of his family, accepted with little hesitation. He believed—as was in fact true at the time—that Thyssen shared his general views on the political situation. He resigned his job as *Reichstag* reporter on military affairs, to avoid any appearance of conflict of interest, since Thyssen held large army contracts. He announced his appointment in the press so that the officials whom he approached on Thyssen business would know that he spoke in the role of company representative and not as a *Reichstag* deputy, though many bureaucrats no doubt failed to make the distinction. The holding of industrial directorships by parliamentarians was contrary to neither the ethics nor the practice of the *Reichstag;* men of unquestioned personal integrity, such as Bassermann and Stresemann, held many directorships.[37]

Erzberger's connection with Thyssen was later used to accuse him of mixing politics and business in an improper manner. He intervened with several governmental officials on behalf of company interests throughout the two years that he remained a director (1915–1917). His interventions, some of which were questionable though none were dishonorable, were discussed at great length in the course of Erzberger's libel suit against Helfferich in 1920. The evidence is summarized in Appendix v. The most serious accusation advanced by Helfferich, that Erzberger was an ardent annexationist while a Thyssen employee only to become a sharp foe of annexationism as soon as he had left Thyssen, broke down completely. The cause-and-effect relationship was the exact reverse. Erzberger became opposed to annexationism in the spring of 1917 for a variety of reasons, all unconnected with Thyssen, which will be discussed below. He knew that his new views must bring about a conflict with Thyssen, and lead to his separation from the firm with a salary loss of 40,000 marks a year. Yet he persisted in his views in spite of the fact that they would deprive him of his main source of income. Thyssen, who remained obstinately annexationist,

[37] Erzberger gave a good account of Thyssen's offer and his acceptance in *Prozess,* pp. 65–68. See also Fritz Thyssen's testimony, pp. 140–51, and August Thyssen's written affidavit, pp. 275–80; also pp. 77–82, 808–10, 863–65, 883–86, 916–20, 999–1000.

deplored Erzberger's newly acquired anti-annexationism but admired a man who refused to have his political conduct influenced by the pocketbook nerve. They parted with mutual expressions of respect, and Thyssen gave the court in 1920 an affidavit that was very favorable to Erzberger.[38]

Erzberger's attitude on war aims remained annexationist throughout 1916, in company with the views of the entire Zentrum Party.[39] Erzberger deplored the internal cleavage of the German people in the war-aims question, and ascribed it to the failure of Bethmann's leadership. He wrote in a memorandum on April 15, 1916: "The government must seize the leadership in the public discussion of war aims. If the government fails to give a lead to public opinion private interest groups will induce the people to oppose the government and voice views calculated to prolong the war. The German people has shown throughout the war that it is eager to follow a government which knows its own mind."[40]

Erzberger suggested to Bethmann a specific program for a unified and inconspicuous manipulation of public opinion. A special office should be set up under the harmless title of *German News Service preparing materials for the coming Peace Negotiations,* to be financed by one million marks from Foreign Office appropriations. Its policy directives would come from the Chancellor. It would mould public opinion in implementation of those directives by influencing the press, setting up a speakers' list primarily composed of university professors, undertaking educational work in the army, and enlisting the help of reputable organizations like the trade unions and the *Volksverein.* Erzberger specifically barred the Navy League, the Agrarians' League, and the Pan-German League from the list of acceptable organizations. Erzberger recommended that his friend Stockhammern, a Bavarian diplomat, be appointed to head the new office. Bethmann refused to accept Erzberger's suggestion since he feared that a specific governmental program at this late date would not unify the nation but rather isolate the government. His views on the crucial questions of Belgium,

[38] *Prozess,* pp. 95–98 (Helfferich's accusation), pp. 279–80 (August Thyssen's statement that the parting was honorable to Erzberger). Thyssen tried to convince Erzberger of the evils of the Peace Resolution as late as October 14, 1917. Erzberger sent him a defense, couched in friendly language, two days later. *Erzberger Papers,* File 27.
[39] F. Wacker, *Die Haltung der deutschen Zentrumspartei zur Frage der Kriegsziele im Weltkrieg 1914–18* (Lohr, 1937), Ch. 1 *passim,* and the study by John K. Zeender, "The German Center Party during World War I," in *Catholic Historical Review,* XLII (Jan. 1957), 441–68, *passim.*
[40] Erzberger's memorandum on the necessity of a Centralized Direction of the War-Aims Discussion, dated April 15, 1916, *Erzberger Papers,* File 4.

Alsace, and Poland remained rather nebulous, and increasingly antagonized extreme annexationists and anti-annexationists alike.

Erzberger had clear-cut views on all three problems though they were to change in the course of the war. He remained rather annexationist on Belgium until the spring of 1917. He both deplored and defended the German violation of Belgian neutrality as a case where necessity (i.e. reason of state) must triumph over international law—while insisting that both apologies and reparations were due to Belgium.[41] He was anxious to alleviate the condition of the population in the occupied country, and vainly sought to check Ludendorff's policy of deporting Belgian workers to Germany. He ridiculed the official view that this was a humane way of solving the problem of Belgian unemployment, and organized a relief fund to mitigate cases of extreme hardship.[42]

Although Erzberger did much to lighten Belgian suffering, and recognized that Germany's initial invasion was an outrage, he nonetheless long desired the veiled annexation of Belgium to Germany. He wrote in a letter to his friend Gerlach, the secretary of Pope Benedict, on July 28, 1915:

> The question of the annexation of Belgium is not acute and is not contemplated by the government. I have repeatedly talked with the Chancellor about it and we completely agree that the incorporation of Belgium into the German Empire is impossible. I am opposed to it from both the German and the Catholic point of view. We Germans lack the faculty for governing foreign nationalities successfully. Perhaps this is due to the Protestant character of the majority of the German people. I contemplate the following terms for the solution of the Belgian question (which are shared in general by the Chancellor): preservation of the Belgian kingdom as a sovereign state, creation of a customs and economic union with Belgium, razing of the Belgian fortifications, integration of German and Belgian railroads, German leasing of the ports of Zeebrugge and Ostende for 99 years, with the provision that the lease is to terminate earlier if Germany and England come to a genuine understanding. Belgium would remain completely independent in all its internal

[41] See, for example, his article in the September 29, 1914 issue of the Dutch newspaper *Tijd*, "The German Zentrum and the Violation of Belgian Neutrality." Copy in *Erzberger Papers*, File 27. Erzberger took the same line in the *Reichstag* as late as Feb. 27, 1918, though he then used it as part of an argument for the complete restitution of Belgium. *Reichstag Debates*, cccxi, 4223.

[42] Erzberger, *Erlebnisse*, pp. 199–201. Erzberger to Ludendorff, June 7, 1917 (misdated June 10 in the paraphrase in the *Erlebnisse*, p. 200), *Erzberger Papers*, File 6. Erzberger commented in connection with Ludendorff's role in the Belgian deportations: "I see the greatest danger in the Supreme Command meddling in purely political affairs." Erzberger to Hertling, Jan. 8, 1917. *Erzberger Papers*, File 32.

problems, especially all questions of an educational and ecclesiastical nature.[43]

Erzberger thought in the spring of 1916 that a somewhat moderated version of this program could be attained by way of separate negotiations between Germany and Belgium. His friend Gerlach at the Vatican had established contact with the Duke and Duchess Vendam, the brother-in-law and sister of the Belgian King Albert. They claimed that King Albert, in contrast to his pro-Entente ministers, wished an early peace with Germany provided that satisfactory terms were offered. Gerlach said that the Vatican would welcome such a peace. Erzberger then sounded out the German government, but secured only a platonic declaration welcoming Papal mediation.[44] The Vatican dropped the matter when Germany did not offer concrete terms and King Albert recognized that he could not win his Cabinet for the policy of a separate peace. An attempt of Erzberger's to open negotiations, this time through the Bavarian Duke Karl Theodor, the father of the Belgian Queen, was vetoed by Bethmann in June 1916, both because it appeared hopeless and because it would give the impression of German weakness.[45]

Erzberger's foreign contacts convinced him by the late spring of 1917 that Belgium was the pivot around which any general peace settlement must inevitably turn short of a total victory for Germany. He began to realize that, so far as English and American opinion was concerned, the Belgian question was primarily a moral matter that could be resolved only by unconditional German restitution. He saw that such a restitution was a prerequisite for negotiations on any other question, and therefore became the most vigorous German champion of such a policy. He began to express this unpopular opinion at public meetings, in the *Reichstag,* and in his conferences with military and civilian officials. Erzberger argued, in conjunction with a group headed by Prince Max of Baden, that a reasonable German offer on Belgium would weaken the English resolve of waging war until Germany was totally defeated. He thought that the opponents of Lloyd George's extremist policy, which included the Left wing of the Labor Party, the Asquith group of Liberals, and the Conservative followers of Lansdowne, would be encouraged by a German renunciation of Belgium.

[43] Erzberger to Gerlach, July 28, 1915. The Pope was horrified by the program and demanded the total restitution of Belgian independence. Gerlach to Erzberger, Aug. 17, 1915. *Erzberger Papers,* File 6. Karl Bachem advised Erzberger to keep the Papal views secret lest they provoke Pan-German anger. Bachem to Erzberger, Sept. 3, 1915. *Erzberger Papers,* File 27.

[44] Gerlach to Erzberger, April 26, 1916. *Erzberger Papers,* File 6. Erzberger to Gerlach, May 6, 1916. Printed in Erzberger, *Erlebnisse,* p. 206.

[45] Naumann, *Profile,* pp. 186–87.

This would allow them to argue that hostilities were being needlessly prolonged only by the French insistence upon Alsace-Lorraine, which was scarcely a British interest. If the British moderates succeeded in overthrowing Lloyd George, a negotiated peace would become possible; even if they should fail, their increasing strength must have a paralyzing effect upon Britain's war effort. In this way moral and Machiavellian considerations merged perfectly in Erzberger's mind as the annexationist Saul of 1914 became the 1917 Paul preaching the restitution of Belgium.[46]

The Alsatian question was, next to the Belgian, the main obstacle to a peace settlement in the west. France demanded the retrocession of the two provinces of Alsace-Lorraine which Germany had annexed in 1871. We have already seen, in connection with the Alsatian constitution of 1911 and the Zabern affair of 1913, that Germany had failed to secure the loyalty of even German-speaking Alsace. Erzberger saw clearly that the Alsatian question must be settled in a manner that would conciliate the population before it could come up for discussion at the peace conference.

He thought, until he suddenly changed his view in July 1917, that this could best be achieved by the rather startling plan of partitioning Alsace-Lorraine between Bavaria and Prussia. The Bavarian Premier Hertling was enthusiastic for this project. Erzberger believed that the sociological structure of Bavaria and Alsace—a political system based on universal franchise, the predominantly agrarian character, the prevalence of small industry, the deep attachment to Catholicism—was very similar, and made assimilation a simple matter, especially since the Alsatians could not look back to any tradition of separate statehood. The Prussian annexation of Lorraine would follow the lines dictated by common economic interests, though Erzberger never pretended enthusiasm for this part of the partition scheme.[47]

Erzberger saw clearly that the only alternative to partition was the creation of a new federal state with full autonomy. He told Colonel Bauer, Ludendorff's right-hand man, in the course of a conversation in early June, 1917:

> The Entente will raise this demand [for status as a federal state] even if we have a favorable termination of the war, and it will have allies in our own country (Socialists, Poles, Progressives.) But Alsace-Lorraine would be an impossible construction if raised into an autonomous federal

[46] Erzberger, *Erlebnisse,* pp. 207–08. Prince Max of Baden, *Erinnerungen und Dokumente* (Stuttgart, 1927), Part II, Sections 5–6.

[47] On the entire Alsation question, see Erzberger, *Erlebnisse,* Ch. XIII, and *Erzberger Papers,* File II.

state. The state would be lost in sentiment for the Empire from the very start and would certainly be lost territorially in the next war. The continued discussion of the Alsatian question in the German press provides fuel and fire for French revanchism. But if Alsace-Lorraine were now partitioned and the appropriate legislation were to go through the *Reichstag* at its next session the question would be settled and revanchism would die down. The press clamor would cease as soon as the Alsatians received the same constitutional rights as all Bavarians and the Lorrainers as all Prussians. The partition would lead to a decline of willingness to make further sacrifices for purely French war aims in Russia. These international reasons require an immediate execution of the partition plans.[48]

Erzberger abandoned this emphatic view only six weeks later after his Peace Resolution had transformed the entire constellation of German politics. His new alliance with the Socialists required his acceptance of their plan of autonomy for Alsace-Lorraine. This tactical consideration was quickly supplemented by insight—a good example of how external pressures had lightning results in promoting Erzberger's advance from folly to wisdom. He sent Michaelis, the new Chancellor, a detailed memorandum on July 20, 1917, pleading for the immediate necessity of elevating Alsace-Lorraine into a new federal state and adding very specific suggestions about its constitutional structure. His earlier view, that such a state would be an "impossible construction," was left unmentioned in this new memorandum.[49] The rather less flexible Hertling, whose heart was set on partition, was startled and angered by this rapid change of view, but his remonstrance brought only the following explanation and consolation from Erzberger:

The July events have made the best possible solution [the partition scheme] impossible; we must now pressure, for both international and domestic reasons, for the creation of an independent federal state. The satisfaction of the wishes of the Alsatian population would have a favorable impact upon peace prospects throughout the entire world, and this is the first of all duties of our policy today. The partition plan cannot, moreover, secure a majority in the *Reichstag* today, even if the Zentrum supported it with all its votes, since there are 189 deputies opposed to it on principle (110 Socialists, 46 Progressives, 19 Poles, 9 Alsatians, 5 Guelphs), to which must be added at least 20 National Liberals. We have established these facts with absolute certainty. The obstacles in the

[48] Erzberger's memorandum about his June 10, 1917 conversation with Colonel Bauer. *Erzberger Papers*, File 18. The conversation is mentioned briefly in *Erlebnisse*, p. 163.
[49] The July 20, 1917 memorandum is printed by Erzberger in his *Erlebnisse*, pp. 164–66.

Bundesrat are well-known. Partition has now been made impossible, exactly as I foresaw would be the case some time ago.

The *Reichstag* will have a considerable majority [by adding the Zentrum votes to the 211 mentioned above] in favor of the creation of an autonomous federal state. The indicated form of government would be a hereditary monarchy, and a Bavarian prince would have a good chance of winning the throne. The solution of the problem will bear no more delays if Germany is to settle it by herself; we must avoid a situation where foreign powers meddle with this internal German question in the style of 1648 and 1806.[50]

The pressure of Erzberger and the *Reichstag* majority in favor of Alsatian autonomy was to prove unavailing in the face of opposition from bureaucrats, soldiers, and successive Chancellors. The question was still unsettled at the time of Germany's collapse in November 1918, when the embittered Alsatian population welcomed the French army as liberators.[51]

The discontent of the Alsatians of the west was matched by the Poles in the east. We have seen how Erzberger had vigorously championed Polish claims against Prussian tyranny before the war. The problem was now enlarged by the German-Austrian conquest of Russian Poland in 1915. Erzberger developed a program of creating an independent Polish state with voluntary ties to the Central Powers. He thought that a friendly Poland would give Germany much better strategic protection in the future than any direct territorial annexations. But a friendly Poland presupposed imaginative policies on the part of the Central Powers. Erzberger thought that these would have to include the cession of Posen and Galicia, two provinces with a predominantly Polish population, to the new state; while Prussia must conciliate her remaining Polish population by repealing all of her anti-Polish legislation. This program was bitterly opposed by Prussian Conservatives who had long hated the Poles and who hankered after a return to the friendship with Tsarist Russia based upon mutual hostility to Polish claims.[52]

In the endless German-Austrian discussions concerning the link which a new Poland should have to the Central Powers Erzberger favored the so-called "Austro-Polish solution." This envisaged the new Polish state as the third partner of an enlarged Hapsburg monarchy. He valued such a settlement as a good solution not only for Polish but also for internal Hapsburg problems. It would end the stranglehold which the Magyars held at present over the entire monarchy, since

[50] Erzberger to Hertling, July 30, 1917. *Erzberger Papers*, File 32.
[51] Erzberger, *Erlebnisse*, pp. 167–69.
[52] Erzberger explains his Polish policy in his *Erlebnisse*, pp. 172–74.

Warsaw could combine with Vienna against Budapest in the future. The detachment of the Polish area from Austria would give the Germans a predominant voice in the remaining part of the state. Erzberger hoped this would be used to bring about a reasonable settlement of the Czech question once the Germans were freed of the fear of Slav domination. Erzberger saw the Austro-Polish solution as part of the general scheme of *Mitteleuropa* championed by Friedrich Naumann. This plan contemplated common military and economic institutions between the German and Hapsburg Empires that would in fact lead to a thinly concealed Germany hegemony.[53]

The most notable feature of Erzberger's career until 1917 is his nearly complete absorption in international affairs. He took little interest in the rising demand for an immediate reform of the Prussian franchise, favoring it in principle but believing it inopportune in wartime. He did not concern himself seriously with the problems of economic organization for war, though economic problems had been one of his specialties before the war. His attention centered on Belgium, Alsace, Poland, and the other problems that held the international stage. His propaganda work contributed to this preoccupation and gave him a professional knowledge of foreign affairs. This knowledge was soon enhanced by his diplomatic missions to Rome, Vienna, Budapest, Constantinople, Sofia, and Bucharest. The first and most interesting of his missions took him three times to Italy in the spring of 1915.

[53] For Erzberger's advocacy of the Austro-Polish solution, see *ibid*. For *Mitteleuropa*, see the excellent study by Henry Cord Meyer, *Mitteleuropa in German Thought and Action 1815–1945* (The Hague, 1955). Erzberger's sympathy with Polish nationalism did not blind him to the larger consideration of the desirability of a separate peace with Russia. Thus he opposed, for example, the Polish Proclamation of November 5, 1916, because it destroyed a promising chance for peace while also being based upon faulty hopes of Polish enlistments in the German army. He wrote to Ludendorff in this sense on November 16, 1916. *Erzberger Papers,* File 29.

CHAPTER VI

DIPLOMATIC ACTIVITIES

The Italian Situation in 1914–1915

ITALY was the only major European power that remained neutral in 1914. Its Triple Alliance obligations did not apply in an aggressive war begun by Austria, but the Central Powers nonetheless had a feeling of having been betrayed by their former ally. They might conceivably have secured Italian participation by offering bribes of French colonial booty, but such offers became unattractive once the German armies had been stopped at the Marne.[1] The Italian government, headed by Premier Salandra, soon demanded concessions from Austria as the price of continued neutrality.[2] It specifically asked for the cession of provinces of the Hapsburg Monarchy that contained large numbers of "unredeemed Italians": the Trentino, the Isonzo valley, Trieste, and parts of the Dalmatian coast. Long negotiations ensued between Vienna and Rome. The Austrians were naturally reluctant to make concessions, so Italy, and especially the strong-minded Foreign Minister Sonnino, threatened war. He believed that Italy must exploit a uniquely favorable international situation to achieve long-standing national aims.[3]

Various sections of Italian public opinion favored a policy of intervention against the Central Powers quite apart from the opportunity of making territorial gains. Liberals and Right-wing Socialists preached an ideological war against the German and Austrian "autocracies," the Freemasons organized agitation for such a crusade, and the rising nationalist movement under the poet D'Annunzio favored action for action's sake, and expected the exhilarating medicine of gunfire and poison gas to purge the decadent Italian soul.[4]

Some influential groups in Italy continued to favor a neutralist policy. Giolitti, the long-time political manipulator who controlled about 300 out of 500 parliamentary seats, correctly foresaw a long and bloody war. He thought that Italy might secure large concessions from Austria without going to war, or that she should at least delay her war entry until Austria should be weakened by her other campaigns. His power

---

[1] Bülow, *Denkwürdigkeiten*, III, 187–91.

[2] Salandra's views appear best in his *Italy and the Great War: From Neutrality to Intervention* (London, 1932).

[3] Bülow, *op.cit.*, III, 219; Salandra, *op.cit.*, p. 145.

[4] A good sketch of pro-war attitudes is in Benedetto Croce *History of Italy, 1871–1915* (Oxford, 1929), Ch. XII.

was, however, small while parliament was not in session, and Salandra ruthlessly used his executive power to create a *fait accompli*.[5] The Left-wing Socialists opposed war on pacifist grounds; but their revolutionary extremism discredited them to such an extent that they injured any cause by their support. The Vatican assumed the leadership of the neutralist forces. Pope Benedict XV specifically feared Italian intervention because of the difficulties which this would create for the Church. The Vatican would be cut off from the Catholics of the Central Powers. In case of Italian defeat, the Papacy might be expelled from Rome by social revolution; in case of victory, Italy would probably become more intransigent still in the Roman question. The defeat of Austria would bring the collapse of the last great Catholic monarchy in Europe. The strongest champions of Italy's entry into the war were the Freemasons, whose main aim was the destruction of Catholicism. For all these reasons the Catholic Church was the real antagonist of Salandra and Sonnino.

The battle between interventionists and neutralists raged from the late autumn of 1914 until May 1915. The Central Powers attempted to strengthen the neutralist party, and the German government sent the former Chancellor, Prince Bülow, on this delicate mission in December 1914. Bülow was especially suited for the role by his Italian connections. He had served in Italy as ambassador before beginning his Berlin career, his wife was an Italian countess, he spoke Italian fluently, and after his fall in 1909 he had taken up regular winter residence in Rome, where he owned the magnificent Villa Malta. If any outsider could influence Italy to maintain her neutrality, he was certainly the man, and this view had at last become prevalent at Berlin after a long succession of remarkable intrigues.

The men around Bethmann, and especially the Foreign Secretary Jagow, were bitterly opposed to sending Bülow to Rome. They feared that success in Rome would inevitably lead to a public demand for his return to the Chancellorship. They resented his manipulation of a newspaper campaign to secure his appointment to the Roman embassy.[6] Their hostility was to go so far—at least in the view of Bülow and Erzberger—as to make them sabotage Bülow's Roman efforts behind his back, on the principle that a hostile Italy was a lesser evil than their

[5] Giolitti's position is best expressed in his *Memoirs of My Life* (London, 1923), Ch. XVI.
[6] Bülow's view that he was reluctantly pressed into accepting the mission need not be taken seriously. *Denkwürdigkeiten*, III, 195–97. Jagow gives his reasons for opposing Bülow's mission in *Front Wider Bülow*, ed. F. Thimme, pp. 212–14. Bülow's hatred of Jagow best emerges in *Denkwürdigkeiten*, III, 33–36.

own displacement from political power.[7] Erzberger was among those who had favored sending Bülow to Italy. He was never a man to bear grudges, and he had readily buried the hostility based upon the 1906 dissolution of the *Reichstag* and his suspicion of Bülow's conduct in 1908 at the time of the *Daily Telegraph* incident. Bülow showed his adaptability by condescending to flatter Erzberger and even apologizing for his 1906 conflict with the Zentrum as "the most stupid thing he had ever done in his life." [8]

Bülow, upon his arrival in Rome, found the political situation to be very unfavorable to the Central Powers, with the Austro-Italian negotiations having come to a standstill due to Austrian procrastination. His first reports to Berlin, like his private letters to Erzberger, were couched in very pessimistic terms. The reaction of the Bethmann circle was characterized by Erzberger as follows: "Bülow deliberately paints a dark picture; one sees how he is preparing himself for all contingencies. If Italy stays out of the war, Bülow will say that he succeeded in the face of overwhelming obstacles. If Italy enters the war he can point to his despatches to prove that the situation was already hopeless at the time of his arrival." [9] Bülow saw that only strong German pressure upon Austria could force the latter to make the kind of concessions that could satisfy the Italian neutralists; and he saw that the Vatican was the center from which neutralism could best be strengthened. He thought that Erzberger was the best man to help him in promoting both developments. Erzberger had good contacts among the Vienna Christian Socialists who might prod Count Burian, the Foreign Minister, into a realistic appraisal of the situation; while as a prominent Zentrum deputy he would have easy access to the Vatican.

Erzberger's First Mission

Erzberger came to Rome in early February 1915 upon the urging of Bülow but with the full approval of Bethmann. He was eager to serve as mediator between these two enemies. Bülow at first thought that Erzberger had been instructed by Bethmann to spy upon him, and in his *Memoirs* tells the improbable story that Erzberger came armed with a special cipher for that purpose.[10] But Erzberger in fact showed all his reports to Bülow before sending them to Berlin, and their co-

---

[7] Erzberger, *Erlebnisse*, p. 23; Bülow, *Denkwürdigkeiten*, III, Chs. xv–xviii, *passim*.
[8] Bachem, *Zentrumspartei*, VII, 81.
[9] Erzberger, *Erlebnisse*, p. 23.
[10] Bülow, *Denkwürdigkeiten*, III, 210. The special cypher is ridiculed by Wahnschaffe in *Front Wider Bülow*, p. 305.

operation soon became so intimate that they frequently sent joint dispatches.[11]

Erzberger's first report gave an excellent survey of the Roman sources that he used to get a comprehensive picture of the Italian political situation:

> I had the opportunity in Rome to establish direct or indirect contact with all influential groups in order to ascertain their views. I was informed of the Vatican's assessment of the situation by the Pope, the Cardinal Secretary of State [Gasparri], the Under-Secretary Pacelli [later Pope Pius XII], Monsignore Gerlach, the German prelates in Rome, the Jesuit General Count Ledochowski, the Provincial of the German Jesuits Father Ehrle, Father Fonck [head of the Biblical Institute], Father von Lossberg, and the Capuchin Father Cölestin [an influential Viennese monk]. Italian governmental views were expressed by prominent deputies and Senators (Capelli, Cirmini, Santini, etc.) whose attitudes can be considered representative. Neutral observers were available in the persons of the Turkish ambassador and Turkish military attaché, the Bulgarian minister and the former Bulgarian Cabinet member Genadiew, and several German journalists. I heard the Austrian view from Ambassador Baron Macchio with whom I had a long conversation at his request. The universal consensus of opinion, apart from the Austrian ambassador, is as follows: *Italy will inevitably enter the war unless a settlement is quickly reached with Austria. The unconditional neutrality of Italy cannot be attained without Austrian concessions. But it can be said with equal certainty that the benevolent neutrality of Italy can be achieved for the entire duration of the war at the price of relatively small Austrian offers. The Austrian concessions can be kept secret [until the end of the war] though Germany would have to assume a guarantee in some form.* These unanimous Italian views appear to be so solidly established so as to make a change appear quite impossible.[12]

Erzberger based this optimistic view, with its assumption that relatively small concessions could secure not only Italian neutrality, but even benevolent neutrality, primarily upon a conversation with Capelli, the Vice President of the Chamber of Deputies, who professed to share

---

[11] The main source materials for Erzberger's missions to Rome are his three reports to Bethmann in the *Erzberger Papers*, File 34, and also in the *Hertling Papers*. They will be cited as *First, Second,* and *Third Report.* They are undated, but judging from internal evidence must have been composed on February 28, April 9, and May 20, 1915. Erzberger used them, with many significant omissions, as the basis of Ch. II of his *Erlebnisse im Weltkrieg.* They fill many gaps left by the most recent study of Italy's entry into the war: W. W. Gottlieb, *Studies in Secret Diplomacy during the First World War* (London, 1957), Chs. xxi–xxiii.

[12] *First Report,* pp. 1–2, partly quoted in *Erlebnisse,* p. 24. Erzberger's italics.

the views of Sonnino, the Foreign Minister. He thought that an early offer of the Trentino alone, when combined with a promise of better treatment of the Italian population within the Austrian Empire, would suffice to assure Italian neutrality. Capelli said that Sonnino was much irritated by Austrian procrastination and evident bad faith, but still hoped for a satisfactory completion of the negotiations.[13] To Erzberger, accepting this view, it appeared nothing short of criminal for Austria to refuse to purchase Italian neutrality quickly at so reasonable a price. He was appalled by the views of Baron Macchio, the Austrian Ambassador, who faithfully took the position of his chief Burian that no concessions whatever were necessary, and that Austria would not be seriously injured even if Italy should decide upon war.[14] Erzberger saw that strong pressure upon Vienna could alone avoid an early Italian entry into the war.

This assessment of the situation was shared by Pope Benedict XV, with whom Erzberger had a long audience on February 23, 1915. It partly dealt with matters unconnected with the Italian situation, such as the Entente charge that German Protestant soldiers had violated 2,000 nuns during the invasion of Belgium (which Erzberger doubted but promised to investigate), and the problem of securing a new occupant for the arch-episcopal chair of Posen-Gnesen (where Erzberger promised to press Papal views upon the German government).[15] But the main topic of the conversation was the best way of preventing Italy's entry into the war. Erzberger wrote to Bethmann-Hollweg the following account of the Pope's attitude: "The Pope attaches the greatest value to the maintenance of peace between Italy and Austria, partly because of the general Catholic interest of his being able to carry out the untrammelled administration of the Church, partly because of his specific interest in Austria, which he wishes to see maintained as a Catholic Great Power." [16]

Erzberger then urged the Pope to make his influence felt in Vienna to produce the concessions which could alone maintain peace:

> It would be a great service to the cause of peace if Your Holiness could in some form make Vienna aware of the seriousness of the situation. Of course one can understand Austrian hesitations, which are based primarily on the following two considerations:

[13] *First Report*, pp. 4–5. The conversation with Capelli is described in *Erlebnisse*, pp. 24–25, without identifying Capelli.

[14] *First Report*, pp. 6–7. *Erlebnisse*, pp. 25–26.

[15] Erzberger, *Erlebnisse*, pp. 41–43.

[16] Erzberger's report to Bethmann about conversation with Pope, undated. *Erzberger Papers*, File 34.

1. Will Italy really be satisfied by minor frontier corrections, or will these only be followed by additional demands, such as the cession of Trieste, which would be intolerable from both the German and Austrian point of view?

2. Can the secrecy of any agreement be absolutely maintained [until the end of the war] so that the various nationalities of the Hapsburg Monarchy will not think that the concessions to Italy constitute the beginning of the complete dissolution of the Austro-Hungarian Empire?

Guarantees on these two questions are the prerequisites for a smooth settlement of the Austro-Italian question.[17]

Benedict XV agreed with Erzberger's analysis which pointed to the main obstacles in the way of a settlement. The Austrians were unwilling to make any concessions on the ground that these would only be taken by Italy as the basis for further blackmail. The Austrian insistence upon secrecy in any agreement that was reached required that any promised cessions would be deferred until the end of the war. Yet on this point—the timing of the cessions, assuming that such could be agreed upon—the mutual distrust which both Italy and Austria felt for each other made agreement virtually impossible. Salandra and Sonnino doubted the good faith of Austria in living up to her promises in case of victory.[18] Burian, on the other hand, thought it impossible to hand over any territory until the completion of hostilities; immediate cession would destroy Hapsburg prestige, would stimulate the appetite of other nationalities for concessions, and would surrender Austria's border fortifications (which naturally lay in the territory contiguous to Italy which would be transferred) to the unrealiable Italians. Might not the Italians, fearing an Austrian victory, declare war after securing Austria's military defenses through negotiations, with the prospect of an unimpeded march to Vienna? Were the countrymen of Machiavelli incapable of such sharp dealings? [19]

Erzberger believed that these obstacles could be overcome. His recommendations to Bethmann, written after his return to Germany from his first journey, envisaged a comprehensive program for applying pressure upon Austria to make concessions that could satisfy Italy without being intolerable to the Hapsburg government.

On the basis of all my information I come to the following conclusions:

1. An agreement between Austria and Italy must at all costs be quickly achieved under the leadership and guarantee of Germany as otherwise the

[17] *Erzberger Papers*, File 34.
[18] Salandra, *op.cit.*, pp. 240–44, 255, 257.
[19] Count Stefan Burian, *Drei Jahre aus der Zeit meiner Amtsführung im Kriege* (Berlin, 1923), Ch. 1.

World War will probably be lost by Germany through the entry of both Italy and Rumania [which was believed to take her cue from Italy] into the war.

2. The Viennese resistance to concessions can be overcome through guaranteeing their secrecy, through sending personalities to Vienna who have sufficient influence among the leading men of the Hapsburg government (Father Cölestim, Father Andlau), through letters which the Pope is willing to send to influential cardinals (Czernoch, Hornich, Piffl) if requested to do so, and through contacting immediately the leaders of the Christian Socialist Party (which I am willing to undertake myself if requested to do so).

3. Germany should be prepared to grant concessions on her own part to Austria, to balance her losses to Italy: (a) the freeing of the Elbe River from shipping dues, which will win over Bohemia and above all its Czechified high nobility; (b) handing over the Sosnowice coal area [the tip of Upper Silesia] after expropriating its present owners, to Austria-Hungary; thus certain Hungarian circles, interested in cheap coal, would become more kindly disposed towards a settlement.

4. The fear that Austria might, while smarting with resentment under the strong German pressure, make a separate peace with Russia, is groundless in view of the fact that Germans, Hungarians, and Poles would be equally opposed to such a policy. I wish to add emphatically that a quick resolution of the entire question is of the utmost importance.[20]

Bethmann was much impressed by the cogency of Erzberger's views, and secured him an interview with the Emperor in order to mobilize William to apply the indicated pressure upon the Emperor Franz Joseph in Vienna (March 1, 1915). Times had changed indeed, when a divine-right Hohenzollern was willing to receive a tailor's son from Buttenhausen. To the remark of an aide-de-camp, who received Erzberger at Castle Bellevue before the audience, "I trust you will only bring good news to His Majesty?" Erzberger replied that he would speak the full truth as he saw it. Karl Bachem gives an account of the beginning of the interview, based upon what Erzberger told him the same afternoon:

The Emperor received Erzberger in a very friendly manner, invited him to sit down, and handed him his cigarette case. Erzberger said, "No, thank you, Your Majesty." Then the Emperor, "What's the meaning of this (Nanu)? In my entire life it has never happened before that someone rejected a cigarette which I offered!" Erzberger replied unperturbed, "But Your Majesty, I really do not smoke!" The Emperor laughed, and a cordial atmosphere was established.[21]

[20] First Report, pp. 7–8. Brief Summary in Erlebnisse, p. 26.
[21] Bachem, Zentrumspartei, VI, 18.

The conversation between Emperor and Erzberger proved rather desultory, but Erzberger succeeded in having William see the necessity of putting pressure on Franz Joseph. William said wistfully that the latter was "his sole surviving friend in the world." Erzberger's general estimate of William was as follows:

> The Emperor was very charming during the entire conversation and spoke rapidly and vigorously. It was not easy to give him a coherent report on any one subject, since he interrupted frequently and often turned the conversation to new questions. Yet I nonetheless had the impression that it was not too difficult for a man with a clear and firm purpose to win the Emperor over to his own point of view.[22]

The Emperor was evidently charmed by his new Swabian acquaintance, and dismissed him with the following words: "Mr. Erzberger, feel yourself free to call on me at any time of the day or night; all you have to do is to announce yourself." Erzberger was sophisticated enough not to take this seriously.[23]

One difficulty in the way of German pressure upon Austria was that such a policy was not endorsed by German public opinion, which naïvely preferred airing its moral indignation against Italy to taking a cool and realistic view of the situation. Erzberger used his press connections in order to educate it into a more reasonable frame of mind.[24] The Austrians were given to feel that their intransigence was considered dangerous by the German government.

German and Papal pressure upon Vienna rose to fever heat in early March, and was successful to the extent of inducing Franz Joseph to recognize the necessity of further negotiations with Italy—though he described the proposed cession of the Trentino as "suicide for the monarchy." [25] The Pope urged Piffl, the Vienna Cardinal, Ledochowski, the Jesuit General, Pacelli, the Under-Secretary of State, and Monsignor Scapinelli, the Vienna Nuncio, to influence the old Emperor, and Katharina Schratt, his actress friend, was mobilized for the same purpose.[26] Bethmann instructed Tschirschky, the German Ambassador to Vienna,

---

[22] Erzberger, *Erlebnisse,* pp. 50–52, a nearly verbal reproduction of a memorandum dated March 1, 1915, in *Erzberger Papers,* File 34.

[23] Bachem, *Zentrumspartei,* VI, 18.

[24] Letter of *Verlag der Kölnischen Volkszeitung* to Bethmann, March 6, 1915, with copy in *Erzberger Papers,* File 34.

[25] Erzberger, *Erlebnisse,* p. 25.

[26] Memorandum by Stockhammern, undated but from internal evidence composed in 1921, printed in Wilhelm Patin, *Beiträge zur Geschichte der Deutsch-Vatikanischen Beziehungen in den letzen Jahrzehnten* (Berlin, 1942), p. 17. Henceforth cited as Patin, *Beiträge.* See also Salandra, *op.cit.,* pp. 232 and 239. Piffl denied that the Pope had urged him to see Franz Joseph. See Karl von Macchio, *Wahrheit! Fürst Bülow und ich in Rom* (Vienna, 1931), p. 63.

to apply pressure upon Burian, and also sent Count Monts, a prominent retired diplomat, to act in the same sense, though Bülow—who was a personal enemy of Monts—thought that the latter did more harm than good.[27] Erzberger himself approached Dr. Albert Gessmann, a former Minister of Public Works, and Prince Alois Liechtenstein, the parliamentary leader of the Christian Socialists, both of whom carried some weight with the Austrian Foreign Office. Both urged the stubborn Burian to show a little more flexibility in negotiating with the Italians. The result was Burian's new proposal of March 9, 1915, which at least had the effect of prolonging the negotiations.

Erzberger proudly took credit for having broken the ice, "more especially by his plan for German counter-concessions to Vienna."[28] He was confirmed in this view by flattering letters from people in close touch with the Roman situation. Mühlberg, the Prussian minister to the Vatican, wrote to Erzberger on March 9, 1915: "You alone deserve the credit for starting the heavy stone rolling." Bülow wrote on March 27: "I am very pleased that you, after examining the situation here in full independence and without prejudice, have come to exactly the same conclusions as I myself. You have served the Fatherland well in forcing your impressions upon Berlin with your accustomed fearlessness."[29]

Erzberger's Second Mission

Erzberger was summoned by Bülow and despatched by Bethmann on a second journey to Rome in the first week of April. He had another audience with the Pope on April 3, where many pending questions were again discussed. Erzberger urged the Pope to restrain the Belgian Cardinal Mercier in his incessant conflicts with the German military administration—a request to which Benedict gave a noncommittal answer. The Pope urged a two-day truce on the bloody Nieuwe Chapelle battlefield to allow burial of the dead, and Erzberger secured the assent of the German military commanders to this within a few days. Erzberger sent the following telegram to Bethmann summarizing Benedict's political attitude:

> Pope has applied pressure upon Cadorna [the bellicose Italian Commander-in-Chief] in favor of peace through an intermediary, and will continue his efforts. He does not view the Austro-Italian situation pessimistically, although England has offered Italy a loan of billions. Wiegand will have audi-

[27] Bülow, *Denkwürdigkeiten*, III, 397.
[28] Erzberger, *Erlebnisse*, p. 27.
[29] *ibid.*, p. 26. Macchio, *op.cit.*, p. 112, denies that Erzberger's pressure had any influence upon the Austrian Court.

ence with Pope and Cardinal Secretary of State tomorrow concerning American shipments of war equipment [to the Entente].[30]

Karl von Wiegand, the famous correspondent of the *New York World,* did have his interview on April 5, and published a sensational article a few days later quoting (or misquoting) the Pope as indicating that he favored an American arms embargo, which would do grave injury to the Entente Powers. This Papal pronouncement, indirectly stimulated by Erzberger, caused grave annoyance to England and France, with England going so far as to lodge an official protest against the Papal remarks.[31] Benedict was probably irritated by this development, and it was perhaps on this occasion that he passed the judgment which Bülow later quoted in his *Memoirs:* "This famous Erzberger may possess considerable parliamentary talents. But why, in heaven's name, does he meddle in diplomacy for which, it seems to me, he is not at all suited." [32] Erzberger was indeed a far cry from the traditional diplomat, and many professionals found his informal approach and excessive zeal annoying. But it must be remembered that Benedict continued to maintain close contact with Erzberger on the latter's third journey to Rome—no matter what his personal reservations—and that Bülow valued his services sufficiently to urge him to return at the very height of the intervention crisis.

Erzberger had a long conversation with Sonnino, the Foreign Minister, on April 6, in order to report to him the German pressure upon Vienna and the German willingness to guarantee Austian compliance with any agreement. The interview had been suggested by Capelli and arranged by Bülow. Erzberger had the correct impression that Sonnino had not yet signed any agreement with the Entente, despite his dissatisfaction with the inadequate Austrian offer of March 9. He used the following approach to persuade Sonnino to maintain neutrality:

My exposition showed that the German people wished to see friendly relations of a permanent nature between Italy and Germany and Italy and Austria. For this reason the German government had done everything in its power, despite almost insuperable obstacles, to prepare the way in Vienna for a settlement. Germany was willing to guarantee the execution of any possible agreement, and it was strong enough to make its guarantee an absolute assurance. Germany's military position was excellent, her armies stood on both fronts deep in enemy territory and were able to hold those fronts no matter how long the war would last. Germany had soldiers,

[30] *Second Report,* p. 1.
[31] Erzberger, *Erlebnisse,* pp. 43–44, quotes the Wiegand article. Letter of Mühlberg to Erzberger, April 22, 1915, in *Erzberger Papers,* File 34.
[32] Bülow, *Denkwürdigkeiten,* II, 170.

munitions, food, and above all money to meet all foreseeable demands. Italy must recognize that she cannot gain more even in the case of a victorious war than she can secure now by way of friendly negotiation. As regards possible claims to Trieste she must take into account that—according to authoritative Russian press utterances—the Slavs will certainly insist upon securing both Trieste and the Dalmatian Coast. The terrific sacrifices in blood and money which entry into the war would entail must therefore be in vain.

Erzberger ended by urging Sonnino to stick to the nationality principle, which dictated moderation in Italy's Adriatic demands. He preached the virtue of moderation by reminding Sonnino of Bismarck's conduct in 1866, when the very restrained Prussian demands upon Austria had prepared the way for prolonged Austro-Prussian friendship. He finally urged the necessity of a quick settlement lest German public opinion become strongly hostile to Italy.

Sonnino replied that the latest Austrian offer was quite unsatisfactory and must certainly be enlarged. He also declared—and this was a very serious matter—that he could not agree to maintain the secrecy of any possible agreement. The Italian parliament and people must see visible results from the present negotiations, or else the demand for war would become irresistible. Only full publication of a treaty, no matter how humiliating this was to the Hapsburg Monarchy, could satisfy Italy.[33]

The Jesuit General Ledochowski was now far more pessimistic than in February, feeling that Italian Freemasonry placed its hatred of Catholic Austria above the attainment of national aims in the Trentino.[34] But others were more optimistic. The prominent Cardinal Lorenzelli considered war to be out of the question if the Trentino were ceded, and he developed the theory that the rapid pace of Italian military preparations was aimed not so much against Austria, but at coercing France in the event of the attainment of Austrian concessions. If Austria was compelled to cede Trentino as the price of Italian neutrality, why should France not be compelled to cede Tunisia or Corsica for the same end?[35] Erzberger's friend Capelli, the Vice President of the Chamber, was still convinced that the government did not want war.[36] On the basis of these talks Erzberger came to the following

[33] Second Report, pp. 3–4. Erzberger gives Sonnino's, but not his own, arguments in Erlebnisse, p. 28.

[34] Second Report, p. 2. Erzberger does not identify Ledochowski by name in his Erlebnisse.

[35] Second Report, p. 2.

[36] Second Report, p. 2. Erzberger does not identify Capelli by name in his Erlebnisse, p. 27.

conclusions at the end of his second Roman journey: "Italy demands from Austria an offer that goes beyond the first; she will make strong counter-demands, but will then be satisfied with a peaceful solution based upon terms half way between the two extremes." [37]

Erzberger stopped in Vienna on his return journey in order to convince the leading figures of the necessity of making an offer going beyond Burian's note of March 9. He had interviews with several members of the House of Parma, whose influence was strong because Zita, the wife of the heir-apparent Charles, was the daughter of the Duchess of Parma. Erzberger won the Duchess and her daughter over to the policy of further concessions to Italy, though they were both resentful of the pressure which Germany was applying in Vienna. He talked with prominent ecclesiastics, Cardinal Piffl, the Capuchin Cölestin, and the Jesuit Provincial Andlau. He saw Morawski, a prominent minister, and his former contacts Gessmann and Liechtenstein. Erzberger's advocacy of a new Austrian offer to Italy ran into a new obstacle: Viennese circles were indignant at Bülow's conduct in Rome, because he was constantly prodding Macchio to make ever greater concessions.

This Austrian attitude was partly the necessary result of Bülow carrying out his assigned task of preserving Italian neutrality at the expense of Austria; but it was strengthened by Jagow, the German Foreign Secretary, who showed Bülow's dispatches from Rome, filled with castigation of Austria's procrastinating diplomacy, to the Austrian ambassador at Berlin.[38] Erzberger probably was also responsible, through incaution rather than malice, for the Viennese hostility to Bülow. He had sent copies of some of his and Bülow's joint dispatches to the Hungarian Archbishop Arpad Varady with the purpose of enlisting his influence on behalf of the policy of concession to Italy—a policy which Hungary, little interested in the Austrian *status quo,* might be induced to support. Varady showed these dispatches—replete with hostile remarks about Hapsburg diplomacy—to his friend Count Stephen Tisza, the Hungarian Premier, who passed them on to Vienna. This brought hostility to Bülow to a fever pitch, with injured personal vanity compounding genuine disagreement on policy. Erzberger himself was treated more leniently as a secondary accomplice without official status.[39] The resentment against Bülow was to have important consequences in July 1917,

[37] Erzberger, *Erlebnisse,* p. 27.

[38] Bülow, *Denkwürdigkeiten,* III, 217. Erzberger hints at Jagow's intrigues in *Erlebnisse,* p. 29.

[39] Bachem, *Zentrumspartei,* IX, 410–11; Count Botho von Wedel, "Diplomatisches und Persönliches," in *Front Wider Bülow,* pp. 251–56; Count Stefan Tisza, *Briefe 1914–18* (Berlin, 1928), edited by Oskar von Wertheimer, pp. 236–44.

when Austrian opposition was one of the reasons why Bülow's hopes of succeeding Bethmann were destined to be frustrated.[40]

Erzberger felt that he had made solid progress on his visit to Vienna, writing to Bethmann: "I think I have attained my objective that Austria will not answer new Italian demands with a flat 'no' and the termination of negotiations." [41] He urged Bethmann to continue his pressure upon Vienna, with Bethmann going to see Burian for a show-down meeting on April 25, 1915. At that meeting Bethmann quoted Falkenhayn the Chief of the General Staff, as saying that Italian entry into the war would inevitably lead to the defeat of the Central Powers. He also told Burian of Germany's total inability to give any help to Austria on any future Italian front. In view of these facts there was no alternative to meeting Italy's terms.[42] The strength of this statement is clear proof that Bethmann himself, whatever may be said of his entourage, gave solid backing to the Bülow-Erzberger policy, though it was regrettable that Bethmann had not done so two months earlier, for the game was to be lost for the Central Powers on the next day.

Erzberger's Third Mission

Italy signed the Pact of London with the Entente Powers on April 26, 1915, pledging entry into the war on the side of the Entente within a month, in return for great promises at Austria's expense. But this pact remained secret for several weeks, and Bülow continued to hope until early May that an Austro-Italian agreement was possible. He summoned Erzberger to Rome for a third time in late April, and the latter arrived for a last visit on May 1. Erzberger immediately threw himself into a series of conferences, sometimes under dramatic and conspiratorial conditions.

> There were daily conversations with many different people, frequently outside Rome because Germanophile Italians felt afraid of being accused of treason by their fellow countrymen if seen [with Erzberger]. Meetings in obscure churches, crypts, remote monasteries and alleys alternated with conferences at the Villa Malta [Bülow's residence], the Palazzo Caffarelli [German embassy], the Villa Bonaparte [residence of the Prussian ambassador] and in the apartment of the Bavarian envoy Baron Ritter.[43]

Erzberger made one last attempt to influence the Italian government by another interview with Sonnino and a first interview with the Pre-

[40] Bülow's peevish hostility to Erzberger in his *Memoirs* may go back to this incident. See also Bachem, *Zentrumspartei*, IX, 381–86.

[41] Erzberger, *Erlebnisse*, p. 29.

[42] Protocol of Bethmann-Burian Conference in *F.O.*, File 1498.

[43] *Third Report*, p. 1.

mier Salandra. Sonnino, whom he saw on May 3 after Cardinal Gas-parri had expressed the suspicion that Italy had already bound herself to the Entente, naturally tried to give Erzberger the opposite impression. Sonnino complained bitterly about the negotiating technique of Macchio, while praising the work of Bülow. Bülow had—no doubt acting in good faith—repeatedly stated that Vienna would make certain concessions which were subsequently watered down when officially presented by Macchio. Sonnino demanded an end of such double-dealing, and Erzberger was so impressed that he sent an alarmist telegram to Bethmann, advising him to give Vienna an ultimatum: "We can no longer hesitate or drift. We must force Austria with decisiveness, and if necessary with ruthlessness, to yield [to Italian demands] within three days. Otherwise our further efforts here in Rome will be hopeless." [44] Erzberger spoke with similar emphasis to Macchio, who promised to secure a final Austrian offer to Italy in the next few days.[45]

Erzberger saw Salandra for a long conversation on May 4, and both men have left an account of their meeting. Salandra found Erzberger "a quick and audacious mind. He was an exuberant talker, astute but somewhat vulgar. Altogether, a complex personality and a remarkable man, if not altogether sympathetic." [46] In the course of their talk Sa-landra, according to Erzberger, repeated Sonnino's complaints about Austria, but then expressed remarkably moderate views, demanding for Italy only a part of Trentino and suggesting a free city status for Trieste.[47] This was presumably calculated to deceive Erzberger, since Salandra had already bound himself to the Treaty of London, which promised Italy the entire Trentino, the entire Istrian Peninsula including Trieste, and several Adriatic islands. Salandra in his *Memoirs* specifically denied the accuracy of Erzberger's account (which had been published in 1920), but the motive of his denial is patent, since Erzberger had exposed him at the game of "lying for the good of his country." Salandra was also annoyed by Erzberger's intimacy with the Vatican, which the Premier knew to be the strongest antagonist of his pro-war policy. "He [Erzberger] continually trafficked with the Vatican, not of course with the Pope personally, although he pretended on many occasions to represent him and to interpret his intentions." [48]

Erzberger and Bülow shrewdly suspected that Salandra and Sonnino were irrevocably committed to war. They now bent their efforts upon

[44] Erzberger, *Erlebnisse,* p. 31.
[45] *ibid.,* p. 32.
[46] Salandra, *op.cit.,* pp. 315–16.
[47] Erzberger, *Erlebnisse,* p. 32.
[48] Salandra, *op.cit.,* p. 36.

overturning their government rather than converting it towards a neutralist policy. This unorthodox behavior for one in Bülow's position of accredited ambassador was dictated by the urgency of events, and his chief collaborator Erzberger eagerly threw himself into the intrigue. The plan of campaign was to approach prominent neutralists with money to finance an anti-war agitation. The Cabinet, which included some members who were hostile to war, was to be split wide open. These efforts would be supported by a further Austrian diplomatic offer, backed by German guarantees, that would satisfy most Italian demands. Erzberger would circulate this offer among opposition politicians—who were completely ignorant of the extent of Austrian willingness to make concessions—to buttress their view that a war policy was unnecessary. The final aim was the replacement of Salandra by Giolitti or some other neutralist politician. The hopes of success rested upon the widespread neutralist sentiment outside of governmental circles and above all in the Chamber of Deputies.

Erzberger began daily morning meetings with a South Italian archpriest by the name of Lopoma on May 4, who assumed responsibility for collecting signatures for a clerical petition opposing war. Sixty bishops signed up in the course of the following week. Lopoma also contacted Grippo, the Minister of Education, who was the main neutralist within the Cabinet. Grippo reported that four ministers: Salandra, Sonnino, Zupelli (War), and Martini (Colonies) were irrevocably set upon war, while seven others were uncertain in their views, with two, Cavasola (Agriculture) and Rissio (Post Office), tending towards his own neutralist views. Grippo promised to promote dissension within the Cabinet, acting from a combination of conviction, Vatican persuasion, and love of Erzberger's money.[49]

Bülow and Erzberger used ruthless methods to secure an Austrian offer that could strengthen Grippo's hand and that of neutralists outside the government. Macchio, tied by Burian's instructions, was unable to provide the offer which he had promised Erzberger on May 3, and he also showed signs of psychological strain under the difficulties of his

---

[49] *Third Report,* diary entries for May 4, 6, 8, 9, 1915. Salandra, *op.cit.,* p. 346, denies there was any Cabinet division, but his account is refuted by Erzberger's description of his close contact with Grippo, and by his statement that the Pope attempted to confirm Riccio's neutralism as late as May 18. Herbert von Hindenburg, counsellor at the German Embassy, remembered that Erzberger had plans for bribing 200 deputies for 100 million lire at this time. *Am Rande zweier Jahrhunderte* (Berlin, 1938), p. 281. Chs. XVII–XIX of these valuable memoirs deal with Hindenburg's years in Rome. Bagdan Hutten-Czapski, *Sechsig Jahre Politik und Gesellschaft* (2 vols., Berlin, 1936), II, 204, states that Erzberger was told by Pope Benedict himself at an evening interview on May 6 that Italy would enter the war before the end of the month. This further explains Erzberger's feverish activity.

situation. This induced Erzberger to demand that full negotiating authority must be placed in Bülow's hands, and he sent the following strong telegram to Bethmann on May 9:

> There cannot be any consideration for Macchio or the Viennese government. His pitiful irresolution can become disastrous for us. He has completely given up the game and has already negotiated with the Americans about safeguarding his personal property [the American ambassador would protect Austrian interests in case of war]. A man who suffers from crying fits when he sees his position tottering must be eliminated ruthlessly. The fate of millions, the fruits of the bloody sacrifices of the nation, the future of our Fatherland, must not be endangered by the incapacity of a single man, who is sabotaging our efforts. I beg Your Excellency to be aware of the responsibility which you assume towards the German people and history if you leave us dependent upon this idiot (*Schwachkopf*). The situation can be resolved by declaring him ill. There is no time for replacement, and therefore negotiating powers will naturally be concentrated in a single hand [Bülow's]. I stand by every word of this dispatch if its substance is criticized by Vienna.[50]

The situation on May 10 appeared so critical that Erzberger decided he could not wait until Macchio's removal before undertaking further action. The Italian neutralists needed to have a specific Austrian offer in order to strengthen their position against the interventionists. Erzberger formulated the terms of such an offer in a talk with Macchio on the morning of May 10. The document accepted the following Italian demands: (1) Trentino, i.e., the Italian part of Tyrol; (2) the Isonzo territory including Gradisca; (3) for Trieste: municipal autonomy, a free port, and an Italian University; (4) Valona; (5) a completely free hand in the rest of Albania; (6) protection of cultural rights of the Italian minority remaining under Austria; (7) further negotiations about the still open questions of Gorizia and the Adriatic islands; (8) German guarantee of the above agreement. Macchio refused to approve these proposals without consulting Vienna first, but this did not deter Erzberger from handing them over to opposition deputies including Giolitti, with whom he maintained contact through Facta, a man later destined to become Premier. Giolitti was naturally distrustful of a purely unofficial document and asked for a copy signed by Bülow and Macchio, which he could use in a pending conference with the King. Erzberger, excited by the prospect of success, got together a quick conference of Bülow, Macchio, and himself at the Villa

---

[50] Erzberger, *Erlebnisse*, pp. 33–34; Macchio, *op.cit.*, pp. 110–12, protests Erzberger's characterization of himself.

Malta, and the two Germans succeeded in intimidating the Austrian into giving his signature—an act which Macchio repented the same evening, when Erzberger pursued him through the hotels and night clubs of Rome in order to secure his signature for additional copies. Giolitti had suggested the impropriety of a diplomatic offer's being handed to the opposition without even being shown to the responsible ministers, and Erzberger reacted by procuring copies for Salandra and Sonnino also.[51]

This far-reaching offer had an electrical effect upon the political situation. Sonnino and Salandra felt the ground slipping under their feet. The interventionist forces thought to discredit the May 10 document by questioning Austria's good faith, and noting the absence of iron-clad guarantees other than the doubtful word of Germany. There were accurate rumors that Burian had reprimanded Macchio for signing the document of May 10, though Burian acquiesced in the proposal on May 12. To counteract these contentions Erzberger drew up the following memorandum on May 12, 1915, aimed at strengthening the confidence of the neutralists in the reliability of Austrian concessions.

> Burian has accepted the joint exposée of the two ambassadors. New Guarantees:
> a. Personal guarantee of German Emperor.
> b. Solemn proclamation of Austrian Emperor.
> c. Immediate establishment of a mixed Austro-Italian commission to supervise the transfer of territory.
> d. Immediate release from the Hapsburg Army of all soldiers who were natives of the ceded territories.
> e. Immediate Italian assumption of the civil administration.
> 3. The Italian demand for the taking over of Austria's frontier fortifications is unacceptable so long as the present war lasts.
> 4. Guarantees for the permanent possession of the newly acquired territories:
> a. Personal guarantee of the German Emperor.
> b. Renewal of the Triple Alliance upon the basis of reciprocal guarantee of the new frontier.
> c. The fact that an Italy which has remained neutral throughout the war will be stronger than a war-weakened Austria.
> d. The fact that military conquest is more likely to lead to a revanchist war than peaceful cessions.[52]

Political passions in Rome had now risen to a fever pitch. Giolitti had left his rural retreat in order to assume personal command of the forces opposing war, and some 300 out of 500 deputies left cards at his

[51] *ibid.*, pp. 34–36, with French text of offer on p. 35.
[52] *Third Report*, p. 27.

house to show their approval of his position. He vainly strove to win the King for the course of peace. The interventionist forces decided to rely upon the power of the mob, with D'Annunzio being brought to Rome to stir popular passions by fervid orations. Huge demonstrations paraded through the streets. Deputies favoring neutrality were terrorized and their families threatened. Giolitti himself could not move in the open without military protection, and his house was nearly sacked by the mob.[53] Erzberger had reason to fear arrest as early as May 9, noting in his diary that day:

A Vatican prelate came at nine in the evening and told me that a deputy friendly to our side, Valenzani, had just told him that I would be arrested and expelled this very evening. Sonnino was supposed to have opposed the arrest since it would cause a great stir. The prelate had also learned at second hand from the French deputy Lasson that I was going to be arrested, and the latter wanted to have me warned. When reporting this to the Villa Malta I was immediately invited to take up residence there, and next day I was formally attached to the German Embassy in order to secure extraterritorial status and be enabled to continue my work.[54]

Bülow in his *Memoirs* describes the latter event as follows:

When Erzberger feared with good reason for his personal safety, because his frequent Vatican visits had aroused much Italian press criticism, I asked him to take up residence with me in the Villa Malta, and I at the same time told the *Consulta* [Italian Foreign Office] that the deputy Erzberger had been attached to the Embassy. The good Matthias seemed to view this as a promising omen for his future diplomatic rise. I gave him two beautiful rooms on the second floor from which he enjoyed a magnificent view of the Eternal City, the dome of St. Peter's and the hills that surround Rome. He proved a pleasant house guest for my wife and myself. Erzberger made himself completely at home, and he was very amusing when he talked about Berlin in his delightful Swabian accent.[55]

The attachment to the Embassy saved him from official expulsion but was no protection against mob violence. On May 13 his car was greeted by a shower of stones thrown by a crowd that shouted "a basso Erzberger."[56] On May 16 his car ran unexpectedly into an Italian military patrol whose "commanding officer swung his naked sword through the roof of our open car; I and the accompanying diplomat were saved from injury only by bending down and ordering a rapid departure."[57]

[53] Giolitti, *op.cit.*, p. 397ff., and Salandra, *op.cit.*, p. 353.
[54] *Third Report*, p. 22, partly summarized in *Erlebnisse*, p. 34.
[55] Bülow, *Denkwürdigkeiten*, III, 210.
[56] Erzberger, *Erlebnisse*, p. 38.
[57] *ibid.*, p. 39. Salandra, *op.cit.*, p. 348, by way of denying the existence of street terror, claims that Erzberger suffered only from imaginary dangers. The British Ambas-

Salandra shrewdly decided to clarify the difficult political situation by a dramatic resignation of his government on May 13, made in the hope that his neutralist opponents would be unwilling or unable to form an alternative government that would keep the peace. When Erzberger met the Archpriest Lopoma for their daily conference at the Lateran Church on May 14, he was greeted with a cry of "Hurra, victory." [58] The expectation was that Giolitti would assume office that very day: the chief remaining obstacle was the continued doubts concerning the authenticity of the Austrian concessions of May 10. The *Corriere della Sera,* the leading interventionist newspaper, carried an inspired story on May 14 that the Austrian concessions had come only after Italy had denounced the Triple Alliance (May 4), and it revealed for the first time the existence of the Treaty of London (signed on April 26, 1915), the repudiation of which must do grave injury to Italy's diplomatic prestige. It also stirred up nationalist passions by the correct charge that the Austrian offer of May 10, by having been made to the opposition rather than to the government, constituted improper interference in Italian internal affairs.[59] There was talk that the Austrian offer was a mere device for bringing down Salandra and that it would be cynically withdrawn as soon as Giolitti had assumed power. Bülow, Erzberger, and the Vatican were at great pains to refute the latter allegation, as can be seen by Erzberger's May 14 dispatch to the German Foreign Office: "Cardinal Secretary of State has just told me that he will tell the Austrian ambassador today that Vienna must not withdraw an inch from the joint offer of May 10, no matter what the new developments; the new [Italian] Cabinet must, on the contrary, receive something additional in some form." [60]

Erzberger completed the dispatch with the following significant request: "Please send immediately to the Monte account at the Nast-Kolb and Schumacher bank the sum of five million lire." [61] The purpose of this money is apparent from the following entry: "In talks the next day we pledged adequate funds for the next elections to deputies who should oppose war." [62] Grippo was a few days later "given every possible guarantee for the financial security of his family." [63]

Erzberger's joy was to be short-lived. The King, pledged to Salandra's

sador admitted the contrary. Sir James Rodd, *Social and Diplomatic Memories.* Vol. III, *1902–1919* (London, 1925), Ch. x.

[58] *Third Report,* May 14 entry.
[59] Salandra, *op.cit.,* p. 13.
[60] *Third Report,* May 14 entry.
[61] *ibid.*
[62] *ibid.*
[63] *ibid.,* p. 40.

war policy, refused to accept the resignation of the government. He feared that the interventionist mob would threaten his life if he should appoint a neutralist to the Premiership. Giolitti disappointed neutralists by his behavior at the height of the crisis. Erzberger claims that he suffered a physical and mental collapse that forced him to leave Rome for his Piedmontese villa, and that fear of violence may have played a part in his failure to press resolutely for office.[64] There were many other reasons for his reluctance to replace Salandra. Giolitti had, furthermore, never favored peace at any price, and he might well have been appalled by the probable consequences of a reversal of the war policy at this late stage—street violence verging on civil war, a possible royal abdication, and the deep enmity of the Entente without winning the friendship of the Central Powers. Giolitti could not be absolutely sure that Austria would really carry out her pledges, and there was great danger of Italy falling between two stools. These considerations did not make Giolitti a champion of war, but they paralyzed his efforts to form a peace cabinet. His failure to go beyond advising against war doomed Erzberger's mission to failure.

When Salandra resumed power on May 17, and Erzberger learned of Italy's definitive pledge to enter the war by May 26 (one month after the Treaty of London), he saw that his further usefulness in Rome was ended. He resolved to return immediately to Berlin because the Vatican was embarrassed by his continued presence. Some of his neutralist friends promised to continue their efforts, and Erzberger left them prodigally supplied with funds, though full payment was to be deferred until a later day. "I signed a promissory note for 50 million marks, payable if Italian neutrality is maintained until the end of the war." [65] His friend Capelli saw that entry into the war had become inevitable but expected it to be a short war of four to eight weeks, with Italian defeats certain to spark a revolutionary outbreak. He pledged himself to lead the prosecution of Salandra and Sonnino for criminal incompetence if this should happen.[66] Erzberger's sanguine temperament may have accepted this view. He wrote to Gerlach, the Pope's Chamberlain, a few days later that the Pope should prepare to go to Einsiedeln in Switzerland as soon as military defeat should threaten Papacy and monarchy alike.[67]

Erzberger found Bethmann incredulous about the Italian decision to enter the war, and the Chancellor asked him on May 22 to return

[64] Erzberger, *Erlebnisse*, p. 38.
[65] *Third Report*, p. 40.
[66] *ibid.*
[67] Erzberger to Gerlach, May 22, 1915. *Erzberger Papers*, File 34.

to Rome for a fourth visit—a useless journey which Erzberger wisely refused to undertake.[68] This constitutes clear proof of the falseness of Bülow's story that Erzberger himself had optimistic illusions about Italian intentions.

When he passed through Munich a few days [sic] before the Italian declaration of war, he visited the mother of my valued colleague Stockhammern. He entered the drawing room like a whirlwind, saying, "I bring you greetings from your son. He will arrive in two days himself. He has helped to preserve the peace which is now absolutely assured." When the wise old woman read twenty-four hours later [sic] the Italian declaration of war in the *Münchener Neueste Nachrichten,* she wrote to her son, "I am very depressed that a man as confused as this excitable Swabian now plays a great role in Berlin." [69]

It is impossible to decide whether this story—like so many others in Bülow's *Memoirs*—is pure invention, or whether Erzberger merely said some encouraging words to Stockhammern's mother, who must have trembled for the physical safety of her son, only to have them blown up into proof of his political frivolity.

The Debate about Austrian Policy

Erzberger's official report to Bethmann, written on May 20 (four days before the Italian war declaration), stated that war had been made inevitable by the following factors:

1. The will of the King, influenced by the Queen and Queen Mother. Italy could not have entered the war without the decision of the monarch. The King told Marchese Capelli that he was forced to wage war as otherwise a revolution would break out and deprive him of his throne. A victorious war offered the possibility of strengthening the position of the House of Savoy.

2. The long years of sapping work undertaken by Masonry, which is financed by French money and knows no other aim than to tear down Austria as a Catholic Power and Germany as a bulwark of order and authority.

3. The dishonest policy of the Salandra-Sonnino government.

4. The failure of Giolitti at the crucial moment when a new Cabinet had to be formed.

5. The fact that Austrian concessions always came too little and too late, and the manner in which the Austrian ambassador in Rome had conducted the negotiations.

[68] Erzberger, *Erlebnisse,* p. 40.
[69] Bülow, *Denkwürdigkeiten,* III, 236.

The majority of the Italian people does not want war, nor does the majority of the Chamber and Senate, though both will vote war credits. The terror of the mob, the open reign of street violence in the last days before my departure from Rome, had so cowed the pro-German and pro-peace elements that they dare not protest any longer. Italy is entering a war created by a few newspapers and lawyers. A number of friendly Italians in very high positions have told me that not only great disappointment, but even revolution, is sure to come after the first military defeats. That will be the point when a rapid peace with Italy can be concluded.[70]

Erzberger took some part in the bitter recrimination between Berlin and Vienna which followed Italy's entry into the war. The Austrians denied that a more flexible policy could have preserved neutrality. They took the line that Italy had been resolved to enter the war all along, and had only played with Austria during the negotiations—thus creating a good alibi for their own procrastination. Erzberger argued against this theory of the "inevitable war" in a twelve-page memorandum, written June 9, 1915. He recognized that some of the Austrian premises were correct: the long-standing Austro-Italian differences, the unique opportunity which World War One presented to Italy to achieve her aims, and the interventionist attitude of Cadorna and Sonnino; but Erzberger nonetheless disputed the correctness of the Austrian conclusions. He noted that the Vatican had not accepted this theory. It had, on the contrary, been very anxious to secure German guarantees of the Austrian proposals because these might turn the tide away from war. He emphasized that Italy had delayed her entry into the war for several months. He further stated that the fear of financial collapse must have played a restraining role in Italy's decision. From these premises Erzberger argued that bungling Austrian diplomacy had missed a real chance of avoiding war. If the offer of May 10, 1915, which he had extorted from Macchio, had been made two months earlier, before Italy had signed the Treaty of London and denounced the Triple Alliance, and if Austria had negotiated in a manner inspiring confidence, instead of replacing intransigence by great concessions only at the very last moment, then Italy might well have maintained its neutrality, if not under Salandra then under Giolitti.[71]

Erzberger's memorandum repeated what had been his attitude in the course of his entire Roman mission. Its correctness cannot be con-

---

[70] *Third Report*, pp. 1–2.

[71] Erzberger's June 9, 1915, memorandum is in *Erzberger Papers*, File 34. The opposite thesis of the inevitability of the entry of Italy into the war is ably argued by W. Petzold, *Italiens Eintritt in den Weltkrieg* (Leipzig, 1934), esp. pp. 54–58.

clusively proved, but one can say that if there was in fact a chance of Italy's remaining neutral, then Erzberger's policy was best calculated to promote it. He deserves credit for clearly seeing that early, far-reaching, and honest Austrian concessions were the key to preserving peace, and that only German pressure could achieve those concessions and only German guarantees make them acceptable to the Italians. The Central Powers had nothing to lose, and much to gain, from such a policy. Even if ultimately unsuccessful in failing to prevent Italy's going to war, it would nonetheless pay dividends in terms of strengthening Italian internal opposition to the war effort. Erzberger's failure in Rome was not due to defective insight or want of vigorous action on his part, but rather to the intrinsic hopelessness of the situation created by Austrian diplomacy. This was also Bethmann's view, who continued to employ Erzberger on many subsequent missions.

Balkan Questions

Bethmann sent Erzberger to Vienna and Budapest in June 1915 to apply pressure upon the Hapsburg government to make concessions to the oppressed Rumanians of Hungary. There was fear that the Rumanians might follow the Italian example and enter the war against Austria in order to "redeem" her co-nationals. Erzberger had a stormy interview with Tisza, the strong man of the Magyar government, on June 4, 1915. He developed a very specific program of small territorial concessions to Rumania accompanied by better treatment of the Rumanian minority remaining in Hungary. The Rumanian language should be permitted in local administrative transactions, the Rumanian minority should receive greater school autonomy, and the franchise should be extended so as to guarantee the Rumanians thirty seats in parliament.[72]

Tisza was unwilling to make these concessions and predicted that the Rumanians would remain neutral in any case. He bluntly told Erzberger to mind his own business. Erzberger refused to be discouraged by Tisza's intransigence, and repeated his proposals in writing (June 8, 1915). Tisza sent him a tart reply (June 12), beginning with, "I have received your essay with thanks. While reading it I have asked myself with amazement how this spiteful mixture of so little truth and so much poetry could be written by a man with whom I have recently discussed this very subject. I do not have time to correct the innumerable errors contained in your essay." Erzberger vainly tried to revive the correspondence by a conciliatory letter (June 15), but Tisza refused

[72] Erzberger, *Erlebnisse*, pp. 104-05; Tisza, *Briefe 1914-1918*, pp. 228-30.

to reply.[73] The Hungarian Premier's view that the cowardly Rumanians would not enter the war even if denied concessions proved true in the short run (until August 1916), because the Rumanians were frightened by the German victories against Russia after the Gorlice break-through (May 1915).

Erzberger traveled to Turkey in February 1916 in order to see what he could do to protect Catholic property which had been confiscated by the Turkish government. The Turks had used the fact that the property was mostly owned by French congregations in order to carry out a long-desired policy of secularization and expulsion of the ecclesiastics. Erzberger urged the Turkish leaders Enver and Talaat to allow German and Austrian Catholics to replace the expelled Entente nationals. The Turks were willing to give permission to carry on educational and medical work, but without using the property of the confiscated French institutions.[74]

The second purpose of Erzberger's journey was to check the horrible Armenian deportations which the Turks had carried on under the pretext of military necessity. Some Germans thought that the threat of cancelling the German-Turkish alliance should be used to force the Turks to mend their ways, and Erzberger seriously contemplated this policy; but he decided that Turkish obstinacy would make such a threat ineffective.[75] He tried instead in his conversation with Enver and Talaat to appeal to Turkish self-interest by pointing out that Turkey's national aims were seriously hurt by her reputation for brutality. The Turks were interested in the abolition of the system of capitulations which allowed foreign nationals to be tried by their own courts. Turkey was just negotiating a treaty with Germany in which the latter was to recognize the end of the capitulations. Erzberger pointed out that the Armenian deportations, along with the hostile treatment accorded Catholic institutions, were creating in Germany a political climate hostile to the ratification of the treaty by the *Reichstag*. He did not hesitate to threaten specific Zentrum opposition, but the Turks were unimpressed. They rejected Erzberger's proposals for the gradual return of the Armenians to their homes. They did, however, allow Erzberger to organize a relief operation for the miserable refugees.[76] Erzberger was very disgusted by the failure of his mission

[73] The three letters are printed in Tisza's *Briefe*, pp. 231–34.

[74] The best account of Erzberger's activities in Turkey is to be found in Chs. v and vi of his *Erlebnisse*. This must be supplemented by Erzberger's report to Bethmann, dated Feb. 25, 1916, in *Erzberger Papers*, File 28.

[75] Erzberger, *Erlebnisse*, pp. 81–82.

[76] On Erzberger and the Armenians, see his *Erlebnisse*, Ch. vi, and File 3 of the *Erzberger Papers*.

to Constantinople. His hostility to the Turks led him to believe in the inevitability of a partition of Turkey after the war, regardless of who should be the victor.[77]

On his return journey to Berlin, Erzberger visited Bulgaria and Rumania to survey the political situation in both countries. He found the Bulgars loyal to the German alliance. Several Cabinet members, especially the Finance Minister Tontschew, expressed the view that German-Bulgar relations could be improved still further if certain steps were taken and certain irritants removed. The able German minister Count Oberndorff, who was to become Erzberger's colleague on the armistice commission in 1918, agreed with this view. Erzberger recommended the founding of a good German-owned newspaper in Sofia, the replacement of certain arrogant German officers by men with a more sympathetic attitude towards Germany's ally, and the organization of an exchange of parliamentary delegations to symbolize the close friendship between the two countries. He took the leading role in making the last proposal a glowing success, and personally participated in the German visit to Sofia on June 1916.[78]

It was on this latter occasion that Erzberger had long interviews with Tsar Ferdinand and Crown Prince Boris on the question of a possible Bulgar ecclesiastical union with Rome. Ferdinand professed to favor this by way of reducing Russian postwar influence, exercised through the Orthodox Church, in his country. A first step would be the establishment of diplomatic relations between Sofia and the Vatican and the negotiation of a concordat. The matter was dropped, however, when the Vatican feared reprisals from the Entente Power and loss of its reputation for neutrality.[79]

Erzberger visited Bucharest from Feburary 18 to 20, 1916, in order to form a judgment on the prospects of Rumania continuing her neutrality. Archbishop Netzhammer of Bucharest, a German Benedictine, arranged a long interview with King Ferdinand, of which Erzberger gives a detailed account in his *Erlebnisse*.[80] The King was certainly more friendly towards Germany than his government, but he was not a

---

[77] The experienced Austrian ambassador to Constantinople, Count Pallavicini, influenced Erzberger in these views. Erzberger, *Erlebnisse*, pp. 62–63.

[78] On Erzberger and Bulgaria, see his report to Bethmann about travel impressions in Bulgaria, Feb. 14–18, dated Berlin, Feb. 25, 1916. *Erzberger Papers*, File 28. Erzberger summarized this in his *Erlebnisse*, Ch. VIII.

[79] Letter of Erzberger to Gerlach, June 30, 1916. *Erzberger Papers*, File 8. Erzberger, *Erlebnisse*, pp. 99–100.

[80] Erzberger, *Erlebnisse*, pp. 106–09. This is based upon the still more extensive account of Erzberger's Report to Bethmann, dated Feb. 25, 1916, in *Erzberger Papers*, File 28.

major political figure. The Liberal Premier, Bratianu, was favorable to the Entente and looked upon the acquisition of Transylvania, the part of Hungary largely peopled by Rumanians, as the natural objective of Rumanian foreign policy. A small party under the former Premier Marghiloman, upon whom Erzberger planted a German mistress with a great deal of money,[81] favored joining the Central Powers, with the primary aim of conquering Bessarabia from Russia. Erzberger had the impression that the King had some sympathy for the latter view but did not feel strong enough to oust Bratianu. This induced Erzberger to make the following clumsy suggestion (which he omitted in his *Erlebnisse*): "To my observation that the interests of Rumania would be best guaranteed by going along with Germany, I added the question whether to attain this purpose outside pressure to force a change of government was desirable. To this the King replied: 'That is your business.'"[82] Erzberger had no scruples about seeking to overthrow a foreign government that was hostile to German interests, as he had shown in Rome the previous year.

The Rumanian government was obviously, like Italy, waiting for a suitable moment to enter the war, though it was made cautious by the failure of Italy's entry to bring about decisive results. Erzberger favored a double policy to thwart Rumanian aims. We have seen him vainly urging Tisza to apply a policy of appeasement that would remove legitimate Rumanian grievances. He now wished to supplement appeasement by coercion. The over-all military position of Germany and her allies was very favorable in February 1916. Erzberger wished to use this strong position in order to force Rumania into either joining the Central Powers (or at least guaranteeing benevolent neutrality until the end of the war) or facing immediate invasion—a policy of a preventive ultimatum that might lead to a preventive war. Erzberger, relying upon Netzhammer's judgment, doubted that the Rumanians would engage in a scorched-earth policy of destroying their grain stores or blowing up their oil wells to injure Germany economically in retaliation for invasion. He thought that an ultimatum, sugar-coated by the promise of Bessarabia and a joint military occupation of the Ukraine, stood an excellent chance of being accepted. The King would certainly acquiesce. The Rumanian government was terrified by the prospect of such a policy, and its continued willingness to supply Germany with grain—which stood in glaring contrast to its generally

---

[81] Hannsen, *op.cit.,* p. 112, where Erzberger brags about planting a mistress on Marghiloman, armed with a blank check on the *Deutsche Bank*.

[82] Erzberger's Feb. 25, 1916, Report to Bethmann. *Erzberger Papers,* File 28.

pro-Entente policy—was based upon this fear. Erzberger warned that Rumanian economic good will, like Rumanian neutrality, was certain to end if Germany's military position should deteriorate—a prediction soon to be fulfilled. Erzberger was disappointed that his repeated entreaties could not win the weak Bethmann to the policy of a preventive ultimatum.[83]

Erzberger's Catholic Projects

The single diplomatic project closest to Erzberger's heart throughout the war never had the slightest prospect of realization. It was the restoration of the Pope's Temporal Power. The position of the Pope as a "prisoner in the Vatican" after 1870 had long been a Catholic grievance; it became intolerable after Italy's entry into the war. Benedict was prevented from communicating freely with German and Austrian Catholics, and the semi-official Vatican newspaper *Osservatore Romano* was placed under Italian censorship. Erzberger felt, both as a patriotic German and a zealous Catholic, that this situation must be remedied while the world situation remained in flux.

He took the lead, after consulting the Munich Nuncio Frühwirth, in organizing the International Catholic Union with headquarters in Switzerland in the winter of 1916–1917. His close friend Georg Baumberger, editor of the *Züricher Neueste Nachrichten,* became general secretary. The association included Catholics from both warring camps and neutral countries. Its main purpose was to stimulate world opinion in favor of settling the Roman question in a manner satisfactory to the Pope, though the Vatican—fearing complications with the Italian government—urged moderation in statement and encouraged the union to concern itself publicly with other problems, such as the social question as well.[84]

Erzberger did not rely exclusively upon public opinion to secure a settlement of the Roman question. He worked out two plans for submission to the German and Austrian governments respectively, which aimed at enlisting their support in a diplomatic solution favorable to the Pope. A thirty-five-page memorandum to the German Foreign Office, submitted in November 1915, anticipated in many ways Mussolini's Lateran Treaty. It argued in favor of restoring the Temporal Power

---

[83] Erzberger, *Erlebnisse,* pp. 109–10.

[84] Erzberger to Frühwirth, Oct. 3, 1915. Gerlach, in a letter to Erzberger on September 26, 1915, had given an evasive reply to Erzberger's request for a draft treaty acceptable to the Vatican. *Erzberger Papers,* File 33. Erzberger's obvious intent was to help the Vatican without compromising it. On Erzberger's role in the Catholic Union, see *Erlebnisse,* pp. 17–18; his correspondence with Baumberger can be found in *Erzberger Papers,* File 27.

on grounds of expediency (the experience of the present war), on the authority of successive Popes (Pius IX, Leo XIII, Benedict XV), and the judgment of enlightened Protestant statesmen (Guizot, Palmerston, Bismarck). Erzberger asserted that historical justice required the restoration of a Papal state extending from the Tyrrhenian to the Adriatic Sea, but he realized that this would be undesirable because it must lead to incessant friction with the Italian state. The ensuing need for support from foreign powers would compromise Papal independence. It would also saddle the Vatican with undesirable administrative responsibilities. Erzberger saw the ideal solution in giving the Pope the sovereignty over a small part of Rome, plus a corridor to the sea. He thought that such an arrangement would be durable since it did not violate any essential Italian interests. It could be placed under international guarantees. The area was sufficiently small so that it would not require any self-governing institutions (parliamentary or municipal), which Erzberger believed to be incompatible with Papal theocracy.

Erzberger wanted this kind of settlement to be attained by direct negotiations between Italy and the Vatican. If these failed, it should be achieved at the general peace conference by the pressure of all the interested powers. Erzberger desired to impose it upon Italy if the Central Powers should win a complete victory, though he realized that only a voluntary agreement could be permanent. He recognized that a country like Germany, with its predominantly Protestant population, could not be expected to make great sacrifices for a primarily Catholic cause, but he ended his memorandum by insisting upon the general importance of the question and urging the government to keep it in mind. He characteristically included a very detailed treaty draft drawn up after close consultation with experts in international law.[85]

The German government treated Erzberger's proposal in a friendly but noncommittal manner, since the question did not require any decision until the end of the war. Erzberger meanwhile prepared a rather startling new plan, this time for submission to the Austrian Emperor. It called for providing Benedict XV with temporal sovereignty by inducing the Prince of Liechtenstein to transfer his sovereignty to the Pope. While not solving the Roman question directly, it would give the Pope a place of refuge and a temporal rank that might

[85] Memorandum concerning the future position of the Holy See, dated Nov. 11, 1915. F.O., File 1498. The treaty draft is printed in Erzberger's *Erlebnisse*, pp. 130–33. Erzberger secured his historical information from G. J. Ebers, *Italien und das Garantiegesetz* (Cologne, 1915).

facilitate subsequent negotiations with the Italian government. Erzberger at first thought of restoring one of the bishoprics secularized in 1802—perhaps Salzburg or Brixen—but the Austrian government would not hear of this. He then hit upon Liechtenstein because this territory was ideally located next to the neutralized Swiss Confederation, hence allowing access for all powers in time of war. He thought that the reigning ducal house could be appointed hereditary regent with the rank of Cardinal Archbishop, thus freeing the Vatican of direct administrative responsibilities while making the Liechtenstein loss of sovereignty one of form rather than substance. Erzberger also sought Austrian concessions to the ducal house to make the entire transaction palatable. In a memorandum written for Franz Joseph he urged the Emperor to enlarge Liechtenstein by elevating some of the landed estates held by the ruling family in various parts of the Hapsburg Monarchy into full sovereign status. The reigning Duke could also be flattered by being admitted into the Order of the Golden Fleece.[86]

Erzberger used a ten-day Easter visit to Vienna (April 17–26, 1916) in order to enlist support for this project. He mobilized such influential people as the Duchess of Parma, the Archduchess Maria Theresia, the Jesuit Andlau, and Cardinal Piffl. The latter was very skeptical about the feasibility of the project, but he nonetheless persuaded the Liechtenstein family, through Countess Fünfkirchen, the sister of the reigning duke John, to give Erzberger a hearing.[87] Erzberger first went to see John's brother Prince Franz von Liechtenstein on April 23, 1916. Franz was dead set against a project which would lead to his house's loss of sovereignty, and would be opposed by the Liechtenstein population. He also thought that a Liechtenstein sacrifice would not benefit the Pope, since Italy would be unlikely to recognize his newly acquired sovereignty. He was unimpressed by Erzberger's argument that the House of Liechtenstein could secure fame exceeding that of Pippin the Short. Erzberger next saw Prince John himself, and reported as follows:

> He made the impression of a weak and sick man and immediately referred to the opinion of Prince Franz. He himself would be glad to surrender his sovereignty but he could not do so in the face of opposition by members of his family. He was too old to assume any initiative and did not wish to provoke family quarrels. He again emphasized that, while seeing many difficulties, he was really willing to transfer his sovereignty

[86] Erzberger's memorandum for Franz Joseph, April 28, 1916, *Erzberger Papers,* File 33. The entire matter is covered in *Erlebnisse,* pp. 134–37.

[87] On Piffl's skepticism, see Naumann, *Profile,* pp. 347–48, and the same author's *Dokumente und Argumente* (Berlin, 1928), p. 201.

to the Pope, but unfortunately was unable to do so. I got the impression from this conversation and subsequent negotiations that Prince Franz was the soul of the resistance [to the project].[88]

Erzberger was not easily discouraged, and continued conversations that sought a formula that would both satisfy Papal needs and also leave sovereignty to the Duke of Liechtenstein—he evidently still hoped that Duke John would overcome Franz' opposition once the obstacle of loss of sovereignty had been removed. His summary of the situation when leaving Vienna was as follows:

> 1. The Liechtenstein family is prepared to surrender its sovereignty over the existing territory of the duchy if its sovereignty can be preserved in some other way.
> 2. Two ways appear to be feasible for preserving the sovereignty of the House of Liechtenstein: one way would be the partition of the duchy, but this I opposed because of the international complications and also because I did not know the views of His Holiness.
> 3. The other way would be the enlargement of the duchy by adding to it the various family properties; the latter could easily be done by Austria, and since parliament is not in session it could be done simply by Imperial decree.[89]

The Austrian government in fact made no efforts to influence the House of Liechtenstein, either by bribery or coercion, and the Duke and his brother remained unwilling to follow in the footsteps of Pippin the Short. Erzberger's optimism remained nonetheless unshaken, and was strengthened when Hertling, ordinarily a very cautious man, wrote him after reading one of his memoranda for Franz Joseph: "When first hearing about the Liechtenstein project I considered it to be rather utopian, but I admit that the considerations advanced in the memorandum have brought its realization much nearer." [90] The Vatican, however, took a more sober view, and probably was never enthusiastic in the first place. Gerlach wrote to Erzberger in early May 1916 that the Liechtenstein opposition was evidently unmovable, and that the Pope considered the matter dead: "The plan of partitioning the country must not even be thought of, since the result would no longer be a sovereign state but a ridiculous artificial structure. The matter would have been attractive if there had been a voluntary offer from the House

---

[88] Erzberger to Gerlach, April 27, 1916, gives a full report on his Vienna conversations. Erzberger had earlier (March 27, 1916) sent Gerlach a detailed draft in 10 articles of a treaty between the Pope and the Duke of Liechtenstein, and urged Gerlach to come to Switzerland for further discussion. *Erzberger Papers,* File 33.
[89] Erzberger to Gerlach, April 27, 1916. *Erzberger Papers,* File 33.
[90] Hertling to Erzberger, May 1, 1916, *ibid.*

of Liechtenstein, but as it stands now it is best to drop it before possible embarrassments are created for the Church." [91] Erzberger was long hesitant to accept this view and he continued to seek to enlist influential people in support of his project. He accepted the impossibility of altering the views of Prince Franz only in the late summer of 1916. In his 1920 *Erlebnisse* he is still almost nostalgic about the plan and notes sourly that "the House of Liechtenstein in any case lost its sovereignty 24 months later without even the association of a great historical act." [92] No single activity of Erzberger's career earned him greater ridicule when it became known after the war than this attempt to give the Pope a Liechtenstein sovereignty; yet none is more characteristic of the man.

Another Catholic project championed by Erzberger was connected with his Oriental journey described above. He proposed that German Catholics should purchase in Jerusalem the Coenaculum, a small mosque on Mt. Zion which was the alleged site of the Last Supper. This matter had already interested Christians for several decades but had aroused Moslem hostility, since the Coenaculum stood on top of a big mosque which was believed (in Erzberger's view erroneously) to contain the grave of David. Erzberger worked out a specific plan which called for German diplomatic pressure to induce the Sultan to purchase the Coenaculum and then to present it to the German Emperor; the *quid pro quo* was to be a German field marshal's commission for the Sultan and the sum of three million francs, which more than covered the purchase price. Erzberger trusted himself to raise this sum quickly among German Catholics. The next step would be for the German Emperor to present the Coenaculum to the King of Bavaria as Germany's leading Catholic sovereign. [93]

Bethmann treated this fantastic plan in an evasive manner, and the Turks were suspicious and hostile. The Vatican was opposed to the German purchase of the Coenaculum, claiming that it meant too great a financial sacrifice. The real reason presumably was that Catholics in the Entente countries, especially France, would be indignant about Germany's acquiring a holy site at the very time when French ecclesiastical influence had been driven out by brutal Turkish measures. In July 1916 the Cardinal Secretary of State told Erzberger through

[91] Gerlach to Erzberger, May 9, 1916, *ibid.*
[92] Erzberger to Prince Henry of Bavaria, June 15, 1916, and to Gerlach, Aug. 18, 1916, *ibid.* Erzberger, *Erlebnisse*, p. 137. Liechtenstein amalgamated its economy and administration to Switzerland in 1919.
[93] Erzberger to Bethmann, March 2, 1916, *Erzberger Papers*, File 10. An abbreviated copy of this letter is printed in *Erlebnisse*, pp. 86–87.

Frühwirth, the Munich Nuncio, that he preferred direct Vatican purchase to the German plan. But Erzberger replied that this was impossible, since German diplomatic pressure was the essential lever for moving the Sultan. Turkey and Germany had finally signed a Treaty ending the capitulations. Erzberger wanted the Zentrum to oppose this treaty, exactly as he had threatened to Enver, unless the Coenaculum matter were settled first. He wanted to tell the Turks that German hostility towards them, based upon the confiscation of Christian properties and the Armenian deportations, could be alleviated only if the Jerusalem site passed to Germany.[94]

Erzberger was disgusted when Jagow, the Foreign Secretary, refused to allow a connection between the acquisition of the Coenaculum and the ratification of the Turk Treaty. The matter dragged on for months without coming to any definite conclusion, and was made increasingly doubtful by the advance of the British armies towards Jerusalem. The Turks continued to emphasize the importance of David's grave in the big mosque under the Coenaculum. Erzberger had the bright idea that this obstacle could be overcome by removing the sarcophagus, on the plea of protecting it against British artillery, to a new mosque which the Sultan could build with money raised by German Catholics.[95] The British captured Jerusalem with all its holy sites before the idea could be implemented, thus ending this episode in Erzberger's career. It was one of the few clear instances where Erzberger placed a specific Catholic interest before the general national interest. When Erzberger made the satisfaction of certain Catholic claims the prerequisite for cordial relations between Germany and Turkey, he provided Protestant patriots with a genuine grievance.

Erzberger maintained regular contact with the Vatican during the war, first by corresponding with Gerlach, the Pope's secretary, later (after Gerlach left Italy) by writing regular reports for the Munich Nuncio Pacelli. He knew that he could rely upon the discretion of the Vatican and he deemed it his duty as a Catholic to keep the Pope as well informed as possible. His relation to Pacelli, the later Pope Pius XII, who resided in Munich after May 1917, were especially close, and led to many acts of kindness on Pacelli's part towards Erzberger's family.[96] Erzberger sent him long memoranda almost every week

[94] See Erzberger's memorandum, dated January 17, 1917, on the steps undertaken towards acquiring the Coenaculum from February to December 1916, in *Erzberger Papers*, File 10.
[95] Erzberger, *Erlebnisse*, p. 89. The entire Ch. VII of this book is devoted to the Coenaculum matter. The narrative is based upon the materials in File 10 of the *Erzberger Papers*.
[96] Pacelli visited Erzberger's daughter Maria at her boarding school when she was

and frequently answered questionnaires on matters that had aroused Pacelli's encyclopedic curiosity. Many of these memoranda can be found in the *Erzberger Papers* in Koblenz; they are one of the best sources of Erzberger's activities during the most influential period of his career.

Erzberger was all the more anxious to write regularly to the Pope because he felt that Vatican policy—perhaps because Benedict was cut off from all regular German contacts—was becoming increasingly favorable to the Entente. He wrote to Hertling on January 8, 1917:

> I have long been reluctant about accepting the view that the Cardinal Secretary of State is not only no friend of the Central Powers, but works systematically against them, but I can no longer resist it. Proof has accumulated in recent months. The Holy Father is, of course, in as difficult a position as can be imagined. [There follow some examples of Vatican discourtesy towards German diplomacy, and of Erzberger's protests to Gerlach; but Gerlach, on the verge of his expulsion from Italy, did not reply, and no longer had access to the Pope.] It is an undignified position for the Supreme Head of the Church that he can no longer freely decide which persons are to be in his immediate entourage. I fear that when Gerlach leaves Rome, the policies of the Cardinal Secretary of State will prevail completely and cause no end of difficulties for Germany. I am not by nature a pessimist, but I nonetheless fear that this will provoke a new tide of anti-Catholicism in Germany which will destroy what we have patiently built up in good will towards the Holy See in the last two years. It is a grave disadvantage both for Rome and for Germany that the last German advisor should be removed from the person of the Holy Father. I have written to Cardinal Frühwirth [who had been transferred from Munich to Rome in early 1916] to ask him to present this point of view personally to His Holiness, because I remain firmly convinced that Benedict XV stands at heart on our side and that many of his acts have resulted from external pressure. But I fear that if he ceases to receive direct information from Germany, the Entente point of view will completely dominate at the Vatican.[97]

This was unusually strong language for Erzberger in criticizing the Papacy. He did not expect the Vatican to favor the German side, though he believed that Germany was engaged in a purely defensive war against predatory enemies. He recognized that the Vatican must seek to stand above the warring parties, and must avoid commitment on controversial issues. When someone suggested that Benedict should mediate in the Belgian question, Erzberger told the following story

planning to become a nun (1920). He sent a special telegram to Mrs. Erzberger upon her eightieth birthday (1955). Dr. Hammer and Mrs. Erzberger mentioned both of these facts in 1956.

[97] Erzberger to Hertling, Jan. 8, 1917. *Hertling Papers.*

with approval: "A Roman countess asked the Pope in February 1915 to declare who was right and who was wrong [in the Belgian question]. His Holiness replied: 'What would you do, my dear Countess, if two of your children quarrelled and beat each other? You would not ask who was right and who was wrong, but would rather separate them and promote peace between them. This is my task between Germany and Belgium.' " [98]

Erzberger, since he expected this attitude to prevail throughout the war, was naturally disturbed when Vatican diplomacy appeared at times to favor Germany's enemies. He sought to explain this regrettable fact by postulating that the Francophil Cardinal Secretary of State Gasparri was imposing his views upon the benevolent Pope Benedict XV only because the latter was isolated from all pro-German advisers. He continued to seek to remedy Benedict's one-sided information by sending the long reports via Pacelli. Erzberger never doubted that, despite Gasparri's policies, the Pope remained if not pro-German at least neutral at heart, and he was confirmed in this when the Pope's attempt to mediate peace between the belligerents in August 1917 aroused the hostility of Entente and German chauvinists alike. His personal relations with Pacelli were never affected by his distrust of Gasparri.

Erzberger was generally unsuccessful in achieving his diplomatic aims. He failed in his efforts to keep Italy out of war. He failed to persuade Tisza to make concessions to the Rumanians. Bethmann rejected the policy of a preventive ultimatum towards Rumania. Erzberger's efforts to protect Catholic property in Turkey and to stop the Armenian deportations ran into a stone wall of Turk opposition. His plan to purchase the Coenaculum won little support at Berlin and was doomed after the British capture of Jerusalem. His efforts for a Bulgar Union with Rome were declared inopportune by the Vatican. His championing of the Liechtenstein project aroused uneasiness at Rome and hostility at Vienna. His hope of promoting a Vatican policy of genuine neutrality was frustrated, in his view, by the ascendancy of Cardinal Gasparri over Pope Benedict.

The reasons for his failure are manifold. Some of his projects, especially those dictated by Catholic zeal, were intrinsically quixotic. The Coenaculum project ignored the fanaticism of Islam and the stubborn suspiciousness of the Turkish government. The Liechtenstein project was both complicated and artificial, and the appeal to imitate the glorious example of Pippin the Short was anachronistic by a thou-

[98] Erzberger to Bergen, July 7, 1916. *Erzberger Papers,* File 5.

sand years. A Bulgar Union with Rome undertaken as a wartime measure devoid of spiritual content was intrinsically worthless for both Sofia and Rome.

Most of Erzberger's other aims were intrinsically reasonable but happened to confront an opposition which a person in Erzberger's position could not overcome. The Salandra-Sonnino government had the power to commit Italy to war beyond the point of no return. Tisza was a fanatical champion of Magyar ascendancy. The irresolute, self-doubting Bethmann could not be won for a strong policy forcing an option upon Rumania. Erzberger's activities give the impression of much effort but few results, except as regards his personal position. They helped him to secure the superb knowledge of the general war situation that proved an important factor in his rise to parliamentary leadership in 1917.

Note: A detailed analysis of one aspect of Erzberger's Balkan policies, his desire for a military campaign against Serbia in the summer of 1915, will be published by the present writer under the title "Erzberger's Political Operations: A Case Study," in the *Journal of Central European Affairs* in 1959.

CHAPTER VII

PRELUDE TO THE JULY CRISIS

Erzberger's Opposition to Submarine Warfare

THE sharpest domestic controversy of wartime Germany concerned the desirability of using the submarine against England without the restrictions imposed by international law. The vulnerability of submarines, when confronted by even lightly armed merchant vessels, made it suicidal to conduct submarine operations in accordance with the generally accepted code of maritime warfare, since these regulations required the warning and safeguarding of crews before a commercial vessel could be sunk. A submarine abiding by these rules would always be in great danger, since the slightest damage to its hull (even if due only to shells from a small gun) was likely to destroy its diving capacity. For this reason, German naval opinion was nearly unanimous in demanding that submarines be allowed to torpedo all vessels approaching England without prior warning or search. They opposed exceptions for vessels flying neutral flags since British vessels used these regularly as a *ruse de guerre*. Yet the torpedoing of American vessels would probably lead to America's entry into the war.

The passions aroused by the issue were due to the fact that the Conservative forces, desperately needing a full German victory in order to maintain their sagging domestic position, believed that the submarine constituted a *deus ex machina* for a speedy end of the war. The naval authorities under Tirpitz did not scruple to unleash a press campaign promising the early starvation of England. They did not hesitate to denounce Bethmann and the Socialist and *Freisinn* forces opposing the submarine as motivated by an unpatriotic Anglophilia. Bethmann, weighed down by the fear that America might enter the war, naturally resented such tactics. He was appalled by the ludicrous situation of a Germany where Conservatives sought to determine basic questions of military strategy by newspaper articles and public meetings—this in a country whose constitution had long been defended on the ground that it left foreign and military policy in the hands of an authoritarian monarchy unswayed by popular passions.[1]

Erzberger had himself supported the inauguration of submarine

[1] Erzberger compares the demagogic submarine agitation with the pro-war reign of terror in Rome in May 1915. *Erlebnisse*, p. 214.

warfare in the winter of 1914–1915 as part of his early wartime follies.[2] He had second thoughts in the summer of 1915 as Germany confronted American hostility in the *Lusitania* crisis, and he supported Bethmann's wise handling of that case while getting very angry about what he thought was the ambiguous role of U.S. ambassador Gerard. He went so far as to urge the Chancellor to declare Gerard *persona non grata,* noting that such action would be cheered by large sections of German public opinion.[3] When Admiral Tirpitz, overruled by Bethmann, threatened resignation in September 1915, Erzberger, again deferring to domestic opinion, was instrumental in patching up a face-saving compromise which left Tirpitz' capacity for mischief little impaired.[4]

Erzberger had become an outspoken opponent of unrestricted submarine warfare by the winter of 1915–1916 when the question was again being publicly agitated. It must be emphasized that his opposition, in contrast to that of many Socialists, was in no way based upon humanitarian grounds or consideration of international law. It was a purely utilitarian hostility against using the submarine so long as it was unlikely, on a sober estimate of the case, to bring decisive results. Erzberger had learned that Germany had only fifty submarines, of which only one-third could blockade England at any given time, since one-third would be on the outward or return journey and another third would need overhauling at German repair docks. This left only 17 submarines to blockade approximately 1,700 miles of British coastline, or one for every 100 miles: a ridiculously small number, especially in view of the foggy climate around the British Isles. Erzberger was most surprised when Tirpitz, at an interview on January 10, 1916, assured him that unrestricted submarine warfare could bring Britain down on her knees in six weeks. Holtzendorff, the Chief of the Admiralty staff, was somewhat less optimistic, and mentioned six months as the required period during a conversation two weeks later. Neither admiral was able to give solid reasons for holding such optimistic expectations.

Erzberger held discussions with two of Tirpitz's close collaborators, Captains Löhlein and Vanselow, during the month of February 1916, at which he demonstrated to them the folly of submarine warfare even if naval claims that 5 million tons of Entente shipping could be sunk in six months were correct. The Entente Powers could build 1 million tons in new ships during this same period, and they would secure the use of the 1.7 million tons of German shipping which was at present in-

[2] Conversation with Bachem, July 31, 1915. Report in *Bachem Papers,* File 90.

[3] Erzberger to Bethmann, Sept. 11, 1915, *Erzberger Papers,* File 32.

[4] Erzberger, *Erlebnisse,* pp. 211–12, based upon a memorandum on Erzberger's conversations with various people, Sept. 4–7, 1915, *Erzberger Papers,* File 44.

terned in neutral, mostly American, ports (if America entered the war). The net Entente shipping loss would therefore be only 2.3 million tons, which was only about one-eighth of the known British tonnage (18 millions): to expect the starvation of the British Isles under these circumstances was to ignore grammar-school arithmetic. Erzberger saw that a total blockade of England was impracticable with the small number of submarines available. He made the specific alternative proposal of proclaiming a blockade of certain ports only, such as the English coal ports of the northwest whose exports were vital to the functioning of the French and Italian economy. All the coal was exported in British and French vessels, thus minimizing incidents involving neutrals. Erzberger made his proposal in a formal memorandum, only to have it rejected on March 14, 1916, in a letter from a high naval official, Widenmann, to Karl Bachem (whom Erzberger had used as an intermediary). The letter stated, in Erzberger's paraphrase

> ... that the blockade of the coal ports was impossible for technical reasons, since the coal ships crossed the Channel under strong escort and then hugged the shallow shore to Le Havre, where the coal was landed for railroad transport into the interior. I replied that if British coal exports, estimated at 30 millions tons per year, could go this way safely, it would be easy for England's grain imports, estimated at only 7 millions, to go the same way safely in the opposite direction; this refuted once and for all the assertion that the submarines could starve out England.[5]

Erzberger was distressed that his arguments made no impression whatsoever upon the naval mind. The submarine enthusiasts preferred invective to sober argument, and Löhlein told him that he was considered to be the sharpest opponent of the use of submarines:

> I replied that I was the warmest adherent of submarine warfare as suggested in my memorandum [limiting it to the coal ports], and that I would become an enthusiastic supporter of unrestricted submarine warfare against all ships as soon as the Navy possessed a sufficient number of submarines to give an absolute guarantee that England would be crushed.[6]

This statement was made to clear himself of the charge that he was motivated by humanitarian or even Anglophile scruples in his views. Erzberger saw that the submarine problem involved, not a technical

[5] Erzberger, *Erlebnisse*, pp. 215–16. The last two paragraphs are based on a 9-page Erzberger memorandum on the submarine question, dated March 20, 1916, in *Erzberger Papers*, File 44. The account in Erzberger's *Erlebnisse*, pp. 212–16, is based upon this.

[6] Erzberger's March 20, 1916, memorandum, in *Erzberger Papers*, File 44.

calculation of tonnage to be sunk, but a political judgment on how to estimate American entry into the war. Here Erzberger, like Chancellor Bethmann, saw clearly that American participation must inevitably spell ultimate defeat for Germany. They were not deceived by the pitiful size of the American army and the civilian temper of the American people—the main factors that led German militarists to hold American power in contempt. Erzberger realized the decisive importance of the American economic potential, and correctly saw America as a sleeping giant, slow to be roused but irresistible once its energies were mobilized for war. He was unimpressed by the fatal question propounded by the champions of submarine warfare to their opponents: "How do you propose to defeat England, if not by using the submarine?" Erzberger did not pretend to have an alternative recipe for victory, but he knew that submarine warfare could not succeed; his thoughts turned towards a negotiated peace based upon the *status quo ante,* which was definitely preferable to bringing America into the war.[7]

Erzberger's views were identical with those of the Chancellor. The question was whether Bethmann could prevail against the powerful forces that stood behind Tirpitz when the problem of whether to inaugurate submarine warfare came up for decision by the Emperor in March 1916. Erzberger attempted to mobilize Hertling in support of Bethmann. He urged the Bavarian Premier to use the official *Bayerische Staatszeitung* to denounce the intrigues against the Chancellor which were being spun by the submarine enthusiasts. Hertling agreed that the fall of Bethmann would be catastrophic and was willing to insert an article written in Berlin provided he was requested to do so by Bethmann. Bethmann was too proud to ask for this kind of support. He proved, in fact, strong enough to win a decisive victory over Tirpitz. The Emperor decided against submarine war and accepted the admiral's preferred resignation (March 17, 1916). The Conservative and National Liberal parties wanted to provoke a *Reichstag* crisis in support of their dismissed hero, but this fizzled out when the Zentrum, thanks largely to Erzberger's winning out over the large body of prosubmarine figures in the party, introduced a motion on the question which was acceptable to Bethmann.[8] The supreme folly of provoking America's war entry was postponed for another year and, while Bethmann deserves the main credit, he was faithfully supported by Erz-

---

[7] Lerchenfeld reported Erzberger's views to Hertling, Feb. 26, 1916. *Hertling Papers.*
[8] Erzberger to Hertling, March 18, 1916, gives a long account of the involved parliamentary maneuvers. Erzberger's initial letter to Hertling was sent March 2, 1916, Hertling's reply March 4, 1916. The entire correspondence is in *Hertling Papers.*

berger throughout the entire crisis—with Erzberger's influence within the Zentrum giving Bethmann protection against a parliamentary stab in the back.

Erzberger unintentionally promoted the ultimate inauguration of submarine warfare by taking a hand in the replacement of Falkenhayn by Hindenburg and Ludendorff in August 1916. He summarized his objections to Falkenhayn in an undated memorandum, probably written in early August 1916. Falkenhayn had failed to foresee Germany's wartime munition needs as War Minister; the 1914 Flanders and 1916 Verdun campaigns had been bloody failures; he had used the War Press Office under its director Deutelmoser to advertise his own glory and cover the achievements of others with silence; while he had eliminated all capable and popular rivals (Generals Beseler, Kluck, Lauenstein, and Mudra) and side-tracked the great Hindenburg-Ludendorff combination when he could not eliminate it altogether. Erzberger ascribed Germany's great 1915 success on the eastern and Serbian fronts to General von Seeckt, and claimed that Falkenhayn had had nothing to do with these. The memorandum ended with the hope that Falkenhayn would soon be replaced by Hindenburg.[9]

Erzberger sent copies of his memorandum to the Bavarian and Württemberg military representatives at Berlin for transmission to their sovereigns. The two South German Kings then pleaded with the Emperor for the dismissal of Falkenhayn, though whether this was due to Erzberger's influence or to other factors it is impossible to say. Their pressure certainly played some role in the advance of Hindenburg and Ludendorff, though this was primarily due to the weight of public opinion clamoring for saviors in the difficult military position of the summer of 1916.[10] The elevation of Hindenburg, who in all important questions was a rubber stamp for his energetic subordinate, Ludendorff, constitutes a watershed in the history of wartime Germany. The Supreme Command was to become the main antagonist of Erzberger's foreign and domestic policies in the last third of the war.

Ludendorff had nearly all the virtues and vices that characterized the Prussian officer corps. He had great professional skill, dedication to

---

[9] Erzberger's memorandum is in *Erzberger Papers,* File 23.

[10] Rechberg, *Reichsniedergang* (Munich, 1919), pp. 62–64. The matter is mentioned, with no source reference, in J. Wheeler-Bennett, *Wooden Titan: Hindenburg in Twenty Years of German History 1914–34* (New York, 1936), p. 69. This account is presumably based on M. Ludendorff, *Als ich Ludendorff's Frau war* (Munich, 1929), pp. 178–81. Mrs. Ludendorff claimed that Erzberger told her he had seen the monarchs of Bavaria and Württemberg, and upon their instigation the Emperor Franz Joseph, before telling William in person that he must dismiss Falkenhayn—an implausible story backed by no other source.

duty, and personal courage. His main vice was an incredible political naïveté which became a great danger when he began to use the threat of resignation, based upon his military indispensability, in order to force decisions in non-military fields. He identified himself completely with Conservative views, demanding vast annexations and opposing internal reforms. His annexationism was primarily due to narrow professional reasons: his main preoccupation was to give Germany a better strategic position at the beginning of the inevitable next war. He demanded control of Belgium to protect the Ruhr against enemy attack and vast annexations in Poland and the Baltic to prevent a future Russian invasion of East Prussia. In domestic affairs he was convinced that the Imperial structure of government was the acme of perfection, its only undesirable feature being the rise of a Socialist Party and the influence occasionally allowed to *Reichstag* deputies. He opposed the democratic franchise for Prussia and feared above all that a parliamentary form of government, by subordinating the army to civilian politicians, would destroy the Prussian military tradition to which he had dedicated his life.

Ludendorff was in a position to make his views prevail after August 1916 because his chief Hindenburg possessed the prestige and moral authority that made him both popular and irreplaceable. He confronted a governmental vacuum produced by an invisible Emperor, a succession of weak Chancellors, and a divided *Reichstag* lacking a constructive program. He filled this vacuum, not because of a brutal lust to rule or a native bent for politics, but rather out of a sense of dedication to what he believed to be the best interests of Germany. His quasi-dictatorship was supported by at least three-quarters of the German people so long as he produced victories, and it was acquiesced in by Emperor, Chancellors, and *Reichstag* alike. It was to lead to a fantastic series of follies that made Germany's defeat inevitable. The fashion among Liberal historians has been to blame Ludendorff personally for these mistakes, but the fault lies rather with a constitutional situation that placed ultimate political decisions in the hands of a soldier completely unequipped to deal with them.[11]

The greatest of Ludendorff's follies was the inauguration of submarine warfare in February 1917. The question had been adjourned, not resolved, by the dismissal of Tirpitz in March 1916. The Right-wing parties raised the matter again in the October 1916 session of the *Reichstag,* and Erzberger was unable this time to hold his own

[11] The best biography of Ludendorff is Karl Tschuppik, *Ludendorff. Die Tragödie des Fachmanns* (Vienna, 1931).

Zentrum Party in line. His old mentor Gröber and his old enemy Spahn were both in favor of beginning the submarine campaign, and there was danger that the party would split openly on the issue. During the debates in the Budget Committee the government revealed deplorable internal divisions. Bethmann was rather feeble in his continued hostility to submarine warfare. Karl Helfferich, the Vice Chancellor, exercised his great pedagogic talent to demonstrate, upon the basis of irrefutable figures, the impossibility of starving England out. Jagow, the Foreign Secretary, was asked by Erzberger by what means Germany could defeat America, if the submarine provoked her entry into the war, even under the favorable assumption that England could be knocked out of the war. Jagow replied that no such means were available, and that this alone was a conclusive reason for not embarking upon a new policy. Capelle, Tirpitz' successor at the Navy Office, took the opposite view for narrow departmental reasons. While pleading for the use of submarines he went so far as to assert that the military effect of an American war entry would amount to exactly "zero." Erzberger greeted this foolish statement with the incredulous interjection "Oho!" but Capelle did not hesitate to repeat his views and place them unmistakably on the record.[12]

The Conservative and National Liberal Party favored while the Progressives and Socialists opposed the inauguration of submarine warfare. The Zentrum leaders, with Erzberger's acquiescence, introduced a compromise resolution on October 7, 1916, calculated to cover up its internal divisions. It stated that the ultimate responsibility for deciding the question must rest with the Chancellor (who was known to oppose submarine warfare), but that he should be guided in his decision by the views of the Supreme Command (which was rightly suspected to favor its inauguration). This hydra-headed resolution pleased everyone except the Socialists, with the bourgeois anti-submarine politicians placating their conscience by the hope that Bethmann might prevail after all, and by the remaining uncertainty of what the views of Supreme Headquarters really were. Ludendorff had opposed submarine war in August 1916, not because it might bring America, but because it might bring Denmark and Holland, into the war. The transfer of the decision to the popular Hindenburg-Ludendorff combination was in any case a convenient method of avoiding responsibility. The acceptance of the October 7, 1916 Zentrum resolution

---

[12] Hannsen, *op.cit.*, gives a good account of Erzberger's October 5, 1916, speech against submarine war, pp. 149–51. See also Erzberger's account in his *Erlebnisse,* pp. 217–18.

proved a dark day for Germany. When Ludendorff demanded in January 1917 that Germany should begin the submarine campaign, Bethmann knew in advance that the *Reichstag* would back Ludendorff rather than himself, and this made him acquiesce against his better judgment. Only a firm alliance between Bethmann and the *Reichstag* would have stood any chance of prevailing against the Supreme Command.[13]

Erzberger's regrettable acquiescence in the October resolution was a sacrifice to party unity, though it must be said in his defence that he led the wing of the Zentrum that opposed submarine war and that he made it clear to the entire *Reichstag* that he opposed the proposals advanced by the navy. He showed his incorrigible optimism by long believing that the Supreme Command really shared his point of view. His friend Dr. Hammer describes a conversation held in December 1916.

> Erzberger wired me one day in December 1916, that he would arrive on the evening train in Friedrichshafen [where Hammer was a schoolteacher] on the way to Switzerland, and that he would like to see me at the ship. My first question was: "Will we begin unrestricted submarine warfare and provoke an American declaration of war?" His reply was, "You need not worry. We will not start a war with America. I talked with Bethmann about this matter once more yesterday, and he told me: 'Never—for provoking America would be an act of madness. Even if we should still be in a position to win a military victory we would be subjected in the postwar period to an organized economic boycott that would force us upon our knees through sheer starvation.' Hindenburg, whom I visited at General Headquarters a few days ago, also expressed himself opposed to submarine warfare. Helfferich demonstrated to us already in October on the basis of precise figures that submarine warfare could not lead to decisive results."[14]

While opposing submarine warfare on political grounds, Erzberger characteristically concerned himself with the technical measures that

[13] An important monograph on the October 7, 1916 resolution is Willy Bongard, *Die Zentrumsresolution vom 7 Okt. 1916* (Cologne, 1937), a dissertation that utilizes the unpublished protocols of the Budget Committee. It is valuable for its careful analysis of the debates in the Committee and the reconstruction of the precise relationship between Bethmann and the Supreme Command from August to December 1916. Its main thesis, that the October 7 resolution was *not* intended to strengthen the Supreme Command in the struggle against Bethmann—though this was its effect—because no such struggle existed in October 1916, is somewhat forced. It requires the assumption that Ludendorff's advocacy of submarine warfare, once certain prerequisites had been met, was not generally known. Erzberger stated in a letter to Hertling on October 8, 1916 that no Chancellor could resist submarine warfare if Hindenburg should demand it. This was a dispassionate recognition of an inescapable fact. *Erzberger Papers*, File 32.

[14] Hammer, *Erzberger*, p. 55.

might make it successful if it should be started contrary to his judgment. He sent to the Admiralty Staff in late December 1916 a memorandum written by a prominent Kiel engineer, H. Bruns, containing detailed proposals for the mass production of submarines. The memorandum showed how 200 submarines could be produced at 12 wharves in the space of 7 to 8 months if submarine construction were given absolute priority over other vessels. A realistic blockade of the British Isles would become feasible upon the completion of the program, with 100 submarines operating at any given moment around the 1,700-mile British coast, with one submarine guarding 17 miles at a time. Erzberger argued that the case for submarine warfare, so weak at present, would at least become technically, though not politically, convincing as soon as the proposed number of submarines were available.[15]

Ludendorff, yielding to naval advice and Conservative clamor, forced a decision in favor of unrestricted submarine warfare in early January 1917. Erzberger, after learning of this decision, wrote a long letter to Bethmann that aimed at minimizing the damage likely to occur. He urged that the beginning of the new policy be postponed for a month until March 1917 in order to allow possible peace moves to ripen. He argued that the stormy month of February was in any case little suited to submarine operations. Erzberger advised that orders be issued to spare passenger liners, whose sinking would cause the most difficulty with neutrals; a submarine commander had told him there would be no technical difficulties, since differentiating liners from freighters was as easy as seeing the difference between an ox and a cat. His final advice was to open a line of retreat by not announcing the new policy openly so that it could be reversed if the early tonnage sinkings did not come up to expectations:

> The beginning of unrestricted submarine warfare should not be announced to the neutral powers. . . . One does not announce in advance when one proposes to use a new type of bomb or gun. An announcement of unrestricted submarine warfare would immediately place us in the wrong in neutral eyes. The neutral governments would naturally issue protests under the pressure of their peoples. These dangerous protests would arrive long before the new warfare would yield any tangible results. There is another matter: no one can make accurate predictions in advance on how much success our subs are going to have. It might

[15] Erzberger to Admiralty Staff, Dec. 23, 1916, enclosing the Bruns memorandum. *Erzberger Papers*, File 44. Erzberger continued to be interested in mass production of submarines, sending Chancellor Michaelis an urgent 10-page letter from Kiel, Aug. 19, 1917. *Ibid*. Erzberger took a continuous interest in the technology of war. He advocated the construction of tanks in November 1914. *Erlebnisse*, pp. 314–15.

be far smaller than our naval experts now think. One would have a definite basis for judgment after some three or four weeks of unrestricted operations. One could procrastinate about replying to neutral protests during this period by stating that the submarine involved in any incident had not yet returned to its home port and that a careful examination of the facts of the case must await its return. If the new operations should not yield the expected results the possibility would still remain open of coming to an understanding with the neutral powers that would eliminate the danger of their war entry [by calling off the submarine war]. An additional advantage would be that the neutrals would not know that we had abandoned the use of our last and strongest weapon because it had not yielded the anticipated and feared success.[16]

This shrewd and Machiavellian advice was not accepted by the German government. Bethmann presumably rejected it as dishonorable, since it jeopardized neutral lives without fair warning; the Admiralty rejected it because what the sailors wanted was an irrevocable decision in favor of submarine warfare. Karl Helfferich aroused Erzberger's special anger by becoming in February a prominent champion of the very submarine policy he had opposed with conclusive reasons in October, a feat made all the more remarkable by his manipulating precisely the same statistics in order to sustain diametrically opposite conclusions.

All of Erzberger's efforts to prevent, postpone, or mitigate submarine warfare were doomed to failure, and Germany made the decision that brought America into the war. Yet Erzberger's efforts had not been completely in vain. It helped him later to secure the reputation of a prophet whose advice had been rejected in an evil hour for Germany. His exposure of the failure of the submarine campaign in July 1917 was enhanced in its effectiveness because his earlier stand opposing the use of the weapon was well known: the impression produced by his exposure was to become the driving force behind the Peace Resolution. Erzberger was justifiably proud of the discernment he had shown in the intricate submarine problem: "It has been shown once again that a 'layman' with healthy common sense will find the truth which a reputed 'expert' often obscures by his artificial calculations with their erroneous conclusions." [17] This sound observation was most unpalatable to the bureaucrats, civilian and military, who ran the German govern-

[16] Erzberger to Bethmann, Jan. 16, 1917. *Erzberger Papers*, File 44. Much of the letter is summarized in Erzberger's *Erlebnisse*, pp. 220–21, but his proposal not to warn neutrals is omitted.

[17] Erzberger to Baron von Schönberg-Thammenheim, March 20, 1918, *Erzberger Papers*, File 44.

ment. Erzberger's confidence in his own judgment, always consider-able, was enhanced when his personal calculations had proved far sounder than the detailed memoranda written by the greatest naval and shipping experts in Germany; and his estimate of his own powers won increasing acceptance among Progressives and Socialists, thus setting the stage for his leadership of the Peace Resolution majority in July 1917.

Erzberger's Intelligence Network

Erzberger's sober estimate of the probable results of submarine war-fare had been influenced by reports which he received from persons stationed in neutral countries. He had built up in 1915 an intelligence network collecting information concerning conditions behind the en-emy lines. His main information centers were located in Switzerland, Holland, Denmark, and Sweden.

Baron von Stockhammern, a young Bavarian diplomat whom Erz-berger had met in Rome in the spring of 1915, was the head of the Swiss office, while being formally attached to the Bavarian embassy in Berne. He collected materials with admirable impartiality from two sources that were bitterly opposed to each other: the Vatican and Ital-ian Masonry. His main Vatican source was an extraordinary adven-turer, the Papal Chamberlain Rudolf von Gerlach, whom we have already encountered as Erzberger's main channel to the Pope. Gerlach was the only citizen of the Central Powers who remained at the Vatican after the Italian declaration of war. He wrote Stockhammern many re-ports that utilized official Vatican information. Gerlach served, unbe-known to the Pope, as Erzberger's paymaster to some Italian news-papers that spread defeatist propaganda. He also acted as a communica-tion channel for a German spy network headed by one Ambrogetti, which had infiltrated into the Italian navy. He was forced to flee to Switzerland in January 1917 when the Italian police were hot on his trail.[18]

Stockhammern's main Masonic source was a former Orator of the Rome Grand Orient, who is referred to in the *Erzberger Papers* as "Seneca." He was evidently motivated to serve Erzberger because of his opposition to Italy's war policy, jealousy against the Grand Master

[18] On Stockhammern and Gerlach, see the valuable but prejudiced study by W. Patin, *Beiträge zur Geschichte der Deutsch-Vatikanischen Beziehungen in den letzten Jahr-zehnten* (Berlin, 1942). The Nazi author had access to Stockhammern's confiscated papers. Many of Stockhammern's reports are in *Erzberger Papers*, Files 41 and 42. The Ambrogetti network was exposed at his trial, reported in *The London Times*, Aug. 8, 1917.

Ferrari (who had prevented his own elevation to the Grand Master-ship), and love of money. He had access to the archives of the Rome Grand Orient, which received innumerable communications from Masonic lodges all over the world. Seneca also established special contacts with agents in Paris, London, and St. Petersburg (labelled 99, 33, etc.) who sent him regular reports. All these reports—giving a detailed analysis of political and economic conditions, and chronicling the activities of influential Masonic lodges—were sent on to Erzberger, and proved of great value to him and the German government in getting an objective assessment of the situation behind the Allied lines.[19]

Erzberger's Dutch office, located at Rotterdam, was headed by F. Stephan, who concealed his activities by serving as a correspondent for several German newspapers. He specialized in getting reports from England.[20] The Copenhagen center was headed by Leo Winz, a Russian Jewish journalist who sympathized with the Central Powers because of the anti-Semitic policies of the Tsarist government.[21] The Stockholm center was headed by R. A. Ziese, a wealthy East Prussian businessman who had owned extensive properties in Russia which had been confiscated during the war.[22] The two Scandinavian offices concentrated upon obtaining intelligence information on Russia. Erzberger was to build upon this information in his most spectacular action as an amateur diplomat—negotiations with Russia looking towards a separate peace in 1917.

Negotiations with Russia

The collapse of the Tsarist autocracy in March 1917 aroused vast hopes in Germany. It was known that the Russian masses were utterly weary of the war. The Provisional government soon encountered strong popular opposition to its declared policy of continuing the war and rejecting any thought of a separate peace with Germany. The opposition to the war centered in the Petrograd Soviet, whose Bolshevik Left wing soon proclaimed the slogan of "peace at any price."

Erzberger was visiting General Hoffmann, the Chief of Staff on the eastern front, when he first heard the news of the Russian revolution. He immediately saw that the prospects for a separate Russo-German peace, which had been dashed by the Polish proclamation of December

[19] On the Masonic network, see Erzberger, *Erlebnisse,* Ch. xii; *F.O.* Files 1498–1500; *Erzberger Papers,* Files 13, 20, 37, and 41; and Patin, *op.cit.,* pp. 55–89.
[20] On Stephan, see *F.O.* File 2024 and *Erzberger Papers,* File 37.
[21] Winz to Erzberger, Feb. 15, 1919, *Erzberger Papers,* File 36.
[22] On Ziese, see an undated memorandum by Erzberger written in the autumn of 1916. *Erzberger Papers,* File 36, and *F.O.* File 2089.

1916, might be revived. His desire for such a peace was enhanced when Hoffmann gave Erzberger and his National Liberal travelling companion, Richthofen, a very pessimistic estimate of Germany's over-all military situation. The General destroyed the few illusions of victory that Erzberger continued to harbor after the inauguration of the submarine campaign, and strengthened the latter's belief in the absolute necessity of securing a negotiated peace in the near future.[23]

An opportunity to work towards this end came earlier than expected. Erzberger was asked through an intermediary around March 20 to come to Stockholm to see, as he described the matter to Bethmann, "the Russian State Councillor Joseph von Kolyschko, formerly Under-Secretary of Finance and a personal confidante of Count Witte [the Russian statesman, who had been opposed to Russia's war policy until his death in 1915], who had lived in Stockholm as a well-known liberal author since the beginning of the war." [24] Kolyschko had long worked for Russo-German cooperation and was married to a German woman. He had just been invited to return to Russia and assume a high position in the Provisional government. He wanted to talk with Erzberger about possible German-Russian peace terms before going to Petrograd.[25]

Erzberger, after securing Bethmann's approval, went to Stockholm for three days (March 26-28, 1917). He reported to Bethmann after his return as follows:

> I immediately had a twelve-hour conversation, with only brief interruptions, with Kolyschko at the private apartment of Gurewicz, a Warsaw industrialist who moved to Stockholm a year ago. The following points were the gist of our conversation: Kolyschko insisted that the renunciation of large-scale annexations was the most important prerequisite for peace. Only frontier corrections could be considered. The new [Provisional] government desired genuine friendship with Germany. Annexations would prevent this friendship and drive Russia completely into the hands of England. My question on what he considered to be frontier corrections was answered by his stating that Russian standards would apply, which means that fairly large areas can be involved. Russia wished to retain a part of the territory which she had conquered (East Galicia).

[23] Max Hoffmann, *Aufzeichnungen*, edited by K. F. Nowak (Berlin, 1929), I, 161–62; Richthofen, in *Erzberger-Heft*, pp. 687–88 and in *U.A.*, VII (2), 217–20.

[24] Erzberger's report to Bethmann on his first 1917 journey to Stockholm, March 26–28, 1917 (7 pages), undated. *Erzberger Papers*, File 36. Henceforth cited as *First Report*.

[25] *ibid.* The Stockholm negotiations are described by Erzberger without details in his *Erlebnisse*, pp. 234–38. They are given passing references by Richard Fester, *Die politischen Kämpfe um den Frieden (1916–1918) und das Deutschtum* (Munich, 1938), p. 69; and E. Hoelzle, *Der Osten im Weltkrieg* (Leipzig, 1944), p. 42; and by Max Hoffmann, *Der Krieg der versäumten Gelegenheiten* (Munich, 1923), pp. 168–69.

Vilna must not be separated from Russia under any circumstances. Any German demand for the annexation of all of Lithuania and Courland would present great difficulties. The Polish question had been complicated by the German proclamation of the Polish Kingdom. I replied that the Polish issue had been raised originally by Russia [in 1914] and that in any case the November proclamation would not constitute an insuperable obstacle [to a peace settlement]. . . . Kolyschko believed that a meeting of minds would be possible. I then asked him to develop the Russian view on some specific points. He said that Russia could agree to the abolition of the capitulations in Turkey, provided it secured the promise of Germany's good services in the Dardanelles and Armenian questions. Russia would never pay any war indemnity, but a long-term commercial treaty between Russia and Germany could be incorporated in the peace settlement.[26]

Erzberger thought these views left the way open for promising negotiations, and he immediately dashed off a letter to Bethmann, who was scheduled to make a major foreign-policy pronouncement in the *Reichstag* two days later. Erzberger urged a very moderate speech which would give encouragement to the Russian peace party:

> The situation today is similar to that of 1866, when Bismarck's much misunderstood moderation—opposed by King and military alike—proved the prerequisite for the founding of the Empire in 1871 and the 1879 alliance with Austria-Hungary. If Germany had annexed Austrian territory in 1866 the two countries would never have entered into alliance.
>
> Either we desire good relations with the new Russia, or we must reconcile ourselves to making her a mortal enemy—there is no third alternative, since all talk of destroying Russia as a major military and political power is utopian. The revanche desire in the West has contributed substantially to the present war, new revanche desires in the East would perpetuate the war danger.
>
> Russia has attained one war aim: the elimination of the autocracy [sic]; Germany can attain one quickly today: to split the Entente.
>
> Not much is required from your Excellency at the present moment in order to attain this goal. We are standing face to face with one of those periods of world history, which Bismarck described so beautifully as the supreme moments of his life when he was content to touch the hem of the dress of Providence passing through world history.[27]

Bethmann's March 29, 1917 speech fitted Erzberger's specification very well.[28]

---

[26] *First Report.*

[27] Erzberger to Bethmann, March 27, 1917. *Erzberger Papers*, File 36. Summarized, without sketching the immediate background, by Erzberger in his *Erlebnisse*, p. 235.

[28] T. von Bethmann Hollweg, *Kriegsreden* (Stuttgart, 1919), pp. 225–27.

Kolyschko also inquired about what Germany's terms would be in the West and Austria's towards Italy—matters on which Erzberger was evasive, though he championed Austria against all Italian demands.[29] Kolyschko's aim was to work for a general peace in which England and France would join Russia. Erzberger doubted that such a peace was attainable at the present moment. He aimed primarily at a separate peace with Russia alone. He exaggerated, with his habitual optimism, the willingness of the Provisional government to contemplate a separate peace. He thought that the revolutionary danger from below must convince the leaders of that government that an immediate peace was imperative, provided it could be attained without dishonor. Erzberger even raised the question whether Germany should wait with peace offers until a Socialist government had replaced the present bourgeois coalition, an event he deemed inevitable if the war should continue. Erzberger opposed a waiting policy

> . . . since it could easily happen that the Socialists would not secure power throughout the entire Empire, that counter-movements would appear in several provinces, and that a great variety of Russian governments would then be established. The war in the east might in that case become bogged down with no end in sight. It would be uncertain whether any one government would feel itself strong enough to make peace. Whoever wants an early peace cannot calculate on a Socialist government bringing it more rapidly [than the present Provisional government].[30]

Erzberger saw that the speedy offer of moderate peace terms by Germany was the prime requirement of the hour. It was arranged that Kolyschko should go to Petrograd to talk with members of the Russian government and that Erzberger should return to Berlin to talk with Bethmann. They planned to meet again in Stockholm for further negotiations on April 20.[31]

The Russian Provisional government issued a vague "Statement about the Ends of the War" on April 9, 1917, which reached Berlin in the early morning of April 12.[32] It was interpreted by the Germans as a veiled peace feeler though it was primarily for domestic consumption. The German authorities immediately went into consultation concerning an appropriate reply. Erzberger saw Bethmann at 9.30 that morn-

[29] Erzberger felt very strongly that no concessions should be made to Italy. See his report to Bethmann about some abortive peace negotiations which he had had at Brunnen, Switzerland, with an Italian officer, July 12, 1916. *Erzberger Papers,* File 17.

[30] *First Report.* Erzberger makes the same point forcefully in a letter to R. A. Ziese, April 25, 1917. *Erzberger Papers,* File 36.

[31] *First Report.*

[32] For text, see W. H. Chamberlin, *The Russian Revolution* (2 vols, New York, 1935), I, 440–41.

ing, Helfferich at 11.00, Zimmermann, the Foreign Secretary, at 12.00, and Stumm, the Under-Secretary, at 1.00. He suggested that Russia should not receive a direct reply but that the Emperor should instead send an open letter to Bethmann welcoming the Russian desire for peace and giving the Chancellor full authority to enter into negotiations. The letter should not explicitly call for a separate peace, since Russia would be offended by the open suggestion of disloyalty to her allies. Erzberger wanted the necessity of making a separate peace to become evident to Russia herself after she had failed to persuade England and France to accept reasonable terms offered by Germany.[33]

Erzberger wrote out a draft of such a letter and sent it to Admiral Müller, the chief of the Naval Cabinet, for presentation to the Emperor. His explanatory note suggested the special advantages of the proposed Imperial letter: it would inform Russia of Germany's willingness to make peace, without dignifying the indirect Russian offer with a direct reply; it would strengthen the monarchy by prominently associating William with the first step leading to peace; and it would buttress Bethmann's position against his internal foes by ostentatiously expressing Imperial confidence in him for the coming peace negotiations.[34] The latter statement shows that Erzberger was far from wishing Bethmann replaced in April 1917, though this was only three months before the July crisis.

The Supreme Command, which was already harboring plans to overthrow Bethmann, vetoed the idea of the Imperial letter. Erzberger then suggested as an alternative that the government should insert a conciliatory statement towards Russia in the semi-official *Norddeutsche Allgemeine Zeitung*. His view was strongly supported by Under-Secretary Stumm, who reported after a trip to Vienna that the Austrian government was insistent upon giving Russia some kind of reply. The statement appeared on April 15, 1917. Erzberger received a message from Kolyschko the same day, urging him to come to Stockholm on April 18. He had a conference with Bethmann on April 17. The Chancellor told him that peace could be promoted no further by *Reichstag* speeches and semi-official newspaper articles. The time had come for negotiations between authorized agents.[35]

Before his second journey to Stockholm Erzberger participated in an event which was to have a greater impact upon world history than

[33] Memorandum, dated April 12, 1917, written by Erzberger on his activities that day. *Erzberger Papers*, File 36.

[34] Erzberger to Admiral Müller, April 12, 1917. *Erzberger Papers*, File 36.

[35] Erzberger's memorandum on his activities, April 13–17, 1917, undated, *Erzberger Papers*, File 36.

anything else he ever did. He was approached by a certain Dr. Parvus, a Socialist acquaintance from the time of their common exposure of colonial scandals, with a proposal from the Swiss Socialist leaders Robert Grimm and Fritz Platten, on behalf of several Russian revolutionaries, including Lenin, who were exiled in Switzerland. They wanted to return to Russia by way of Germany. Erzberger welcomed the proposal and pressed for its acceptance at the German Foreign Office. Baron von Maltzahn, a high official in the Eastern Section, was easily won over. They made a joint call on Bethmann and secured his approval, which was endorsed by Ludendorff. The German envoy in Berne, Romberg, was then authorized to sign an agreement with Lenin (April 6, 1917). The Entente Powers had refused Lenin's request to pass through their territories, since they felt that his presence in Russia would undermine the continuance of the war effort against Germany. Erzberger favored Lenin's passage for this very reason and proved an accurate short-run prophet. He could not foresee the long-range consequences of Lenin's return.[36]

Erzberger had his second conference with Kolyschko at Stockholm on April 19, 1917. Kolyschko spoke warmly of Germany's peace actions since their previous meeting on March 26: Bethmann's speech on March 29, the return of Lenin to Russia, and the newspaper declaration of April 15. But he wished more vigorous press support for a conciliatory peace with Russia, to convince the Provisional government that German public opinion stood behind Bethmann's desire to resist the Pan-German clamor for punitive terms. This complaint prompted Erzberger to suggest to the Chancellor the summoning of a conference of influential editors to mobilize the required newspaper backing. Kolyschko reported to Erzberger on Russian conditions, and described them as very unpredictable in the question of peace or war. The Entente was applying strong pressure to strengthen the pro-war party through a special mission headed by the French Socialist Albert Thomas. Miliukov in the government and Plekhanov among the Socialists favored continuance of the war, while Kerensky was described as heading the peace forces. Kolyschko urged Germany to strengthen the latter by conciliatory statements and by abstaining from military attacks that would provoke Russian chauvinism (as a recent German offensive in

[36] The Erzberger Papers contain nothing about Erzberger's intervention for Lenin. His action is mentioned by Max Hoffmann, *op.cit.* II, 174. Margarethe Ludendorff, *op.cit.*, pp. 180–81, purporting to be Erzberger's own statement at a dinner party, contains some inaccuracies. On Alexander Helphand *alias* Parvus, see Fester, *Die politischen Kämpfe*, pp. 62–66, and the laudatory memoir by K. Haenisch, *Parvus* (Berlin, 1925). His collaboration with Erzberger's colonial campaign is attested in Parvus, *Die Kolonialpolitik und der Zusammenbruch* (Leipzig, 1907).

the Stochod sector had done). Erzberger promised to do his best to promote both objectives.[37]

The two men then drew up a detailed armistice agreement for submission to their respective governments. A draft in Erzberger's handwriting survives among his papers, with the delightful heading: "Councillor of State von Kolyschko and Matthias Erzberger pledge themselves to work with all their power to induce the governments of Russia and Germany to accept the following agreement." The document is the most concrete unofficial peace proposal that was worked out by any two of the belligerents in the entire course of the war. For this reason it deserves to be printed in full. A paraphrase of Erzberger's commentary to Bethmann will be inserted in brackets at the appropriate points:

A general six-weeks armistice between all the armed forces of Germany and Russia with Rumania shall be effective from the . . . of May 6.00 a.m. until the . . . of June 1917 6.00 a.m. It is understood that the troops of both sides will remain in the position they occupied the day that the armistice became effective. The purpose of the armistice is to negotiate an honorable peace settlement upon the following basis:

[Germany is understood to secure Bulgar, Turk, and Austrian concurrence.]

1. The Russian Boundaries will be restored as of August 1, 1914, except for frontier corrections.

["Frontier corrections" are understood to be on a Russian, i.e., considerable, scale. Erzberger warned Bethmann against talking of "annexations"].

2. The frontiers of a new Polish state will be determined by agreement between Russia, Germany, and Austria. A plebiscite of all male Polish inhabitants above the age of 25 is to be held before the . . . of June 1917 to decide if the Poles wish to remain under Russian sovereignty or become a free republic or a hereditary monarchy.

[Erzberger noted that the influence of the Polish clergy would bring a result favorable to Germany, i.e., for a hereditary monarchy closely tied to the Central Powers.]

3. Russia agrees to the abolition of the Turkish capitulations, while Germany will offer her good services in the Dardanelles and Armenian questions.

4. All private legal relationships between Russian and German citizens will be restored as they existed on August 1, 1914. If they cannot be restored *in natura* there is to be full replacement *in natura;* if this proves physically impossible both parties will submit their claims to the Swiss Supreme Court sitting at Lausanne.

[37] Erzberger's report to Bethmann on his second 1917 journey to Stockholm, dated Berlin, April 20, 1917. Henceforth cited as *Second Report. Erzberger Papers,* File 36.

[Erzberger noted that points 2, 3, and 4 had already been arranged during his March 26 conference with Kolyschko.]

5. The commercial treaty in force between Germany and Russia on August 1, 1914, will be continued until a new treaty can be negotiated. Both states are prohibited from enacting emigration restrictions, export embargoes, or transit difficulties.

[Erzberger was told by Kolyschko that Russia would insist upon negotiating a new commercial treaty because she had signed the old one under the unfavorable circumstances of her defeat in the Russian-Japanese war. Erzberger desired the complete abolition of export taxes but Kolyschko insisted that Russia must tax her grain exports for fiscal reasons.]

6. Each of the two countries will bear its own war costs and repair its own war damages.

7. All other questions will be settled in the definitive peace treaty.

8. Russia and Germany obligate themselves to support an international limitation upon armaments.

9. Both states agree for the future to submit any question at dispute between them to international arbitration before taking any measures preparatory to war (proclamation of war emergency, mobilization, etc.)

[Kolyschko wanted to make this more concrete by naming specific arbitrators: the Spanish King, the Pope, and the President of Switzerland, but Erzberger rejected this.]

10. Germany declared herself to be willing, upon the behest of Russia, to sign an armistice with the other belligerent powers at any time for the purpose of negotiating a general peace settlement.

[This point was especially important to Russia for the sake of avoiding the odium of signing a separate peace. Erzberger described Points 8 to 10 as being vital for securing the concurrence of the "idealistic" Russian peace party centering around Kerensky.]

The properly authorized instruments embodying this treaty are to be exchanged as quickly as possible at Stockholm, but in no case later than in four weeks, that is May 18, 1917.[38]

In his general commentary on the terms, Erzberger added that Russia would insist upon Germany keeping her present level of forces on the eastern front during the period of the peace negotiations, since a German attack in the west with troops drawn from the east would poison Russia's relations with her old allies. Kolyschko had agreed that Russo-German trade could be resumed during the armistice period, with Russia providing grain and manganese in return for German coal and chemicals. But he refused to include this offer in the written

[38] *Second Report.* The armistice terms are given in a special appendix.

terms for fear that England and France would immediately complain about Russia aiding their common enemy.[39]

Erzberger returned to Berlin on April 20 in a jubilant mood. He conferred with Zimmermann, the Foreign Secretary, and Bergen, the Foreign Office specialist on Austria, during the morning of April 21, and found both enthusiastic about the Stockholm draft. Zimmermann's desire for an early peace had been much enhanced by the recent arrival of a pessimistic report which Count Czernin, the Hapsburg Foreign Minister, had written about Austria's prospects for the Emperor Charles (April 12, 1917). Czernin predicted that Austria would collapse if the war should continue for another winter. This made a deep impression upon Erzberger. It is important to note, in view of the subsequent role played by this famous report, that—according to Erzberger's strictly contemporary account—Zimmermann (with Bethmann's approval) instructed Bergen to let Erzberger read this document the same afternoon.

Erzberger saw Bethmann at noon that same day. The Chancellor expressed his concurrence with the Stockholm agreement while noting that its one weakness was the imprecision about future frontiers—a point that had been kept deliberately ambiguous since it constituted the biggest obstacle to a settlement.

> Bethmann desired a definition of the term "frontier corrections" prior to the completion of the armistice agreement. I [Erzberger] referred to Point 2 dealing with the joint determination of the future boundaries of Poland. The Poles throughout the entire world would demand that Vilna and Grodno be included in the new state. Russia would never accept this. We should support Russia in her opposition and use our support to secure large parts of Courland and Lithuania for ourselves. This would give us two irons in the fire and would guarantee our success.[40]

Erzberger told Bethmann that he was travelling to Vienna that very evening to see his Austrian friends. "The Chancellor asked me not to mention the Stockholm agreement in my Viennese conversations; and also asked me to see to it that certain false conceptions concerning [the lack of success] of our submarine war spread no further." [41] The above

---

[39] *ibid.*

[40] Erzberger's memorandum on his April 21, 1917 Berlin conversations, written that same evening. *Erzberger Papers,* File 36. Erzberger stated again that Bethmann had given specific instructions to Bergen to show him the Czernin Report in a memorandum dated September 5, 1917 in *ibid.,* File 18.

[41] Erzberger's April 21, 1917 memorandum. *Erzberger Papers,* File 36.

instructions showed that Erzberger went to Vienna with the full concurrence of Bethmann.[42]

Erzberger spent Sunday and Monday, April 22–23, in Vienna with
the purpose of counteracting the Austrian war-weariness as documented by Czernin's report, widespread strikes and riots, and rumors
concerning an Austrian attempt to secure a separate peace. This was
the time of the Prince Sixte of Bourbon affair, when Charles toyed
with the idea of deserting Germany. His brother-in-law Sixte had made
his first visit to Vienna in late March.[43] Erzberger's first conferences
were with his court contacts: the Archduchess Maria Theresa, the
Duchess of Braganza and the Duchess of Parma, in order to enlist their
support in keeping the Imperial couple, Charles and Zita, loyal to the
German alliance. He next had a long interview with Count Czernin,
who explained to Erzberger the difficulties of the Austrian situation,
but minimized the immediate dangers from the recent strikes. The
two men found themselves in agreement on the necessity of securing an
early peace, and decided to remain in regular contact through a friend
of Czernin's, Wassilko, who travelled regularly between Berlin and
Vienna. Erzberger faithfully carried out Bethmann's instructions to
emphasize that the submarine campaign had been a great success in
the first two months and that its real impact could be judged only in
midsummer.[44]

Erzberger conferred next day with Cardinal Piffl, who assured him
that Austria stood in no immediate danger of revolutionary outbreaks.
Erzberger next saw Weisskirchner, the Mayor of Vienna, who also was
confident about maintaining law and order. But the main business of
the day was a long interview with the Austrian Emperor. Charles assured Erzberger of his complete loyalty to the German alliance while

[42] Erzberger's claim that he went to Vienna with instructions from Bethmann became controversial at the time of the libel suit against Helfferich in 1920. The latter
charged Erzberger with deliberate untruthfulness, arising from a desire to inflate his
own importance. Bethmann—embittered against Erzberger for being the main instigator
of his fall from power—corroborated Helfferich's accusation, but Erzberger's contemporary notes show that Bethmann suffered a lapse of memory. The court declared that
the matter was a misunderstanding. *Prozess,* pp. 735–39, 848–49, 904, 1042–43.

[43] The best account of this is still Richard Fester, *Die Politik Kaiser Karls und der
Wendepunkt des Weltkrieges* (Munich, 1925), which is based upon the official German
documents which were at the time made confidentially available to the *Reichstag* Committee of Inquiry, and were leaked to Fester by Dietrich Schäfer, one of its professional
advisors.

[44] Erzberger's Report to Bethmann on his journey to Vienna, April 22–23, 1917, dated
Berlin, April 24, 1917. *Erzberger Papers,* File 36. Erzberger described the conversation
with Czernin in his *Erlebnisse,* pp. 117–18. Wassilko was a Ruthenian member of the
Austrian parliament, and became in 1918 Ukrainian ambassador to Vienna. K. Werkmann, *Deutschland als Verbündeter* (Berlin, 1931), p. 179.

insisting that Austria could not continue the war much longer. To document this contention he handed Erzberger a copy of the Czernin report, with the authorization to use it any way he considered suitable to promote their common aim of an early peace. This was the basis on which Erzberger subsequently read the memorandum to a Zentrum Party meeting at Frankfurt. The entire conversation between Charles and Erzberger was extremely friendly. "At its termination the Emperor asked me to stay in touch with him and send him information regularly." [45] The subsequent storm about Erzberger's use of the Czernin report was to make this their last interview for several months.

Erzberger returned to Berlin on April 24 to find that his Stockholm armistice draft had aroused a hornet's nest of controversy. He had sent a copy to Admiral Müller at General Headquarters before going to Vienna, with the label "strictly confidential and only for your personal information." [46] Müller clumsily showed the document to the Foreign Office representative at General Headquarters, Grünau, who used it on his own authority in some conferences with General Ludendorff, without preparing the ground in advance. Ludendorff was outraged by the fact that the terms of a tentative armistice agreement had been drawn up without prior consultation with himself. He denounced Erzberger as an amateur civilian who had no business meddling in his own military sphere, forgetting that Erzberger had acted as Bethmann's authorized agent and that the Stockholm negotiations were an essentially political matter. He was also angered by the leniency of the terms proposed by Erzberger, especially the vagueness involved in the term "frontier corrections."

Admiral Müller apologized to Erzberger on April 27 for the unintended consequences of his carelessness, excusing himself by saying that "I acted on the assumption that the draft (*Aufzeichnung*) was not an agreement (*Abmachung*), but only a report (*Referat*) concerning steps desired by Russia preliminary to the holding of peace conversations." He criticized Ludendorff for his opposition to "your entire activity for which you deserve nothing but thanks." [47] Erzberger wrote Müller a soft reply since he felt that the admiral might yet prove useful in bringing Ludendorff into a more reasonable frame of mind:

[45] Erzberger's Report to Bethmann, April 24, 1917. Erzberger's *Erlebnisse*, pp. 118–19, gives a nearly complete reproduction of his contemporary account of his talk with Charles. The fact that Charles gave Erzberger the Czernin Memorandum is implicit in *Erlebnisse*, pp. 119–22, though Erzberger chivalrously refused to assert the fact in the Emperor's lifetime. Kühlmann asserts it from personal knowledge in his *Erinnerungen* (Heidelberg, 1948), pp. 491–93.
[46] Erzberger to Admiral Müller, April 21, 1917. *Erzberger Papers*, File 36.
[47] Admiral Müller to Erzberger, April 27, 1917, *ibid.*

I hope you will influence Ludendorff in the sense that it [the Stockholm draft] can under no circumstances be considered a definitive agreement, but only an exploration of the terrain. It only seeks to establish the prerequisites for armistice and peace negotiations. Such an exploration is always indispensable. I cannot say yet whether it will lead to the desired result, but I am very hopeful. Let Ludendorff be assured that the [military] interests which he represents will in no way be injured, and that no violation of his [military] jurisdiction is intended.[48]

Ludendorff had known about Erzberger's secret Stockholm negotiations even before receiving a copy of the armistice draft by way of the incautious Müller. The Admiralty maintained an elaborate spy network that kept tab on all of Erzberger's contacts with the Scandinavian states, and shared its knowledge with the Supreme Command. Detailed reports about Erzberger's negotiations had reached the general through this channel, as Erzberger was to learn through the bragging indiscretion of a naval officer some weeks later.[49] Ludendorff had immediately sent the industrialist Hugo Stinnes, who agreed with the extreme annexationist views of the Supreme Command, to Stockholm in order to induce Kolyschko to desist from further negotiations with Erzberger. The Stinnes mission documented the peculiar relationship existing between the Supreme Command and the civilian government in Imperial Germany. Stinnes offered Kolyschko money to serve as a German agent in promoting Russia's disintegration. This was indignantly rejected by the Russian, as was a proposal to set up a pro-peace newspaper in Petrograd. Stinnes' main purpose was to discredit Erzberger (and indirectly Bethmann) by stating—what was indeed the truth—that the Supreme Command would never accept the moderate proposals for a general peace contained in the Stockholm agreement. The clear implication was that negotiations with Erzberger were a waste of time, and that he—Stinnes—represented the powers that really counted in Germany, and that all Russo-German negotiations should henceforth be with himself alone.[50]

Erzberger first learned about Stinnes' operations in the form of complaints from Kolyschko that he was confused about the views held by

[48] Erzberger to Admiral Müller, April 28, 1917. *Ibid.*

[49] Erzberger Memorandum, dated April 27, 1917, about his friction with Stinnes. *Ibid.*

[50] Erzberger to Zimmermann, May 12, 1917. This long letter chronicles Stinnes' action and Kolyschko's response to them. *Erzberger Papers*, File 36. Stinnes' contacts with Kolyschko are not mentioned in the various biographies. H. Brinckmeyer, *Hugo Stinnes* (Munich, 1921); G. Raphael, *Hugo Stinnes* (Berlin, 1925); Kurt Heinig, *Stinnes und seine 600,000 Arbeiter* (Berlin, 1925); E. Ortner, *Gott Stinnes* (Hannover, 1922).

the German authorities. He wished all further negotiations to be exclusively with Erzberger, and wanted to terminate his futile contacts with Stinnes. The latter had already travelled to Stockholm several times in 1916 to try to negotiate a German-Japanese separate peace (which Russia might be invited to join), and had seen Kolyschko upon these occasions.[51] Stinnes' spasmodic contacts with the Russians had become regular only after Erzberger had begun his own far more promising efforts. Erzberger was indignant about the desire of both Admiralty and Supreme Command to sabotage all steps leading to a reasonable peace. He denounced Stinnes to Zimmermann as unsuited for any kind of negotiations (April 27, 1917):

> Kolyschko has told me that it is utterly impossible for him to negotiate with Stinnes successfully, since their views are poles apart. They cannot reach any meeting of minds. There is a further consideration. The Russian government is undoubtedly turning to the Left. If the Russian Socialists should learn that the German government is using Stinnes as a negotiator they will, in my view, immediately break off contacts. Stinnes is notorious abroad for his ruthless attitude towards his workers during strikes, and every Russian Socialist would refuse to speak to him. It is also known that the forcible deportation of Belgian workers was largely undertaken upon his initiative. . . . He is further known as a man with far-reaching annexationist plans and a foe of our present Chancellor.[52]

Ludendorff formally protested to the Foreign Office about Erzberger's activities after seeing the armistice draft, with Zimmermann replying weakly that the Stockholm protocol represented only an exploratory operation and that Ludendorff would be consulted in the later stages of the negotiations—instead of firmly telling the Supreme Command to mind its own business.[53] But Ludendorff's remonstrance resulted in the issuance of an "unclear declaration" by the Foreign Office that was far less satisfactory to the Russians than earlier statements (April 25, 1917).[54] Kolyschko wired immediately from Petrograd that "it made further negotiations nearly hopeless unless a clarification were issued immediately."[55] Erzberger answered the same day

[51] On these German-Russian negotiations, and Stinnes' part in them, see the definitive article by Erwin Hoelzle, "Deutschland und die Wegscheide des ersten Weltkrieges," in *Otto Becker Festschrift,* edited by M. Göhring and A. Scharff (Wiesbaden, 1954), pp. 266–85; also Erzberger, *Erlebnisse,* pp. 231–32.

[52] Erzberger to Zimmermann, May 12, 1917. *Erzberger Papers,* File 36.

[53] Erzberger's memorandum, dated April 27, 1917, about a conversation with Zimmermann the previous day. *Ibid.*

[54] Erzberger, *Erlebnisse,* p. 236.

[55] Erzberger memorandum, dated April 27, 1917, chronicling his activities that day. *Erzberger Papers,* File 36.

that the April 25 declaration did not alter the bases of the April 20 armistice draft, and that he was working very hard to secure its acceptance.[56]

Erzberger's efforts were in fact made hopeless by the ascendancy of General Ludendorff and the weakness of Bethmann-Hollweg. The Emperor had summoned a secret war-aims conference to Bad Kreuznach on April 23—while Erzberger was in Vienna—between the Chancellor and the Supreme Command. Here Bethmann had agreed, presumably under the pressure of Ludendorff's threat of resignation, to extreme annexationist aims that precluded any kind of negotiated peace. The Bad Kreuznach protocol demanded in the west: military control of all of Belgium and the direct annexation of Liège, the Flemish coast, Luxemburg, and the Briey-Longwy area; in the east, annexations of Courland, Lithuania, and the islands in the Gulf of Riga, plus considerable frontier corrections in Poland. Russia would be allowed compensations in Galicia and Moldavia at Austrian and Rumanian expense, with Austria receiving her compensation in the form of large parts of Serbia and Rumania.[57] Bethmann knew how fantastic these aims were, especially in the west. He explicitly stated both then and later that he did not feel bound by them under all contingencies, but it was nonetheless an act of weakness on his part to assent to them, however tentatively and provisionally.[58]

The promising contact to Kolyschko was broken in mid-May when it became clear that Erzberger could not induce the Berlin government to accept the Stockholm draft. He pleaded with Bethmann on May 14 to give at least lip service, in his *Reichstag* speech scheduled for next day, to a modified version of the Socialist formula of "no annexations and indemnities" as the basis for a general peace between all the powers. Erzberger argued that a probable rejection of the formula might clear the way for a separate peace with Russia alone. He wrote:

> The rejection of the Socialist demands would drive the Russian Socialists completely into the arms of England. This would mean the greatest misfortune for Germany and possibly the loss of the entire war. I believe that the following formula, which I take the liberty of sending to you, to be a suitable means, in view of the general war situation, of circum-

[56] *Ibid.*

[57] E. O. Volkmann, in *U.A.,* Vol. xii (1), pp. 200–02.

[58] Bethmann's view that his concurrence with the Bad Kreuznach war aims was provisional is brought out forcefully in a letter to Hertling, Jan. 26, 1918. *F.O.* File 1499. See also his Chancellery notations printed by Westarp, *Konservative Politik,* ii, 85. I have analyzed the war aims controversy in the spring of 1917 in "The Development of German-Austrian War Aims in the Spring of 1917," *Journal of Central European Affairs,* Vol. xvii, Nr. 1 (April 1957), pp. 24–47.

venting such fatal consequences. . . . "No annexations, no indemnities, but compensation for the occupied territories." This formula surrenders nothing, rejects the idea of a war of conquest, unifies the German nation at home, and is suited to become a world slogan.[59]

Bethmann rejected this ambiguous formula, despite the fact that it was preferable to having no formula at all, and preferred to speak in vague platitudes.[60] The reaction in Russia was understandably hostile, with public opinion interpreting his silence on the Socialist formula as a practical rejection.[61] Erzberger thought the speech a great disservice to the cause of peace, and began to wonder if a man like Bethmann was strong enough to undertake negotiations in the face of Ludendorff's hostility.[62]

It is probable, though documentation is lacking in the Erzberger Papers, that Kolyschko was experiencing difficulties in Russia with the Provisional government similar to Erzberger's. The pro-war forces in that government accused Kolyschko of serving as a German agent and threatened him with arrest. It had never been clear to Erzberger exactly what Petrograd forces Kolyschko had represented. It is certain that his credentials were never as specific as Erzberger's, though several cabinet ministers had at least tolerated his negotiations. When Erzberger travelled to Stockholm for the third time (May 20, 1917) Kolyschko refused to see him for another meeting. The fact that Stinnes had continued his sabotaging activities, seeking to influence Mrs. Kolyschko while her husband was away at Petrograd, may have played a role.[63]

Erzberger's desire for peace had a curious aftermath in the middle of June. We have seen how he arranged for Lenin's passage through Germany after the Swiss Socialist Robert Grimm had approached him. Grimm went to Russia himself in late April 1917 in order to arrange for the return of other exiles, and he offered to survey peace prospects. Erzberger, with Zimmermann's approval, valued getting a second contact to check on Kolyschko's soundings. Grimm saw several leading Russian figures, including two Menshevik Cabinet members, Tseretelli and Skobelev, Ministers of Posts and Labor respectively, after his arrival

[59] Erzberger to Bethmann, May 14, 1917. *Erzberger Papers,* File 32.

[60] Bethmann-Hollweg, *Kriegsreden*, pp. 238–45.

[61] Erzberger gives extracts from Russian press articles collected by his Copenhagen office in his *Erlebnisse*, p. 238.

[62] Erzberger, *Erlebnisse*, pp. 237–38. P. Hannsen, *op.cit.*, p. 262, quotes Loretz on Erzberger's anger at Bethmann's weakness.

[63] Erzberger to Mrs. Martha Schiftan (his Stockholm agent), May 1 and May 9, 1917. Mrs. Schiftan to Erzberger May 11, 1917. *Erzberger Papers,* File 36. Alexander Kerensky, when asked about Kolyschko in 1957, had only vague recollections. He said that Kolyschko actually had been arrested but was released under an amnesty in September 1917. I owe this information to Professor Michael Karpovich of Harvard University.

at Petrograd. They asked him for an authoritative statement of German peace terms before committing themselves to a peace policy—a reasonable request since Germany had done nothing to implement the Kolyschko-Erzberger armistice draft, and Bethmann's May 15 speech had been very vague. Grimm then used the Swiss diplomatic wire with the permission of Arthur Hoffmann, Swiss Foreign Minister, and Odier, Swiss Minister to Petrograd, in order to ask Hoffmann if he could send him a statement of German war aims (May 25, 1917). Hoffmann, in his anxiety to end a war which was imposing grave economic hardships upon his country, was eager to comply. He received a copy of Germany's eastern war aims in an ambiguous form representing a compromise between Ludendorff and Erzberger on May 31, through Romberg, the German Minister in Bern, and he cabled these to Grimm on June 3, 1917. The Russian government, still dominated by the war faction, intercepted and deciphered this cable, and published its content in a pro-Entente Swedish newspaper while simultaneously expelling Grimm as a German agent. The Entente Powers immediately protested at Bern about Hoffmann's unneutral conduct. It was indeed improper for a neutral Foreign Minister to promote a separate German-Russian peace to the detriment of the other Entente powers. Hoffmann resigned immediately (June 18, 1917), while affirming that he had aimed only at promoting Swiss interests. He was replaced by Gustav Ador, a French-speaking Swiss who was inclined towards the Entente cause as Hoffmann had been somewhat inclined towards the Germans —though both were good Swiss at heart who knew that neutrality best served their country's interests. Erzberger's Right-wing critics were to denounce his role in the entire so-called "Grimm-Hoffmann affair" as a typical piece of clumsiness upon the part of a diplomatic amateur. It was nothing of the kind. To enlist the Swiss Foreign Minister for steps promoting German interests was a great stroke upon Erzberger's part, while the interception of diplomatic cables was an accident that could not reasonably be foreseen. The replacement of the pro-German Hoffmann by the pro-French Ador proved a minor misfortune for Germany without damaging consequences.[64]

Erzberger's attempt to promote a separate peace between Germany and Russia in the spring of 1917 proved unsuccessful. Was the failure inevitable? One must note, in the first place, that Erzberger's policy of offering a general "peace of conciliation" to the entire Entente as a

---

[64] On the Grimm-Hoffmann affair, see Ruchti, *op.cit.*, I, 229–66; Fester, *Die Politischen Kämpfe*, pp. 71–75; Olga Gankin and H. H. Fisher, *The Bolsheviks and the World War* (Stanford, 1940), pp. 613–29.

prelude to making Russia willing to contemplate a separate peace, was never tried. Ludendorff and Bethmann must share the responsibility for Germany's refusal to renounce all annexations, even if for tactical purposes only. Their mistaken policy must be partly ascribed to their individual faults; but it must also be remembered that their annexationism was shared by much of German public opinion.

The general obstacles to any kind of negotiated peace were very great throughout World War One. Europe had entered into a period of popular nationalism, which bred a spirit of total war aiming at total victory. Cosmopolitan diplomats of an earlier age could fight limited wars with limited resources for limited ends. They never conceived of arousing mass emotion to promote mass sacrifices, and they never stimulated mass appetites that would be frustrated if the rewards of victory were incommensurate to the efforts of a total mobilization. Yet deep popular frustration confronted the powers during the First World War if they should consent to a reasonable negotiated peace. For France to accept peace without Alsace, for Italy without Trentino, for Austria without crushing Serbia, for England without curtailing the German navy, for Germany without increased securities against future wars, for Russia without the control of the Dardanelles, was close to being impossible in the inflamed state of public opinion.

Germany, as a semi-absolutistic state where the masses exercised no direct influence over foreign policy, was theoretically in a position to act in accordance with the dictates of Reason of State. If it had possessed a strong and clear-sighted Chancellor, it would have offered a *status quo* peace in defiance of the clamor of the annexationists. Such a peace, if accepted by the Entente Powers, would in fact have been tantamount to a German victory. A Germany that had survived an Anglo-French-Russian coalition would have held European hegemony even if it had not secured any territorial accretions.

The Entente was for this reason quite unable to accept a *status quo* peace. Germany should have exploited this fact in order to throw the onus of prolonging the war upon her enemies. This would not only have given Germany a great propaganda advantage, but would have strengthened peace forces in all the Entente countries. There was little hope that these could influence policy in stable countries like England and the United States, or even France; but a German peace move might have been decisive in the chaotic Russian situation of the spring of 1917. There the diplomatic intransigence characteristic of popular nationalism was cracking under the strain of incessant military defeats. An influential section of public opinion, organized by the Soviets, was clamoring for a peace of conciliation. A generous German offer acceptable to Russia while unacceptable to the Entente would have seriously embarrassed the pro-war Provisional government, and might have led to its early overthrow in case of rejection. Germany had much to gain and nothing to lose from such an offer.

It is to Erzberger's great credit that he saw Germany's chance of splitting the Entente and getting Russia out of the war. He probably overestimated the strength of the forces in the existing Provisional government that could be won for a peace policy; but this was no reason why they should not be encouraged as much as possible by a generous German peace offer. This was certainly Bethmann's view when he authorized the Stockholm negotiations and before he surrendered to Ludendorff's unreasonable war aims at Bad Kreuznach. The annexationists in Germany, acting through the Supreme Command and industrialists like Stinnes, refused to recognize Germany's great opportunity, both because they were hypnotized by the thought of new conquests and because they lacked the wisdom to assess Germany's real position. Bethmann proved too weak to resist their disastrous influence, and this was to induce Erzberger to want a new Chancellor a few weeks later. He looked upon the Russian negotiations as a great opportunity muffed by military intransigence and civilian incompetence.

CHAPTER VIII

THE PEACE RESOLUTION (JULY 1917)

Introduction

T HE *Reichstag* crisis of July 1917, which produced the Peace Resolution and the fall of Bethmann-Hollweg, marks the turning point in the wartime development of Germany. It signalized the approaching end of the bureaucratic-authoritarian regime and the advance of the liberal-parliamentary system. The crisis that brought such great results had its background in the equally bleak foreign and domestic situations that confronted the country in the early summer of 1917. The submarine war, begun in February with the expectation of defeating England within six months, was clearly failing in its purpose. America's entry into the war had given the Entente Powers a great psychological boost. England under Lloyd George was dedicated to the policy of the "knockout blow." France appeared to stand firm despite the failure of Nivelle's spring offensive. Russia had remained loyal to her Western allies despite the strains of two years of nearly continuous defeats. How could Germany expect to win the war militarily against such a ring of enemies? And was not time working on the side of the Entente, as American resources became mobilized? These questions were bound to raise deep anxieties among all *Reichstag* members willing to face reality.

The German domestic situation was also one of increasing difficulty. The pressures of the prolonged war were leading to deep frustration and bitterness. Food shortages, coal shortages, and endless casualties were testing human endurance to the breaking point. The disciplined unity of the Social Democratic Party broke under the strain. All of Germany's difficulties were compounded by the split between the Majority wing under Ebert and Scheidemann, which continued to support the war effort, and the Independent Socialists under Haase and Ledebour, which went into opposition and ruthlessly exploited every popular discontent.[1] The grievances arising from material sufferings were beyond remedy, but those arising from Germany's anachronistic internal structure could have been attacked by the government. Yet Bethmann's call for "internal reorientation" consisted of noble phrases rather than constructive achievements. The government at last prom-

[1] Carl Schorske, *German Social Democracy 1905–1917; the Development of the Great Schism* (Cambridge, 1955) brilliantly develops the thesis that the wartime split was the natural culmination of prewar intra-party controversies.

ised a reform of the Prussian franchise in the Easter message of 1917, but the implementation was adjourned until after the end of the war, and the government carefully refrained from committing itself to a completely democratic suffrage system.[2]

A *Reichstag* Committee began to discuss constitutional changes looking towards increased parliamentary influence in March 1917, but its talk of subordinating the army to the civilian government aroused the anger of Emperor and military caste alike. The Majority Socialists found it increasingly difficult to justify their patriotic policy to broad groups among their usual supporters. Their problem was made more difficult by the continued ambiguity of Bethmann in the question of war aims. The Independents began to agitate on the theme that the war was being needlessly prolonged by the annexationist ambitions of the ruling class. Hugo Haase, in his generally impressive philippics against Bethmann's policies, suggested that a "peace of reconciliation" was possible at any time if only Germany would forswear annexationist aims. He greatly exaggerated the potential influence of people of his own views in the various Entente countries.[3] But his false assessment of the foreign situation did little to curtail the effectiveness of his agitation. He was right in his main point that Germany's annexationists were a major obstacle to peace negotiations. The bitterness of millions of Germans against their own government became so intense as to constitute an obstacle to the successful prosecution of the war. The Majority Socialists, threatened by their Independent competitors, felt by July 1917—when a new vote for war credits was coming up in the *Reichstag*—that they must vote against the credits, which symbolized general support of the war, unless they could assure the masses that Germany was fighting a purely defensive war. Erzberger devised the Peace Resolution, meeting Socialist needs, partly with the purpose of strengthening Ebert's position against Haase.

The unfolding of the July crisis may be briefly summarized. The Main Committee of the *Reichstag* met in the first week of July 1917 in order to prepare the vote for war credits. Erzberger, after a preliminary attack on the naval administration on July 4, which pointed out the failure of the submarine war, made a great speech on the condition of Germany on July 6. It caused widespread panic because of its somber

[2] On the Prussian franchise question during the war, see *U.A.,* VIII, 180–97 and L. Bergsträsser, *Die preussische Walhrechtsfrage im Kriege* (Tübingen, 1929).

[3] Hugo Haase, *Reichtstagsreden gegen die deutsche Kriegspolitik* (Berlin, 1919). For a trenchant criticism, see Hans Herzfeld, *Die Deutsche Sozialdemokratie und die Auflösung der nationalen Einheitsfront im Weltkriege* (Leipzig, 1928), though this book goes too far in the direction of the "stab-in-the-back" legend.

and detailed portrayal of desperate military prospects. He called upon the *Reichstag* to pass a resolution opposing annexations to serve as preparation for a negotiated peace, which he believed to be Germany's sole remaining hope. Helfferich, speaking directly after Erzberger, and Bethmann, speaking the next day, carried little conviction when they opposed such a move as inopportune and likely to be interpreted as a sign of weakness abroad. An Interparty committee, composed of National Liberals, Zentrum, Progressives, and Majority Socialists—excluding the two extremes of Conservatives and Independent Socialists—was set up on the afternoon of July 6 in order to draft the kind of resolution which Erzberger had suggested. Political excitement rose to a fever pitch the next day when Ludendorff came to Berlin to exploit the looming friction between the *Reichstag* majority and the government for the purpose of felling Bethmann. The Emperor, loyal to his Chancellor and outraged by direct military meddling in political affairs, ordered Ludendorff to return to his post at the front. The general left his confidante Colonel Bauer behind in Berlin to continue the intrigue against the Chancellor. The known views of the Supreme Command strengthened the position of Bethmann's foes. The Conservatives and National Liberals, who had long clamored for his resignation, were now joined by the Zentrum, acting under Erzberger's influence, in their call for a new Chancellor.

The Interparty Committee demanded at the same time the rapid introduction of the democratic franchise in Prussia and an advance towards parliamentary government by the admission of prominent deputies to executive offices in both the Prussian and Reich governments. Bethmann was willing to accept these demands. He secured the Emperor's concurrence at a Crown Council on July 9. This concession seemed to strengthen Bethmann's position despite the fact that Stresemann, speaking for the National Liberals, openly called for his dismissal in a *Reichstag* speech that same day. The prospect seemed to be that Bethmann would remain in office, supported by a Left-wing coalition of Zentrum, Progressives, and Majority Socialists, with a program of implementing domestic reforms while accepting a slightly watered-down version of Erzberger's Peace Resolution.

The situation was altered when the Crown Prince appeared at Berlin, ostensibly to consult his father on the Prussian franchise reforms, but really as Ludendorff's delegate to bring down Bethmann (July 11). He worked closely with Colonel Bauer, who arranged interviews with selected party leaders, including Erzberger, for the purpose of showing that the Chancellor had little backing in the *Reichstag* (July 12). The

Crown Prince used Bethmann's parliamentary weakness in order to induce the Emperor to fire the Chancellor, but the decisive step was Ludendorff's imperative ultimatum that either he or Bethmann must go (July 12). The Chancellor, aware of the popularity of the Supreme Command and in any case not the man to fight for his position, resigned the next day (July 13). The Emperor then appointed the inexperienced Dr. Georg Michaelis, previously Prussian Food Commissioner, to succeed Bethmann, after Count Hertling had turned down the appointment. The Interparty Committee, indignant at the Emperor's failure to consult them about the new Chancellor, and suspecting that Michaelis was an annexationist at heart, then pressed all the more vigorously for the passage of the Peace Resolution in the *Reichstag*. Ludendorff, on a second trip to Berlin, vainly attempted to prevent or at least to alter the Resolution in conferences with the party leaders. He allowed himself to become the spokesman for the annexationist minority (July 13–14). But the majority proved adamant in defense of its policy, and Ludendorff, having achieved his primary objective of felling Bethmann, and confident that Michaelis could be counted upon to sabotage Erzberger's policy, acquiesced. The *Reichstag* then passed the Resolution on July 19 by 212 to 126 votes, with Zentrum, Progressives, and Majority Socialists voting in support, and Conservatives and National Liberals voting against. The Independent Socialists opposed the Resolution because they felt it was not quite anti-annexationist enough. The new Chancellor accepted the Resolution with the fatal emendation "as I interpret it"—a *caveat* that revealed his coming conflict with the *Reichstag* majority. The result of the crisis was a new Chancellor who was much worse than his predecessor, a frustrated *Reichstag* majority that was unable to enforce its will upon the government, and the continued dictatorship of Ludendorff.[4]

Erzberger's role in these events is the most controversial part of a career that was rarely free from controversy. His conduct had a decisive impact upon Germany's development, yet his aims and motives are very difficult to disentangle. They puzzled both friendly and unfriendly observers at the time, and his own account was to lead to several charges of perjury at the 1920 trial against Helfferich.

The Reasons behind Erzberger's Action

What considerations were in Erzberger's mind when he made his dramatic attack upon the annexationists and proposed the Peace Reso-

[4] There is no adequate monograph on the July crisis. The pertinent material is spread over a great many memoirs and biographies. The best general accounts are Bredt, *U.A.*,

lution in the course of his July 6 speech? He was acting primarily under the impression of the failure of the submarine war. Erzberger wrote in a memorandum drawn up at the end of the crisis (July 15, 1917):

> I became completely convinced after my last trip to Sweden (May 20, 1917), after a conversation with Nuncio Pacelli (June 6, 1917), after receiving reports from my agents 99, 33 and 32, and collating these with the reports from the German legations abroad, that the calculations of the Admiralty and other governmental bodies that showed that unrestricted submarine campaign would bring peace by the end of July or the beginning of August, were completely wrong. The Chancellor and Helfferich and Zimmermann agreed completely with my own point of view.[5]

When Erzberger presented his own tonnage figures, assembled on the basis of his foreign sources, to the Admiralty (June 16, 1917), he pointed out at the same time the basic error that vitiated all the calculations of the submarine enthusiasts. They reckoned only with English shipping, not with the world shipping total, ignoring the fact that England could force neutrals to make their shipping available to her. On July 3 Erzberger received an evasive reply from the Admiralty which claimed that his figures had been examined and rejected by a great expert, Chief Engineer Müller of the Hamburg Vulkan Shipyard. There was no attempt to refute Erzberger's elaborate calculations on substantive grounds.[6] He was never impressed by expert opinions that contravened his own common sense, and he was convinced that the submarine could not bring victory for Germany. He drew the inevitable conclusion: Germany could no longer hope to win the war militarily; therefore she must strive for a negotiated peace as her sole remaining chance to come out of the war intact.[7]

Erzberger's pessimistic assessment of Germany's difficult military position was not exclusively due to his recognition of the submarine failure. It had been promoted by his visit to General Hoffmann at Brest in March.[8] It was now confirmed by an important talk with Colonel Bauer (June 10, 1917), whom Erzberger described to Hertling the next day as "Ludendorff's right hand in political questions."[9] Bauer

---

VIII, 69–131; J. Hohlfeld, *Geschichte des deutschen Reiches 1871–1924* (Leipzig, 1924), pp. 531–54; and Rosenberg, *op.cit.,* Ch. v.

[5] Ten-page memorandum, dated July 15, 1917, drawn up by Erzberger to document his own conduct during the July crisis. *Erzberger Papers,* File 18. Henceforth cited as *July 15 Memorandum.*

[6] Erzberger, *Erlebnisse,* pp. 222–24.

[7] *ibid.,* pp. 266–67.

[8] *Supra,* Ch. VII.

[9] Erzberger to Hertling, June 11, 1917. *Erzberger Papers,* File 32.

told him that Ludendorff did not share the naval optimism about an early termination of the war, and was instead preparing for a winter campaign. He painted a gloomy picture of Germany's military condition by stating that the Entente possessed a superiority in munitions of 4–1. Erzberger replied that the Supreme Command had previously given the impression that it shared the optimism of the Admiralty, and that the German people had been grossly misled about the true condition of their affairs. When Bauer admitted that this was the case, they both began to formulate plans for creating a "spiritual war food office" (*eine Art geistiges Kriegsernährungsamt*) that would prepare the people to face a fourth winter of war.[10]

Erzberger reported Bauer's startling views to Bethmann on June 16, 1917, in a long and cordial letter, which shows that their personal relations were excellent only three weeks before the July crisis.[11] Bauer reiterated his views in a second conference on June 19, and again made a deep impression upon Erzberger.[12] The plan for the "spiritual war food office" was accepted by Ludendorff but treated by Bethmann with his habitual procrastination. This must have been one reason inducing Erzberger to use shock tactics in his July 6 speech to awaken the *Reichstag* to the urgency of the situation. Ludendorff's support and Bethmann's indifference helped to prepare the way for Erzberger's alliance with Ludendorff against Bethmann.[13]

Erzberger's pessimistic assessment of the condition of Austria strengthened his conviction of the imperative necessity of an early negotiated peace for the Central Powers. Czernin's flat statement in the April 12, 1917 memorandum that Austria must quit before the end of the year left an indelible impression upon Erzberger, especially since this was also the view of the Emperor Charles. Erzberger had maintained regular contact with Czernin since his April visit to Vienna, and he knew of Czernin's hope that the *Reichstag* would place a bridle upon the annexationism of Germany's military leaders. Czernin was

[10] Erzberger's memorandum, dated June 10, 1917, on his conversation with Bauer. *Erzberger Papers*, File 18. Summarized in *Erlebnisse*, p. 252.

[11] Erzberger to Bethmann, June 16, 1917. *Erzberger Papers*, File 18.

[12] Memorandum by Erzberger on his June 19, 1917 conversation with Bauer. *Erzberger Papers*, File 18.

[13] *July 15 Memorandum*. Bauer ran into trouble with Ludendorff when Bethmann complained to the Emperor that Erzberger's new political course was the result of Bauer's pessimism in the conversation of June 10. The Emperor passed this on to Ludendorff. Bauer, in a letter to Erzberger, July 6, 1917, asked "to be cleared of this charge," and wanted Erzberger to state that their conference had been private and "that he had not spoken with the authority of the Supreme Command." Erzberger replied on July 8 with an obliging letter with the key sentence, "Your information about our munitions supply has had no influence upon my political views"—a statement that was true only in a Pickwickian sense. *Erzberger Papers*, File 18.

later to claim credit for inspiring Erzberger's sponsorship of the Peace Resolution.[14] This became the basis of the subsequent charge that Erzberger had promoted defeatism as an Austrian agent.[15]

Erzberger also intended to promote an atmosphere favorable to the Papal Peace Note, which he knew was to be issued in early August. He had seen Pacelli, the new Munich Nuncio, at Luzern on May 27 when visiting Switzerland in connection with the Grimm-Hoffmann affair. He saw him again in Munich on June 6 and in Berlin on June 26, where Pacelli had come for preliminary conversations with Bethmann about the coming Papal Note. Erzberger explicitly denied in his *Erlebnisse* that he had learned in advance of the specific peace terms proposed by the Pope; but he never denied that he had a good idea that some sort of Papal action was coming.[16] His friend Müller (Fulda), whom he saw on July 2, later recollected that: "He—Erzberger—mentioned the intended peace mediation of the Pope and said that the urgent task of the moment was to support this by a *Reichstag* Resolution in favor of a peace without annexations."[17] Nationalist historians have distorted these facts to accuse Erzberger of being a Vatican as well as an Austrian agent. They forget that Papal mediation offered the best, albeit only a small, chance for ending the war through negotiations, which constituted Germany's only hope. There was nothing unpatriotic about a German politician doing his best to induce his government to give a favorable reception to Papal efforts. The Vatican, though it helped inspire the July action, was far from satisfied with its results. The replacement of Bethmann by Michaelis, who was far less disposed than his predecessors to cooperate with Vatican diplomacy, was a severe blow to the success prospects of the Papal Peace Note; while the Peace Resolution proved of no value at all since Michaelis did not feel himself bound by it.[18]

[14] Ottokar Czernin, *Rede über die Politik während des Weltkriegs* (Vienna, 1919), p. 16. Also Czernin's *Im Weltkrieg* (Vienna, 1919), p. 211.

[15] R. Fester, *Politik Kaiser Karls*, pp. 135–42.

[16] Erzberger, *Erlebnisse*, p. 274. See also his important newspaper article, "Neues zur päpstlichen Friedensvermittlung im Jahre 1917," in *Germania*, April 22, 1921, refuting an article by the Jesuit Robert Leiber, "Die Friedenstätigkeit Benedikts XV," in *Stimmen aus Maria Laach*, LI (Jan. 1921), 267–80.

[17] *U.A.*, VII (1), 384. Johannes Bell, a Zentrum colleague, wrote Karl Bachem in two letters, dated February 5 and 22, 1932, that he knew for a fact that Erzberger knew about the Papal action in advance and wished to support it. *Bachem Papers*, File 90. Erzberger, when denying that he had acted under Papal directives, never went so far as to disclaim advance knowledge of Papal action. See, for example, a strong letter to Pfeffer, editor of a newspaper in Mrs. Erzberger's home town, August 30, 1917, who had asked him about his relations with the Vatican at the time of the July crisis: "There was no suggestion, no order, no mutual understanding." *Erzberger Papers*, File 21.

[18] For an example of a nationalist attack on the "Papal inspiration" of Erzberger's move, see Fester, *Die politischen Kämpfe*, pp. 87–90.

Erzberger's long-standing desire to strengthen the position of the *Reichstag* within the framework of the Imperial constitution also made him favor a statement about war aims on its part. He thought it undignified that the people's representatives should not be heard on the paramount question facing the nation, especially since it was known that the government and the Supreme Command did not see eye to eye on war aims. Erzberger thought that a peace appeal supported by a solid *Reichstag* majority would carry considerable weight abroad, while also implying greater influence for the *Reichstag* at home. The participation of parliament in the formulations of foreign policy would also take the edge off Wilson's democratic crusade against Prussian autocracy.[19]

Erzberger realized that a peace of conciliation would create much frustration in view of the "wasted sacrifices" of the war, and he knew that if the *Reichstag* Peace Resolution led to this result much of the odium would fall upon the *Reichstag*. He argued—at least *ex post facto* —in a letter of February 6, 1918, that this was one of the advantages of his policy:

> The *Reichstag* has assumed the responsibility for peace terms that do not correspond with the expectations of large parts of the nation. It thereby protects both the Crown and the government. All the indignation directed against the Peace Resolution today would be directed against the Crown after the end of the war. The *Reichstag* Resolution provides the strongest protective wall for the Crown, and it is especially valuable that the Social Democrats are part of that wall.[20]

The strongest consideration in Erzberger's mind, apart from the recognition that a negotiated peace was Germany's only hope of emerging intact from the war, was the desire to promote domestic harmony and keep the Majority Socialists loyal to the war effort. To this must be added the partisan motive of preventing the Socialists from monopolizing the increasingly popular anti-annexationist slogan. Erzberger told a Zentrum meeting on July 7 when defending his action of the previous day:

> The people expect action from the *Reichstag* before it votes the war credits. The Social Democrats have declared that they cannot support the new credits until clarity has been created about war aims and certain reforms have been achieved. It would be dangerous to leave the peace move-

[19] Erzberger, *Erlebnisse*, pp. 230 and 267, also *July 15, 1917 Memorandum*.
[20] Erzberger to Bergen, Feb. 6, 1918, who had asked him officially to summarize the motives that induced him to promote the Peace Resolution. *Erzberger Papers*, File 18; *Erlebnisse*, p. 267.

ment solely to the Social Democrats—indeed this would bring disadvantages for the state, the Church, the bourgeoisie, and the Zentrum Party. The yearning for peace throughout the world is as great as the fear of a new winter of war, and everyone is waiting for the saving word. The *Reichstag* cannot avoid a decision in any case since the Social Democrats will introduce a motion (opposing annexationism). They will oppose the new credits if their motion were rejected, with very great disadvantages for Germany (impression abroad, strikes at home).[21]

Thus Erzberger aimed both at inducing the Majority Socialists to support the war credits (by refuting the Independent charge that the war was being perpetuated for annexationist ends) and at associating the Zentrum with the rising demand for an early negotiated peace.

The Element of Surprise

The various considerations analyzed above give an adequate explanation of Erzberger's action. What surprises the later observer is not that Erzberger made his call for a negotiated peace, but rather that his call had such a tremendous impact upon the hundred odd *Reichstag* members who heard him speak. The explanation lies in Erzberger's reputation for possessing inside information, based upon his position as Bethmann's intimate, as Germany's propaganda chief, and as a man with unusually good foreign contacts. When he spoke, he spoke with the authoritative air of a man who knew much that had been concealed from ordinary *Reichstag* members. The fact that he had once held annexationist views himself gave him the zeal of a recent convert. His caustic attitude towards his former allies won the plaudits of the Left: "One cannot pay any attention to the Pan-Germans, let them go berserk. It is cheaper to build sanatoria for them than to continue the war for another year." [22]

Both the Main Committee of the *Reichstag* and the government were surprised by the sharpness of his attack and the precision of his figures on the submarine issue. His case was strengthened by its essential simplicity. The Right had demanded the inauguration of submarine warfare six months previously on the plea that it was the only method by which Germany could still secure a military victory. The weapon had been tried, and had failed. Germany must, therefore, forswear all hopes of victory, and seek a *status quo ante* peace while she was still in a strong bargaining position. Erzberger's bluntness in stating unpleasant facts was a new experience for the deputies. One of them wrote:

[21] *July 15 Memorandum.* See also *Erlebnisse*, p. 267.
[22] A paraphrase of Erzberger's speech is printed in *U.A.*, VII (1), 111.

No one had previously expressed the naked and brutal truth so clearly. What most members felt but did not yet dare to express was placed convincingly in front of their eyes. For the Left what happened here was a kind of declaration of bankruptcy, for the Right a kind of sacrilege. For the government it was a blow that it was scarcely able to parry, since there were no new facts to introduce and the old consolations had lost their potency.[23]

The government was completely surprised by Erzberger's assault, and its defense was feeble in the extreme. It was argued later by Erzberger's enemies that he ought, in view of his intimate relations with Bethmann, to have given advance warning to the Chancellor. To this Erzberger replied that he had, in fact, expressed his dissatisfaction with the government to several highly placed figures—including Bethmann and Helfferich—in the month of June. He wrote on July 15 in defense of his conduct: "I pointed out the seriousness of the situation and called for a positive governmental program. I told the [above-named] gentlemen: 'I shall place myself at the head of the opposition.' The present program is completely unsatisfactory, we must create absolute clarity [on war aims and the failure of the submarine war]." [24] The officials approached by Erzberger did not take his statements sufficiently seriously to make preparations for a major *Reichstag* explosion.[25]

[23] V. Bredt in *U.A.*, vii(1), 73.
[24] *July 15 Memorandum. Prozess*, pp. 698–709. See also Erzberger's letter to Michaelis, Aug. 1, 1917, in *Erzberger Papers*, File 5.
[25] Other people approached by Erzberger included Solf (Colonial Secretary), Roedern (Treasury Secretary), and several high officials of the Foreign Office (Zimmermann, Stumm, Bergen). Solf and Bergen confirmed Erzberger's story at the trial in 1920 and the subsequent perjury investigation. *Prozess*, pp. 718–20; Löwenstein, *op.cit.*, pp. 58–67. Helfferich charged Erzberger in 1919 with deliberately concealing his plans from the government. He recalled a meeting at the Interior Ministry on June 30, 1917 at which Erzberger had expressed his deep concern about the failure of the submarine war. Helfferich had asked him if he proposed to raise the matter at the coming *Reichstag* session, and Helfferich recalled receiving a negative reply. Two witnesses who were present, the Zentrum leader Spahn and Helfferich's Undersecretary Lewald—both hostile to Erzberger—recalled both Helfferich's question and Erzberger's answer. Erzberger claimed that he had told Helfferich that he did not intend to raise the matter at the moment, but might change his mind if the Admiralty gave him an unsatisfactory reply to the memorandum he had submitted on June 16. We have seen that the Admiralty reply of July 3, showing a total disregard for reality, in fact became a primary cause of Erzberger's speech on July 6. Erzberger was embarrassed during the 1920 trial by the fact that Helfferich, Spahn, and Lewald all remembered his negative reply without the condition which he claimed to have attached. The court convicted Erzberger of perjury. It rejected any explanation in terms of a misunderstanding, though this was made rather plausible by the personal antipathy of all the witnesses towards Erzberger. The court also ignored the probability that Erzberger planned his specific assault upon the government only at the very last moment, and therefore could not speak specifically about his intentions for July 6 on June 30. Erzberger's relationship to the government just before the July crisis may be sum-

Whom did Erzberger consult before embarking upon the speech that triggered the entire July crisis? His confidence in his own judgment is revealed by the fact that he conferred about his plans with only a few personal friends and ignored the official leadership of his party. Erzberger consulted with his friend Müller (Fulda) as early as July 2, and asked him to sound out the Progressive leaders about the possibility of cooperating in an Interparty Committee to put pressure upon the government in the question of war aims. He followed this up by a personal approach to Haussmann, one of the most influential Progressive leaders, on July 5, revealing his plans in detail and calling for close cooperation between the Zentrum and the Progressive parties. Haussmann followed up Erzberger's suggestion by securing the selection of four party leaders to serve on the proposed Interparty Committee at a Progressive caucus that same afternoon. The Zentrum members of the Main Committee (6 in number), including Spahn, learned from Erzberger about his plan to expose the submarine fiasco on July 3. Several of them were hostile to his proposed action. This may have confirmed Erzberger's hesitation about revealing his full plans for the speech that shook the Main Committee on July 6.[26]

Erzberger did talk over his plans with four prominent Zentrum deputies: Gröber, Giesberts (a trade union friend of twenty years' standing), Dr. Pfeiffer (prominent in the *Volksverein*), and Count Praschma (a member of the conservative wing), pledging them all to secrecy. He claimed that he won the approval of each of them for strong *Reichstag* action.[27] Erzberger also attempted to secure a general political discussion at a Zentrum Party caucus on July 5. He wrote ten days later: "I supported the motion of Becker to enter into an immedi-

marized in this way: Erzberger expressed his general dissatisfaction about governmental policies to several high officials at various times in June. He did not give specific warning about his July 6 action. The problem of when precisely Erzberger turned against Bethmann is insoluble since his conduct showed some ambiguity even during the July crisis. Some disillusionment took place in late May 1917 when the negotiations with Kolyschko collapsed because of Bethmann's weakness towards Ludendorff. Stockhammern wrote Erzberger on May 3, 1917, warning him against becoming too closely identified with a Chancellor who was increasingly unpopular, lest they topple together. Erzberger replied on May 15, thanking him for his frank advice, but insisted that Bethmann must be supported against his Pan-German assailants. *Erzberger Papers*, File 41. It is possible that Erzberger's conduct in July was partly motivated by the desire to leave a sinking ship.

[26] Letter of Richard Müller (Fulda) to Karl Bachem, July 12, 1930. *Bachem Papers*, File 90. This letter is the basis for the statement in Bachem, *Zentrumspartei*, IX, 450. Conrad Haussmann, *Schlaglichter, Reichstagsbriefe und Aufzeichungen*, edited by U. Zeller (Frankfurt, 1924), p. 96. Erzberger, *Erlebnisse*, p. 255. Also *July 15, 1917 Memorandum*. Spahn was completely surprised by Erzberger's action, and indignant on that account. See "Der Fall Spahn-Erzberger," in *Kreuzzeitung*, Jan. 17, 1918.

[27] *July 15, 1917 Memorandum*.

ate discussion about the political situation, with the urgent plea that important matters must be resolved and haste was imperative. But the party meeting rejected the motion and decided to discuss the question of Prussian electoral reform instead." [28] Erzberger, while making no secret of his over-all views, valued the tactical element of surprise. He consulted enough Zentrum deputies to make sure that he could count upon party support after creating a *fait accompli*. His soundings with the Progressives showed him that he could rely on their support, while the Social Democrats could be taken for granted. Together these three parties possessed a two-thirds majority of the *Reichstag,* thereby assuring the success of Erzberger's proposal.

The Fall of Bethmann-Hollweg

The most notable result of the July crisis was the downfall of Bethmann-Hollweg. Erzberger's role in this event is one of the most controversial questions of his career. Did he intend to bring Bethmann down from the moment that he made his sensational speech on July 6? Or was this an unintended by-product of a crisis which he had provoked for quite different reasons? At what point did Erzberger join the Right-wing critics of Bethmann whom he had previously opposed? What motives governed his conduct? These issues were debated at great length at the time of the libel suit against Helfferich in 1920. They can be answered for the most part from the trial testimony and the evidence preserved in the Erzberger Papers.

Bethmann had not attended the committee session at which Erzberger made his sensational attack. The Chancellor summoned him as soon as he heard reports of Erzberger's speech, and complained about being surprised. Erzberger then reminded him of his earlier warnings about his dissatisfaction with governmental policies. Bethmann had not understood them as heralding any *Reichstag* action. Erzberger then said—according to Bethmann's recollection—that the purpose of his speech was to strengthen the Chancellor against his Pan-German opponents, by rallying a *Reichstag* majority in defense of his reasonable stand on war aims. This was intrinsically plausible since everyone knew that Bethmann was a moderate at heart. Bethmann then read to Erzberger the paragraphs dealing with war aims in his forthcoming *Reichstag* speech, and Erzberger approved the draft. They parted on amiable terms. Bethmann showed his lack of political instinct by his failure to understand the crisis situation created by Erzberger's action. At an interview with the Emperor the next day he belittled the entire *Reichs-*

[28] *ibid.* Erzberger, *Erlebnisse,* p. 255.

tag excitement, and predicted that it would calm down as soon as he made the speech that was scheduled for two days later.[29]

If Erzberger had intended to buttress Bethmann's position on July 6, he changed his views as soon as he thought through the implications of his policy. The Interparty Committee which was formed upon his suggestion met almost daily after July 6 and drafted the so-called Peace Resolution. Soon serious questions arose whether Bethmann was the right man to implement the new policy. It is certain that he agreed with it at heart and had long resented the follies of the annexationists; but he and his chief subordinate Helfferich had opposed the idea of any Resolution in the *Reichstag,* and it was difficult for the government to swallow it without loss of face. There were other objections to Bethmann's continued tenure of power. He was distrusted abroad because he had been Chancellor upon the outbreak of war, was formally responsible for the violation of Belgian neutrality and the inauguration of submarine warfare, and he had made very ambiguous statements on war aims. He had shown deplorable weakness towards the Supreme Command, as Erzberger knew only too well from the fate of his Stockholm armistice draft. The implementation of the Peace Resolution required a man who could break the political influence of General Ludendorff. Erzberger, in his search for an alternative candidate, thought that Prince Bülow was the only man equal to the task. He thought that Bülow combined the necessary qualities of strength, prestige, and flexibility—all of which Bethmann lacked.[30]

Erzberger's desire to see Bülow replace Bethmann was probably reinforced by purely tactical considerations. For the success of his peace policy he required an overwhelming *Reichstag* majority. The intransigent Conservatives were certain to oppose any Resolution, but the National Liberals might be won in addition to the Zentrum, Progressives, and Social Democrats. The National Liberals were deeply divided on what to do; a majority of the party continued to favor large annexations. A minority under Erzberger's friend Richthofen favored a nonannexationist peace. With Stresemann's rise to influence in the party it had become more favorable to parliamentary government and Prussian franchise reform than it had been before the war. Stresemann's primary desire was to eliminate Bethmann-Hollweg, whom he disliked as a weak and irresolute character. His candidate for the succession was also Prince Bülow, for whom he retained an inordinate admiration through-

[29] Erzberger, *Erlebnisse,* pp. 257–58. *Prozess,* pp. 712–18. *U.A.,* VIII, 71.

[30] There is remarkably little detailed material about Erzberger's advocacy of Bülow, though the fact is repeatedly stated as a commonplace. For example, *U.A.,* VII (2), 304 (Stresemann), 358 (Bell), 361 (Dittman). Westarp, *Konservative Politik,* II, 354–55.

out life.[31] Erzberger knew of this common ground. He apparently wanted to utilize it in order to induce the National Liberals to support the Peace Resolution. The terms of the bargain would be Liberal support of the Peace Resolution, in return for Zentrum support in felling Bethmann. Specific proof of Erzberger's intention to strike such a bargain cannot be found, but this hypothesis gives the best explanation of his conduct during the July crisis. It is certain that Erzberger saw Stresemann on July 7 and discussed with him the fate of Bethmann.[32]

The two men had dinner at a Berlin restaurant that evening with Colonel Bauer. This meeting had a significant genesis. General von Stein, the War Minister, summoned Hindenburg and Ludendorff to come to Berlin as soon as he realized the tremendous impact of Erzberger's speech upon the deputies. The generals arrived on the morning of July 7 and planned to meet several deputies after making a call upon th Emperor. Colonel Bauer arranged for an evening meeting among Ludendorff, Erzberger, and Stresemann. Bethmann was furious about Ludendorff's arrival in the midst of crisis, and rightly suspected the general of wishing to intrigue for a change in the Chancellorship. Bethmann filled the Emperor with the same sentiment. William, to demonstrate his support of his Chancellor, gave Hindenburg and Ludendorff a rather cool reception and ordered them to return to the front immediately. This forced Ludendorff to cancel his appointment with the deputies. Erzberger could not be reached in time by the general's messenger. Erzberger, when he arrived at the appointed place, was surprised to find only Stresemann and Colonel Bauer present. He was indignant that Bethmann should have frustrated this meeting with Ludendorff. He stated later that this incident had been primarily responsible for his change of view on the desirability of Bethmann's continued Chancellorship. He discussed the future political situation with his two dinner companions and pressed Stresemann to support the Peace Resolution.[33]

It is uncertain to what extent Erzberger pledged himself to work for Bethmann's overthrow as a *quid pro quo* that evening. He could not reveal his real motives to Stresemann and Bauer. They wanted Bethmann replaced because of his anti-annexationism and because his moderation often made difficulties for the Supreme Command. They

---

[31] Stresemann discussed his 1917 attitude towards Bethmann in *U.A.*, vii(2), 302–05.
[32] *Prozess*, pp. 723 and 827–30. Stresemann remembered a meeting at 7:00 a.m., which Erzberger did not recollect. If it did take place it puts Erzberger in an unfavorable light, as he would have intrigued against Bethmann within sixteen hours of assuring him of his support.
[33] *ibid.*, pp. 722–24, 730–33.

thought that Bülow would cooperate smoothly with them. Erzberger, on the other hand, wanted Bülow in order to curb the annexationists and to subordinate the Supreme Command to the civilian government. Erzberger definitely favored the elimination of Bethmann after July 7, both for substantive and tactical reasons. His primary aim remained the securing of *Reichstag* support—preferably including the National Liberals—for the Peace Resolution. Whether Bethmann remained in power was to him an important but secondary consideration. This explains his refusal to join the National Liberals in openly clamoring for a new Chancellor, and his later statements that his action had not aimed at overthrowing Bethmann. Erzberger gave the impression of irresoluteness, of not knowing precisely what he wanted in the question of the Chancellorship, in the further unfolding of the July crisis.

Erzberger defended his speech of July 6 to an initially hostile Zentrum Party caucus the same day that he dined with Stresemann. He won nearly unanimous support for the Peace Resolution policy. But the party made this support conditional upon the National Liberals acting likewise. The position of Bethmann did not come up for debate at the Zentrum meeting, since Erzberger's speech had been directed against the navy and the Pan-Germans rather than the Chancellor.[34] Erzberger first publicly attacked Bethmann at a meeting of the Interparty Committee on July 8. He criticized him for not understanding the severity of the parliamentary crisis and insisted that the external and internal situation confronting Germany had aroused deep anxiety among parliamentarians. The time had come for resolute action rather than soothing words. He also complained about Bethmann's thwarting the proper contact between deputies and the Supreme Command.[35]

The Chancellor's position began to totter on July 9, when Stresemann, in a speech in the Main Committee, openly called for his resignation as a weak incompetent. Bethmann at last recognized his vulnerability. He called Erzberger into a corner of the room to ask whether he could still count upon the support of the Zentrum. Erzberger answered evasively that his colleagues were divided on the question and that no official decision had been reached. In a speech that same day, Erzberger emphasized again the supreme desirability of the Peace Resolution, but left the question of the Chancellorship ambiguous. He did, however, insist that the effect of the resolution depended upon its wholehearted acceptance by both Chancellor and *Reichstag*. Erzberger foresaw the

[34] *July 15 Memorandum.* Haussmann, *Schlaglichter,* p. 112.

[35] Haussmann, *op.cit.,* pp. 106–07. Haussmann's report proves that Erzberger's story in 1920 of why he turned against Bethmann was not an afterthought. See also Scheidemann, *Der Zusammenbruch* (Berlin, 1920) p. 87.

uselessness of any resolution if it were sabotaged by the German government. He argued that to achieve close cooperation between government and *Reichstag* required the immediate admission of deputies into the government as a first step towards the introduction of the parliamentary system. This argument expressed Erzberger's deep convictions but was also calculated to help woo the National Liberals, in view of Stresemann's known sympathy for the parliamentary system.[36]

Bethmann asked for an official Zentrum statement on how the party stood on his continuance in the office of Chancellor that same afternoon. A special party meeting then took place at 5.00 p.m., which resulted in an ambiguous declaration that was on the whole unfavorable to Bethmann: "The Zentrum Party in the *Reichstag* looks upon Bethmann's retention of the Chancellorship as an obstacle to the attainment of peace, in view of the fact that he held office at the time of the outbreak of the war; but it desires that the date of his retirement be left to his own sense of duty."[37] The party was in fact divided between those who wished his immediate resignation and those who wanted him first to carry the Prussian franchise reform and the admission of parliamentarians into the government. The party decision was influenced by the fact that Colonel Bauer had circulated the news that Ludendorff wanted Bethmann's dismissal. Erzberger kept himself in the background during the discussion. This uncharacteristic conduct may have been due to uncertainty about what he really wanted, but it is more likely that he recognized that the decision he considered right would be all the more valuable if it owed nothing to his direct advocacy. There was considerable testimony at the 1920 trial that many of his colleagues did not think that he wanted to see Bethmann dismissed at this time.[38]

Bethmann had meanwhile won a Crown Council decision in favor of the democratic franchise for Prussia, perhaps in order to strengthen his position, but also in implementation of his known views (July 9). His position was further strengthened when the Emperor rejected his proferred resignation on July 11. Erzberger was summoned that same day by the influential Chief of the Civil Cabinet, Valentini, to receive an explanation of the Emperor's decision. Valentini said that the absence of a suitable successor was a sufficient reason for retaining Bethmann, and that William intended to keep his Chancellor until the end

[36] *U.A.*, VIII, 125–31; Erzberger, *Erlebnisse*, p. 259; full text of Erzberger's July 9 speech in *Erzberger Papers*, File 32. A paraphrase can be found in *Erlebnisse*, pp. 259–60.
[37] Erzberger, *Erlebnisse*, p. 261.
[38] *Prozess*, pp. 756–70, 825–27, 830–33, 836–38. Both Giesbert (one of his closest party friends) and David (his main contact among the Socialists) testified to this effect.

of the war. Erzberger suggested Prince Bülow as the best man for the job. Valentini replied that the Emperor would not have him because their personal relations had been broken by the 1908 *Daily Telegraph* Incident. Erzberger, who had himself patched up a bitter quarrel with Bülow, thought that Reason of State should override the Emperor's private peeves. Erzberger also learned from Valentini that Prince Hohenlohe, the Austrian ambassador, had protested energetically against Bülow's appointment because of Viennese resentment against his Roman conduct in 1915. Erzberger, though he wanted to defer to Austrian sensibilities as much as possible, thought that yielding to such a veto would go much too far.[39]

No one can tell whether Bülow's appointment in 1917 would have brought good results for Germany. Bülow had a skill at handling men which Bethmann lacked. His lack of the three moral virtues of scruple, seriousness, and deep political conviction would have been an advantage in a difficult situation calling for maneuver and manipulation. Bülow was quite willing to cooperate in the evolution of the parliamentary system in Germany and to base his position squarely upon the *Reichstag* majority. His realistic appraisal of the international situation had made him a foe of annexationism on purely pragmatic grounds. His prudent concealment of his views would have protected him at least temporarily from the hostility of the Right. If any civilian could put the leash upon Ludendorff, he was certainly the man.[40]

Ludendorff had decided to seize the opportunity, while the political situation was still fluid, to force the Emperor to dismiss Bethmann. The Crown Prince came to Berlin for this specific purpose and held a series of conferences with prominent parliamentarians to see whether Bethmann could be dismissed without offending the *Reichstag* leaders (July 12). The Conservative and National Liberal leaders demanded, as expected, the immediate dismissal of the Chancellor. Payer of the Progressives and David of the Social Democrats wanted to keep Bethmann without pretending any enthusiasm for him. Erzberger spoke decisively against the Chancellor. He emphasized his unsuitability for making peace along the lines of the Peace Resolution, since President Wilson was known to have a strong prejudice against him on account of the submarine war. Erzberger put this graphically by stating that "Bethmann, soiled by his dirty (*bekleckert*) vest, could not possibly

[39] Erzberger, *Erlebnisse,* p. 262. Cf. Bülow's story of his failure to secure the chancellorship in *Denkwürdigkeiten,* III, 115. Valentini describes the July 11 conversation in *Kaiser und Kabinettschef* (Oldenburg, 1931), p. 163. Erzberger had repeatedly visited Bülow at Luzern in the spring of 1917, and it can be assumed that he acted with Bülow's full approval. *U.A.,* VII (2), 365–66.

[40] Bülow's 1917 plans are described in his *Denkwürdigkeiten,* III, 266.

sit at the peace table" (if Bülow's account can be trusted).[41] He denounced his procrastination in the question of domestic reforms, and also called him an obstacle to cordial relations between the *Reichstag* and the Supreme Command. The cancelled meeting of July 7 still rankled. Erzberger evidently did not believe that the Imperial veto upon Bülow was final, for otherwise his sharp hostility towards Bethmann becomes unintelligible.

Erzberger's opinion, which Bauer immediately wired to Ludendorff, must have strengthened the general in his resolve to force Bethmann's dismissal by an ultimatum. This gives Erzberger a major share of responsibility for Bethmann's overthrow. If the Zentrum had supported the Chancellor as the Progressives and Social Democrats did, Bethmann would have possessed a parliamentary majority. Even Ludendorff might have hesitated to provoke a sharp conflict over the Chancellorship with a *Reichstag* firmly resolved to back Bethmann.[42]

Erzberger reported his conversation with the Crown Prince to a party meeting that had been called to make a final decision upon the Peace Resolution. It was now clear that the National Liberals, perhaps because they were certain that the Supreme Command would secure Bethmann's fall in any case, had decided to oppose the Resolution despite the efforts of Richthofen's Left wing and the wooing of Erzberger. But the majority of the Zentrum felt that Erzberger's position must be supported on its merits nonetheless, even if it implied participation in a new coalition with the Left. Even Spahn was reluctantly tending towards this view, though he had openly spoken up for large annexations only five months previously. His voice ceased to count in any case because he suffered a complete physical collapse in the midst of the meeting, which took him out of active politics. Gröber, who was still an annexationist, was also ill at this time. Thus effective party leadership fell in Erzberger's lap. The party meeting endorsed both his hostility to Bethmann and the policy of the Peace Resolution with virtual unanimity. The annexationists in the party were so delighted by the fall of Bethmann that they were willing to acquiesce in the Peace Resolution. This may have been an additional reason why Erzberger wanted a change in the Chancellorship.[43]

On July 12 Ludendorff sent his ultimatum to the Emperor that Bethmann must go or else he would resign his post in the Supreme

[41] *ibid.,* p. 265.
[42] Ludendorff, *Urkunden der Obersten Heeresleitung* (Berlin, 1920), pp. 409–10.
[43] Erzberger, *Erlebnisse,* p. 262; Haussmann, op.cit., p. 124; Bachem, *Zentrumspartei,* IX, 455. An excellent description of the July 12 party meeting can be found in a letter of Richard Müller (Fulda) to Bachem, July 14, 1929, in *Bachem Papers,* File 90. The Zentrum attitude towards Bethmann was uncertain until the crucial meeting. The

Command. The Emperor resented this unheard-of pressure from a member of the military caste that had always prided itself upon its monarchical sentiments. Bethmann was not the man to fight for his position and the existing constitutional order against Ludendorff's arrogance. A stronger personality might have insisted that Ludendorff rather than himself go. He might have fanned William's indignation against the general, and thrown himself upon the Left-wing *Reichstag* majority by accepting the Peace Resolution. He might have discredited Ludendorff by castigating his wild annexationism and his primary responsibility for the submarine war. He might have capitalized upon the royal promise of the democratic franchise for Prussia, which he had just carried through the Crown Council. He might have strengthened his position by calling parliamentarians into the government. A skillful man might even have succeeded in separating Hindenburg from Ludendorff, as was to be done in October 1918, retaining the former in his figurehead position. This would have dampened the popular explosion which Ludendorff's dismissal would have provoked in Right-wing quarters. The combined support of Emperor and *Reichstag* majority would have made Bethmann's position politically impregnable, since German traditions precluded a military *coup d'état*. But Bethmann was not the kind of man for a showdown with the general. He resigned as he had ruled, revealing impotence and lack of political flair. Erzberger had made the Chancellor's position difficult by creating the panic of July 6 and leading the Zentrum Party into opposition against Bethmann, but the primary responsibility for Bethmann's acquiescence in Ludendorff's ultimatum belongs to himself and cannot be blamed upon Erzberger. His weakness in a sense justified Erzberger's desire to have him removed from office. Yet his successor was to prove much more incapable still.

Bethmann resigned on July 13, the day after Ludendorff's ultimatum. He had a talk with his friend Theodor Wolff, the Liberal editor of the *Berliner Tageblatt,* a few days later, which gives the best description of the Chancellor's view of the July crisis. Bethmann said about Erzberger's action on July 6:

> He yielded to impulsive panic. I—Wolff—replied that my first impression had been that he [Bethmann] must have agreed in advance to Erzberger's action as a suitable step for promoting peace possibilities and creating room for diplomatic maneuver, but I knew now that this had not been

---

National Liberal Schiffer was told by Trimborn that morning that the party stood behind the Chancellor. He next saw Erzberger to secure confirmation. Erzberger told him "with sardonic laughter to wait and see what would happen at the 3:00 p.m. meeting that afternoon." Schiffer, *Ein Leben für den Liberalismus* (Berlin, 1951), p. 196.

the case. He said: "I knew nothing about it. I admit that much of his speech was quite good. It did no harm to expose the hollowness of the nationalist phrases and to speak some unpalatable truths, but he went too far and acted like a bull in a China shop!" He then spoke of the Peace Resolution: "I hope that it will not remain completely without influence upon our enemies!" He thought it possible that peace might come in the autumn, because the English would not wish to wait until they were completely overshadowed by the Americans. This would be contrary to their interests. Perhaps the submarines might, after all, have some influence. Although Bethmann had plenty of cause to be bitter against Erzberger, he could not hide his fundamental sympathy for the man. Erzberger appeared to him, despite all his faults, as one of the few active parliamentarians capable of great deeds, a political force that could be used to good advantage.[44]

The Emperor selected Dr. Georg Michaelis, a complete political nonentity, to be Bethmann's successor on July 14. A more grotesque appointment could scarcely be imagined and it demonstrated, even more than Ludendorff's ultimatum, the complete bankruptcy of the Imperial constitution. Michaelis had played no previous political role. He had been a conscientious Prussian bureaucrat, who had won some public attention by a vigorous *Landtag* speech made in his role as wartime food administrator, in which he promised to crack down on chisellers. Ludendorff, who often thought firm language a substitute for wisdom, had been impressed and thought this an adequate qualification for the Chancellorship. The Emperor had never met Michaelis personally prior to his selection. It has never been clearly established who originated the idea of appointing Michaelis; no one was willing to admit responsibility after the fiasco of his brief tenure. Bethmann was not consulted. The *Reichstag* leaders were deliberately ignored for fear of creating precedents that might promote the parliamentary system. Their weakness was that they lacked an obvious candidate upon whom the majority could agree. Prince Bülow, who could have won *Reichstag* approval, was put out of the running by the Imperial veto. Count Hertling, the aged Bavarian Premier whom the parties were to accept in October, rejected the post when he received an offer prior to Michaelis' selection. The authoritarian monarchical system, though heavily diluted by irresponsible military influences, certainly died hard.[45]

[44] Theodor Wolff in an Erzberger obituary in the *Berliner Tageblatt,* Aug. 29, 1921. Copy in *Erzberger Papers,* File 43.
[45] Magnus von Braun, at that time Press Chief in the Interior Ministry, has recently admitted responsibility for suggesting the name of Michaelis to Ludendorff, though it is unclear whether this suggestion was decisive. *Von Ostpreussen bis Texas* (Stollhamm, 1955), pp. 113–17.

Michaelis, to do him justice, had some hesitation about assuming a post for which he was obviously unsuited. But a misguided sense of duty, reinforced by his religious faith, induced him to accept. He described his thoughts just before Valentini arrived at his home to make the formal offer of the Chancellorship in the following words:

> It was the most difficult hour of my life. No man was with me, but God was. The text for the day in the manual of the Protestant brotherhood (*Brüdergemeinde*) to which I belonged, which gave me, like thousands of others, daily advice for the pilgrimage of life, was verse nine from the first chapter of Joshua: "Have not I commanded thee? Be strong and of a good courage; be not afraid, neither be thou dismayed; for the Lord thy God is with thee whithersoever thou goest." [46]

Michaelis interpreted this as a divine call to accept the Chancellorship. The party leaders, somewhat less illumined, were both surprised and indignant at the unexpected appointment. Erzberger's failure to secure Bülow's accession must have caused bitter second thoughts about his contributory role in felling Bethmann. He immediately predicted to Haussmann, who had first brought him the bad news, that Michaelis would remain "a provisional Chancellor—a two-months child, as they say at Court." [47] Erzberger strove, meanwhile, to minimize the evil of Michaelis' accession by securing passage of the Peace Resolution in the hope that the new Chancellor would make it the guidepost of his foreign policy.

The Passage and Meaning of the Peace Resolution

Erzberger was too busy with party conferences to take a personal part in the drafting of the Peace Resolution. It emerged with the following wording from the Interparty Committee on July 12:

> The *Reichstag* declares: as on August 4, 1914, so on the threshhold of the fourth year of the war, the word of the speech from the Throne holds good for the German people "We are not impelled by lust of conquest." Germany resorted to arms in order to defend her freedom and independence and the integrity of her territorial possessions. The *Reichstag* strives for a peace of understanding and the permanent reconciliation of peoples. Forced territorial acquisitions and political, economic, and financial oppressions are irreconcilable with such a peace.

[46] Michaelis, *Für Staat und Volk* (Berlin, 1922), p. 321.
[47] Haussmann, *op.cit.*, p. 129. Erzberger on one occasion could not resist bragging about his political influence and boasted about having "made" Michaelis. This throws an unfavorable light upon his character, but does himself a substantive injustice. Bachem, *Zentrumspartei*, IX, 386.

This was followed by planks condemning economic discrimination in the postwar world and advocating the freedom of the seas and "international judicial organizations" (*Rechtsorganisationen*). It then warned all enemy governments that so long as they maintained their plans of conquests and refused the proffered hand of peace "the German nation will stand together as one man and steadfastly hold out and fight until its own and its allies' right to life and development is secured."[48]

The terms of this resolution were criticized, both at the time and later, by the opposite extremes of Conservatism and Independent Socialism. The former denounced it as a cowardly renunciation of conquest. The latter denounced it as hypocritical for appearing to oppose annexations while in fact leaving the door open to them. There was some substance in the Socialist view. The resolution did not explicitly favor a peace based upon the *status quo ante* and did not explicitly accept the Socialist formula of "no annexation or indemnities." It only condemned "forced territorial acquisitions and political, economic, and financial oppressions." Erzberger did not intend to slam the door on territorial exchanges produced by negotiations, and there could be various interpretations of the terms "forced acquisitions" and "oppressions," depending upon the actual conditions prevailing at the time when negotiations got underway. Michaelis was to seize upon this opening when he accepted the resolution only "as I interpret it" on July 19. Erzberger himself told Max of Baden at the time that Germany could acquire the Briey-Longwy mining area under its terms through a mutually satisfactory exchange.[49] When his Bulgar friends protested that the resolution seemed to preclude their major war aim of unifying all Bulgars, i.e. conquering Macedonia from Serbia, he calmed them by referring to the sentence about the "right to life and development" of Germany and its allies, adding, "Be assured that unification of all Bulgars remains a German war aim."[50] Erzberger also wrote to Michaelis on July 20, the day after the resolution was adopted, urging the rapid creation of an independent Lithuanian state. He said that this could not properly be described as a violation of the resolution, because it would not constitute a "forcible annexation."[51] A similar freedom of interpretation was to lead Erzberger the next year to de-

[48] R. H. Lutz, *Fall of the German Empire* (Stanford, 1932), II, 282–83.
[49] Max of Baden, *op.cit.*, p. 114.
[50] Oberndorff (German minister to Sofia) to Foreign Office, July 18, 1917, and Erzberger's undated reply to Oberndorff (probably telegraphed the same day) in *F.O.* File 1499. Erzberger, *Erlebnisse*, p. 265.
[51] Erzberger to Michaelis, July 18, 1917. *F.O.* File 1499.

clare that the terms of the Treaty of Brest-Litovsk were compatible with his resolution.

Erzberger was never opposed to the idea of annexation on moral grounds. He was now, as later, quite eager to secure economic and strategic gains for Germany, provided that the international ill will engendered did not exceed the tangible gains secured by Germany. By 1917 he rejected wild annexationist schemes such as those he had propagated in the early years of the war, but he still hoped that Germany could make profitable exchange bargains. The Independent Socialists were, from their point of view, justified in voting against Erzberger's resolution. Erzberger was, unlike them, not interested in bearing testimony to noble moral principles. He pursued the more limited aim of strengthening the German government against its annexationist foes who would embarrass it in any peace negotiations that might ensue. He thought that prudential considerations dictated a peace based upon the *status quo ante* as the best that could be attained in the summer of 1917. Yet he did not wish to foreclose all annexations if by chance the over-all war situation should improve for Germany, or if the bait of annexations was necessary to keep allies faithful to Germany (e.g. Bulgaria). He thought that the prospects for territorial changes were far better in the east than in the west, where they could take the form of genuine self-determination of formerly Russian territories such as Poland and Lithuania. In the west he realized, apart from occasional illusions about Briey-Longwy, that Germany must accept the prewar borders. Pacelli had told him, shortly before the July crisis, that "Germany can now have peace if she makes a clear-cut declaration of the unconditional restoration of Belgium." [52] Papal diplomacy believed consistently that German renunciation of Belgium was a prerequisite for the beginning of any peace negotiations between Germany and England. Erzberger had for some time pressed such a declaration upon Bethmann, and he desired an explicit renunciation of Belgium in the Peace Resolution; but he could not prevail in the face of the combined opposition of those who wished to retain control of Belgium and those who thought it a poor tactic to surrender any trumps prior to the beginning of negotiations. [53]

Erzberger and his colleagues on the Interparty Committee were uncertain whether Michaelis was in sympathy with the Peace Resolution. They resolved to be all the more insistent upon its *Reichstag* passage without any further watering down. Their task was made more difficult when Hindenburg and Ludendorff came to Berlin, for the

[52] Bachem, *Zentrumspartei*, IX, 449.
[53] Erzberger, *Erlebnisse*, p. 207.

second time in a week, in order to meddle in political affairs. The two generals now expressed open hostility to any anti-annexationist resolution, a hostility they had concealed when their primary purpose had been to bring down Bethmann and they still needed Erzberger's help in this task. Erzberger, in company with Mayer (Kaufbeuren) of the Zentrum and the two Socialists Ebert and Scheidemann, saw Ludendorff in the late afternoon of July 13. The general tried to reassure his visitors about the military situation. Erzberger was gratified that on this occasion Ludendorff, still testing his ground, offered only minor objections to the Peace Resolution. He was horrified when, at a private meeting the next morning (July 14), the general spoke sharply against its terms. He proved completely oblivious to the force of Erzberger's arguments on the submarine failure and the consequent necessity of abandoning annexationist policies.[54]

Michaelis was introduced to the *Reichstag* leaders at a garden party held under Helfferich's auspices on July 14. Hindenburg and Ludendorff also attended. The social festivities were interrupted by a sharp altercation between the generals and the parliamentarians on the wording of the proposed *Reichstag* Resolution. Erzberger insisted that the Resolution must be adopted as drafted by the Interparty Committee, while Ludendorff demanded changes in wording that would have negated all of Erzberger's purposes. Michaelis, caught in the crossfire, made himself ridiculous by stating that he would never have accepted the Chancellorship if he had not been under the mistaken impression that there existed full harmony between the *Reichstag* and the Supreme Command. He had told Scheidemann a short time previously that he must find his way gradually in political affairs since he had hitherto "been so absorbed in his professional work that he had only run as a contemporary (*Zeitgenosse*) along the side of the cart of politics." [55] The discussion between the party leaders and the generals about the Peace Resolution proved inconclusive, with Ludendorff wanting another meeting the next day. Scheidemann, acting on his own responsibility, ruthlessly terminated the discussion by leaking a copy of the text as determined by the Interparty Committee for publication to the *Vorwärts* that same evening. This action, while naturally resented by Michaelis and the generals, could not be repudiated by them without creating a disastrous impression at home and abroad.[56]

The *Reichstag* adopted the Peace Resolution on July 19 and Michaelis

[54] *July 15 Memorandum.* Also *Erlebnisse,* p. 264. Scheidemann, *Zusammenbruch,* pp. 92–94.
[55] Scheidemann, *op.cit.,* p. 100.
[56] The best account of the garden party is in Haussmann, *op.cit.,* pp. 130–37. Also Scheidemann, *op.cit.,* pp. 98–102.

made his first speech as Chancellor that same day. He had consulted with Erzberger and Scheidemann in advance about the paragraphs on foreign policy and had won their approval since his text called for a flat endorsement of the resolution.[57] Yet he added in his delivered speech the crucial qualification "as I interpret it" to his endorsement. This addition was no mere slip of the tongue but was intended to leave the way open for the whole annexationist program of the Supreme Command. The significance of the qualification was not immediately noticed in the excitement of the *Reichstag* plenary session;[58] but it soon became apparent that Michaelis looked upon himself primarily as the agent of Ludendorff and that he had no intention of being a parliamentary Chancellor. He wrote to the Crown Prince on July 25: "My interpretation has removed the greatest danger from the notorious Resolution. One can, after all, now make any peace that one likes under its terms."[59]

The Frankfurt Zentrum Meeting

The Peace Resolution, while having little impact abroad, caused intense internal controversy within Germany. It succeeded in its main purpose of securing continued Socialist support of the war effort, but this was offset, so far as national harmony was concerned, by a wild agitation of the annexationists in the newly founded Fatherland Party. They accused Erzberger of undermining the German will to victory and stabbing the glorious army in the back. This view was shared by the right wing of the Zentrum Party, though more in the party apparatus than among the deputies who had heard Erzberger. A special conference was called at Frankfurt for July 23 to give Erzberger a chance to explain his policy. It was attended by both the Zentrum Central Committee (*Reichsausschuss*) and the presidium of the Catholic press organization (*Augustinusverein*), with 64 men attending. The introductory speech was made by Fehrenbach, leader of the Baden Zentrum, who approved of Erzberger's action. Then Held, one of the Bavarian leaders, attacked. Erzberger replied in a two-hour oration that repeated many of the facts that he had first revealed in Berlin two weeks before. The impression made upon the audience was again devastating. Erzberger, to convert the few participants that still doubted the desperate position of the Central Powers, read the Czernin memorandum, which the Emperor Charles had given him in April

[57] Scheidemann, *op.cit.*, pp. 100–05.
[58] *U.A.*, VIII, 86–88.
[59] Michaelis to Crown Prince, July 25, 1917. *U.A.*, VII (2), 390–91.

to use as he saw fit. Bachem, who was present, reports that Erzberger insisted upon stringent security precautions, realizing that a leakage of the memorandum would promote consternation in Germany and jubilation in the Entente countries. "Erzberger stated that nothing in the memorandum must be allowed to reach the public. All members present gave their word of honor to preserve secrecy. All doors were locked and guarded from the outside. Erzberger warned against taking any notes. He read the memorandum with extreme rapidity so that it was difficult to follow." [60]

Erzberger's shock tactics scored immediate success when the party meeting unanimously endorsed the Peace Resolution policy. This triumph was, however, purchased at too great a price for Erzberger's reputation. To read such an important document to 64 people and expect absolute secrecy was naïve. When the Czernin memorandum became known to the Entente sometime in mid-1917 Erzberger's foes began to denounce him as a traitor for leaking vital official information to the enemy. Whether Erzberger was motivated by English bribery or mere imprudence they professed themselves unable to decide. No proof was ever advanced that the Entente had received the Memorandum via Frankfurt, though Erzberger's accusers continued to assert this as a categorical fact. The accusation that Erzberger was an indiscreet man who irresponsibly used top-secret information to protect his personal party position, if not for worse purposes, stuck to him until the end of his life.[61]

The reading of the memorandum must be criticized as an act of faulty judgment rather than of dishonor, though it should be noted that Erzberger faced an audience which it was extremely important for him to win over. Erzberger had, however, received the Memorandum in a completely legitimate way, and had been authorized to use it in any way he thought appropriate to help promote a negotiated peace: to win Zentrum Party approval for the Peace Resolution was certainly a purpose covered by Emperor Charles' intentions. Erzberger took maximum precautions to avoid leakage. It must also be remem-

[60] Bachem, *Zentrumspartei*, IX, 439. The entire meeting is described pp. 437–41. Another good account by a participant is Hugo Baur, "Mein politischer Lebenslauf," in *Deutsche Bodensee Zeitung,* March 2, 1929. Copy in *Bachem Papers,* File 90.

[61] The leakage of the Czernin Memorandum led to considerable discussion in the summer of 1919, when Czernin joined the ranks of Erzberger's accusers. Erzberger wrote Czernin July 30, 1919, demanding proof that the memorandum had gotten to the Entente via Frankfurt. Czernin replied on August 8, 1919, that he had no proof, but believed that nothing known to a great number of people could remain secret. Erzberger replied on August 18, 1919, pointing out some errors in Czernin's last letter. Czernin then preferred to end the correspondence. *Erzberger Papers,* File 8.

bered that the memorandum was already three months old when Erzberger read it, and that it contained no specific facts that were not already known to Entente intelligence. The Entente had, moreover,
other possibilities of securing the report. Erzberger's foes could never
document their contention that he was responsible for the memorandum's reaching London and Paris. Their further assertion, that it
destroyed promising peace chances existing in 1917, by stimulating
Entente willingness to continue the war by prospects of an early victory, was also incapable of proof. The latter accusation came with
rather poor grace from the foes of the Peace Resolution. They usually
argued that Erzberger and the Socialists engaged in a dangerous illusion when they believed in a negotiated peace, asserting that Entente
intransigence would never rest until the total defeat of Germany. Yet
they at the same time criticized Erzberger's alleged leakage of the
Czernin Memorandum for destroying a promising peace possibility by
stimulating the supposedly flagging Entente zeal to continue the war.[62]

The Results of the July Crisis

A judgment upon Erzberger's conduct during the crisis of July 1917
involves the evaluation of some imponderables upon which there will
never be full agreement among historians. What were the prospects for
a negotiated peace in the summer of 1917 if the German government
had made a serious offer consonant with the Peace Resolution? One
must repeat what was said about the general peace prospects at the
time of the Stockholm negotiations three months before: they were
not very promising. England, France, Italy, and America were unwilling to accept peace based upon the *status quo ante* so long as they
saw the prospect for a complete military victory. The hopes for a
German separate peace with Russia had dimmed since Ludendorff and
Stinnes had sabotaged the Erzberger-Kolyschko negotiations. The
probability that the Entente would be willing to accept the Erzberger
program was very slim, but the July resolution at least offered the German government the support of the *Reichstag* to seize whatever opportunity existed.

The small chance of complete success did not mean that Erzberger's
policy was intrinsically mistaken. It was justified even if the Entente
governments rejected any reasonable German peace offer. Partial success, in terms of encouraging anti-war sentiment in the various Entente
countries, was certain *if* the resolution was taken seriously abroad. Un-

[62] For an example of this essentially inconsistent charge, see K. Helfferich, *Fort mit
Erzberger* (Berlin, 1919), pp. 6, 45.

fortunately this "if" loomed very large. Foreign opinion believed (not incorrectly) that the voice of the *Reichstag* was not decisive in German affairs and that it had no direct authority in the field of foreign policy. The significance of Michaelis' "as I interpret it" was immediately understood abroad. He was rightly suspected of speaking for a powerful body of annexationist public opinion which would be backed in any showdown by the Supreme Command. Any success for Erzberger's policy—even in the limited sphere of promoting the feeling in Entente countries that the war was being needlessly prolonged by the Entente lust for conquest—presupposed a constitutional revolution in Germany. It presupposed the development of the parliamentary system, or at least complete harmony between the *Reichstag* majority and the executive government on war aims. It also required the complete subordination of the Supreme Command to a Chancellor who firmly believed in the Peace Resolution.

It is to Erzberger's credit that he recognized these facts. His desire for the appointment of Bülow and the entry of parliamentarians into the government was intended to give Germany a strong civilian Chancellor who could use *Reichstag* support to curb Ludendorff's annexationism. The retention of Bethmann, if accompanied by the dismissal of Ludendorff, would have served almost as well; while the appointment of Michaelis immediately destroyed most of the positive effects that might otherwise have resulted from the Peace Resolution. It is ironical that Erzberger should have contributed to this result by his campaign against Bethmann in cooperation with Stresemann. He was for once in his life outmaneuvered, and he allowed himself to be used by his fellow-intriguers to bring down the man who at least agreed with his policy. His hope that he might use Stresemann and Ludendorff for his own purposes, both by elevating Bülow and securing National Liberal support for the Peace Resolution, failed on both counts. Erzberger made the worst political mistake of his career when he joined hands with Bethmann's Right-wing enemies without making sure in advance that a better man would get the Chancellorship. He should have realized that his hopes for Bülow would remain illusory unless he could impose the prince upon the Emperor. To do so required a cohesive *Reichstag* majority united by common principles, a strong will to power, and unity behind the Bülow candidacy.

Erzberger attempted to create such a majority composed of Zentrum, Progressives, and Social Democrats. To unite them behind the common policy of the Peace Resolution was a great achievement, and meant a fundamental reconstruction of German political affairs. It broke the previous Conservative–National Liberal stranglehold over *Reichstag* policy and for the first time won the Social Democrats for responsible political activity in cooperation with other parties. The Zentrum, previously the left wing of a Right coalition, was brought by Erzberger into the position of being the right wing of a Left coalition. The cooperation of the three parties prepared the way for the establishment of the parliamentary system and the termination of the unfortunate prewar alienation of most of the working class from the existing state system. The new coalition was a constructive attempt to overcome the structural flaws of Bismarck's political system.[63]

But the new majority was not yet strong enough to impose the parliamentary system upon Germany. The Emperor ignored the *Reichstag* leaders when selecting Michaelis, and the leaders could not challenge the appointment after it had been announced. They could insist upon Michaelis' swallowing the Peace Resolution much against his own inclination, but they were not strong enough to immediately challenge his phrase "as I interpret it." They were unwilling to use their budgetary power, which was made more potent by the incessant demand for war credits, in order to impose their will and policy upon the state.

The cumulative heritage of the undistinguished history of German parliamentary institutions serves to explain their weakness. The *Reichstag* parties were accustomed to act as pressure groups, not responsible coalition partners—hence their inability to agree upon a joint program covering all problems of German life. Erzberger had secured agreement in the crucial question of war aims by the formula of the Peace Resolution, but this was capable of divergent interpretation. The Zentrum, Progressives, and even some Social Democrats rediscovered their annexationist desires as soon as the military situation improved. The majority parties were not united upon the desirability of the parliamentary system, much less upon the expediency of forcing its introduction at that particular moment. They also lacked an authoritative spokesman who could voice their common views and lay claim to the Chancellorship on their behalf. Erzberger, although seemingly the natural candidate, was still considered too young, too controversial, and too much the *enfant terrible* of his own party. His manner of engineering the July crisis had augmented his influence rather than his reputation.

The general circumstances of July 1917 appeared as unpromising for achieving great results as the inherent weakness, division, and

[63] For an appreciation of Erzberger's "revolutionary achievement," see A. Rosenberg, *Entstehung*, p. 156.

lack of leadership of the majority parties. The war, by requiring frequent votes of credit, had given the *Reichstag* its opportunity, but it also militated against the use of that opportunity. To secure the introduction of the parliamentary system by forcing the appointment of a parliamentary Chancellor meant a constitutional revolution in the midst of national danger. There were many timid and some ultra-patriotic men, even within the ranks of the *Reichstag* majority, who felt that the accompanying internal strife would distract from the paramount obligation of fighting Germany's foreign enemies. They forgot that the maintenance of the decadent Imperial constitution stimulated discontents that also compromised the effective prosecution of the war. They forgot that the failure to achieve a parliamentary form of government left political power in the hands of General Ludendorff. Many also felt that a *Reichstag* assertion of authority would be met by defiance rather than submission on the part of the Supreme Command, with the result of sharp constitutional friction followed perhaps by an open military dictatorship. But it is doubtful whether Ludendorff would have gone to such an extreme. It must be remembered that he had a real aversion to politics and that he meddled in it from a sense of disgust with the existing leadership rather than to achieve far-reaching political aims. He was not a man cast in a Napoleonic mould. He had yielded on the passage of the Peace Resolution, which he disliked intensely, and probably would have yielded on other questions if confronted by an unpleasant alternative. The *Reichstag* erred in not exploiting his unwillingness to engage in a major political conflict. Many of its members continued to be hypnotized by the prestige of the Prussian General Staff.[64]

[64] Bredt's criticism of the timidity of the *Reichstag* majority, the main theme of his book published as *U.A.*, VIII, assumes that the majority parties were something other than what history and the circumstances of 1917 made them. See especially p. 85.

The criticism which Arthur Rosenberg, in *op.cit.*, pp. 156–58, directs against Erzberger—that he erred in not creating a firm majority coalition that could make its views prevail in the state—ignores the party materials with which Erzberger had to work. It was a great enough achievement to secure their temporary cooperation in the Peace Resolution. To demand more is to apply a perfectionist standard that is irrelevant under the conditions of 1917. Rosenberg's other major criticism—that Erzberger ought to have fired his oratorical blasts at Ludendorff, the real culprit, rather than Bethmann, the innocent accomplice in the submarine question—also misunderstands the realities of the situation. To secure Ludendorff's dismissal in July 1917 was certainly beyond the powers of any German party politician. The organization of a *Reichstag* majority against Ludendorff might have been possible for Bethmann, supported by the Emperor and the prestige of the Chancellor's office, after the general had sought to force his dismissal by an ultimatum. A party leader like Erzberger could not succeed in such a task, even if he had been armed by the same degree of provocation. What Erzberger could do and did was to achieve the passage of the Peace Resolution in the teeth of Ludendorff's opposition, thus giving any Chancellor a weapon for fighting the annexationism of the Supreme Command.

Erzberger failed to achieve the foreign objectives of his Peace Resolution: a negotiated peace, or at least the fanning of war weariness in
the Entente countries. But he succeeded in his secondary domestic objectives. The Majority Socialists continued to vote for war credits. Their
position against the Independents was at least temporarily strengthened. The constitutional position of the *Reichstag* was considerably enhanced despite its failure to influence the selection of the new Chancellor. Two parliamentarians, the National Liberal von Krause and the
Zentrum leader Spahn, became heads of the Imperial and Prussian
Ministries of Justice respectively, a small step in the direction of giving
Reichstag men a greater role in the executive government. The new
majority coalition of Zentrum, Progressives, and Social Democrats was
a force with which the government must henceforth reckon. Its influence was to be considerably greater in the next Chancellor crisis
three months later.[65]

The worst result of the July crisis was that it did not produce clear-
cut decisions. It created a powerful *Reichstag* coalition, yet one that
could not shape executive policy. It made a weak and incompetent man
Chancellor, yet this man was strong enough to thwart the *Reichstag*
will. It humiliated the Emperor by his yielding to a military ultimatum,
yet left his prerogatives unimpaired. It enhanced General Ludendorff's
position because the success of his political intervention whetted his
appetite for more actions of the same kind, yet left his constitutional
position as undefined as it had previously been. No one knew what
Germany's war aims were, or whether the *Reichstag,* Chancellor, Emperor, or Supreme Command had the authority to define them if an
occasion for peace negotiations should arise. Germany's internal situation remained in complete flux: a reform of the Prussian franchise
had been promised but not implemented. A *Reichstag* majority existed
that favored the enlargement of parliamentary powers, yet it was
paralyzed by internal divisions and the fear of provoking a constitutional struggle in the midst of war. A deep, latent conflict existed between the new democratic-parliamentary forces and the old authori-
tarian-bureaucratic military state, yet both sides were hesitant to enter
into an open clash. The result was a hopeless confusion that prevented
Germany from developing any coherent foreign or domestic policy.

The effect of the July crisis upon Erzberger's personal position was
both exhilarating and disastrous. On the one hand, he emerged as Germany's most powerful deputy, while his name became a symbol for the

---

[65] Erzberger, always an incorrigible optimist, exaggerated the positive results of his
resolution in a February 6, 1918 memorandum to von Bergen. *Erlebnisse,* pp. 266–68.

attempt to end the war by a negotiated peace. This gave him great popularity in the country, above all among the lower classes. On the other hand, he became the most hated man in Germany among all those elements—primarily in the upper classes—who wanted an annexationist peace and no tampering with Germany's social and political structure. He was attacked with incredible ferocity as a British or Austrian or Vatican agent. Old accusations, based upon his campaign of colonial exposure and his unfortunate part in the Pöplau and Janke cases, were revived and embellished for public consumption. A whispering campaign denounced him as a draft dodger, war profiteer, and man who used his propaganda work for personal enrichment, and his foreign travels to get around rationing restrictions. No charge was too silly to be levied against Erzberger, and millions began to believe that he was the evil genius of Germany. The seeds were being sown for his later assassination by young idealists, whose minds had been poisoned against their victim by an agitation supported by groups that felt themselves threatened in their traditional control of Germany.[66]

[66] The first major anti-Erzberger pamphlet, F. Hussong, *Matthias Erzbergers Wege und Wandlungen,* appeared in Berlin in early September 1917. Erzberger denounced the scurrilous and ludicrous attacks against him in *Reichstag Debates,* cccxi (Feb. 27, 1918), 4226–28.

CHAPTER IX

FROM MICHAELIS TO HERTLING (JULY–OCTOBER 1917)

After the Peace Resolution

ERZBERGER was irritated by the appointment of Michaelis, but he made up his mind to cooperate with the new Chancellor in the optimistic hope that he would support the policy of the Peace Resolution. Michaelis himself did not quite know how to handle Erzberger when the latter came to see him privately in late July in order to ask if his confidential relationship to the Foreign Office would continue under the new administration. The Chancellor at first answered evasively. He called in three Zentrum deputies (Spahn, Porsch, and Giesberts), to ask them about Erzberger's qualities and position (August 7), presumably to find out if he could drive a wedge between Erzberger and his party. All three praised his conduct (the former two placing party loyalty above their personal convictions) and warned Michaelis against driving Erzberger into opposition.[1] Michaelis then decided to permit Erzberger continued access to Foreign Office files; but he withdrew Erzberger's general passport, which had allowed him hitherto to travel anywhere abroad without seeking specific permission for each trip. Since passports were granted by the military (who were generally hostile to the author of the Peace Resolution) Erzberger's enemies secured an opportunity for harassing him. When, for example, he wanted to accept an invitation by the Budapest branch of the Catholic *Volksverein* to speak on peace prospects in September 1917 he was flatly refused permission to go.[2] Some soldiers wanted, indeed, to go further, and seriously contemplated silencing Erzberger by drafting him into the army. This punitive wish was frustrated when the Foreign Office continued to insist upon his deferment.[3]

Erzberger, exhausted from the strains of the last few months, went

---

[1] Memorandum by Dr. Pfeiffer, Aug 11, 1917, who learned the facts from Spahn. Also letter from Giesberts to Michaelis, Aug. 8, 1917. *Erzberger Papers,* File 18.

[2] *U.A.,* VII (2), 108 (Michaelis' testimony). Erzberger, *Erlebnisse,* p. 268. The Emperor approved this passport deprivation. Grünau to Michaelis, Oct. 5, 1917. *F.O.* File 1499.

[3] This fact was first revealed by Erzberger's enemies when they stole his draft records from the *Kriegsersatzamt* (in charge of military manpower). *Kölnische Volkszeitung,* Aug. 8, 1919. It is confirmed by the memoirs of the Prussian War Minister, Ernst von Wrisberg, *Erinnerungen an die Kriegsjahre* (Leipzig, 1921), Vol. II, p. 93.

on a brief vacation to Switzerland in late July. Before settling down at Brunnen, Erzberger spent a few days at Zurich. There he made an unfortunate statement that was to add to his reputation for arrogance and frivolity. He had a talk with Lord Weardale, an Englishman active in the exchange of prisoners of war, about terms of peace, and evidently received a false picture of English moderation. He thought that English reasonableness plus the Peace Resolution could give Europe an early peace, and his optimistic temperament refused to believe that Michaelis could be an obstacle. Erzberger then talked with his friend Georg Baumberger, editor of the pro-German *Neue Züricher Nachrichten,* who, according to the story of one of Erzberger's friends,

> congratulated him upon his powerful campaign for peace. But he did not conceal his view that the appointment of Dr. Michaelis was interpreted to mean an intensification of the war spirit. Erzberger replied: "The judgment that the new Chancellor is a 'war Chancellor' is completely false. He considers it his mission to become the 'peace Chancellor.' This is also the view of the *Reichstag,* which possesses adequate guarantees that its views will prevail. The appointment of Dr. Michaelis does not mean a weakening of the Peace Resolution, it on the contrary strengthens it in all its parts." Erzberger then gave the following assessment of peace prospects: "If I had an opportunity in the near future to have a talk with Lloyd George or Balfour or one of their authorized agents, we could probably agree in a few hours upon a basis of peace and reconciliation, so that official peace negotiations could then follow immediately." Baumberger then said: "These last sentences are of such importance, I want to ask you to allow their *verbatim* publication." Erzberger: "You may do so, I will confirm their accuracy." [4]

Erzberger's statement led to a great outcry in Germany, and was denounced by Right-wing circles as stimulating illusions that must undermine Germany's war effort. The Conservatives asked him in the *Reichstag* what terms he would have suggested to Lloyd George; to this he gave an evasive answer.[5] The Conservatives added to their already hostile stereotype of Erzberger the image of a frivolous man who thought that a few hours of personal diplomacy could alter the entire outlook of European affairs.

[4] Arnold Rechberg in *Tägliche Rundschau,* July 25, 1919, quoted by F. von Lama, *Die Friedensvermittlung Papst Benedikt XV und ihre Vereitelung* (Munich, 1932), p. 57, note 12. The last two sentences are included in a contemporary account in the *Kölnische Volkszeitung,* July 28, 1917. Copy in *Erzberger Papers,* File 5.

[5] The Conservative inquiry was made in the Main Committee on Aug. 28, 1917. See *Kreuzzeitung,* Aug. 31, 1917. Copy in *Bachem Papers,* File 89.

Erzberger and the Papal Peace Note

The diplomatic stage was dominated in the late summer of 1917 by the attempted Papal Peace Mediation. Pacelli had come to Berlin for a second visit immediately after the Peace Resolution in order to resume with Michaelis the exploratory conversations he had begun with Bethmann. This time he brought a set of detailed peace proposals which became the basis of the subsequent Papal Note: (1) freedom of the seas; (2) disarmament; (3) judicial arbitration of disputes; (4) evacuation of Belgium, occupied France, and German colonies; new guarantees for Belgian neutrality; (5) postwar economic cooperation between nations; (6) amicable settlement of territorial disputes between Germany and France (Alsace-Lorraine) and Austria and Italy (Trentino); (7) restoration of Poland, Serbia, Rumania, and Montenegro.[6] Erzberger approved these terms when Pacelli asked him for comment on July 24. His only suggestion was that some of the points should be made more specific, with Point 5, for example, being changed to call specifically for the open door. These terms give a faithful record of Erzberger's ideas of a peace settlement only five days after the passage of the Peace Resolution.

The Papal Note was published to the world in mid-August. Michaelis discussed it with the *Reichstag* leaders on August 20, and at this meeting the Majority parties first realized from his general remarks that the new Chancellor did not believe in the policy of the Peace Resolution. A sharp clash ensued. Michaelis then tried to pacify the *Reichstag* suspicions by agreeing to the appointment of a Committee of Seven from its ranks—including Erzberger—to advise the government about the German reply to Rome. While Germany procrastinated, the English Foreign Secretary Balfour sent a letter to Count deSalis, the English ambassador to the Vatican, stating that a final English reply to the Papal Note could not be formulated until Germany had first revealed her plans about Belgium (August 21, 1917). The French associated themselves with this letter on August 23. This Anglo-French move was distorted in subsequent controversy into a "peace offer," though the term is too specific for describing a request for a unilateral German declaration on one of the several questions that must be discussed at the peace table. The Papacy recognized the reasonableness of the Anglo-French request, and Pacelli sent a special letter to Michaelis (August 30) pointing out the supreme importance of including a specific German renunciation of Belgium in the German reply to the Vatican. This important

[6] Copy of Pacelli's terms, with annotations by Erzberger, in *Erzberger Papers,* File 18.

letter was concealed from the Committee of Seven which the Government had promised to consult.[7]

This Committee met formally on two occasions with Kühlmann, who had just been selected Zimmermann's successor as Foreign Secretary. Michaelis had wanted to appoint Helfferich to the post, but Erzberger had successfully objected on the score that Helfferich was *persona non grata* to the *Reichstag,* and had made annexationist statements in the past which were incompatible with the Peace Resolution.[8] Kühlmann had, on the other hand, the reputation of a moderate, and Erzberger treated him with what was later shown to be excessive trust.

The German reply to the Pope was formulated in an atmosphere dominated by President Wilson's letter to Benedict (August 30), which had accepted most of the Papal program but had hinted that the abdication of William and the breaking of German military power was a prerequisite for making Germany a reliable negotiating partner. This intervention in her internal affairs naturally caused great indignation throughout Germany, with the Conservative leader Heydebrand and the Pan-German journalist Reventlow leading a campaign of personal abuse against Wilson. Erzberger, on the other hand, emphasized that many of Wilson's ideas were acceptable to Germany (disarmament, arbitration, etc.) and added a very sensible comment in an interview with a Hungarian journalist (which was widely reprinted in German newspapers at the time):

> One must never yield to indignation and emotion in statecraft. Political decisions must be made by cold reason that calculates consequences closely. One must, of course, reject humiliating insults and unjustified interference in one's domestic affairs with vigor and decisiveness. But one must nonetheless examine the reply of an enemy more for its material content [than its insulting form]. Besides, Wilson will remain President until 1921. Will Reventlow and Heydebrand demand that he leave office before the expiration of his term? I do not believe that these two gentlemen take the view that we must continue the war against America until America should elect a new President. The simple fact is that Germany will have to negotiate the peace settlement with Wilson. This simple consideration forces every German capable of reasonable thought to avoid, while of course

[7] On the entire Papal peace move, see Lama, *op.cit.,* a passionate but scholarly attack upon Michaelis; *U.A.,* VIII, 132–55, an admirable survey by Bredt; John Snell, "Benedict XV, Wilson, Michaelis and German Socialism," in *Catholic Historical Review* XXXVII (1951), 151–78, a recent American account. A revival of the controversy can be found in Ernst Deuerlein, "Zur Friedensaktion Benedicts XV," in *Stimmen der Zeit,* CLV (Jan. 1955), 241–55, and Wilhelm Michaelis, "Der Reichskanzler Michaelis und die päpstliche Friedensaktion," in *Geschichte in Wissenschaft und Unterricht,* VII (1956), 14–24 and 128. The latter is a defense of Michaelis by his son.

[8] Erzberger, *Erlebnisse,* p. 288.

emphasizing the German point of view, using insulting words which can only bring bitterness into the difficult task of peace-making and thereby disturb and endanger it.[9]

The decisive conference between Kühlmann and the *Reichstag* Committee took place on September 10. Erzberger, along with four of the other members, pressed Kühlmann to include a specific renunciation of Belgium in the German answer to the Pope. Erzberger did not know the content of Pacelli's letter of August 30, but he was in spontaneous agreement with Vatican views.[10] His own views had been confirmed by a conversation with Czernin on September 6, who had urged the extreme desirability of offering full restitution to Belgium.[11]

Kühlmann, on the other hand, argued against an explicit reference to Belgium. He supported his arguments by the threat of resignation if the Committee should refuse to yield to his views. The Committee members were reluctant to quarrel with the new Foreign Secretary, because he was known to be generally opposed to annexations. Their reluctance was strengthened when Kühlmann accepted a suggestion of Erzberger's to include an explicit reference to the Peace Resolution in the German reply. The Majority parties interpreted this as involving the restitution of Belgium, though they should have known that a different interpretation prevailed abroad. Kühlmann also promised to let the Vatican know confidentially what Germany's views on Belgium were. The *Reichstag* leaders got the impression that this meant that Germany would privately renounce all annexations in the west. With this assurance they agreed to Kühlmann's draft of a very general answer to the Pope, which was despatched on September 19. It is hard to blame them for their conduct in view of their complete ignorance of both the specific Anglo-French inquiry about Belgium of August 23, and Pacelli's letter of August 30. The responsibility for the German failure to make

[9] *Rheinisch-Westfälische Zeitung*, Sept. 9, 1917. *Bachem Papers*, File 89. Ernst Reventlow's articles were reprinted in Berlin in 1941 under the title *Die Neutralität der USA 1914–1918*.

[10] Michaelis mistakenly believed that Erzberger knew about the content of the Papal letter, and that his later criticism of the German reply was unjustified since he had participated in drafting it with full knowledge of the content. This led to a bitter controversy. Erzberger stated in his *Reichstag* speech of July 28, 1919, that he had known the fact, but not the content of the correspondence between Pacelli and Michaelis (Aug. 30 and Sept. 24, 1917). He said that he had promised Pacelli absolute discretion and had not even informed other Zentrum leaders. *Reichstag Debates*, cccxxviii, 2026–27. Pacelli confirmed this in the *Augsburger Post Zeitung*, July 30, 1919. Quoted in Lama, *op.cit.*, p. 157, note 19. Michaelis based his view upon the fact that Erzberger had asked at the Chancellery on Sept. 4 whether an important letter from Munich had arrived. *U.A.*, vii (2), 108–09.

[11] Erzberger, *Erlebnisse*, p. 278.

the necessary pledges on Belgium rests squarely upon the shoulders of Michaelis and Kühlmann.[12]

Erzberger showed his vigorous support of a "peace of conciliation" at this time in a controversial speech at Biberach (the center of his *Reichstag* district) that aroused the anger of the naval authorities (September 16, 1917). It was his first visit to his constituency since 1913. His local importance was symbolized by the fact that the Württemberg railroad administration provided a special train from Ulm to Biberach when an earlier delay made it uncertain whether he could reach Biberach on time for a scheduled meeting. Erzberger's anger had been aroused by the inauguration of the so-called Fatherland Party a few days previously—a party that aimed at rallying all the annexationist groups in Germany against the policy of the Peace Resolution. Erzberger was the favorite target of their attack. He was accused not only of fainthearted defeatism in general but of having sabotaged the beginning of submarine warfare in the spring of 1916 (when prospects of success were supposedly greatest). Erzberger hit back hard at the annexationists in his Biberach speech, denouncing them for fostering illusions and hurting Germany's war effort by alienating the broad masses from the government. He refuted the accusation concerning submarine warfare by revealing that Germany had owned less than fifty seaworthy submarines in the spring of 1916. The advocates of the submarine had spread the rumor at the time that Germany had 300.[13] The military censor refused to permit the publication of Erzberger's remarks in Germany. When the *Germania* printed extracts on September 19, the entire issue was confiscated by the government.[14] The naval authorities accused Erzberger of revealing military secrets to the enemy, though the so-called secrets were already eighteen months old. They attempted to

[12] On the committee meeting of September 10, see Erzberger, *Erlebnisse*, pp. 278–79. Protocol of the session, with copy in *Erzberger Papers*, File 14. Kühlmann, *Erinnerungen*, pp. 478–79; Scheidemann, *Zusammenbruch*, pp. 113–14; *U.A.*, VIII, 145–46. Erzberger praised the evasive German reply to the Pope in the Main Committee of the *Reichstag* on September 28, 1917, but only because he believed that Michaelis would find another way to inform the Vatican about Belgium, as Kühlmann had already promised. Erzberger also claimed that Michaelis had told him just before the debate: "You need not worry about the failure to mention Belgium explicitly in our Reply Note. The Entente Powers will receive full knowledge of our Belgian position through another channel." Erzberger admitted in 1919 that he ought to have insisted more firmly upon a specific mention of Belgium in the Committee of Seven, but mentioned Ludendorff's ascendant position and the threat of a treason prosecution against himself (see below) as extenuating circumstances. *Reichstag Debates*, CCCXXVIII (July 28, 1919), 2025 and 2028.

[13] Erzberger, *Erlebnisse*, p. 227.

[14] H. Frenzel, *Erzberger der Reichsverderber* (Leipzig, 1919), p. 11. For a full account of the Biberach meeting, see *Augsburger Post Zeitung*, Sept. 18, 1917. Copy in *Bachem Papers*, File 89.

initiate a prosecution for treason against him, but this was prevented by the public prosecutors' office.[15]

Erzberger made a comprehensive defense of his entire peace policy in a great speech at Ulm before a Württemberg Zentrum Party Congress a week after the Biberach meeting (September 23, 1917). It is worth summarizing at some length. He spoke of the Peace Resolution, the Papal Peace Note, and the German official reply as the "three cornerstones of peace," and proclaimed his belief that peace negotiations would commence as soon as the Entente Powers had made their reply to the Pope. He praised Kühlmann as a diplomat well suited to negotiate a mutually acceptable settlement. Erzberger then explained for the first time, in public, the motives that had induced him to introduce the Peace Resolution: the impossibility of securing a full victory over a "world of enemies" in view of their geographical location and economic resources; the necessity of rebuilding European Christian civilization upon the basis of compromise and conciliation, not of brute conquest; the weakness of Austria; the desire to stimulate the peace movement in Entente countries; and the necessity of disavowing annexationism in order to retain Socialist support for the war.[16]

Erzberger was unable to mention the submarine fiasco as the major reason for his action. Ulm was a fortress town under direct military jurisdiction, and the garrison commander had warned him before his speech that any mention of the submarine issue would be followed by his immediate arrest.[17] Erzberger had chosen the course of prudent reticence, in view of the fact that a prosecution for treason was already pending since his Biberach speech. The whole episode throws a glaring light upon the conditions governing political controversy in wartime Germany.

The main part of Erzberger's speech was a vigorous defense of the Peace Resolution and a refutation of the arguments which were being advanced against it. Opponents said that it expressed the desire for a dishonorable peace of renunciation (*Verzichtfrieden*). But Erzberger emphasized that renunciation of conquests was expected from all the belligerents—England, for example, would be forced to restore Germany's colonies and Asiatic Turkey. Germany did not need more industrial areas in Europe; she rather needed access to overseas raw materials, freedom of the seas, prohibition of Entente plans for postwar eco-

[15] Erzberger, *Erlebnisse*, p. 227. Magnus von Braun, *Von Ostpreussen bis Texas*, p. 144.
[16] Erzberger, *Der Verständigungsfriede* (Stuttgart, 1917), pp. 3–13. This is a printed version of his Ulm speech, published by the Württemberg Zentrum Party.
[17] Erzberger, *Erlebnisse*, p. 227.

nomic warfare, and perhaps an enlargement of her colonial empire through amicable negotiations. All these aims were attainable within the framework of the Peace Resolution. The opponents of the Peace Resolution also attacked it for giving an impression of weakness abroad, thereby strengthening the Entente will to victory. Erzberger was impatient with an argument that precluded any kind of peace offer at any time short of total victory. He argued that Germany, precisely because she was in a position of impregnable defensive strength, could well afford to make a peace offer. He cited the repeated peace offers which Bismarck had made to France in the course of the 1870-1871 war.[18]

Erzberger then lauded the Papal Peace Note and claimed that the Peace Resolution had prepared the way for giving it a favorable reception in Germany. He hailed the German reply of September 19 for setting the basis for negotiations with the Entente. He said that it clearly implied the complete renunciation of Belgium, while not precluding the establishment of new national states at Russia's expense in the east (Poland, Lithuania, Courland)—a matter that will be discussed in detail below. He thought that the acceptance of the principle of national self-determination by the new Russian government allowed a considerable territorial reorganization in Eastern Europe without precluding a "peace of conciliation" between Germany and Russia.[19] The meeting ended with a unanimous resolution approving Erzberger's policies and a sharp condemnation of the conduct of the Fatherland Party.

Erzberger's optimistic tone at Ulm was due to his mistaken faith in Kühlmann. That the latter would evade his pledge of pressing for peace on the basis of renouncing Belgium never occurred to Erzbeger, since Kühlmann was known to be a man without illusions and a statement, open or secret, on Belgium was the obvious prerequisite for starting negotiations. The reasons for Kühlmann's evasive reply to the Pope are obscure even today, and his memoirs, published in 1948, only add to the mystery.[20] Erzberger may be pardoned for not understanding a line of conduct that is still puzzling historians.

The Accession of Hertling

The *Reichstag* Majority had been suspicious of Michaelis' foreign-policy views since the conference of August 20, 1917, mentioned above,

[18] Erzberger, *Verständigungsfriede,* pp. 14-19.
[19] *ibid.,* pp. 19-26.
[20] Kühlmann, *Erinnerungen,* pp. 486-87.

and their wrath was not appeased by the appointment of the Committee of Seven. What was mistakenly believed to be the favorable reply to the Pope was ascribed to Kühlmann rather than to the Chancellor. The personal inadequacy of Michaelis, and his inability to cooperate with the *Reichstag,* could not be long concealed from the Emperor, public opinion, or even the Supreme Command. The occasion of his early and inevitable fall was a poorly documented attack (October 9, 1917) of his Navy Secretary, Capelle, upon the leadership of the Independent Socialist Party for allegedly fomenting a recent naval mutiny. An accompanying hint that the entire party should be outlawed was interpreted as a dangerous symptom of the old authoritarian mentality.

Erzberger was indignant about Capelle's speech, not primarily because of the injustice done to the Independents—whose attitude on the war he deplored—but rather because the prominence given to the relatively insignificant naval mutinies would do Germany incalculable harm abroad and injure peace chances. He wrote to his friend, Dr. Hansen, editor of the Stuttgart *Volksblatt* (on which he had served his journalistic apprenticeship twenty years earlier) a few days after the crucial *Reichstag* session:

> The entire political situation makes the position of the present Chancellor untenable. He is simply not up to his difficult task. The replacement of some of his subordinates [such as Capelle] is no solution, for it does not enhance his own capacity. . . . The incomprehensible conduct of the Chancellor and of Capelle will cost us several additional months of war. It means the greatest conceivable injury to all peace actions. People abroad believe now that all discipline is gone in the German armed forces and that it will take only a brief period until the German army will collapse. This is, of course, an error, but it is not surprising that foreigners should come to this conclusion if the government itself inflates the importance of a few Kiel mutineers. In this way the government has created new obstacles to peace at the very time when it is a difficult enough task to eliminate the obstacles erected by our enemies.[21]

The Interparty Committee met on October 22, 1917, in order to draft a joint demand to the Emperor for the immediate dismissal of Michaelis —a constitutional innovation that showed that Germany was advancing towards the parliamentary system. The party leaders were, however, unable to agree upon a suitable candidate for the succession, or even upon the propriety of pressing a candidate upon the Emperor. Erzberger again promoted Bülow, but the Socialists were doubtful whether he could be made acceptable to their party. There was agreement that

[21] Erzberger to Dr. Hansen, Oct. 17, 1917. *Erzberger Papers,* File 18.

Dr. Helfferich was absolutely unacceptable.[22] A delegation was selected the next day to see Valentini, the Chief of the Civil Cabinet, to call for Michaelis' dismissal, but "it was stated explicitly that the delegation should not name any candidate for the succession, to avoid interfering in any form with the free decision of H.M. the Emperor." [23] A later meeting decided that if the Emperor would call upon the parties to nominate a man—a most unlikely prospect unless the *Reichstag* applied pressure—they would suggest Fehrenbach, one of the respectable but rather colorless leaders of the Zentrum.[24]

The Interparty Committee could not make up its mind to press for the appointment of a parliamentary Chancellor, but it did urge Valentini that any prospective Chancellor should have "an official discussion with the parties in order to agree upon a joint program that could provide a basis for cooperation until the end of the war," prior to his definitive appointment.[25] The Interparty Committee accepted Erzberger's suggestions concerning a four point program upon which the parties should insist in such a discussion:

1. In foreign policy the new Chancellor must accept the German reply of September 19 to the Peace Note of the Pope.
2. Prussian electoral reform must be carried through rapidly and loyally.
3. Political censorship must be eliminated and army meddling in political affairs cease.
4. In social legislation, the government must pledge itself to introduce a law concerning *Arbeitskammern* (management-labor councils) and the repeal of par. 52 section 2 of the industrial code [prohibiting boycotts in labor disputes].[26]

The last point may seem picayune in the midst of a great war, indeed a black-mailing attempt to exploit a difficult national situation to achieve a plank of the Socialist Party program. Erzberger had included it upon the demand of the Socialists, who were hard pressed by their Independent competitors despite the Peace Resolution. There were important *Reichstag* elements, including the Right wing of the Zentrum Party, who wanted to break up the July majority and restore the traditional hostility of all bourgeois parties to the Socialists that had characterized Imperial politics before 1917. Erzberger was opposed to any combination that would drive the Socialists back into opposition:

[22] Protocol of the Oct. 22, 1917, session of the Interparty Committee. *Erzberger Papers*, File 18.
[23] *ibid.* of the Oct. 23, 1917 session.
[24] Erzberger, *Erlebnisse*, p. 291.
[25] *ibid.*, p. 290.
[26] *ibid.*, pp. 289–90.

Such a policy would mean the ruin of the Empire, and would prolong the war by driving the Socialist leaders and the working masses into passive resistance. . . . The Socialists have, until this moment, set no conditions for further party cooperation which the bourgeois parties cannot accept of their own free will; the bourgeois parties must do everything in their power to meet the Socialist willingness to be incorporated into the existing state. It would be a crime against the Fatherland to pursue plans which preclude further Socialist cooperation.[27]

Erzberger must be criticized, along with the rest of the Interparty Committee, for not using their strong political position to force a satisfactory solution of the Chancellor crisis. Both the Emperor and the Supreme Command shared in the discredit provoked by the incompetence of Michaelis and were in a weaker position than they had been in July. The fall of Michaelis came, moreover, unlike that of Bethmann, neither suddenly nor unexpectedly. The party leaders had the opportunity to develop plans at leisure, and could not be confronted by a new Chancelor as a *fait accompli*. Their direct responsibility for Michaelis' dismissal—whereas Bethmann had yielded to an ultimatum from Ludendorff—placed a special obligation upon them to secure a suitable successor. Neither the Emperor nor Ludendorff could wish a major constitutional crisis at that moment. The party failure to nominate a suitable man was perhaps excusable in view of the absence of an obvious candidate; but the failure to insist upon an absolutely clear-cut program was inexcusable. To require that the German reply to the Papacy serve as a basis for the new Chancellor's foreign policy was not enough. Erzberger should have insisted upon an explicit acceptance of the Peace Resolution and a specific pledge to restore Belgium. To require support of Prussian franchise reform was not enough. Erzberger should have insisted upon a pledge to carry the reform at any price, even including the dissolution of the refractory *Abgeordnetenhaus* in the midst of war. To call for the elimination of military influences in politics was laudable but meaningless unless accompanied by the subordination of the Supreme Command to the civilian government. The social demands had symbolic value only. The entire four-point program drafted by Erzberger was utterly inadequate in the crisis confronting Germany in October 1917. To make this program the basis of negotiations with the new Chancellor meant a perpetuation of the ambiguity which existed in foreign and domestic policy alike.

This unfortunate prospect was realized when the Emperor appointed the seventy-four-year old Count Hertling Chancellor on October 28,

[27] *ibid.,* p. 291.

1917, again without consulting the *Reichstag* leaders. At an earlier time this appointment would have represented a political revolution, for Hertling had made his career as a Zentrum Party leader and *Reichstag* politician—whereas Chancellors were previously selected from the army, diplomatic service, or bureaucracy. To make the Chancellorship a possible object of parliamentary ambition created a disturbing precedent for the Imperial order. To appoint a deeply pious Catholic to Bismarck's office was also a great political innovation; [28] it showed that the *Kulturkampf* era was in the past. Yet Hertling was at least half a bureaucrat himself, and his political principles were not too far removed from those of Prussian Conservatism. He was, in fact, a transition figure, whose appointment retarded rather than accelerated constitutional development. His views had not changed from those analyzed in Chapter III, thus making him more than ever an anachronism. He still had a deep contempt for parliamentary bodies. He believed that an authoritarian monarchy that appointed the executive was far preferable to a government based upon *Reichstag* parties. This belief had been strengthened by his experience as Bavarian Premier, when he had been forced to cooperate with a difficult legislature in the years after 1911. His Munich associations had also confirmed his faith in federalist principles with the corollary abhorrence of a unitarian parliamentary system. He hated democracy as destructive of the orderly aristocratic world which he cherished, and his acceptance of Prussian franchise reform fell far short of a passionate conviction. Hertling was also out of tune with social reform demands despite his deep study of the social question. He took the anachronistic view that original sin made economic evils fundamentally ineradicable. He accepted the principle of state intervention only for the purpose of protecting certain human rights, such as Sunday rest; he rejected the view that it could be justified in order to promote the general welfare. His foreign policy views were also out of tune with the needs of 1917. He was a strong nationalist, all the more fervidly because his nationalism had come comparatively late in life after the wound of 1866 had healed. He had ridiculed the popular demand for international disarmament before the war. His over-all political record was most unfortunate for a Chancellor who was compelled to rely upon cooperation with the July *Reichstag* majority, and who was expected to initiate peace negotiations with the enemy. All of his inadequacies were compounded by his advanced age and failing physical powers. He was almost blind, so that his son had

[28] Prince Hohenlohe, Chancellor from 1894 to 1900, had been a nominal Catholic only, and an especially virulent foe of the Jesuits.

to read nearly everything to him. His daily schedule had to be closely regulated in order to avoid excessive strain or excitement. Evening conferences with him were virtually out of the question no matter how pressing the business at hand.[29]

We have seen that Erzberger had shared many of Hertling's views on foreign and domestic policy until 1917, and had been on cordial terms with him until the Peace Resolution. Their personal relations had cooled thereafter but were still intact in October 1917. Hertling reluctantly accepted the demand of the Interparty Committee that the prospective Chancellor should consult with *Reichstag* leaders before giving his final decision to the Emperor. Erzberger was the first deputy to be summoned for a conference (October 28). Hertling told him that he felt he could not refuse the Chancellorship after it had been offered him the second time within a year. He proposed, however, to lighten his burden by retaining Michaelis in the Prussian Premiership to carry through the franchise reform. Erzberger immediately opposed the separation of the two offices on constitutional, political, and personal grounds.[30] Hertling was impressed by his arguments and asked him to present them in a written memorandum. This Erzberger did the next day (October 29), stating the following objections against the separation of the two offices: it would reduce the power of the Chancellor and damage the interests of the Empire by depriving him of direct control over the hegemonial Prussian state; the two previous attempts at separation (1872, 1892) had both been failures; Hertling would be embarrassed in his treatment of Imperial problems whenever they impinged directly upon Prussia, as in the Polish and Lithuanian question; suspicions against Hertling's government would be raised both at home and abroad, since Michaelis' retention of the Prussian Premiership would be interpreted as a continued predominance for Conservative views; a struggle between the plutocratic *Landtag* and democratic *Reichstag* over the franchise question would become likely. All these considerations suggested the certainty of continued political friction, whereas Germany needed above all domestic harmony for the concluding phase of the war. Erzberger also suggested that Hertling's prestige required holding both offices at the same time. The downfall of Michaelis was inevitable in the near future even if he should resign the Chancellorship and retain only the Prussian Premiership. His fall

[29] For bibliography on Hertling, see footnote 9 of Ch. III. On Hertling's impaired working powers, see Kühlmann's *Erinnerungen*, p. 511, and the revealing admissions of his son Karl von Hertling in his *Ein Jahr in der Reichskanzlei* (Freiburg, 1919), pp. 45–47.

[30] Erzberger, *Erlebnisse*, pp. 292–93.

might drag down Hertling as well, thus bringing a third Chancellor crisis within half a year. The difficulty which Hertling complained of —his fear of too many burdens and his unsuitability for carrying Prussian franchise reform—could best be resolved by creating a Vice-Premier who would do all the detailed work under Hertling's direction. The Right-wing National Liberal deputy von Friedberg would be well suited for this position.[31]

Erzberger's reasoning was so conclusive that the thought of separating the two offices was removed from Hertling's mind, thereby sealing the fate of Michaelis. Erzberger succeeded in his primary aim of preventing a completely unworkable arrangement. He may possibly have pursued the further aim of persuading Hertling by indirection to decline the Chancellorship by emphasizing its severe and unavoidable burden; if this was his purpose he did not succeed. Erzberger did not want Hertling in the Chancellorship, but could not work against him openly because of their common Zentrum membership and close previous association. Erzberger's friend Richthofen, who saw him daily in the critical days of the crisis, testified before the 1926 *Reichstag* Committee of Inquiry exploring the crisis of October 1917:

> There can be no doubt that Erzberger was strongly opposed to Hertling's appointment. He did not consider him to be a suitable person for the Chancellor's office. In the first place he was much too old. He did not think that Hertling possessed the physical stamina to perform the required duties. He thought, furthermore, that Hertling's political conceptions were so much rooted in the past that he would be unable to meet the problems of the present either at home or abroad. Erzberger was convinced that Hertling would not muster the energy necessary to control the Supreme Command, which Erzberger and I, along with many others, considered to be the most important function of the Chancellor. Erzberger desired the appointment of Prince Bülow. . . . There was a period when the appointment of Count Hertling had become very questionable. There were two kinds of difficulties, namely getting Hertling to agree to certain political conditions, of which the future of Alsace Lorraine created the greatest problem, as well as questions of personnel.[32]

The two difficulties mentioned by Richthofen prolonged the political crisis by several days. Hertling had readily agreed to the four-point program drawn up by Erzberger on October 22. This was now expanded to include a fifth point, autonomy for Alsace-Lorraine, which

[31] Erzberger's 8-page memorandum, dated Oct. 29, 1918, is in *Erzberger Papers*, File 22. Summarized in *Erlebnisse*, p. 293.

[32] *U.A.*, VII (2), 222. Erzberger naturally does not mention the matter in his *Erlebnisse*, Ch. XXI.

had been demanded by the *Reichstag* majority since July. It is possible, but cannot be proved, that this demand was presented with the deliberate purpose of inducing Hertling to withdraw his candidacy. His preference for the alternative partition scheme was well known. There was much opposition to Hertling that could not express itself openly and must aim at defeating his appointment by indirect means. Protestant bigots were opposed to any Catholic Chancellor, and thought one especially inappropriate in the year of the Reformation anniversary.[33] Some Catholics were unhappy about the prospects of a Catholic scapegoat if the war should not come to a victorious conclusion. The leaders of the *Reichstag* Majority showed at a meeting of the Interparty Committee on October 29 that they were appalled by Hertling's fundamentally conservative outlook, but they also felt that they could not oppose a man who was one of their own and who had introduced the constitutional innovation of consulting them before giving his final acceptance to the Emperor.[34]

Hertling at last agreed to grant autonomy to Alsace-Lorraine, a meaningless promise since he succeeded in sabotaging it until the end of the war. Agreement on the personnel of his government proved more difficult, because here acceptance of *Reichstag* wishes could not be negated through subsequent procrastination. Hertling wished to retain the able but unpopular Karl Helfferich in the post of Vice-Chancellor, a plan which the *Reichstag* majority, headed by Erzberger, rejected. They demanded the appointment of the Progressive leader Friedrich von Payer, who possessed the confidence of both his own party and that of the Socialists. The making of this demand heralded the advance of the parliamentary system. The simultaneous National Liberal demand that von Friedberg be given the Prussian Vice-Premiership was also supported by the other parties.

Hertling did little to hide his indignation at the *Reichstag's* seeking to control, contrary to established constitutional practice, the selection of his closest subordinates. He thought seriously of refusing the Chancellorship altogether, and on October 31 stated his intention of actually doing so to some deputies. The Interparty Committee then selected Erzberger to see Hertling "to ask him to tell the Emperor the real reasons for his refusal, as the parties lacked confidence in the persons surrounding the Emperor at Court [who misinformed him frequently], and to thank Hertling for having respected the *Reichstag* wish of being

[33] See the open expression of this view in Paul Hoensbroech, *Graf Hertling, Reichskanzler und Ministerpräsident. Ein offener Brief* (Leipzig, 1918).

[34] Protocols of October 29, 1917 meeting of the Interparty Committee, in *Erzberger Papers*, File 22. Summarized in *Erlebnisse*, pp. 293–94.

consulted." [35] Erzberger was prepared to congratulate Hertling on the escape from a severe burden, but found to his surprise that Hertling had changed his mind and was now willing to make the necessary concessions to the Majority party. Kühlmann told Erzberger that Hertling's elevation was desirable for foreign-policy reasons, and that he thought a fruitful cooperation between Chancellor and *Reichstag* would not be too difficult. Erzberger then promised to support Hertling's appointment under the following conditions: the firing of Michaelis and Helfferich, the appointment of Payer, and full satisfaction in the Alsatian question. He cooperated henceforth with Kühlmann in smoothing away all remaining difficulties, while insisting that his terms be met in every particular. [36]

While Erzberger had believed that the Hertling candidacy was finished he had sent Richthofen to see Prince Bülow, whom Erzberger considered now, as in July 1917, the best candidate for the post of Chancellor. Bülow, who had come to Berlin to intrigue for his return to power, told Richthofen that Kühlmann was the crucial man in the current negotiations, because he alone possessed the confidence of the Emperor, Hertling, and *Reichstag* leaders alike. Richthofen then went to Kühlmann to discuss the situation; the Foreign Secretary described himself as personally sympathetic to Bülow but declared that the obstacles with the Emperor were insuperable. [37] Kühlmann used his considerable negotiating skill to bridge the gap between Hertling and the *Reichstag* parties in the following days. Hertling yielded readily on Friedberg and Alsace, while proving most difficult on the appointment of Payer. [38]

The *Reichstag* leaders proved absolutely adamant upon the last point. Erzberger and Richthofen (the latter acting upon the instructions of his party leader Stresemann) finally called at the Bavarian Embassy, where Hertling was staying, on the evening of November 7 to force an end of the prolonged bickering. They were told by Lerchenfeld, the ambassador, that Hertling was too exhausted from the day's conferences to receive any more visitors. The two *Reichstag* leaders then left a stern ultimatum: grave consequences would ensue if Hertling did not accept Payer's appointment by the next morning. Hertling, angered

[35] Erzberger, *Erlebnisse,* p. 294.
[36] Erzberger's memorandum on conversations with Hertling and Kühlmann, Oct. 31, 1917, in *Erzberger Papers,* File 22. Summarized in *Erlebnisse,* pp. 294–95. Erzberger's opposition to Hertling was not shared by many other Zentrum leaders; Trimborn had urged him strongly to accept the Chancellorship. Valentini, *op.cit.,* p. 180.
[37] *U.A.,* VII (2), 223–24.
[38] See the protocols of several conferences between Kühlmann and the *Reichstag* leaders, especially on Nov. 6 and 8, 1917, in *Erzberger Papers,* File 22.

by this conduct, sent Lerchenfeld to the two deputies to complain that a loaded pistol had been placed against his breast, but Erzberger and Richthofen only renewed their ultimatum. Hertling was shrewd enough to know when he was beaten, and Payer's appointment as Vice-Chancellor was announced on November 9, thereby completing the Hertling-Friedberg-Payer ministry.[39] This combination was to govern Germany until October 1918.

The entire incident did much to worsen Erzberger's personal relations with Hertling. Hertling had valued Erzberger's friendship until 1917 because it gave him contact with a man who possessed much inside information and who shared his general political outlook. He had been surprised by Erzberger's complete reconstruction of his views at the time of the July Crisis, and appalled by the triumph of the Left wing within the Zentrum Party and the construction of the new *Reichstag* majority. Erzberger's role in forcing Payer and the Socialist alliance upon him was the last straw. He resolved to make the undermining of Erzberger's political influence one of the primary objectives of his Chancellorship. He accepted the Pan-German view that Erzberger was the evil genius of Germany, telling Count Galen, a Right-wing member of the Zentrum: "Erzberger is ruining the Zentrum. His conduct is disastrous not only for the party, but also for our Fatherland and above all for the Catholic Church. Fifty years from now [in 1968] people will still reproach both the Zentrum and the Church for the actions which Erzberger undertook during the war against the Fatherland."[40]

Hertling's anger against Erzberger became still more virulent when he convinced himself in January 1918, contrary to the facts, that Erzberger had taken a secret journey to Vienna in December 1917 to intrigue against himself at the Austrian court. He denounced Erzberger to his entourage as a liar for denying that he had taken such a journey or seen the Emperor Charles. Hertling was annoyed when Erzberger reminded him that he had reported to him after returning from an open trip to Vienna in December 1917. Hertling remained convinced that Erzberger had in fact taken a second trip and had seen Charles. He told various Zentrum leaders that he would never receive Erzberger at the Chancellery again. Erzberger was stung by the accusation of untruthfulness, which was quickly exploited by his numerous enemies.

[39] *U.A.*, VII (2), 225–26. Erzberger hints at the incident in his *Erlebnisse*, p. 297.
[40] Dr. Eisele to the editorial staff of the *Kölnische Volkszeitung*, Mar. 22, 1918. *Bachem Papers*, File 90.

He immediately penned an outspoken letter to the Chancellor, summarizing his conduct and adding:

> Your Excellency must admit that it is painful for me to hear, despite these obvious facts, that Your Excellency continues to believe that . . . I consciously told you an untruth in a political matter. Your view is all the more unreasonable because it would be foolish for anybody, in view of wartime regulations governing the crossing of borders, to deny having gone abroad if he had in fact done so. It would also have been foolish to deny to you having made a trip in January about which I had reported to you in December after my return. I am also surprised that you should think me guilty of such hostile and disloyal conduct, especially in the light of my role . . . in smoothing away the considerable misunderstandings at the time of your call to Berlin [referring to Erzberger's negotiations with Kühlmann].[41]

Erzberger then threatened to bring the entire matter up at the next party meeting unless Hertling should refresh his memory and retract his charges.

Hertling then began to make excuses to Gröber and Fehrenbach about a "misunderstanding," but Erzberger deemed these excuses insufficient. He sent Hertling an even more outspoken letter a week later, and got Hertling to acknowledge the baselessness of his accusations (March 4, 1918).[42] But this confession of error could not heal the personal breach with the Chancellor. Erzberger was henceforth no longer a person with good inside connections, and the Chancellor's name continued to be used against him. The general tranquillity of German internal politics during most of the Hertling period militated even more against Erzberger's influence than the loss of official contacts. His power was always at a maximum in time of intense crisis, as in July and October 1917. He was pushed off the center of the stage for most of 1918, returning to major influence only when military defeat loomed in October 1918.

[41] Erzberger to Hertling, Feb. 23, 1918. *Erzberger Papers*, File 32.

[42] Erzberger to Hertling, Mar. 1, 1918. *Ibid*. The entire matter was discussed in an article obviously inspired by Erzberger in *Deutsches Volksblatt*, June 14, 1918. Copy in *Bachem Papers*, File 90. See also the brief account in *Erlebnisse*, p. 300.

CHAPTER X

ERZBERGER DURING THE HERTLING GOVERNMENT (OCTOBER 1917 TO SEPTEMBER 1918)

The Period of Brest-Litovsk

THE achievement of surface political calm was the major political success of the Hertling government. The latent conflict
between *Reichstag* majority and Supreme Command over
both internal policy and war aims was prevented from breaking into
the open. Hertling sided with the Supreme Command on most issues.
He used his considerable prestige to coddle the *Reichstag* into an attitude of passive acquiescence in Ludendorff's wishes. He introduced
Prussian franchise reform in the *Landtag* but refused to carry matters
to extremes when the Conservative-dominated body proved hostile.
The introduction of the semi-parliamentary regime of Hertling, Friedberg, and Payer had temporarily stilled the clamor for the introduction of the full parliamentary system. The Zentrum, National Liberal,
and Progressive parties were directly represented in the government,
though in every case by men who stood on the extreme Right wing
of their respective parties. The Socialists, while still opposed to assuming direct governmental responsibilities, looked upon Payer to represent their views. Yet the appearance of a close cooperation between the
executive and the legislature was deceptive. Hertling looked upon himself as an appointee deriving his authority from the Emperor, not as
the servant of any *Reichstag* majority. He had not been a member of
the *Reichstag* since 1911. Payer and Friedberg were forced to resign
their parliamentary seats on account of the constitutional provision
which prohibited simultaneous membership in the *Reichstag* and
Bundesrat (art. 9, par. 2). Their admission into the government led
to an immediate decline of their influence in the *Reichstag*. The new
ministry was clearly one of transition between the authoritarian system
of the past and the parliamentary democracy of the future.

Hertling's task of achieving domestic tranquillity was facilitated by
the lack of firmness shown by the majority parties of the *Reichstag*.
We have seen how they shunned constitutional strife, and lacked an
adequate program, during both the July and October 1917 crises. They
weakened in their anti-annexationism—the original reason for the

construction of the July majority—when vast conquests beckoned in the east after the Russian military collapse. They showed a similar lack of firmness in the face of Hertling's procrastination in dealing with domestic reforms. The country rallied all its energies for the final year of war. *Reichstag* passivity, the continued prestige of Ludendorff, and Hertling's capacity for moderating conflicts all contributed to the general tranquillity. The alternative possibilities of a military dictatorship and the completion of the parliamentary system were both avoided.

The winter of 1917–1918 was dominated by the peace negotiations between Russia and the Central Powers at Brest-Litovsk. The Bolsheviks, exploiting the failure of the Kerensky government to make peace with Germany, seized power in November 1917. Lenin saw the immediate necessity of ending the war. The German government was anxious to secure a formal peace treaty that would allow the despatch of troops to the crucial Western Front. There was much difference, however, between the civilians, led by Kühlmann, and the soldiers, led by Ludendorff, on the terms to be imposed upon Russia. Kühlmann, anxious to appease the *Reichstag* majority which had passed the Peace Resolution, and mindful of the bad impression which open German imperialism would create abroad, wanted to achieve German hegemony in Eastern Europe through the genuine implementation of self-determination for the Poles, Lithuanians, etc. Ludendorff, on the other hand, wanted direct annexations extorted by the naked sword. The Kühlmann policy required patience and subtlety in negotiations, and a reform of the composition and enlargement of powers of the self-governing bodies (*Landesräte*) which the Germans had set up in the occupied territories. The Ludendorff policy was one of forcing the Russians to sign on the dotted line, and pretending that the existing unrepresentative *Landesräte* gave a faithful reflection of public opinion.

The terms of the Treaty of Brest-Litovsk (March 3, 1918) substantially accorded with Ludendorff's views. Russia renounced all rights in the German-occupied territories of Poland, Lithuania, and Courland, which remained under direct German military administration. Russia also promised to evacuate her troops from Finland, Esthonia, Livonia, and the Ukraine, and it could readily be foreseen that the ensuing military vacuum would soon be filled by German troops on one pretext or another. The sole alleviating feature of this victor's peace was that there was no demand for reparations.[1]

[1] The background and terms of Brest-Litovsk are presented brilliantly in John Wheeler-Bennett, *The Forgotten Peace: Brest-Litovsk, March 1918* (New York, 1938).

Erzberger had given strong backing to Kühlmann's position at conferences held between government leaders and *Reichstag* deputies during the prolonged period of the Brest negotiations (December 1917 to March 1918). He was anxious above all to see that the terms of the Peace Resolution were not violated. He saw that the prewar *status quo* had passed irretrievably, and that extensive boundary changes were inevitable. In seeking to reconcile conscience with reality, he made a sharp distinction between direct German annexations and the detachment of Russian border areas in the name of self-determination. Erzberger went so far as to assert a German mission to champion the liberty of the hitherto oppressed Eastern nationalities.[2]

His celebrated and often-quoted statement on the compatibility of the Brest-Litovsk Treaty and the Peace Resolution in a *Reichstag* speech of February 27, 1918 must be understood in this context. His exact words were as follows:

> Germany can make the peace which it has just negotiated in the east so durable that it cannot subsequently be revised, but only upon one presupposition: that the program of the July majority towards the Eastern nations is faithfully carried out. *The peace treaty falls completely within the framework of our Resolution insofar as this is done.* [My italics.] Germany can make this peace lasting if it uses the time between now and the general peace settlement to promote the general contentment (*Zufriedenheit*) of Russia's western border nations. If she does this there will be no protest to the general peace conference on the part of the Poles, Lithuanians, Courlanders, or the Estonians and Livonians (though the latter are not really our business) [since they lie beyond the German lines]. If there are no plaintiffs at the time of the general settlement, the peace conference will not arrogate to itself the position of judge. The great task which confronts us now in the east can be achieved only upon the basis of the self-determination of the affected nations. I hold the firm conviction that any other principle—be it annexationism or the exercise of brute force (*Vergewaltigungsprinzip*)—will inevitably lead to shipwreck and will prevent us from holding the gains permanently which we have achieved in the present fluid situation.[3]

Erzberger emphatically repudiated any "master race" theories as applied to German relations with Eastern Europe, which lay (though much less explicitly than twenty-five years later) at the bottom of much Right-wing annexationism: "Germany can never deprive other nations

---

[2] For Erzberger's attitude, see, for example, protocol of a conference held between Roedern, Treasury head, and the leaders of the Interparty Committee, on Jan. 18, 1918. *Erzberger Papers,* File 36.

[3] *Reichstag Debates,* cccxi (Feb. 27, 1918), p. 4218.

of the right [of self-determination] which she claims for herself. Other peoples have exactly the same right to existence as we. I know no better justification for Germany's rights than that I demand for every other people what I claim for my own. The full implementation of this sentence can alone protect Europe against the recurrence of the horrors from which she is now suffering." [4] Erzberger showed throughout 1918 that he meant serious business when he proclaimed this principle.

The bitterness of the German masses against the annexationism of the ruling class reached fever pitch in the course of the Brest conference, when it seemed for a while that Ludendorff's intransigence might lead to a collapse of negotiations. The workers in Berlin and other cities engaged in a protest strike. The leaders of the Majority Socialists, Ebert and Scheidemann, placed themselves at the head of the strikers. Erzberger was at first shocked by their conduct, but accepted their explanation that they were motivated by the desire to prevent the working class from turning to the Independent Socialists.[5]

The Conservatives sought to exploit this incident to bring about a renewal of the political ostracism of the Socialists—a reversion to the pre-July 1917 situation. Erzberger, on the other hand, insisted upon a policy that would facilitate the difficult task of keeping the workers loyal to the war effort:

Is it politically wise, to allow the working millions who had felt themselves to be alienated from the state in the prewar period—as was proved at each successive election—to remain in this position during the present war? Now the war, with all its sufferings, created the great opportunity where the workers and their political leaders approach the leaders of the other parties and say: we stand with you in the same position and wish to become spiritually incorporated into the state. We wish to abandon our fundamental opposition against the state and wish to work together with you. Should not a patriot answer: we shall meet you halfway to allow cordial cooperation? Only in this way can we secure victory for our German banners. I do not shrink from the following sentence: We, who are cooperating today with the Social Democrats, which we can do without violating our principles—they have never demanded this of us—are carrying out a state-preserving, conservative policy in the best sense of the word. Our opponents, with their policy of alienating the Socialists and their

[4] *ibid.*, p. 4219.
[5] Erzberger denounced the Socialists in a letter to Hommerich, editor of *Germania*, Feb. 5, 1918, calling for close cooperation between Zentrum, Progressives, and National Liberals in view of the unsatisfactory conduct of the Socialists. But he changed his mind after hearing Scheidemann's defense in the Interparty Committee the same day. Both the letter and the Committee protocol are in *Erzberger Papers*, File 21. See also Erzberger's *Erlebnisse*, pp. 299–300.

huge working-class following, are conducting the most radical and an-
archical policy that could be conceived.[6]

Erzberger pleaded for the immediate introduction of the parliamentary system, and warned the Conservatives that they must get used to
the fact that non-Conservatives could become ministers even in Germany. He called Prussian franchise reform the paramount necessity of
the hour, stating bluntly that everyone knew that the Prussian ministry
was the real ruler of Germany, and that cooperation between two
bodies as different as the Prussian *Landtag* and German *Reichstag* was
becoming increasingly impossible.[7] Erzberger warned that big internal
reforms were necessary in order to maintain popular morale in the face
of economic hardships and disappointed hopes of an early victory:

> It is best to tell our people the whole truth about the war situation—
> they are mature enough to face the facts. Then Germans will not be dis-
> appointed at being forced to make further sacrifices in the face of the
> bellicosity and imperialism of our enemies. We cannot give our people
> more bread, more potatoes, or more fat-stuffs, because we cannot increase
> our inadequate stocks. But we can give them something else. We can give
> them freedom, the right to express their political convictions, and the
> satisfaction of their religious demands. These concessions would buttress
> the willingness of our people to bear all the further hardships of war.
> Whoever opposes these popular demands, which have the ardent support
> of the greater part of the nation, is doing a disservice to the Fatherland.[8]

Erzberger and Lithuania

Erzberger's main concern in the months after Brest-Litovsk was to
press for the genuine grant of self-determination to the eastern nationalities. He was especially interested in the fate of Lithuania because it was a predominantly Catholic country. Erzberger had established contact with Lithuanian emigrés in Switzerland early in the
war. He approved of their proposed creation of a Lithuanian kingdom
with an elected German prince. They commissioned him in August
1917 to look over possible candidates. Erzberger hit upon a fellow
Württemberger, the Duke of Urach, a distant relative of the monarch
reigning in Stuttgart, as the best choice. Urach, an able and willing
man, was a Catholic; he was blessed with a numerous progeny; he
laid no claims to any other throne. He thus possessed the qualities desired by the Lithuanians, who feared above all any dynastic union with

---

[6] *Reichstag Debates,* cccxi (Feb. 27, 1918), p. 4229.

[7] *ibid.,* p. 4230. Erzberger stated on this occasion that he had acquired Prussian citi-
zenship and therefore could not be accused of meddling in other people's business.

[8] *ibid.,* p. 4231.

another country (which had once before, in 1386, led to the loss of independence) or the uncertainties produced by a possible failure of blood heirs. A meeting between Urach and the Lithuanian National Committee, arranged by Erzberger, proved completely successful, though Urach was unwilling to pursue his candidacy unless it won the full support of the German government. This Erzberger found impossible to procure. The Supreme Command wanted William II to assume the Lithuanian crown in personal union as the best way of assuring direct German control of the new state. The Saxon monarchy announced its own claims on the basis of the 18th century connection between Saxony and Poland-Lithuania. Several federal states protested any decision that might disturb the existing German political equilibrium. These petty dynastic squabbles prevented any direct progress towards settlement of the question.[9]

Erzberger pressed for the creation of a Lithuanian state in a motion introduced in the *Reichstag* on August 28, 1917. The government obliged by setting up a nominated Lithuanian *Landesrat* in late September but refused to grant it any powers. Erzberger encouraged the Lithuanians to take a strong line with the German military administration. The *Landesrat* responded by issuing a declaration of Lithuanian independence in December, but the Hertling government refused to take cognizance of its declaration. A delegation sent to Berlin was not received by the Chancellor despite Erzberger's efforts. The Supreme Command, affronted by Erzberger's contact with the Lithuanians (who were technically enemy aliens), wanted to initiate another prosecution for treason against Erzberger, but the public prosecutor's office declared this to be ridiculous.[10]

Erzberger was very angry about Hertling's attitude towards Lithuania, and at a meeting of the Chancellor with the leaders of the Majority parties on March 12, 1918 (ten days before the final ratification of the Brest Treaty) he spoke his mind:

> The eastern peace will not be worth the paper on which it is written if the right to self-determination of the Poles, Lithuanians, and Courlanders is not implemented quickly, loyally, and honestly. The main point about the east is this: the military officials are working openly and demonstrably against the declared policy of the Chancellor. To speak very bluntly: Lithuanian independence would be recognized immediately if the *Landesrat* would only declare itself in favor of personal union with the Emperor.

[9] On Erzberger and Lithuania, see his *Erlebnisse,* Ch. xv and *Erzberger Papers,* File 26.
[10] Erzberger, *Erlebnisse,* p. 190.

But the Lithuanians rightly do not wish that. They desire to have a Catholic ruler. They reject the idea of a personal union for constitutional and historical reasons. The pro-German elements in Lithuania have become disgruntled through our policy of procrastination and vacillation. Every further day of delay [in recognizing Lithuanian independence] does great injury to Germany's interests.[11]

Germany formally recognized Lithuanian independence eleven days later, but no progress was made in the Urach candidacy. Erzberger advised the Lithuanians to make a detailed agreement with Urach and to elect him their monarch, as Mindaugas II, without waiting for German approval (July 11, 1918). Hertling woodenly refused to accept either Urach or the reality of an independent Lithuanian state, and the unhappy people remained under German administration. The result was bitterness throughout the country and a complete atrophy of the friendly feelings towards Germany which the liberation from Russian tyranny had originally aroused. The future of the country remained in flux so long as Hertling remained in power, and the Max of Baden government did not have enough time to repair all the earlier mistakes.[12] The Lithuanian state was to crystallize finally under Entente auspices following Germany's collapse. Yet its institutions were built upon the *Landesrat* set up under Erzberger's pressure in September 1917, and Lithuanians hailed Erzberger as one of their benefactors during the brief life of the new state (1918–1940).

Erzberger's ardent championing of self-determination did not blind him to the fact that the "national will" is always as much a manipulated as a spontaneous product. He was not opposed to German hegemony in Eastern Europe; he only wanted it to be based upon friendly cooperation with the eastern nationalities rather than their brutal suppression. He wanted pro-German groups to determine the future of Poland and Lithuania, and was quite willing to use some German pressure to achieve this result. Erzberger had written to General Hoffmann a year previously explaining how self-determination could be manipulated to serve Germany's purposes:

How do matters stand in Lithuania? Would its people vote in our favor if they were called to make a decision today? I wish to make the question more precise: have we taken all steps that could help to bring

[11] Protocol of Mar. 12, 1918, conference in *Erzberger Papers,* File 21. Partly summarized in *Erlebnisse,* pp. 300–01.

[12] Erzberger insisted upon the removal of von Falkenhausen, who had mishandled Lithuanian matters for the Foreign Office. Falkenhausen later became Chief of the Chancellery for the Kapp government. Erzberger, *Erlebnisse,* pp. 192, 196. Falkenhausen protested Erzberger's account in the *Kreuzzeitung,* Oct. 6, 1920, but received a very sharp reply from Erzberger, Oct. 7, 1920. *Erzberger Papers,* File 31.

a decision in our favor? A few skillful agitators will play the crucial role in view of the low cultural level of the Lithuanian people. I see it as our main task to secure, by all means at our command (including bribery) and with the greatest possible speed, a decision favorable to us. We must cultivate especially lawyers, doctors, and clergymen. The [German] district chiefs must receive strict orders to establish personal contact with prominent Lithuanians and to win them for our side. The district chiefs should invite the leading clergymen for dinner at least twice a month. They must fulfill even small wishes of prominent Lithuanians. In this manner we can easily secure a reliable cadre of people which can assume leadership at the appropriate moment so that a result favorable to us emerges from the principle of self-determination.[13]

Erzberger's Attack on Germany's Ukrainian Policy, May 8, 1918

Erzberger was also, as we have seen earlier, much interested in the fate of Poland, and he continued to press for giving the Poles complete autonomy—preferably as part of an Austro-Polish solution—throughout 1918.[14] But his special interest in the period after Brest centered upon Poland's new eastern neighbor, the Ukrainian state, which became a classic battleground between the rival principles of self-determination and German militarism. Ludendorff had sent an army of half a million men into the Ukraine to protect its newly-won independence against the Bolsheviks and to secure foodstuffs for Germany. The German troops were received by the population as conquerors rather than liberators, and the peasants were not anxious to deliver grain to the army of occupation. The Ukrainian government in Kiev, though it had signed the peace and been saved from Bolshevik conquest by Germany, refused to act as a pure satellite and rather sided with the peasantry against the German army. The German military then arranged a *coup d'état* for the benefit of ultra-reactionary and pro-German forces under the Hetman Skoropadsky, which Erzberger descibed as follows:

All the parties in the Rada [legislature] opposed a decree of General Eichhorn [the German military commander]. Towards three o'clock one afternoon, as the Rada was sitting, German soldiers with armored cars and machine guns drew up before the Rada building to close it. A German officer appeared in the Assembly hall with a file of German soldiers, and gave the order in Russian, "Hands up, in the name of the German government!" On being repeatedly required to do so, the deputies obeyed this order. The President, Hrushevsky, who did not obey it, was threatened

[13] Erzberger to General Hoffmann, May 25, 1917. *Erzberger Papers,* File 23.
[14] Erzberger, *Erlebnisse,* pp. 179–83. *Erzberger Papers,* File 29. The latter contains considerable correspondence with Nuncio Pacelli on Polish matters.

with a revolver. All the deputies were searched. Members of the Rada were not arrested, but members of the Ukrainian government were.[15]

This scene was followed by the appointment of General Skoropadsky, "the little Boulanger," as Chief of State, and the installation of a completely reactionary new ministry. Erzberger continued: "The consequences are, however, very regrettable for Germany. A German soldier can no longer show himself unarmed in Kiev. . . . The railway men and workmen are planning a general strike. The whole population was in the highest degree dissatisfied because Skoropadsky's new decrees were issued to the advantage of the great landowners. The peasants would not deliver any grain, and bloodshed must be reckoned with in the event of requisitioning. That is not the way to attain the first object of our intervention, namely securing the surplus grain supplies for the German people." [16] Erzberger favored the policy of weakening Russia permanently by detaching the various nationalities living on the frontiers of the Empire, but he knew this could be done only by winning the friendship of the peoples involved.

Erzberger was indignant about the brutal German meddling in the internal affairs of the Ukraine. It was not the only case of Germany's going beyond the terms of Brest-Litovsk. The Supreme Command also supported the demands of the German aristocratic landowners in Esthonia and Livonia for help against the Bolsheviks.[17] Hertling was too weak and apathetic to keep the military under control in their Imperialist policy. Erzberger thought it was the duty of the *Reichstag* to prod the government to observe its treaty obligations scrupulously, especially when the Peace Resolution was being torn to shreds. He therefore proposed (May 8, 1918) the following motion in the Main Committee, which won the support of all the Zentrum members present (Gröber, Nacken, Pfleger, and Rechenberg):

1. Political and economic decisions in the eastern territories may be taken only with the explicit approval of the Chancellor.
2. The peace treaty of Brest-Litovsk is to be observed in the letter and spirit. . . .
3. The German political and military organs are to abstain from any intervention in the internal affairs of these countries.[18]

[15] Erzberger's newspaper article, "Mein Vorstoss im Hauptausschuss des *Reichstages*," was printed in many newspapers. *Vossische Zeitung*, May 14, 1918. English translation in R. H. Lutz, *Fall of the German Empire 1914–18*, I, 852–58. The passage is from p. 854.
[16] *ibid.*, p. 855.
[17] Erzberger, *Erlebnisse*, p. 245. Lutz, *op.cit.*, p. 856.
[18] The motion was printed by Josef Wirth in an article defending Erzberger in the *Freiburger Tagespost*, May 15, 1918. Copy in *Bachem Papers*, File 90.

Erzberger supported these seemingly self-evident principles in a strong speech in the committee that same day. He called primarily for more information on the recent happenings in the Ukraine, while excoriating the *coup d'état* described above. He accused the military of annexationism, brutality, and complete want of subordination to the civilian government. But his main target—though more by implication than direct statement—was the Hertling-Payer government which tolerated such nefarious actions, and he called upon the *Reichstag* to set things right.[19]

Erzberger's exposure caused a sensation that reminded men of his speech of July 6, 1917, with its impact upon the fate of Bethmann-Hollweg. It was thought that Erzberger wanted to bring Hertling down, especially since he had told some friends that further revelations would follow in the very near future.[20] Stresemann played, however, on this occasion a role very different from his cooperation with Erzberger ten months earlier. Speaking shortly after Erzberger, he stated that the acceptance of the motion would be disastrous, since it imputed to the government either insincerity about its treaty obligations or hopeless weakness in the face of the Supreme Command. The result would be a weakening of Hertling's prestige at home and a confirmation of Wilson's point that Germany was a military autocracy with which the Entente powers were unable to negotiate.[21] Stresemann was evidently not bothered by the fact that all these points were completely true, and that Erzberger had wished—however diplomatically—to call attention to this very fact.

Hertling prudently avoided answering Erzberger himself. He sent his deputy Payer to calm *Reichstag* members. Payer took the view that Erzberger's motion was intrinsically acceptable because it consisted of nothing but truisms, but that Erzberger's supporting speech had given it a sharp edge against the government. He threatened to resign immediately if the motion were not withdrawn, and used his influence with the Progressive Party to make it dissociate itself from Erzberger's action.[22] The Zentrum leaders got cold feet when they saw the possible effects of Erzberger's action, and regretted having permitted Erz-

---

[19] The protocols of the Main Committee have not yet been published. The gist of Erzberger's speech is summarized in his newspaper article cited in footnote 15.

[20] Eisele to the editors of the *Kölnische Volkszeitung*, May 8, 1918. *Bachem Papers*, File 89. Eisele claimed he had gotten his information directly from Gröber and Fehrenbach. See his article in *Neues Mannheimer Volksblatt*, May 21, 1918. Copy in *Bachem Papers*, File 90.

[21] Letter of Dr. Pfleger to Eisele, May 21, 1918. *Bachem Papers*, File 89.

[22] Two of its members, Haas and Gothein, who were favorable to Erzberger's stand, were withdrawn from the Committee upon Payer's insistence.

berger to initiate it. Gröber and Fehrenbach succeeded in persuading Erzberger to withdraw his motion, and thereby ended the looming crisis.[23]

Erzberger felt he had achieved his objectives by calling attention to a crying scandal. When he saw that he could not marshal further support in the *Reichstag,* he gave a very innocuous interpretation of his speech. He now claimed that he had never intended to either overthrow Hertling or attack the Supreme Command, but only to put pressure on both to alter their misguided policies:

> As regards the malicious imputations to which my relation to the army and its glorious leaders are subjected, I am anxious in this connection to point out emphatically that the Supreme Command was not in any way included in my criticism. Hindenburg and Ludendorff, to whom our whole nation rightly looks up with gratitude and confidence, are to me, as to all of my countrymen, great and revered personages. The name of Eichhorn is forever linked with a succession of great military achievements in the difficult years of the Russian war. But we must remember that we are no longer at war with Russia, and particularly not with the Ukraine. We are supposed to be living on "terms of peace and friendship." Therefore, in criticizing the measures adopted by military officials in Kiev, I had exclusively in mind political questions. . . . Measures of a purely political nature, such as those I spoke of on May 8, cannot possibly be immune from all discussion, simply because they emanate from military quarters. It is the right and duty of every deputy to make up his mind about them. . . . To reproach me with enmity to the military is a deliberate misconstruction of my intentions, which aim no less at the greatness of the German Empire and at bringing about an honorable, lasting peace safeguarding Germany's cultural, political, and economic future, than do those of any of my open and secret adversaries.[24]

The entire statement was a good example of Erzberger's skill at retreating from an advanced position. He did not apologize for any of the charges which he had made. He only denied the intention of drawing the corollaries which could be drawn from his charges. His statement of devotion to Hindenburg and Ludendorff was part of the ritual of German wartime politics.

The Right-wing forces in Germany, including the conservative wing of the Zentrum, refused to accept Erzberger's explanations and continued to insist that Erzberger had wanted to bring down Hertling. Karl Bachem's *Kölnische Volkszeitung,* the main organ of conserva-

---

[23] Gröber described his attitude in a long talk with Eisele. Eisele to editors of *Kölnische Volkszeitung,* May 22, 1918. *Bachem Papers,* File 89.

[24] Lutz, *op.cit.,* pp. 857–58.

tive Catholicism, ridiculed Erzberger's attempts to portray his action as completely innocuous. It pointed out the facts that Erzberger's speech had been very sharp in its tone, that Payer had threatened his resignation if the motion should pass, that Gröber had feared that Erzberger wanted to depose Hertling, and that the Zentrum Party had applied great pressure upon Erzberger to withdraw his motions—all facts that were incomprehensible if Erzberger had not been engaged in an action threatening the life of the government.[25] It also accused Erzberger of having secured his incriminating materials from the Ukrainian Embassy, a rather unusual proceeding when attacking the policy of one's own country.[26]

The personal virulence of the *Kölnische Volkszeitung* against Erzberger caused much adverse comment in the Zentrum Party.[27] Bachem excused it in a private letter by arguing that nothing short of a full-scale action could save Hertling and get the party to shake off the Erzberger incubus. He was very critical of the Zentrum leadership, especially of Gröber, for their failure to curb Erzberger. This made it necessary for the *Kölnische Volkszeitung* to undertake this task:

> We have now begun the struggle because our conscience prohibited further silence. We will continue it in a calm and objective manner but with deep determination. We consider it necessary because the party is unable to apply a remedy. If the party does not find the strength to remove Erzberger and [his colleague] Rechenberg from the Budget Commission, as the Progressives have withdrawn their frondeurs [upon Payer's insistence], it remains the duty of the Zentrum press to check the progressive disintegration of the party.[28]

Bachem thought that an independent newspaper like the *Kölnische Volkszeitung* must take the lead, since "Erzberger's rule of terror over the press increases from day to day. A great number of Zentrum jour-

[25] *Kölnische Volkszeitung,* May 15, 1918. *Bachem Papers,* File 90.

[26] *ibid.* Erzberger denied receiving Ukrainian embassy materials in a "correction" which he forced the *Kölnische Volkszeitung* to insert May 19, 1918. The Ukrainian ambassador Sewrjuk supported Erzberger's denial in a message to the same paper, May 21, 1918. The denial was plausible since the Ukrainian Embassy had, due to the chaotic circumstances in Kiev, lost contact with its government from April 28 to May 8. *Bachem Papers,* File 90.

[27] The *Germania,* May 23, 1918, opened its columns to Erzberger for a vigorous reply to the *Kölnische Volkszeitung* under the title "Macht oder Recht," in which Erzberger accused the Cologne paper of a pagan worship of power in preference to a Christian conception of justice. Copy in *Bachem Papers,* File 90. This led to a sharp reply in the *Kölnische Volkszeitung,* May 26, 1918 under the title "Ein vergeblicher Rechtfertigungsversuch Erzbergers." Copies in *Bachem Papers,* File 90.

[28] Bachem to Eisele, May 16, 1918. A further letter of May 22, 1918, admitted the probable hopelessness of the campaign, since two thirds of the parliamentary party appeared to stand behind Erzberger. Copy in *ibid.*

nalists are so closely tied to Erzberger personally that they are compelled to support his policies whatever they are." [29]

The opponents of Erzberger knew that they were a minority both in the *Reichstag* Zentrum and in the party press. They saw that their only chance to break Erzberger was to mobilize anti-Erzberger sentiment in some of the local Zentrum associations. This led to a rash of hostile resolutions in late May and early June, of which the following from Paderborn, accepted by a vote of 27 to 8 after several hours of debate, may serve as an example:

> The Zentrum voters are watching with increasing perturbation the busybody activities and peculiar policies of deputy Erzberger. The cleavage created within the party by the events of July 1917 threatens to become ever larger. Only energetic action within the party can resolve the crisis and restore the much-needed unity of the Zentrum. The assembled party committee of Paderborn hereby petitions the executive committee of the *Reichstag* party to take prompt action in the Erzberger matter and to resist Erzberger's party-destroying activities with all the power at its command. Its minimum demands are Erzberger's removal from the Main Committee and the termination of his role as official party spokesman.[30]

The *Reichstag* Zentrum Party held a meeting on Erzberger's action of May 8 and the ensuing controversy on June 9, 1918. It proved a personal triumph for Erzberger since it vindicated him on every point. Wilhelm Marx, Josef Wirth, and Josef Giesberts, all rising Zentrum men, were especially vigorous in defending Erzberger. He was commended for having consulted the party leaders, including Gröber, in advance of his *Reichstag* speech, and the principles embodied in his motion were proclaimed as Zentrum principles. The critics of Erzberger, and above all the *Kölnische Volkszeitung,* were condemned as guilty of conduct damaging to the party. A resolution was approved which urged moderation in intra-party dissensions. This in effect aimed at screening Erzberger since only the outvoted minority had an interest in maintaining a virulent tone in further polemics. The conservative wing of the party was able to save face by asserting that the resolution was aimed as much at Erzberger (whose rough polemical methods were well known) as at itself. But Erzberger had every reason to be satisfied with the backing he had found at the caucus.[31]

[29] Bachem to Pichler, the conservative Bavarian Zentrum leader, May 18, 1918. Copy in *ibid.*

[30] *Kölnische Volkszeitung,* June 3, 1918. Copy in *ibid.*

[31] For text of Resolution, see *Kölnische Volkszeitung,* June 15, 1918. Eisele gave a full account of the meeting in a letter to the editors of the *Kölnische Volkszeitung,* June 13, 1918. *Bachem Papers,* File 89. Dr. Fortmann, Erzberger's successor in the management of the *Zentrumskorrespondenz,* sent out a confidential account very favorable to Erzberger on June 19, 1918. Copy in *ibid.*

Mounting Attacks upon Erzberger

A mere party resolution could not stop the continuous personal attacks which had been levied against Erzberger ever since the July crisis, because his worst assailants were Protestant Pan-Germans not subject to Zentrum discipline. Erzberger refuted and ridiculed many of the charges made against him in a speech in the *Reichstag* in late February, though ridicule could not kill in wartime Germany. Most of the accusations had been summarized in a pamphlet published by Friedrich Hussong in September 1917, of which an enlarged second edition appeared in July 1918.[32] But many other accusations circulated in ephemeral single-sheet publications where libel suits were practically impossible. Erzberger mentioned among others the following stories current about him in the spring of 1918: that he had spent the large sum of 28 million marks in his propaganda work after Bethmann had given him a blank check; that he was a bribed agent of the English secret service; that he had concocted the Peace Resolution at a meeting with the Jesuit General Ledochowsky on Lake Thun in May 1917, and had then gone to Rome disguised as a monk to receive final orders, stopping in Vienna before his return home; that he aimed at destroying the "Protestant" Hohenzollern Empire by detaching the South German states for the greater glory of the "Catholic" Hapsburg monarchy; that he had acquired a huge personal fortune serving on various wartime economic agencies; that he had led a foreign-inspired campaign for the removal of Hindenburg and Ludendorff; and many other tales of an equally ludicrous nature.[33]

Attacks on Erzberger were sometimes humorous. He took a brief vacation in Bavaria in April 1918 and received the following reception from the local newspaper *Alpenbote:*

HE HAS ARRIVED

The neighboring village of Schliersee has become overnight the center of the diplomatic world, the veritable navel of the earth. The Grand Mogul of Buttenhausen, President of the German Republic, Duke of Albania and Lithuania, yellow coward *(Gelbfüssler)* of Biberach . . . and Count Spider-Web, Matthias Erzberger, has arrived with his retinue. Lord Balfour is expected shortly, and Clemenceau will arrive *incognito.*

[32] Friedrich Hussong, *Matthias Erzbergers Wege und Wandlungen* (Leipzig, 2nd edition, 1918). The military authorities showed their hostility to Erzberger by tampering with his private mail. Many of his correspondents complained that their letters did not reach Erzberger or that his letters showed signs of having been opened. See, for example, letters from E. Fischer (a Swiss editor) to Erzberger, July 10, 1918, and from Leo Winz (a Copenhagen agent) to Erzberger, Feb. 15, 1919. *Erzberger Papers,* Files 36 and 37.
[33] *Reichstag Debates,* cccxi (Feb. 27, 1918), 4226–28.

It is said that Erzberger will dictate peace terms in the Hotel *Seehaus*. Privy Councilor Falschhausen from Parma has already visited him. He is the same man with whom he had under-the-table dealings in Switzerland in June of 1917.

Contact with the Vatican is maintained through the constant use of carrier pigeons. It is considered questionable whether the terrifying *Gelbfüssler* will allow the German Empire to continue to exist.

The ruler of the world exhibits himself daily from 12 to 3 o'clock. Whoever wishes to view the biggest Swabian braggart *(Fotzmaul)* of all time can do so cheaply now.[34]

How did Erzberger himself explain these violent attacks? He was asked this question by Nuncio Pacelli in early May, and sent the following forthright reply:

The attack against myself is organized primarily by the Pan-Germans and the Evangelical League. At the head of the assailants stands F. Hussong, the editor of the *Tägliche Rundschau*. This current unhappily finds support among certain annexationist Pan-German circles within the Zentrum Party, more especially among members of the Catholic nobility. The crux of the matter is always this: my enemies seek to destroy me politically because I am the father and the strongest champion of the Peace Resolution. . . .

The agitation is at the present moment carried out with special virulence, because the Pan-Germans believe that the great victories in the west provide a good opportunity for abandoning the idea of a peace of conciliation and reasserting the principle of a power-peace *(Machtfrieden)*, involving annexations for Germany and the suppression of foreign nationalities. I stand in the way of these Pan-German aims, and that is why they assail me with the secret approval of the Supreme Command.

I foresee that the present period of intense attack will continue for some time and that a change will come only after the military situation has been clarified. A further purpose of these attacks is to put pressure on me to abandon the principle of a peace of conciliation and to sacrifice publicly the resolution of July 1917. I will, of course, not do either under any circumstances, since I cannot be untrue to my convictions. I continue to believe that the July principles provide the only basis for a satisfactory peace. The attacks are especially vehement because I am a Catholic. Both liberal and orthodox Protestantism have proved very accessible to the idea of a peace based upon power and might *(Die Idee des Machtfriedens und Machttums)*.[35]

Erzberger was accustomed to rough political controversy, and gave as good blows as he received; but he did resent attacks upon his per-

[34] The *Alpenbote* greeting was reprinted by the *Casseler Tageblatt*, April 18, 1918. Copy in *Bachem Papers*, File 89.
[35] Erzberger to Pacelli, May 4, 1918. *Erzberger Papers*, File 21.

sonal honor when they emanated from supposedly reputable people. A prominent Right-wing member of the Zentrum Party, the Saxon Count Schönburg-Wechselburg, called him a "lying pig-dog" (*verlogener Schweinehund*) at a Zentrum Party meeting at Dresden in April 1918. Some of the members present protested this description, and the count was willing to retract the "pig-dog" and replace it first by "subject" and finally by "man"; but he refused to withdraw the adjective "lying." [36] Erzberger immediately started a libel suit, and secured the services of his party friend Fehrenbach as lawyer. The matter was discussed at a secret meeting of the national committee of the party at Berlin on June 29, 1918. Pressure was applied upon both sides to avoid a public scandal. Erzberger was willing to withdraw his suit if Schönburg would apologize and make a large donation to Zentrum funds to compensate the party partially for the damage caused by his accusations. Count Schönburg refused this characteristic Erzberger offer. The case never came to trial because Schönburg possessed parliamentary immunity as a member of the Saxon First Chamber, which could be lifted only after that Chamber had finished its long summer vacation. Erzberger's lawyer Fehrenbach was elected *Reichstag* president in June, thus making it inopportune for him to appear in a controversial libel case. A court examination of Erzberger's work and character was to be delayed for another year and a half.[37]

The Fall of Kühlmann and Hintze's Eastern Policy

The spring of 1918 saw the collapse of Germany's offensive on the western front. This meant that the defeat of Germany could be only a question of time unless she first used her still formidable defensive power to seek a negotiated peace. Kühlmann, recognizing this fact, made a very sensible speech in the *Reichstag* on June 25, 1918, stating that military means alone could not end the war for Germany. The annexationists regarded this truism as a combination of pessimism and treason, and Ludendorff demanded Kühlmann's immediate resignation. Erzberger urged the Foreign Secretary to fight for his position, mobilized the Interparty Committee in his support, and pleaded with Payer, the Vice Chancellor, for his retention in office. He was appalled by the bad impression that would be created abroad by the retirement of Kühlmann. But the latter, believing that Ludendorff was still omnipotent, offered his resignation.[38] Erzberger regretted this action and de-

[36] *Berliner Tageblatt*, April 30, 1918. Copy in *Bachem Papers*, File 90.
[37] Bachem left notes on the meeting and the further disposition of the case in his *Papers*, File 89.
[38] Erzberger's memoranda on conversations with Payer (July 7, 1918) and Kühlmann (July 9), in *Erzberger Papers*, File 21. Also *Erlebnisse*, pp. 303–04.

fended his general record until the revelations of 1919 showed his mishandling of the reply to the Papal Peace Note.

Admiral von Hintze, a man much less able, became the new Foreign Secretary. His first task was to complete negotiations with Russia on certain supplementary treaties, and to decide upon future relations with the Bolsheviks. The Brest-Litovsk Treaty had left many matters to be settled by subsequent negotiations, and these were completed in early August 1918. Germany now demanded complete control of Livonia and Estonia, the expulsion of the British from Murmansk (which they occupied as part of the Russian intervention), and reparations of six billion marks. The Germans promised in return to evacuate several areas occupied in violation of the Brest Treaty (Black Sea area, Don basin), to stop supporting Russian separatist and counter-revolutionary movements, and to recognize the abolition of private property decreed by the Bolsheviks (in return for compensation to Germany). The Bolsheviks were willing to sign an unfavorable treaty because they were literally on their last legs and needed a respite at any price. They lacked popular support in the country and were threatened by White Russian movements supported by both the Central and the Entente Powers. The German government wanted to extort a signature to the treaty now because it felt that no fuure Russian government would ever be so weak as to accept such utterly humiliating terms.[39]

Erzberger was opposed to these treaty provisions on a variety of grounds. The recognition of the abolition of private property was contrary to natural law and constituted a dangerous precedent. The demand for reparations constituted an unmistakable violation of the Peace Resolution. The proposed detachment of the Baltic states from Russian sovereignty could never be accepted permanently by any Russian government—whether Tsarist or Bolshevik—because it reduced Russia's access to the Baltic to the small area around Petersburg. The treaties were, therefore, a fatal barrier to future Russo-German reconciliation. Erzberger also thought that Germany's violation of the Brest terms and her ruthless exploitation of her military superiority further blackened Germany's already very bad reputation in the Entente countries. He was also indignant that Germany had negotiated the treaties without bothering to even consult her allies Austria, Bulgaria, and Turkey—an example of provocative arrogance that helped prepare the breach in her alliances a few weeks later.[40]

---

[39] On the supplementary treaties, see Wheeler-Bennett, *Forgotten Peace,* Ch. VIII. There were important secret clauses in an exchange of letters between Hintze and Joffe, printed in *Europäische Gespräche,* IV (1926), 148–53. Erzberger, *Erlebnisse,* pp. 245–49.

[40] Erzberger's objections to the treaties are stated in a letter to Hintze, Aug. 21, 1918, and a conversation with Kriege, Aug. 30, 1918. Copies in *Erzberger Papers,* File 56.

The Foreign Office tried to assuage Erzberger's opposition—a serious matter since *Reichstag* ratification of the treaties was necessary—in a long conversation which Erzberger had with Kriege, the head of the Legal Section. Kriege admitted that the treaties were bad, and that the provisions about the Baltic States were especially unfortunate. But, he argued, the Foreign Office had no choice in the face of the policy of the generals in the east, who fancied they were empire-building in the style of Alexander the Great. Erzberger reported this part of the conversation as follows:

> The political leadership had no choice in this matter. If these territories were not removed from Russian control by way of a treaty the military would seize them in violation of treaties. He had pressed for rapid completion of the negotiations because of the danger that the generals might create a *fait accompli* any day. To my remark that the generals at the moment ought to have other preoccupations [in view of the Entente seizure of the military initiative in the west], Kriege replied: "The more they are pressed in the west the madder they get in the east." I retorted that his explanation had made the completion of the treaties intelligible for the first time. But the consideration which appeared to weigh most heavily with the officials of the Foreign Office could not be decisive for me as a politician.[41]

Erzberger had a further reason for opposing the treaties: he had become a convert to the policy of smashing the Bolsheviks in preference to entering into further treaty relations with them. The horror of Bolshevik rule had become apparent to all except the Independent Socialists. Bolshevik propaganda was systematically fomenting revolution in the Central Powers, and Lenin's government had observed the treaty terms of Brest-Litovsk no more than Germany had. The murder of the German ambassador to Moscow, Count Mirbach, had provided an excellent pretext for German military intervention (July 6). Mirbach's successor, Karl Helfferich, became the most outspoken champion of the policy of breaking with the Bolsheviks, and Erzberger for once agreed with his old enemy. There can be no doubt that the Bolsheviks could have been overthrown by a minor military demonstration.[42]

General Hoffmann was a strong champion of Helfferich's policy. He developed it in a talk with Erzberger on September 3, 1918, pointing up the danger which Bolshevik propaganda presented to German

---

[41] Erzberger's memorandum on his talk with Kriege, dated Aug. 30, 1918. *Erzberger Papers,* File 56.

[42] For Helfferich's policy, see his *Weltkrieg,* III, 442–93; and above all two valuable articles by Kurt von Raumer, using Helfferich's private papers: "Das Ende von Helfferichs Moskauer Mission," in *Srbik Festschrift.Gesamtdeutsche Vergangenheit* (Munich, 1938), pp. 392–99, and "Zwischen Brest-Litovsk und Compiègne: die deutsche Ostpolitik vom Sommer 1918," in *Baltische Lande,* IV, 1–14 (Leipzig, 1939).

military discipline in the east. Hoffmann was convinced that the triumph of the counter-revolution was inevitable, and wanted it to take place under German rather than Entente auspices. He claimed to have established contact with several possible pretenders (the Archdukes Michael and Dmitri and even the Rasputin murderer Prince Jussupoff), and to have found that they were willing to cooperate with Germany. Erzberger stated his general agreement with Hoffmann's views:

> I told him that I was, of course, unable to check the accuracy of his information, but that if it was correct Germany must act immediately. The German government had unhappily established much too close ties with the Bolsheviks. For this reason he had been an opponent of the supplementary treaties. It would indeed be funny if Germany should use a provision of those very treaties [the Russian obligation to expel the English from Murmansk, which they were unable to do] as a pretext for destroying the Bolshevik government [as Hoffmann proposed]. But Germany must above all end her support of the Bolsheviks. It had made a great mistake in the treaties when it accepted the abolition of private property in return for alleged and purely temporary advantages.[43]

Erzberger's Book on the League of Nations

Erzberger used his period of political impotence—when he was unable to exercise any real influence upon Germany's policies—in order to write a book about a future League of Nations that he hopefully expected to dominate the postwar world. He showed his remarkable political instinct by being the first major politician in Germany to take up a theme which was to be on everyone's lips a few months later. The book documents Erzberger's glowing vision of the future. It was to gain wide currency because Erzberger had become a *Staatssekretär* in the government of Prince Max of Baden by the time it appeared, in October 1918.[44] It supported what he declared to be the nearly universal demand of mankind for guarantees against the recurrence of the horrors of war. Erzberger praised Wilson's advocacy of the League, and specifically repudiated the popular notion that the American President was a hypocrite. Erzberger saw clearly that Wilson's idealism was

[43] Erzberger's memorandum on conversation with General Hoffmann, dated Sept. 2, 1918. *Erzberger Papers*, File 36. Summarized in *Erlebnisse*, pp. 248–49. Erzberger, torn between his hatred of Bolshevism and fear of Germany's imperialist ventures in the east, had been a late convert to the policy of a "march upon Moscow." He had written a letter to Bergen on July 23, 1918, opposing the sending of troops to Moscow to avenge the Mirbach murder, for fear of provoking new hostilities in the east. *Erzberger Papers*, File 4.

[44] Erzberger, *Der Völkerbund. Der Weg zum Weltfrieden* (Berlin, 1918). English translation by Bernard Miall under the title *The League of Nations, the way to the world's peace* (New York, 1919).

deeply rooted in America's democratic and anti-militarist traditions. He emphasized to his German audience the strength of League sentiment in England and France, while deploring its frequent identification with plans to perpetuate the anti-German alliance in the postwar world (by excluding the Central Powers from the future League). Erzberger deplored that the League conception had many open enemies among annexationists and militarists in Germany, but he emphasized that it had won public endorsement from both Chancellors Bethmann and Hertling, and was supported by the great majority of Germans who endorsed the principles of the Peace Resolution. Erzberger saw the road clear for a League in which former enemies could cooperate as conciliated equals.[45]

Erzberger asserted that a League was in full accord with both Christian principles and the traditions of the German people. He praised the long-standing Papal policy of promoting international peace, and the specific support given by Pope Leo XIII to the principles of arbitration. Erzberger endorsed the dictum of Pope Benedict XV that World War One was the natural result of the modern rationalist-democratic-liberal heresy—a curious attitude for a man who was just then engaged in the democratization and liberalization of Germany as the prerequisite for a lasting peace with the western democracies. Erzberger, whose political ideals required the assimilation of Germany's constitutional structure to that of England and France, recognized the polemical force of the nationalist-militarist argument that both democratic and League of Nations ideas were alien imports from western Europe. He therefore attempted to show that the arbitration principle was deeply rooted in Germany's past, and relied upon his friend Hommerich, the editor of the *Germania,* to gather together precedents.[46] These were the Hanseatic League, the League of Rhenish cities, the Electors' League of Rense, the 1495 Edict of Perpetual Peace, Article 11 of the 1815 Federation, and Article 76 of the 1867 Constitution. International arbitration had also been supported by Kant, Germany's greatest philosopher. Erzberger enlisted the Königsberg sage as a valuable ally in the struggle for European cooperation in a loose federation, open diplomacy, the restriction of armaments, the principle of non-intervention, and the development of liberal constitutionalism in Germany.[47]

Erzberger's specific proposal for a League advocated general acceptance of the following principles: (1) obligatory arbitration of all dis-

[45] Erzberger, *Völkerbund,* Ch. I.
[46] A. Hommerich, *Deutschtum und Schiedsgerichtsbarkeit, ein geschichtlicher Beitrag zu einer grossen Gegenwarts-und Zukunftsfrage* (Freiburg, 1918).
[47] Erzberger, *Völkerbund,* Ch. IV.

putes by specially appointed boards with the rule of law replacing the rule of force, (2) disarmament eliminating fear and suspicions, (3) freedom of the seas, (4) a world-wide open-door policy preventing economic discrimination, (5) a common European program for the economic development of Africa, (6) special guarantees for perpetually neutral states. To these principles, to be discussed in detail below, he added the points of (7) non-intervention in the internal affairs of neighboring states (8) international guarantee of minority rights, and (9) the penalization of chauvinistic insults delivered against other nations.[48]

Erzberger attached special importance to the compulsory element in arbitration, attacking the existence of "saving clauses" that reserved freedom of action in cases affecting the national honor. Erzberger recognized that many international disputes were not capable of a purely judicial solution, and for this reason wanted to keep the work of the world court separate from the arbitration boards which he was proposing. The latter should be composed of three arbitrators, with one to be appointed by each side with the approval of its parliament, while the third man would be appointed by mutual agreement. In case the two parties could not agree upon a third man, Erzberger desired that he be appointed by the Pope.[49]

Erzberger saw far-reaching disarmament to be both the prerequisite for and the corollary of the compulsory arbitration of disputes. He saw the impracticability of the total abolition of standing armies because of the permanent threat of social revolution in modern communities. His specific plan postulated a negotiated settlement ending World War One without victors or vanquished: an agreement to scrap a high proportion of the existing arms, guarantees against a new arms race, and the general abolition of conscription. He expected favorable results from these measures, both in creating a new climate of confidence and in diverting the resources wasted upon armaments to more profitable uses.[50]

Erzberger attached great importance to the principle of the freedom of the seas, interpreting it in a way that was quite unacceptable to England. He desired a drastic modification of existing conceptions of blockade, contraband, and the right of seizing property at sea without compensation. He evidently had some doubts about the ability of his arbitration procedure to prevent war, and aimed for a minimum objective of civilizing warfare if it could not be abolished completely. He

[48] *ibid.*, Ch. vi.
[49] *ibid.*, Ch. vii.
[50] *ibid.*, Ch. viii.

was willing to surrender the submarine weapon as Germany's contribution to the formulation of a new code. He had impracticable notions on naval disarmament, arguing that effective freedom of the seas required the breaking of English naval preponderance through abandonment by the English of strategic naval bases that in fact controlled world traffic (Gibraltar, Aden, etc.), and the internationalization of key waterways like the Suez and Panama Canals.[51]

Erzberger advocated economic equality between nations and the principle of the open door in order to prevent Entente postwar economic warfare against the Central Powers. He realized that Germany was very vulnerable to economic ostracism, but thought that she could survive in view of her special relationship to eastern Europe made possible by the Brest Treaty. He further favored specific measures of international economic cooperation, such as a controlled allocation of scarce raw materials based upon 1913 imports, reciprocal penetration of the economic life of the major nations through an exchange of stock ownership, and international agreement upon social legislation.[52]

Erzberger looked upon a joint European economic approach to African development as a relatively innocuous way for Germany to secure colonial opportunities proportional to her capital resources. He thought Germany entitled to an enlarged role on the basis of her proved colonial capacity since the time that his own exposures had led to Dernburg's reforms. Erzberger also thought that Germany's honor required that her role be at least as great as that of Belgium or Portugal. He argued that Africa should be neutralized in the future and regretted that the Entente powers had broken the neutrality guaranteed in the Congo Acts of 1885 by their invasion of Germany's colonies.[53]

He showed special concern for the rights of neutral states in his League of Nations draft. He recognized that the concept of uniquely neutral states would lose its theoretical validity after the general outlawry of war, but he stated that it would probably retain some practical importance. In this connection Erzberger again defended Germany's violation of Belgium as an unjust but necessary act, while insisting that the injustice required complete restitution and reparations as well. He hoped that the new League would create a situation where statesmen in Bethmann's position would no longer be forced to choose between doing wrong and violating the dictates of national security. This

[51] *ibid.*, Ch. ix.
[52] *ibid.*, Ch. x. Erzberger was a firm believer in a plan for exchange of stock advanced by his friend Arnold Rechberg in *Weltfragen* (Berlin, 1918).
[53] *ibid.*, Ch. xi.

would not be the least advantage of replacing power politics by the rule of law.[54]

Erzberger placed all these suggestions in a detailed League draft of forty articles that might be submitted to the future peace conference. He pleaded for a simple, understandable plan which could be enlarged after experience of its working, and warned against all utopian schemes of world government which aimed at annihilating national sovereignty. Some further features of his draft deserve to be mentioned. Erzberger required that League membership be universal and permanent, and accepted the principle of "one state, one vote"—a concession to the principle of the equality of unequals that could safely be made because the crucial arbitral decisions were not left to majority votes. French should be the language of business since it had long been the medium of diplomacy, a proposal revealing a laudable freedom from linguistic chauvinism. He favored a strong executive who would enforce arbitral decisions by diplomatic, economic, and finally military sanctions. Erzberger doubted that the latter would ever be necessary in view of the enormous power of world public opinion (which Erzberger warned his fellow Germans not to underestimate) and the potential economic and military strength of the League against any potential aggressor. He thought that public opinion in all civilized states, whose internal structure he expected to conform to a relatively homogeneous Christian-democratic pattern, would overwhelmingly support the League, thereby making adherence to League principles safe since it did not put any power at a comparative disadvantage. He anticipated such near-unanimous support because the only alternative was the prewar pattern of rival alliances, an armament race, and military and economic warfare.[55]

Erzberger ridiculed the opponents of the League as either foolish or wicked or both. There were a few stubborn adherents of power politics (*Machtpolitiker*) who refused to recognize the bankruptcy of the existing international system. A few romantic admirers of war refused to revise their views despite the horror of four years of trench warfare, but they were hopelessly out of touch with the spirit of the age. Then there were a few Social Darwinians who believed that conflicts were the destiny of man and that the race would atrophy if no longer confronted by martial challenges. These pseudo-biologists were incapable of understanding the idea of the interdependence of men taught both by the Christian tradition and the modern democratic

[54] *ibid.*, Ch. xii.
[55] *ibid.*, Chs. xiii–xv.

movement. Erzberger was unimpressed by these various opponents of League principles, but he admitted that some reputable arguments could be advanced against his League. It would tend to freeze the territorial *status quo,* but this would matter less than previously because frontier corrections would no longer be required for either military or economic reasons. Arbitral decisions would not necessarily be based upon justice—but neither was victory in war. Indeed, arbitration was far more likely to lead to justice than the possession of the bigger battalions. Erzberger's optimism about the future of the League was based largely upon his view that all hostile arguments were weak, and that no attractive competing system of international life was available.[56]

Erzberger's enthusiastic vision was shared by the best and most enlightened men in all countries at the time, but it nonetheless proved a very faulty preview of the shape of things to come. It assumed that the war would be ended by a negotiated settlement between equals and with a universal desire for international conciliation, whereas the Entente victory proved the prelude to a victor's peace of Versailles. It provided for the establishment of a League from which Germany was long excluded, and whose main duty was to perpetuate what was for Germany an undesirable *status quo.* Erzberger's hope that territorial disputes would prove of little significance in the future was completely mistaken. His assumption that the League would secure such near-unanimous support as to make anti-League defiance suicidal proved much too optimistic. In fact, nationalism proved a far stronger force than League principles; the defiance of the League was generally supported by public opinion in the offending states (Japan, Germany, Italy); states favoring League principles proved unwilling to make any sacrifice upon their behalf; and the moral force of the world proved totally unavailing.

Erzberger viewed the postwar world in far too idyllic terms. He did not foresee the evil forces of revanchism (since he expected a negotiated peace), irredentism fed by unsatisfactory boundary settlements, and economic chaos produced by faulty reparations policies. His belief that all postwar states would become Christian democracies adhering

---

[56] *ibid.,* Ch. xiv. For important discussions of Erzberger's book see Adolf Grabowsky, "Die Grundprobleme des Völkerbundes," in *Zeitschrift für Politik,* xi (1919), 377–451; A. Mendelssohn-Bartholdy, "Deutsche Literatur zur Völkerbundsfrage 1919–21," in *Schmollers Jahrbuch,* xlvi (Berlin, 1922), 543–55, especially 549, praises the historical sections of Erzberger's book; and Alfred Frachon, *Les Opinions allemandes sur la Reconstruction du Droit internationale* (Paris, 1921), pp. 191–384, a hostile treatment, that takes up Erzberger's book in detail chapter by chapter. A widely circulated popularization of the book was Fidelis (H. Popert), *Erzbergers Grundgedanken* (Hamburg, 1919).

to common standards of law, decency, and parliamentary government proved wide of the mark. He believed that Communism would prove a purely temporary phenomenon, since it appeared to be on the verge of collapse in 1918.

His conception of a League suffered from a fundamental flaw quite apart from his specific misreading of the future. He underestimated the traditional tenacity of the international system based upon competing national states. His faith in the "judicialization" of international disputes, whether through court judgments or arbitral decisions, assumed the existence or development of a universally accepted code of international law which was in fact unlikely to occur. He failed to see that the policeman enforcing judgments or decisions would in fact be unavailable, and he overestimated the degree of voluntary compliance that could be expected. A world public opinion deeply dedicated to the rule of law and international cooperation developed only in a very few countries, and was abandoned even there in favor of a reversion to narrow conceptions of national self-interest as soon as adherence to League ideals required personal sacrifices rather than noble words.

Erzberger's glowing vision was to sustain him through the chaos which was descending upon Germany. The Hertling government was tumbling down as he was composing his book. The new government was to appoint him to the onerous job of armistice commissioner, and in this role he was to experience the worst recrudescence of the practices of power politics in his negotiations with the Entente Powers. Germany, far from developing into a Christian democracy, experienced the danger of a Communist dictatorship through the winter of 1918–1919. Erzberger was in the thick of the diplomatic and domestic struggle during these crucial months. He never despaired, no matter how bleak the prospects before him. His strength must be ascribed to his Christian principles, his naturally buoyant temperament, but also to his vision that a better world order was on the verge of being created, no matter how much it was distorted by the continued vitality of the forces of the past.

CHAPTER XI

FROM THE FALL OF HERTLING
TO THE ARMISTICE
(OCTOBER–NOVEMBER 1918)

The Fall of Hertling

THE Entente armies seized the initiative on the western front in July 1918, thereby ending the German dream of a military decision before the arrival of large bodies of American troops in France. The defeat of the Central Powers became a foregone conclusion. Erzberger was among the first to understand the turn of events. He saw that time was working against Germany, and that her chances for still securing a tolerable peace were much better now than they would be a few months later. In an acute memorandum written on July 16, 1918, which is printed in Appendix VI, Erzberger called for the immediate formation of a new government, which must be based upon the *Reichstag* majority that had voted the Peace Resolution. The new government must make a peace offer that would include large concessions to the Entente, such as the cession of Alsace-Lorraine. A negotiated peace might still be possible, so long as Germany's defensive might was still formidable and once she possessed a government that inspired confidence abroad. The sole alternative confronting Germany was unconditional surrender after further defeats in the field. Erzberger stated in July what was to become the basis of the government of Prince Max of Baden in October.[1]

By that time Germany's military position had deteriorated so disastrously that the foundations of Erzberger's policy had collapsed. The octogenarian Hertling, who stayed in power until September 29, 1918, was responsible for the prolonged paralysis of German policy. He was incapable of curbing Ludendorff or of undertaking new departures in the paramount quest for an early peace. His prestige began to wane only in the late summer as the period of German hopes for victory— the basis of his continued annexationism and sabotage of internal reforms—came to an end. The Majority parties were angered by his procrastination in the question of Prussian franchise reform. They also disapproved of his acquiescence in the wild imperialism of the generals in the east, with the complete failure to implement the principle of self-

[1] Erzberger's memorandum, dated Aug. 12, 1918, is in *Erzberger Papers,* File 14.

determination. His prestige was further shaken by the Austrian Peace Note of September 14, 1918, which was sent to all the belligerents. It called for the immediate initiation of peace negotiations. The Austrians had dispatched their note over the stiff protests of Germany.[2] The Turkish front in Syria collapsed under English attack on September 19. This was followed by a Bulgar call for an armistice on September 25, 1918, signalizing the end of the Quadruple Alliance. All of Germany's allies were trying to save what still could be saved. The Hertling government was utterly impotent in the face of all these catastrophes.

Erzberger saw in the entry of the Socialists into the government the key to both internal stability and success in negotiations with the Entente Powers. Yet the Socialists were unwilling to enter any Cabinet headed by Hertling, and the antipathy was entirely mutual. They also demanded the introduction of the full parliamentary system as the prerequisite for their participation in the government; a demand which Hertling rejected categorically. The Socialists demanded, specifically, the repeal of Article 9, clause 2, of the constitution which forced all ministers (by virtue of their membership in the *Bundesrat*) to resign their *Reichstag* seats. The Progressives completely agreed with the Socialist view. The Zentrum was naturally more cautious in advancing a demand that must bring about Hertling's fall from power. But Erzberger used all his influence to meet the Socialists' terms at a crucial Zentrum Party meeting on September 23, 1918. Gröber pleaded with his colleagues to stand behind Hertling. Erzberger replied that "he did not desire the fall of Hertling, but that it was absolutely indispensable to have the Socialists enter the Cabinet. The Zentrum must meet their wishes for repeal of Article 9 clause 2. If Hertling rejected this he could no longer be supported; for if the Socialists should go into opposition the Hertling Cabinet would fall in any case, since Payer [who represented both the Progressives and the Socialists] would be forced to resign." [3] Erzberger won the party over to his point of view, thereby creating a parliamentary majority for what was to become the governing coalition under Prince Max of Baden. It was but a continuation of the Peace Resolution majority of July 1917.

The necessity for Hertling's retirement began to be openly discussed during the meetings of the Interparty Committee in mid-September. The National Liberal leader Stresemann approached Erzberger at this

[2] Erzberger told the Foreign Office that "a German government that has allowed this moral breach in the alliance cannot continue to hold office, and is unable to guide the future destiny of our people." *Erlebnisse*, p. 318.

[3] Protocol of Sept. 23, 1918 Zentrum meeting, in *Erzberger Papers*, File 21. This is the basis of the narrative in *Erlebnisse*, p. 308.

time about the return of his party to the Committee, which it had left at the time of Brest-Litovsk. Erzberger was reluctant to have Stresemann rejoin, since "during his previous participation he had always informed Ludendorff about its proceedings, thereby making the work of the Majority more difficult."[4] Erzberger required, as a prerequisite, unconditional acceptance of the Peace Resolution, which the National Liberals were as yet—in mid-September 1918!—unwilling to grant. They were to change their minds a few days later. This became apparent in their assent to a program for a new government which Erzberger drafted at the request of the Majority Parties on September 30, 1918. His program, which was to become the basis of the next government, contained the following points: (1) full acceptance of the Peace Resolution and the German reply to the Papal Peace Note, (2) support of a League of Nations, (3) a clear-cut promise of Belgian restitution with full reparations, (4) the Brest Treaty to be subject to revision by the general peace conference, though this would probably prove unnecessary if Germany promoted genuine self-determination, (5) Alsace to be raised to a position of equality with the other federal states, (6) rapid completion of Prussian electoral reform, (7) admission of deputies into the government and elimination of all surviving relics of absolutism, and (8) immediate relaxation of the state of siege.[5]

While Erzberger was drafting the outline of these new policies, decisive events took place at Supreme Headquarters. Ludendorff had his famous failure of nerves on September 29, 1918.[6] In mid-August he had been so optimistic as to hope to retain parts of Belgium for Germany in any peace settlement. Yet at the end of September he suddenly became convinced that the western front might collapse at almost any moment. He therefore demanded, without any preparation whatsoever, that an immediate armistice request be sent to President Wilson, not merely a note offering to enter into peace negotiations. Ludendorff simultaneously insisted upon a broadening of the basis of the German government both as the prerequisite for a successful appeal to the Entente Powers and to rally the German masses for a last-ditch effort if negotiations should fail. His new domestic program parallelled that being advanced by the Interparty Committee under Erzberger's leadership at

---

[4] Erzberger, *Erlebnisse,* p. 307.

[5] *ibid.,* pp. 309–10, where the program is printed in full.

[6] The most judicious study of the background of the issuance of the armistice request, emphasizing Ludendorff's responsibility, is to be found in Ludwig Beck, *Studien* (Stuttgart, 1955), Ch. VII. Ludendorff's responsibility for the armistice request of October 4 is proved beyond doubt by the documents in *Amtliche Urkunden zur Vorgeschichte des Waffenstillstandes 1918* (2nd enlarged edition, Berlin, 1924), Ch. V. Cited henceforth as *Amtliche Urkunden.*

Berlin. Hertling was unwilling to adjust himself to the new needs confronting Germany. He refused to contemplate the introduction of the parliamentary system, and his annexationist record made him unsuitable for signing a peace appeal to Wilson. His resignation was accepted by the Emperor on September 29, thus ending a political career that had had decisive impact upon Zentrum policies for over twenty years. Hertling's spirit was soon to be broken by the German Revolution, and he died, almost unnoticed in the turmoil of the hour, on his Bavarian country estate in early January 1919.

The Government of Max and the Armistice Appeal

The appointment of Prince Max of Baden to succeed Hertling in the Chancellorship was announced on October 2. The intervening days were filled with feverish negotiations among party leaders about the distribution of seats in the new government. The *Reichstag* leaders were, again, unable to present a candidate for the highest post to the Emperor, and they acquiesced in Max *faute de mieux*. The armistice appeal to Wilson demanded by Ludendorff absorbed the attention of the government leaders, although Prince Max was, ironically, sharply opposed to any precipitate appeal. He thought it would reveal Germany's utter weakness to her enemies and simultaneously promote a psychological collapse at home. The German people had been fooled by their leaders, who in turn had fooled themselves, about the true condition of affairs. The energies of the nation had been galvanized in the face of cumulative exhaustion by the continued hopes of victory. A sudden armistice request—without a preceding gradual preparation of public opinion—must lead to such shock and paralysis as to preclude a final rally of the German people if the Entente powers should refuse to grant peace on reasonable terms. Prince Max foresaw these catastrophic developments and opposed Ludendorff's demands by the alternative program of forming a government on a basis calculated to invite confidence at home and abroad. This government could issue, after a sufficient interval to avoid the impression of panic, a request for peace negotiations in a dignified form without simultaneously asking for an armistice.[7]

The new Chancellor showed his weakness by yielding to Ludendorff's pressure for an armistice request. He must not be judged too harshly since the Emperor, the Foreign Secretary Hintze, and the Vice-Chancellor Payer all agreed with Ludendorff, and had in effect yielded to the general prior to Max' arrival at Berlin. Yet the initial

[7] Max, *op.cit.,* Pt. III, Ch. I, *passim.*

mistake of the armistice request was to predetermine all the major political decisions of his brief Chancellorship, and it is tragic that he had to bear all the consequences of a step that had been taken contrary to his own wishes. Max was an attractive rather than a forceful figure, a man, like Bethmann, more noted for his correct insights than for his capacity to make them prevail. While generally opposed to annexations during the war, he had privately criticized the Peace Resolution as the product of a temporary panic. He had backed Bethmann's efforts of internal reorientation but had never hidden his contempt for parliamentary government and party politicians. His greatest fault had been a refusal to intrigue to secure power when his sensible ideas could still help Germany. His friend Haussmann finally persuaded him to offer his services to William in early September 1918 with a program of (1) forming a new government appointed upon the initiative of the Emperor, (2) avoiding the full parliamentary system, and (3) making a peace offer to the Allies after the western front had stabilized. Max advocated this plan of a new government on the specific ground that it was the sole alternative to an otherwise inevitable parliamentary government which would be dominated by Erzberger and Scheidemann. The Emperor rejected this program when it was first suggested. When Max was finally summoned to the Chancellorship in early October his three wishes had all become impossible to achieve.[8]

Erzberger had no influence upon either the appointment of Max or the precipitate armistice request. He told Maximilian Harden that he opposed Max because his princely status was a poor advertisement of Germany's democratization, both for Wilson in America and the increasingly radical masses in Germany.[9] Erzberger deplored the inability of the *Reichstag* to nominate a better man. The *Reichstag* could not select the head of the new government, but it showed its power by the successful insistence upon excluding the Conservatives from the new Cabinet. This breach of the principle of national solidarity was necessitated by the primary goal of securing a unity of outlook within the Cabinet in pressing for both peace and internal reform.[10] The *Reichstag* majority was able to dictate, to the chagrin of the new Chancellor, the specific composition of the cabinet, including the appointment of

[8] Max's Sept. 7, 1918 memorandum to the Emperor is printed in *ibid.*, pp. 308–311.
[9] Harden described his October 2, 1918 dinner with Ballin and Erzberger in the Berlin *National-Zeitung* on Aug. 28, 1921. He noted that Erzberger, always a model of punctuality, phoned twice because important party conferences made him three quarters of an hour late. Harden was impressed by Erzberger's optimism despite all the disasters descending upon Germany.
[10] Max, *op.cit.*, pp. 344–45.

several Zentrum, Progressive, and Socialist *Staatssekretäre,* of which Erzberger was one.

Erzberger's entry into office was possible only after severe obstacles had been overcome. Max had a snobbish contempt for him and had asked Haussmann in early September: "Can one get around appointing Erzberger to office?" receiving the reply: "Only at the price of his hostility." [11] Berg, the Chief of the Civil Cabinet, discussing with party leaders the distribution of posts in the new cabinet, told them he hoped they would spare the Emperor's feelings by not insisting upon Erzberger. Gröber indignantly defended his party colleague against Berg's ill-timed remark.[12] The Zentrum favored Erzberger's appointment and delegated Gröber to tell Max that his exclusion from office would be resented.[13] Erzberger did not hide his eagerness for responsibility, provided he would secure a role proportionate to his talents. He demanded that he be appointed at the same time as the other *Staatssekretäre*—there was talk of a plan of delaying his appointment by several days to allow time for overriding obstacles—to conceal the fact that there were special difficulties in his case. Payer, who was conducting the negotiations for Max, wanted to make him only an Undersecretary in the new government. Erzberger wrote on October 4:

> Bergen [of the Foreign Office] informed me at 12:30 that Solf would become Secretary of State for Foreign Affairs, and asked me if I were willing to accept the post of Undersecretary. I said that I would have to consult my political friends first. I soon informed him through the deputies Gröber and Pfeifer that I could not accept this office, both because the Zentrum Party had been promised a full Secretaryship and also because I could not work under Solf, who was totally ignorant of political affairs.
>
> Payer then told me at 6:30 that the Emperor had appointed me *Staatssekretär* without Portfolio. He said I would shortly receive a specific sphere of duty.[14]

Erzberger's appointment had really been inevitable despite the hostility of Max, Berg, and various people prominent at Court. He had been the main architect of the coalition first formed in July 1917 which

---

[11] Haussmann in *Aus Haussmanns politischer Arbeit,* edited by his friends (Frankfurt, 1923), p. 109.

[12] Memorandum of Erzberger about conversation with Gröber, Oct. 1, 1918, in *Erzberger Papers,* File 21. Berg had only expressed his own views. Erzberger's friends at the Foreign Office, Bergen and Rosenberg, checked with the Emperor and the Supreme Command on whether Berg's statement had been authorized. They secured diplomatic denials from both, and immediately informed Erzberger at the *Reichstag.* Memorandum by Erzberger, Oct. 2, 1918, in *Erzberger Papers,* File 32.

[13] Protocol of Zentrum meeting, Oct. 3, 1918. *Erzberger Papers,* File 32.

[14] Erzberger memorandum, Oct. 4, 1918. *Erzberger Papers,* File 56.

was now at last assuming control of Germany. His name had become a symbol for a peace of conciliation, at home if not abroad. He was the only bourgeois politician who had a popular following among the masses, an urgent matter at a time when their loyalty to the new order had to be buttressed against the propaganda of the radicals on the Left. His own party, with its Right-wing elements temporarily silenced, recognized his claim to power. The new government urgently needed his executive energy and love of responsibility that never shirked any disagreeable duty.

Gröber and Trimborn became *Staatssekretäre* along with Erzberger as representatives of the Zentrum Party. Of the four Zentrum leaders discussed in Chapter III, two now entered the national government. Hertling had retired from politics, while Spahn had become Prussian Minister of Justice. This would have deprived the *Reichstag* party of all its leaders prior to the introduction of the parliamentary system, since the Imperial Constitution prohibited the simultaneous holding of an executive office and a *Reichstag* mandate. The constitutional reforms proposed by Max's government prevented this intolerable situation. The Chancellor, preoccupied with questions of foreign policy, placed Gröber in charge of steering the constitutional legislation through the *Reichstag*. The old Zentrum leader performed this task to everyone's satisfaction. The full-scale parliamentary system, advocated by Erzberger since 1909, was introduced at last. Trimborn assumed the Interior Ministry and proved a failure in the face of a very difficult situation. He had little understanding of the explosive subterranean currents of German political life, and had become rather stuffy with advancing years. He neither foresaw nor crushed the revolution in early November and tolerated subversive activity that ought to have been smashed mercilessly.

Prince Max placed Erzberger in charge of propaganda activities on October 21, 1918. Erzberger could not make a real mark in this office since he became armistice commissioner only two weeks later (November 6). In his role as propaganda chief he controlled the War Press Office (which had until recently attacked him bitterly), the general censorship (which had been used to harass spokesmen of the Majority parties), the *Zentrale für Heimatdienst* (in charge of internal propaganda), and the *Vaterländischer Unterricht* (which had given instructions to the troops in political questions, often with a marked Right-wing tendency). Erzberger instructed all these agencies to give unified support to the policies of the government, and ended the military stranglehold over Germany's communication network. Conservatives have accused him of failure to rally the nation against Wilson's terms of peace, but this would have run counter to governmental views. When the demand for the Emperor's abdication entered public controversy, Erzberger gave instructions to screen William against attack. It was the fault of circumstances rather than Erzberger that this defense could no longer be successful.[15]

Erzberger's restless energies were by no means absorbed by his propaganda tasks. He busied himself with the main foreign policy problem confronting the government: the diplomatic exchanges with President Wilson. Erzberger had insisted, even before his appointment as *Staatssekretär*, that Germany's first note include a specific acceptance of the Fourteen Points, when Max himself wanted to make these only the basis for subsequent discussions.[16] Erzberger, along with Scheidemann, became the chief spokesman in the Cabinet for the policy of accepting the progressively sharper demands which Wilson made upon Germany. Max characterized their attitude in contemptuous terms:

> Erzberger and Scheidemann were without any experience of the foreign countries and the peoples which they wished to influence, but they had an unlimited confidence in their own common sense and their own intuition since the day when they made the timely recognition that we must emphasize the strictly defensive character of our war aims [in contrast to the predominant annexationists]. Thus they joined my Cabinet in a spirit of complacency, with the feeling that they had already proved their capacity in foreign politics. In the deliberations of October and November they were not lacking in good ideas and apposite phrases. But in the decisive questions of foreign politics their instinct led them astray. They had an exaggerated fear that they might irritate Wilson by a dignified tone of speech, and would not believe that peoples who like the Anglo-Saxons are accustomed to rule, only become harder when they meet with servility. An unkind fate had impressed upon these two gentlemen the conviction that they owed it to themselves and to their parties to play their part in the drafting of documents of state.[17]

The German government was relieved when President Wilson consented to negotiate with it in a series of diplomatic exchanges. Wilson

[15] On Erzberger's propaganda responsibilities, see Nicolai, *Nachrichtendienst, Presse und Volksstimmung* (Berlin, 1920), pp. 134–36; Payer, *op.cit.*, p. 126; Erzberger, *Erlebnisse*, p. 313; Vogel, *op.cit.*, pp. 59–60. The new definition of responsibilities was originally discussed at a conference on October 11, 1918 between Payer, Erzberger, Scheidemann, and Deutelmoser, the Chancellor's press chief. Erzberger's official appointment was delayed until the formalities of his designation as a *Staatssekretär* were completed.

[16] Erzberger's talk with Haniel at the Foreign Office, Oct. 3, 1918. Erzberger Papers, File 56.

[17] Prince Max, *Memoirs*, transl. by W. M. Calder and C. W. Sutton (New York, 1928), II, 45.

showed great courage in seeking a negotiated peace in the face of Allied opposition—based upon distrust of his idealism—and the unreasonable Republican clamor, fanned by Theodore Roosevelt and Senator Lodge, for unconditional surrender.[18] Majority public opinion in all the Entente countries refused to believe that the new German government meant the dethronement of the Prussian military caste, and looked upon Max's peace appeal as a device for sowing dissension between German's enemies. Wilson was forced to make concessions to this point of view by issuing the following stiff demands to the Germans as prerequisites for an armistice: they must accept the Fourteen Points without reservations; they must evacuate all occupied territories; they must give guarantees for the maintenance of the existing Entente military superiority; they must immediately abandon submarine warfare; and they must give guarantees that the new German government was a trustworthy negotiating partner by eliminating all autocratic influences (which was interpreted as a hint for William's abdication). These demands were not unreasonable from the Entente point of view, though their expression in successive notes (instead of all at once) had the unfortunate effect of prolonging the negotiations. The impatient German masses, fearing that peace was being unduly delayed, drifted into an unnecessary revolution which destroyed the continuity of the German political tradition.[19]

Erzberger insisted at successive cabinet meetings upon speeding up negotiations with Wilson. His political instinct made him aware of the psychological repercussion provoked by the precipitate armistice request of Ludendorff. He recognized that the demand for a new national rally—the corollary of ending the negotiations—would be expecting too much of an exhausted and disillusioned nation. Erzberger became angry when Ludendorff refused to endorse Germany's third note to Wilson (October 20) because it accepted the "dishonorable" demand for abandoning submarine warfare. Ludendorff had suddenly resumed his cocky self-assurance and wanted to reverse the fatal policy he had inaugurated in late September. The cabinet was in despair since it was not yet accustomed to override the Supreme Command. The question of what to do about Ludendorff came up for discussion on

[18] Harry Rudin, *Armistice 1918* (New Haven, 1944), Ch. IV. This solid and comprehensive book provides an excellent guide through the intricate events of October and November 1918. It is especially good in correlating German with English, French, and American sources.

[19] See the contemporary criticism of Wilson by Max Weber in the *Frankfurter Zeitung* in mid-October. Marianne Weber, *Max Weber, Ein Lebensbild* (Tübingen, 1926), p. 638.

October 21. One of Max's close collaborators, Kurt Hahn,[20] suggested that an open divergence between Cabinet and Supreme Command would not only not be disastrous but be positively advantageous, for advertising the newly won supremacy of the civilian authorities. Hahn told Haeften, Ludendorff's liaison man with the Foreign Office, that

> there could be no greater proof of the Cabinet's power than if General Ludendorff would have to give way even when he was not convinced. This idea struck Haeften, he hurried back to the [Cabinet] conference room, where he took the most energetic *Staatssekretär*, Herr Erzberger, into a corner and explained to him that now political power was concentrated in the hands of the government, and the Supreme Command was no longer a power in politics. There was no reason why the Supreme Command and the government should always be of the same opinion; what mattered was that the government should always get its own way. The scales fell from Erzberger's eyes; "There I think you are quite right; it can only be for the good of the world to know that we are really and truly masters in our own house!" and he quickly resolved to seize the opportunity of being the man to allay the crisis. He fetched Scheidemann over and conversed with him for a quarter of an hour. Then he asked to be allowed to speak, and made an impassioned speech; he said it would damage the prestige of the whole Cabinet, if it was known to have required the enforced consent of the Supreme Command to cover its actions. Scheidemann seconded him.[21]

Erzberger became the architect of a temporary compromise between the government and the Supreme Command that involved Ludendorff's explicit renunciation of any political role, while relieving him of the necessity of approving what he deemed to be contrary to a soldier's honor. But this kind of compromise could not suffice for maintaining permanent cooperation. Most members of the Cabinet had begun to question Ludendorff's military judgment when the western front became stabilized contrary to his panicky anticipations of September 29; and they naturally wanted to secure the independent judgment of other generals about the military situation. Erzberger had already urged this in early October, though the matter was dropped when Ludendorff threatened resignation.[22] The inevitable conflict between the government and the general came to a head when the Supreme Command issued an army order on October 24 denouncing the

[20] This remarkable man largely composed Max's *Memoirs* for the prince. He secured fame as an educator in the 1920's while headmaster of the Salem school, and opened a boarding school in Scotland after the Nazi accession to power.

[21] Prince Max, *Memoirs*, Engl. edition, II, 163.

[22] *Amtliche Urkunden*, pp. 77 and 92. (Meetings on Oct. 6, and 10, 1918.)

terms of Wilson's third note which had arrived that same day. This order was a flat violation of the terms of the October 21 compromise. The government now induced the Emperor to fire Ludendorff (October 26), while skillfully keeping the popular hero Hindenburg in his post. The retention of the Field Marshal did much to allay popular anxieties at a time when psychological shocks had become cumulative for the German people. General Wilhelm Groener was appointed Ludendorff's successor. The change in the Supreme Command was expected to convince the Entente countries that the power of the military clique had been broken at last.[23]

Erzberger approved of the explicit acceptance of the Fourteen Points, of the evacuation of the occupied territories, and of the abandonment of submarine warfare. He proved adamant, however, on one matter demanded by Wilson (in veiled terms): the Imperial abdication. Erzberger realized, indeed, that a change in the throne was inevitable in the face of the widespread impression—whether true or false—that Germany would secure better peace terms if it chased the Emperor away; but he felt that he was precluded by his oath as *Staatssekretär* from applying direct pressure to achieve this result.[24] The National Liberal Party urged Erzberger in early October (after the arrival of Wilson's first note) to raise the matter himself with the Emperor, but he replied that he was unable to take responsibility for such a step.[25] He hoped that William would recognize the inevitable by himself, but thought it undignified for the German people to cast mud in time of trouble upon the man they had adored in happier times. Erzberger took refuge in the view that Wilson had not explicitly demanded abdication. The American President had only asked for securities against autocratic influences; these securities had been provided by the far-reaching constitutional changes recently accepted by the *Reichstag*. Erzberger summarized his objections to putting pressure on the Emperor to abdicate in a letter to Pacelli on October 31, 1918:

> The considerations speaking against an abdication at this moment are that the present governing majority would be seriously shaken [with many Zentrum members sharing Erzberger's scruples]; that there would be difficulties about a new oath of loyalty for the army; and that the throne would presumably pass to the oldest son of the Crown Prince [the Crown Prince himself was obviously impossible], a boy of only twelve years. The near-

[23] On Ludendorff's dismissal, see Max, *Erinnerungen*, Pt. III, Ch. VIII.

[24] Richthofen in *Erzberger Heft*, p. 689. On Erzberger's attitude towards the Imperial question, see Bachem, *Zentrumspartei*, IX, 483–85.

[25] Erwin Gugelmeier, *Das Schwarze Jahr (1917–1918). Erlebtes aus dem letzten Kriegsjahr* (Freiburg, 1926), p. 94.

est Prussian agnate, Prince Eitel Friedrich, the oldest brother of the Crown Prince, would presumably become Regent though he is a political cipher. The abdication would weaken Germany by leading to deep internal friction. For these reasons I share the view of all the members of the government that an abdication would at this moment harm, not help, Germany. The abdication must be a matter for the voluntary decision of the Emperor and not the result of popular pressure upon him. The latter becomes conceivable only if there were incontrovertible proof that Germany could secure a better peace without the Emperor.[26]

Erzberger shares responsibility for the serious results which flowed from the government's failure to force William's abdication. An abdication in mid-October probably would have saved the monarchy, thus preserving the external continuity of Germany's constitutional development. It would have improved her negotiating position abroad by advertising the fundamental nature of Germany's political changes. Above all it would have convinced the German masses themselves of the reality and extent of those changes, thereby making a revolution unnecessary. Max's policy of peace and democratization expressed everything that the majority of the German people really wanted; the elections of January 1919 were to show that there was no majority for the further step to socialism. The government could not tell the masses how near the negotiations with Wilson had brought the country to an armistice, for fear of creating the impression of weakness abroad; but it ought to have done a better public-relations job in convincing the masses that all their political demands at home had been met, thereby making revolutionary violence senseless. The extent of the changes achieved was concealed by Max's princely status, a poor symbol for democratization; by the unspectacular nature of the constitutional legislation; and above all by the absence of any great dramatic development (such as the Imperial abdication would have been) that could capture the popular imagination. The revolution came in November because many people, headed by the mutinous sailors, mistakenly believed that Germany was still ruled by the old clique that had throughout the war opposed both democratic advances in Prussia and a Wilsonian peace of reconciliation.[27]

[26] Erzberger to Pacelli, Oct. 31, 1918, *Erzberger Papers,* File 56. See also Max, *op.cit.,* p. 540, on Erzberger's attitude during the October 31 Cabinet meeting. Erzberger called for counterpropaganda against the abdication agitation, and emphasized the monarchical sentiments of the Christian Trade Unions, pp. 540, 549. A year later Erzberger, when Finance Minister, helped the Emperor financially by agreeing to pay 40 million marks for two Hohenzollern palaces. William used the money to buy his Doorn estate. Rudolf Nadolny, *Mein Beitrag* (Wiesbaden, 1955), p. 70.

[27] The best statement of this theme is in Rosenberg, *Entstehung,* Ch. VII.

Erzberger experienced the saddest days of his personal life shortly after joining the government. His only son, Oskar, had finished his high-school education in June 1918, with special distinction in history and mathematics. He showed many of his father's extraordinary qualities. Oskar entered the army in mid-summer and was sent to an officers' training school at Karlsruhe in early October. Most of his class came down with influenza a few days later, and Oskar's case was so serious that the doctors summoned Erzberger on October 14. He left Berlin while the Cabinet deliberated on Germany's third vote to Wilson. Erzberger found his son barely conscious when he arrived, and Oskar died in his father's presence on October 16. Erzberger's official duties did not allow for any period of mourning. The most tragic days of his political life were to follow immediately upon this personal tragedy.[28]

Erzberger's Selection as Armistice Commissioner

Erzberger was outraged by the mutiny of the German sailors in early November. His patriotic nature could not understand how sailors could refuse to do their duty while the war was still going on. The Cabinet sent Haussmann, the Progressive leader, to Kiel to calm the mutineers; Erzberger would have preferred sending troops—if reliable troops had been available—to crush them without mercy. He saw clearly that Germany's prospects of securing a peace based upon the Fourteen Points rather than unconditional surrender were being undermined by indiscipline. Haussmann, despite assistance from the Socialist Noske, could not stop the spread of the disorders throughout Germany. Erzberger showed his mettle by opposing a general amnesty for the sailors when this came up for Cabinet discussion on November 5.[29]

Haussmann's mission to Kiel was to have fateful personal consequences for Erzberger, for Haussmann had been in charge of armistice preparations for the government. This made him the natural man for serving as the civilian member of the Armistice Commission which was preparing to go to the headquarters of Marshal Foch. But Haussmann returned to Berlin from his Kiel negotiations on November 5 in a state of complete physical and nervous exhaustion, obviously unfit to assume the strenuous job of Armistice Commissioner. The extension of the

[28] Erzberger, *Erlebnisse*, p. 323. Hammer, *Erzberger*, p. 98.
[29] Max, *op.cit.*, p. 586; H. Müller, *Die November-Revolution* (Berlin, 1928), p. 25. Some of the mutineers considered Erzberger a hero. A naval officer on the battleship *Thüringen* was puzzled by the demands of the sailors, and asked them, "What do you really want?" receiving as a reply, "We want Erzberger." F. Fickentscher, "Die Wahrheit über den Zusammenbruch der Marine," in *Politische und Militärische Zeitfragen*, No. 29 (Berlin, 1920), p. 23.

naval mutiny into a nationwide revolutionary movement during the first November days made the early completion of an armistice imperative. General Groener reported in this sense to the Cabinet on November 6, and he was probably the first who suggested Erzberger's appointment in place of Haussmann. Erzberger noted in his diary that same evening about the Cabinet session:

> There was complete agreement, after extensive reports on the situation by the Chancellor and the First Quartermaster [General Groener] that a German armistice delegation must leave for the west the very same day. The negotiations must start Friday morning [November 8] at the latest. In case we do not have a reply from Wilson by that time [on making arrangements for the reception of a German commission] our delegation must raise the white flag in order to secure an armistice or if necessary even a capitulation.[30]

Prince Max then suggested to the Cabinet that Erzberger replace Haussmann as governmental representative on the Armistice Commission. Max's suggestion came as a complete surprise to all members of the Cabinet and a most unwelcome one for Erzberger. He realized that Marshal Foch would set very stiff conditions, and that his signature under them would compromise his entire political future. Erzberger's reluctance to accept the onerous task, which is universally attested by his Cabinet colleagues, was undoubtedly sincere. But they all appealed to his patriotism, with his Zentrum friends Gröber and Trimborn applying the strongest pressure. They both declared themselves too old and exhausted to take the strenuous trip through the enemy lines; whereas Erzberger was still a young and vigorous man. Erzberger at last agreed to accept the appointment. His acceptance of a politically suicidal mission speaks well for his willingness to place his duty to Germany above purely personal considerations. He thought that his championship of the Peace Resolution might make him especially *persona grata* to the Entente, though this was to prove an illusion.[31]

[30] Erzberger's detailed 91-page report in diary form, for the days Nov. 6–13, 1918, is in *Erzberger Papers*, File 48. It served as the basis for Ch. XXIII of the *Erlebnisse*. Henceforth referred to as *Armistice Report*.

[31] On Erzberger's appointment, see the excellent summary of the evidence in Bachem, *Zentrumspartei*, IX, 456–67, which prints much of the primary evidence. The main sources are Erzberger's *Erlebnisse*, pp. 325–26; Max, *op.cit.*, p. 594; Payer, *op.cit.*, p. 157; Haussmann, *Schlaglichter*, p. 264; an article by Dr. Arnold Brecht, who had drawn up the protocol of the November 6 Cabinet session, in *Berliner Tageblatt*, Sept. 13, 1921; an anonymous article in the *Vossische Zeitung*, Sept. 12, 1921, purporting to express Erzberger's own view; and two letters written in 1931 by Generals Groener and Haeften to Karl Bachem. For an example of the frequent charge that Erzberger pushed himself to become armistice commissioner, see Bülow, *Denkwürdigkeiten*, I, 357. Gündell's account in the *Militärwochenblatt*, November 5, 1921, unconvincingly challenges the accuracy of Erzberger's account.

Erzberger's appointment was made at noon on November 6, and he prepared to leave for Spa (the seat of the Supreme Command) a few hours later. The arrival of Wilson's fourth note in the course of that afternoon ended the thought of raising the white flag. It stated "that Marshall Foch has been authorized by the government of the United States and the Allied governments to receive properly accredited representatives of the German government, and to communicate to them the terms of an armistice." [32] The Entente Powers, moreover, declared their acceptance of the Fourteen Points (with two exceptions) as the basis for peace. This greatly relieved Erzberger. His only instructions from Prince Max were that any armistice, however harsh, must be accepted in view of Germany's desperate situation. Max advised Erzberger to take with him Count Brockdorff-Rantzau, German ambassador to Copenhagen, as Foreign Office representative, but the difficulties of wartime transportation, and the urgent necessity of a speedy departure, made this impossible. Erzberger then talked over alternative candidates with Solf, the Foreign Secretary, and settled upon his old friend Count Alfred Oberndorff, the wartime ambassador to Bulgaria. [33]

Before leaving for Spa, Erzberger still needed formal credentials from the Chancellor enabling him to sign the armistice for the government. He telephoned the Chancellery at 3:00 p.m. to ask when the proper documents would be ready—there were to be two, as will be explained later—but was referred to Kriege, the head of the Legal Section of the Foreign Office. Erzberger then telephoned Kriege, who

was deeply hurt that he had not been consulted during the earlier discussions [about Erzberger's appointment]. He claimed he was completely out of the picture and was presently engaged in a dispute with the head of the Political Section. The entire course of world history knew no precedents for making out the kind of document that was required (*Eine solche Urkunde sei bisher in der Weltgeschichte noch nicht ausgestellt worden*) [i.e. a Foreign Office authorization to sign a military armistice]. Erzberger replied: There were no precedents for a World War in the Foreign Office files either. He must have the documents before his departure, the train was leaving at 5:05 p.m. Kriege agreed in principle to get the documents ready. [34]

When Erzberger arrived at the railroad station at 5:00 he found neither Count Oberndorff nor the necessary documents. The former arrived ten minutes, the latter fifteen minutes, late. As soon as the train

[32] Quoted in Rudin, *Armistice,* p. 322.
[33] *Armistice Report* (Nov. 6).
[34] *ibid.* (Nov. 6).

left the station, Erzberger, in his other role, that of propaganda chief, began to dictate directions to the *Zentrale für Heimatdienst* on how the press should deal with Wilson's last note. He emphasized the mutual acceptance of the Fourteen Points (with two exceptions) as constituting a pre-armistice contract, and asserted that this refuted the widespread notion that peace terms could be improved if the Emperor should abdicate. Erzberger thus defended his Emperor to the last. He then had a late supper with General Groener (who was returning to Spa on the same train) to discuss the general situation, and retired early for his last continuous night's sleep for several days.[35]

Erzberger arrived at Spa on the morning of Thursday, November 7. He immediately conferred with Admiral von Hintze, who had become Foreign Office liaison officer to the Supreme Command after being replaced as Foreign Secretary by Solf in early October. Hintze advised Erzberger to put himself at the head of the Armistice Commission—at the moment he was only the governmental representative on it—replacing as Chairman General von Gündell, the representative of the Supreme Command. Erzberger accepted this advice, which was immediately endorsed over the telephone by Prince Max at Berlin.[36]

The reason why Erzberger replaced Gündell—a step which was to expose him to much odium and ridicule from his enemies—has a somewhat complicated history, important both because it was to lead to many legends and to the novel historical fact that a military armistice was negotiated and signed by a civilian. It has been argued by critics of the German military tradition that the use of a civilian was the result of a militarist maneuver designed to create a scapegoat so that the Supreme Command could escape responsibility for Germany's defeat. This was the effect rather than the intention of Hintze's advice. Erzberger's signature was to become a chief exhibit of the so-called "stab-in-the-back" legend.

The actual explanation of the primacy of a civilian in completing the armistice is quite different. The Supreme Command had appointed an Armistice Commission under General Gündell in early October, at a time when Ludendorff mistakenly believed that his panicky armistice request would bring results immediately. We have seen that Ludendorff soon repented of his panic and then aimed at frustrating the negotiations with Wilson, a course that led to his dismissal. The government continued to distrust the Supreme Command even under Groener and feared that a purely military delegation sent to Foch might behave in-

[35] *ibid.* (Nov. 6).
[36] *ibid.* (Nov. 7).

transigently in order to sabotage negotiations. To prevent this, Erz-berger had won support at a cabinet meeting, on November 2, for the idea that a civilian *Staatssekretär* should accompany the military dele-gation, with Haussmann being the natural choice. The initiative for civilian participation in the Armistice Commission came, therefore, from the government rather than the Supreme Command.[37]

One other consideration played a decisive role in the attitude of both soldiers and civilians towards Erzberger's appointment. They both feared that the Entente Powers might refuse an armistice altogether, and they felt that the Entente crusade against Prussian militarism might make them unwilling to negotiate with a member of the German offi-cer corps. They attached great importance to a report sent to the Su-preme Command by a Bern agent on October 25, 1918, concerning the Allied plans of dealing with Germany. The crucial section read as follows:

A discussion concerning armistice terms to be presented to Germany is taking place at this moment at French military headquarters between Haig, Pershing, and Foch. It is not yet completed, but the following con-ditions have been formulated: (1) Strict rejection of any negotiations with Ludendorff or another representative of the Supreme Command. But willingness to negotiate with a commission selected by the *Reichstag* for this purpose [four other conditions follow].[38]

[37] Gordon Craig, in his excellent book on *The Politics of the Prussian Army 1640–1945* (New York, 1956), p. 347, argues that Groener was anxious to leave the signature of the armistice to the civilians in order, in his own words, to "keep our weapons clean and the General Staff unburdened for the future." Wilhelm Groener, *Lebenserinnerun-gen* (Göttingen, 1957), p. 466. But Groener's view may very well be an *ex post facto* contemplation. The initiative of the government in appointing a civilian to the Armi-stice Commission, and the fear that the Entente might not negotiate with a soldier (both discussed below), were the primary facts in November 1918. It is possible, but not certain, that the military desire to "pass the buck" also played a significant role already at the time. Walter Obkircher, *General Erich von Gündell* (Hamburg, 1939), p. 309, gives some support to the "passing the buck" theory. Gündell, noting in his diary his removal from the commission November 7, added "Personally I prefer this solution. It may perhaps have the additional advantage of giving the government the responsi-bility." Lersner, Foreign Office representative along with Hintze, is quoted on p. 310 as saying many years later that he deliberately wanted to place the responsibility upon the government and not the army. Erzberger advocated the membership of a civilian (Haussmann) on the Commission as early as November 2. *Amtliche Urkunden*, p. 237.

[38] *Amtliche Urkunden*, p. 230. Hintze telegraphed the full text to the Foreign Office on Oct. 30, 1918. Cf. also the sentence in Wilson's third note to Germany, Oct. 23, 1918. "If it [the U.S.] must deal with the military masters and the monarchical autocrats of Germany . . . it must demand, not peace negotiations, but surrender." The text is con-veniently available in Rudin, *op.cit.*, p. 173. The October 25 telegram referred to the Senlis conference that same day, and it was quite accurate in its account of the armistice conditions, as formally proposed by Foch to Clemenceau on October 26. But Foch's proposals do not include any refusal to deal with the German military, the point that was to have such crucial consequences. On the Senlis conference and Foch's report, see Rudin, *Armistice*, pp. 177–81.

Hintze had sent this report to Berlin on October 30, where it had made a considerable impression though it did not immediately lead to the replacement of General Gündell. But it had led to Erzberger being given two authorizations on November 6—one to act as a member of the Armistice Commission under Gündell, the other giving him blanket authority to place himself at the head of the Armistice Commission. A final decision was evidently postponed until Erzberger could judge the latest information available at Spa. Hintze convinced him that Gündell —or indeed any soldier—would make an unfavorable impression upon Foch, and Erzberger was resolved to take no unnecessary chances with the coming negotiations.[39] It is immaterial whether he was right or wrong in his belief that the Entente would negotiate only with a civilian. The important point is that this was the paramount consideration in his mind and in that of the soldiers. Erzberger believed until the time of his death that the Entente would have refused to deal with a soldier at the head of the Armistice Commission. This belief added to his consciousness that he had performed an onerous duty patriotically and well.[40]

Erzberger found at Spa that a dozen officers had prepared themselves to accompany the armistice delegation to Foch's headquarters. He believed that it was inadvisable to take such a large group in view of Entente hostility to the German officer class, and he resolved to take only two: General Detlev von Winterfeldt, a prewar military attaché at Paris, and Captain Vanselow, a naval officer of exceptional ability. Erzberger then conferred briefly with Hindenburg, Groener, Hintze, and Admiral Scheer. He gives the following account:

> Hindenburg told me that this must be the first time that politicians rather than soldiers negotiate an armistice. But he agreed with this entirely, especially since the Supreme Command no longer issued political directives. The army required an armistice above all else. He said good-bye with the following words: "May God travel with you, and see that you succeed in attaining the best that can still be secured for our Fatherland." [41]

The Compiègne Negotiations

The Armistice Commission, composed of Erzberger, Oberndorff, Winterfeldt, and Vanselow, left Spa and headed for the front in several automobiles around noon on November 7. The first car (in which

[39] Erzberger, *Erlebnisse,* pp. 326–27.
[40] See article in *Vossische Zeitung,* Sept. 12, 1921, quoted in Bachem, *Zentrumspartei,* IX, 461–62.
[41] Erzberger, *Erlebnisse,* p. 327.

Erzberger sat with Oberndorff) soon had a serious accident: it failed
to make a sharp curve and smashed into a house, whereupon the second
car hit the rear end of the first. The street was littered with glass and
both automobiles were totally disabled. Erzberger and Oberndorff
miraculously escaped injury. Oberndorff spoke of the accident as an
"unfavorable omen"; Erzberger replied with the German proverb,
"Broken glass brings good luck." The journey was continued in the
three remaining cars. Progress was slowed since the roads were filled
with endless columns of retreating German troops. Erzberger admired
their constancy in the face of the overwhelming Allied superiority. Arrangements had been made with Foch's headquarters for a cease-fire in
the front sector where the delegation was to cross the German lines.
Erzberger placed a big white flag on the hood of the first car and secured a trumpeteer from the nearest regiment to herald his arrival to
the French. The last German soldier whom Erzberger saw turned out
to be a fellow-Swabian, who asked in his provincial dialect: "Where
are you going?" Erzberger replied, "To conclude an armistice." The
Swabian replied incredulously, "You really think the two of you can do
that? (*Das werdet ihr zwei gerade fertig bringen?*)." [42] Erzberger's
diary records his thoughts when crossing the German lines on Thursday, November 7, at 9:20 p.m.:

> Three weeks ago I travelled to Karlsruhe to the death-bed of my only
> son. My wife and daughter were at the same time seriously ill with the
> grippe in Berlin. My feelings on the journey to Karlsruhe, which any
> father can readily understand, were no more depressed and painful than
> my feelings at the present moment. The words of the Schumann song
> about *The Two Grenadiers* went through my head.[43]

The German delegation was courteously received by the French, who
supplied new automobiles for the further journey, this time through
territory devastated by the fighting and by the German retreat. Supper
was served at one in the morning at an isolated farmhouse that served
as the headquarters for an army command. The Germans were transferred to a railroad car a few hours later which then carried them with
blinds turned down to an undisclosed destination, which turned out
to be the Forest of Compiègne. The train stopped there in the early

---

[42] *ibid.,* pp. 328–29.
[43] *Armistice Report* (Nov. 7). Erzberger quotes the song: "Nach Frankreich zogen
zwei Grenadier, die waren in Russland gefangen, Und als sie kamen ins deutsche Quar-
tier, da liessen die Köpfe sie hangen. Da hörten sie beide die traurige Mär, dass Frankreich verloren gegangen, Besiegt und geschlagen das tapfere Heer, und der Kaiser, der
Kaiser gefangen!"

morning and Erzberger found a similar special train standing on some tracks about a hundred yards away.[44]

The other train turned out to be the headquarters of Marshal Foch. Negotiations started at 10:00 a.m., Friday, November 8—exactly the time that Groener and Max had demanded at Berlin two days previously. Marshal Foch, accompanied by General Weygand, his Chief of Staff, and two senior British Naval Officers, Admiral Wemyss and Admiral Hope, gave the Germans a frosty reception with the intention of raising their fears that an armistice might not be granted. Erzberger handed his credentials for signing an armistice "subject to the approval of the Chancellor," to the Allied officers, who then went into an adjoining room to examine them carefully while the Germans cooled their heels. Marshal Foch soon returned and opened formal proceedings with the questions: "What brings these gentlemen here? What do you wish of me?" Erzberger answered that he awaited proposals for an armistice. "I have no proposals to make," Foch stated. This was his way of saying that he would not offer proposals that were subject to negotiations, but only terms that must be accepted without further ado. Erzberger, fearing at first an Entente refusal to negotiate altogether, had Oberndorff read the text of Wilson's fourth note, with its concluding sentence, which stated that Foch had been authorized to communicate armistice terms to a German delegation. Foch then relented and ordered Weygand to read the terms that had been worked out at inter-allied conferences between November 1 and 4.[45] The Germans were asked to accept the terms within seventy-two hours. They requested facilities for telegraphic communication with Spa and Berlin, which were readily granted. Foch declared that negotiations concerning the terms were impossible since he was bound by instructions from the various Allied governments, but he declared that informational conversations could be held if requested by the German delegation and that he was willing to receive written communications. Erzberger and his colleagues then withdrew to study the conditions in detail and to plan strategy for securing possible modifications.[46]

[44] Erzberger, *Erlebnisse*, pp. 329–30.

[45] The Allied conferences of Nov. 1–4, 1918, are summarized in Rudin, *Armistice,* Ch. xii.

[46] On the scene and negotiations at Compiègne, see Erzberger, *Erlebnisse,* Ch. xiii; F. Foch, *Memoirs* (New York, 1931), Ch. xiv; T. Plivier, "Im Walde von Compiègne," in *Neue Deutsche Blätter,* 1 (Nov.–Dec. 1933), 145–56, 219–29; P. C. Ettighoffer, *Moskau, Compiègne, Versailles* (Gütersloh, 1936), Pt. ii; W. Wemyss, *Lord Wester Wemyss* (London, 1935), pp. 389–95; Jules Sauerwein, "Le Marèchal Foch raconte l'armistice," in *Le Matin,* Nov. 8, 1920. An excellent summary of the published material is Rudin, *Armistice,* Ch. xv. It must be supplemented by Erzberger's *Armistice Report* cited above.

The terms demanded by the Entente Powers were exceedingly stiff, being aimed at making a resumption of hostilities impossible. The main items were (the numbers refer to the armistice text):

2. German evacuation of Belgium, France, and Alsace within 14 days, all troops remaining behind to become prisoners of war.

4. Immediate surrender of 5,000 guns, 30,000 machine guns, 3,000 minethrowers, and 2,000 airplanes.

5. German evacuation of the entire left bank of the Rhine, as well as bridgeheads opposite Mainz, Koblenz, and Cologne, within 25 days. A neutralized zone 30–40 kilometers broad to be created on the right bank of the Rhine.

7. Surrender within 14 days of 5,000 locomotives, 150,000 railroad cars, and 10,000 trucks.

9. Immediate repatriation, without reciprocity, of Allied prisoners of war.

12–14. Withdrawal of Germany's eastern armies behind the prewar frontiers, meaning the evacuation of the Baltic Countries, Poland, the Ukraine, and Rumania.

15. Annulment of the Treaties of Brest-Litovsk, Bucharest, and of the Supplementary Treaties.

17. Unconditional surrender of the German troops in East Africa.

22–23. Immediate surrender at allied ports of 160 submarines, 6 battle cruisers, and 50 destroyers.

26. The Allied maritime blockade of Germany to continue.

34. The armistice to be limited to 30 days, but with the possibility of extension.[47]

Erzberger and his colleagues felt that these terms were not only very onerous but in some instances literally incapable of being fulfilled, thus opening the way for still further extortions on the pretext of violation of the terms. They took some comfort in the fact that Foch had prohibited publication, thus allowing modifications without Entente loss of face. The text was sent by courier to the Supreme Command at Spa while the main points were sent by wireless to allow early transmission to Berlin, where the Chancellor would have to give his approval before Erzberger's credentials allowed him to sign. Erzberger's subordinates conferred with Allied officers during the next two days to see what concessions could be obtained. The two delegation heads, Foch and

---

[47] The terms can best be studied in the official German publication, *Der Waffenstillstand. Das Dokumentenmaterial der Waffenstillstandsverhandlungen,* edited by E. Marhefka, 3 vols. (Berlin, 1928). Vol. I, pp. 22–57, gives in parallel columns the Allied proposals, the German replies, the Allied counter-replies, and the final texts, thus facilitating the study of the modifications attained by Erzberger.

Erzberger, did not personally participate in these discussions. Oberndorff and Winterfeldt saw Weygand about the military terms and Vanselow saw the British sailors about the naval terms. The Germans concentrated their efforts upon extending the brief deadlines allowed for the evacuations, in view of the millions of men who might otherwise become prisoners; the elimination of the demilitarized zone on the right bank of the Rhine, since the latter left the way open for a Bolshevik reign of terror by denuding the Ruhr industrial districts of troops; an honorable surrender in East Africa; a scaling down of the demand for rolling stock to prevent a complete paralysis of German economic life; and above all a lifting of the Allied blockade in order to end the semi-starvation conditions prevailing in Germany.[48] These were the very points on which the Supreme Command urged Erzberger to secure revisions in a telegram that arrived only on the evening of November 10, though Hindenburg's telegram concluded: "The armistice must be signed even if these modifications cannot be attained."[49]

The main argument used to secure an improvement in the armistice was stated by Count Oberndorff to General Weygand when discussing the questions of evacuation deadlines, the continued blockade, and the surrender of rolling stock:

> I told the general that Germany, if driven to despair, would oscillate between two extremes. Either there would be a revival of bellicose passions leading to a resolute fight to the finish, whose result could not be foreseen; or Bolshevism would triumph and turn the country into a chaos like Russia's. In case of renewed fighting France risked the further devastation of her countryside, in case of Bolshevism the danger of contagion and the loss of Germany's solvency for payment of reparations. It seemed to me that France had a real interest in preventing the triumph of Bolshevism in Germany. But this required an orderly withdrawal of the German troops and a guarantee of adequate food supplies for the German population. The contemplated evacuation deadlines and the simultaneous surrender of all of our rolling stock made both of these protections against Bolshevism completely impossible.[50]

This argument made little impression upon the Entente officers, many of whom genuinely believed that the German armistice request was a clever trap to allow the German armies to withdraw under cover of a truce from their over-extended lines, in order to resume fighting under better auspices upon Germany's frontiers. They felt that the se-

[48] Erzberger, *Erlebnisse*, pp. 331–34. Detailed reports on all the conferences can be found in *Armistice Report*, entries of Nov. 8, 9, and 10.
[49] *Amtliche Urkunden*, p. 263.
[50] *Armistice Report* (Nov. 8).

vere military and naval terms were necessary to prevent a resumption of hostilities. They rightly doubted that Bolshevism could win in Germany, and they refused to believe that it could constitute a danger to their own victorious countries.

The most recent news from Germany also made them discount the possibility of a renewed outburst of military passions. The revolutionary movement sparked by the naval mutiny—an act of criminal folly in its effects upon Erzberger's negotiating position—was spreading like wildfire through Germany. The Independent Socialist Eisner overthrew the Bavarian monarchy on November 7 and threatened to break up the unity of Germany if peace was not made immediately. The leaders of the Majority Socialists, fearing loss of influence among the masses due to competition from the Independents, withdrew from Max's cabinet on November 8, and brought it to a fall. A provisional government was formed under Ebert and Haase the next day, composed exclusively of Socialists. Scheidemann proclaimed the German Republic on November 9 and the Emperor's withdrawal to Holland came a few hours later. Germany was soon dotted with Workers' and Soldiers' Councils that arrogated to themselves governmental responsibility. The authority of the Berlin government was challenged by both Spartacist and separatist forces, the big cities were terrorized by lazy and vicious mobs, and hunger was stalking the land. No one could reasonably expect success in foreign negotiations under these conditions of total internal collapse.

Erzberger heard only general rumors of these developments while he was isolated in the Forest of Compiègne. He did not know whether he was representing an Empire or a Republic, and there was some doubt about the validity of his credentials now that Ebert had replaced Max as Chancellor.[51] But he resolved, in view of Germany's desperate need, to complete the armistice without attending to technicalities. The discussions with Weygand and Hope showed that minor improvements in the terms were possible despite Foch's initial intransigence. An open despatch—not in cipher—arrived in the late evening of November 10, authorizing Erzberger to sign the armistice as originally proposed. Erzberger was angered at the careless omission of cipher. He wrote:

> The result of two days of negotiations was seriously compromised. The despatch had been signed *"Reichskanzler Schluss"* (Chancellor period.)

[51] The Entente was also wondering whether Erzberger's signature still had any value. See H. Mordacq, *L'Armistice* (Paris, 1937), pp. 17–18, on the doubts of Clemenceau and Foch; Wemyss, *Wemyss,* pp. 392–93, on those of the British admiral.

The French interpreter asked if Schluss was the name of the new Chancellor and who this gentleman might be; he was completely unknown to both the French Supreme Command and the government in Paris. I enlightened him that "Schluss" at the end of the telegram meant "period." [52]

The incident reveals the Entente bewilderment at German developments.

Erzberger asked for another session with Marshal Foch for 2:15 a.m., November 11, in order to beat the 11:00 a.m. deadline set three days previously. He fought valiantly for final modifications of the terms though the written German counter-suggestions (delivered by Oberndorff to Weygand in the early afternoon of November 9) had received a generally negative reply from Foch. Erzberger again raised the question of the blockade, and he scored the triumph—later to prove hollow —of the insertion of a sentence that "The Allies and the United States contemplate the provisioning of Germany during the armistice as shall be found necessary" (Art. 26). Erzberger and his colleagues secured several other improvements that demonstrate his negotiating tenacity: the number of machine guns to be surrendered was scaled down from 30,000 to 25,000, of airplanes from 2,000 to 1,700; the neutral zone on the right bank of the Rhine was reduced from 30–40 kilometers to 10; the evacuation deadline of the Rhineland was extended by six days from 25 to 31; the number of trucks to be surrendered was halved from 10,000 to 5,000; the surrender deadline was extended from 15 to 36 days, thus making them available for the crucial period of the German retreat; the evacuation of German troops from the eastern territories was not to be immediate but to occur only "as soon as the Allies think the moment suitable, having regard to the internal situation of these territories" (Art. 12), thus preventing the Bolsheviks from filling the vacuum; the unconditional surrender of the East African troops was changed into "evacuation within a period specified by the allies" (Art. 17); and the period of the armistice was extended from 30 to 36 days.

Erzberger also succeeded in securing specific promises on two points of vital importance to the population of the occupied Rhineland. The administrative unity between the left and right bank was to be maintained, thus theoretically barring Allied encouragement of Rhenish separatism. The prosecution of German industrialists for their participation in the plunder of machines from German-occupied Belgium and northern France was prohibited. An agreement was reached to set up a joint Armistice Commission with headquarters at Spa to supervise the implementation of the terms. The conference that brought

[52] Erzberger, *Erlebnisse,* p. 335.

these results lasted for nearly three hours until 5:00 a.m. Then the signatures were affixed to the armistice document, and World War One was over.[53]

Before leaving Foch, Erzberger read a declaration which asserted Germany's intention to carry out the onerous terms, while protesting against their severity and warning that Germany might be unable to keep her word:

> The German government will, of course, seek to fulfill the obligations imposed upon it with all the resources at its command. . . . But it wants to make it clear that the brief evacuation deadlines as well as the surrender of much rolling stock threatens to create a situation where the fulfillment of some of the conditions may prove impossible without any bad faith on the part of the German government or people.
>
> The German delegates . . . also wish to reemphasize their view that the consummation of this armistice must throw the German people into anarchy and famine. They had a right to expect conditions which, while guaranteeing the full military security of our enemies, would at least end the suffering of non-combatant women and children.
>
> The German people, who stood steadfast against a world of enemies for fifty months, will preserve their freedom and unity no matter how great the external pressure. A nation of seventy millions can suffer but it cannot die.

This proud language, more suitable to be cheered at German beer-tables than to promote the implementation of the armistice, was requited by Marshal Foch with a laconic "Très bien." [54] It shows, incidentally, how ridiculous Erzberger's Right-wing enemies were in charging him with lack of patriotic feeling or of signing the armistice with a light heart.

The Return to Berlin

The German delegation returned to Spa accompanied by the cheers and curses of the French and Belgian populations who were overjoyed

---

[53] A full protocol of the November 11, 1918 session is in Marhefka, *op.cit.,* pp. 61–73. Erzberger summarized the improvements achieved by himself in *Erlebnisse,* pp. 336–38. They appear most clearly in Marhefka, *op.cit.,* pp. 22–57.

[54] Erzberger's statement to Foch is printed in Marhefka, *op.cit.,* pp. 72–73. It was first suggested by him in a telegram to the Supreme Command on November 8 when transmitting the armistice terms, and was authorized in the November 10 telegram signed *Reichskanzler. ibid.,* pp. 58–60. The latter telegram was really composed by the Supreme Command and approved by Ebert only *ex post facto. Erlebnisse,* p. 338. The new Cabinet had met with party leaders on November 10, 1918, discussed the terms cabled by Erzberger, and had seen no alternative to acceptance. R. Künzer, "Die Aussenpolitik des Zentrums," in *Nationale Arbeit,* edited by K. A. Schulte, (Berlin, 1929), p. 84, citing the unpublished memoirs of Fehrenbach.

by the completion of the armistice but in no mood to forgive and forget. Erzberger arrived at Supreme Headquarters on the morning of November 12. He was congratulated by Hindenburg and Groener for having secured modifications in Foch's original terms that exceeded their expectations. The Field Marshal thanked Erzberger "for the extremely valuable services he had rendered to the Fatherland," a statement in notable contrast to Hindenburg's later identification with the "stab-in-the-back" legend. Erzberger then appointed the German section of the International Armistice Commission and placed his colleague General Winterfeldt at its head.[55]

Conditions at Spa were, meanwhile, nearly as chaotic as they were throughout revolutionary Germany. Erzberger reports in his *Erlebnisse:*

> A Workers' and Soldiers' Council had been formed; there had been a real danger that it would arrest the Supreme Command; mobs tore the epaulets from the shoulders of officers. I could see myself that soldiers no longer saluted officers and that all the automobiles carried red flags. Hindenburg had declared that he placed himself behind the new Ebert government, and he asked me to do the same. . . .
>
> Around one o'clock two delegates of the Hannover Soldiers' and Workers' Council arrived at Spa on a special train. They wanted to go on to Brussels in order to proclaim the world revolution there, and they surprised me with the "absolutely reliable news" that Marshal Foch had been assassinated the previous afternoon. . . . They described the aim of the German Revolution to be the proclamation of Liebknecht as President of the German Republic. This aim had not yet been attained but was expected soon. I persuaded them not to continue their journey to Brussels, where riots were taking place. Since they were in possession of a locomotive and it was imperative for me to get back to Berlin as quickly as possible we arranged to travel together. We left Spa, which was decked in the Belgian national colors, at 4:00 p.m. All the trains that we passed were crowded with soldiers. They sat on the footboards and even on the roofs of the railroad cars, exactly as had happened in Russia [at the time of the revolution].[56]

Erzberger arrived in Berlin in the late afternoon of Wednesday, November 14, exactly a week after his departure for Spa and Compiègne. "Returned to my fatherland, I found it completely transformed. Even my car carried a red flag, which I replaced by Black-Red-Gold." [57] Erzberger was immediately received by the Council of People's Com-

[55] Erzberger, *Erlebnisse*, p. 339.
[56] *ibid.*, pp. 339–40.
[57] Erzberger, *Erlebnisse*, p. 340.

missars (the new Ebert-Haase government) to report on his armistice mission. They thanked him for his services "rendered to the German people in times of exceptional difficulty" and decided to prolong the life of the Armistice Commission. It was assigned the task of implementing the Compiègne terms. Erzberger accepted reappointment as chairman, thereby consenting to serve under the new all-Socialist government which was the product of the revolution. He did this in the hope of helping Ebert to restore orderly conditions at home and to give Germany a government which the Entente powers would accept as negotiating partner in the coming peace discussions.[58]

Erzberger's chairmanship of the Armistice Commission, both at Compiègne and in all the subsequent negotiations, was to prove a terrible liability in his subsequent career. Nationalist and Conservative circles had long hated him as the architect of the Peace Resolution and leader of the Left wing of the Zentrum, and they had openly questioned his patriotism. Their case was now strengthened in the eyes of millions by the popular identification of Erzberger with the very severe armistice terms. The odium directed against Erzberger was magnified by the popular belief that he had intrigued in order to become Armistice Commissioner, had signed everything that Foch had demanded, and had done so in a frivolous spirit untroubled by concern for the national honor. The facts—that he had been pressed into accepting the job by his Cabinet colleagues, that he had secured the maximum modifications attainable from Foch, and that he had finally signed with a heavy heart under the specific instructions of both government and Supreme Command—made little headway in the public mind in the face of the nationalist slanders.

[58] *ibid.*, p. 340. Also *Armistice Report* (Nov. 14).

CHAPTER XII

WEIMAR AND VERSAILLES (NOVEMBER 1918 TO JUNE 1919)

The Winter of 1918–1919

THE Ebert-Haase government, called the Council of Peoples' Commissars, was formed on November 9, 1918, while Erzberger was negotiating with Foch in Compiègne. It was a coalition of Majority and Independent Socialists, and therefore deeply divided from the very beginning. Ebert and his Majority colleagues had long stood on the Right wing of the party, and were primarily reformist democrats who looked upon Socialism as a distant rather than immediate goal. Their immediate concern was to end the existing chaos and danger of a Communist coup by holding early elections for a democratic Constituent Assembly. Haase and his Independent colleagues also favored a Constituent Assembly, but they wanted to postpone elections while using the interval to create a series of Socialist *faits accomplis*. They were embarrassed by being tied to an unruly Left wing that maintained cordial relations with the Communists. The latter used their mob following in Berlin to organize riots and demonstrations that made life unsafe for the members of the Council of Peoples's Commissars. The government was helpless since it lacked any reliable police or body of soldiers that could guarantee its physical safety. The regular army was melting away in a disorderly demobilization. No one knew what the real constellation of public opinion was, with the extreme Leftist elements being believed to be far stronger than they turned out to be in the elections of January 1919.

Ebert, recognizing his weakness in the face of the Communist danger, was eager for support from the Liberal and Zentrum parties. He urged Solf to remain as Foreign Secretary and Erzberger as Armistice Commissioner. He selected the Left Liberal Professor Hugo Preuss to draft a constitution for submission to the future National Assembly. Preuss's draft was, incidentally, to shock the Zentrum by its advocacy of centralization, Church-State separation, and prohibition of confessional schools. Solf, Erzberger, and Preuss all accepted appointment because they knew that Ebert was a man of reliable democratic views who would never countenance a proletarian dictatorship for Germany. Erzberger felt very uneasy about serving under a cabinet in which the Independents carried great weight, but he foresaw that they would soon be forced to choose between breaking with their Left wing or leaving the government. Erzberger was far from sorry when Haase decided upon the latter alternative after less than seven weeks of power.[1]

Erzberger saw two primary tasks confronting Germany upon his return from Compiègne: the restoration of order and the early election of a Constituent Assembly. These were prerequisites both for realizing democratic principles and negotiating with the Entente powers. Erzberger wrote:

> Law and order no longer existed in Berlin. The War Minister, who visited me at my request in my apartment late one evening in civilian clothes, told me that it was impossible to safeguard public safety. I began to organize a small body of reliable troops with the help of a few resolute men. We hopefully waited for the arrival of soldiers loyal to the government. The danger that new riots would lead to a purely Independent or even Communist government was ever-present.[2]

This danger was to exist for another three months until Gustav Noske, newly appointed War Commissar after the Independents left the government, formed the famous Free Corps. These succeeded in disarming the Communist mobs and ending the terror of the street. The Free Corps were soon to prove, however, something of a Frankenstein monster to their Majority Socialist creators. Their bourgeois membership had little enthusiasm for the emerging Weimar Republic, and their suppression of the Spartacists was marred by needless brutality. Their formation has been generally condemned by liberal and democratic historians, but it is doubtful whether Ebert and Noske could have formed any other body of troops that would have smashed the Communists. The formation of a reliable anti-Communist Socialist militia was practically precluded by the long-standing cult of proletarian solidarity.[3]

The revolution had made the Independent Socialist Adolf Hoffmann Minister of Culture. A fanatical atheist, he immediately began to decree the whole Socialist anti-clerical program (separation of Church and State, abolition of confessional schools, etc.). Cardinal Hartmann of

---

[1] Erzberger's activities in the winter of 1918–1919 are covered briefly in his *Erlebnisse*, p. 340. The *Erzberger Papers* begin to fail at this point of the story.

[2] Erzberger, *Erlebnisse*, p. 340. These activities caused Eisner, the Bavarian Independent Premier, to denounce Erzberger as the "fountain of counter-revolution" (along with Solf) at a Premiers' Conference on November 25, 1918. But Ebert defended Erzberger vigorously. W. Ziegler, *Die deutsche Nationalversammlung 1919–1920* (Berlin, 1932), p. 10.

[3] The standard book on the Free Corps movement is Robert Waite, *Vanguard of Nazism* (Cambridge, 1952).

Cologne wrote to Erzberger to express his deep anxiety, and received a reply pledging the Zentrum to fight Hoffmann's schemes. Erzberger said that this could be done only after a Constituent Assembly had restored some kind of order to political life: "The decisive task of the moment is to secure a bourgeois majority for the National Assembly. This goal can be attained if the bourgeois strata of the population pull themselves together."[4] Erzberger wrote the cardinal that he was pressing the government to call early elections (as was finally done on December 16, 1918). Ebert's promise to do so had been the prerequisite of Erzberger's willingness to continue as Armistice Commissioner.

The Zentrum Party found it comparatively easy to adjust its election campaign to the new revolutionary situation. Catholic political thought, though tending to prefer the principle of monarchy to republicanism and opposed to extreme statements of popular sovereignty, was not intrinsically hostile to the parliamentary democratic republic that was Germany's sole alternative to a proletarian dictatorship. Some Catholic sections of the German population, like the Bavarian peasantry, had never pretended much enthusiasm for the Hohenzollern Monarchy. The precipitate flight of the Emperor to Holland had further weakened monarchist sentiment. The traditional Zentrum horror of the Socialists had been much relaxed since Erzberger had formed the Peace Resolution majority in July 1917. The Right wing of the party had now become a small and sullen minority, and it could not offer any real opposition to the policy—advocated by Erzberger—of protecting Catholic interests and Zentrum principles by cooperation with the Majority Socialists. The task of smashing Bolshevism took precedence over monarchist sentiments and the traditional hostility to the Socialists.[5]

Erzberger's preoccupations as Armistice Commissioner prevented his taking a leading role in the electoral battle that ended on January 19, 1919. The Ebert government had introduced a new voting system based upon proportional representation on a regional level to replace the

---

[4] Erzberger to Cardinal Hartmann, November 21, 1918, replying to a letter dated November 18. *Erzberger Papers,* File 45.
[5] For Zentrum acceptance of the Republic, see K. Bachem, *Zentrumspartei,* VIII, 256–62 and F. Sell, *Die Staatspolitik des Zentrums* (Berlin, 1924). Erzberger's part in reorganizing the Zentrum Party in the winter of 1918–1919 is mentioned briefly in Bachem, *Zentrumspartei,* VIII, 253–54. The party secured a national secretariat for the first time, with Erzberger appointing his friend Maximilian Pfeiffer first general secretary in November 1918, a post he retained until his appointment as German Ambassador to Vienna in April 1920. The secretariat set up a speakers' bureau, organized courses in political education, and issued pamphlets and short articles. The latter service was organized by Friedrich Sell, himself an able and prolific pamphleteer. On these party questions see Zentrumspartei, *Offizieller Bericht des 1. Reichsparteitages* (Berlin, 1920), especially pp. 74–82 (report by Dr. Brauns).

286

old system of single-member constituencies. Erzberger received second place on the Württemberg Zentrum list after Gröber, thereby assuring his return to the *Reichstag* without any local campaigning.[6]

Erzberger's main national objective—the prevention of a Marxist majority—was attained when the Majority and Independent Socialists together secured only 45 percent of the vote. The Zentrum secured 20 percent, the Progressives (who renamed themselves Democrats and absorbed the Left wing of the National Liberals) nearly 19 percent, while the two parties identified with the old Imperial order (Conservatives, renamed the German Nationalist People's Party, and the National Liberals, renamed the German People's Party) received less than 15 percent together. It was an auspicious beginning for the new parliamentary system. Erzberger was relieved by the termination of the danger of wild Socialist and anti-clerical experiments. He hoped, on the other hand, that the Majority Socialists, properly tamed by bourgeois coalition partners, should participate in the new government, and resisted the idea of forming an anti-Socialist coalition extending from the Nationalists to the Democrats (which theoretically could have won the support of 55 percent of the Constituent Assembly).

The task of forming a parliamentary Cabinet to replace Ebert's purely provisional government confronted the Assembly when it convened at Weimar (in safety from the Communists that still terrorized Berlin) in early February. At the first meeting of the Zentrum deputies, Erzberger took the initiative in securing the reelection of the old leadership headed by Gröber and Trimborn.[7] The party then voted, 64 to 5 over the opposition of some Bavarians, to enter into a coalition with the Majority Socialists. Erzberger insisted that the fact of a "bourgeois majority" in the elections made a Socialist majority in the new Cabinet unthinkable, and the Zentrum leaders were instructed to be tough in coalition bargaining. They were to insist upon a program of three points: (1) the creation of an army that could break any resistance that the Soldiers' and Workers' Councils might offer to the Constituent Assembly, (2) a constitution under which the rights of the Catholic Church would be safeguarded, and (3) the preservation of the federal structure of Germany in opposition to the Socialist and Democratic demand, headed by Preuss, for the unitary-centralized state. This

---

[6] On the Württemberg elections, see Max Miller, *Eugen Bolz* (Stuttgart, 1951), pp. 101–04.

[7] Mayer-Kaufbeuren was also reelected. The addition of a working class leader was proposed, with Adam Stegerwald, the Christian Trade Union leader, being suggested. But Erzberger vetoed him because of his wartime chauvinism and close association with Walter Rathenau. Becker-Arnsberg was elected instead. Report on Zentrum meeting of Feb. 5, 1919, in *Erzberger Papers*, File 14.

Zentrum program was to be completely achieved by the Weimar Assembly.[8]

Scheidemann became Chancellor after Ebert was elevated to the Presidency on February 11, 1919. He appointed a coalition cabinet of 7 Socialists, 3 Democrats, and 3 Zentrum members (Erzberger, Giesberts, Bell). Brockdorff-Rantzau became a non-party Foreign Minister while Erzberger entered the cabinet as Minister without Portfolio in charge of armistice affairs.

Erzberger wrote a justification of the Zentrum participation in the government in a long letter to Pacelli on February 24, 1919, replying to a specific inquiry:

> The Zentrum is predestined by its entire history to be a party of positive work rather than negative opposition. It cannot refuse to undertake responsible work for the Fatherland in the present period of difficulty. The specific reasons [dictating coalition with the Socialists] were the following: foreign policy considerations require Zentrum participation in the governing coalition. Its participation will impress all the enemy states with the stability of the German government, as it will be supported by more than 75 percent of the National Assembly. Our enemies cannot impose new burdens upon us on the plea that the German government is not strong enough to guarantee the implementation of its pledges. I have been informed by English sources that the entry of the Zentrum into the government will have considerable influence upon the course of the peace negotiations.
>
> To this must be added that the Zentrum can do nothing to champion the rights of the Holy See at the peace conference if it is not a participant in the government.
>
> The domestic reasons are the following: The Cabinet would stand on very precarious foundations if the Zentrum were in opposition. Partisan struggles would increase in vigor, and the country would not quiet down. . . . The National Assembly would soon be reduced to impotence and the nation would become victim to anarchy. The entry of the Zentrum into the government has, on the other hand, already yielded good results. The original constitutional draft, which required the obligatory separation of Church and State in all the federal states, has been modified. The revised draft, which has now been submitted to the National Assembly, contains nothing about the separation of Church and State, while guaranteeing freedom of religious observance. This will give much needed protection to Catholic minorities in predominantly Protestant areas. The original draft also contained a provision in favor of inter-confessional schools (*konfessionslose Simultanschule*) throughout Germany. This has been cancelled in favor of leaving the question up to the individual states.
>
> These two successes must be esteemed all the more since a further political development to the Left must be expected in the near future before we

[8] *Ibid.*

can expect the inevitable return to the Right. Great injury to the Church can be prevented by the Zentrum in this present period of maximum danger. If Church-State separation were once put into effect it would be almost impossible to return to the earlier condition. The Zentrum will, of course, do its best to continue to champion the rights of the Church and the confessional schools in the coming constitutional debates.[9]

Erzberger had reason to look back with satisfaction upon the winter of 1918–1919. The temporary chaos created by the naval mutiny, the revolution, the flight of the Emperor, and the overnight collapse of the entire Imperial regime had been terminated by the election of a democratic parliament that in turn elected a democratic government. His faith in Ebert as the savior of Germany from anarchy and Bolshevism had proved fully justified. The Workers' and Soldiers' Councils had been unable to give Germany orderly administration, and were replaced by the old efficient bureaucracy, subordinated now—in theory at least—to the democratic National Assembly. The Communist mobs had been crushed by the Free Corps—an effective instrument whose ultimate danger was little appreciated. The Courts had resumed their normal functions. Various wild schemes for expropriation of Junker lands and nationalization of key industries, which would have thrown Germany into economic chaos and political civil war, had been averted. The Zentrum Party had rejected a policy of sulking sterility and entered into fruitful cooperation with the Socialists.

The result was to be the Weimar constitution with its realization of the democratic program which Erzberger had advocated for more than a decade. It was achieved without being accompanied by either Socialism (which he distrusted) or anti-clericalism (which he abhorred). Erzberger—along with other Weimar politicians—failed to understand that Germany's democratic foundations remained insecure because of the failure to achieve far-reaching social reforms. The preoccupation with the Communist danger had led to the optimistic view that the pillars of the old Imperial order had accepted the Republic at heart. The old bureaucrats, old soldiers, old judges, old Junkers, and old industrialists retained most of their influence, and their recovery from the shock of November 1918 was bound to lead to a revival of Right-wing intransigence.

Work of the Armistice Commission

Erzberger did not take a prominent part in the constitution-making of the Weimar Assembly. He had never been primarily interested in pure constitutional questions. The Zentrum did not send him into the

[9] Erzberger to Pacelli, Feb. 24, 1919. *Bachem Papers,* File 89.

special Constitutional Committee.[10] His main task throughout the winter and spring was rather the negotiation and implementation of successive armistice agreements. The Armistice Commission which he headed mushroomed by late November into an organization with hundreds of employees engaging in a great variety of tasks. Erzberger maintained over-all direction from his Berlin office.[11]

The implementation of the armistice dealt with such miscellaneous matters as the surrender of military and naval equipment, the return of machines and other objects which the Germans had taken from Belgium and northern France, relations between occupied and unoccupied German territory, the handing over of locomotives and trucks demanded by the Entente on rigid datelines, and negotiations about the lifting of the blockade and the supplying of Germany with foodstuffs. Erzberger's activities required close cooperation with most of the regular ministries of the government, and this led to many jurisdictional conflicts. Erzberger's impatience with regular bureaucratic procedure frequently embittered the inevitable frictions. This was especially the case in his dealings with Brockdorff-Rantzau, the Foreign Minister.

Their relations had gotten off to a very bad start in early January. Rantzau, upon entering his office, learned that Erzberger was just about to offer to the Entente the surrender of the Russian revolutionary Radek, who had been arrested in Berlin. The new Foreign Minister was horrified by such unorthodox diplomacy, which would degrade Germany in the eyes of the world, threaten future relations with Russia, and cause a domestic explosion on the part of the Independent Socialists. He also thought that the matter should be handled by the Foreign Office rather than by the Armistice Commission. Rantzau held a rather stormy conference with Erzberger on January 5, 1919, which Rantzau later considered the starting point of their bitter personal antagonism.

[10] The Zentrum members were Gröber, Spahn, Trimborn, Stegerwald, and Beyerle. Ziegler, *op.cit.*, p. 111.

[11] For the personnel of the Armistice Commission, see Marhefka, *op.cit.*, III, 411–19. The organization is briefly described by Stockhammern in Erzberger and others, "Der Waffenstillstand," *Europäische Staats-und Wirtschaftszeitung*, Vol. IV [n.d.], special numbers 12 and 13, pp. 330–35. This publication, written from internal evidence in March 1919, is a valuable contemporary commentary on the armistice and its implementation by the leading members of the Commission. (Henceforth cited as *Waffenstillstand*.) The General Staff representative at Spa was Major Theodor Düsterberg, later notorious as one of the leaders of the *Stahlhelm*, the reactionary officers' organization. He was fired by Erzberger after one of his letters to the War Minister, which had been intercepted for Erzberger, showed that he was intriguing against Erzberger. *Prozess*, pp. 583–89, 856–57, 902, 936–37.

Erzberger declared that he was willing to cooperate with Rantzau in a friendly fashion, but that this was made very difficult by intrigues against him in the Foreign Office. The count [Rantzau] then drew his watch from his pocket and said: "It is now 12 o'clock; please give me the names of those of my subordinates who are intriguing against you. I promise that they will all be suspended by eight o'clock this evening." Erzberger became very embarrassed and said that the intrigues were laid so skilfully that he could not give names. Rantzau then declared that he must urgently request Erzberger to abstain from slandering his officials in the future.[12]

The friction between the two men received new fuel because of the necessity of negotiations with the Entente for prolonging the armistice (which had been limited to 36 days at Compiègne). Erzberger as Armistice Commissioner was in charge of these negotiations with Marshal Foch, which were held at Trier on December 12–13, January 15–16, and February 14–15. The last two meetings took place after Rantzau assumed office, and he questioned the necessity of Erzberger's acquiescence in the increasingly onerous terms imposed by Foch.

The Trier conferences centered around the four topics of German failure to fulfil the armistice terms on schedule, German complaints about harsh Allied policies, the lifting of the blockade of Germany to relieve starvation, and the establishment of a demarcation line between Germans and Poles in the east. The Entente had the whip-hand over the Germans, with Foch having as instruments of coercion the German prisoners of war, the refusal to lift the blockade, and the fact that all armistice extensions until February were deliberately made short term to allow the extortion of further demands. The Allied threat to march into unoccupied Germany hung as a constant sword over Erzberger's head, with Germany being in no condition to resume hostilities.

The mood of the victors was symbolized by the refusal of ordinary courtesies to the German delegation. Erzberger and his colleagues were received at the Trier railroad station (when arriving for the first negotiations) by a large body of American troops who escorted them to the automobiles which were to take them to the hotel Zur Post. Erzberger describes what followed:

[12] Erich Brandenburg, *Brockdorff Rantzau* Ch. v, p. 1. This valuable manuscript biography, whose publication was prevented by the German Foreign Office, is available on microfilm in *F.O.* File 1083. Henceforth cited as Brandenburg, *Rantzau*. Erzberger and Rantzau signed a formal agreement delimiting their sphere of influence in peace preparations on February 21, 1919, in which Erzberger received authority in questions involving the occupied Rhineland, the League, and the reconstruction of the devastated territories. Erzberger soon complained that Rantzau had not kept to his side of the bargain. *Ibid.*, pp. 50–51.

Some of my companions expressed themselves gratified by this honor escort; but it soon became apparent that the soldiers were intended to limit our freedom of movement in an intolerable way. When I expressed the wish, soon after our arrival at the hotel, to visit some friends in the city I was told that orders had been given that no one was to leave the hotel. A Trier official who had been helpful in planning our accommodations was prevented from returning to his home by the remark that only the American captain in charge could allow exceptions from the general rule. The captain was nowhere to be found. We were told that the fact that the gentleman did not belong to our delegation was of no consequence whatever. He finally secured, very late in the evening, permission to communicate with his family so that his pyjamas could be brought for the night. American soldiers were stationed in the halls and on the stairs of the hotel. The wife of the proprietor was alone permitted to go out in order to buy food; her children were not allowed to go to school during the days that the Armistice Commission was quartered in the hotel.

The bishop of Trier sent a letter to Erzberger on a pressing matter. Erzberger's reply was returned by the American city commandant with the remark that "Marshal Foch has prohibited all contact between the Armistice Commission and the population of the occupied territories." The American soldiers on duty were, to do them justice, very unhappy about their role as jailors, one of them telling Erzberger, "It is outrageous the way you are imprisoned here." But he stated that Foch had personally ordered the degrading treatment. Erzberger's first demand after the start of the negotiations was that his delegation should be granted "all the rights and liberties which have hitherto been customary in international dealings between representatives of different governments." The Marshal accepted this demand so far as the four armistice commanders (but not their subordinates) were concerned, having succeeded in impressing the Germans with their utterly hopeless condition.[13]

Each of the three Trier meetings began with Foch's complaints that the Germans had not fulfilled the terms of the armistice. There were arrears in the delivery of locomotives, industrial equipment, and submarines. The Germans were also slow about returning Allied prisoners of war. Erzberger excused the delays by pointing out the intrinsic unreasonableness of many of the Allied schedules, as he had already done at Compiègne, and the compounding of all difficulties by the chaotic conditions existing in Germany. He insisted upon the good faith of the German government in seeking to honor all of Germany's obligations. He was indignant when Foch penalized Germany's arrears by

[13] Erzberger, *Erlebnisse*, pp. 342–45.

compelling him to agree to the surrender of 58,000 agricultural machines in the near future—a most unusual provision in a military agreement that showed how much the armistice foreshadowed the future peace terms.[14]

Erzberger was not slow to reply to Allied charges by protesting against Allied violations of the armistice agreement and practices contrary to the dictates of humanity. The Allies refused to return the German prisoners of war, preferring to hold them as hostages to force Germany to accept the final peace treaty. This was no violation of the armistice terms but was certainly contrary to the high moral principles which the Allies professed. The Allies sealed off the left from the right bank of the Rhine, to the great detriment of the economy of both. They expelled Germans resident in Alsace-Lorraine with unnecessary cruelty. They arrested Germans living in the occupied territories for alleged crimes committed during the war (especially industrialists who had participated in the removal of machinery from Belgium), contrary to the specific terms of the armistice. They, above all, refused to implement Article 26 under which they had promised to supply Germany with food.

The problem of the continued blockade, with the related shipping and fiscal questions, was to produce the most heated controversy both between Germany and the Allies and Erzberger and his domestic foes. The Americans and British were eager to conform to the armistice promises; the French were not. Herbert Hoover, in his role as director general in charge of food shipments, was eager to get supplies to Germany: humanitarian considerations, the fear of Bolshevism, and the wish to get rid of wartime American agricultural surplusses all supported his position. A major obstacle in the way of supplying Germany was the world-wide shipping shortage created by Germany's submarine war. The Allies demanded that Germany, as a condition before receiving food imports, should make her merchant fleet (which had lain idly in her ports since 1914) available to the world shipping pool that was being directed from London. Erzberger and the other German negotiators saw in this demand the surrender of the ships to Allied ownership as part of the armistice, and an anticipation of the terms of the peace treaty. They refused to see that the Allies were certain to demand the ships in the final treaty in any case, and that it was better to lose the ships as a *quid pro quo* for urgently needed foodstuffs

---

[14] The best brief account of the three Trier negotiations is in Ch. xxiv of Erzberger's *Erlebnisse*. The protocols of the meetings are printed in Marhefka, *op.cit.,* i, 95–260, with Erzberger's introductory speech at the meetings being especially interesting.

in January than to lose them for nothing in July. Erzberger stubbornly fought for guarantees that the ships should remain in German possession. He secured a pledge that making them available did not mean surrender of ownership, and a suitable sum was to be paid to the German shipowners by way of lease. A German representative was added to the Allied Shipping Council. These concessions loomed big at the time, but proved worthless at the time of the treaty. The German insistence upon these points delayed a shipping agreement until March 14, 1919. The long delay suggested, at least to the Allied negotiators, that the German food shortage was not as desperate as the German negotiators portrayed it. In fact it only proved the weakness of the German government in the face of the German shipping lobby, whose ferocious campaign against Erzberger will be described below.

The financing of the food imports proved, next to shipping terms, the greatest obstacle to ending the blockade of Germany. Erzberger insisted that the work of the special commissions set up for shipping, food, and finance be synchronized so that Germany's vessels were made available only after agreement had been reached on both shipment of supplies and terms of payment. The Allies were ready to start supplies rolling as soon as the agreements were signed. Hoover was soon to succeed in sending 1.26 billion metric tons of food to Germany between April and August 1919, or 29 per cent of all the food distributed by him after the armistice. These food supplies prevented a serious hunger crisis in the summer of 1919. The Germans had hoped, initially, to finance the imports by securing an American loan, being obtuse to the fact that the continued public antipathy to Germany made a loan requiring Congressional approval completely out of the question. They then reluctantly decided to offer gold and foreign investments, only to run into French objections that this would reduce Germany's ability to pay reparations, and would therefore feed Germany at the expense of France's legitimate claims. The British and Americans finally overcame French objection, and food shipments began to enter Germany in April 1919. The haggling on both sides had not been very edifying in what ought to have been treated primarily as a humanitarian matter. Most Germans believed that the Entente had deliberately sought to perpetuate the blockade.[15]

[15] On the entire blockade question, the most sprightly account is that of J. M. Keynes, "Dr. Melchior: A Defeated Enemy," in *Two Memoirs* (London, 1949), pp. 11–71. Keynes was the representative of the British Treasury in the negotiations. The pertinent documents are printed in S. L. Bane and R. H. Lutz, *The Blockade of Germany after the Armistice 1918–1919* (Stanford, 1942), and in Marhefka, *op.cit.*, II, 3–229. The shipping problems are covered in Paul Kollbach, *Deutsche Handelsflotte und Versailler*

Another urgent problem concerned the relationship between Germans and Poles on Germany's eastern frontiers. The Poles were elated by the simultaneous defeat of Russia and Germany in 1918 and dreamed of exploiting this unique opportunity by restoring a Polish state with the extensive frontiers of the eighteenth century. Many Poles wished to utilize Germany's temporary weakness in order to create a *fait accompli* going in its territorial settlement beyond what the statesmen at Paris were likely to concede. Volunteer armies occupied large parts of West Prussia, Posen, and Upper Silesia. Their invasion was met by a mounting resistance, at first only by the local German population, but soon also by Free Corps from the rest of Germany who rushed to defend the "bleeding Eastern border" against the hated and despised Poles. The Supreme Command under Hindenburg and Groener, after establishing itself at Kolberg, assumed command of German operations in mid-winter 1918–1919 and quickly placed the Poles upon the defensive. The French trembled about the fate of their Eastern protégé. Foch demanded, in the course of the third Trier negotiations (February 14–15, 1919), that the German forces in the East stop operations against the Poles on a demarcation line set by himself. Erzberger, as always confronted by the threat of an Allied invasion of Germany, was forced to accept Foch's terms. His surrender was bitterly assailed by both the Supreme Command and large sections of the frontier population.[16]

Erzberger was more successful in another Polish matter. The Poles, while invading Germany in the west, were themselves threatened by Russian invasion from the east. A Polish volunteer army under General Haller had fought with the Entente on the western front against Germany, and wanted to return to the homeland in order to parry the Russian danger. The Entente had secured the right in the first armistice

---

Vertrag (Berlin, 1927). Bernhard Menne, *Armistice and Germany's Food Supply* (London, 1944), written under the impact of the World War Two view of the eternally wicked German, denies the existence of a German food shortage and almost criticizes Allied zeal for getting food to Germany too fast. Erzberger was co-responsible for a German attempt to define the damage done to the health of the German people by the enemy blockade in monetary terms. He asked Dr. F. Bumm, the country's leading health officer, for a memorandum on December 16, 1918. Bumm calculated the damages at 56.4 billion marks. This sum included a birth shortage of 1 million babies that was ascribed to the blockade. The capital value of a new-born baby was estimated at 8,400 marks, which, multiplied by 1 million, amounted to 8.4 billions. Other damages were assessed in a similar spirit. Luckau, *op.cit.*, p. 39. The memorandum is printed in *U.A.*, vi, 389–442.

[16] On the demarcation line, see Erzberger, *Erlebnisse*, p. 360, and his speech of defense in the National Assembly. *Reichstag Debates*, cccxxvi (Feb. 17, 1919), pp. 127–30. General Groener was hostile to Erzberger because of the demarcation line. See his letter to Bachem in Bachem, *Zentrumspartei*, ix, 466, and D. Geyer, *Groener* (Frankfurt, 1955) pp. 133–34.

(Article 16) to send troops by way of Danzig and the Vistula into the eastern territories evacuated by Germany. Foch now proposed to send the Haller army to Poland by this route. Erzberger protested against the plan, fearing that Haller would use his presence in Danzig to secure control of the city for the new Poland. General Groener gave Erzberger some unasked-for advice on the entire question, entreating him to be firm and emphasizing that the Allies needed Germany against Bolshevism:

> I do not consider it impossible that Foch will make us proposals for joint operations against the Soviet army. We must tell him in that case that joint action is possible only if (1) the Allies renounce plans for a vindictive peace (*Gewaltfrieden*), (2) the Allies help us in overcoming our internal problems by evacuating the Rhineland and helping us rebuild our economy, (3) the Allies do not fetter us unnecessarily in the rebuilding of our army.[17]

Erzberger never shared these fantastic illusions held by even a comparatively reasonable man like Groener. He devised, instead, as a practical expedient a plan for transporting the Haller army by railroad through Central Germany rather than by ship across the Baltic. He took a special trip to Spa on April 2–4, 1919, to negotiate the matter with Foch. Erzberger secured a personal interview with the Marshal who accepted the railroad proposal as a practical matter while refusing to surrender the theoretical right of passage through Danzig. Erzberger succeeded in the formal negotiations, which took place in the Villa Neufbois—the wartime residence of Emperor William where the abdication had been signed less than six months previously—to have Stettin rather than Danzig selected as the supply port for the Polish army. The city assembly of Danzig voted a resolution of thanks to Erzberger for his vigorous defence of their German status.[18] It was his one unquestioned success during the armistice negotiations.

The Attack upon Erzberger as Armistice Commissioner

Erzberger was not a member of the German Peace Delegation. He felt he had undertaken his share of onerous tasks as Armistice Commissioner, and knew that the crucial decision of acceptance or rejection of the Allied terms would be made in Weimar rather than in Versailles. His handling of the armistice negotiations had been sufficiently controversial to make it desirable to leave the Peace Delegation uncompromised by his membership. The initial popular feeling of ela-

[17] Groener to Erzberger, Mar. 31, 1919, in Geyer, *Groener,* pp. 135–36.
[18] Erzberger, *Erlebnisse,* pp. 363–65. Marhefka, *op.cit.,* II, 335–70.

tion in Germany induced by the end of the war yielded to widespread despair as the full weight of the armistice terms began to be felt. Erzberger had originally shared the illusion that a bad armistice, dictated by Foch, need not necessarily preclude a good peace, negotiated under the paramount influence of President Wilson.[19] This illusion evaporated in the face of the ever more rigorous armistice extensions and the rumors about the harsh terms being prepared by the Paris Conference. Broad sections of German opinion were searching for a scapegoat, and Erzberger fitted the role perfectly. Had he not undermined the German will to victory through his Peace Resolution? Had he not created a solid majority for the anti-militarist forces by swinging the Zentrum into alliance with the Social Democrats? Had he not placed himself at the head of the Armistice Commission with an utter lack of patriotic shame? And had he not bungled the successive armistice negotiations with Marshal Foch?[20]

Erzberger's record as Armistice Commissioner was attacked by Vögler, a steel magnate belonging to Stresemann's People's Party, in the National Assembly after the completion of the last Trier meeting (February 18, 1919).[21] He denounced the armistice as heralding a violation of Wilson's Fourteen Points in the coming peace treaty. His main accusation against Erzberger was that he had negotiated in an autocratic fashion without bothering to seek the advice of experts. Vögler said that an agreement affecting the steel industry (completed at Luxemburg December 25, 1918, in pursuance of the first Trier conference) had been signed without consulting the representatives of the Ruhr industrialists.[22] The shipping arrangements, likewise, had been made without properly consulting the Hanseatic shipowners, who had arrived at Trier at 4:30 p.m. one afternoon only to find that the agreements must be completed by 5:00 p.m. that same day. Vögler ridiculed Erzberger's plea that Germany could not secure better terms because she was negotiating from a position of weakness, quoting the influential *Frankfurter Zeitung:*

> Mr. Erzberger constantly seeks to prove that Germany cannot secure better terms. It is, of course, difficult to show *ex post facto* that the presence of experts would have affected the end result. But Erzberger is responsible for

[19] For Erzberger's initial belief that a bad armistice could be followed by a good peace, see Max, *op.cit.,* p. 506.

[20] For a contemporary anti-Erzberger diatribe, see A. Friedrich, *Die Wahrheit über die Waffenstillstandsverhandlungen. Wie Erzberger das deutsche Volk abfertigt* (Berlin, 1919).

[21] On Vögler, see the favorable sketch by Louis Lochner, *Tycoons and Tyrant* (Chicago, 1954), pp. 56–59.

[22] On the Luxemburg agreement, see Marhefka, *op.cit.,* II, 233–61.

the fact that the experts were not even given a chance. Erzberger, with his habitual delusions of grandeur, believes he can do everything better than anybody else.[23]

Erzberger replied to these accusations by a characteristic combination of defense and counter-attack. He ridiculed his assailants (and the industrial groups which they represented) for their very belated enthusiasm for Wilson's Fourteen Points; during the war they had wanted to annex everything from the English Channel to the Caucasus; now they waxed indignant when the Entente did not stick closely to Wilson's principles. Vögler's conversion to a Wilsonian peace of reconciliation was very suspect. "I am delighted by anyone travelling from Jerusalem to Damascus, provided he does not take a round-trip ticket." Passing to Vögler's specific charges, Erzberger admitted that the Ruhr magnates had not participated in the Luxemburg conference, but he explained that this was because they had selected Hugo Stinnes to act as their spokesman. Erzberger felt that Stinnes was a very unsuitable person to engage in delicate international negotiations. He had been one of the worst annexationists during the war and one of the main beneficiaries of Belgian forced labor (as Erzberger had pointed out to Zimmerman in 1917). For this reason Erzberger vetoed his appointment as adviser to the German delegation. The steel industry then refused to select anyone else and Erzberger replied to this blackmail by appointing high officials from the Ministry of Economics and dispensing with experts drawn from private industry. He was quite unrepentant about his action, telling the Rightist parties of the *Reichstag:* "You gentlemen think you can influence the government by this kind of terror. But, believe me, your period of power is over." Erzberger regretted the inability of the shipping experts to arrive at Trier earlier, but put the blame upon the difficulties of transport in Germany and Foch's insistence upon rigid datelines.[24]

Erzberger accused his assailants of failure to understand the difficulties of his situation. "One thread was apparent throughout Vögler's speech. He forgot the inconvenient fact that we have unfortunately lost the war." [25] Foch held all of the trump cards in the negotiations, and there were influential Entente groups who wanted Germany to refuse her signature in order that they might have an excuse to march into un-

[23] Vögler's attack is in *Reichstag Debates,* cccxxvi (Feb. 18, 1919), 132–36.
[24] Erzberger's defense is in *ibid.,* pp. 136–45, and Feb. 19, 1919, pp. 171–73. His attack on Stinnes is discussed by G. Raphael, *Stinnes,* pp. 96–98.
[25] *Reichstag Debates,* Feb. 18, 1919, p. 144.

occupied Germany.[26] A resumption of hostilities would free the Allies of their obligations, expressed in Wilson's November 5, 1918 Note prior to Compiègne, of basing the Final Peace upon the Fourteen Points.[27] It would create intolerable conditions in Germany, with Erzberger arguing:

> If we reject an extension of the armistice, the territory now occupied by the Entente armies will become enemy territory, the entire Rhineland will be lost, the German people would be forced to feed a large army of occupation out of its scanty foodstocks, the entire male population of military age would be treated as prisoners of war, and the economic and financial enslavement of the German people would be carried out in the literal sense of the term.[28]

This ghastly prospect paralyzed Erzberger's negotiating position. His difficulties were increased by the general feebleness of the German government and the Cabinet dissensions that left him without clear directions. Erzberger had to brave Communist bullets on his way to the Berlin railroad station to catch the train for his second trip to Trier.[29] He attempted to maintain close telephonic contact with the government in the course of the negotiations, but was unable to secure clear instructions within the short periods allowed by Foch's methods of issuing ultimata. Erzberger described his contact with Berlin on January 16, 1919 (the day of the second armistice extension):

> Telephonic communications were very poor. We finally understood that the following declaration should be made: "The German government takes notice of the new demands of Marshal Foch [about the surrender of agricultural machines] but believes that they cannot be fulfilled." Repeated inquiries finally established the point that I was instructed to enter this as a reservation before signing the new armistice agreement. If Foch should refuse to accept this reservation and should ask whether the German government considered the armistice extended by this kind of qualified signature [without his explicit acceptance] I was to say that I had nothing to add and had to return to Berlin right away. If Foch then declared that hostilities would resume next morning I should nonetheless break off negotiations. Instructions for each of these contingencies could be extracted

[26] This view was forcefully presented by Haniel, Foreign Office representative on the Armistice Commission, in a report to Erzberger and the Foreign Office, Jan. 15, 1919. *F.O.*, File 2031.

[27] *Reichstag Debates,* cccxxvi (Feb. 18, 1919), 160.

[28] *ibid.,* p. 136. Vögler quoted these words to denounce Erzberger as a bad negotiator because he exposed Germany's weakness. Erzberger faced the impossible task of simultaneously forcing his countrymen to accept harsh realities yet of not weakening Germany's external negotiating position.

[29] Erzberger, *Erlebnisse,* p. 349.

from Berlin only with the greatest difficulty. My inquiry concerning which of Foch's demands was considered incapable of fulfillment yielded the answer: surrender of the agricultural machines within the brief period proposed. My further question, if I could sign if concessions were made on this one point, was answered affirmatively. All the other demands were explicitly described as not incapable of fulfillment. These telephonic instructions, with the constant alterations of attitude by the Berlin government, cannot be described as a political masterpiece.[30]

Erzberger was forced to rely upon his own judgment in the face of an evasive and confused Cabinet, but he was not the man to shirk responsibility. He believed that Germany could not afford a resumption of hostilities, and, after appealing in vain to the victor's sense of justice, he accepted the inevitable in every case. He thereby saved Germany from invasion at the expense of his own good name.

Erzberger aroused intense hostility by his conduct, but this hostility was augmented by his personal characteristics. A journalist described his parliamentary manner in the spring of 1919:

Erzberger almost always provokes contradiction even when one does not really disagree with him. Is this due to his external appearance? Many people confess an unconquerable aversion to the physical figure of the minister, although they cannot give reasons for their aversion. Quite on the contrary—an objective observer has to admit that Erzberger appears, with his ruddy face and well-tailored clothes, the most youthful and lively of all the ministers. But his rather square Swabian head on top of a medium-sized thickset body, his small eyes and his thin moustache cause annoyance despite a certain surface amiability. When he begins to speak one thinks after the first sentences: "What a cunning orator!" but one's second thought is, "Is there solidity beneath the glittering surface?" Erzberger's greatest single source of strength, whether sitting on the ministerial bench or standing before the speaker's rostrum, is his imperturbability. He sits as if all the attacks against him could not possibly make the slightest impression, indeed that he found them rather diverting by way of distraction from more important matters. On some occasions, when the attacks become very severe, a friendly smile runs across his face. This smile is always a red rag for the anger of members of the Right. . . .

[30] *ibid.*, pp. 353–54. The protocol of the Cabinet meeting discussing the new Trier terms (Jan. 16, 1919), in *F.O.*, File 2030, confirms Erzberger's account of the chaotic helplessness of the government. See also Payer, *op.cit.*, pp. 292–95 and Brandenburg, *Rantzau*, Ch. v, pp. 6–9. Rantzau quotes Erzberger to the effect that he had secured permission to sign from Ebert himself over the telephone. Erzberger's acceptance of the last armistice extension nearly led to Rantzau's resignation (February 16, 1919). The latter argued that the Entente terms were intolerable, that murder was preferable to suicide, and that the Entente would be embarrassed by Germany's rejecting the terms. The Cabinet had originally accepted his view but had caved in after consultation with party leaders. Brandenburg, *Rantzau*, Ch. v, pp. 13–22.

Erzberger usually sits on the ministerial bench with his glance half towards the speaker, half towards the other deputies. His left arm leans over the back of the chair, his right arm is busy taking notes. Every once in a while Erzberger returns, by a characteristic gesture, his pincenez to the nose from which it is constantly falling off. Erzberger rushes to the rostrum as soon as an assailant has finished. His opponent must then prepare himself to withstand a heavy barrage. Erzberger's smile is gone, one sees that the man is a born polemicist who is always able to defend his own skin. Every member of the House knows that it is perilous to tangle with Erzberger. He knows all the [Reichstag] protocols and commission reports by heart, always has citations available, and is especially fluent on foreign affairs, where most speakers are rather inexperienced. Erzberger considers any doubt about anything that he says quite impossible for any reasonable man. Even his obvious contradictions between yesterday and today do not perturb him in the least (when they are pointed out). Erzberger's voice always sounds a bit excited after the first sentences. He retains a noticeable Swabian accent which is also apparent in his pronunciation of occasional French words, leading to very humorous effects. When he speaks he is accompanied at proper intervals by a chorus of his faithful Zentrum lackeys, who interject either an understanding "very good" or an emphatic "hear, hear." [31]

The Treaty Terms and the Conger Mission

The main preoccupation of the German government in the spring of 1919 consisted, apart from the paramount task of restoring domestic order, in making preparations for the Peace Conference. The main burden of the work was carried by Count Bernstorff, the former Ambassador to Washington, who headed a special section within the Foreign Office created for this purpose. Erzberger cooperated with him in a friendly fashion until they began to differ on policy in May. The cooperation was a matter of importance in view of the close intertwining of the armistice conditions and the future peace terms. Bernstorff recognized that jurisdictional conflicts were inevitable. He rather appreciated Erzberger's direct approach in resolving these by frequent oral consultation.[32]

Count Brockdorff-Rantzau, the Foreign Minister, took a less lenient view of Erzberger. The two men were made to misunderstand and dislike one another even apart from their jurisdictional and policy differences. Rantzau was an aristocrat to his fingertips, the scion of a

[31] Kölnische Zeitung, March 9, 1919. Copy in Bachem Papers, File 89.
[32] Bernstorff's recollection of their cooperation includes a rather favorable judgment upon Erzberger. Erinnerungen, p. 183. Erzberger describes their common work in Erlebnisse, pp. 366–67.

distinguished Holstein family that had long served the Kings of Denmark. Holsteiners are not only geographically but also temperamentally far from the Swabians: they are cool, reserved, and obstinate, where Swabians tend to be warm, impulsive, and flexible. Rantzau had enjoyed a brilliant career in the Imperial diplomatic service, rising to the post of minister to Denmark during the First World War. Here he had been privately critical, long before Erzberger's Peace Resolution, of the annexationism of the German government, and had established cordial relations with the leaders of the Majority Socialists on their frequent trips to Scandinavia. Ebert and Scheidemann had selected him for the post of Foreign Minister in December 1918. Rantzau had set stringent conditions when he agreed to accept office in the midst of the revolutionary chaos: the Communists must be smashed and the peace terms of the Entente must be rejected if they violated the "pre-armistice contract." Erzberger heartily favored the first, but was to take a completely divergent attitude on the second question.

Their conflict over policy was exacerbated by ill-concealed personal antipathies. Erzberger had no respect for the metier of diplomacy, and he believed that Rantzau was unsuited for the role of parliamentary statesman. Rantzau was completely lacking in parliamentary skill, and his inability to speak without notes often embarrassed the government. For Erzberger, with his marvellous fluency, this must have been a source of annoyance. Rantzau was morbidly suspicious of his colleagues, and thought that Erzberger engaged in many more intrigues than he actually did. His personal sensitivity made him impatient of contradiction, while Erzberger had almost grown to love the tumble of political controversy. Rantzau resented Erzberger's restless, incautious, and meddling activity; Erzberger resented Rantzau's *noblesse oblige* attitude towards parliamentarians and his ill-concealed disdain for amateurs in diplomacy. He also thought, when it became clear that Rantzau favored defiance of the Entente Powers, that this policy expressed quixotic conceptions of aristocratic honor ill-suited to the democratic age. Erzberger was reported to have told intimates in a Weimar beer house, "This man must be removed from office as quickly as possible. His policy constitutes a danger to the state." [33]

[33] Brandenburg, *Rantzau,* Ch. VIII, p. 36. On Rantzau, see also his *Dokumente und Gedanken um Versailles* (3rd edition, Berlin, 1925); Edgar Stern-Rubarth, *Graf Brockdorff-Rantzau. Wanderer zwischen zwei Welten* (Berlin, 1929); M. J. Bonn, *Wandering Scholar* (London, 1949), pp. 228–31. Rantzau's relations with Erzberger are analyzed in Bernstorff, *Erinnerungen,* p. 184, and Stern-Rubarth, *ibid.,* pp. 89–92. Brandenburg quotes some of Rantzau's untranslatable characterizations of Erzberger, such as "gemeingefährlicher Schädling" (to Ebert, June 22, 1919), Ch. VIII, p. 48, "ein Hans Dampf in allen Ecken und apolitischer Mann" (to Scheidemann, April 22, 1919, Ch. VI, p. 53). Rantzau said on the same occasion, following a press indiscretion, that

The German Peace Delegation, headed by Count Rantzau himself, went to Paris in late April to receive the terms worked out by the Entente Powers. The document of peace was handed to the Germans at a brief ceremony on May 7, with Rantzau replying to Clemenceau's ill-tempered presentation remarks with a strong speech of defiance. All the members of the German delegation were shocked by the severity of the terms. Germany was to be excluded from the League of Nations, to be deprived of all her colonies, to be saddled with an astronomic but unspecified reparations debt, and to lose her military sovereignty by a restriction of her army to a professional force of 100,000 men. Germany was to lose Alsace-Lorraine to France, Eupen-Malmedy to Belgium, North Schleswig to Denmark, and parts of West Prussia, Posen, and Upper Silesia to Poland in the name of national self-determination; yet the Austrian and Bohemian Germans were at the same time deprived of the right of joining Germany on strategic and economic grounds, in violation of self-determination. The Rhineland was to be occupied for a period of fifteen years, while the Saar was to be administered by the League of Nations for a similar period. Germany was also required, by Article 227, to hand over her so-called war criminals, including the Emperor, for trial to the Entente Powers. Worst of all was Article 231 of the treaty, which the Germans interpreted, probably erroneously, as an admission that Germany alone was responsible for the outbreak of war. German indignation was to center upon these two articles, collectively known as the "articles of shame" (*Schmachparagraphen*). Their inclusion in the treaty was to make the German debate on acceptance of the treaty one of honor versus dishonor rather than one of conflict between positions held on prudential grounds alone. The irony was that the surrender of the war criminals was never to be implemented, and that the "war guilt" clause assumed practical importance only after the Germans had made its refutation the basis of revisionism.[34]

---

he would be unable to remain responsible for foreign policy "wenn ein so brutaler Bursche wie Erzberger mir ununterbrochen ins Handwerk pfusche" (p. 52). An additional source of friction between Erzberger and Rantzau was a difference of opinion on Russian policy. Erzberger, reversing his attitude from the time of his wish to hand over Radek to the Entente, wanted a regular armistice with Russia to end the fighting in the Baltic in April 1919, to be followed by a resumption of commercial relations. Rantzau opposed this at the time as likely to harm relations with the Entente. Erzberger curiously anticipated the very policy of cooperation with the Bolsheviks of which Rantzau became the main spokesman in the 1920s. See Count Rüdiger von der Goltz, *Meine Sendung in Finnland und im Baltikum* (Leipzig, 1920), pp. 25, 89, 272, and F.O. Files 1665 and 2049. My attention was called to the latter by the courtesy of Mr. Douglas Unfug of Emory University.

[34] A superb account of the work of the German delegation is A. Luckau, *The German Delegation at the Paris Conference* (New York, 1941), which includes all the major documents in translation. The atmosphere is conveyed by Victor Schiff, *So war es*

Both the Peace Delegation and German public opinion were angered and surprised by these terms, a fact explicable only because of the widespread belief that Wilson was in a sufficiently strong position to prevail against Clemenceau. The Postmaster-General, Josef Giesberts, a close friend of Erzbergers since their joint role in founding the Christian Trade Unions twenty years previously, represented the Zentrum Party on the German Delegation. Walter Simons, the Commissioner General, described him in a letter to his wife as staggering into a delegation conference on the evening of May 7, yelling:

> Gentlemen, I am drunk. That may be proletarian, but with me there was nothing else for it. This shameful treaty has broken me, for I had believed in Wilson until today. When I talked to him in America, that Puritan said to me that the parochial schools in America were the best. From that day I believed him to be an honest man, and now that scoundrel sends us such a treaty. Right now if I had those fellows here, who this afternoon were sitting opposite me—Wilson, Lloyd George, and Clemenceau—they would hit the ceiling so hard that they'd stick to it. But I am telling you this, gentlemen [and with that he jumped up and banged his fist on the table so hard that it spilled a glass of cognac] if those fellows think that the German laborers are going to work hard for that capitalist gang, they're wrong, and when they march into the mining district, the few hand grenades that'll be needed to flood every mine, will be on hand! [35]

This outburst was not an untypical reaction. The German National Assembly called a special indignation session at Berlin, in which Chancellor Scheidemann, speaking for the government, called the Paris terms "unbearable, unrealizable, and unacceptable," and prophetically predicted that "the hand should wither" which signed a treaty placing Germany in such intolerable fetters. His stand was solemnly supported by every party except the Independent Socialists. Erzberger valued the expression of national near-unanimity against the treaty because it would strengthen Rantzau's position at Versailles, but he opposed the inclusion of the irrevocable word "unacceptable" at the Cabinet meeting where Scheidemann's declaration was drafted. The Democratic ministers insisted upon inclusion of the word. Erzberger's *Erlebnisse* describe his position.

> I argued, supported by two Socialist Ministers, against the word "unacceptable" with the remark: Scheidemann will have a tremendous popular

in Versailles (Berlin, 1929). Schiff accompanied the delegation as a Socialist journalist. The thesis that the Germans misunderstood the "war guilt" clause is stated forcefully in Hajo Holborn, "Diplomats and Diplomacy in the Early Weimar Republic," in *The Diplomats 1919–1939*, edited by G. Craig and F. Gilbert (Princeton, 1953), pp. 141–44.
[35] Luckau, *op.cit.*, p. 124.

success today if he includes the word. But the government must contemplate the situation which will arise in three or four weeks. . . . The words "unbearable" and "unrealizable" are strong enough. If they—supported by a strong popular movement—cannot impress our enemies the word "unacceptable" will not change their views either.[36]

Erzberger foresaw correctly that Scheidemann's demagogic speech would only compound Cabinet difficulties when the final decision on whether the terms should be accepted would have to be made; but he was forced to yield to the Democratic threat of resigning from the Cabinet if their wishes were not accepted. Their resignation would have undermined Rantzau's position completely.[37]

The German Delegation at Versailles meanwhile embarked upon a campaign of written notes against the draft treaty since oral negotiations were not permitted. The German notes were models of legal reasoning and stylistic trenchancy, but they made singularly little impression upon the Entente statesmen. Erzberger, in Berlin, thought that the aggressive language employed by Rantzau was inappropriate, and that the technique of piece-meal notes, contesting nearly every provision of the treaty instead of making constructive counter-offers, was unlikely to yield results. He thought he had done rather better himself in his negotiations with Foch on the successive armistice extensions. Erzberger knew that the German delegation at Versailles was practically imprisoned in a hotel, and must find it very difficult to develop informal communication channels with the Allies. He feared the intransigent spirit prevailing in Rantzau's entourage, which was clearly prepared for a policy of defiance of the Allies, daring them to occupy all of Germany.

These facts induced Erzberger to attempt a characteristic piece of amateur diplomacy. When the Versailles negotiations had bogged down in a campaign of notes and counter-notes, he sought to establish an indirect contact with President Wilson by inviting Colonel Arthur Conger, an intelligence officer on General Pershing's staff, to come to Berlin in the middle of May. Colonel Conger, whose significant diplomatic role in the spring of 1919 has only recently been discovered, was a very untypical American officer.[38] He had graduated from Harvard College, not West Point, in 1894 after specializing in classical

[36] Erzberger, *Erlebnisse*, p. 368.
[37] Schiff, *op.cit.*, pp. 74-75.
[38] Fritz T. Epstein, "Zwischen Compiègne und Versailles," in *Vierteljahrshefte für Zeitgeschichte*, Vol. III (Stuttgart, 1955), pp. 412-45. Conger's contact with General Groener from December 1918 to March 1919 is described in Craig, *op.cit.*, pp. 364-65. The American documents were first printed in *Foreign Relations of the United States, Paris Peace Conference*, XII (Washington, 1945), 124-35.

philology, Eastern religions, and music. He entered the army at the time of the Spanish-American War, and decided to become a regular officer. Conger soon rose to become an instructor at the Army Staff College as an expert on Germany. He spent the war on General Pershing's staff and was sent into Germany shortly after the armistice to survey political and military conditions. He saw Groener, Erzberger, Rantzau, and many other figures in the early spring. At that time the German government, with the approval of both President Ebert and Foreign Minister Rantzau, sought to use him to establish direct contact with President Wilson. Walter Loeb, a native of Frankfurt, who later became President of the *Thüringische Staatsbank* (state bank of Thuringia), served as regular intermediary. He had frequent conferences with Conger throughout March, April, and early May. The American colonel rather misled the Germans, intentionally or unintentionally, about the peace terms that were to be expected. For this reason Rantzau refused to have further dealings with him after the Allied proposals had been formally made.[39]

Erzberger thought that Conger was the best available channel for communicating a specific offer of acceptable peace terms to President Wilson, which might yet inaugurate a process of genuine negotiations. He invited Conger and a fellow-officer, Major Frederick Henrotin, to come to Berlin on May 17, 1919. Erzberger arranged to have Bernstorff present during his first conference with the Americans on the morning of May 18, since he knew that at heart Bernstorff agreed with his own view that the treaty must be accepted no matter how harsh the terms. The two Americans were at great pains to destroy certain German illusions concerning internal Allied disagreements, which led to the expectation that a policy of defiance might secure an improvement in the terms of the treaty. They stated that President Wilson was in full sympathy with the terms presented to Germany; that the American army would join the French march into Germany if the Germans should refuse to sign; and that there could be no doubt that the French were willing, and indeed anxious, to occupy further parts of Germany in order to extort maximum terms. Conger stated in his official report that

> During the elucidation of the above points, Count Bernstorff maintained a running fire of comment and of protest, making such statements as that under no circumstances would Germany sign the present treaty, and that

[39] Epstein, *op.cit.,* pp. 415–28, *passim.* Rantzau's last conference with Conger was on the train while Rantzau was on his way to Paris (April 29, 1919). For Rantzau's report, see Brandenburg, *Rantzau,* Ch. VII, pp. 8–10.

the Allies could do what they pleased. He appeared much agitated and several times on the point of having lost his temper. Mr. Erzberger, on the contrary, appeared calm and unmoved, glad to have the information, and seemingly glad to enjoy Count Bernstorff's discomfiture.[40]

The Americans received a very unfavorable impression of Bernstorff, who had talked too much and who had ostentatiously ignored Erzberger. The conversation had been carried on mostly in English, which Erzberger did not understand. Bernstorff had thought it his duty to give aggressive support to Rantzau's views regardless of his private convictions.[41]

Erzberger did not think this joint interview very profitable, and he resolved to see the Americans the second time alone in order to see if an alternative policy to Rantzau's defiance could not be developed. Conger continued his report:

> The next morning, by appointment [May 19, 10 a.m.], Major Henrotin and myself . . . met Herr Erzberger alone. He began the conversation with the statement that it was perfectly patent to everyone that Germany must have peace, and the German government cordially and even anxiously desired peace. But the German government could not accept the present proposed terms, and therefore wanted to meet the Allies and inform them of the difficulties of the German government in meeting the demands of their people, in the hope that a compromise could be made which Germany could accept. Herr Erzberger's attitude during this statement seemed to indicate that he was making the proposal *con gusto,* and that he had his way about it in making it in the Cabinet meeting which we were informed was held the preceding evening. The proposals he made were taken down in writing by Major Henrotin and are transmitted herewith.[42]

Erzberger's proposals were the following:

1. Germany's immediate entry in the League.

2. The reduction of the army to 100,000 men must be delayed for at least two years, in order to cope with the Bolshevik menace. But "he stated that the military terms would not constitute an obstacle to signing the treaty."

3. "Germany would need to retain a portion of her merchant fleet in order to resume the economic life of Germany." He stated that British and American capital might be given stock ownership in the German shipping lines.

[40] Epstein, *op.cit.* The interview is described on pp. 429–30 (Conger), 433–34 (Henrotin), and 434–35 (Bernstorff).
[41] *ibid.,* p. 433.
[42] *ibid.,* pp. 430–31.

4. All territorial questions to be settled by secret plebiscites held under neutral supervision after withdrawal of all troops. "This is to include territory already in the hands of the Poles."

5. Instead of League rule of the Saar, Erzberger proposed guaranteed coal deliveries to the French and French partnership in German mines.

6. Termination of the Rhineland occupation within 6 months. As the Allies claimed that occupation was necessary for security reasons and to guarantee reparation payments, Germany was willing to offer instead that "no military forces would be maintained within a distance of 50 kilometers of the east bank of the Rhine" (the idea later realized at Locarno). Reparation payments could be guaranteed through "receipts of railroads, public forests and lands, customs duties, internal revenues, etc." (as was later done under the Dawes Plan).

7. On colonies, "Erzberger wishes that Germany be made mandatory for her colonies, or part of same, in order to satisfy public opinion in Germany, so that her people would think that she was a nation possessing colonies."

8. On finance, Erzberger made detailed suggestions that aimed at a reduction in Allied demands for indemnities. "Speaking of reparations, he stated that Germany was in a position to rebuild France and Belgium, and that two months after the peace treaty was signed, 100,000 workingmen could be sent for that purpose and that six months later, 500,000 men could be devoted to this work, and that in two and a half years, all would be restored. The work would be modern and sanitary."

9. The extradition of the Emperor and the so-called war criminals to the Allies was unthinkable. "He stated that he agreed that all guilty parties should be punished, and that he understood that the Allies could not accept the proposal that they should be tried before German courts. He suggested that a neutral tribunal should be instituted at The Hague, or elsewhere, and that the accused should appear before this court with the allies acting as plaintiff." Erzberger also protested the war guilt clause.

Henrotin concluded his report with the significant words:

Mr. Erzberger stated that they [the government] would sign the treaty, and that he wishes it to be signed, and to be observed sincerely. However, he could not sign a treaty which departed too far from the 14 Points of President Wilson. He stated further that he could have the treaty accepted in Germany, although he let it be understood that it would require a certain amount of camouflage to put it over, but promised he could do it.

Henrotin ascribed Erzberger's conciliatory approach in the treaty question to the impression made by his and Conger's firm statements on the American attitude during the conference with Bernstorff on the previous day.[43]

Conger ends his official report with the following significant remark:

> Erzberger stated that he had sent a message to Lloyd George by a British officer who called on him two days ago. He also made reference to numerous conversations which he had had with French officers, who were constantly protesting the friendliness of the French government to Germany, which was said with an expressive shrug of the shoulders indicating lack of credence on his part.[44]

Conger and Henrotin returned to Trier after their interview with Erzberger, and immediately despatched a full report on their mission to the American Peace Delegation. This report was sent by Christian Herter, Delegation Secretary, to President Wilson on May 21, with a letter of transmission, emphasizing the importance of Conger's mission, and ending, "beg to call your attention particularly to the report by Major Henrotin on the second interview which he had with Mr. Erzberger in which the latter made certain definite suggestions in regard to amending various articles of the proposed treaty." [45]

Erzberger's offer secured no reply from President Wilson. The President probably thought it dishonorable to engage in negotiations behind the back of his Allies, and he knew that he had no leverage for making the French accept the kind of terms proposed by Erzberger. The inter-Allied compromises embodied in the treaty draft submitted to the Germans were too fragile to allow for a complete reopening of fundamental controversies. Colonel Conger was instructed to tell the Germans that there was no alternative to accepting the treaty as it stood. The colonel saw Walter Loeb, acting as Erzberger's intermediary, at Trier on June 5–6, and again aimed at destroying the German hope that President Wilson was prepared to help them get better terms. He also warned Loeb to have no illusion that an American military occupation would be pleasant, going so far as to cite the record of American brutality in the Philippines when the natives behaved in a provocative manner.[46] Erzberger was disappointed at the total failure of his diplomatic effort. His inability to secure treaty modifications did

[43] *ibid.,* pp. 439–41.
[44] *ibid.,* p. 431. The story of Erzberger's contacts with Lloyd George was told by Melchior to Lord Keynes with great bitterness. See *Two Memoirs,* p. 69.
[45] Epstein, "Zwischen Compiègne und Versailles," pp. 443–44.
[46] Loeb to Erzberger, June 6, 1919. *Erzberger Papers,* File 46.

not, however, alter his fundamental conviction that the treaty must be signed.

What light do Erzberger's contacts with Conger throw on his personality and his political techniques? He has been criticized both for negotiating with the Allies behind the back of the Foreign Minister, in a sense at variance with official policy, and for bragging about dishonorable practices in which he intended to engage (e.g., his statement that he could secure ratification of the treaty by using the necessary camouflage). He is further charged with revealing to the Allies the deep internal fissures of the German government on the basic question of whether or not to accept the Treaty of Versailles. He represented himself as the leader of a group that favored acceptance, whereas Rantzau never wavered in emphasizing that he was irrevocably opposed. Erzberger's statement that he could get the treaty ratified with the proper camouflage was certain to weaken Rantzau's negotiating position, since Rantzau's only trump card was the plea that the National Assembly would never ratify a treaty embodying the Allied terms.[47]

There is much force in these criticisms, but they ignore certain factors and conditions influencing Erzberger's judgment in the specific circumstances of May 1919. His contact with Conger was obviously incompatible with the normal canons of Cabinet solidarity and diplomatic intercourse. It would stand condemned *prima facie* in ordinary times, but times were not ordinary in Germany in 1919. The entire future of the country depended upon the kind of peace treaty which it was able to secure. Rantzau was precluded, both by his known intransigence and by the Allied refusal to engage in genuine negotiations at Versailles, from performing the ordinary functions of a Foreign Minister. With Rantzau paralyzed, there was much to be said for attempting, by means however unorthodox, to see if an indirect appeal to Lloyd George and Wilson could not lead to further negotiations. The substance of the terms offered by Erzberger certainly constituted the limit to which any German government could voluntarily go. It was desirable to let the Allies know what those limits were, even though in fact it did not lead to a change in Allied policies.

It is not the substance but the particular method of Erzberger's diplomacy that is vulnerable to attack. It is certain that Rantzau, assuming that he knew of Erzberger's approach, would have disapproved of it for both substantive and departmental reasons. German foreign policy must have appeared chaotic to the Allied statesmen, with Rantzau at Versailles taking one line and Erzberger at Berlin quite another. Con-

[47] Epstein, *op.cit.*, p. 445.

ger and Henrotin believed that Erzberger spoke to them after securing formal Cabinet authorization the previous evening (May 18), a belief that Erzberger must have fostered to enhance his negotiating authority; but this belief is not born out by Cabinet records. There was no Cabinet meeting on May 18; the last previous meeting had been held on May 17. At that session the Cabinet had tentatively approved formal counter-proposals to be despatched to Rantzau in Paris for submission to the Allies, which became the basis of the German note of May 29, 1919. The substance of this note, in whose formulation Erzberger took a major part, largely coincided with Erzberger's specific proposals to Conger on May 19. Erzberger correctly foresaw that the note, when presented at Paris to all the Allies, must secure a general rejection. He hoped, though in vain, that private negotiations with the Americans, accompanied by a frank avowal of his domestic difficulties, would lead to better results.[48]

The exceptional situation of 1919 made the maintenance of Cabinet solidarity very difficult. It must also be remembered that this kind of solidarity was not required by German political traditions. Erzberger could not be expected to feel bound by the rules that govern old estab-lished Cabinet systems. The German tradition had rather allowed for high officials working at cross purposes with little sense of loyalty to-wards their colleagues. One only has to recall Tirpitz' sabotage of Bethmann's efforts towards a naval understanding before the war, and Ludendorff's sabotage of Erzberger's negotiations with Kolyschko in 1917 despite their authorization by Bethmann.

The justification for Erzberger's conduct can be found, if at all, in his deep conviction that Rantzau's policy of bravado and defiance, cul-minating in a refusal to sign the treaty, must lead to disastrous conse-quences for Germany (Allied invasion, mass famine, partition, etc.), as will be described in detail below. These consequences were of such weight that to avoid them warranted a breach of the principle of Cab-inet solidarity, which while valuable cannot be assigned an importance equal to the prevention of invasion, starvation, and disunity. Whether the contact with Conger was in fact likely to help Germany was a question of political judgment on which men were bound to differ. It

---

[48] *ibid.,* pp. 431 and 441. The protocol of the Cabinet session held at 5:00 p.m. on May 17, 1919 can be found in *F.O.* File 1665. It does not include any reference to any coming approach to Conger. The next Cabinet meeting, held on May 19 at 11:00 a.m. immediately after Erzberger's conference with Conger, saw Erzberger mentioning his first interview with Conger, at which Bernstorff had been present, but not the crucial second meeting. If Erzberger had been authorized to approach Conger he naturally would have reported back about the results.

must be noted, however, that success, the great justifier of many political irregularities, cannot be pleaded in Erzberger's favor.

Erzberger's approach to Wilson used two arguments: his domestic difficulties in securing ratification of the treaty, and the incompatibility of the Entente draft with the Fourteen Points to which Germany was entitled under the "pre-armistice contract." It suggested one simple conclusion—the return to the Fourteen Points—as the prerequisite for overcoming the ratification difficulty. The appeal to Wilson was both to his sense of honor and his practical desire to get the treaty ratified by Germany. It was accompanied by Erzberger's stating that he—because of his strong political influence—could in fact get the treaty ratified, provided concessions were made: a prerequisite, in Erzberger's view, for establishing his value as a negotiator, since the Allies would look ridiculous if they first modified the treaty only to have it rejected by Germany anyway. Erzberger told Wilson in effect: "I recognize that our weakness compels us to sign the treaty and have no illusions on this score. But I appeal to you as an honorable man to abide by the Fourteen Points, which the present treaty violates. Please remember, also, that I am having great difficulty with my own people in securing approval for the ratification policy. You would make things a little bit easier for me if you relaxed some of the rigors of the treaty and stuck as closely as possible to your own Fourteen Points. You must recognize that a negotiated peace will prove more permanent than a dictated peace, and both honor and policy require that you accept the treaty modifications that I have indicated." Rantzau could not make this kind of appeal, because he was at heart committed to opposing the treaty, and known to be so. If this kind of appeal offered any prospect of success, Erzberger was the right man to make it.

His talk about putting the treaty over by "camouflage" is not very edifying, but again must be viewed in the context of 1919. If the policy of acceptance of the treaty was objectively required by German self-interest, and parliamentary opinion was too obtuse to recognize this fact, then a certain amount of camouflage was justified by the circumstances. Erzberger used the unfortunate term primarily to impress the Allies with the difficulty of his domestic situation, a perfectly legitimate device in private international negotiations; he also wanted to impress the two Americans with the extent of his own political influence.

The most vulnerable part of Erzberger's strategy was that it required the revelation of the internal dissensions of the German Cabinet. It meant a breach in Rantzau's policy of united defiance, which presented the Allies with the supposedly unpleasant alternatives of modification of their terms to assure German acceptance or of occupying the entire country in the face of German obstinacy. The trouble with Rantzau's policy was that it ignored the fact that France was eager to march into Germany in order to go beyond what she felt to be the minimum terms of Versailles (as stated correctly by Conger). Rantzau's policy of ostentatious defiance had, moreover, the undesirable consequence of enhancing British and American solidarity with French aims. Erzberger's conciliatory approach, while no more successful than Rantzau's, was at least worth trying in Germany's desperate situation. Erzberger did not promise Conger that he could or would get the treaty ratified as it stood. He assured him only of being able and willing to guarantee ratification if the Allies should make the broad concessions which he suggested, concessions which went, incidentally, beyond Rantzau's hopes at Versailles. The implication of Erzberger's remarks was that the treaty could not possibly be ratified as it stood. Yet Erzberger probably could not completely conceal his intention of working for ratification regardless of the degree of Allied concessions. This must have confirmed Allied hopes of compelling German acceptance of the treaty as it stood.

The Allies knew, in any case, that there were deep German differences of opinion on what to do about the treaty. The Independent Socialists had refused to participate in the national proclamation of defiance on May 12, 1919, and threatened insurrection if the government should refuse to sign the treaty. The alternatives confronting Germany, whether signing or not, were so desperate that men were bound to take divergent views. The physical and moral exhaustion of the country from four years of war practically precluded the heroic policy of united defiance. These facts could not be concealed from the statesmen of the Entente, no matter how loud the shouting when Scheidemann declared the treaty to be unacceptable. Entente journalists circulated freely in Germany, and were able to judge currents of public opinion. Newspapermen emphasized the existence of two groups in the government, one for ratification headed by Erzberger, one against ratification headed by Rantzau. The appearance of national unanimity required by Rantzau was objectively unattainable.[49]

[49] Erzberger's critics accused him of inspiring newspaper stories stating that Germany would accept the treaty in any case. The Liberal editor Theodor Wolff accused him in the *Berliner Tageblatt,* June 10, 1919, of contacts with Gentizon, a Berlin correspondent of the *Le Temps.* Erzberger categorically denied having spoken about his attitude to foreign journalists after the treaty draft had been submitted. *Erlebnisse,* p. 369. Wolff also accused Erzberger of sending his friend Prince Ysenburg to the Hague to assure English circles that the treaty would be ratified. See also *Prozess,* p. 39.

The Struggle for Ratification

An attempt was made to reconcile divergent views within the government shortly after Conger's mission. A conference was held at Spa between members of the Cabinet (Scheidemann, Erzberger, Dernburg) and members of the Peace Delegation headed by Rantzau (May 23). Here plans were laid for Germany's final reply to the Allied Treaty draft to supplement the succession of notes on particular points despatched by the delegation to the Allies during the preceding two weeks. The conferees agreed, upon Erzberger's insistence, to place little importance upon revising the military clauses of the treaty, but to concentrate upon economic and territorial improvements. It was decided that Germany should make a reparations offer of 100 billion gold marks interest free, provided certain territorial and economic prerequisites were met. Erzberger was at first opposed to this offer, despite the fact that the vast sum might make an initially favorable impression. He argued that Allied mathematicians would quickly figure out that an interest-free sum, paid over a long period of time, was no larger than a much smaller sum with compound interest added. He feared an unfavorable reaction once the real total offered by Germany had been explained to Allied public opinion by emphasis upon the words "interest free." Alternatively there was danger that the words "interest-free" might get lost in later negotiations. The same might happen to the stringent prerequisites which the German delegates were instructed to require. Erzberger did not prevail, but his opposition to the offer of a large fixed sum was to anticipate his later stand on reparations. The question was to prove of no immediate importance since the Allies, unable among themselves to decide upon a reparations sum, insisted that Germany sign a blank check in the treaty.[50]

The antipathy between Erzberger and Rantzau was ill-concealed at the Spa conference. Bernstorff had to use considerable persuasion to get Rantzau to agree to shake hands with his antagonist.[51] The Versailles

[50] Erzberger, *Erlebnisse,* pp. 369–70. Schiff, *op.cit.,* pp. 85–87; Protocol of Spa Conference, in *Erzberger Papers,* File 14; Craig, *op.cit.,* p. 368. Erzberger and Rantzau, while disagreeing on nearly everything else, agreed in making the modification of the Entente's military terms a minor priority. For this they both earned the enmity of Seeckt. F. von Rabenau, *Seeckt: Aus seinem Leben 1918–1936* (Leipzig, 1940), pp. 175–76. The limitation of the German army to 100,000 later created intense frustration among officers for freezing promotion possibilities; when Erzberger, as Finance Minister after 1919, further sought to insist upon rigid military economies, he became the *bête noir* of the entire officer corps. Harold Gordon, *The Reichswehr and the German Republic* (Princeton, 1957), p. 85 and 338.

[51] Bernstorff, *Erinnerungen,* p. 187. Rantzau, in a letter to his cousin Langwerth, June 1, 1919, prided himself on literally turning his back on Erzberger at Spa. He was

delegation had heard of Erzberger's view that the treaty must be signed, and was generally contemptuous of the Berlin politicians who did not stand in the thick of the diplomatic battle with the Allies. Simons, whose description of Giesberts was quoted above, expressed to his wife the delegation sentiment about the government: "The Cabinet is really like a poultry yard over which a hawk is hovering. It is restless, nervous, irresolute, and is almost always making the wrong decisions." [52] He described Erzberger, "whom we call *Archimonteur* (arch climber)," as "constantly throwing stones in front of the wheels" of the efforts of the Peace Delegation.[53] He stated that Erzberger had planted several spies in the delegation to know what it was doing, by which he meant that several of its members reported regularly to Erzberger about their work. Rantzau unceremoniously sent these members home whenever he learned about their correspondence.[54] Personal relations within the German government had become completely impossible as the hour of decision on whether to accept the final Allied terms approached.

Erzberger knew that Rantzau and his delegation would recommend rejection of the treaty after their return to Germany. He did not want the final decision to be made under the time pressure of an Allied ultimatum, and therefore forced a Cabinet discussion of the question, "to sign or not to sign," on June 3 and 4, 1919, while the German delegation was still exchanging notes with the Allies at Versailles. Scheidemann asked Erzberger to present his views in a written memorandum, which served as a basis for the discussion. Erzberger's memorandum stated the alternatives forcefully and tersely:

I. *If the Treaty is signed.*

Terrible burdens will be placed upon the German people.

1. *Foreign policy consequences:* The state of war and the blockade will

especially furious because Erzberger had sent a letter to Scheidemann on April 26, 1919, just before Rantzau's departure for Paris, regretting the absence in the German peace delegation of any diplomat with experience in France, England, Italy, or Belgium. Rantzau took this as a slur on his judgment and previous diplomatic career. Scheidemann, in reply, had promised to try to get Erzberger to apologize, but Erzberger had failed to do so by the time of the Spa meeting. Brandenburg, *Rantzau*, Ch. VI, pp. 55–60, and Ch. VII, pp. 43–45.

[52] Luckau, *op.cit.,* p. 127.

[53] *ibid.,* p. 126. For another unflattering view of Erzberger's diplomatic efforts, see a letter by Wilhelm von Bülow, the future *Staatssekretär,* to Friedrich Wilhelm von Prittwitz, June 3, 1919, quoted in the latter's *Zwischen Petersburg und Washington* (Munich, 1952), p. 236.

[54] Luckau, *op.cit.,* p. 127. The *Erzberger Papers,* File 46, contain a good many letters to Erzberger from Versailles, especially from Major Boetticher and the industrialist Röchling. One of the men sent home was Otto Driesen, a close collaborator of Erzberger's. Brandenburg, *Rantzau,* Ch. VIII, p. 21.

be terminated. The borders will be opened, food and raw materials will enter Germany, and our merchants will again secure private credit. Exports will revive. The prisoners of war will return. Poland will be forced to terminate its aggressive designs. The unity of Germany will be preserved:

2. *Domestic policy consequences:* The tax burden will be crushing, but this will be compensated for business by the fact that imports will revive and internal order will be restored. Employment will rise, with output for both export and the domestic markets returning to normal. Bolshevism will lose its attraction. Working morale and working efficiency will be restored. Increased coal production will end the transportation bottleneck. . . . The present government will presumably remain in power, though the Right and a part of even the Liberal bourgeoisie will oppose it vehemently. It is even possible that there may be a military putsch [against a pro-ratification government] organized in eastern Germany. One must reckon on the east opposing the implementation of the treaty by force of arms, and starting a general agitation to this effect. But this movement will probably collapse quickly on account of the deep yearning for peace among the vast majority of the people and the visible improvement in the general situation once the treaty has been accepted.

II. *If the Treaty is Rejected*

1. *Foreign policy consequences:* Active warfare will be resumed three days after the Allied denunciation of the armistice. The Allied armies, the Americans included, will advance at least up to Kassel in a line parallel to the Rhine. The entire Ruhr area will be occupied. There are also reports that the Allies will create a corridor from Frankfurt to Prague to separate north from south Germany. The blockade will be sharpened, the borders will be sealed hermetically. . . . The Poles will advance from the east.

2. *Domestic consequences:* A general shortage of food and raw materials throughout Germany. The border population will flee before the advancing armies and will concentrate in the interior of Germany, leading to a catastrophic famine. The loss of the Ruhr will mean an end to Germany's coal supplies, meaning a collapse of transport and consequent paralysis in all big cities. The hour of Bolshevism will come. Plunder and murder will be the order of the day. The communications system will cease to function in the general anarchy. Hence the atomization of Germany. The civil service will be paralyzed in the absence of instructions from higher authority. The shortage of goods will lead to a crazy inflation and complete worthlessness of the currency. Russian conditions will come to Germany. Numerous bourgeois elements will be driven by sheer terror into the arms of the extreme Left. The rest will go to the extreme Right. The result will be civil war, especially in Berlin and the other big cities.

The unity of the German nation will be destroyed. The individual states will not be able to withstand Allied pressure to sign separate treaties of peace. Separatist tendencies have already shown themselves in Bavaria, the Rhineland, and the east. These tendencies will be much strengthened following the total disintegration of the German state. A Rhenish Republic would be proclaimed within a few days. The Allies will attach the individual states to themselves by bonds so firm that a German national state will cease to exist. Several smaller German areas would also seek independence to secure the favor of the Allies. The map of Germany would again become a crazy patchwork quilt, thereby realizing the dream that has long guided French ambitions. The unoccupied part of Germany would soon be forced to seek terms from the Allies as an exhausted and ruined country. Even if the consequences of an Allied advance were less catastrophic than here assumed, the Rhineland would in any case be lost and German unity destroyed. A still worse peace than the present one would be imposed upon the German people within a short period. The hope that the Allies would be willing to assume the administration of an utterly ruined Germany is probably mistaken. A powerful current in France and England wishes the total impotence of Germany. The Allies would partition the country and leave each part to stew in its own juice.

The results of the failure to sign the treaty and the consequent military advance of the Allies can be summarized briefly:

1. The dissolution of national unity and the establishment of several German states. The hatred of the various states against Prussia, which is widely blamed for the present catastrophic situation, would make the separation a permanent one.

2. Peace would have to be signed after a brief interval, but it would be signed by the several different states separately. They would be obligated, under imposed terms, to pledge themselves not to enter into any future German national state. Such a peace would be still worse than that now proposed.

3. Overthrow of the government and its replacement by Independent Socialists and Communists, dissolution of the army, and anarchy throughout the entire country.[55]

The majority of the Cabinet was sharply opposed to acceptance of the Treaty of Versailles at the meetings on June 3 and 4. This was the

---

[55] Erzberger, *Erlebnisse*, pp. 371–73. Erzberger's preoccupation with the separatist danger, so evident in this memorandum, was paramount in his mind throughout the spring of 1919. He vigorously opposed the view of some Rhenish Zentrum figures that a Rhenish state, more or less closely linked to France, was desirable to escape from Prussia, Bolshevism, and heavy reparations burdens. Scheidemann and Erzberger met with Rhenish deputies on March 13, 1919 to warn them against the plan of breaking away from Prussia though they intended to remain loyal to Germany. G. Senger, *Die Politik der Zentrumspartei zur Frage Reich und Länder von 1918–1928* (Hamburg, 1932), pp. 37–38.

view of both Chancellor Scheidemann and of President Ebert (who sometimes attended Cabinet sessions). Erzberger took the view, for the reasons stated in his memorandum, that there was no alternative to acceptance. The opponents of the treaty argued that it would be dishonorable to accept terms which were objectively incapable of being fulfilled, but Erzberger replied that:

> There was no dishonor if we signed under clear duress, provided we announced the fact that we were signing under duress. Suppose someone tied my arms and placed a loaded pistol against my chest, and asked me to sign a paper obligating me to climb to the moon within 48 hours. As a thinking man I would sign to save my life, but would at the same time say openly that the demand simply could not be fulfilled. The moral situation presented by [the Entente demand to sign] the treaty was exactly of the same kind.[56]

Erzberger's arguments did not prevail in the Cabinet: only three of his colleagues, the Socialists David, Noske, and Heine, agreed with his view. The Democratic ministers were especially vehement against ratification.[57]

The Cabinet did not, however, accurately reflect the views of the parties composing it. Most Democratic deputies shared the view of the Democratic ministers that ratification was unthinkable, but a small minority under former Vice Chancellor Payer, coming mostly from the southwest (an area directly exposed to French invasion), favored acceptance of the treaty.[58] A large majority of the Socialists favored acceptance despite the strong opposition of Scheidemann. This left the decision up to the Zentrum Party. A majority for ratification could be obtained only by a Socialist-Zentrum coalition, while an anti-treaty majority coalition could reach from the Zentrum to the Nationalists. Erzberger worked very hard, at a series of party meetings beginning June 13, to rally the Zentrum to the cause of ratification. He found general agreement that renewed military resistance was unthinkable, but many deputies took the view that they could not vote for a treaty which included the dishonorable articles 227 and 231. Erzberger then suggested a formula that proved to be the wedge that broke up the anti-treaty majority in the National Assembly. He got the Zentrum Party

---

[56] Erzberger, *Erlebnisse*, p. 374.

[57] The Cabinet sessions of June 3 and 4 are described in *Erlebnisse*, pp. 373–75, an account based upon Cabinet protocols in *Erzberger Papers*, File 14. The moon analogy was deemed too frivolous for inclusion in the Cabinet protocols. Scheidemann gives his account in *Zusammenbruch*, pp. 248–51, and in *Memoiren eines Sozialdemokraten* (Dresden, 1928), pp. 370–72.

[58] Payer, *op.cit.*, Ch. XVII.

leadership to agree to ratification of the treaty provided the Entente would agree to make concessions on the two dishonorable articles.[59]

Did Erzberger have the illusion that the Entente might agree to such modification of the treaty? The approach to Conger had proved fruitless. Erzberger tried a second time in mid-June to obtain concessions from the Allies by pleading his domestic difficulties. This time he approached Clemenceau through two French agents stationed in Germany, Professors Haguenin and Hesnard. Both were personally opposed to the vindictive features of the Versailles settlement. Haguenin wrote to the Entente leaders in Paris on June 21, 1919, urging concessions in the questions of war guilt and war criminals, but found Clemenceau obdurate. Haguenin and Hesnard also assured Erzberger that the treaty would be less harshly enforced than its terms warranted. They argued that the important thing was to accept it now in order to end bellicose attitudes. They argued that this would promote lenient interpretations of what admittedly were very harsh terms. This proved an accurate prophecy as regards the surrender of the war criminals, which was in fact never carried out. Erzberger attached considerable importance to the views of the French professors, and used them freely in drumming up support for the treaty. He found the assurances a valuable tool at a time when desperate men were willing to clutch at straws. They helped him to persuade many deputies to favor conditional acceptance of the treaty, provided concessions were made on articles 227 and 231. Once men had committed themselves to this position it was difficult for them to oppose the treaty solely on the two points of honor if the Allies should continue to prove obdurate. The stimulation of unrealistic hopes of modification may have been part of the "camouflage" that Erzberger had mentioned to Conger on May 19, but it is equally likely that Erzberger believed the not unreasonable predictions of the two Frenchmen.[60]

The Entente presented Germany with a seven-day ultimatum on June 16, 1919, either to accept the treaty (with only very small modifications achieved by Rantzau) or to face invasion. The German Peace Delegation returned to Weimar determined to reject the Allied ultimatum, while Erzberger continued his efforts to organize a majority in favor of acceptance of the treaty. The crucial Cabinet meeting of June

[59] Erzberger, *Erlebnisse,* p. 375.
[60] Haguenin's letter to the Peace Delegation, June 21, 1919, is printed in James M. Read, *Atrocity Propaganda 1914–19* (New Haven, 1941). The role of Haguenin and Hesnard is discussed in K. F. Nowak, *Versailles* (Berlin, 1927), pp. 283–87, 320–24. For a portrait of Haguenin, see Vallentin, *Stresemann* (Leipzig, 1930), pp. 63–72. Erzberger freely admitted his contact with the Frenchmen in his *Erlebnisse,* p. 379, and in *Prozess,* p. 744.

18 showed that Erzberger had made some progress since the meetings two weeks earlier. The vote then had been 10 to 4 against ratification. It was now 7 to 7, with the two Zentrum members (Bell and Giesberts) and one additional Socialist now converted to Erzberger's view. Erzberger pleaded in favor of ratification by a pointed analogy with Kerensky's failure to make peace on time, and called Rantzau the champion of a "Vabanque Policy." The advocates of ratification were much strengthened by the virtually unanimous support of the Premiers of the various German states, especially those from the south who feared being driven into a position where they would have to sign separate treaties of peace. Scheidemann, who remained opposed to accepting the treaty and felt himself bound by his pledge of May 12, 1919, then announced the resignation of the Cabinet to President Ebert (June 19). This left Germany without a government while only four days remained until the Allies would begin their march into Germany.[61]

Erzberger then took the leading hand in the organization of a ministry willing to meet the Allied demands. Bauer, a Socialist who had previously been Minister of Labor, was appointed new Chancellor by Ebert. Erzberger wanted to become head of a new Ministry of Transport in order to carry out the great work of railroad nationalization contemplated by the National Assembly, a work that he believed particularly well-suited to his executive gifts.[62] The new government was to be based upon the Majority Socialists and the Zentrum, but Erzberger favored the inclusion of individual Democrats in the Ministry, not as delegates of their party (since it was opposed to the treaty) but as private individuals. Their inclusion would have heralded the future return of the Democrats to the Weimar coalition once the treaty issue was out of the way. Erzberger pressed Bernstorff, who saw the necessity of accepting the treaty, to accept the Foreign Ministry, despite their quarrel at the time of the Conger mission; but Bernstorff refused out of loyalty to Rantzau and the Democratic Party, and also because American public opinion still mistook him for a circus master of spies and saboteurs.[63] Erzberger urged Dernburg, the former Colonial Secretary who had become one of the founders of the Democratic Party, to remain as Finance Minister to implement the great tax reforms which were being planned. But the Democratic Party sternly prohibited its members from participating in the government. Dernburg's refusal left the Finance Ministry unoccupied at a time when Germany's desperate

[61] Erzberger, *Erlebnisse*, pp. 376–78. Stern-Rubarth, *op.cit.*, p. 107. Schiff, *op.cit.*, pp. 112–13.
[62] Erzberger, *Erlebnisse*, p. 378.
[63] Bernstorff, *Erinnerungen*, p. 192.

financial situation made it the most important office in the government. Both Ebert and Bauer told Erzberger that he was the natural man for the job because of his energy, imagination, and expert knowledge of fiscal problems. Erzberger knew that the drastic new taxes that were required were bound to make any Finance Minister odious to the propertied classes, and felt that he already had enemies enough. But his party friends urged him to make, exactly, as he had done when becoming Armistice Commissioner, another personal sacrifice for the sake of the Fatherland. Erzberger then accepted the offices of Finance Minister and Vice Chancellor while resigning as Armistice Commissioner.[64]

The immediate problem for the new government was to secure the ratification of the treaty by the National Assembly. The government sought and secured on June 22 an authorization to sign the treaty, provided modifications were made on articles 227 and 231 as required by the Zentrum Party decision opposing unconditional ratification. The government won the support of the National Assembly by 237 to 138, with the Zentrum Party voting 78 for and only 9 against. This conditional ratification was immediately cabled to Paris in the hope that it would secure Allied acceptance. But the Allies rejected all concessions whatsoever and demanded unconditional acceptance of the treaty within 24 hours. The deadline was 7:00 p.m. on June 23, 1919.[65]

Erzberger and his Zentrum Party colleagues were shaken by the Entente reply, which endangered the solidarity of the pro-ratification coalition. They were also disturbed by specific rumors concerning the plans of some officers to start a revolt in case Germany should sign the dishonorable treaty. A scheme was afoot to set up a new military state in Eastern Germany, which would secede from the rest of Germany and defy the Allies.[66] Noske, the Minister of Defense, who had previously been Erzberger's closest ally in the struggle for ratification, changed his mind under the threat of mass action by his officers—be it military revolt or collective resignation. A Zentrum Party meeting on the morning of June 23 declared, by an overwhelming majority against only 14 votes, that the treaty must be rejected in view of the Allied in-

---

[64] Erzberger, *Erlebnisse,* pp. 378–79. The Armistice Commission got a new head in Von Simson, and was now subordinated to the Foreign Office. Erzberger urged its rapid dissolution as a separate body, suggesting August 1, 1919, as a terminal date. Erzberger to Stockhammern, July 4 and 17, 1919. *Erzberger Papers,* File 50.

[65] Erzberger, *Erlebnisse,* p. 380.

[66] The Prussian Minister of War, Reinhardt, favored plans of resistance in the east. Groener spent much time checking him. See Geyer, *Groener,* pp. 151–64, and Craig, *op.cit.,* pp. 368–73. Carl Goerdeler, the later head of the resistance against Hitler, was actively engaged in a conspiracy to set up a separate state in the east. G. Ritter, *Goerdeler* (Stuttgart, 1954), pp. 21–25.

transigence. Erzberger acquiesced in a decision he felt at first powerless to change.[67]

The Zentrum vote created a theoretical majority opposed to the ratification of the Versailles terms. The situation was desperate. The government, formed for the specific purpose of accepting the treaty, was breaking apart. An alternative government was unavailable, since both the Democrats and the Zentrum, however great their dislike of the treaty, were unwilling to form a coalition with the Nationalists against the Social Democrats. They felt that Germany could not be governed against the wishes of 45 percent of its population represented by the two Socialist parties. The Allies were set to march into Germany in the early evening if the treaty was not unconditionally ratified by that time. A conference of party leaders met at noon under the leadership of President Ebert to see whether the situation could still be saved. Erzberger put the question squarely to the opponents of ratification: were they willing to form a government that would face renewed hostilities? The answer was a clear "No" from the Democrats and People's Party and an evasive "No" from the Nationalists. The opponents of ratification lacked the courage of their convictions. Many of them had been shocked by the last-minute Zentrum reversal which deprived them of the agreeable position of protesting against the treaty as patriots while being (secretly) relieved that their opponents accepted the odium for what they recognized to be an inevitable decision.[68]

A decision in favor of unconditional ratification was promoted by two unexpected developments. Ebert asked the opinion of General Groener on whether the treaty should be ratified. Groener, speaking over the telephone from Kolberg, made a curious distinction: he recommended acceptance not as an officer, but as a German. He also believed that he could prevent both a mass resignation of officers and the crazy plan of a military state in the east seceding from the rest of Germany. Groener's assurances calmed one of the two apprehensions that had

[67] On the Zentrum Party meeting, see Erzberger, Erlebnisse, p. 380, A. Koehler, Deutsches Zentrum-deutscher Rhein (Trier, 1932), pp. 44–47. The best account of the Zentrum meeting is in a memorandum drawn up by two Zentrum ministers, Wilhelm Mayer and Johannes Bell, printed by A. Luckau, "The Unconditional Acceptance of the Treaty of Versailles by the German Government June 22–28, 1919," in Journal of Modern History, xvii (Sept. 1945), 218. Noske explains his change of view in Von Kiel bis Kapp (Berlin, 1920), p. 153. See also his Erlebtes aus Aufstieg und Niedergang einer Demokratie (Offenbach, 1947), pp. 107–08, and Wilhelm Keil, Erlebnisse eines Sozialdemokraten (Stuttgart, 1948), ii, 184–86.
[68] Erzberger gives a contemptuous account of the behavior of the anti-ratification parties in his Erlebnisse, pp. 381–83. See also Payer, op.cit., pp. 300–04 and Luckau, op.cit., pp. 218–19.

governed the Zentrum caucus vote against unconditional acceptance.[69]

The difficulty about the points of honor remained, however, unresolved. It threatened to classify supporters of the treaty as less honorable than opponents. Karl Heinze, a leader of the People's Party that was supposedly adamantly against ratification, produced a formula that aimed at meeting the problem. He suggested a parliamentary maneuver whereby the authorization given to the government the previous day to sign the treaty conditionally would be enlarged to convey an authorization to sign unconditionally as well. This would avoid a new vote on the treaty itself in which its supporters would be forced to go on record as approving the points of dishonor. Heinze also suggested that the parties opposing ratification should agree to make statements that they recognized that the supporters of the treaty were animated by motives as patriotic as their own. These declarations were an honest if unsuccessful attempt to avoid future political embarrassment for the parties supporting ratification. The Democratic, People's, and Nationalist Parties showed their true colors by giving their support to Heinze's maneuver. Their mood is perhaps not unfairly characterized by Friedrich Naumann, who told Erzberger in the course of the parliamentary session on the afternoon of June 23: "Today we still need you, but in a few months, when the over-all situation will have changed, we will get rid of you." Erzberger replied: "I shall be satisfied with having sacrificed my personal reputation today for the Fatherland in its hour of greatest trial." [70]

The treaty was accepted on June 23 and Germany was spared a further Allied invasion. Erzberger's policy had succeeded in bringing the decision in favor of ratification despite great obstacles. He had never wavered in his conviction that the treaty must be signed. He was almost alone in refusing to yield to pessimism about Germany's future, and he did not participate in the mood of doom and gloom that was sweeping the country. He carried his incorrigible cheerfulness to an incautious extreme when drinking his beer with some Zentrum friends at the *Goldener Adler* Inn on June 14—a week before the acceptance of the treaty. The proprietor asked all the members of the party to write something in his guest book, and Erzberger obliged with: *"Erst mach dein*

---

[69] Geyer, *Groener*, p. 161; Erzberger, *Erlebnisse*, p. 381.

[70] *Ibid.*, pp. 382–83. Heuss, in his biography of *Naumann*, p. 494, doubts that his hero used the words reported by Erzberger, but there is no reason why Erzberger should have invented them. Naumann, who had become a sick and irritable man under the strain of the war, engaged in personal invective against the proponents of treaty ratification at the first Democratic Party Congress four weeks later. Heuss, *op.cit.*, p. 495.

Sach—dann trink und lach" (Attend to your business first, but drink and make merry afterwards).[71] This provided easy ammunition for his enemies, and large sections of the public believed in the stereotype of a beer-consuming, portly Erzberger laughing while the Fatherland was sinking into ever greater misfortunes.

Erzberger's policy of supporting the treaty had, in fact, arisen from a serious and responsible consideration of the desperate alternatives confronting Germany. The decision had been made in complete disregard of the consequences for himself. He knew that his advocacy of ratification would sharpen the hostility aroused by his work as Armistice Commissioner. The enmity was soon to take a violent form. Erzberger wrote:

> An assassination plan worked out by some members of the army on the evening that the treaty was ratified failed. Some shots were fired through the windows of my office in the Finance Ministry a few days later. A room that was believed to be my bedroom was wrecked by a hand grenade. . . . But all this hatred on the part of my opponents cannot shake my conviction that the signing of the peace treaty was the only way to save the German people at that time.[72]

Was acceptance of the treaty the best policy for Germany in 1919? The consequences of acceptance can be described only as catastrophic. The treaty, especially in its blank-check reparations provisions, was incapable of being fulfilled by Germany, a fact that was certain to lead to incessant future controversy between Germany and her former enemies, not only about Germany's obligations but also about her good faith in seeking to live up to them. These controversies were bound to take the form of future ultimata like the one which had led to the acceptance of the treaty in the first place. Germany was destined to go from humiliation to humiliation, while her default must lead eventually to the French imposition of sanctions. This was to happen in 1923 with the occupation of the Ruhr and its attendant consequences: the total collapse of the currency, renewed attempts at Communist insurrection, Hitler's Beer Hall Putsch, and the progressive demoralization of German society.

The worst effect of the acceptance of the Versailles Treaty by the

---

[71] Graefe, *Damals in Weimar* (Berlin, 1929), pp. 27, 28. Graefe was so enraged by this that he entered in the same guest book a few days afterwards:

> Als Deutschland noch in Ehren und Macht,
> Hab nach der Arbeit ich gerne gelacht.
> Doch seit ein Judas in Deutschland erstand,
> Das Lachen von meinen Lippen schwand!

[72] Erzberger, *Erlebnisse*, p 383.

National Assembly was the complete discrediting of the Weimar Republic among broad strata of the population, especially among the upper and middle classes. They identified the democratic Republic with the external humiliation of Germany, and exploited the fact that the parties that had carried the acceptance of the treaty (Socialists, Zentrum, and some Democrats) were also the parties that supported the new constitution. The Right parties found the promise of June 23, 1919 —to respect the patriotic motives of their opponents—convenient to escape responsibility for resuming hostilities with the Allies, but forgot it speedily afterwards. The democratic parliamentary tradition in Germany, already burdened by the failure of the *Paulskirche* in 1848 and the success of Bismarck in 1870–1871, was further saddled with responsibility for one of the most humiliating peace treaties known in European history. The Weimar Republic never established solid roots in German national life, and for this its unsuccessful foreign policy, from Versailles to the Ruhr, was mainly responsible. The terrible inflation of 1922–1923, among whose causes the impossible reparation load and the Ruhr invasion are most prominent, further embittered the attitude of the moneyed classes towards a Republic that had tolerated the destruction of their social substance. Both the inflation and the humiliation were the natural consequences of a policy that accepted the treaty.

But would a policy of rejection of the treaty not have been more catastrophic still? It has been argued, on the contrary, that the Entente Powers were really bluffing, that they were desperately anxious to have some German government sign a treaty, and wanted to avoid an Allied occupation of Germany at almost any price. It is further asserted that the Allies, prodded on by Lloyd George who personally thought the treaty much too severe, would have met a united German refusal to sign by concessions bringing a considerable improvement in terms. No solid evidence has ever been presented to buttress these arguments and assertions.[73] The inevitable result of a German refusal of Allied terms

[73] Rantzau's sympathetic biographer, Brandenburg, admits that his hero's attitude was motivated not so much by rational argument but by an instinct that defiance would secure better terms for Germany, and a deep feeling of irritation at having foreign policy questions decided by party caucusses. His friend Walther Simons, in a memorandum drawn up in late June 1919, gives the best summary of what went on in Rantzau's mind. He did *not* expect that a German policy of defiance would lead to (1) immediate Entente acceptance of the German counter-proposals of May 29, or (2) immediate open dissension between the Allies or (3) the United States' preventing a French occupation of the Ruhr and an English seizure of the Kiel Canal. But he *did* expect that (1) the Entente would at last enter into oral negotiations between experts and that (2) Entente dissensions would break out as soon as military actions had been undertaken. Rantzau believed the United States would not tolerate a renewal of rigid blockade practices, and that she wanted normal commercial relations with Germany. England, he believed, needed a strong Germany as a counterweight to France and Russia and as a desirable

would have been the horrors which Erzberger described in his memorandum of June 3, 1919—Allied advance up to the Weser River, the separation of north from south Germany, separate peace treaties between the Allies and several German states, and the permanent partition of Germany.[74] This gloomy prospect would have been accompanied by famine, disorder, and Bolshevism, with Moscow being more than eager to exploit the desperate plight of the German lower classes. The Allies would scarcely have been deterred by either moral scruples or economic self-interest. The latter really required the preservation of a prosperous Germany from which reparations could be milked. But the French valued security more than reparations.

The analogy of 1945 is sometimes invoked to show that Allied occupation of all of Germany would not have been a bad thing in 1919, especially so far as the future of German democracy was concerned. The present-day democracy of Western Germany is, indeed, a more sturdy plant than was Weimar democracy, despite the fact that it is burdened by the bitterness stored up by the primitive conditions of life during the early years of the military occupation (1945–1948)—conditions which certainly would have been equalled in the years after 1919 if Germany had been occupied after the First World War. The analogy ignores two fundamental differences between 1919 and 1945. In 1919 the French government would have had the paramount voice in German affairs. The United States assumed this role after 1945. The restoration of civilized living conditions after 1945—the prerequisites for the emerging democratic structure—was the result of American rather than French policy. An Allied military government under Foch, taking orders from Poincaré in Paris, would have carried out a policy in 1919 of partitioning Germany and prolonging economic chaos.

The analogy of 1945 is misleading in another respect. Germany was internally far better prepared for democracy in 1945 than she had been in 1919. The defeat of Nazism in 1945 had finally discredited German chauvinist and anti-democratic attitudes by a most powerful pragmatic

---

customer. He was convinced that public opinion in England, France, and Belgium—especially in Liberal and Socialist circles—was rapidly turning against a vindictive peace, and would swing even farther after violence had been imposed upon Germany. Rantzau felt certain that Germany's over-all position would, therefore, soon improve even if defiance should lead to Anglo-French military operations. If worst came to the worst, Germany could still sign the treaty later under direct compulsion, as the Russians had signed Brest—her moral position would be better if she signed in the face of military operations rather than the mere threat of such operations. Brandenburg, *Rantzau,* Ch. VIII, pp. 56–64.

[74] The Allied Plans, which Erzberger guessed with remarkable accuracy, are described in the discussion of the Council of Four, printed in *Foreign Relations. Paris Peace Conference,* VI, 501–50.

argument—failure. The extent of the catastrophe in 1945, and the obvious responsibility of the Nazis for starting and prolonging the war, made a later glorification of the Nazi era quite impossible, and militated against the spread of any "stab-in-the-back" legend. All these considerations were absent in 1919. The democratization of Germany had then advanced *pari passu* with military defeat, and the hostility of part of the working class to the war effort gave some plausibility to the "stab-in-the-back" legend. The Imperial period could easily secure the reputation of a golden age, and did so increasingly as the Weimar Republic had to cope with impossible tasks set for it by the victors. In 1945 there appeared to be no alternative to democracy—apart from Communism—for the German people, with Nazism standing completely discredited. To reason about 1919 in terms of the results of 1945 is to ignore the major differences in both the internal and external conditions of Germany between the two dates.

To secure the ratification of the treaty in 1919 was Erzberger's greatest single achievement, yet it was one for which public monuments will never be erected to honor his name. He thwarted the policies of those who, misled by nationalist phrases, quixotic conceptions of honor, or failure to foresee consequences, would have driven Germany into famine, partition, and military occupation. The harshness of the treaty was the natural result of the popular passions provoked by modern war and the utter helplessness of Germany. The necessity to accept the treaty arose from the simple fact of German defeat in war. This defeat had been the result of the prewar and wartime folly of the Imperial regime, for which its generals, bureaucrats, Junkers, capitalists, and professional patriots must bear the primary responsibility. It is ironic that these five groups screamed loudest against the Weimar politicians for accepting the treaty, and talked as if Erzberger were personally responsible for the onerous terms dictated by the Allies. Erzberger and his colleagues were, in fact, only administering an estate which their assailants had thrown into bankruptcy. The wild rage of Erzberger's enemies was soon to be further provoked when he led a campaign to expose the mistakes of Germany's wartime leadership, and inaugurated financial reforms that taxed the propertied classes with unparalleled severity.

CHAPTER XIII

FINANCE MINISTER (JUNE 1919 TO MARCH 1920)

The Political Situation in July 1919

THE acceptance of the Treaty of Versailles brought a temporary relaxation of tension. The National Assembly continued its work of constitution-making, while also serving as the regular legislature. The new government under Bauer, with Erzberger as Vice-Chancellor and Finance Minister, proposed a policy of economic revival in domestic policy and loyal fulfillment of the Treaty of Versailles in foreign policy. It condemned the continued agitation of the Independent Socialists and Communists, who called for the dictatorship of the proletariat and incited endless strikes that prevented economic recovery. It condemned with equal vigor the policy of the extreme Right, with its program of restoring the monarchy and a foreign policy based upon armed revanchism. The extreme Left could be crushed by Noske after bloody street fighting. The extreme Right was far less vulnerable, because it was entrenched in the army, bureaucracy, and judiciary, and had the sympathy of much of the capitalist and landlord class. The latter groups had been paralyzed in the first weeks after the revolution, but they soon recovered their nerve and began to attack the government which had just saved them from Bolshevism. Their theme was that the parties of the Weimar coalition were responsible for Germany's present plight by their defeatism during the war, and had even desired Germany's collapse to place themselves in positions of power. They questioned both the patriotism and the integrity of many of the Republican leaders, and stopped at nothing to discredit them in the eyes of the German public. Their special phobia was Erzberger, who appeared particularly vulnerable because he had signed the armistice and been responsible for getting the Treaty of Versailles accepted by the National Assembly.[1]

Erzberger was not the man to suffer in silence. He always thought counterattack the best political defense. The government decided to strike a vigorous blow against the parties of the Right by issuing revelations about their wartime follies with the aim of showing that they, and

[1] For the program of the Bauer-Erzberger government, see the government declaration of July 23, 1919, in *Reichstag Debates*, CCCXXVIII, 1843–59. For a Right-wing attack on the government and especially Erzberger, see speech of A. von Graefe, a member of the Conservative Party, in *ibid.*, July 25, 1919, pp. 1912–25.

not the Zentrum and Socialists, were primarily responsible for Germany's unfortunate present condition. Erzberger played the leading role in a speech in the *Reichstag* on July 25, 1919, that caused a sensation. Erzberger denounced the Imperial government, the Conservative Party, the Pan-Germans, and the Supreme Command for their chronic illusions about a military victory, their annexationism, their submarine policy, and above all their sabotage of a peace of reconciliation by their insistence upon retaining control of Belgium. In this connection he used his access to Foreign Office files to first reveal the inside history of the Papal peace move of the summer of 1917 and its unsatisfactory treatment by Kühlmann and Michaelis. He exposed the plans of some German industrialists for controlling the Belgian economy with the help of Helfferich. Erzberger also pinned down Ludendorff's responsibility for the panicky armistice request of October 4, 1918, by way of refuting the "stab-in-the-back" legend. Erzberger denounced the campaign against Zentrum and Socialist leaders undertaken by the motley assortment of militarists, nationalists, bureaucrats, and plutocrats as a camouflage maneuver to distract attention from their own crimes and follies. The government proposed establishing a Court of Inquiry to investigate who was responsible for the military defeat of Germany. This proved the genesis of the *Reichstag* Committee of Inquiry. The immediate effect of Erzberger's revelations was devastating. The *Reichstag* majority fell into a collective fit of indignation against Germany's former rulers and voted the printing of the speech at public expense for circulation throughout Germany. Some mothers in the spectators' galleries, who had lost sons in the war, were seen shaking their fists at Conservative deputies, yelling "Give us back our murdered sons!"—referring to the governmental failure, under Conservative pressure, to make peace in 1917.[2]

Erzberger's revelations (especially about the Papal peace note) did not remain unchallenged in the ensuing debate, and his opponents were able to point out inaccuracies of detail that took some of the luster from Erzberger's initial oratorical success. His Right-wing assailants also developed the *tuquoque* argument, stating that Erzberger's annexationism in the early war years deprived him of the right to criticize other annexationists, and that his public approval of Michaelis' handling of

[2] *ibid.*, pp. 1926–43. The scene is described by Hans Goslar, a government official, in *Germania,* Sept. 3, 1921. See also the vivid and generally accurate political novel by Karl Widmaier, *Erzberger, Ein Kulturroman der Gegenwart* (Dillingen, 1922), pp. 252–67. Widmaier was a Württemberg schoolteacher with few literary gifts but great political penetration. His portrait of Erzberger in the years 1918 to 1921 is very valuable. The Right-wing organizer of Erzberger's assassination in the novel, Count Sassin, is overdrawn and unconvincing, and does not represent any historical figure.

the Papal note in September 1917 made his criticism purely *ex post facto*. Erzberger freely admitted his annexationist follies in the early stages of the war, but took pride in his abandoning them as impracticable while his antagonists persisted in their folly until the end of the war. He excused his action on the Papal note by Michaelis' failure to give him full information. Erzberger then warned the critics of the government to moderate their attacks lest the government be forced, in self-defense, to publish material in German files about the wartime activities of Right-wing politicians, soldiers, and industrialists. Such publication might have unfortunate consequences for the affected individuals, since the Allies had still not drawn up a final list of German war criminals to be extradited. Erzberger's opponents, like Helfferich, interpreted this statement as a threat that the government would hand them over to the Allies unless they stopped their attacks. Erzberger insisted, on the contrary, that he had only pointed out the logical consequences that would probably ensue if the government were pressed to give, for example, details about Helfferich's plan to exploit the Belgian economy (which he had mentioned in his speech of July 25). Both Erzberger's statement, and the indignation provoked by it, indicate the deplorable tone of German political warfare in the summer of 1919.[3]

The entire debate was unfortunate in arousing public passions without leading to constructive results. The anti-Republican elements in Germany (especially those entrenched within the governmental apparatus) ought to have been attacked by methods stronger than speeches of exposure. The greatest mistake of the Bauer-Erzberger government was its failure to weed out unreliable elements in the army, bureaucracy, and judiciary. The explanation of its failure lies in its preoccupation with immediate administrative and legislative tasks, and its con-

[3] Erzberger's supplementary speeches can be found in *Reichstag Debates*, CCCXXVIII (July 28, 1919), 2022–31; (July 29, 1919), 2057–61. His main Right-wing opponents were Graefe, pp. 1912–25 and Riesser, pp. 2050–56. The alleged threats to hand his opponents over to the Allies occur on pp. 2031 and 2061. There is considerable doubt what Erzberger actually said. A version in the *Deutsche Allgemeine Zeitung*, July 30, 1919, quoted by Helfferich in *Prozess*, p. 22, included a clear threat. Erzberger, in *Prozess*, pp. 42–43, declared this version inaccurate, and was supported by the *Reichstag* protocol of July 29, p. 2061; but the latter had been checked over and possibly corrected by some officials of the Finance Ministry, though not by Erzberger himself. The textual controversy centered around whether a comma or a colon was the correct version. In the former case, Erzberger would be giving his own views; in the latter, those of another man whom he had just referred to (Dr. Riesser of the People's Party). The controversy could not be settled since both commas and colons are inaudible. The question was discussed at length in *Prozess*, pp. 740–51, 854–55, 902, 959. Riesser admitted that Erzberger was quoting him, pp. 748–51, and the Court, though generally hostile to Erzberger, ruled in Erzberger's favor, pp. 1046–49. Helfferich's belief that Erzberger was trying to hand him over to the Allies is symptomatic of the pathological political atmosphere of 1919, though Erzberger should have taken greater care not to be misunderstood.

centration upon the paramount Bolshevik danger. The belief that its opponents on the Right were an anachronistic and fading group, while sanctioned both by Erzberger's optimism and the Socialist philosophy of history, proved a dangerously mistaken view. Erzberger had, meanwhile, made the political mistake of provoking his enemies without crushing them. He had assumed the leading partisan role in a campaign concerning past events at the very time when his new job as Finance Minister required that he play a national rather than a partisan role. His drastic tax program was bound to be resisted by the upper classes in any case; it was unfortunate that he had further stirred their anger by taking the lead in blackening their wartime record.

Germany's Financial Needs

Germany's financial situation appeared nothing short of catastrophic when Erzberger took over the Finance Ministry on June 21, 1919. The national debt, which had stood at 5 billion marks in 1913, had risen to 153 billions, of which 72 billions were floating debt necessitating either early repayment or a gigantic funding operation. The responsibility for this condition must be charged to the men who managed German finances during the war, especially Karl Helfferich, Treasury head from 1914 to 1916, whom Erzberger was soon to call "the most frivolous of Finance Ministers." Helfferich had advocated the comfortable principle that Germany's enemies should pay for the whole cost of the war after their defeat (which did not prevent his expressing moral indignation when the Allies applied a far more lenient principle to Germany after 1918). He had placed all of Germany's military expenses (including even the sums spent for peacetime maintenance of the army) in an "extraordinary budget," which was covered by loans and Treasury bills to be repaid out of reparations. This allowed him to brag about a surplus in the "regular budget" despite the fact that the yields from the regular taxes (tariffs, excises, railroad surplusses, etc.) had declined during the war. Helfferich failed to introduce new taxes in the spring of 1915 when the cost and unpredictable length of the war ought to have been apparent: his excuses were a continued faith in an early victory, the undesirability of controversial legislation in the midst of war, and the political difficulties arising from the federalist limitations upon Germany's national finance. It will be recalled from the discussion of the prewar fiscal controversies that direct taxes, and especially the income tax, were considered the preserve of the individual states. The anachronistic structure of the Imperial constitution is revealed by the fact that Germany attempted to fight a major war without a national income tax, the one flexible and readily expansible tool of modern finance. A great Finance Minister would have overcome all federalist obstacles and achieved an adequate centralized tax system during the war; but Helfferich did not even attempt this task, and it was left to Erzberger when he assumed management of the near-bankrupt Treasury in 1919.[4]

Helfferich finally yielded to pressure from the *Reichstag* in the spring of 1916 and introduced some new taxes on war profits, turnover (a general excise), and tobacco (all of which were to be retained by Erzberger in 1919). Count Rödern, who succeeded Helfferich in 1916, extended the war profits tax with the aim of capturing a substantial part of all increases in income secured in the course of the war. This meant that some portion of the costs of the war was henceforth financed out of taxes, instead of relying exclusively upon loans; but the damage done during the Helfferich years could not be undone. The national debt skyrocketed thirty-fold, as we have seen; the circulation of paper money (including *Reichsbank* notes) increased from 2 billion in 1913 to 45 billion in 1919. The way was being prepared for the catastrophic inflation of the postwar years.[5]

The revenue and expenditure outlook in 1919 was, if anything, even more discouraging than the size of the national debt. The total expenditure of the Reich in 1913 had been 2.4 billion marks; by 1919 this had multiplied seven-fold to 17.5 billions. The annual interest on the debt now stood at 10 billions, which was more than four times the total peacetime budget. Payments to veterans and war widows and orphans required 4.3 billions. There were completely new expenditures, such

[4] The characterization of Helfferich is in Erzberger, *Reden zur Neuordnung des deutschen Finanzwesens* (Berlin, 1919), p. 6, with citations from Helfferich's wartime speeches on p. 22. This useful collection of Erzberger's financial speeches will be cited henceforth as *Reden*. Ezrberger's criticism of Helfferich was *ex post facto*, since he had praised Germany's financial management in a long memorandum to the Pope, *Wie steht es um Deutschland?* Feb. 24, 1916. Erzberger had then stated: "The Central Powers hold pledges (*Faustpfänder*) of such great value, and their military situation is so favorable, that Helfferich's expectation that 'the lead weight of billions' will be assumed at the peace table by those who have frivolously provoked the war [i.e., the Entente Powers] appears to be justified by the military and economic situation." *Bachem Papers*, File 89.

[5] The standard treatment of German war finance is Walter Lotz, *Die deutsche Staatsfinanzwirtschaft im Kriege* (Stuttgart, 1927). The treatment of financial topics in this chapter is based primarily upon Paul Beusch, *Die Neuordnung des deutschen Finanzwesens* (M. Gladbach, 1920), a brilliant popular exposition henceforth cited as *Neuordnung;* Heinrich Brüning, "Die Arbeit der Zentrumspartei auf finanzpolitischem Gebiet," in *Nationale Arbeit,* pp. 354–88; Johannes Popitz, "Die deutschen Finanzen 1918–28," in *Zehn Jahre Deutscher Geschichte* (Berlin, 1928), pp. 179–202. For technical treatments, see J. Jastrow, "The New Tax System of Germany," in *Quarterly Journal of Economics,* xxxvii (1923), 302–41, and Erwin Respondek, *Die Reichsfinanzen auf Grund der Reform von 1919–20* (Berlin, 1921).

as payments to the unemployed (a wartime innovation that could not be discontinued); subsidies for food and housing necessitated by inflation; and compensation for Germans who had lost private property through enemy action during the war or in the territories ceded by Germany under the Treaty of Versailles. The as yet unspecified Allied reparations demands hung as a further cloud over Germany's financial future. The expenditures of the individual Länder and communities had risen in the years since 1913 from 3 to 7.5 billion. This created an additional headache for Erzberger since he was about to deprive these units of many sources of revenue in favor of the Reich and had to make some provision for them to meet their legitimate needs.

While expenditure mounted, the yield from the regular peacetime taxes declined. The taxable wealth of the country was diminished by the loss of valuable territories (such as Alsace with its textile mills), the surrender of the merchant fleet, and the Allied confiscation of all of Germany's foreign assets. The continued paralysis of foreign trade led to decline in tariff revenues. The railroads, which had regularly earned surpluses before the war, all operated in the red under the impact of excessive wartime use, neglect of capital investment, and surrender of rolling stock to the Allies. The so-called matricular contributions, paid by the individual states to the Reich government as a symbol of the federalist principles embodied in the constitution, had become an impossible burden upon the states, whose financial situation was nearly as desperate as that of the Reich. The taxes introduced in the latter half of the war brought revenue up to about 7.5 billion marks despite the declining yield from the prewar taxes. Since expenditure had swollen to 17.5 billions Erzberger was confronted with the need for finding 10 billions in permanent new taxes, or about four times the normal prewar budget. In addition he must seek to collect steep one-time levies in order to scale down the crushing burden of floating debt, with its permanent threat to Germany's credit position.[6]

Some fiscal theorists considered Erzberger's problem to be insoluble, and they advocated a declaration of national bankruptcy in order to get a clean start. This would have meant a repudiation of Germany's huge internal debt. Erzberger set himself sternly against this course, partly to save Germany's credit, partly to protect the rights of millions of small bondholders. He emphasized that patriotism must not be penalized:

Debt repudiation would injure those who have helped the Fatherland in its hour of need. The war profiteers and black marketeers, who did not put their money into war bonds, would be twice favored; in the first place

[6] For a lucid survey of the financial position in 1919, see Beusch, *Neuordnung,* Ch. I.

they made big money during the war, in the second place they would not be affected by the repudiation of the debt.[7]

Erzberger looked instead to levying heavy, indeed confiscatory, taxes upon the rich. He felt that this was morally justified because of the scandalous failure to raise adequate taxes during the war.

> The basic mistake of our wartime economic policy can be expressed in the following formula: we mobilized living bodies through our universal military service, but we neglected to draft capital and property as well. We exacted blood but refused to demand sacrifices of property without payment of interest.

He drew in the same speech a somber portrait of the conditions created by this mistaken policy:

> We see on the one hand ethical and physical devastation in human life and human strength . . . impoverishment and misery on the part of the middle and lower classes, who have borne the main brunt of the war. We see on the other hand huge profits, the consolidation of capital, luxury, ostentatious living, and no diminution in wealth among the greater part of those who have hitherto constituted the ruling class. . . . The crazy, destructive, and completely negative theory of Bolshevism raises its ugly head in the midst of the ruin of our existing political and economic order, drawing its power from the fact that it embodies, in an extreme form, the violated conscience of the nation. The only medicine against this Asiatic disease is the creation of a social order based upon justice, in which wise leadership gives expression to justified demands.[8]

Erzberger looked upon his tax plans not only as devices to avert bankruptcy and to restore orderly finances. He looked upon them primarily as a way to build up a genuinely democratic order in Germany in which the rich shared sacrifices along with the poor, and in which Bolshevism would lose its attractiveness to the lower classes.

Erzberger's Organizational Reforms

Erzberger's greatest achievement as Finance Minister was the establishment of the fiscal sovereignty of the Reich at the expense of the individual states. The Reich acquired the power to levy all kinds of taxes and to prohibit the Länder and communities from raising any taxes that interfered with its own. It also established a national tax-collecting machinery that largely superseded that of the states. This constitutional revolution was explained and justified by Erzberger in the following words:

[7] Erzberger, *Reden*, pp. 4–5.
[8] *ibid.*, pp. 5–6.

The Reich has completely changed its structure [since the collapse of the Imperial regime]. It is no longer a federal state, created in response to the wishes of a group of monarchs. A great step in a unitary direction has been made [by a democratic parliament working out a new Constitution]. The present structure of the Reich has been created by the will of the German people as a whole [rather than the individual states]. In this fact lies a strong centripetal tendency. The constitutional changes require a comparable change in the authority to tax. The individual states have been until now the practical tax sovereign in Germany. The Reich was, to be sure, theoretically in a position to raise direct taxes, but the hostility of the *Bundesrat* made this a practical impossibility. . . . The Reich will become the primary tax sovereign in the future. The introduction of tax-collecting machinery under its direct control will reflect the changes in the structure of the German constitution.

There are, in addition, compelling practical reasons that require the creation of national tax machinery and the transfer of the most important revenue sources to the Reich. . . . The relationship between the tax needs of the Reich on the one hand and the states and the communities on the other hand has been altered completely. Before the war the Reich required about 40 percent of the total tax yield, the Länder and communities about 60 percent. Today the Reich needs some 75 percent, the Länder and communities only about 25 percent, meaning a complete reversal of the earlier proportions. When the payments required under the peace treaty become fully effective, the Reich will require at least 80 percent of the total yield. With such a shift in tax needs it is inevitable that we secure a similar shift in tax authority, namely to give the Reich control over all important revenues while making it responsible for meeting the needs of the Länder and communities.[9]

These arguments could not convert the federalists, who saw in fiscal centralization the death-knell of their political principle. Reich control of all major revenues was bad enough, but the corollary drawn by Erzberger—that the Reich must collect its own taxes through its own officials—was still worse. Yet Erzberger knew that no tax system can be better than its collecting machinery, and he succeeded in establishing Reich collecting offices throughout Germany (*reichseigene Finanzämter*). The purpose was to secure uniformity, rigor, and equity where variety, laxity, and injustice had previously prevailed. Income tax rates had differed from state to state, and assessment practices had differed still more. There were several tax-free islands that had competed for becoming the legal residence of wealthy persons, as the states of the American Union once competed in granting charters to corporations. The East Elbian officials had long been known for their low assessment

[9] *ibid.*, p. 112.

of property owned by Junkers. Erzberger swept away all this historic variety of favor of a unitary system directed from Berlin. He created a uniform tax code that was applicable to all Germans, regardless of their local residence. A great increase in yield was expected from the fact that the new Reich collectors would be free from local pressures.

Erzberger's reforms gave Germany a modern, efficient, and economical tax system that has stood the test of time. The new system represented the greatest advance towards national unification achieved since 1867, and Erzberger hailed it as a powerful rivet of the Reich (*Reichsklammer*) at the very moment when Germany's enemies hoped for a revival of the centrifugal particularism that had marred so many centuries of German history. The result of Erzberger's legislation was to make the once independent states little more than provinces of a centralized state. The old system which had kept the Reich dependent upon the financial contributions of the Länder (the so-called matricular contributions) was replaced by one where the states became completely dependent upon the Reich as the latter monopolized the major sources of revenue. Erzberger did not intend to starve the Länder financially. He deprived them of fiscal sovereignty rather than revenue, for he generously placed large percentages of the yield from several new Reich taxes at their disposal. They were to receive 57 percent of the new income tax, 20 percent of the new inheritance tax, and 50 percent of the new land transfer tax. This gave the states an estimated federal contribution of 5.3 billion marks, whereas their total 1913 revenues had been only 2.4 billions. Erzberger also left them in control of some of their traditional taxes—such as those on amusements, real estate, buildings, and crafts—but he insisted that they must meet certain norms set by the Reich in the administration of these taxes. These norms were set for a common minimum of equity and efficiency, and they also served to strengthen the position of the Finance Ministers of the individual Länder in dealing with their often very parochial parliaments. Erzberger also urged the states to show some ingenuity in developing new sources of revenue. These hopes were largely disappointed, and the virtual atrophy of state fiscal sovereignty was one of the results of Erzberger's tax reforms. For this federalists, especially Bavarians, never forgave him.[10]

[10] On the reorganization of Reich-Länder relations in the tax field, see Erzberger, *Reden,* pp. 113–19, and Mabel Newcomer, "Fiscal Relations of Central and Local Governments in Germany under the Weimar Constitution," *Political Science Quarterly,* LI (1936), 185–214. Erzberger insisted upon the abolition of the financial privileges accorded to the South German states in 1870 (the so-called *Reservatrechte*). These represented particularism rather than federalism, and appeared all the more odious in the

The nationalization of the railroads was another great step towards centralization. The railroads had been hitherto administered by the individual states. Bismarck had wanted to nationalize them, but had been defeated by a combination of the federalist (Zentrum) and *laissez-faire* (Liberal) forces in the *Reichstag*. The war had shown the advantages of centralized administration of the network as a whole, and it appeared desirable to carry these advantages into peacetime.

When Germany faced a transport crisis in November 1919 in potatoes and coal, the government ordered an embargo upon passenger travel: the Bavarian railroad administration, proud of its autonomy, openly defied this embargo, thus providing a further argument to the proponents of nationalization. The general shortage of rolling stock, resulting from losses under the armistice terms, also suggested the need for consolidation and centralized direction. The individual states were much less averse to nationalization than they had been before the war, because all the roads were in a desperate financial position. The Prussian railroads, for example, had earned a surplus of 463 millions in 1913; they ran up a deficit of 4.3 billions in 1919. The railroad employees were eager for nationalization because they wanted to benefit from the very generous pay scales passed by the National Assembly for government employees (the *Reichsbesoldungsreform*), effective April 1, 1920.

Erzberger had become interested in the railroad problem while Armistice Commissioner, and we have seen his ambition to become first Minister of Transport when the Bauer government was formed in June 1919. When Erzberger became Finance Minister instead, the job went to his Zentrum colleague Johannes Bell. Elaborate negotiations between Bell and the various state railroad administrations took place in January and February of 1920, but ended in a complete deadlock due to the extravagant financial demands of the states. The problem was then handed to Erzberger as Finance Minister, though he was at the same time absorbed by the great tax reforms and his libel suit against Helfferich.

Erzberger was in a strong negotiating position because the Weimar Constitution called for a transfer of the railroads to the Reich by April 1, 1921. It provided that the German Supreme Court should assign com-

light of Erzberger's unitarian principles. He backed his colleague Giesberts in abolishing the South German postal privileges as well. Erzberger went rather too far in needlessly provoking federalist enmities. In a speech in the *Reichstag,* on October 8, 1920, he labelled the Länder obsolete and called for the substitution of *Reichsprovinzen. Reichstag Debates,* cccxxx (Oct. 8, 1920), 2938. Erzberger earned the special enmity of the Bavarians by his strong unitarian views, and the Bavarian Zentrum Party went so far as to secede from the main body of the Zentrum Party.

pensation to the states if a voluntary agreement between Reich and
Länder was not reached by October 1, 1920. The Länder knew that they
would get better terms by negotiation than by adjudication. Erzberger
supplemented the threat of a court decision by a divide-and-conquer
technique that worked Länder claims off against one another. A settlement was promoted by his inclination to be generous about assuming
railroad debts incurred since 1916, which were estimated at 30 billion
marks. He defended this generosity on the grounds that the real value
of the sum was bound to be diminished by future inflation, that the
health of the finances of the Länder was of genuine concern to the
Reich, and that it was desirable to deprive the foes of nationalization of
any financial argument. An agreement between Reich and Länder was
reached in March and was ratified by the National Assembly on April
24, 1920. By that time Erzberger was no longer in office, but his colleague Bell carried out his policies faithfully.

Erzberger gave Germany a single, unified railroad system whose
efficiency was soon to become the envy of the world. It further promoted the trend towards unitarian centralization which had been the
keynote of Erzberger's policy since the revolution. The Reich government now ran a railroad system extending over 53,000 kilometers and
employing more than 1 million officials and laborers. The economical
management of the network soon led to surpluses which were to play
a significant role in the first constructive approach to the reparations
problem at the time of the Dawes Plan of 1924.[11]

Erzberger's Taxes

When Erzberger became Finance Minister he found that his predecessors in office, the Democrats Schiffer (November 1918 to April 1919)
and Dernburg (April to June 1919), had prepared several tax proposals
which were ready for submission to the National Assembly. The
very able *Staatssekretär* Moesle had done a good job of technical preparation. Hence Erzberger cannot claim credit for originating the taxes
that he introduced in July 1919. His job was the more difficult one of
pushing the new taxes through parliament before the summer recess.
His political flair, zest in debate, and technical proficiency made him
the perfect man for dealing with his fellow-deputies. His manner of
driving the bills through the Finance Committee has been described by
an observer:

[11] On the railroad nationalization, see K. Hildenbrand, "Der Minister" in *Erzberger
Heft*, p. 696; W. Ziegler, *Nationalversammlung,* pp. 232–36. The success of the Reich
administration of the railroads is analyzed in Gerhard Lassar, "Reichseigene Verwaltung unter der Weimarer Verfassung. Zwei Studien," in *Jahrbuch des öffentlichen
Rechts,* xiv (1926), 1ff.

The scene is set in the main room of the Finance Committee [meeting at Weimar in the summer of 1919]. The debate is heated, the room is filled. The small, bespectacled *Staatssekretär* Moesle has a difficult position in the cross-fire of attacks and questions. The Right-wing experts are headed by the skillful Dr. Becker from Hessen, the finance specialist of the People's Party, assisted by the old *Geheimrat* Riesser. Hampe, the finance expert of the Nationalist Party, assists them as a valiant swordsman. The room is filled with cries of "Finance dilettantism," "strangulation of capital," etc. Erzberger arrives the moment the debate gets really hot. Moesle, visibly relieved, sits down in his chair while Erzberger jumps into the fray with his customary radiance and carefree manner. The entire picture changes. Erzberger, who has been on his legs since eight o'clock in the morning, and who has already appeared before several other committees, intervenes in the debate with his marvelous elasticity. He immediately attacks his strongest antagonist, Dr. Becker, despising attack where resistance would be weak. He follows the formula that counter-attack is the best defense. Moesle has informed him with a few words about the tactical situation and the preceding debate. This suffices for Erzberger to drive back Becker point by point. The nervous and melancholy Adolf Braun, the Socialist expert, gives support to the minister. The corpulent figure of Dernburg arises with difficulty from its chair, seeking to calm the passionate debate by the introduction of some technical consideration. Then a side door opens and Dr. Südekum, the Prussian Finance Minister, appears straight from Berlin, his red face flushed with anger. He is loaded with explosives against the Reich Finance Minister, and immediately begins a sharply accentuated and temperamental attack. The Right also renews its assaults. Erzberger is not in the least dismayed. He gives out blows in a most friendly and joyful fashion, while sometimes surrendering, in an almost imperceptible manner, small bits of ground. Erzberger, in the joy of combat, loses control of his tongue. He indiscreetly makes several announcements about future tax plans that had previously been kept top-secret, having been discussed only with a few high officials of his Ministry that very same day. Three or four *Geheimräte* at the government table turn white with horror and cast despairing glances at each other. All the committee members turn to the sensational revelations, and a new battle begins.[12]

Erzberger forced the committee to remain at work despite the sultry summer heat of Weimar. When the committee wanted to go on a parliamentary vacation,

Erzberger appeared suddenly, asked to speak, and within five minutes he had kneaded the tired committee, previously bent upon adjournment, like clay in his hands. The friendly, corpulent man appeared as the very em-

[12] Hans Goslar, "Erzberger in Weimar. Einige Erinnerungen," in *Germania*, Sept. 3, 1921.

bodiment of energy, he radiated such a fascination that serious opposition was impossible. Erzberger urgently demanded that the committee complete the discussion of at least one of his tax proposals. Several heads drooped with resignation and intimidation, but the question had really been settled by this speech. The chairman, the soft spoken and somewhat unctuous Mr. Mumm, a clergyman by profession, can only say "yes" and "Amen." Erzberger smiles with happiness, shakes a few hands, and then disappears to another committee meeting. The chairman, who had really planned to send his committee home on vacation today, distributes the new printed material, and announces with one eye smiling and the other in tears: "Well, gentlemen, let us get started. The title of the new law is." [13]

Erzberger's first tax proposals, submitted in July 1919, consisted of five main parts. The first was a war profits tax (*Kriegsabgabe*) for 1918 that followed principles already introduced by Rödern for the years 1916 and 1917. It taxed any increase in income which persons or corporations had over 1913, on the assumption that such an increase constituted a war profit. The tax affected only wealthy people, the incidence starting at 13,000 marks. The first 10,000 marks were taxed at 5 percent, the next 10,000 at 10 percent, and so up to 70 percent for millionaires. The increased profits of corporations were taxed at 80 percent, though this could be cut in hardship cases down to 40 percent. Payment was facilitated by the Treasury's accepting war bonds at face value for payment, but only if they were turned in by the original purchaser. The latter provision was aimed at speculators who had manipulated the value of the bonds at the bourse. Erzberger hoped to raise no less than 10 billion marks by this tax.

Erzberger's second tax was aimed at fortunes which had swollen during the war (*Kriegsabgabe vom Vermögenszuwachs*). Erzberger set January 1, 1914 (when assessment had been made for the *Wehrbeitrag*), and June 30, 1919 (i.e., immediately after the signing of the peace treaty) as the two dates on which fortunes were to be compared. The gains in those five and a half years were to be taxed progressively, with the initial exemption being set at 10,000 marks total property and 5,000 marks gain. The first 10,000 of taxable increase were taxed at 10 percent, the next 10,000 at 15 percent, and so on. All increases exceeding 172,000 marks were taxed at 100 percent, thus setting a theoretical top limit to war profiteering. The parties of the Right opposed any such absolute ceiling, while the Socialists thought it scandalous that any one should be allowed to keep any wartime gains at all. Erzberger defended his bill against the criticism of the Left by arguing that small gains

[13] *ibid.*

were usually the result of thrift rather than of speculation, and that these gains were usually made in the form of repayment of business debts. To tax these small gains would handicap postwar economic reconstruction by throwing many small businesses back into debt. Erzberger expected to collect 2 billion marks from this tax, which, when added to the 10 billion from the *Kriegsabgabe* for 1918, would theoretically allow an immediate reduction in the debt by 12 billion marks, with the result of an improvement of credit and an annual saving of 600,000 marks (5 percent of 12 billion) in interest alone.[14]

Erzberger's third tax was an inheritance tax of great technical beauty (*Erbschaftssteuer*) which was expected to yield 700 millions. It introduced three principles to govern the very steep progression: distance of family relationship (with wives and children paying least, remote relatives most), size of the bequest, and previous wealth of the beneficiary. The main incidence of the tax was intended to fall upon individual bequests, though taxes upon the estate as a whole and gift taxes were retained for control purposes. Erzberger's proposal was bound to raise partisan controversy in view of the earlier Zentrum hostility to inheritance taxes. Erzberger explained that his own main objection to the 1909 law—the ease of evasion by mobile capital—was no longer valid, in view of the availability of the assessments made for the 1913 capital gains tax (*Vermögenszuwachssteur*) and the certainty of firm administration by the new Reich collecting offices. The tax was, in fact, accepted with relatively little opposition. A drastic reorganization of the tobacco tax also enjoyed smooth passage. Erzberger's fifth proposal was a completely new land transfer tax of 4 percent, of which half the proceeds were to go to the states and communities. This last tax was an example of Erzberger's unitarian centralization, since it gave the Reich exclusive tax authority in a field that had previously been a tangled chaos of state and communal jurisdiction.[15]

These five taxes—the two *Kriegsabgaben* on increases in income and property, the new inheritance tax, the tobacco tax reorganization, and the new land transfer tax—were all completed before the summer recess. The total revenue from the first two would be a one-time yield of 12 billions. The three other taxes, which were intended to be permanent, were expected to yield about a billion annually. This was only

---

[14] An excellent description of the two *Kriegsabgaben* can be found in Paul Beusch, *Die ausserordentliche Kriegsabgabe für das Rechnungsjahr 1919 und die Kriegsabgabe vom Vermögenszuwachs* (M. Gladbach, 1920). A popular attack upon the two taxes, aimed at the working class, is a pamphlet by Wilhelm Henning, *Habt acht auf Erzberger! Das neue Steuerprogramm und der Vorschlag der Vermögensabgabe eine Täuschung des deutschen Arbeiters!* (Osnabrück, n.d. [1919]).

[15] On the last three taxes, see Beusch, *Neuordnung,* Ch. II.

about one-tenth of the new taxes required in order to balance the budget.[16]

To raise the remaining nine-tenths became the main business of the National Assembly in the winter of 1919–1920 after its work of constitution-making had been completed. Erzberger's most controversial proposal was to raise a one-time capital levy, called a *Reichsnotopfer* (Sacrifice to the Reich in Its Hour of Need). The once controversial *Wehrbeitrag* of 1913 was nothing compared to what Erzberger now demanded from the German taxpayer. The exemption of all small fortunes, exactly as in the two *Kriegsabgaben* of 1919, showed that the main aim was to tax the wealthy. Erzberger allowed a personal exemption of 5,000 marks, with an additional exemption for each family dependent except the first child. This meant that a married man worth 30,000 marks was exempted from the levy altogether if he had five children. The rates applied to taxable wealth were very stiff. The first 50,000 were taxed at 10 percent, with the rate rising to 50 percent for those worth 3 millions. It must be remembered that these were taxes on capital, not on income. Lump-sum payment was completely out of the question without throwing the entire economy into hopeless confusion. Payments were, therefore, scheduled to extend over thirty annual installments stretching from 1920 to 1949. The possessor of 3 millions would, for example, have to pay 50,000 marks every year for the next thirty years. The tax was intended to hit personal fortunes without causing major injury to industry. Corporations were taxed leniently at 10 percent on their reserves alone, not the value of their capital issues. It was felt that the latter were already taxed through their individual owners, with Erzberger arguing that double taxation (of the corporation as a whole and its stockholders individually) should be avoided.[17]

It was hoped that the capital levy would reduce the inflationary danger by checking new investment (with surplus funds going into tax payments) and reducing the quantity of money in circulation (by the Treasury withdrawing Treasury bills, as they were used for tax payment, from circulation). The hope turned out to be a poor prophecy. The *Reichnotopfer* did nothing to check the mounting inflation, and probably did something to stimulate it. Wealthy people saw in inflation a convenient way of sabotaging the capital levy. The largest fortunes were the most difficult to assess fairly, and by the time assessments were finally made, the inflation, galloping after 1921, had made them meaningless. The owners of smaller fortunes had in most cases begun pay-

[16] *ibid.*, Ch. II.
[17] *ibid.*, Ch. III.

ments when money was still worth something, thus giving a regressive
character to the levy. Erzberger would have done better to collect
much smaller sums, preferably in gold, much earlier. But the inflation,
without precedent in modern times, was foreseen by no one in the
autumn of 1919.[18]

Erzberger's other taxes were intended to become permanent features
of the German fiscal system. His main achievement was the Reich income tax of 1920, whose constitutional consequences were already mentioned above. It superseded all Länder income taxes and abolished the
right of the communities to add their levies to income taxes (*Zu-
schlagrecht*). The latter had led to fantastic tax differentials, with industrial communities with low incomes and many needs sometimes adding
300 percent while residential communities with high incomes and few
needs made almost no additions at all. Erzberger's income tax also
introduced for the first time the principle of payment at the source by
deduction from wages. This proved both a great convenience and the
basis of high tax morality. The rates introduced by Erzberger were, at
the time, considered to be very steep, with a bachelor earning 10,000
marks being taxed 12.6 percent. The personal exemption was set at
1,000 marks, which was popularly considered to be the "existence minimum," with allowance of exemptions for all family members (500
marks for wife, 300 for each child) being a new feature of German tax
law. Erzberger introduced many socially valuable features into the tax,
such as deductions permitted for serious illness and expenses incurred
in a wife's working. But the most important aspect of the tax was its
unitarian character, its ending the chaotic diversity of taxation throughout Germany, and its stern enforcement, without fear or favor, by the
newly established Reich collectors working under the direct control of
the Finance Minister.[19]

Erzberger proposed a capital gains tax to supplement the general income tax, consisting of a 10 percent tax upon dividends prior to their
distribution to stockholders. He spoke of dividends as unearned income
that should be taxed on the same principle that increased land and
housing values should be taxed—in all three cases the owner had made
no personal effort to increase the value of his property. He rejected, exactly as he had done in the case of the capital levy, the taxation of the
stock value of corporations, preferring to tax dividends instead; for to
tax stock issues at their face value, irrespective of whether they earned

[18] The *Reichsnotopfer* is criticized by both Brüning and Popitz in the articles cited in
footnote 5.
[19] Beusch, *Neuordnung,* Ch. IV.

3 or 30 percent in dividends, would throw the entire stock market into confusion. Erzberger hoped to raise 1.4 billion marks from his capital gains tax. He feared that even the moderate 10 percent tax rate might divert capital into consumption, and proposed to deal with this by taxing the excess consumption of the very rich (*Aufwandsteuer*). The principle suggested was to add a surtax on all high income taxpayers who claimed they were not liable to the capital gains tax because their total property had not increased. Suppose a man stated 70,000 marks as his annual income, and claimed that he had spent every last pfennig. The government should decide that, for example, 50,000 marks was all that a man should resaonably spend, and that he ought to have saved and invested the remaining 20,000. If he had done so he would have paid capital gains tax on the 20,000. Erzberger now proposed that he should be penalized for failure to save, by taxing the 20,000 for excess consumption at a rate considerably higher than the capital gains tax for an equivalent sum. This was certainly a dangerous invasion of the state into the private sphere of how a man should spend his own income.[20]

So far, all of Erzberger's taxes had been mainly levied upon the rich, but he realized that indirect taxes must also be substantially increased. Erzberger raised the turnover tax (a tax upon every turnover in the ownership of every article from production to retail sale) to 1½ percent, which amounted on the average to a 7½ percent general excise (with goods being turned over on the average five times). This tax, unknown in Anglo-Saxon countries, had been introduced initially by Helfferich under the prodding of the *Reichstag* parties in 1916. Erzberger preferred it, from both a moral and administrative point of view, to clamping innumerable individual excises upon different goods. He sought to eliminate its regressive character by supplementing it by a 15 percent manufacturers' excise upon all luxury goods. Erzberger expected to raise 4 billion marks from the turnover and luxury excises combined.

Erzberger also raised several other indirect levies. He placed tariffs upon a gold basis by executive order in July 1919, a step calculated both to check imports and to raise the real value of customs receipts, which were expected to run to 1.5 billions. He raised transportation taxes, on both persons and goods, so as to lead to a yield of about 1 billion. He raised the coal tax, falling equally upon domestic and industrial users, to lead to a yield of 2 billion marks. Various other taxes on consumption (sugar, salt, matches, etc.) were raised to yield 2.5 billion

[20] Erzberger, *Reden,* pp. 106–07.

marks annually. Altogether Erzberger expected to raise no less than 11 billion marks through indirect taxation:

Turnover and luxury	4.0 billions
Tariffs	1.5 billions
Transportation	1.0 billions
Coal	2.0 billions
Miscellaneous	2.5 billions
Total	11.0 billions

Erzberger expected to raise about 14 billion in direct taxes, divided as follows:

Income tax	8.0 billions
Capital gains on dividends, land transfer, etc.	2.4 billions
Inheritances, etc.	1.0 billions
Capital levy (annual proceeds)	2.6 billions
Total	14.0 billions

These figures show that Erzberger sought a surplus of 2.2 billions for debt reduction or future reparations, since an income of 25 billions would be matched by an expenditure of only 17.5 billions by the Reich plus 5.3 billions transferred to the Länder and communities.[21] The budget does not include the 12 billion marks raised through the one-time levies of 1919, which were to be used for immediate debt reduction. Erzberger also emphasized the extreme arbitrariness of many of the figures of estimated yield. No one knew how Germany's foreign trade (and customs receipts) would develop, or how the revolutionary upheavals and the beginning inflation had affected the distribution of income (and hence of income tax receipts). Erzberger's main aim was to establish, on paper at least, a balanced budget that would restore confidence in Germany's financial management at home and abroad. He was also satisfied that the centralized fiscal institutions which were being created would allow a rapid adaptation of the tax system to future needs if his estimates of tax revenues should prove mistaken. Erzberger succeeded in temporarily restoring confidence, though this eroded again when the Allied reparations demands became known in 1921. He rightly predicted that his organizational reforms would prove adequate to meet the exigencies of the future.

The heavy taxes upon income and property levied by Erzberger

[21] All these figures are, of course, very rough, and aim at giving a general picture rather than technically accurate information. Erzberger analyzed the quantitative side of his budget in *Reden,* pp. 100–10, with a table on p. 110.

aroused deep indignation among the upper class. A feeling of panic swept through financial circles, and capital attempted to flee abroad to escape the new taxes. Erzberger, foreseeing this, had taken the most drastic steps against the flight of capital, both in terms of rigid frontier controls and draconian punishments for violators.[22] These increased the bitterness of the upper classes against Erzberger. The hatred of pluto-cratic and Pan-German circles, already rooted in Erzberger's Peace Resolution and the armistice negotiations, was now reinforced by the pocket-book nerve. Erzberger was depicted as the head of an octopus-like organization spying upon the private habits of all Germans in order to collect new taxes to hand over as reparations to the Allies. The fact that tax proceeds would (not in 1920, but in future years) go to the Allies rather than to meet German needs gave a patriotic coloration to tax evasion. The fact that the high taxes were the price that Germany had to pay for the misconduct of the war by the very classes that screamed loudest against the taxes was easily lost sight of.[23]

Erzberger vainly called for a new attitude towards property. His moral preachments anticipated the doctrine of Christian Solidarism that he was to advocate after his fall from power:

> We must be clear that our reforms are conceived in the spirit of a new age. An exaggerated individualism distorted our conception of property before the war. It emphasized the rights of property while neglecting both its duties and its limitations. I accept, of course, the view that property is rooted in natural law, that it constitutes a basic category of social ethics. But its justification cannot lie in the natural right of each man to own property without restraints. It lies rather in the fact that the social well-being of mankind appears to be impossible without private property. . . . The property concept denies its own justification whenever it leads to an excessive accumulation of wealth, whenever a powerful plutocracy de-velops, and whenever the broad masses of the people, the real creators of wealth, do not participate fairly in the general development of material well-being and culture.
>
> The natural result of such conditions is social disintegration, class hatred, and the corrosive struggle of pressure groups. If a mammonistic spirit accompanies exaggerated conceptions of property, the entire development of a nation will be down a blind alley (*Irrweg*). The proper limits of prop-erty are not observed when the ruling class uses its political power to impose most of the tax burden upon those least able to pay [as had hap-pened in Imperial Germany]. They are not observed when wealth is put to a disorderly use, contrary to the requirements of true culture, in the

[22] For Erzberger's treatment of this problem, see *Reden,* pp. 46–48.

[23] For a bitter attack on Erzberger in a financial debate in the *Reichstag* session of December 9, 1919, see the widely circulated pamphlet by Alfred Hugenberg, *Hugenberg gegen Erzberger* (Berlin, 1919).

support of an artificial culture, which places vulgar ostentation in the place of internal solidity. Then the danger exists that the best potentialities of a nation, its spiritual resources, are suffocated in the pursuit of sensual pleasures. Whenever such conditions prevail, society has a duty to restore more proper conceptions of property. To place the matter in a nutshell: private property finds both its justification and its limitation in the welfare of all. The interests of the nation as a whole must override the interests of its individual citizens. This is the principle underlying the present demand for socialization. It must also be our guiding star in the present tax reforms. We must replace the conception of property and acquisition as autonomous ends by the old Christian conception that man must be both the basis and the goal of all economic activity. But, this can happen only if an organic view of society replaces the prevalent individualistic view. The ideas of Solidarism must be led to triumph.[24]

These ethical appeals met no response from Germany's upper classes. Erzberger's taxes assumed a high order of tax morality which in fact did not exist in Germany. The flight of capital could not be checked completely, and this fact naturally increased resentment among honest taxpayers. The propertied classes were intimidated by measures emanating from what they resented as a hostile government. The capital market was thrown into confusion to the detriment of Germany's postwar reconstruction. It is probable that Erzberger could have collected almost as much, and avoided the unfortunate consequences described above, if he had set his tax rates substantially lower. The moral puritanism revealed by Erzberger was better suited to a revivalist preacher than a Finance Minister. The indiscriminate condemnation of wealth was ill-advised for a man who operated within a social framework that remained capitalist, where the Finance Minister required considerable voluntary cooperation from the upper classes if he were to conduct his office well.

The criticism gains special force when one looks at the fate of the capital levy. We have seen above how it created a powerful class of people who were interested in inflation in order to depreciate the real value of their tax obligations. Erzberger's taxes all assumed that the purchasing power of the mark would remain relatively stable, and when this failed to be the case Germany's finances fell again—after Erzberger's fall from office—into chaos.[25] His successors proved unable to restore orderly finances until 1923.

[24] Erzberger, *Reden*, pp. 121–22 (Dec. 3, 1919).
[25] Erzberger declared in the autumn of 1919 that price levels were unpredictable, and he tried to scare the National Assembly by warning that a failure to cope with the problem of the floating debt might lead to a depreciation of the mark by 90 percent. He clearly did not expect a run-away inflation. *Reden*, p. 46 (Aug. 12, 1919) and p. 102 (Dec. 3, 1919).

A major factor in promoting the inflation—apart from the self-interest of part of Germany's upper class—was the intolerable reparations burden imposed upon Germany in 1921. Erzberger's budget had been based upon the belief that reparations would be based upon Germany's capacity to pay. When this proved a mistaken assumption it was useless to work for a balanced budget or orderly finances. We shall see later how Erzberger proposed to deal with reparations in the spring of 1921. For now it suffices to say that his failure to foresee both the intolerable reparations burden and the unprecedented inflation danger reduced the value of the new taxes he introduced. He shared this lack of foresight with all the politicians and economists of the day, and criticism is inevitably of an *ex post facto* nature.

Erzberger's great permanent achievement lies in the creation of the centralized financial system that survived the inflation. The Reich was henceforth undisputed fiscal sovereign in Germany. The Länder became financial dependents of the national government. The clumsy system of matricular contributions was abolished. An efficient tax-collecting machinery was established in every part of Germany. It administered a comprehensive and uniform tax code. The Länder and communities were forced into a minimum degree of uniformity in the collection of the revenues that remained in their hands. The railroads were integrated into a single, coordinated network owned and operated by the Reich.

These great achievements were completed in the short span of eight months. They give a measure of Erzberger's capacity for constructive legislation. Erzberger achieved his reforms under the difficult circumstance of leading a minority party within a coalition Cabinet that was in frequent danger of breaking apart. He worked in the face of incessant personal attack which he knew would soon lead to a political trial that might ruin his entire career. He worked while immediate fiscal difficulties—an empty till and a mammoth load of floating debt—would have kept a man of lesser capacity from undertaking broad reforms. Yet Erzberger refused to remain enmeshed in the difficulties of the present, and sought rather to attack the revealed deficiencies of the past in order to provide Germany with a better future.

CHAPTER XIV

THE ERZBERGER-HELFFERICH TRIAL
(JANUARY–MARCH 1920)

Helfferich's Campaign

RZBERGER's tax reforms were not the only source of excitement in the winter of 1919–1920. The monarchist, militarist, and nationalist forces, temporarily cowed by the fear of Bolshevism after the military collapse, had resumed much of their intransigence after the ratification of the treaty. The Allied demand for the surrender of the war criminals stirred Germany into seething excitement. No German government was willing or able to fulfill this part of the treaty, or indeed willing to give the accused a serious trial in Germany.[1] Erzberger won, through an intermediary, Foch's assurance that, in return for some minor financial concessions to France, he would not press the matter.[2] No bad consequences in fact followed when the German government pleaded its inability to fulfill Allied demands.

Many of the so-called war criminals were increasingly hailed as national heroes, especially as the "stab-in-the-back" legend gained currency. The decision of the government to investigate the policies of the Imperial regime unintentionally promoted this end. The original proposal, at the time of Erzberger's revelations of July 25, 1919, was to set up a court to try some Imperial officials. This was changed into a standing *Reichstag* Committee of Inquiry into the Causes of Germany's Defeat, which was to engage in valuable historical research for the next ten years. Its value to future historians was much greater than its contemporary effectiveness in strengthening the Republic. Hindenburg and Ludendorff were summoned at an early session, and used its forum for proclaiming the "stab-in-the-back" legend. Helfferich, the former Treasury Secretary and Vice Chancellor, was also summoned to testify,

---

[1] E. Eyck, *Weimarer Republik*, I, 254–55, effectively ridicules the German trial of war criminals at Leipzig.

[2] Erzberger wrote to Müller, the Foreign Minister, on August 8, 1919, enclosing a report on a conversation between Stockhammern and the French General Dupont, in which the latter had said Foch would not insist upon the surrender of the war criminals in return for certain secret financial concessions to France: "The Marshal finds this Treaty clause [surrender of criminals] odious and contrary to his military conceptions of honor. He has said repeatedly that France attaches no value to the *mise en pratique* of this provision of the Treaty, which was placed there purely because of the demand of England. The provision can be explained only with reference to the narrow puritanical British mentality, which wishes *replacer le bon Dieu* in the punishment of the guilty." *Erzberger Papers*, File 53.

and created a sensation when he ostentatiously refused to answer any questions put by an Independent Socialist member of the Committee. Helfferich asserted that a patriotic German could not properly be interrogated by an internationalist Marxist who had prepared the revolution with the help of Russian gold. The majority of the Committee, accepting the curious position that Independent members differed in their rights from other *Reichstag* deputies, punished Helfferich with only a nominal fine.[3]

Karl Helfferich had become the intellectual leader of all of the foes of the Republic. He concentrated his attack upon Erzberger's personality and policies. Helfferich's career presents an interesting contrast with Erzberger's. He was born in 1872, the son of a small textile manufacturer, and he received the best in university education that Germany could offer. His success was meteoric in the three fields of scholarship, business, and politics—it may, indeed, stand comparison with that of John Maynard Keynes, though he lacked the humane spirit and artistic culture of the Englishman. At age twenty-three he made his debut as a fiscal pamphleteer defending the gold standard against the silver heresy, and followed this up at age thirty by a scholarly treatise on *Money* that was translated into every civilized language and gave him a world-wide reputation.

Helfferich was far too ambitious to be satisfied with mere scholarly laurels. He sought a bureaucratic career and entered the colonial office in 1901. Here it fell to his lot to answer Erzberger's charges in the *Reichstag.* Erzberger caused him considerable embarrassment when his official position required him to defend the indefensible. The deep personal antipathy between Helfferich and Erzberger dated from this period.

Helfferich left the colonial office to become head of the Constantinople bureau of the Anatolian Railroad in 1906, when he was only thirty-four years old. He identified himself completely with the German economic imperialism symbolized by the project of building a rail network stretching from Berlin to Bagdad. His virulent nationalism was stimulated by his role as empire-builder. The *Deutsche Bank,* one of the four giant German banks, made him a director in 1908, and used him as a negotiator at various international conferences. Bethmann selected him as the best man to manage German wartime finance in 1915, and promoted him to the posts of Interior Secretary and Vice-Chancellor in 1916.

[3] On the Committee of Inquiry, and especially Helfferich's conduct, see E. Eyck, *op.cit.,* pp. 184–91.

Helfferich's intellectual gifts and prodigious working capacity made him the work-horse of the Bethmann government. His social charm made him a favorite with the Emperor, and there appeared to be no ceiling to his future political ambitions. His one failure lay in his *Reichstag* relationships. Helfferich did not suffer fools gladly, and he hated the aimless debating that characterizes all parliamentary bodies. Helfferich treated the deputies like a professor addressing a class of schoolboys, saw few of them socially, and gave the *Reichstag* the impression that attending its meetings distracted him from more important labors. He soon became *persona non grata* to the Majority parties, and when Hertling wanted to keep him as Vice-Chancellor in November 1917 he had to abandon this project under *Reichstag* opposition. Helfferich, who until recently had been considered a candidate for the Chancellorship itself, must have been mortified by being henceforth confined to the minor job of first directing preparations for the peace negotiations and later becoming German ambassador to Moscow. Erzberger had organized the parliamentary veto against Helfferich's retention in high office.

Helfferich's wartime career was brilliant but sterile. We have already noted the failure of his tax legislation and his belief that Allied reparations could be counted on to pay the whole cost of the war. He failed in his opposition to the submarine war, and lost much credit when he publicly supported the policy he had previously opposed. He failed to prevent the outbreak of the crisis of July 1917. He failed to curb the disastrous influence of the Supreme Command and opposed the only possible remedy of an advance to parliamentary government. He failed to heal the internal schism of the German people by carrying a generous program of domestic reforms, whose necessity did not escape his acute perception. He failed to win the government for his policy of smashing the Bolsheviks in the summer of 1918. He failed above all in his ambition for a commanding position in Imperial politics.

His failure was partly one of character and partly one of conviction. His personality was cold, arrogant, and pharisaical, and always more concerned about achieving his ends than adjusting himself to the follies and eccentricities of his fellow-men. He fully appreciated his own remarkable abilities. Rational and calculating himself, he could not appreciate an exuberant and impulsive temperament like Erzberger's. Helfferich was incapable of engaging in any minor vice, and was very strait-laced in passing sharp judgments upon the moral frailties of others. Someone called him a "Jesuit in a frockcoat." His sense of duty to his country and to himself was perfectly matched. He always considered it an injustice for Germany to be deprived of his own remarkable talents in a leading position—hence his deep antipathy to the parliamentary system, which was incompatible with rule by professorial bureaucrats like himself; hence his aversion to Erzberger, a mere parliamentarian, who thought that the education of a grade-school teacher sufficed for filling the post of Finance Minister. Helfferich's hatred of Erzberger resulted from arrogance, frustrated ambition, embitterment, and cumulative friction, but it was combined with the sincere conviction that Erzberger was ruining the Germany that he loved. He thought that the example of Erzberger—whose personal faults he exaggerated—was spreading moral ruin in Germany. He was convinced that Erzberger's tax policies were a sure road to economic collapse. He asserted that Erzberger's foreign policy from the Peace Resolution to the Treaty of Versailles was incompatible with the national honor, and called for a simple remedy: "Away with Erzberger!" [4]

Helfferich began a series of newspaper articles under this title in the *Kreuzzeitung* immediately after the signing of the Peace Treaty. In these he brought together all the charges developed piecemeal by Erzberger's enemies over the years. He was bent upon forcing Erzberger to sue for libel in order to get a judicial verdict upon the points at issue. Erzberger, then busy with his finance reform, did not answer the articles himself; but he encouraged two of his young assistants, Otto Driesen and Heinrich Hemmer, to mount a journalistic counterattack.[5] The tone of the controversy became increasingly bitter on both sides, with Helfferich finally summing up his charges in the following statement:

Erzberger was during the war one of the worst annexationists while serving on the board of directors of a steel firm. Yet after his sudden and involuntary removal from the board of directors he could scarcely find

[4] For Helfferich's career, see the laudatory biographies by Rudolf Fischer, *Helfferich* (Berlin, 1932) and Adolf Scheffbuch, *Helfferich: Ein Kämpfer für Deutschlands Grösse* (Stuttgart, 1934); also the brief sketches by Kurt von Raumer, "Karl Helfferich," in *Deutscher Westen-Deutsches Reich,* edited by K. von Raumer and K. Baumann (Kaiserslautern, 1938), I, 185–220, and Kuno Westarp, "Helfferich," in *Deutscher Aufstieg,* edited by G. von Below and Hans von Arnim, pp. 371–85. Helfferich's own works are the best introduction to the man, especially his monumental *Der Weltkrieg* (Berlin, 1919) and his *Reden und Aufsätze aus dem Kriege* (Berlin, 1917), *Reichstagsreden 1920–1922* (Berlin 1922), and *Reichstagsreden 1922–1924,* edited by J. W. Reichert (Berlin, 1925). Helfferich had a brilliant career after his campaign in bringing down Erzberger had succeeded. He entered the *Reichstag* in 1920 as a Nationalist and soon won a dominant position in that party. His polemic against the "policy of fulfillment" was vain but added to his prominence. Helfferich played a constructive and perhaps a decisive role in the stabilization of the mark in 1923. He died under tragic circumstances in a Swiss railroad wreck in 1924, aged only 52, when he stood on the threshold of a great second career in high official positions.
[5] The carelessness and inaccuracy of Hemmer and Driesen was discussed at the trial. See *Prozess,* pp. 246–58, 1043–44.

sufficiently strong words of condemnation to express his hostility to the steel industry and annexationism.

Erzberger, when confronted on all sides by accusations against his personal and political conduct, makes no attempt to answer the irrefutable accusations. He relies instead upon false and defamatory accusations against his accusers.

Erzberger has been accused of deliberate untruthfulness not two or three times, but ten or twenty times. He has been accused of mixing his political activity with the pursuit of private financial gain. Yet Erzberger refuses to sue for libel to refute these accusations, preferring instead to escape by muddying the waters in the manner of a cuttlefish.

Erzberger seeks to reply to the accusations levied against him by threatening to denounce his accusers to the Entente as suitable candidates for surrender in accordance with the shameful paragraph 227 of the Erzberger-Treaty.

Erzberger does not hesitate, in order to protect his own skin, to throw the German people into political turmoil by falsifying a useless Papal peace feeler into a serious British peace offer. He knew of the Papal feeler for the last two years, but has only now proclaimed as a new discovery that it was sabotaged by the Supreme Command, the former government, heavy industry, the Pan Germans, and all his other enemies.

Erzberger cannot wash himself clear of the unexpiable guilt of having destroyed a promising peace possibility in the summer of 1917. He allowed himself to be used by the Austrian Emperor and even more by the Emperor's Bourbon-Parma relations in order to sabotage the German will to further resistance, at the very time when our enemies were softening up under the impact of the submarine war, our military successes, and the beginning of the Russian collapse.

Erzberger stabbed German policy in the back with his July action at the decisive moment of the war, acting upon the instigation of his Hapsburg-Bourbon employer. He destroyed the faith in victory and thereby the power to achieve victory of the German people, while restimulating the fading faith in victory and the will to victory among our enemies. He received from the Austrian Emperor behind the back of the Hapsburg Foreign Minister the secret report prepared by the latter for the specific purpose of influencing the German Emperor. He read this disastrous secret report to party assemblies and thereby brought it, according to Count Czernin, to the knowledge of our enemies; thereby giving them, according to their own testimony, the certainty of victory and eradicating once and for all any tendency which may have existed to negotiate an honorable peace with us.

Erzberger's name very properly stands under the miserable armistice.

Erzberger helped the Entente in the period of the armistice to paralyze us financially and steer our entire merchant fleet into Entente ports.

Erzberger led us to Versailles by expressing to our enemies during the course of the peace negotiations his willingness to sign unconditionally the shameful treaty that reduces us to slavery. He has on his conscience the promise to surrender the Emperor and other German men. Knowing his own handiwork he evaded signing the treaty personally.

Erzberger's name is nonetheless attached indissolubly to Germany's suffering and Germany's dishonor.

Erzberger will soon lead Germany to complete ruin by squandering the little moral, political, and economic capital that has survived her collapse, unless his political power is finally broken.

One thing only can save the German people. A single demand must be sounded with irresistible force everywhere in the country: "Away with Erzberger!" [6]

Erzberger could not ignore such charges, coming from a man of Helfferich's prominence, and he filed a libel suit despite the fact that the coming trial would, regardless of its outcome, divert him from his pressing political tasks for several months. He also did so in the knowledge that the peculiarities of German libel law would enable Helfferich to undertake a fishing expedition through his entire past. Helfferich charged him with three kinds of crimes: (1) offenses against propriety (*Anständigkeit*), (2) habitual untruthfulness, and (3) mixing his political with his business affairs. We shall see that Helfferich had comparatively little material on each of the three points at the beginning of the trial, but that he accumulated additional evidence in the course of the judicial proceedings. German libel law allowed the accused to seek to establish completely new facts (not mentioned in the initial libel) if they in any way corroborated his original accusations. Helfferich's charges were of a general nature concerning Erzberger's character; e.g. that he mixed politics with business. The court allowed any aspect of Erzberger's life (whether mentioned in Helfferich's articles or not) to be examined if it threw some light upon whether or not Erzberger mixed business with politics. Since Erzberger was by the nature of the circumstances forced to be the main witness, this left the way open for cross-examination about any and all aspects of his previous life. It would be ungracious for a historian using the valuable trial transcript to complain on this score, but Erzberger was placed in an intolerable situation. Statements introduced in court during the trial were immune from libel action, while being printed in every German newspaper. Thus Helfferich had every advantage in conducting a campaign of character assassination.[7]

[6] Karl Helfferich, *Fort mit Erzberger!* (Berlin, 1919), pp. 81–83.
[7] The difficult legal situation confronting Erzberger is analyzed by Löwenstein, *op.cit.*, p. iff. Helfferich's anxiety to be sued for libel is apparent in his two letters to President

The public prosecutor's office declared that there was a public interest involved in the case, and automatically took over the formal task of prosecution. This proved a great disadvantage to Erzberger, as the two prosecutors, *Oberstaatsanwalt* Krause and *Erster Staatsanwalt* von Clausewitz, became convinced in the course of the trial that Helfferich's charges were substantially accurate. Their summing-up speeches sounded more like an indictment of Erzberger than of Helfferich, though the latter was supposed to be on trial. There was nothing formally irregular in this, since prosecutors are considered in Germany to be impartial state officials rather than parties to the case; but the shift of the prosecutors from attack to defense of Helfferich nonetheless made a deep impression upon the public mind. Such a shift would have been inconceivable under the Empire in a case involving the libel of a minister by a private citizen.[8]

The Beginning of the Trial and Hirschfeld's Murder Attempt

The Erzberger-Helfferich trial took place before a court in Berlin-Moabit (*Strafkammer des Landgerichts I Berlin*) from January 19 to March 12, 1920. The scene has been described as follows: "The court room was dominated by an oil canvas of Frederick William III, the least imaginative of the Hohenzollerns. The spectators' chairs were closely packed with members of the upper classes, with a prevalence of the female element ranging from the high conservative Lutheran nun (*Stiftsdame*) to the fashionable society woman (*Kaffeeschwester*). . . . Erzberger compared the giggling ladies with the Capitoline geese, who thought to save the Fatherland by their cackling."[9] The presiding judge, *Landgerichtsdirektor* Baumbach, conscientiously aimed at keeping political passions out of the courtroom, but his efforts were completely unsuccessful. The spectators frequently cheered Helfferich and laughed at Erzberger, despite repeated admonition from the bench. The threat to clear the galleries was never implemented. The personnel of the court consisted of men hostile to the parliamentary republic.

Ebert, August 17 and September 5, 1919, complaining about the failure of Erzberger and the government to start suit. *Prozess,* p. 986. Erzberger's lawyers denied that there had been any delay in filing suit, and characterized Helfferich's search into all of Erzberger's previous life as an assault upon personal freedom. *Prozess,* pp. 25-26, 939-40.

[8] Eyck, *op.cit.,* pp. 197ff. Eyck's description is the best short account of the trial, combining excellent scholarship with a lucid analysis of the legal problems involved. The main sources for the trial are the 1,050-page stenographic transcript, cited as *Prozess;* S. Löwenstein, *Der Prozess Erzberger-Helfferich* (Ulm, 1921), a legal brief on Erzberger's behalf; and "A" [Adolf Stein] *Gerichtstage über Erzberger* (Berlin, 1920), a brilliant account by a Right-wing journalist.

[9] Fritz Zinnecke, *Erzberger gegen Helfferich* (Berlin, 1920), p. 8.

Judges and prosecutors alike had been raised in a strait-laced bureaucratic tradition which was utterly ignorant of the realities of parliamentary life. They did little to hide their contempt for a party politician, and were horrified by any conduct on the part of a deputy that did not conform to their accustomed bureaucratic codes of honor. They were, specifically, hostile to a deputy engaging in business affairs that would be unbecoming in a state official. "It is not easy to escape one's own skin, and the skins of our high officials have been shaped in an earlier political era. Perhaps the example of the sergeant at arms (*Gerichtsdiener*) Kassube of Moabit is typical. Whenever Bethmann or some other great figure of the old Empire was summoned as a witness, he left the room and returned personally with the man who had been called; but if the witness was a minister of Republican Germany he ripped open the door and yelled through the hallway in a stentorian voice, 'Minister—.' " [10]

The day's session usually opened with a carefully prepared statement of accusation by Helfferich, which was distributed to the press in advance. Yet Helfferich managed to give the impression of spontaneity. He combined an encyclopedic knowledge of the inextricable maze of detail thrown up by the trial with sharp logic and ready wit. His passionate hatred of Erzberger and the new Republican regime gave an emotional force to his arguments and made them all the more convincing to those who were prepared to accept his premises. Helfferich aimed his speeches at least as much at the galleries as at the court. He knew that he had little chance of a technical victory in the trial, since he had without doubt formally libelled Erzberger. He aimed at a moral victory consisting of court acceptance of the substance of his charges, and was willing to accept a nominal fine if he achieved his larger political aims. He never forgot that the real battle was fought out before the forum of public opinion. His free time during the trial was given to briefing journalists. Helfferich was ably assisted by Dr. Max Alsberg, the most effective criminal lawyer in Germany, who proved himself a genius at organizing the ever-mounting volume of new materials that was sent to the Helfferich defense from all parts of Germany as the trial proceeded. [11]

Helfferich's accusation would usually be followed by a defense by

[10] *ibid.*, p. 7.
[11] *ibid.*, pp. 8–9. Helfferich received some material from a certain Semer, a Papal chamberlain, who pretended to be a close friend of Erzberger's, walked behind his coffin in 1921, and took the lead in collecting money for a memorial chapel. Erzberger never suspected his dishonorable activities. See an article by J. André in the *Deutches Volksblatt*, Feb. 1, 1925. Copy in *Erzberger Papers*, File 27.

Erzberger—a procedure that effectively concealed the fact that Helfferich was the man who, technically, stood on trial. Erzberger's courtroom manner often lacked his customary effectiveness. Having busied himself with his great financial reforms until the eve of the trial, he did not have Helfferich's mastery of detail. His style of public speaking required a favorable response from the audience. His temperament felt cramped when he talked to a hostile group of people who met his strongest points with frosty silence or incredulous laughter. He had always been more effective in attack than defense. His main lawyer, the venerable von Gordon, had advised him to avoid political duels and to stick to the facts of the cases under discussion. This may have been sound courtroom advice, but it prevented Erzberger from matching Helfferich's impact upon newspaper readers. His second counsel, Dr. Friedländer, advised him to engage in political counter-attack, with the aim of exposing the reactionary attitudes of Helfferich, judges and prosecution alike. Erzberger, by yielding to this advice only on a few occasions, lost the opportunity of winning a moral victory among the Republican forces outside the courtroom. His optimistic temperament, confirmed by his subjective feeling of rectitude, clung to the hope that he might secure a fair trial despite the fact that the court was bound to be prejudiced against him.[12]

The trial nearly came to a premature end when a half-crazed demobilized officer candidate, Oltwig von Hirschfeld, attempted to assassinate Erzberger as he was leaving the court session on January 26, 1920. His attempt and subsequent trial for murder throw a glaring light on the atmosphere of the time. Hirschfeld had sat in the court as a spectator that day and had followed the Minister out to his waiting automobile. Erzberger had just sat down in the rear seat next to his personal assistant, Dr. Hemmer, and was exchanging a few last words with his lawyer, Dr. Friedländer, when Hirschfeld stepped up on the running board. The young man fired two shots at Erzberger before he was knocked down by the bystanders. The first bullet caused a painful wound in Erzberger's right shoulder. The second pierced his vest, but was deflected from the lung by Erzberger's gold watch chain. The Minister suffered considerable loss of blood and was rushed off to the hospital. He felt that he had escaped death by a miracle.[13]

Hirschfeld was placed on trial on February 21, 1920. His previous history was developed by his lawyer to establish his idealistic motiva-

---

[12] Zinnecke, op.cit., pp. 9–10.

[13] A good description of the crime can be found in the *Hamburger Nachrichten*, Feb. 21 and 22, 1920, reporting the Hirschfeld trial nearly *verbatim*.

tion. Hirschfeld was born in 1899 the son of a merchant. His parents destined him for the army and he received his officers' training at an old cadet school. He saw action towards the end of the war and was twice wounded while on patrol duty. Hirschfeld then joined the government troops that cleared Berlin of the Spartacists in January 1919 but was at a loss when order was restored in Germany. His ambition to become an officer was frustrated by the disarmament provisions of the Treaty of Versailles, and he vaguely thought of preparing to become a merchant like his father.

Hirschfeld told the court that he had begun to read newspapers and pamphlets in 1919 in order to learn who was responsible for Germany's sorry plight. His search was illuminated when he hit upon Helfferich's pamphlet, *Away with Erzberger!* which convinced him, in his own words, that Erzberger "was the chief person responsible for Germany's collapse, and that he knowingly worked against the public welfare." Hirschfeld also believed that Erzberger was paid by the British government for his unpatriotic actions. He felt that Helfferich's call for the removal of Erzberger should be taken literally, and he planned the assassination without any accomplices.

The presiding judge at the trial asked him how he, with his tender years and lack of education, could be sufficiently sure of his opinions to justify implementing them by murder. Hirschfeld replied that he had searched for the truth as best he could, and had been confirmed in his convictions by the fact that they were shared by a famous man like Dr. Helfferich. He insisted upon placing the concluding pages of the Helfferich pamphlet in the trial record as pertinent for explaining his motives.

Hirschfeld's lawyer secured character testimonials from the teachers and commanding officers of his client, which were uniformly favorable. He placed on the witness stand Hirschfeld's mother, who praised her boy and quoted some commendatory letters she had recently received concerning her progeny. A professor at Heidelberg had written her: "All great historical deeds are always done by a single individual." The defense lawyer compared Hirschfeld's action with Cicero's campaign against Catiline. He did, indeed, go so far as to condemn political murder *per se,* but coupled this with an attack upon Erzberger as the man responsible for creating political conditions in Germany where murder inevitably occurred with increasing frequency.

Hirschfeld did not pretend to regret his action while on the witness stand; many of the spectators, mostly ladies with a day off from the Helfferich trial (which had adjourned to allow Erzberger to testify about the attempted murder), approved of Hirschfeld's manly sentiments. He did, however, yield to legal advice to the extent of pleading that he had intended only to wound, not to kill, Erzberger, a suitable excuse for his poor marksmanship. He claimed that Germany was being visibly injured every day that Erzberger continued in power, and he feared that the Helfferich trial, though certain to ruin Erzberger eventually, might yet take months; hence he believed in the necessity of direct action in order to promote the welfare of Germany. Hirschfeld convinced the court of the nobility of his motives, and he was sentenced to the grand total of eighteen months in jail. This ridiculous verdict was not calculated to discourage further assassination attempts against Republican ministers.[14]

The End of the Trial

Erzberger could have forced an indefinite postponement of the Helfferich trial after the assassination attempt by staying away from court for a period of three days (the maximum permissible period of adjournment). Public sympathy had shifted towards him (though far from unanimously) after Hirschfeld's action, and would have approved his seeking full recovery from his wounds before resuming judicial combat. But Erzberger dragged himself out of bed in defiance of doctor's orders in order to allow the trial to come to a finish. He was always eager to get through as quickly as possible any matter that he had started, and probably continued to believe in a favorable verdict.[15]

No attempt can be made here to discuss all of the cases discussed at the trial. Helfferich had charged Erzberger with offenses against propriety, citing the theft of the Naval League letters in the Janke case and his alleged threat to deliver his opponents over to the Entente in July 1919 as primary examples. These cases have already been discussed in Chapters III and XIII. The court decided against Erzberger on the first charge but cleared him of the second. Some further items of impropriety are discussed in the Berger case below.[16]

Helfferich's second main charge against Erzberger was that he habitually and knowingly departed from the truth. The charge was supported by Erzberger's alleged perjury in the Pöplau affair already discussed in Appendix II. The second accusation of perjury dealt with a statement of Erzberger's at a party meeting concerning Bethmann's views on wartime finance, which is examined in Appendix VII. Helfferich's three other examples were all drawn from the political conflicts

[14] All the trial details are taken from *ibid.*
[15] Löwenstein, *op.cit.,* pp. I–VIII.
[16] *Prozess,* pp. 1046–53.

of 1917, and the evidence has already been summarized in Chapter VIII. Some further cases of possible perjury occurred in the course of the trial, and were also deemed relevant by the court in sustaining the accusation of Erzberger's habitual untruthfulness.[17]

The greatest amount of time during the trial was spent in a discussion of some forty-two cases alleging that Erzberger improperly mixed business with politics. The court found him guilty in seven and innocent in thirty-five of these. The most important case, involving his relationship with August Thyssen, has already been discussed in Chapter v and Appendix v. The details of many other cases, which often throw interesting sidelights upon Erzberger's character, can be found in Appendix VII. The discussion here will center around three cases where the court found Erzberger guilty: his relations with the Berger, Hapag, and Rechberg firms.

Julius Berger, a Berlin businessman, owned an engineering firm that specialized in building underground structures on contract from the government. He had built some sections of the Kiel Canal and was engaged in arbitration with the government about terms of payment and the quality of the work performed. He appointed Erzberger arbitrator in several cases against the government between October 1915 and May 1917. Helfferich thought it improper for any deputy to accept arbitration cases against the government, and he noted that Erzberger had spoken up for claims similar to Berger's (though involving another firm) in a meeting of the Budget Committee of the *Reichstag* on February 17, 1914. Helfferich inferred that Berger had appointed Erzberger to the well-paid arbitral position as a reward for the opinions expressed in the course of his parliamentary duties, and he called this an improper mixing of business with political affairs. Berger, when asked the reasons for the selection of Erzberger, replied that he had valued his expert knowledge of canal-building and his reputation for moral integrity in the face of bureaucratic pressures. The court accepted the validity of Helfferich's charges, with their underlying purism about the role of deputies in business affairs. The judges ignored the fact that several other deputies, including the Democratic Party leader Schiffer, had also sat on arbitration cases without evoking unfavorable comment.

Some other aspects of Erzberger's relations with Berger gave rise to more legitimate criticism. Erzberger had, according to the testimony of two disgruntled former Berger employees, received secret information from the firm while sitting as company representative on the arbitration

---

[17] *ibid.*, pp. 1032–46. Löwenstein, *op.cit.*, pp. i–viii, includes a discussion of the failure of the perjury proceedings.

board, a practice which, though no doubt it occurs frequently, is inadmissible in principle. Much worse was the fact that Berger had approached Erzberger with the offer of a seat on the board of directors of the firm while Erzberger was still sitting as arbitrator. Erzberger had failed to reject the proposal categorically, replying instead that he had to consult Thyssen before accepting. Thyssen gave his approval even before the last arbitration case was settled on May 24, 1917. Erzberger joined the board of directors on June 14, 1917, only three weeks after completing his arbitral tasks, a questionable step made even more questionable by the conditional rather than negative reply given to Berger's initial inquiry. There is no reason to believe that Berger intended to bribe Erzberger or that Erzberger was influenced in his decisions by the prospect of joining the board. Berger had many reasons for wishing Erzberger in his firm: his expert knowledge of canal business, his close contact with Thyssen from whom Berger bought his steel, and his influential position, which could facilitate business in the face of bureaucratic regulations. These reasons make the bribery hypothesis completely unnecessary, but they cannot exculpate Berger from making, and Erzberger from not rejecting, an intrinsically improper proposition. It must be remembered, however, that Erzberger's arbitral decision was unfavorable to the Berger firm, a fact that proves that his conduct was improper rather than corrupt.[18]

Erzberger's relation with the Hapag shipping firm showed extraordinary lack of judgment. We have seen how he had promised, in the course of the Trier armistice negotiations, to make the German merchant fleet available to the world shipping pool as part of a bargain to supply Germany with food. His domestic enemies had denounced this as a frivolous and unnecessary surrender, and predicted correctly that the ships would never be returned to Germany. Erzberger thought otherwise. To document his faith he bought 40 shares of stock in the Hapag shipping firm on January 27, 1919, when they stood at 94, and

[18] The Berger case is discussed in *Prozess*, pp. 312–88, 813–18, 867–68, 892–95, 921, 952–53, 957–58, 1011–15. Erzberger's conduct is defended in Löwenstein, *op.cit.*, pp. 15–21. Several of Helfferich's minor accusations in the case were found trifling. Erzberger had urged the War Minister Scheuch to include Berger on a list of recipients of the Iron Cross Second Class on October 8, 1918, while he owned stock in the company. The most serious charge against Erzberger was that he had written a letter to the Prussian Minister of War, Reinhardt on January 27, 1919, supporting some Berger compensation claims against the government. The letter had been handed to Helfferich by some enemies of Erzberger employed in the War Ministry, a questionable proceeding that led to much *tuquoque* talk when Helfferich denounced Erzberger's methods of securing information. *Prozess*, pp. 794–98. Reinhardt rejected the Berger claims, but they were fully sustained by an arbitral decision on January 8, 1920. Erzberger had not asked for a favor for the company; he had only called attention to what the arbitration tribunal declared to be an indubitable legal claim.

60 additional shares on March 28, 1919, at 92. He urged his friend
Giesberts, the Postmaster General, to do likewise, and did nothing to
conceal the fact of his purchase—indeed he later claimed that he had
made his purchase widely known in order to bolster public confidence
in the return of the ships. Erzberger's conduct was questionable on two
counts. He knew, as a Cabinet Minister, what was not known with the
same precision to the general public, that the government would pay
generous compensation to the shipowners if the Allies should refuse
to return the ships. Moreover, as Finance Minister, he soon played a
role in the compensation negotiations with the shipowners following
the loss of the ships in the Versailles Treaty. He therefore should have
sold his stock in July 1919 at the latest, but in fact did so only on November 26, 1919, when they stood at 114. The rise since March was
largely due to inflation, but was also helped by the prospect of early
Reich compensation. The shipowners had received emergency aid for
the prior few months, with regular compensation scheduled to begin
in December (which presumably explains Erzberger's sale on November 26). Erzberger emphasized in court that he had induced the shipowners to put the emergency payments into construction rather than
dividends—hence that he could not personally benefit from them. But
the fact remained that he had, as Minister of Finance, negotiated with
a company in which he personally held stock. There is no reason to
believe that he was influenced by corrupt motives, but his conduct was
highly improper nonetheless, and it showed culpable carelessness in a
matter important for any public official—avoiding even the appearance
of a conflict of interest. Erzberger's friends found it difficult to defend
his conduct in the Hapag case, though they emphasized that his initial
purchase had not been speculative (since the shares did not stand especially low when he bought them), that he had done nothing to conceal
his conduct from public scrutiny, and that he sold the stocks when they
were on the verge of a great advance in value as soon as he saw a clear
conflict of interest.[19]

Erzberger's connection with the Rechberg firm, which produced a
special type of leather called Anhydat, arose from his friendship with
Arnold Rechberg, a man with interesting political connections. Arnold's brother Ernst owned a plant in Hersfeld in Hessen, which had
developed a new tanning process that aroused Erzberger's curiosity. An
interest in new inventions, and invariable optimism about their future
prospects, was one of Erzberger's most characteristic traits. The Rech-

---

[19] The Hapag case is discussed in *Prozess,* pp. 568–89, 822–23, 870–71, 921–23, 954,
1029–30. For a defense of Erzberger's conduct, see Löwenstein, *op.cit.,* pp. 36–43.

berg brothers offered Erzberger 40 shares of the firm's stock at par in August 1916, when the firm stood on the threshold of large profits. A contract with the Kassel Clothing Office of the Prussian War Ministry was signed on September 29, 1916. It guaranteed a reliable supply of raw materials in return for a promise to sell the entire output of the firm to the War Ministry. This contract allowed Rechberg to pay out 12 percent dividends in both 1916 and 1917, and 20¼ percent in 1918. Thus Erzberger made a great deal of money on his initial investment of 40,000 marks, and his dividends increased still more when he received 60 additional shares when the firm enlarged its capital structure in 1917.

Why did the Rechberg brothers decide to let Erzberger in on their lucrative profits at a time when their stock was not for sale to the general public? He was no expert on the leather business and he could not help them with their technical problems. Claims of friendship may have played a part. The court decided, however, that the main reason must have been a desire to enlist Erzberger's political influence, and declared this to be proof of Helfferich's charge about the mixture of business and politics.

Did Erzberger in fact use his political influence to secure favors for the firm? Rechberg did not need his help in securing contracts, but he once asked his help on a patent matter. Erzberger wrote, at Rechberg's request, a letter to the Reich Ministry of the Interior on December 30, 1916, asking for permission to sell the Anhydat patent to Scandinavia (in spite of the fact that an earlier request had been refused under wartime regulations as not in the national interest). Permission to sell was finally granted in June 1917, and it is possible that Erzberger's letter may have carried some weight in the decision of the Interior Ministry. In actual fact the sale never took place. Erzberger's letter about the patent constituted his only service for the Rechberg firm, and it was the kind of service that he willingly performed for dozens of companies every month. He did not think that it was in any way improper for him to call the attention of bureaucrats to the problems of all those who had asked him for recommendations or introductions. He unwisely ignored the fact that Germany's timid bureaucrats were deeply afraid of him, and saw a threat of parliamentary action attached to every letter of recommendation that emerged from his office.[20]

[20] The Anhydat Leather Case is discussed in *Prozess*, pp. 429–40, 519–56, 820–21, 869, 924–26, 1021–24. Erzberger's conduct is defended in Löwenstein, *op.cit.*, pp. 25–36. Erzberger was technically vulnerable because he sat, after 1917, as a parliamentary representative on the War Leather Corporation, though his was a purely decorative post. He did not sit on the committee that allocated raw materials between the producers.

The discussion of several other cases showed that Erzberger had spent much of his time helping individuals and firms in their tangles with the wartime bureaucracy, without looking too closely at the objective merits of the claims he was forwarding. Erzberger's desk contained a box full of cards of introduction, which he readily gave to anyone asking for them. The court found this quite unedifying, and was even more antagonized by Erzberger's lack of repentance in his final speech:

> I have entered this courtroom with a good conscience and I leave it with an erect head. My entire life has been thoroughly examined. I plead guilty to possessing the faults of a good character—excessive eagerness to be helpful—or, to put it more precisely: love of my neighbor (Nächstenliebe) on the one hand, confidence in the statements of those seeking help on the other hand. . . . In my role as deputy I have occasionally been credulous when people asked my support. I fear, however, that I will take these "shadow sides" of my character into the grave as an incorrigible part of myself, because I do not wish to despair of mankind. I know that I have been misused and exploited but I shall never cease to work for the helpless among our people, the widows, orphans, disabled, and veterans. Many fellow-deputies have approached me in the last few weeks with the offer to testify here in court that the aspects of my activities that have been discussed do not constitute even 1 percent of my total activities, and that the part here discussed gives a distorted picture, indeed a caricature, of my whole personality. The code of court procedure does not allow their testimony; but it remains true nonetheless that I have been for years the most accessible of all Reichstag deputies, and that the disinterestedness of my political actions cannot properly be questioned.[21]

Erzberger emphasized, moreover, that he was not a rich man, and that he had neglected many opportunities of becoming one:

> I have repeatedly rejected offers to join company boards. I could easily have earned hundreds of thousands, or even millions, without becoming vulnerable to legitimate attack, if I had been primarily interested in money. I have rejected all these opportunities and have instead built up a small fortune through solid work, not the abuse of my parliamentary position. The imagination of my enemies has invented millions that do not exist. . . . What I have added to my fortune during the war is mostly being taxed away by the laws which I have introduced as Finance Minister. I shall leave the Finance Ministry a poorer man than I entered it. I was until 1918 a free deputy and must be judged by standards applicable to a deputy. Where I assumed business connections, as in the cases of

21 Zinnecke, op.cit., pp. 66–67.

Thyssen, Berger, and Anhydat Leather, I acted within the limits of what is permissible, customary and proper.[22]

The holding of directorships was not unusual for a deputy, with some 10 percent of the total membership of the *Reichstag,* including Stresemann, Haussmann, and Trimborn, doing the same.[23]

Erzberger did not deny that he had sometimes approached government officials on behalf of firms in which he or his friends held a financial interest. But he denied that this constituted improper conduct:

> I have always looked upon the task of mediating between bureaucrats and citizens as one of the most attractive aspects of a deputy's duties. I have always enjoyed helping where others could not help, and I shall continue this enjoyment even if my conduct arouses suspicions. I have helped thousands of people, whether known or unknown to me. It would have been improper to deprive my friends of my help; this would have placed them in a special category with fewer rights than people unknown to myself. I never asked for special favors but only for the satisfaction of legitimate wishes within the framework of the general interest.[24]

Erzberger ridiculed the view, held by the prosecutor and presumably by the judges, that it was his duty to examine carefully the merits of any request before recommending it to the proper authority:

> The prosecutor has no idea of the number of requests that flood a deputy's office, or of the work-load carried by a deputy. The sending of such requests to the authority concerned does not constitute improper intervention. The deputy has the right to assume that an official would not be deflected from doing his duty by a card of introduction, a letter, or even a personal visit from a deputy.[25]

The court found Erzberger's apologia unconvincing, and condemned him for improperly mixing politics with business in seven out of forty-two cases advanced by Helfferich. His carelessness about the maintenance of appearances could not be denied even by his friends, and his sometimes peculiar use of his money, as in investing in new inventions of dubious merit, caused mirth among his enemies. Yet the latter were rather disappointed by the results of the trial, since they had expected sensational revelations about Erzberger's having illegally amassed a huge fortune and having transferred it to neutral countries in defiance of his own regulations against the flight of capital.

[22] *ibid.,* p. 67.
[23] *Augsburger Postzeitung,* Aug. 24, 1917.
[24] Zinnecke, *op.cit.,* p. 72.
[25] *ibid.,* p. 71.

Erzberger's enemies, partly cheated of their prey, decided upon an alternative method of ruining Erzberger. They stole his personal tax returns with the complicity of some officials of the Berlin revenue office, and published them in photostat in the Right-wing newspaper *Hamburger Nachrichten* on February 22, 1920. The returns seemed to give *prima facie* evidence of tax evasion, though later investigation was to show that the charge was groundless. But the immediate sensation was tremendous: Erzberger, who had preached the sternest kind of tax morality since becoming Finance Minister, appeared unmasked as a chiseler and hypocrite. He immediately asked for a suspension from his ministerial duties pending a full investigation of the charges (February 24). The suspension lasted until his formal resignation a few weeks later, following the damaging verdict in the Helfferich trial.[26]

Some of Erzberger's friends, recognizing the inevitability of a hostile court decision, urged him to prevent a formal judgment by withdrawing his initial libel suit, and inducing the government to do the same, shortly before judgment. This might have had a favorable political effect if it had been done immediately after the two prosecutors had gone over to the defense, and if accompanied by a blast against the reactionary attitudes of the Imperial holdovers in the judicial system. It certainly would have hurt Erzberger less than a hostile verdict. But Erzberger disdained all such advice.[27]

Erzberger decided instead to yield to the advice of his junior counsel Friedländer and make a belated political counter-attack. He included a vigorous assault upon Helfferich and his other enemies in his final speech before the court. He called Helfferich

> a typical representative of the happily superseded absolute bureaucracy and plutocracy, who fights with all conceivable, permissible and impermissible methods against a representative of the young German democracy. . . . Why [asked Erzberger] does he concentrate his fire upon myself? He wants to injure our new democracy and fears our political forward movement. He wants to eliminate the present government and to reinstate a reactionary regime, being undeterred by the fact that this will mean an inevitable civil war and the total collapse of Germany. The same political blindness that governed in the form of a military dictatorship from 1914 to 1918 believes that the time has come to resume rule by eliminating myself. And why am I the prime target? My enemies fear what even they acknowledge to be my energy, my constructive capacity,

[26] *Hamburger Nachrichten,* Feb. 22, 1920. For a discussion of Erzberger's finances and taxes see Appendix VIII.

[27] Haussmann reported his advice, given through Fehrenbach, in the *Berliner Tageblatt,* Sept. 7, 1921.

my consolidation of all progressive forces, and my democratic outlook. Some circles also hate me because of my Catholic religion. Others claim that a former schoolteacher is unqualified to be Finance Minister, though I taught school for but two and a half years and have been an active politician for twenty-five.[28]

Helfferich, in his brilliant concluding speech following Erzberger's, denied that he was motivated by personal hatred of Erzberger or the democratic Republic *per se*. He stated that he wanted to defend his personal honor, but also scorned to deny the political motivation of his suit. He was impressed by the perfect identity between his own interest and the public interest, with both calling for the immediate removal of Erzberger from office. He expected a great national revival once the Erzberger cancer had been removed. His final speech, like all his earlier speeches, showed him at once passionate and calm, impulsive and logical, anxious and self-confident. He had every quality needed to play the role of Cato in the young German Republic.[29]

The court delivered its verdict on March 12, 1920. It judged Helfferich guilty of both formal libel and making several false accusations. It ordered him to pay 300 marks to Erzberger and to carry the whole cost of the trial. The presiding judge, Baumbach, explained that the smallness of the penalty was justified by the fact that Helfferich had proved the substantial accuracy of his charges, had acted largely from patriotic motives, and had been provoked in his sharp language by Erzberger's counter-attacks. The main part of the judgment declared Erzberger guilty of many of Helfferich's accusations: namely, of three cases of impropriety, six of perjury, and seven of mixing politics with business. Baumbach passed the following general verdict upon Erzberger: "A man of undoubted ability, exemplary industry, enviable memory, great energy, and extraordinary activity, but on the other hand of a regrettable lack of judgment and a really surprising imprecision in all matters." [30]

The outcome of the Erzberger-Helfferich trial ended Erzberger's political career. He resigned immediately from the Finance Ministry to devote himself to the rehabilitation of his personal honor. An appeal to a higher tribunal, the *Reichsgericht,* failed since disputes about the case concerned questions of fact rather than of law (December 21, 1920). The verdict of habitual untruthfulness injured Erzberger most, and he demanded an indictment for perjury so that the cases could be

[28] Zinnecke, *op.cit.,* pp. 62–63.
[29] *Prozess,* pp. 978–88.
[30] *ibid.,* p. 990.

examined in detail. A preliminary investigation showed that the evidence did not warrant the initiation of court proceedings (June 29, 1921), thus throwing a significant light upon the prejudice of the earlier court. The charge of tax evasion, popularly identified with the trial record, was also found on further investigation to be groundless.[31] There remained the charges of impropriety and of mixing political and business affairs.

Erzberger's friends argued that a regular court was an unsuitable tribunal for judging cases of this kind, because of the inability of regular judges to understand the realities of political life. This was especially true of judges trained in the Prussian tradition, which deified the state as the embodiment of reason while ignoring its reality as the arena of social conflicts. The Prussian tradition also supported a double standard in the matter of industrial participations. No one objected in Imperial Germany if deputies who owned Junker estates voted for higher agrarian tariffs or state subsidies to horse-breeders. Yet deputies who were connected with industrial enterprises were treated with grave suspicion.[32]

Erzberger's judges refused to accept the fact that a modern parliament is naturally a representation of conflicting social forces, and that deputies reflect this both in legislation and in applying pressure upon the executive. The pressure applied by Erzberger upon bureaucrats on behalf of groups and individuals was improper only if carried beyond a certain point. Whether he often, or ever, transgressed this point is difficult to decide. There is ample evidence that many bureaucrats feared him, much less evidence that they frequently yielded to his real or imaginary threats. A court was, in any case, not the best organ for judging the extent of Erzberger's pressures, since the judges disapproved of any deputy pressuring bureaucrats *per se*. A Select Committee of the *Reichstag* would have provided a better tribunal. The English example of the investigation of the Marconi Affair could have provided a suitable precedent.[33]

The prejudice of the court is not the only reason for doubting the justice of the judgment. The trial took place in the midst of ferocious political passions, and the judges would have been super-human if they had remained completely immune to the sentiments of the upper classes from which they had sprung. The peculiar state of German libel

[31] On Erzberger's efforts for a re-trial and a perjury investigation, see Löwenstein, *op.cit.*, pp. i–ix.

[32] The double standard is discussed in Eyck, *op.cit.*, I, 200–01.

[33] On the Marconi Case, see Marquess of Reading, *Rufus Isaacs* (New York, 1940), pp. 267–315.

procedure was a further disadvantage to Erzberger, since it placed him completely upon the defensive and allowed Helfferich to rake through his entire private life.

It speaks rather well for Erzberger, under these circumstances, that so little was brought out by the trial which could permanently damage his reputation, or prevent his return to politics once he had been cleared of the perjury and income-tax evasion charges. Erzberger was shown to be impulsive, energetic, careless, imaginative, and imprecise. His virtues and his vices were closely connected. Impulsiveness led to many errors of judgment, but was the source of that love of responsibility which did not prudently calculate consequences. His energy was the root of his political power, but it also led to that busybody quality which involved Erzberger in many unnecessary conflicts. His careless-ness, imprecision, and power of imagination led to some questionable financial dealings and to patronage of useless inventions, but it also lay at the root of his grand conceptions and political achievements. Bureau-crats and judges were bound to be horrified by his vices and frightened by his virtues. Both are essential for explaining Erzberger's career. That career must be judged on his political achievements and not on the de-tails of his relationship to particular companies. His moral faults were great, but they fell far short of Helfferich's conception of an indelibly dishonorable man. His lawyer, Friedländer, ended his final defense speech with the words: "I claim for Erzberger that he has always sought what was good and just, and that he has frequently attained it. He has sometimes erred in his choice of means, but his entire life, so devoted to the service of the people, makes it outrageous to stamp him as a pro-fessional political criminal." [34]

[34] Zinnecke, *op.cit.,* p. 62.

CHAPTER XV

AFTER THE TRIAL (MARCH 1920 TO AUGUST 1921)

Erzberger's Struggle for Rehabilitation

THE Erzberger-Helfferich trial ended on March 12, 1920. The very next day saw the Kapp Putsch undertaken by the enemies of the Republic. The legitimate Ebert-Bauer government fled to Stuttgart, though a successful general strike organized by the Socialists soon allowed a return to Berlin.[1] Erzberger, no longer a minister, remained in the capital. When warned that Kappist rowdies were out to assassinate him, he took refuge in the monastery Zum Guten Hirten behind the Tempelhof airport.[2] His enemy Helfferich, despite his hatred of the Republic, was too intelligent to identify himself with the hopeless *coup d'état*. He was, in fact, distressed that the counter-revolution distracted attention from his judicial triumph over Erzberger.[3]

Erzberger's political vigor was sorely missed by the Republican forces after the collapse of the Putsch. The latter episode had shown that influential elements in the army, bureaucracy, and judiciary were hostile to the Republican regime, or at least unwilling to take a clear-cut stand against the Putschists. A drastic purge was obviously called for, and Erzberger would have been a good man for the job. But he was preoccupied with fighting for his personal honor when his energies would have been of great use to strengthen democratic institutions in Germany.

The attitude of the Zentrum Party towards its most controversial member was ambiguous after his resignation from office. The *Fraktionsvorstand* urged him to resign his *Reichstag* seat by 7 votes to 3, with 2 abstentions; only Wirth, the coming Chancellor, Schofer, the Baden leader, and Müller-Fulda, Erzberger's colleague on the Budget Committee, stood resolutely behind the fallen minister. Erzberger re-

---

[1] The best contemporary work, hostile to Kapp but including most relevant documents, is Karl Brammer, *Fünf Tage Militärdiktatur* (Berlin, 1920).
[2] "A" [Adolf Stein], *Sieben-Tage-Buch. Kappregierung und Generalstreik* (Berlin, 1920), p. 11.
[3] Unpublished *Erinnerungen* by G. Traub, a prominent Right-wing Protestant clergyman, p. 194. Quoted in Lewis Hertzman, *The German National People's Party (DNVP) 1918–24* (Harvard Thesis, 1954), p. 302.

jected this advice but agreed to abstain from appearing in the *Reichstag* until his judicial appeal to the *Reichsgericht* had been decided.[4]

The executive committee of the Zentrum Party in his native Württemberg urged Erzberger, by a vote of 20 to 10 with 5 abstentions, to retain his seat.[5] It placed him at the head of the party list for the elections scheduled for June 6, 1920, thus guaranteeing his reelection. This decision was endorsed by a Württemberg party congress which met at Stuttgart on May 14, 1920. Erzberger made a long defense of his conduct that won the approval of the numerous delegates. The vote in his favor was 356 to 27, thus showing that the party delegates were far more favorable to him than the party committee. The leaders feared that Erzberger might be a party liability, but the rank and file were loyal to the man who had long championed their interests.[6]

In the summer of 1920 Erzberger published as part of his campaign of rehabilitation *Erlebnisse im Weltkrieg,* the book that described his experiences in World War One. It was composed with his customary rapidity during a brief vacation at Jordanbad, a resort near Biberach, following the completion of the trial. Erzberger was forced to be reticent on many matters because the events described were so recent. For this reason he did not mention his intelligence network at all, and the account of his diplomatic missions was sketchy. Many persons whom Erzberger had dealt with were described in vague terms as "a man of world-wide reputation" or "an important personage" rather than named. The Kolyschko-Erzberger negotiations at Stockholm in April 1917 were only hinted at. His close ties to the Vatican were concealed to avoid antagonizing German Protestants. His aggressive championing of Catholic aims, in such matters as the Roman question and the Jerusalem Holy Sites, was, on the other hand, stressed. This aspect of the narrative was directed at those elements of the Zentrum Party who—in their blind rage at Erzberger's Leftist orientation—had even questioned the sincerity of his Catholicism. The book must be judged in the context of 1920; it was certainly one of the most valuable war memoirs published up to that time. Apart from the omissions mentioned above, it gave a faithful and full account of Erzberger's conduct from the outbreak of the war to the acceptance of the Treaty of Versailles.[7]

A meeting of the *Reichsausschuss* of the Zentrum Party on June 24,

---

[4] Sincton Upclair, *Erzberger kommt wieder!!!* (Berlin, 1920), p. 24.
[5] *ibid.*
[6] *Schwäbischer Merkur,* May 15, 1920.
[7] A French translation of the *Erlebnisse* appeared under the title *Souvenirs de guerre* (Paris, 1921), with a preface by M. Muret. For a hostile review see H. von Liebig, *Reichsverderber* (Berlin, n.d. [1922]), pp. 36–76.

1920, was deeply divided on what stand to take on Erzberger. It decided to adjourn the matter until Erzberger's appeal to the *Reichsgericht* should be decided. The latter rejected a revision of the verdict on December 21, 1920, as had been generally foreseen. This left Erzberger without any further legal remedy. The *Reichsausschuss* then persisted, contrary to its intention in June, to maintain its silence about the case. Erzberger obliged his party enemies by continuing to abstain from attending *Reichstag* sessions. He demanded, however, that the government open a perjury proceeding against himself. The *Reichstag* lifted his parliamentary immunity at his request on March 4, 1921. The ensuing thorough investigation, completed on June 29, 1921, showed that there was insufficient evidence to warrant court prosecution. It thus cleared Erzberger of the charge of perjury which had been sustained by the court at the trial. A meeting of the Zentrum *Reichsausschuss* that same day opened the door to Erzberger's return to politics, though Trimborn and Fehrenbach continued to oppose him. Wirth and Giesberts spoke strongly in his favor.[8]

The charge of income-tax evasion still hung over Erzberger's head, the last obstacle in the way of his return to power. He pressed for an early and thorough investigation, which took place in the summer of 1921. It covered the charges made concerning both tax evasion and illegal export of capital, and included the interrogation of the Swiss bishops of Chur and Lugano who knew about his transfer of ecclesiastical funds during the war. The examination was so searching that it aroused the protest of the Foreign Office for fear that Erzberger's intelligence contacts might be placed in jeopardy. Erzberger learned a few days before his death that the investigation had cleared him of all charges. He planned to attend the *Katholikentag* in late August 1921 as a first step in his formal return to politics.[9]

[8] On Erzberger's campaign of rehabilitation, see Löwenstein, *op.cit.*, pp. i–viii; Bachem, *Zentrumspartei*, IX, 473–74; and a memorandum by Karl Bachem on the meeting of the *Reichsparteiausschuss* on June 29, 1921, in *Bachem Papers*, File 89. The lifting of Erzberger's immunity was debated in the *Reichstag* on Jan. 25, 1921 (for perjury), and on May 4, 1921 (for income tax evasion). *Reichstag Debates*, CCCXLVII, 2089–95, and CCCXLIX, 3589–3622. Erzberger demanded the lifting of the immunity in letters dated Dec. 15, 1920 and Feb. 24, 1921.

[9] For details on Erzberger's tax case and personal finances, see Appendix VIII. Libels concerning both abounded. The *Hamburger Nachrichten*, Oct. 12, 1920, claimed, for example, that he had recently paid 4 million francs taxes in Switzerland. Erzberger refused to sue for libel on the grounds that (1) the provocation of libel suits was a device of his enemies to prevent his return to politics, (2) the excitement of a trial exposed him to the daily danger of assassination, and (3) the Helfferich trial showed that judges were prejudiced against him. Letter of Erzberger to W. Bosbach, a Munich Trade Union secretary, Oct. 30, 1920, printed in *Anzeiger vom Oberland*, Nov. 6, 1920. Copy in *Erzberger Papers*, File 31. On the latter point Erzberger thought he had specific evi-

Erzberger's Political Attitudes, 1920–1921

Erzberger would not have been himself if he had completely abstained from engaging in political activity during the intervening period. He consolidated his hold over the Württemberg Zentrum Party by a tour of the countryside in the spring of 1921. A Democratic politician, who had sometimes crossed swords with him, described his manner as follows:

> Erzberger made not only the official speeches planned in his program, but he joined his fellow-citizens at the beer-table of the village inn. His close friends and the local party big-wigs gathered around him, and he had no objection if the group was joined by members of other parties. Indeed their presence made the meetings more lively, and Erzberger was not sparing in self-criticism. He declared on one such occasion: "I am the first politician in Germany that admits openly that I have made mistakes in my political career. During the course of the war I began to realize gradually, and not without severe internal struggles, that many things in which I had previously believed and for which I had previously fought, were mistaken. I began to realize the need for a fundamental alteration in our national education, institutions, and political goals."
>
> This represented his honest conviction, which he repeated on frequent occasions. He possessed a great deal of *Zivilcourage,* that is the courage to say what he believed at the moment, even at the risk of contradicting earlier statements. In party struggles, especially when preparing for elections, it was almost a joy to tangle with such a clear head that always grasped the essentials of any position rapidly. His South German democratic attitudes were the fixed pole in a nature otherwise free of rigid principles. This meant that he was usually able to secure a common ground even with debating antagonists from other parties [if they shared his democratic premises], who at the end of an evening liked him almost as well as did the Württemberg peasants that cheered him on his way.[10]

Erzberger had used the leisure brought by his partial withdrawal from politics to think through the social problems confronting Germany. He became converted to the principles of Christian Solidarism enunciated by the Jesuit Heinrich Pesch as an alternative to both Capi-

---

dence against Judge Baumbach. He wrote to his lawyer Dr. Werthauer on December 18, 1920 that a certain Mr. Sklarz had declared that he knew two witnesses, including a former public prosecutor named Fabian, who were "willing to testify that the presiding judge at the Helfferich Trial, Baumbach, had said some time before the trial, when it had not yet been decided which judge would try the case: 'If Erzberger comes under my hands, he will be finished.' " *Erzberger Papers,* File 31.
[10] Unsigned "Erinnerungen eines Parteigegners," in *Berner Tageblatt,* Aug. 31, 1921. Copy in *Erzberger Papers,* File 43.

talism and Socialism.[11] Erzberger's previous political career had shown many traces of the Christian Solidarist spirit, but his practical preoccupations had hitherto prevented his theoretical consideration of the problems involved. By the spring of 1921 his views were introduced to the public in a series of speeches that were soon printed in pamphlet form. They aroused considerable controversy and impressed men by their great precision. Erzberger was never the man for fuzzy generalities. His penchant was for making concrete proposals that spelled out all details.[12]

Erzberger was equally sharp in his condemnation of capitalism and socialism. His attack upon Capitalism equalled Marx's in intensity:

> The capitalist system has deprived the worker of his soul. It has cut the tie between the personality of the worker and his place of work, a tie which is the indispensable prerequisite for joyous creativity, energy, and the highest development of human capacities. I intentionally use very pointed language in order to penetrate the wall of prejudice erected in the course of decades. The modern worker has been treated as a mere cipher, as a kind of economic jailbird, who appears at the appointed time, receives his number, works his regular hours with repugnance, and leaves his place of torture, that ought to be a place dedicated to joyous labor. He has no influence upon the management of the factory in which he works. He finds himself confronted by an abstract capitalism, and never sees the capitalist, who therefore becomes the embodiment of oppression and exploitation.[13]

Erzberger thought capitalism not only horrible but utterly discredited because of its failure to solve crying social problems (unemployment, housing, etc.) and its identification with World War One. Erzberger accepted the Marxist view that monopoly Capitalism and imperialist wars were related phenomena.[14]

He thought that Socialism was just as undesirable as Capitalism. He believed that it contravened human nature by denying the role of self-

[11] Heinrich Pesch, 1854–1926, became a Jesuit in 1876, lived four years in England where he studied social movements, and received a thorough training in economics under Schmoller and Wagner at Berlin. His fundamental work was *Liberalismus, Sozialismus und christliche Gesellschaftsordnung,* (Freiburg 1896).

[12] The sources for Erzberger's doctrines are his pamphlets *Christlicher Solidarismus als Weltprinzip* (M. Gladbach, 1921) and *Der Solidarismus. Europas Rettung und Zukunft* (M. Gladbach, 1921). See also Alfons Winz, *Erzberger zu den neuen Problemen der Gegenwart* (Singen, 1921). A former Socialist Minister of Economics, Rudolf Wissell, wrote a favorable review of these pamphlets under the title of "Sozialismus und christlicher Solidarismus," in *Die Glocke,* edited by Parvus, VII (July 11, 1921), 402–09.

[13] Erzberger, *Christlicher Solidarismus,* pp. 7–8.

[14] *ibid.,* pp. 2–8.

interest. It was based upon materialist principles of science which the best scientific minds were rapidly abandoning. Its Muscovite version had led to a combination of political tyranny and economic chaos unique in modern history. Erzberger clearly saw the fundamental difference between Communists and Socialists, praising the latter for their recognition of the impracticality of socializing all economic life. He looked upon the German Socialists as a constructive force in German political life, and even considered them possible allies in the establishment of Christian Solidarism. His anti-Socialist strictures were directed against Socialist theory (and its implementation in Moscow) rather than the practice of the Revolutionary Socialists of Western Europe.[15]

The elimination of Capitalism and Socialism left the way open to Christian Solidarism, which Erzberger praised for its recognition of the dignity of man (denied by both the capitalist exploiter and the Communist bureaucrat), its harmonizing of freedom with authority, and its aim of maximizing the distribution of private property.[16] He praised Solidarism for possessing the key to industrial harmony by its advocacy of the two principles of co-determination (*Mitbestimmung*) and of corporations partly owned by the workers themselves (*Werksgenossenschaften*). Erzberger thought of co-determination as a systematization of the German institution of workers' committees (*Arbeiterausschüsse*) established under the Empire and the workers' councils (*Betriebsräte*) that were contemplated by the Weimar constitution. He also welcomed profit-sharing schemes based upon distributing stock among the workers of a given factory, but thought it unlikely that this would bring a real solution to social problems.[17]

Erzberger's pet scheme was the development of *Werksgenossenschaften*. He proposed that the workers of a given factory should own, corporately rather than individually, 50 percent of the stock of a firm, and secure a proportionate voice in the stockholders' assembly and on the board of directors. The remaining 50 percent would be retained by the existing owners. How was the workers' corporation to secure ownership of so much stock without violent revolution? Erzberger made the following proposal. Companies were to be required, by law, to pay half of their annual dividends above 6 percent into the treasury of a newly-formed workers' corporations. This money was to be used, in the first year, to purchase stock in the company; this stock would pay dividends in subsequent years exactly as did all other stock. If profits

[15] *ibid.*, pp. 8–11.
[16] *ibid.*, pp. 11–15.
[17] *ibid.*, pp. 26–31.

were less than 6 percent the company would be required to pay 2 percent for 10 years into the workers' treasury, and 1 percent in each of the succeeding 30 years. Thus the workers' corporation would own half of the company stock in 40 years at the latest, without the company suffering any major inconvenience.

The result of the scheme would be that the workers would identify themselves with the company instead of looking upon it as an exploiter. Erzberger saw an automatic ending of the class struggle while retaining the advantages of entrepreneurial initiative and increasing productivity by maximizing incentives. He spoke in glowing terms of the *Werksgenossenschaft:*

> It is the embodiment of Christian Solidarism in the individual factory. It pushes the idea of solidarity (*Gemeinschaftsgedanke*) into the foreground, whereas the plan to distribute shares of stock among the individual workers is rooted in outdated liberal-individualist economic principles. The *Werksgenossenschaft* accords with the ancient German principle of mutual cooperation (*Genossenschaftprinzip*). It embraces all the workers in a given factory and conceives of them as a collective entity in the productive process, but also makes them co-owners of the entire enterprise. . . .
>
> The *Werksgenossenschaft* is created by way of organic development. The way of revolution is avoided in favor of natural growth within the confines of the enterprise. The creation of the capital of the *Werksgenossenschaft* out of dividends is justified, because the dividends are only a different form of wages. . . . The capital assembled in this way for the *Werksgenossenschaft* should be indivisible and inalienable. It creates what might be called the entailed property of labor. The capital will grow naturally from year to year. It will grow rapidly in those enterprises where profits are greatest.[18]

How would the *Werksgenossenschaften* use the dividends that they would receive? Erzberger thought there might be some dividend distribution to individual families, but he thought the money should primarily be used for social purposes (housing, care of children, etc.). The *Werksgenossenschaft* would be administered by officials elected by the workers and their wives. Erzberger valued all experiments in self-government, and thought the workers' corporations would stimulate democratic life throughout Germany. He also thought that they would kill what remained of a demand for nationalization of industries, a fact that should make capitalists favorable to the idea in their own enlightened self-interest.[19]

[18] *ibid.*, pp. 31–33.
[19] The *Werksgenossenschaften* are described in *ibid.*, pp. 31–41. Detailed statutes are given on pp. 46–49.

Erzberger believed that his proposal was so reasonable that it must prevail, regardless of the fact that it was sure to be opposed by both Capitalists and Socialists. He was unimpressed by the theoretical objections that could be advanced. Capitalists said it would reduce profits to coupon-clippers, but Erzberger thought this was desirable in an impoverished country where luxury had become morally intolerable. Socialists argued that it would not bring equality, that indeed it would perpetuate differences existing between workers in prosperous and in marginal factories, but Erzberger thought equality an abstract and undesirable ideal. The so-called educated classes doubted whether workers were really capable of managing great financial affairs, but Erzberger condemned this as mere snobbishness and anti-democratic prejudice. Economists argued that it would reduce the mobility of labor, but Erzberger thought this desirable to check the demoralizing nomadism of the modern proletariat; besides, mobility could easily be retained by allowing for transfer of membership from corporation to corporation. Erzberger found all objections frivolous or based upon false social values, and believed that his scheme must have a great future.[20]

Erzberger wanted to supplement self-government in individual enterprises by self-government of industries as a whole. We have seen how he had favored the curtailment of competition before the war, but opposed cartels run purely in the interest of Capitalists. He wanted the election of working class delegates to the boards that managed cartels. He recognized the danger of labor-management collusion in setting high prices at the consumers' expense, and suggested representation for both consumer groups and the state as a remedy. The latter would insist upon setting prices to cover costs for a medium, not the least efficient, firm, thus cutting undesirable profit margins.[21]

The Christian Solidarist school feared an unbalanced industrial development such as had occurred in England under the reign of *laissez-faire,* and was resolved to buttress German farming. Erzberger's proposals combined a concern for agriculture with a strong bias against landowners who benefitted from unearned increment. He wanted to set a maximum sale price for land at the value given at the last tax declaration, with anything beyond this going 100 percent to the State. Erzberger knew that the profiteering and black-marketeering practiced by farmers during the war had caused deep bitterness among the urban classes, and he wanted to diminish this in the future by state control of all farm prices at cost of production plus 4 percent return upon the

[20] *ibid.,* p. 40.
[21] *ibid.,* pp. 41–43.

value of land. Erzberger was deeply concerned about the condition of the farm laborer. He favored the introduction of collective bargaining into the countryside, but wanted to prohibit strikes at harvest time in favor of compulsory arbitration. He feared the drain of farmers' sons into the big cities, and wanted to check such migration by making it contingent upon the permission of the village authorities—an extraordinary curtailment of freedom of individual movement. No other feature of his social program showed more clearly how hostile he was to the principles of *laissez-faire*.[22]

An equally drastic proposal of Erzberger's was to institute an 18 months' period of compulsory labor for all Germans between the ages of 18 and 25, a so-called *nationaler Arbeitsdienst*. This plan was remarkably similar to that later introduced on a voluntary basis in the last years of the Weimar Republic and later made obligatory by the Nazis. Erzberger conceived of it as a substitute for the military service prohibited by the peace treaty. He saw in it an excellent way of overcoming labor shortages in such fields as farming, housing, and coal mining. Germany suffered a special shortage of mine workers, but Erzberger realized the impracticability of compelling young people to work in this dirty and dangerous industry. He preferred to rely upon incentives to get mine volunteers among those subject to labor service, namely premiums of 4,000 marks and a shortening of their work obligation from 18 to 12 months. Erzberger looked upon the *Arbeitsdienst* as much more than an expedient for solving immediate economic problems. He thought that individual *Arbeitsdienst* groups should administer their own affairs, thus securing training in self-government. An additional advantage would be the curtailment of adolescent delinquency. He also wished to strengthen the devotion of young people to the Weimar Republic by political lectures and discussion groups.[23]

Erzberger expected that the spirit of Christian Solidarism would transform German political life. It would prevent both the recurrence of such an upperclass government as had disfigured the Empire and the emergence of a Left-wing dictatorship as desired by the Communists. It would maintain and extend the just system of taxation established by himself, with its heavy taxes upon war gains, capital, inheritances, and unearned increment. Erzberger expected the development of genuine self-government in the local units, and excoriated the dead hand of bureaucracy.[24] But he heartily disliked the federalist call for

[22] *ibid.*, pp. 51–52. The parallel of the old Russian *mir* system may be noted.
[23] Winz, *op.cit.*, pp. 21–24, with fourteen specific suggestions on pp. 25–28.
[24] Erzberger, *Christlicher Solidarismus*, pp. 22–26.

complete decentralization that refused to meet the realities of 1921. Erzberger was proud of his centralizing achievements in the field of finance and railroad management. He sought to terminate the identification of centralization with Prussianization, which had marred German constitutional life since 1866. He favored the breakup of Prussia into its constituent provinces as part of a general reorganization of governmental units: this could create a healthy federalism that was emancipated from historical provincialism and was not blind to the claims of a strong central government.[25]

Erzberger's Foreign Policy Conceptions, 1921

Erzberger's most controversial application of the principles of Christian Solidarism was in the field of foreign policy. He did not hide his disappointment at the League of Nations as established at Versailles, but nonetheless remained faithful to the principles enunciated in his 1918 book. He believed that the French use of the League as an instrument to keep Germany in bondage would prove a temporary phenomenon. Erzberger characterized the Treaty of Versailles as the negation of all Solidarist principles: it placed power before justice, was imbued with vindictiveness, and was maintained by brute force. Erzberger's denunciation of Versailles as the "work of the devil" yielded to no other German in its passionate indignation. He especially excoriated the unilateral application of the principle of self-determination in favor of Entente claims, while Austria's wish to join Germany was vetoed. He also denounced the reparations demands as astronomic and completely incapable of fulfillment.[26]

Erzberger looked upon the revision of the treaty as the main objective of German foreign policy, but he thought that a flexible policy of concession—not a nationalist policy of defiance—was the only feasible way of attaining the desired goal. He opposed the emotionalism that surrounded the issue in German discussions, and implicitly characterized his own attitude as follows:

> Only the man who recognizes political facts for what they are and who has the courage to draw the logical conclusions from the facts, can carry out successful policies and tear the veil off the future, insofar as this can be done by ordinary mortals at all. One must recognize facts no matter how hard, cruel, and disastrous they may be. . . . A statesman must, much more than a private citizen, ignore considerations of emotions and sentiment and follow the hard dictates of reason alone. He must try to look at affairs with perfect calm and detachment, and then do the right

[25] Winz, op.cit., pp. 16–18.
[26] Winz, op.cit., pp. 6–16. Erzberger, Der Solidarismus. Europas Rettung, pp. 15–36.

thing without any thought of securing either the approval or hatred of his fellow-citizens. He must rely upon his conscience to justify drawing ruthless conclusions from inescapable facts.[27]

Erzberger applied this austere attitude in his championing of the so-called "policy of fulfillment" (*Erfüllungspolitik*) of the Treaty of Versailles against those who favored a policy of defiance. "We do not improve matters by clamoring noisily for 'revision of the peace treaty'; we must rather choose means more appropriate for attaining this end. What are these means? We must, first of all, seek to fulfil all the treaty provisions, however horrible, that can be fulfilled; only in this way can we make the world realize that those provisions that we cannot fulfil are, indeed, objectively impossible."[28] Erzberger criticized the German government for its failure to bring the so-called war criminals to trial. "Either these men have been falsely accused, in which case the German courts must speedily restore their honor; or they are in fact guilty of war crimes, in which case they deserve to be punished."[29] The German government had won a great victory (through Erzberger's initiative) in winning the Entente's acquiescence in having these men tried before German rather than Entente courts; this victory was imperilled by the government's cowardly policy of postponing the trials for fear of nationalist demagogy. The government was equally negligent in its failure to live up to the disarmament clauses of the Versailles Treaty, especially in the case of the Bavarian Citizens' Army.[30]

Erzberger took an equally unpopular stand on the question of reparations. He affirmed Germany's moral obligation to pay some reparations, both because of the unprovoked invasion of Belgium and the voluntary acceptance of the pre-armistice contract with its reparations clause.[31] Erzberger's attitude was that Germany should press for a provisional settlement to cover the next five to ten years, instead of demanding—as the German government was doing—a fixed and final settlement. "I consider a policy of maneuver and of elastic defense to be correct, while a policy of the direct collision of conflicting positions is disastrous for Germany. The world will not long remain in the condition of 1920 and 1921; the governing constellations will change completely within ten years. I do not speculate upon divisions within the ranks of our enemies; if I did so I would not proclaim the fact publicly."[32] Erzberger

[27] Winz, *op.cit.*, pp. 4–5.
[28] *ibid.*, p. 15.
[29] *ibid.*, p. 16.
[30] *ibid.*, p. 16.
[31] Erzberger, *Christlicher Solidarismus*, pp. 18–21.
[32] Speech at Kempen, reported in *Niederrheinische Volkszeitung*, April 18, 1921. Copy in *Bachem Papers*, File 90.

in fact expected that public opinion in the Entente countries would not tolerate forcible collection of reparations from Germany after a few years. He speculated upon this fundamental change of attitude, and hoped that if Germany could get over the next ten years time would moderate further Entente demands.[33]

The German government that was installed following the elections of June 1920, with Fehrenbach as Chancellor and Simons as Foreign Minister, pursued a reparations policy that earned Erzberger's sharp criticism. Fehrenbach, once a close friend, had now become a leader of the Right wing of the Zentrum. He failed to take any initiative at all in the reparations question. When the British and French negotiators suggested a provisional five-year settlement in the autumn of 1920, the German government should have jumped at the proposal; instead, it woodenly replied that Germany, under the terms of the treaty, had a right to learn the total sum demanded by the Entente. The latter replied in January 1921 with a demand for the astronomic sum of 226 billion marks plus 12 percent export taxes for the next 42 years (until 1963). The Fehrenbach-Simons government rejected this to the accompaniment of shouts of nationalist approval, and made a ludicrous counter-offer of a mere 30 billions. This was rejected by the Entente at a conference in London. The German government failed to make a further offer, and received a jubilant reception in Berlin for its ostentatious defiance. Since an Allied ultimatum was imminent, the government then made an appeal to President Harding (April 20, 1921) to mediate the reparations question, agreeing in advance to pay any sum that Harding should suggest. Erzberger condemned this appeal, and rejoiced at Harding's refusal to intervene. "The entire action [of the German government] was not only a complete reversal of its previous attitude—an act of political harakiri in the worst sense of the term—but it was an act of despair, emanating from the mistakes of the last few months, the bewilderment of the moment, and the cowardice that would not acknowledge previous mistakes." [34]

The Entente sent an ultimatum on May 12, 1921, demanding that Germany pay 132 billions plus 26 percent in export taxes over the next 42 years, and also requiring the immediate trial of war criminals and the implementation of the disarmament clauses of the treaty. Erzberger had long warned about the danger of willfully defying the Entente on the last two points. The sum of 132 billions was no improvement over the January figure of 226, because the demands over the next ten years

[33] Conversation of Erzberger with Hammer, reported in Hammer, *Erzberger*, p. 78.
[34] Erzberger's article "Politik oder—?" in *Das Tagebuch*, edited by Stefan Grossman, Vol. II, Nr. 18 (May 7, 1921), pp. 545-51.

(which Erzberger considered the only important point) were 20 billions plus 26 percent export taxes and 35 billions plus 13 percent export taxes respectively, with Erzberger calculating that the doubling of the export taxes would amount to much more than the 15 billion subtracted from the fixed payments. The Allies demanded acceptance of their ultimatum on pain of immediate occupation of the entire Ruhr.

The Fehrenbach-Simons government, despite its histrionic demagogy of the last months, resigned in the face of the Allied demands. The Nationalist Party, despite its specialization in defiance of the Entente, proved no more willing to form a government than it had been in June 1919. A new government dedicated to the policy of fulfillment was formed under the leadership of Erzberger's friend Josef Wirth, with the Zentrum resuming its former alliance with the Socialists. It assumed a somber legacy which Erzberger characterized by writing an epitaph upon its predecessor.

> An iron age is beginning. The terrible mistakes of the recent past tell us daily in our hour of trial of what not to do if our people are to be saved. Our government has once again yielded only to the military threats of our enemies, thereby providing new weapons for all the militarists in the Entente countries. Our unhappy zig-zag policy since January . . . has once again cost us billions of marks. Our see-saw policy has once again lowered our international prestige. The entire world has been strengthened in its conviction that Germany will pay only when a fist clutches its throat. We have had the most expensive ministry in the world from a financial, economic, political, and moral point of view.[35]

Erzberger announced his coming return to politics at a meeting of the Zentrum *Reichsparteiausschuss* on June 29, 1921, shortly after the formation of the Wirth government. He was generally believed to control this government from behind the scenes.[36] His hope was to enlarge the Weimar coalition to the Left by drawing that part of the Independent Socialists which had refused to join the Communists into governmental responsibility.[37] It was rumored that he had collected material about discreditable financial operations on the part of General Lundendorff, and threatened to publish these if personal attacks against himself continued—a questionable method of self-defense if true, though it showed a quality of ruthlessness that most Weimar politicians unhappily lacked.[38] Erzberger's main preoccupation was to strengthen

[35] Erzberger's article, "Das teuerste Ministerium in der Welt" in *Das Tagebuch*, Vol. II, Nr. 20 (May 21, 1921), pp. 609-17.

[36] The *New York Times*, Aug. 27, 1921, spoke of this as an "open secret."

[37] Article by Erzberger's friend Dr. Herz in a Schweinfurt newspaper, *Der Volkswille*, Aug. 23, 1946.

[38] *Basler National Zeitung*, Aug. 19, 1921. Copy in *Erzberger Papers*, File 30.

the left wing of the Zentrum. The death of three of the party leaders who were opposed to Erzberger's return to politics—Trimborn, Hitze, and Burlage—in the summer of 1921 left the way open to a rapid second ascent to party leadership.[39]

His main party antagonist was Adam Stegerwald, who had, like himself, emerged from the Christian Trade Union movement but had evolved in a conservative and nationalist direction. His ascetic personality differed as much from Erzberger's exuberance as did his political views. He had become Premier of Prussia in 1921, and his administration had won the plaudits of the Right. Stegerwald conceived of the prevention of Erzberger's return to power as his main party aim. He called a meeting of 240 Christian Trade Union functionaries at Essen on July 16, 1921, and harangued them for two and a half hours on the evils of Erzberger. His main theme was that Erzberger, as a man of the Left and a symbol of Ultramontanism, was an obstacle to the Zentrum's winning new voters on the Right and among Protestants generally. Stegerwald told the audience that he would try to undermine Erzberger's political position in Baden and Württemberg during a coming vacation in South Germany. In the ensuing debate Giesberts spoke up energetically for Erzberger, and the meeting was so divided that Stegerwald left it in a bad mood. His aim of a Rightist coalition of the Zentrum with the Conservatives and People's Party appeared to be doomed to failure.[40]

Giesberts advised Erzberger to neutralize Stegerwald's intrigues by mobilizing André and Schofer, the Württemberg and Baden leaders, on his behalf, and to keep himself cautiously in the background to avoid becoming vulnerable to attack. Schofer, upon Erzberger's urging, immediately wrote to Stegerwald that he would be *persona non grata* if he visited Baden.[41] Erzberger was in any case resolved to keep himself out of the limelight until the results of the investigation into his income taxes were announced in the late summer. His plan was to attend the *Katholikentag* in Frankfurt in late August, and to resume his *Reichstag* duties in the autumn session. Friend and foe alike believed that he would soon resume a prominent political role, and Erzberger himself thought he was predestined to become Chancellor in the near future.[42]

[39] Article by Haussmann, in *Berliner Tageblatt*, Sept. 7, 1921.
[40] Johann Giesberts to Erzberger, July 19, 1921, and Dr. Burgbacher to Erzberger, July 21, 1921. *Erzberger Papers*, File 30. On Stegerwald, see the excellent biography by Josef Deutz, *Stegerwald* (Cologne, 1952). His penchant for an alliance with the Right in the Weimar years is analyzed on pp. 106-19.
[41] Schofer to Stegerwald, July 23, 1921. Copy in *Erzberger Papers*, File 30.
[42] Stefan Grossmann, "Erzberger," in *Das Tagebuch*, Vol. II, Nr. 35 (Sept. 3, 1921), pp. 1041-48.

The Assassination

Erzberger vacationed with his family at Jordanbad in July and early August 1921. Gabriele, his youngest daughter, now aged six, secured her lasting impression of her father on long walks through the Swabian countryside. The oldest daughter, Maria, was no longer with the family; she had entered a Carmelite nunnery in Holland the previous April. Erzberger approved of her desire to devote herself to a religious life. Dr. Hammer described Erzberger's attitude as follows:

> Erzberger was imbued with the idea of sacrifice [as taught by the Catholic Church]. He deeply loved his children but was willing to accept their entry into monastic orders if God so willed. Erzberger once told his daughter Maria: "I would not have raised any objections if Oskar had decided to enter the Jesuit or the Benedictine Order." Maria added in her report [written for Dr. Hammer]: "How serious he was in this attitude was made clear when he made no attempt to prevent my decision to become a nun, despite my youth. . . . When the hour of separation from my family came, my father said only that I should be sure to return if I found that I did not find real happiness [in my probationary period]. The family would be very glad to have me back at any time. His last letter to me began with the words: "I write you today in the spirit of love and homesickness," and ended with, "I have written the homesickness off my chest, but the love remains." My mother told me when I saw her again after my father's death: "I never saw him so helpless (*fassungslos*) as he was the moment after the monastic gate had closed behind you." [43]

Erzberger knew from police warnings that various assassins were planning to kill him, and that the chances of his violent death increased as his return to politics became imminent. He told Maria shortly before she entered the convent, "The bullet that will kill me has already been moulded." He had been advised to carry a revolver and learn how to shoot, but he had replied "I do not want to learn how to kill." [44] He believed that his escape from Hirschfeld's bullets had been providential, and impressed his friends by his calm composure in the face of threats, saying: "I am prepared. My life is in the hands of God." [45] Erzberger was convinced that God would summon him at the appointed time. His whole view of life had always been deeply theocentric, and his religious convictions deprived death of most of its terrors.

[43] Hammer, *Erzberger*, p. 102. Maria became an exemplary nun under the name of Sister Gertrude Teresia. For a full-length portrait of Maria, see J. N. I. van Hilsum, *Maria Erzberger Zuster Maria Gertrudis* (Bilthoven, 1956).

[44] Hammer, *op.cit.*, p. 109.

[45] *ibid.*

On one of their last days at Jordanbad, Erzberger and Hammer took an excursion to the baroque parish church at Aulendorf, where Erzberger was much moved by a picture of the veil of Veronica with the bloodstained face of Christ. He returned twice as if unable to separate himself from the picture. The family then left Jordanbad on August 8, 1921, to spend ten days at Beuron, living in a hotel near the fine Danubian monastery. From here Erzberger took his last trip to Berlin to check on the state of the investigation into his income tax difficulties. He was told that the inquiry had gone completely in his favor and had removed the last barrier to his second political ascent.[46] When Erzberger returned to Beuron he learned of a suspicious telephone call concerning his whereabouts received by the hotel during his absence. This was a clear sign that his enemies were on his trail.[47]

Erzberger and his family moved on to Bad Griesbach, a small vacationing resort in the Black Forest, on August 19. It is located at the foot of the Kniebis mountain near the headwaters of the Rench River, which enters the Rhine near Strasbourg. The peasants of this area still wear picturesque costumes: the women long black dresses with white ruffs and elaborate head gear, the men green jackets with brown hats decorated by black feathers. Each town is dominated by one or more Catholic churches, expressing the unquestioned and uncritical faith of a people with little contact with the secularism and materialism of the modern world. It was perhaps proper that Erzberger, who had never experienced a crisis in faith, should die among such people.

Erzberger stayed in a hotel run by Catholic nuns. He took daily walks with his wife and daughter up the Kniebis road, which winds in a series of loops up the mountain. A fellow guest named Köhler recalled the evening of August 25:

> Erzberger returned with his wife, his small daughter Gabriele, and a Jesuit Father quite late in the evening. . . . Shortly after supper a heavy thunderstorm caused a short circuit in the hotel electricity. For a moment all was dark. But the sisters who ran the hotel quickly came with candles lighted in shining silver candlesticks. They placed them on the table, the wax began to steam, and their honey-sweet smell brought a festive mood into the room. The guests became a single large family, and many began to sing, as Germans always do when they are ashamed of their emotions. Old tunes echoed through the room while there was rain, thunder, and lightning outside. At a table next to ours a group of Rhinelanders, led by Dr. Hommerich, a skillful dialectician and former editor of *Germania*,

[46] Hammer, *op.cit.*, p. 102. H. Baur, "Erzbergers Werdegang," in *Allgemeine Rundschau*, Apr. 18, 1931, p. 248.
[47] Hammer, *op.cit.*, pp. 109–10.

sang the familiar round, "Today is today," when Erzberger, holding the hand of his six-year old Gabriele, entered the dining room. He was a man who could easily enter into simple fun, and he joined the group and sang, "Today is today" as his turn came. Then Erzberger, his small daughter, and his delicate, quiet, and proud wife, who constantly trembled for his safety, retired for the night. . . .

Next morning, August 26 [continued Köhler] we arose early to go to Church. Four Sisters of the Holy Cross sang songs devoted to the Virgin Mary. The pious Erzberger knelt in front of the altar with his wife and child, absorbed in deep thoughts, which may have concerned his other daughter, who had taken the Carmelite veil only a few weeks previously. When the harmonium had played its final chords Erzberger left his last divine service, and joyfully greeted his friend Diez, a *Reichstag* deputy [from Constance], who had just arrived for a visit.[48]

Erzberger and Diez soon started on a walk up the Kniebis mountain. Erzberger conversed with his usual animation about his Solidarist scheme for social improvement. When about an hour out of Bad Gries-bach they were overtaken by two young men, but paid no attention to them, being engrossed in conversation. The downpour of the night before, and the continuous drizzle, made the road slippery, and shortly before eleven Erzberger and Diez decided to turn back. A few minutes after they commenced their return, the two strangers, who had mean-while taken a short-cut through the woods, suddenly reappeared and stepped up to Erzberger. They pulled their revolvers and fired at his chest and forehead from a distance of only six inches. Their victim, completely surprised, jumped some thirty feet down a slope by the side of the road. He instinctively sought to arrest his fall by clutching at some tree roots. These tore from his finger the ring which Pope Benedict had given him; it was later found at the bottom of the slope. The assassins fired three further shots at Erzberger which pierced his lungs, stomach, and upper thigh. Erzberger vainly sought shelter be-hind a pine tree before collapsing. The murderers then stepped down the slope, bent over the dying man, and fired three final shots to make sure of their handiwork.

Diez had, meanwhile, sought to repel the assailants with his um-brella, but he collapsed immediately from a shot through his chest. When he regained consciousness a few minutes later, he found his friend lying dead at the bottom of the slope. He saw the two murder-ers walking down the road towards Bad Griesbach. With Erzberger beyond help, Diez, though weakened by loss of blood, tried to drag

[48] From diary notes published by Heinrich Köhler in *Kölnische Volkszeitung*, Aug. 27, 1921. Copy in *Erzberger Papers*, File 43.

himself back to the hotel. He soon encountered a fashionable lady vacationer from Hamburg who assisted him. But when he told her his story she only made the laconic comment: "How *could* you go walking with a man like Erzberger!" [49]

Köhler describes the scene at the hotel:

The young children had just finished singing the popular tune about the "Sweet Fairy with a Bell" when we heard a strange commotion and mingling of voices in front of the house. Then we saw Diez, his body covered with blood, run into the hotel lobby. He told the assembled group that Erzberger had been shot at, but warned them not to break the news suddenly to Erzberger's wife. All the young men of the village and many vacationers immediately ran up the lonely mountain road. . . .

Mrs. Erzberger expected her husband back around noon. She frequently stepped up to the window and looked at the excited crowd, which grew silent whenever the small woman with the sorrow-filled eyes appeared. Gabriele played in carefree fashion in front of the house. No one was able to explain the terrible news to her. Soon Mrs. Erzberger ceased to appear at the window. She instinctively knew what had happened, and when she was told that her husband lay wounded in the forest, she replied with the calmness of a woman whose wounds only bleed internally: "I know he is dead." [50]

Erzberger's body remained at the site of the murder overnight to allow the police to make an accurate record of the external evidence of the crime. It was then carried down the valley to the little town of Oppenau, where the required autopsy was performed in the district hospital. The body had been pierced by eight bullets, of which the first two, through the forehead and the lung, were alone sufficient to cause death. The autopsy also showed that Erzberger suffered from an enlarged heart and contracted kidney at the time of his death, and that he did not have long to live in any case. A requiem mass was celebrated in the village church of Oppenau on Sunday, August 28. The Catholic community of Biberach, the center of Erzberger's *Reichstag* constituency, wanted the burial to take place in their cemetery, and the body was transferred there on August 29. The burial service took place the next day with an attendance of 30,000. The Chancellor, Josef Wirth,

[49] Hammer, *op.cit.*, pp. 110–11. This account draws heavily upon Karl Diez's own description in Civis Radolticensis, "Die Lebensgeschichte eines Menschen," Installment 21, in *Deutsche Bodensee Zeitung*, Konstanz, July 29, 1929. Diez survived the Nazi period by becoming a farmer. Keil, *Erlebnisse*, II, 546. He lived to become a high official in the Ministry of Agriculture in South Baden after the Second World War. See also F. W. Heinz, "Politische Attentate in Deutschland," in *Deutscher Aufstand*, edited by Curt Hötzel (Stuttgart, 1934), pp. 202–05.

[50] Köhler, same as in footnote 48.

found strong words of indignation against the political crime, and he hailed Erzberger as a martyr for the cause of the German Republic. He evoked the spirit of his dead friend to call for a rally of all decent men who cared for Christian and democratic principles.[51]

The indignation expressed by Wirth was, however, far from unanimous in Germany. The *Kreuzzeitung,* the favorite organ of the most respectable Junker families in the Prussian east, wrote the day after the murder:

> Nothing is cheaper than to condemn the assassins, whose motives are still unknown. Charlotte Corday, who murdered the Republican Marat, was guillotined in Paris, but German poets have nonetheless glorified her terrible deed. There is really no reason why only the deeds of revolutionary murderers, like Brutus and Wilhelm Tell, should be celebrated in song and story. Those who now praise Erzberger and attack his enemies seem to forget completely that the entire campaign against Erzberger has been essentially a defensive struggle.[52]

With the *Kreuzzeitung* expressing these views, one can imagine the sentiments of the provincial nationalist press with its less select audience. One example must suffice. The *Oletzkoer Zeitung,* always a staunch champion of the German National People's Party, wrote on the day after the murder:

> Erzberger . . . has suffered the fate which the vast majority of patriotic Germans have long desired for him. Erzberger, the man who is alone responsible for the humiliating armistice; Erzberger, the man who is responsible for the acceptance of the Versailles "Treaty of Shame"; Erzberger, the man whose spirit unhappily still prevails in many of our government offices and laws, has at last secured the punishment suitable for a traitor. Regardless of one's feelings concerning political murder (for there can be little doubt that this was not an ordinary crime) there can be no doubt that the majority of the German people breathe a sigh of relief at this moment. A man like Erzberger, who carried the primary responsibility for the misfortunes of our Fatherland, was a standing menace to Germany so long as he was alive. It may sound brutal and heartless to throw such words at a dead man, but we cannot restore Germany to

---

[51] Hammer, *op.cit.,* pp. 111–12. Bachem, *Zentrumspartei,* p. 481. For the Chancellor's funeral oration, see Josef Wirth, *Reden während der Kanzlerzeit* (Berlin, 1925), pp. 169–74. Rightist circles voiced resentment when Wirth and other Leftist leaders called the murder the direct result of the agitation against Erzberger. See Germanicus (pseud.), *Matthias Erzberger. Ein politischer Mord?* (Berlin, 1921). Some Rightist newspapers developed the crazy theory that Erzberger had been murdered by members of the Zentrum Party who feared that (1) his Solidarism might lead to a party split and that (2) he was a political liability in future campaigns. *Der Erzberger Mord. Dokumente menschlicher und politischer Verkommenheit* (Brühl, Baden, 1921), pp. 62–64.
[52] *Kreuzzeitung,* Aug. 28, 1921. Quoted in *ibid.,* p. 41.

greatness with mere sentimentality (*Gefühlsduselei*). We must sow
hatred! We must learn to hate our enemies abroad, but we must also
punish the domestic enemies of Germany with our hatred and our contempt. Compromise is impossible. Only extremism can make Germany
again what it was before the war.[53]

[53] *Oletzkoer Zeitung,* Aug. 27, 1921, quoted in *ibid.,* pp. 15–16. The murderers were
two young former officers, Heinrich Schulz and Heinrich Tillessen. Their motives were
exclusively political, as is proved by the fact that they neglected to kill Diez, though
their own safety required his elimination as a witness. Schulz and Tillessen fled to Hungary with the help of nationalist elements of the Bavarian police, which sabotaged the
efforts of the Baden authorities to track them down. They returned to Germany in 1933
to be hailed as "Erzberger judges," but were tried for murder after the Second World
War, and sentenced to long prison terms. Both were out on parole by 1956. On their
motives leading to murder and their careers after 1921, see the account of the Tillessen
postwar trial in the *Badische Zeitung,* Nov. 29 and Dec. 3, 1946, and Feb. 28, 1947.

CHAPTER XVI

CONCLUSION

ERZBERGER's violent death made him a martyr to the German Republic, and gave his name a popularity among the masses of the Left that he had not enjoyed in his lifetime. His businesslike personality could not be glamorized. His followers admired him chiefly for the enemies he had made, and for his outspoken stands on controversial issues. A journalist, when describing Erzberger's oratorical qualities, gave a good characterization of the man:

> He wins the soul of the small man on account of his candid simplicity, his democratic convictions, his unpretentious way of speaking, his healthy common sense, his homely wisdom, and his far from sardonic sense of humor. What Erzberger says could readily be said by every last voter five minutes later. . . ; but his effectiveness must be explained by this very fact. He only expresses with a refreshing plainness what broad groups in the party or among the people are already thinking: hence he can usually count upon a favorable response. It must be added that all his achievements are the product of hard labor, not spontaneous combustion. He is a craftsman rather than an artist.[1]

Erzberger's prominence arose from his personal qualities, and it is therefore natural that they should have aroused considerable controversy. He was in many ways ill-suited to the social milieu of the Germany of his time, especially before the war. His great role after 1914 was made possible only by the political fluidity created by war and revolutionary chaos. He seized upon the opportunities that were offered to an energetic deputy. His most striking trait was the willingness to assume onerous responsibilities. This explains Erzberger's propaganda and intelligence work, his leadership in the crisis of July 1917, his signature of the armistice, his manipulation of a parliamentary majority that ratified the Treaty of Versailles, and his acceptance of the Finance Ministry in June 1919. What gave Erzberger the courage to undertake tasks from which other men flinched? His buoyant and optimistic temperament played a large part. He could not conceive of either hopeless situations or insoluble problems. He was never embarrassed for want of an expedient to get around an immediate difficulty. He refused to despair, and believed that public displays of melancholy—a specialty of Bethmann's—never served a useful purpose. Erzberger was

[1] Article "Erzberger," in *Der Friede.Wochenschrift für Politik, Volkswirtschaft und Literatur,* edited by Dr. Benno Karpeles, May 31, 1918, p. 453.

free from doubt concerning his own role; he always gave his very best to the task at hand, and was willing to leave the rest to Providence. He usually slept soundly at night in the midst of the gravest preoccupations, and he rarely engaged in self-critical post-mortems. The force of his personality was never weakened by internal friction.

Erzberger's love of responsibility and his customary optimism were reinforced by a monumental self-confidence which arose primarily from his consciousness of possessing very unusual powers. His memory was phenomenal, and gave him a great advantage over other men in debate and negotiation. His lucid and assimilative intelligence enabled him to enter quickly into any subject matter at hand. He had the gifts of a great administrator. His office was run with superb efficiency. Subordinates were given broad independent responsibilities, and consulted their chief only on matters of real importance. This fact alone enabled Erzberger to assume a great variety of tasks.[2]

Erzberger's power of work amazed friend and foe alike. He rarely worked less than sixteen hours a day, and until the war never took a vacation. He was tied to Berlin by the obligations of his *Zentrumskorrespondenz*. When parliament was in session, Erzberger was the first deputy to appear in the library of the *Reichstag* in the morning. He briefed himself for the day's work by a careful perusal of newspapers, magazines, and committee reports. He had few preoccupations outside of politics, apart from his faithful attendance at religious services. His business activities were carelessly handled, and took up very little of his time. His family life gave him a refuge from political controversy, but it interfered only very rarely with his political work. He was a strictly political animal, and his private life was almost non-existent.[3]

---

[2] Hammer, *Erzberger,* p. 93, has a good account of Erzberger's methods of work, using a memorandum prepared by Erzberger's daughter Maria.

[3] The well-known German graphologist Ludwig Klages claimed, on the basis of a single short specimen of Erzberger's handwriting dating from 1911, that Erzberger's activity mania resulted from internal frustration. He guessed that this frustration was probably sexual in nature. He claimed to detect the following traits in Erzberger: "The peculiarity of his ambitions arises from the fact of a central frustration (*Gehemmtheit*), which gives a tone of the forced and the exaggerated (*Krampfhaftes und Übertriebenes*) to the chronic tension from which the writer suffers. The restlessness of the pursuits of his will (*Willensdranges*) appear in the light of his internal harassment (*Gehetzheit*), with his constant craving for external activity and overcoming of obstacles being calculated to conceal an internal feeling of inadequacy (*Knickes und Mangels*). One is tempted to compare this incessant activity with the succumbing to drink, with the same attempt at being stupefied (*Betäubung*). Activity serves to prevent the inward turn towards self-examination. A weaker constitution would be threatened by collapse and disintegration, but the tough personality of the writer only proceeds to ever more extensive plans. It would be a grave mistake to confuse the confidence in success and mania for activity with self-satisfaction or even happiness (*Euphorie. . . .*" Ludwig Klages, "Charakterbild auf Grund der Handschrift Erzbergers," in *Zeitschrift für Menschenkunde,* Vol. I, No. 3 (Heidelberg, 1925), pp. 31-37.

Erzberger's self-assurance in whatever he undertook was not curbed by factors that have often restrained men of similar talents. He had missed the kind of good education that makes a man skeptical of himself and self-conscious about his role in a given social and political milieu. He had never served an apprenticeship under an acknowledged master, or received instructions in making haste slowly. Erzberger's career was a conspicuous success from the tailor's house in Buttenhausen to the chair of the German Finance Minister. He suffered few disappointments that might have encouraged introspection. Erzberger had risen by his personal ability alone. He felt that there was no natural ceiling to his ambition.

Erzberger's cocksureness was especially dangerous in a man of his impulsive temperament. He frequently took a position without consulting friends or thinking out all the consequences. When his enthusiasm was aroused he could pursue impracticable objectives with a total want of rational judgment. Examples can be found in the Liechtenstein project, the plan to acquire the Coenaculum for the King of Bavaria, and the belief that a brief talk with Lloyd George could lead to an early peace in 1917. He irritated and amused men by his obstinate pursuit of the quixotic.

Yet in most cases Erzberger's impulsiveness led to the exact opposite of obstinacy. His close rapport with the mind of the common people gave him a superb political instinct. His freedom from dogmatic preconceptions—apart from certain fundamental beliefs—gave him an unusual adaptability to new political situations, which his enemies denounced as opportunism. Erzberger's rapidity in changing his mind and his carelessness about appearances gave plausibility to the charge. Two examples were his development from extreme annexationism to the principles of the Peace Resolution in 1917, and from passionate defense of the monarchy to an equally fervid republicanism in 1918. Erzberger was quite unperturbed by the accusation that he had changed his mind, and often expressed surprise that other people had not changed theirs with equal good judgment. He loved to quote the German poet Rückert to the effect that wise men travel from error to truth, while fools show their folly by persisting in error.[4] When a Zentrum colleague taxed him with inconsistency, he replied: "I am not a petrifact." When someone mentioned to him that things happened contrary to his predictions, he replied, "Who said I was a prophet?" [5] Erzberger's

[4] "Die durch Irrtum zur Wahrheit reisen,
Das sind die Weisen.
Die bei dem Irrtum verharren,
Das sind die Narren."
[5] Bachem, *Zentrumspartei,* IX, 424.

capacity for continuous growth helps to explain his achievements, but this quality gave him a reputation for political unsteadiness and aroused much enmity.

Erzberger's impulsiveness led to an unfortunate habit of bragging and indiscreet conversation. His regular table *(Stammtisch)* at the Restaurant Krziwanek, at the corner of Dorotheen and Mittel-Street, was one of the gossip centers of Berlin. Erzberger did not hide his light under a bushel, and when he had attained some major *coup* he wanted people to know about it.[6] He sometimes even claimed credit for things with which he had nothing to do: his bragging about playing a role in the appointment of Michaelis was an especially unfortunate example. There were many reports about his careless talk when staying in Swiss hotels during the war. His trusting nature would not permit him to believe that the waiters were probably bribed by the Entente to spy upon him.[7] Erzberger's indiscretion must, however, not be exaggerated. When he was told a specific matter in confidence, his lips were sealed. He never revealed, for example, the fact that he had received the Czernin Report from the Emperor Charles himself, though this extenuated his much-criticized conduct at the Frankfurt Zentrum meeting.

His indiscriminate helpfulness to all kinds of people also resulted from his impulsiveness. He sympathized with the sufferings of others and always saw the concrete hardships in individual cases. He disliked Germany's stuffy and self-inflated bureaucrats, and was ever ready to believe that they had not given a fair deal to people who came to him with complaints. His time did not allow for a personal investigation of grievances, and he developed the habit of urging sympathetic reconsideration of bureaucratic decisions regardless of the merits of a given case. This added to his reputation as a busybody and made him the *bête noir* of the Berlin bureaucrats.

Erzberger's personal integrity in money matters was never doubted by those who had intimate knowledge of the man. His very carelessness about appearances constituted the best proof of his subjective rectitude of intent. It is extremely regrettable that he should have made himself so vulnerable to the charge of mixing his political with his business life. At his death millions of his countrymen believed that he was a sordid and venal politician, if not a paid British agent. A careful examination of his personal finances leads to the conclusion that this view was completely mistaken. He was an honorable man in his pocket-

---

[6] *ibid.*, p. 421.
[7] Letter of Professor Krebs to K. Bachem, June 2, 1918. *Bachem Papers,* File 89.

book as well as his heart, and he was quite indifferent to money. But he 'forgot that men are judged by external appearances, not by subjective intent, and he needlessly compromised his political usefulness by laying himself open to the charge of impropriety.

Erzberger was quite ruthless in his choice of means to attain ends he believed to be valuable. His impulsiveness was quite free of sentimentality. His specialty, from the time of his campaign against the colonial scandals, was exposure. Erzberger cared little whom he antagonized while he was promoting the public welfare. He was almost proud of the number of enemies he made. He infuriated his opponents by being almost impossible to catch, no matter how vulnerable the position he had assumed in political combat. He had a wonderful capacity for extricating himself whenever he appeared cornered. His retreat after his assault on Hertling on May 8, 1918 is a good example.

His slipperiness and adaptability in political tactics stand in sharp contrast to his unshakable conviction in fundamentals. The combination of tactical opportunism with an underlying consistency explains much of his success. Erzberger was deeply attached to Catholicism, democracy, and social justice throughout his entire career. His religion, while never fanatical, gave him deep serenity. It brought him composure in the face of assassination threats. He went to mass every morning unless there were pressing other obligations. He took communion at least once every four weeks. His daughter Maria became a Carmelite nun with his encouragement. Erzberger's Catholicism led to his aggressive championing of all Catholic grievances, his promotion of Catholic candidacies for vacant offices, and his pursuit of the interests of the Holy See during the war.[8]

Erzberger's democratic principles arose from his Swabian environment and humble birth. He believed in opening careers to talents like his own. He hated any authoritarian or bureaucratic structure, whether in party or state affairs. This placed him in fundamental antagonism to the ruling tendencies of both the Zentrum Party and the German Empire before 1914. He had the vision that saw the inevitability of the development of democracy and parliamentary government, and worked as leader of the Zentrum Left wing to swing his party towards supporting these objectives. Erzberger had little success at first, and was constantly frustrated by the entrenched power of the old party hierarchs; but after 1917 he succeeded in winning the Zentrum for a working coalition with the Social Democrats. This provided the parliamen-

[8] On Erzberger's religion, see Bachem, *Zentrumspartei*, IX, 497–98, and Hammer, *Erzberger*, p. 10.

tary basis for the political transformation of Germany from 1918 to 1919. His achievement is all the greater because his ascendancy in the party was never secure. The neutralization of his Zentrum foes always required a major share of his political energy, though he was very adept at intrigue, persuasion, and intimidation. He did not succeed in dedicating the party to a permanent alliance with the Left. It reverted to its traditional conservative tendency after his death. He probably could have kept it on a Leftist course if he had lived, and thereby strengthened the Weimar Republic.

Erzberger's concern for social justice constitutes a continuous thread from his work as a Stuttgart *Arbeitersekretär* to his legislative achievements as Finance Minister. His reform measures arose from concrete knowledge of avoidable human suffering, not from adherence to any over-all social theory. He was an instinctive foe of all exploitation and degradation. His religion forbade any hope that utopia could be established on earth, and he never despaired because progress was slow. Erzberger was convinced, however, that substantial social improvements were possible in the Germany of his time, and he kept the Zentrum on the reformist course originally set by Windthorst. In his last year he began to work for an over-all reorganization of society in the name of Christian Solidarism.

His attitude towards international problems shows an evolution that cannot be found in his approach to religion, democracy, or social justice. He accepted the European diplomatic system uncritically until 1917, and joined the chorus of ridicule that dominated German public opinion on international arbitration and disarmament. Erzberger's chauvinism was, however, restrained by certain considerations of justice —for example, in his championship of the Poles against German misgovernment. Yet the tension between universalism and nationalism, so important in the Catholic tradition, scarcely existed in Erzberger's mind. A great change took place in 1917 when he recognized Germany's desperate military position following the failure of the submarine war. Erzberger suddenly realized the anachronistic nature of an international system based upon sovereign states that inevitably led to bloody and fruitless wars. He then discovered for himself the universalist side of the Catholic tradition and became a champion of a League of Nations, arbitration tribunals, and disarmament. He still believed in the principle of nationality, and wished, indeed, to build up new states on its basis in the liberated parts of Russia. But he now subordinated the welfare of any one nation, his own included, to the general interests of a new international order. His language became free of any nationalist arrogance. He did not yield to any German in his love of country and ardent patriotism. He rather felt that to subscribe to certain international canons of conduct was henceforth the best way of promoting national interest properly understood.

Erzberger stood, at the height of his career from 1917 to 1920, in fruitful concord with the advancing causes of democracy, social justice, and international cooperation—though these continued to be thwarted by bureaucratic authoritarianism, upper-class privilege, and militaristic nationalism. He became a person of historic importance at the time of the July crisis in 1917. By pledging the majority of the *Reichstag* to the policy of the anti-annexationist Peace Resolution, Erzberger provided Germany's rulers with a platform for negotiating a peace of conciliation after victory had become unattainable. It was not Erzberger's fault that the German government, dominated by Ludendorff and blinded by annexationist desires, refused to implement this policy. It offered Germany's sole chance—admittedly not more than a chance —of extricating herself from the war short of a total military collapse.

The realignment of parties promoted by Erzberger at the time of the Peace Resolution had permanent importance. The coalition of Zentrum, Democrats, and Right-wing Socialists, joined at times by the National Liberals, isolated the Conservatives on the Right and the Independent Socialists on the Left. The new coalition pressed for a solution of Germany's long-standing internal problems by demanding the introduction of parliamentary government on the national and the democratic franchise on the Prussian level. It did not achieve either before the military catastrophe of 1918. But it both foreshadowed and prepared the way for the government of Prince Max of Baden.

The signing of the armistice at Compiègne, the most striking and humiliating event of Erzberger's career, made him a marked man for the rest of his life. Erzberger obtained the best terms possible in a very trying situation, and he refused to abandon his new international ideals despite the vindictiveness of the Entente Powers. He promoted the democratic cause by consenting to serve as armistice commissioner under Ebert, thereby leading a rally of the moderate bourgeois parties to the Right-wing Socialists. Erzberger strengthened Ebert in his resolution to smash the Communist terror in Berlin and to end the revolutionary chaos by calling democratic elections for a National Assembly. His adaptation of the traditional Zentrum program to the new conditions of German political life helped to prevent a Socialist majority in the new Assembly. Such a majority would have meant reckless social experimentation, an attack upon the position of the Church, and probably civil war. Yet Erzberger, while resisting socialist domination, wanted to give the Socialists a prominent role in the government that guided the work of the Weimar Assembly. His ideal was a coalition of all the democratic forces of Germany against the anachronistic forces of the Right and the proletarian dictatorship of the Left.

Erzberger assumed leadership of the forces that insisted upon the ratification of the Treaty of Versailles in June of 1919. He yielded to no one in his excoriation of the humiliating treaty, but he saw that nationalist gestures of defiance would only provoke a French occupation of most of Germany. He envisaged the dangers of partition, chaos, and starvation. Erzberger used every possible political stratagem—persuasion, cajolery, and perhaps even deception—to prevent these horrors by getting the treaty ratified. His success was the greatest single achievement of his life.

Erzberger's concern for the unity of Germany had been his main motive when pressing for the acceptance of the treaty. He aimed at strengthening this unity—threatened by old particularism and new separatism—by a vigorous policy of centralization. The nationalization of the German railroad system was largely his work. His greatest achievement in this line was, however, the complete reorganization of Germany's fiscal system. Erzberger gave Germany a centralized system of tax collection. Her new tax structure based upon national income and inheritance taxes was in full accord with democratic ideals of social justice in the fiscal field.

Erzberger's tax program brought to a climax the ferocious hostility which Nationalists had felt towards him ever since his exposure of colonial scandals in 1906. Their attacks on him had risen to fever heat after his promotion of the Peace Resolution, his signing of the armistice, and his advocacy of the acceptance of Versailles. The groups associated with the former Wilhelmine Empire—bureaucrats, officers, Lutheran clergymen, Junkers, and industrialists—hated him as a parvenu and feared his energy and vigor in pursuing Republican policies. They required a scapegoat upon which they could unload their cumulative frustration about Germany's defeat in war and democratic evolution at home. Erzberger's prominence in the events since 1917, his ardent championship of democracy and international conciliation, and his vulnerable personal qualities made him a perfect symbol of hate for all the foes of the Weimar Republic.[9] The campaign of character assassination against him led naturally to his murder in 1921. He died a

[9] For the view that Erzberger's enemies were really attacking the Republic *per se*, see Ernst Troeltsch, *Spectator-Briefe*, (Tübingen, 1924), p. 209.

martyr in the Republican cause, and German democracy was deprived
of one of its most energetic champions.

The jubilation which greeted his assassination in many quarters
showed that millions of his countrymen did not share his ideals. His
career was filled with many striking achievements, but it failed to set
Germany irrevocably on the road towards democracy, social justice,
and international conciliation. Erzberger was not the kind of great
historical figure who can shape an entire era in his own image. It
must be remembered that German affairs had assumed an incredible
complexity in Erzberger's age, with powerful rival forces locked in
internal combat and the shadow of external danger increasing the
difficulty of applying rational solutions to Germany's problems. Even
a Bismarck or a Richelieu could have secured only limited success
under circumstances of this kind. Erzberger, while an able and honorable man, fell short of real political genius. An acute journalist wrote
in 1918:

> Erzberger is an industrious, energetic, and shrewd deputy, but he gives
> the impression of being primarily a political operator. What he lacks is
> the quality of genius. He is not one of those men of whom the poet says
> that they contain music in themselves. In his inner life there is no rhythm,
> only mechanism. The glow of a dominant creative fire does not radiate
> through all his work. He lacks the divine spark. Even the most benevolent
> observer finds in him only a busy master craftsman who does not tran-
> scend a certain humdrum commonplaceness.[10]

[10] *Der Friede,* May 31, 1918, p. 453.

APPENDICES

APPENDIX I

Erzberger's Role in Founding the Christian Trade Unions

THE Christian trade unions were a response to the Marxist stranglehold over the regular trade union movement. Their *raison d'être* is explained by Erzberger in his pamphlet, *Christian or Socialist Trade Unions?*[1] which is a good defense against both Conservative critics of the Right and Socialist critics of the Left. The following is a paraphrase that retains the catechistic exposition of the original.

Erzberger begins by answering conservative Catholic objections. Does the worker have the right to organize? Erzberger bases his affirmative view upon natural law, Holy Scripture, Papal encyclicals, paragraph 152 of the *Reichsgewerbeordnung* (the 1869 law code governing industrial relations), and the dictates of common sense. One's impression is that the latter factor was paramount in Erzberger's mind, but the appeal to multifarious authority is one of his favorite methods of persuasion.

Why do the Socialist trade unions not meet the needs of the working class, thus necessitating the creation of rival Christian organizations? Because they are servile puppets of the Social Democratic Party and are even used to distribute atheistic propaganda. They act as the economic wing of the two-pronged economic-political Marxist movement, despite the fact that the Socialist leaders are skeptical about the possibility of working-class amelioration within the existing monarchist-capitalist state. Erzberger cites many complaints by trade-union executives at Socialist congresses on this score— he was always a close reader of opposition protocols, and soon became known as the possessor of the most deadly quotation box in Germany. But worse than trade-union servility towards utopian politicians is the frequent violation of the conscience of Christian workers through trade-union newspapers that openly express contempt for Christianity. Erzberger cites as an example an article from the 1897 Christmas issue of *Steinmetz* (the masons' journal): the contributor ridicules the Virgin birth of Christ in a manner worthy of adolescent pseudo-scientific atheism. Yet this journal was sent to every member of the mason's union.

What are the Socialist objections to Christian unions, and how can they be refuted? They attack the Christians as late-comers in the field—but this is unjust in view of long-standing Catholic preoccupation with the social question which Erzberger, citing the work of Bishop Ketteler, shows to go back to the 1850's. The Socialists ridicule the existence of a Christian conception of labor requiring a Christian approach to industrial problems—but here they only uncover the materialist emptiness of their souls. They accuse the Christian unionists of serving the capitalist class by splitting the trade-union movement—but the Socialist unions have organized only 6 percent of the

[1] Erzberger, *Christliche oder sozialdemokratische Gewerkschaften* (Stuttgart, 1898).

working class so far, leaving plenty of room for Christian organizers; moreover, the charge of splitting sounds strange if made by Socialists, who never hesitate to split any union whenever it proves insufficiently red. They reproach the Christian unions with including in their leadership Catholic priests, who represent an alien element in the working-class movement. No single charge aroused Erzberger to greater anger, and he replied with an anti-Semitic counter-attack which must, however, not be taken out of the specific time and controversy:

> The Catholic workers are proud of their leaders in whom they can have complete confidence. But who are the Socialist leaders? The fathers of Social Democracy were the Jews Marx and Lassalle. Today Social Democracy is under strong Jewish influence (*stark verjudet*). We see at the head of the Social Democratic Party in Germany the Jews Singer, Arons, Goldstein, Stadthagen, Wurm, Dr. David, Katzenstein, Bernstein, Haase, etc.; in Austria the Jews Dr. Adler, Dr. Ellenbogen, Dr. Ingwer, Austerlitz, Dr. Morgenstern, Kohn, Dr. Verkauf, Dr. Berstel, the brothers Grimm, Hirsch, Beer, Brod, Diamant, Berner, Seligmann, Aaron, Rubinstein, etc., etc.; in Hungary the Jews Schwarz, Baron, Pfeiffer, Schlesinger, Maier, Stern, Kugler. The stiuation is similar in France, Belgium, Italy, etc. The Social Democratic press is almost completely controlled by Jews, starting with the *Vorwärts* and going down to the *Münchener Post,* which has its Cohn, and the *Schwäbische Tagwart,* which has its Stern. The *Vorwärts* has the following Jewish contributors: Frankl in Paris, Jakoby in Switzerland, Aveling in England, Victor in Austria. Among leading Socialist authors are the Jews Perri and Lombroso in Italy, Lafargue in France, E. Marx in England, Iglesias in Spain, and so on. We merely wish to state the facts, while of course leaving it completely to the Social Democrats to select their own leaders; but we would graciously ask them to also allow us the freedom of choosing *our* own leaders.[2]

What are the functions of a Christian trade union? Primarily to serve as agent in collective bargaining, which is made imperative by the disparity in power between labor and capital. It must also serve in miscellaneous ways to improve the condition of working people by the extension of trade skills, instruction in the elements of social legislation, the setting up of labor exchanges, and, in cooperation with municipalities, the support of the unemployed. But the most important function of the trade union is to voice workers' grievances through petitions, appeals to public opinion, and the organization of strikes as a last resort—with Erzberger reminding conservative readers that Pope Leo XIII has approved of strikes under certain circumstances. Erzberger favors work stoppages only when the grievance is great and success is probable, and shows his common sense by advocating

[2] Erzberger, *ibid.,* pp. 29–30.

ad hoc cooperation with Socialist unions whenever required by a given situation.

Erzberger's pamphlet evades the controversy that was to bedevil the Christian trade-union movement until the war, whether its composition was to be purely Catholic or inter-confessional, that is, open to Protestants and Catholics alike. This conflict gave a foretaste of the similar struggle that was to rock the entire Zentrum Party a decade later; it must be analyzed for that reason. One group of Christian workers, under the leadership of the Aachen editor Hubert Immelen, wanted unions upon a purely local and completely confessional Catholic basis. In practice this would lead to tame organizations under cautious clerical leadership. Another group, led in North Germany by the Essen miners' leader August Brust, and in South Germany by Erzberger, favored the creation of industry-wide interconfessional unions. In practice this would mean aggressive organizations under lay leadership. Erzberger was brought to his position by his practical assessment of trade-union problems and not by radical intentions or distrust of the clergy. A private meeting of leaders interested in founding a national movement was held in Krefeld at the time of the August 1898 *Katholikentag* (the annual Catholic congress). Here the two parties still sought a common basis. The people invited were: Dr. August Pieper, a high official of the *Volksverein;* Hessdorfer, a Cologne priest; Michels, the leader of the Krefeld textile workers; Brust and Erzberger, the two leaders of interconfessionalism; Immelen, their antagonist, could not find the appointed meeting place in a city turned chaotic by the *Katholikentag* crowds; while Franz Hitze, the great Zentrum expert on the social question, was prevented from attending by another engagement. The Marxist historian of the Christian trade unions ridicules these seven men as "two workers, two Zentrum editors, and three priests." Yet these men were soon to organize a movement that belied the Socialist claim of having a monopoly on effective working-class organization.[3]

Immelen's lieutenants wanted an immediate national conference where the problem of confessional as opposed to inter-confessional unions could be debated. Erzberger and Brust vetoed such a public exposure of disagreement and instead summoned two regional conferences. One was to be for North Germany at Cologne, and the other for South Germany at Ulm. These they intended to commit to their position and thus use them to pack the coming national congress with their adherents. The Ulm meeting took place on December 8, 1898, with Hans Braun (1861–1907), a Munich stonemason who had become leader of the Bavarian Christian transport workers, as chairman.[4] Forty-six delegates from Bavaria, Württemberg, and Baden attended.

[3] August Erdmann, *Die christlichen Gewerkschaften, insbesondere ihr Verhältnis zu Zentrum und Kirche* (Stuttgart, 1914), p. 68. A more sympathetic account in Gasteiger, *Christliche Arbeiterbewegung*, p. 250ff.
[4] Gasteiger, *op.cit.*, pp. 283–85. Erzberger had met him at the Zurich 1897 Congress.

Erzberger, in his opening speech, proposed a formula of organization drawn up by himself and Josef Giesberts.[5] The crucial first paragraph read:

> The trade unions shall be inter-confessional, that is, to include members of both Christian confessions while standing squarely upon Christian principles. The discussion of confessional questions is strictly prohibited. The Trade Unions shall, moreover, be politically neutral, that is, they shall not attach themselves to any political party. The discussion of party questions should be kept out of the unions, but this is not to preclude the discussion of reforms to be achieved by constitutional means within the existing framework of society.[6]

The last two sentences were difficult to reconcile, but Erzberger's intention is clear. He wanted interconfessional trade unions; by attachment to any party he meant the Zentrum Party; he knew that Protestant trade unionists would never accept subordination to a predominantly Catholic party; hence interconfessionalism required a political neutrality in a party sense. Yet he knew that political and economic questions could not be sharply segregated, and he therefore specifically encouraged political discussion oriented towards Catholic thinking on the subject of reform, namely "by constitutional means within the existing framework of society." He secured the substance of his wishes while verbally respecting the scruples of those with whom he desired to cooperate.

The Erzberger-Giesberts statute was accepted after a lively discussion, and in the following year became the basis of the resolutions of the first national congress. This met at Mainz on May 21, 1899, and brought a complete victory for the views of the inter-confessional party, since Brust, at his Cologne conference, had been as successful as Erzberger had been at Ulm. Erzberger was selected to give the opening speech to the congress. A rear-guard action by Immelen, proposed in the seemingly innocuous form of a motion requiring the editors of trade-union journals to be men with academic degrees (which in practice meant priests), was defeated. A *Zentralauschuss* (executive board) composed of twelve men was selected to lead the new confederation of Christian trade unions. Erzberger was the Stuttgart representative until he entered the *Reichstag* in 1903.[7]

[5] *Prozess,* p. 582.

[6] Erdmann, *op.cit.,* p. 35.

[7] For a general account of the Mainz Congress and aftermath, see Alfons Gornik, *Die Entwicklung der nichtsozialdemokratischen Arbeiterbewegung in Deutschland* (Halle, 1909), pp. 41–57.

APPENDIX II

The Pöplau Case, 1905–1907

THE facts of this case, which became a constant theme in all attacks upon Erzberger, were as follows. O. Pöplau was a minor official in the *Kolonialabteilung* (the colonial section of the Foreign Office) who made a hobby of compiling dossiers on colonial atrocities, drawing his materials largely from classified files. His relations with his superiors were poor: he had thrice suffered small fines for disciplinary offenses, and had been denied a promotion to which he felt himself entitled. His motives in subsequent proceedings appear as a mixture of querulousness and zeal for justice. He had sent reports about colonial atrocities to both the Chancellor and the director of the *Kolonialabteilung* since 1902, but had never received any answer. No steps were taken to eradicate the evils he had exposed. His superiors chose to consider his well-substantiated charges as the product of a diseased imagination. They began an administrative action to secure his compulsory retirement on grounds of mental incapacity. Pöplau thought this was proof that reforms could not the initiated within the administrative apparatus, and he then took his materials to a prominent *Freisinn* deputy. The deputy brought the dossiers to Bülow with the request for an investigation into the abuses. The Chancellor was more shocked by the leakage of documents to a deputy than by the horrors exposed by Pöplau, and he ordered disciplinary proceedings against him on the charge of divulging official secrets to unauthorized persons. Pöplau naturally thought this the consummation of an official cover-up, and reacted by taking his materials to Erzberger on the very eve of his administrative trial (September 1905). The latter soon used the materials in some of his attacks upon the government, but before doing so he had a controversial conversation with Friedrich von Loebell, Bülow's chief of chancellory, on September 26, 1905.

There are two versions about the ensuing conversation, which took place without witnesses. Loebell, basing his recollection upon a memorandum which he wrote two days later, claimed Erzberger had proposed a dishonorable bargain: the disciplinary proceeding against Pöplau, scheduled to start in two days, was to be dropped through Bülow's intervention, with Pöplau offering to return his dossier to the department and cause no further trouble. Erzberger also allegedly threatened a *Reichstag* explosion if this proposal were rejected. Loebell asserted that he had categorically refused to discuss any such proposition. Erzberger's version of the conversation was very different. He specifically denied that he had proposed calling off the trial, a contention supported by the fact that it was quite impossible for the Chancellor to order a cancellation once a trial had been scheduled, though he could have prevented a trial initially by settling the case by administrative action. Erzberger claimed that his purpose in calling upon Loebell was to secure an investigation into the abuses uncovered by Pöplau. If such an investigation revealed the accuracy of the charges, it would throw a favorable light upon Pöplau, and his disciplinary failings would appear in a more lenient light. Erzberger claimed that he had intervened for Pöplau only in this indirect way, and his version was sustained by Pöplau, who said at the subsequent trial that he knew that his disciplinary case could not possibly be called off by the Chancellor, and that therefore he had never commissioned Erzberger to propose the bargain alleged by Loebell.

The Pöplau case led to considerable controversy in later years for the light it threw upon Erzberger's character. Erzberger could not deny that Pöplau's fate had been discussed at the conference along with the general problem of colonial abuses. Loebell cited a statement which Erzberger had made under oath (July 10, 1906) during a further investigation into the Pöplau case, to the effect that he had gone "to see if the matter involving Pöplau could not be settled in some way other than the disciplinary proceeding" (*um zu versuchen, ob die ihn betreffende Angelegenheit nicht auf andrere Weise als durch ein Disziplinarverfahren beendigt werden könne*). This appeared to give substance to Loebell's charge of the proposed bargain, though it presupposed that Erzberger did not know about the limits of the Chancellor's jurisdiction once a case had been put on the regular docket. Loebell sought to discredit Erzberger by contrasting the sworn statement (quoted above) with Erzberger's several subsequent (but unsworn) statements denying any proposal to bargain—an argument based upon the hypothesis, comparatively flattering to Erzberger, that though capable of lying he was incapable of perjury.

The whole matter was probably a case of genuine misunderstanding between two honorable men. Erzberger's primary aim had been to help Pöplau, whom he believed to be persecuted because of his zeal for justice. The fact that he gave Loebell the impression that he wanted to intervene in a pending judicial case was certainly unfortunate, though it may show more about Loebell's suspicions than about Erzberger's conduct. Erzberger's view that a general examination of Pöplau's charges would place Pöplau's technically improper conduct in a favorable light was certainly right. It will never be known whether his intervention went further than this. His hatred of bureaucratic cover-ups, his loyalty to a valued informant, and his occasional reckless imprudence makes it quite possible, but the proof is far from conclusive. His interest in the case certainly did not help Pöplau, who, after dismissal from the service, was later sentenced to three months in jail (December 2, 1907). Erzberger's enemies were henceforth convinced that he was capable of using his political power to influence a purely judicial decision, and to engage in falsehoods in order to screen his improper conduct. This view was to become part of the widespread conception that Erzberger was the incarnation of all evil.

The case was paralleled by a disgruntled Togo official, Wistuba, who carried secret materials to Erzberger's Zentrum colleague Hermann Roeren. Since Pöplau and Wistuba worked in collusion the public talked of a Pöplau-Wistuba case.[1]

[1] The best discussion of the entire matter is in Crothers, *The German Elections of 1907*, pp. 41–44, with a valuable bibliographical note. It was discussed at the 1920 trial. See *Prozess* pp. 899–900 and 1032–34; S. Löwenstein, *Der Prozess Erzberger-Helfferich*, pp. 84–87; Pehl, *op.cit.*, pp. 69–70, and *Reichstag Debates*, ccxviii (Nov. 28, 1906), 3959 (Bülow); (Dec. 3, 1906), 4084–96 (Dernburg and Roeren); ccxxvii (March 4, 1907), 201–04, (March 5, 1907), 242–49 (Loebell and Erzberger). Erzberger firmly believed that Pöplau had suffered injustice, and that his failure to secure promotion was a breach of promise. *ibid.*, ccxviii (Dec. 4, 1906), 4149; ccxiv (Dec. 14, 1905), 523–24. Two significant matters related to the Pöplau case were Erzberger's acquiescence in a search through his *Reichstag* desk by the public prosecutor's office on July 11, 1906, discussed in *Reichstag Debates*, ccxviii (Dec. 3, 1906), 4095–96; and his willingness, after prolonged hesitation and consultation with his friend Hammer, to testify about receipt of confidential information from Pöplau, when threatened by a jail term. Hammer, *Erzberger*, pp. 25–26.

APPENDIX III

Karl Bachem's Memorandum on Erzberger's Relationship with the Vatican, 1914–1915

THE following memorandum was written on May 21, 1918. At this time Bachem and his *Kölnische Volkszeitung* stood in a bitter personal feud with Erzberger, a fact that explains some of the hostile language employed but that also substantiates the accuracy of Bachem's grudging admission of Erzberger's services. Bachem learned most of the facts from Erzberger himself when their personal relations were still friendly.

"It cannot be denied that Erzberger performed extraordinary, valuable services for the newly elected Pope Benedict XV during the first months of the war, and that the Pope was very grateful for these, despite the fact that Erzberger's efforts were sometimes marred by lack of both caution and tact. The Pope overlooked these since Erzberger saved him from a condition of mortal danger (*lebensgefährliche Stellung*). The finances of the Vatican were completely exhausted upon the death of Pius X, with the treasury being literally empty. Pius X had known nothing about the management of money. Benedict, in consequence, was not able to pay the salaries of his court officials during the first period of his pontificate, although they needed these for their daily living expenses. The salary that he was able to offer to his private secretary, Msgr. von Gerlach, was ludicrously small, and Gerlach was able to accept the position only because he had private sources of income. Erzberger saved Benedict from this undignified condition by organizing a money collection among wealthy Germans for the benefit of the Vatican—this at a moment when Papal revenues from France had suddenly come to a total stop. Erzberger also supported the Pope with the funds which the Foreign Office had made available to him [for propaganda abroad]. He provided a large credit for the Pope at the banking house of Nast, Kolb, and Schumacher just before Italy entered into the war, and there is no question that the Pope drew upon this credit. Erzberger's intervention made the Pope financially independent and allowed him to maintain his neutrality in the face of Entente pressure. For someone acquainted with the situation and the history of the Holy See, it cannot appear surprising that the Pope succumbed more than had previously been the case to Entente influences, and especially French prelates, after the above-mentioned sums were exhausted, and after the Pope's direct contact with German prelates and politicians had been interrupted by the war."

The Pope was later embarrassed by some of Erzberger's activities. Yet in 1914–1915 he had been deeply impressed by Erzberger. Bachem continued his memorandum: "Benedict overwhelmed him with proofs of gratitude, presenting him with the one and only red cardinal's hat which he had ever possessed. He gave Erzberger a very high decoration, the Grand Cross of the

Order of Sylvester, if I remember correctly. He gave a precious needle, with his name engraved, as one of several later presents. Erzberger exhibited all these gifts in a glass case in his living room, which I remember as a very impressive exhibit. In the course of his collection of money for the Pope he approached not only Catholics, but also Protestants, and it is probable that he received contributions from the latter; what sums were involved I cannot say. I told him at the time that the subsequent revelation of this fact might prove embarrassing for the Pope, but Erzberger replied that the main task was to help Benedict quickly.

"Erzberger, in the course of his collection efforts, gave indications that Prussian titles and decorations might be bestowed in return for large contributions. When I asked him about this he said that he had been assured that careful consideration would be given to any recommendations that he might make. I then told him that methods of this kind ought to be employed only with great caution and discretion in order to avoid scandal. He replied again in an unconcerned manner that the desperate financial plight of the Pope did not permit delays in the collection of the necessary funds."

APPENDIX IV

The Article "No Sentimentality," February 1915

THE following article, here translated with only minor omissions to avoid repetition, shows Erzberger as the advocate of ruthless methods of warfare. It is the most regrettable piece that Erzberger ever wrote. In judging it one must remember Erzberger's penchant for extreme statements, his hasty methods of composition and habit of never revising his articles, and the fact that his second thoughts were often better than his first. In February 1915 Bethmann and his intimates were accused by Pan-German and naval circles of special tenderness towards England in the matter of submarine warfare, and this specifically provoked the virulent tones of Erzberger's counter-blast.

"The waging of war is a rough and brutal craft, and sugar candy and toy torpedoes are not suitable tools for such serious business. The British Admiral Fisher has said with brutal frankness that war must be carried on with the maximum ruthlessness. Why should we become indignant about this? I should consider it far better and more humane if we Germans translated the same sentence into practice. The greatest ruthlessness in the conduct of war, provided it is applied rationally, actually constitutes the greatest humanity. It would be more humane, if one had the chance, to destroy all of London with one blow, than to allow a single fellow-German to bleed to death on the battlefield; the application of drastic measures (*Radikalkur*) is the quickest road to peace. Procrastination and hesitation, softness and consideration [for the enemy] all constitute inexcusable weakness. Resolute, ruthless action is the earmark of strength and the certain road to victory. England has shown during the first five months of the war that it desires a ruthless conduct of the war. It violates international law, and agreements which it has signed are no more than a scrap of paper which it tears to pieces. England knows no consideration for the legitimate interests of neutral states. England does not wage war against soldiers alone, but rather against the German people as a whole, including children, women, and old people. For this purpose it has mobilized its allies and satellites in all the five continents. England accepts 1,000 pounds from the hands of a Kaffir chief in order to wage war against Germany 'in the name of culture.' England raises auxiliary troops from the white, yellow, brown, red, and if it were possible, even the mixed (*gefleckte*) races and sends them against Germany 'in the name of civilization.' . . .

"England wages war not only against our army, not only against our navy, but it acts like a thief and ruffian on the high seas, plundering not only what our army and navy needs, but also what is required for the feeding of German non-combatants. England made endless difficulties when America wanted to send bread to the Belgian population. America has now declared herself ready to supply foodstuffs to the war-ravaged parts of Poland, but

England procrastinates about a decision; it wants to punish the entire world by its brutality.

"Only German ruthlessness can overcome English brutality; the excitement and retaliatory threats of the English press will leave Germany cold. On the contrary, the noisier English newspaper clamor, the more effective is Germany's conduct of the war. When Tirpitz announced that we would answer English blockade practices by submarine warfare, the islanders at first pretended to be deaf. But now at last we have begun business. Let us continue on this road! English commerce will be threatened by the subsurface monsters of the sea, day in and day out. And when Germany decides to proclaim a real blockade, let it be without loopholes, let it mean the ruthless sinking of every English merchant ship. We will see how many English sailors will still dare to go aboard the threatened English steamers. If England had a weapon like our submarines it would unhesitantly be used in the present war. England knows no restraints where it is a matter of exercising or preserving its power position. We must follow this English example, for our salvation and England's destruction, in the question of the submarine. The same may be said for our airplanes and dirigibles. It is comic and laughable to watch English indignation whenever our dirigibles throw bombs upon unfortified English towns and villages. But have the English not tried to do the same towards Düsseldorf? Has not the influential English publication *The Engineer* stated openly that British airplanes must wipe the Rhenish Westfalian steel industry off the face of the earth? And would England hesitate for a moment to bomb Cologne, Hannover, or Berlin, if the flying range of its airplanes permitted this? It is but a typical case of the eternally new English hypocrisy to become indignant about a dictate of German self-defense when one praises identical actions if undertaken for the sake of English greatness. This double standard cannot be justified even to the blindest neutral observer much longer.

"England has stolen 400 of our merchant ships. The proper reply should be the demolition by air bombardment of at least one English city or town for each one of our ships. Every day that England continues to cut off the foodstuffs of our people by her naval blockade should be answered by our dirigibles bringing terror and death into the ranks of the English people. It is entirely incomprehensible and unjustified that some people wish to exercise restraint in these matters. Any methods that German technology and chemistry can provide for the defense of the Fatherland should unhesitatingly be used to carry the horrors of war to the English enemy. If we understand how to make fire pour down from the heavens, why should we not do so? Experience shows that the victor is always denounced as a barbarian, even when the vanquished has mobilized all the hordes of Asia and Africa against our white warriors. It is better for our people to be denounced by England, France, Russia, and all their satellites as barbarians, than to be pitied by them as the vanquished nation. War toughens men and it must toughen us. We are on the defensive in a war which has been imposed upon us by evil aggressors, and our defensive needs justify the most ruthless measures. . . . *Softness and sentimentality in this war would be inexcusable and hopelessly stupid. Let the enemy say about us what he will, one thing he must not be allowed to say: that the Germans acted stupidly.*" [Erzberger's italics.]

APPENDIX V

Erzberger's Activities for Thyssen

ERZBERGER's activities for Thyssen in promoting certain war aims and approaching certain bureaucrats on company business must be related in some detail, since they became the main item in the later campaign of character assassination directed against him. A great amount of factual material relating to Erzberger's championing of Thyssen interests was thoroughly discussed at the 1920 Erzberger libel suit against Helfferich. The question in each case was whether Erzberger had abused his position as a powerful *Reichstag* deputy to threaten bureaucrats with his political power unless they yielded to Thyssen demands; and also whether the Thyssen demands which he supported were or were not compatible with the public interest. It is regrettable that intelligent men were forced to raise such questions and that Erzberger was not above suspicion, but it must be emphasized that of all the charges made not a single one reflected upon the integrity of Erzberger's character. The charges discussed, and the 1920 court verdict on each of them, were as follows:

1. Erzberger and Thyssen both favored the annexation of the French Longwy-Briey iron region, which bordered upon German Lorraine, where Thyssen held considerable properties. The French government had expropriated Thyssen's vast holdings in Normandy, and he was naturally looking for compensation. His eye fell upon the great *Droit aumont* mine, a valuable French property adjoining one of his own steel works lying directly on the border. He expected to acquire it as soon as Germany should annex the area. He was, indeed, impatient for the German government to expropriate for immediate sale to himself the particular mine even while the war was still going on. Thyssen's confidence in Germany's victory was such that this appeared as a safe investment to him. His legal experts told him, however, that expropriation of private property in enemy territory was contrary to international law, and he therefore never formally applied for such expropriation. But one of his memoranda to the Interior Ministry, then headed by Karl Helfferich, could easily be misinterpreted as requesting immediate purchase of *Droit aumont,* presupposing prior expropriation (May 23, 1916). Helfferich and his *Staatssekretär* Max Richter did so misunderstand it when Erzberger called at Helfferich's office to support the memorandum. This became the basis of Helfferich's charge, seconded by Richter, that Erzberger had promoted a private Thyssen interest in open violation of international law. The court in 1920 declared that the entire matter had been an honest misunderstanding.[1]

[1] *Prozess,* pp. 60–62, 72–75, 77–95, 115–40, 165–70, 189–96, 279, 810, 867, 1000–1003. The confusion created by the May 23, 1916 memorandum was due to the similarity between the German words *Übereignung* (transfer of ownership) and *Überweisung* (securing permission to operate without necessarily implying change of ownership).

2. Erzberger supported Thyssen's demand for the right of exploiting, with no change in ownership, the *Droit aumont* mine for the duration of the war, with the profits going to the French owners. He supported this because he believed that private operation would be more efficient than the present operation by a military administrator. Thyssen had made the same request in a November 12, 1914, memorandum long before Erzberger joined the firm. It was fully in accord with Germany's war needs, since Thyssen was in a position to maximize production by using some of the equipment from his adjoining property. The demand was in no sense a special favor for Thyssen, as the Longwy-Briey area was studded with other iron mines that could be given to Thyssen's competitors upon similar terms. It is true that Thyssen thought that operation would create a *fait accompli* for subsequent ownership, but this was not the reason why Erzberger's request was rejected. The military objected to Thyssen's plan because they wanted to keep the mine, lying in the area immediately behind the front, under their own direct control. It was also feared that labor might be drawn into the area (which was suffering from a severe food shortage) from nearby Lorraine. Many officials of the Interior Ministry favored the acceptance of Thyssen's request, but they were unable to prevail over the military, and Erzberger's advocacy proved unavailing. The court in 1920 found nothing improper in Erzberger's activity.[2]

3. Erzberger, at a conference on July 15, 1916 with Gemmingen, a high official of the Interior Department who was in charge of the Briey-Longwy civilian administration, unsuccessfully asked that captured French iron supplies be distributed to various German firms in accordance with a formula which would have given Thyssen 50 percent of the 800,000 tons involved (by limiting distribution to Lorraine producers and allocating the supplies on the basis of declared deficiencies). He also urged that Thyssen be allowed to join a seven-man civilian council set up at Metz to advise the military administrator of French industrial property. The court established the fact that Erzberger believed, rightly or wrongly, that Gemmingen had welshed upon a promise made to Thyssen in 1914 involving the very formula. Thyssen was already experiencing at that time shortages while other firms had abundant supplies. Erzberger's action in no way violated the national interest. The court also held that Thyssen's request to join the advisory board was entirely reasonable in view of his being the only one of Germany's leading steel magnates who was not represented.[3]

4. Erzberger successfully intervened with the personnel section of the War Office to get Fritz Thyssen released from military service, since he was needed to help run the family business. The court judged this action to be neither unreasonable nor improper.[4]

[2] *Prozess*, pp. 72–75, 189–96, 279, 1003–4.
[3] *Prozess*, pp. 133–34, 169–72, 290–95, 811, 1004–5.
[4] *Prozess*, pp. 601–10, 1005.

5. Erzberger successfully opposed in the *Reichstag* a government proposal made in July 1916 to tax the bills of lading of private railroads extending more than ten kilometers. The Thyssen firm owned several such railroads and stood to gain from the defeat of the government measure, which would have cost it about 200,000 marks per year. Yet the court held that objective considerations, such as the difficulty involved in collecting the tax, were adequate to explain Erzberger's opposition.[5]

6. Erzberger unsuccessfully intervened with Colonel Giessler, head of the export-import section of the War Ministry, to grant Thyssen a license for the export of some protective screens to Holland in the winter of 1915–1916. Giessler rejected the Thyssen request as injurious to the government because the low price proposed by Thyssen would deprive Germany of needed foreign exchange. The court censured Erzberger's intervention as an example of his using his political influence for Thyssen ends. But it must be remembered that the export of the screens was not necessarily harmful to Germany (which indeed would get no foreign exchange whatsoever if the license were refused), and that Erzberger dropped the matter as soon as Giessler had given a firm negative. If Erzberger used political threats he certainly did nothing to implement them—and empty bluff was not part of his nature.[6]

7. The French government had expropriated Thyssen's properties in Normandy at the beginning of the war, acting within its legal rights since they were located on home, not occupied enemy territory (in contrast to the situation at Briey-Longwy). It was natural for Germany to retaliate by expropriating French properties in German Lorraine, and that the expropriated properties should be used to compensate those German industrialists who had suffered from the French action. This view was held by Thyssen and Erzberger, with both having a special eye on the extensive domain owned by the Wendel family. Erzberger, in a memorandum written on May 7, 1917, to the Interior Department, unsuccessfully advocated the liquidation of the Wendel properties in accordance with a formula that would benefit Thyssen. He argued, exactly as he had done in the earlier case of the distribution of ore supplies, that the allocation of the expropriated properties should be limited to German firms located in Lorraine, and that the share of each should be in proportion to its lack of ore supplies—the old point of turning the Thyssen weakness in raw materials into a bargaining advantage. The court censured Erzberger's pressure upon the Interior Department because the above formula favored his employer Thyssen—though it is by no means clear that it was intrinsically unreasonable, and equity in the distribution of wartime loot is always difficult to define. Erzberger's proposal did not violate any clear national interest, and it fell far short of Thyssen's personal desire for the acquisition of the entire Wendel complex for himself. Erzberger

[5] *Prozess,* pp. 661–65, 1006.
[6] *Prozess,* pp. 601–10, 812, 1005–6. For a defense of Erzberger, see S. Löwenstein, *Der Prozess Erzberger-Helfferich. Ein Rechtsgutachten* (Ulm, 1921), pp. 4–8.

claimed that the Alsatian population wanted the allocation of expropriated plants to be limited to those firms already in the province.[7]

8. The court found Erzberger's felony compounded by his vehement opposition to all industrial liquidations in Lorraine in a Budget Committee debate of December 1917, two months after he resigned his Thyssen directorship. The court accepted the *prima facie* evidence that Erzberger championed a policy favoring Thyssen while employed by him while supporting its exact opposite as soon as he had left Thyssen's service. It forgot that the general constellation of affairs had been altered in the seven months between May and December, and that the Peace Resolution had intervened. Erzberger, now preoccupied with securing a negotiated peace based upon genuine conciliation, naturally wanted to avoid all actions that intensified French hostility. The administration of the Wendel properties had recently been placed in the hands of a semi-autonomous corporation established by the government, whose production record was very good. Erzberger did not wish to disturb its smooth operation.[8]

9. The court cleared Erzberger on Helfferich's accusation of a second change of view allegedly caused by the termination of his Thyssen employment. Erzberger opposed a government proposal to tax iron and coal exports in June 1916 (while a Thyssen director), yet led a sharp Budget Committee campaign in favor of such taxes in February, 1918 (after he had left Thyssen). The facts of the case were as follows: Helfferich, in his role as Secretary of State for Finance, decided in the first days of June 1916 that the export of coal and iron ought to be taxed. A kind of taxation existed already because a general embargo had been clamped down on such exports, with fees being charged for exemptions (which were readily granted). Helfferich thought he could tighten the fees collected from exporters by securing formal legislation to replace the existing administrative practice. He sent a *Ministerialdirektor* (section chief) of the Finance Ministry, Gustav Müller, to the *Reichstag* to sound out the various parties on whether they could guarantee smooth passage of such legislation (June 4, 1916). He wanted a noiseless passage arousing a minimum of public attention because export taxes were specifically prohibited by Germany's commercial treaties with several neutral states, and a public debate could easily provoke foreign retaliation by drawing attention to the treaty violation. Müller had a brief conference with Erzberger and Südekum, the main spokesmen on tax questions of the Zentrum and Socialist parties, respectively, at which Erzberger opposed Helfferich's proposal as undesirable. According to the testimony of all three participants—Erzberger, Südekum, and Müller—Erzberger opposed only the opportuneness, not the substance, of the proposed tax. He feared

[7] *Prozess*, pp. 62, 75–76, 811, 1009–11. For a defense of Erzberger, see S. Löwenstein, *op.cit.*, pp. 8–15. Erzberger wrote a long letter to Zimmermann, Jan. 30, 1917, favoring the Lorraine expropriation. *Erzberger Papers*, File 4.

[8] *Prozess*, pp. 62, 75–76, 1009–11. For a defense of Erzberger, see S. Löwenstein, *op.cit.*, pp. 8–15.

retaliation from neutrals who scarcely noticed the existing administrative arrangement. He doubted whether the proposed legislation would yield sums substantially higher than the present system of administrative fees—certainly not enough more to justify provoking foreign retaliation. He also resented the government's springing such a proposal upon the *Reichstag* four days before scheduled adjournment. Erzberger was always a staunch defender of the budgetary powers of the *Reichstag*. Müller returned to Helfferich reporting the failure of his mission, and the matter was dropped. The administrative collection of fees was, of course, continued.

Helfferich was both surprised and angered when Erzberger made a strong attack upon the government in the Budget Committee in February 1918 for its failure to tax coal and iron exports adequately. Erzberger had been aroused by revelations during a secret session in late 1917 about the tremendous difference in coal and steel prices at home and abroad, and the huge profits that were consequently being made by German exporters. The fees charged for export licenses had captured only a small proportion of these profits, and Erzberger calculated that an additional 644 millions could easily have been levied over the last few months. He proposed that this sum be collected retroactively. Erzberger asserted in 1920 that the new facts which he had learned between June 1916 and February 1918 were responsible for his change of view. It must be remembered that his 1916 opposition had been based upon grounds of expediency alone. Erzberger brushed aside Helfferich's contention that his 1916 opposition to legislation had made it impossible for the government to collect the very sums for which he clamored in 1918. He also showed that Thyssen was interested in exports only to an infinitesimal degree, and that his directorship could for this reason alone exercise no influence upon his earlier views. The court was satisfied by Erzberger's explanation.[9]

10. Erzberger's vigorous championing of the German annexation of Longwy-Briey was the most obvious instance of Erzberger the politician supporting what was in the clear interest of Erzberger the Thyssen director. It must be remembered, however, that this had been part of his war-aims program long before he joined the Thyssen firm. He cooperated with Thyssen in drawing up a memorandum for Zimmermann, the Undersecretary for Foreign Affairs, that summarized all the advantages, for both Germany and Thyssen, that would accrue from a Longwy-Briey annexation (September 28, 1915). Germany's economic greatness would be assured by the acquisition of a domestic iron supply that would free her from Swedish exports. This would enable her to defy the British-organized postwar economic warfare that was generally expected. Thyssen would secure compensation for his vast Normandy properties. The Germanization of the ownership of the industry of the annexed area would promote the Germanization of its

[9] *Prozess,* pp. 62–63, 76–77, 98–103, 151–57 (Südekum's testimony), 157–65 (Müller's testimony), 182–89, 812, 1008–9.

French population, thus avoiding a second Alsace-Lorraine whose hostility to Germany was in part promoted by the continued French influence over its economy. The last argument was presumably *ad hoc* unless Erzberger had a temporary lapse from his ordinarily sane outlook upon nationality problems.[10]

Erzberger organized a press agitation for the annexation of Briey-Longwy, financed by several German steel magnates, in May 1917, only two months before the Peace Resolution that was to cause his breach with Thyssen. At the 1920 trial Helfferich attempted to show that Erzberger continued this agitation even after promoting the anti-annexationist Peace Resolution, and drew two conclusions unflattering to his opponent: that Erzberger became anti-annexationist in July 1917 upon all questions except Longwy-Briey, where his pocketbook was personally involved; and that this constituted a vain attempt to forestall being fired by Thyssen, who was becoming very angry with Erzberger because of his increasing collaboration with the Socialists. Erzberger answered these charges by claiming that his post-July 1917 support of the Longwy-Briey propaganda had not been for annexation pure and simple, but had rather looked forward to a territorial exchange with France, where Germany received Briey-Longwy while France received the French-speaking Château-Salins area of Lorraine. This was admittedly a poor bargain for the French, who would trade a rich industrial for a poor agrarian area, but it was calculated to spare French prestige. Erzberger favored a commercial treaty, with France guaranteeing German access to French iron and French access to German coal, which in many ways foreshadows the Schuman Plan after World War II. He thought of this either as a supplement or a substitute for the proposed territorial exchange. In any case, he had never intended the Peace Resolution to mean a prohibition of any and all territorial changes.

Helfferich argued that the plan of exchanging Château-Salins for Briey-Longwy was an *ex post facto* alibi to refurbish Erzberger's tarnished reputation for consistency and integrity, but Erzberger was able to produce two witnesses, neither of them generally friendly to himself, who told the court that he had mentioned the exchange plan to them in the summer of 1917. Helfferich's charge that Erzberger had tried to cling to his directorship was refuted by both August Thyssen and his son Fritz; both deplored his political evolution in 1917 but admired his courage in deliberately choosing a course that he knew must lead to his resignation of the directorship, with its sizable 40,000 mark salary. He made no attempt to cling to his directorship, and he resigned in what was a friendly parting that left personal relations unaffected.[11]

[10] The 12-page memorandum, "The Interests of the Thyssen Firm in France and Its Colonies and the Importance of the Briey Basin for the German Iron Industry," is in *F.O.*, File 1498.

[11] *Prozess*, pp. 49–54, 57–60, 69–72, 95–98, 125–29, 281–90, 1006–08.

Erzberger's activities for Thyssen appear to merit a Scotch verdict. He did nothing that was dishonorable, much less anything illegal, but he did sometimes get himself into the twilight zone between what is undoubtedly proper and what is perhaps questionable. The bureaucrats with whom he dealt on Thyssen business were sometimes apprehensive of his *Reichstag* power, and feared political retaliation if they should reject his wishes. His reputation was that of being "the most powerful man in Berlin. With his recommendation one gets everywhere, without it one gets nowhere," as Alfred Hugenberg, the later Nationalist leader, said.[12] Yet the record shows that his reputation for influence was worse than his actual influence. He was unsuccessful in most of the interventions on behalf of Thyssen described above: Helfferich refused Thyssen the exploitation of *Droit au mont;* Gemmingen refused to distribute the French iron supplies according to the formula suggested by Erzberger; Giessler rejected the export licenses to Holland; and the Wendel properties in Lorraine were not expropriated for Thyssen's benefit. If Erzberger threatened political retaliation in all these matters, his threats were singularly unsuccessful. The particular officials were evidently not terrorized by him, though they were no doubt annoyed by his pressure: a chronic feeling among bureaucrats whenever they are approached by parliamentarians, whether on legitimate or illegitimate business. There is no evidence that Erzberger's pressure was ever improper, or that he promoted private business interests at the expense of the general welfare. Yet on this as on other occasions Erzberger did not watch the appearance, as opposed to the substance, of what he did. The same can be said about his change of attitude in the questions of the Lorraine expropriations and the export duties on iron and coal. The change of circumstances in the intervening period constitutes in both instances an adequate justification for Erzberger's reversal of his earlier position, but an instinct for the impression that his reversal would create ought to have dictated letting others take the lead on behalf of Erzberger's new views. Instead, he rushed into the fray with his customary fighting temper and gave the impression, at least to hostile critics, of having been dominated by mercenary motives in the first place and being later under the sway of vindictiveness towards his former employer Thyssen.

[12] H. Class, *Wider den Strom* (Leipzig, 1932), p. 329.

APPENDIX VI

Erzberger's Memorandum of July 16, 1918

THE following memorandum, circulated on August 12, 1918, shows Erzberger at his best, both in its acute foresight and its constructive suggestions:

"How can we bring the war to an end? It is senseless to continue fighting until our exhaustion in men and materials forces us to capitulate unconditionally. If we fight to the bitter end we lose not only our economic substance and our most vigorous young men, we risk not only our political and economic future for a century, but we endanger the very future existence of our state. The victors will humble us as no other people has been humbled before. Deep internal upheavals, terrible political and social crises will become unavoidable. A naval commander, when defeated by superior forces, may go down proudly with his flag flying; a people of 70 millions cannot do this, and if its leaders call for this kind of effort the masses (*Pöbel*) will drag the flag through the mud.

"There exist, in enemy countries as in ours, reasonable men unaffected by the fanaticism of war, who have long had enough of the bloody slaughter, and wish to end it by a reasonable peace of compromise if given the chance. But they do not get the chance because of the universal belief in Entente countries—be it right or wrong—that we are governed by a small military clique which holds power over the people as Napoleon once held power over the French. It is believed that this clique must be overthrown—exactly as the Corsican usurper was overthrown a hundred years ago—before negotiations are possible.

"Power in wartime is always concentrated in few hands. So long as things go well the majority of the people is quite satisfied with this condition. But in situations like ours today the question becomes urgent: can we leave things this way? Our responsible leaders, who were by no means exclusively civilians, have certainly made many mistakes. The attempt to decide the war through unrestricted submarine warfare was a mistake; the view that American armies could not interfere in time was mistaken; the faith that the enemy could be defeated in the west this summer was mistaken; and the belief that the Treaty of Brest-Litovsk could free us in the east and relieve our economic needs was the worst mistake of all.

"It would be foolish to question the good faith of our leaders or to assail them as evil men. Since we willingly followed their leadership we are accomplices in their errors. But the question must be asked whether these men are suited to lead us through the difficulties that now confront us. If our leaders should now seriously decide to negotiate with the enemy their decision would be received with incredulity in the West. They do not have the authority which is indispensable for conducting negotiations. For that we need men who have long sought a genuine peace of conciliation. Whether they be deputies, diplomats, or other officials is a minor matter.

"We need, in order to get to the negotiating table, a new government which is supported by the great majority of the *Reichstag*. The new government must declare its willingness to make fairly large concessions in order to secure peace. It is painful for any German to think of concessions, not only in the question of colonies but also that of Alsace-Lorraine, which would have been inconceivable even a few months ago—but the offer of substantial concessions is a prerequisite for getting negotiations started. It is also necessary to accept the fact that the Hapsburg Monarchy will not survive the war in its present shape. We must get over the dream of *Mitteleuropa* by recognizing that Austria-Hungary lost its vitality long ago, and that Europe will know no peace so long as it continues to exist [with the suppression of legitimate national aspirations]. But we may also cherish the hope that from the disintegration of that monarchy will arise the union of Germany with Austria which our fathers sought but did not secure in the period of the so-called wars of unification (especially the events of 1866). Our difficult but rewarding task, as soon as peace is secured, will be to build on the ruins created by war a new Germany, capable of great new achievements.

"These prospects are far from pleasant. But they are rosy compared to our lot in the case of unconditional surrender. We can achieve the more favorable alternative only if we make peace *now*. An early peace is more than a pious wish; it is the prerequisite for our future existence. To achieve it now, if necessary by overriding all obstacles that stand in the way, is the immediate task of the German *Reichstag*."

APPENDIX VII

Additional Cases Discussed at the Erzberger-Helfferich Trial

1. *The Angele Case*

Eugen Angele was the co-owner of a malt factory located in Erzberger's *Reichstag* constituency. He had been appointed local agent of the Reich Barley Administration (which bought the entire harvest under wartime controls) early in the war, but was dismissed from this post in August 1916 after a new regulation had made malt manufacturers ineligible for appointment (since they might be tempted to divert barley under their official control to use in their own factories). The new regulation explicitly allowed for exceptions, and Erzberger wrote several letters to *Geheimrat* Hagedorn (in charge of appointments in the Barley Administration) and his superior Von Oppen, President of the War Food Office, urging that Angele be restored to his post. Erzberger argued that an exception in his favor was both equitable and desirable because (1) Angele had just enlarged his storage facilities upon the request of the Reich Barley Administration, and (2) Angele's reappointment was strongly recommended by local officials, the elected assembly of his district and local opinion generally. Erzberger urged the desirability of deference to local sentiments, in view of the cumulative Württemberg resentment against the Prussian-dominated war agencies. Hagedorn was not convinced by these arguments, and resented what he considered to be a threat by Erzberger to attack the Barley Administration in the *Reichstag* unless his wishes were met. Oppen proved more accommodating and devised a compromise whereby Angele secured reappointment but withdrew formally from the management of his malt firm, thereby avoiding a direct conflict of interest: this compromise proved satisfactory to Angele and Erzberger, and was reluctantly endorsed by Hagedorn. The court declared that the settlement was due to Erzberger's direct intervention on Angele's behalf, but found nothing improper in this intervention.

The case became compromising for Erzberger because of two subsequent developments. Angele was indicted in June 1917 for malfeasance in the conduct of his office, with the specific accusation that he had illegally retained a large share of the 1915 local barley harvest for use in his own factory. This fact was, of course, unknown to Erzberger when he intervened on behalf of Angele in September 1916, but it threw an unfavorable light upon his judgment concerning men whose interests he tried to support.

Angele had tried to call upon Erzberger at his Berlin apartment in August 1916, to interest him in his case, but found only Mrs. Erzberger at home. Their conversation turned to the difficult food situation, with Angele telling Mrs. Erzberger that prices were lower and supplies more plentiful in Württemberg than in Berlin. He then offered to send Mrs. Erzberger food packages at Württemberg prices, and this provided the Erzberger family with regular supplies of sugar, butter, geese, wheat, flour, ham, and eggs for the remainder of the war. Mrs. Erzberger was especially eager to secure eggs because they enabled her to cook Erzberger's favorite meal, *Spätzle* (the Württemberg gastronomic specialty). The court took the view that these food shipments (for which Erzberger paid, of course, in full) were an act of gratitude on Angele's part for Erzberger's intervention to have him restored to his post, not a bribe accepted by Erzberger for services rendered. The food shipments involved some violation of rationing laws, and Mrs. Erzberger was convicted and fined 200 marks by a local Charlottenburg court on March 25, 1918, for illegal receipt of food. Angele was indicted at Ravensburg (in Württemberg) on October 9, 1918, for the unauthorized sale of food products, but the case was never brought to trial. The revelation of Erzberger's contacts with Angele had a very unfavorable effect upon his public standing, by contributing to the popular stereotype that Erzberger had lived a gluttonous life in Berlin while his contemporaries lived on potatoes and turnips in the trenches.[1]

2. *The Kowastch Case*

Ambrosius Kowastch was a mining engineer who had invented an explosive that used fluid air rather than dynamite in mining operations. He believed that its introduction would promote mine safety while its production would lead, as a desirable byproduct, to a cheap supply of oxygen for use in hospitals. He had first thought of introducing his new process in the United States, but desisted when he learned on a visit that (1) the U.S. dynamite trust could easily crush his invention, (2) U.S. patent officials were certain to be bribed by the dynamite trust, and (3) American industrialists and workers, being pure dollar chasers, would show no interest in safety devices. Kowastch, who also had literary ambitions, wrote a book about his American experiences, but had trouble finding a publisher. A childhood friend, who knew Erzberger, introduced him to the Zentrum deputy in 1910. Kowastch talked with Erzberger about his book for two and a half hours, and also mentioned his invention of the new process. Erzberger promised help in finding a publisher and was also attracted by the humanitarian implications of the new explosive. He soon invested 2,200 marks in a new company formed by Kowastch, who had no capital himself.

The chief competitor of the Kowastch process was the so-called Marsit process developed by the Marsit Company. There was some question as to which process had the higher safety factor, with Erzberger believing that Kowastch was superior in every respect. He wrote in this sense to Polensky, the expert for explosives in the Prussian Ministry of Commerce, who was in charge of deciding which device was to be used in the state mines. The Marsit Company feared that Erzberger's influence might lead to a judgment hostile to their interests, and they then agreed to a merger with the Kowastch

[1] On the Angele case, see *Prozess*, pp. 442–65, 818–19, 928.

firm on terms favorable to the latter in 1915. Hans Berckmeyer, the General Director of the Marsit Company, testified that fear of Erzberger's influence had been his main consideration in agreeing to the merger. He had also heard reports (never verified) that the powerful Potash Trust had paid the Kowastch company 50,000 marks for the mere option of using its process— an option never used. It was alleged that this payment was made purely out of fear of Erzberger's influence.

The combined Kowastch-Marsit Company decided, after further experimentation, to use the Marsit process alone, since it proved more economical and had no significant difference in safety. The old shares of Kowastch stock rose in value as a result of the merger, and a Swedish firm soon offered 900,000 marks for the purchase of the patent. Kowastch complained to Erzberger that his own lack of stock ownership deprived him of any share in the rising profits. Erzberger, who always sympathized with the plight of inventors, then sold Kowastch his own shares for what was considered to be the cheap price of 30,000 marks. Kowastch was satisfied and Erzberger could look upon his initial 2,200 marks as an excellent investment. His interest in the process was humanitarian rather than financial. The court was distressed by the fact that the actions of the Marsit Company had evidently been motivated by fear of Erzberger, and wondered whether Erzberger had revealed his own financial interest in Kowastch at the time when his letters to Polensky aimed at discrediting the competing Marsit process. Polensky was unfortunately dead, thus making it impossible to determine the latter question. The court declared Erzberger innocent of improper conduct in the absence of conclusive proof.[2]

3. The Pnigodin Case

Richard Erfurt was an apothecary in North Berlin. A customer came to his store one day in 1909 and showed him a plant that had helped him against asthma. The Erfurt family happened to be suffering from whooping cough, and Erfurt thought that what helped against asthma might also help against whooping cough. He gave the plant to his children and was surprised by the rapid cure effected. Erfurt then approached Dr. Peter Scharz, a man who played some role in Zentrum politics in North Berlin. Scharz suggested the formation of a new company to produce the plant commercially with a sugar admixture to make it attractive to children. He suggested Pnigodin as a good name for the new product. Scharz then called upon Erzberger to seek advice about raising the necessary capital. He found Erzberger enthusiastic about the prospective cure for whooping cough: "It would be wonderful (*grossartig*) if this medicine should prove successful because whooping cough is a nasty matter, as I know full well from cases in my own family." [3]

[2] On the Kowastch case, see *Prozess*, pp. 389–429, 665–70, 819–20, 868–69, 895, 926–28, 954, 1017–20.
[3] *Prozess*, p. 225.

Erzberger tried the medicine on himself while suffering from an ordinary cough, and was satisfied with the result. He then persuaded various Zentrum leaders (Count Praschma and the two Bavarians Heim and Held) to make investments in the new company, and contributed 4,000 marks himself (buying 4 shares of stock at 1,000 marks face value apiece). Erzberger became chairman of the board of directors of the new company in 1910 after a patent had been secured for Pnigodin.

The company did not prosper, and Erzberger tried to retrieve its fortunes by selling the patent to an established pharmaceutical firm, the *Sächsische Serumwerke* in Dresden, in 1912. The latter agreed to pay to the Pnigodin company 10 pfennigs per bottle of Pnigodin sold after the first 40,000. Erfurt, convinced of the revolutionary nature of his own medical discovery, thought that the terms were very unsatisfactory, and resented the fact that no compensation was given to him as inventor. The other members of the board were, however, satisfied with the contract, and relieved that a large firm now took an interest in what increasingly looked like a quack product. The *Serumwerke* were rather more optimistic and insisted upon a clause in the contract limiting dividend payments to Pnigodin shareholders to 50 percent.

The *Sächsische Serumwerke* wanted to acquire some Pnigodin stock in order to participate in board meetings. It bought two of Erzberger's shares at 115 some time in 1915, paying 2,300 marks for 2,000 marks face value. The sale was approved at a board meeting at which, however, only three men were present due to wartime conditions. The purchase price was not an unreasonable sum, since the future prospects of Pnigodin were as yet uncertain, and the expected early peace made production difficulties appear insignificant (whereas, in a long war, the sugar shortage—with sugar being an indispensable ingredient—would make output problematical). Helfferich, always suspicious of Erzberger, suggested a connection between the inflated purchase price and a motion which Erzberger had introduced in the *Reichstag* on May 11, 1914. Erzberger had studied the Balkan Wars (just completed) closely, and was impressed by the danger of typhus and dysentery breaking out in modern armies. He proposed a Reich subsidy of 25,000 marks to various pharmaceutical houses in order to induce them to stockpile sera for future use. This proposal was rejected when medical experts declared that the sera would lose their potency during any prolonged storage period. The *Sächsische Serumwerke* was one of the plants that would have benefited from the proposed subsidy. Helfferich's charge that the purchase of Erzberger's stock at 115 constituted a *quid pro quo* for his attempt to secure a Reich subsidy was sharply denied by Friedrich Bethge, the Director of the *Serumwerke*. Helfferich was unable to adduce any proof for his accusation.

The *Serumwerke*, meanwhile, began the production of Pnigodin on a serious scale, and sold 20,000 bottles by the spring of 1918. The Reich Sugar

Office, still suspicious of the new product, made difficulties about supplying further sugar. The firm then asked Erzberger to write to Professor Adolf Juckenack, a high official of the Sugar Office, to ask for a continued allocation of sugar. Erzberger obliged in a letter dated February 3, 1918, which was much resented by Juckenack as constituting parliamentary pressure upon his bureaucratic judgment. Juckenack, after swallowing his anger and seeking the advice of medical authorities, decided that Pnigodin was a genuine medical discovery after all, and granted the request of the *Serumwerke* championed by Erzberger. Helfferich accused Erzberger of concealing his own financial interest in the Pnigodin product when he approached Juckenack. The court ruled, however, that this interest was so infinitesimal that it could not affect Erzberger's judgment. The Pnigodin company would secure royalties only after 40,000 bottles had been sold, whereas production in the last five years had amounted to only half that number. Erzberger owned only two-seventieths of the total Pnigodin stock of 70,000 marks, and royalties were to flow only at the rate of 10 pfennigs per bottle. Erzberger had, incidentally, resigned as chairman of the board of the Pnigodin company in 1917, and no successor was ever elected. There was some doubt in 1920 whether the company still continued to exist. Erzberger's initial investment was clearly the result of his exuberant optimism rather than a sober judgment on the medical value of Pnigodin.[4]

4. *The Kolk Case*

Fritz van der Kolk was a Dutchman who worked in Erzberger's propaganda office as a translator. He had difficulty maintaining his large family on his meager salary of 400 marks a month, and founded a company that imported oils and fats from his native Holland in order to supplement his income. Kolk ran into the usual difficulties connected with wartime bureaucratic regulations, and wrote to Erzberger in November 1917, seeking advice on how to grease the bureaucratic wheels. His letter contained the following remarkable paragraph: "Should you, Mr. Erzberger, be of the opinion that it is necessary for our purpose to give some influential personality a financial interest in our firm, we would be entirely willing to make available 3 percent of our turnover, to be transferred in any manner that you would consider suitable. We would also be willing to settle for a 10,000 mark annual guaranteed minimum if said personality provided the solution for our problem." [5]

Erzberger showed his carelessness by passing this letter on to the Interior Ministry while urging sympathetic consideration of Kolk's difficulties. He

[4] On the Pnigodin case, see *Prozess,* pp. 214–38, 260–71, 311–12, 812–13, 869, 895, 928–29, 1015–17. There was considerable disagreement on the number of shares originally held by Erzberger, and about the precise time when he sold shares to the *Serumwerke.* The figures given in the text appear to be the most probable, and the details are unimportant.

[5] *Prozess,* p. 498.

had, presumably, not found time to read the letter himself. When the Ministry expressed its horror at the terms of the enclosure, Erzberger summoned Kolk to his office and gave him a reprimand. He was, however, sympathetic to the excuse advanced by Kolk: he had lived for several years in the Dutch East Indies, where all business was transacted with the help of bribery, and he found it difficult to adjust to the very different European milieu. Erzberger, who was completely devoid of pharisaism, did not break personal relations with Kolk, and did not fire him from his translator's job. A man of Helfferich's self-conscious virtue found this kind of conduct quite incomprehensible. The court was startled by Erzberger's behavior, but there was obviously nothing illegal about it.[6]

5. *The Richter Case*

Van der Kolk was not taken over by the Foreign Office when Erzberger's propaganda office folded up in the summer of 1918. His oil import business was not going well, so he decided to branch out into railroad safety devices. He met a locksmith by the name of Richter, who had just invented a new kind of hand lock that could be used with railroad switches. They decided to found a company capitalized at 100,000 marks. Kolk approached Erzberger for a financial contribution, with Erzberger deciding to help Kolk, in his own words, "because I considered him to be a decent man, though he had some peculiar notions based upon his origin and earlier activities."[7] Erzberger agreed to buy 40,000 marks worth of shares and gave Kolk a personal loan of 20,000 marks as well—a rather remarkable use of money to help a man whom he had called on the carpet for seeking to bribe officials of the Reich only a few months earlier. Erzberger wanted to withdraw from the company when he became *Staatssekretär* in October 1918, but Kolk and Richter pleaded with him to stay lest the entire company fold up. When Richter had difficulty securing a personal conference with *Geheimrat* Otto Hoogen, the official in charge of safety devices in the Prussian railroad ministry, to demonstrate the value of his invention, Erzberger wrote him a card of introduction on January 23, 1919 which immediately opened all doors. Erzberger did not mention his personal financial interest in the Richter company on his card, but even the court found this unnecessary in what was only a request for an interview. Erzberger stated during the trial that he literally handed out dozens of cards of introduction every day. Richter was unable to convince railroad officials of the value of his invention, and he did not secure a sufficiently large trial order to make it worthwhile to begin production. Erzberger applied no pressure on behalf of the firm. He recognized that his investment was a total loss, and had little hope of even having his loan of 20,000 marks repaid. Richter gave him an I.O.U. for 15,000 marks in November 1919 (when Erzberger severed all connections with the

[6] On the Kolk case, see Kolk's testimony in *Prozess,* pp. 504–07.
[7] *Prozess,* p. 502.

company), but this was still unpaid at the time of the trial. The entire case lost Erzberger a clear 60,000 marks and reveals a culpable recklessness in the management of his personal finances.[8]

6. *Transfer of Money Abroad*

Helfferich levied the broad accusation against Erzberger that he had transferred money abroad in violation of the foreign exchange regulations—an especially odious matter in the light of Erzberger's Catonian denunciation of capital flight when introducing his tax legislation. Helfferich had hired a number of detectives who scoured through bank records in foreign countries (especially Switzerland) and even attempted to bribe bank employees to open secret files to their scrutiny. They found fairly sizable funds deposited in several accounts under Erzberger's name, but could not prove that personal money transactions were involved. Erzberger explained to the court that he had transferred funds abroad for both propaganda and ecclesiastical purposes, and that the former funds especially could not be sent through the regular channels. Much of the testimony on these points was given *in camera* to avoid embarrassment for former German agents. The financing of the propaganda operations had also involved Erzberger in pressure upon the Commissar for Licensing Exports and Imports. Erzberger often wanted to pay foreign firms or individuals for services rendered in export and import permits, which were ordinarily hard to get in wartime Germany. The court felt itself incompetent to decide whether the advantages to propaganda exceeded the fiscal disadvantage in any particular case. Much of the testimony on these points was secret also. Helfferich was completely unable to prove that Erzberger's administration of funds had served his personal enrichment or violated any national interest, while the evasion of exchange regulations had taken place with the approval of Bethmann and the Foreign Office.[9]

Helfferich made much of the fact that Mrs. Erzberger and her two daughters had spent the months from January to August 1919 in a pension (soon inflated in the popular imagination to a luxury hotel) at St. Moritz in Switzerland. Helfferich asked how Erzberger was able to finance such a prolonged vacation without violating German currency restrictions. Erzberger was visibly angered by this attack: he had become rather immune to abuse directed against himself, but he resented having his family dragged into the political arena. He explained that his wife and daughter Maria (then aged 16) had been very ill with the grippe in the winter of 1918-1919. The doctors, warned by the death of Oscar and the tubercular tendencies in Mrs. Erzberger's family, insisted that a prolonged stay in the Swiss mountains was the only way of saving their lives. Erzberger then sent them to St.

[8] On the Richter Case, see *Prozess*, pp. 496–512, 822, 869–70, 920–21, 1020–21.
[9] On the transfer of funds abroad, see *Prozess*, pp. 629–37, 645–85, 824–25, 896, 930–31, 954–55, 1030–33. On pressure to grant export and import licenses, *Prozess*, pp. 593–97, 610–29 *passim*, 770–85 *passim*, 823–24, 921, 930, 1026–27.

Moritz, with Gabriele, the youngest daughter (aged 4), going along to be with her mother. Erzberger secured a loan of 100,000 francs from a Swiss banker friend to pay for the vacation, with the stipulation that it should be repaid as soon as the transfer of capital from Germany to Switzerland became possible again.[10]

Erzberger denounced the vicious whispering campaign that portrayed his family as living in the lap of luxury while Germany suffered. These accusations were of a piece with the stories that Erzberger ate at the fashionable Berlin restaurant Hiller three times a day—a story started because he occasionally transacted business at breakfast conferences there while his family was away in Switzerland. The court found nothing censurable in Erzberger's activities, but some of the mud thrown at Erzberger inevitably stuck. Working-class fathers could not send their families to Switzerland on doctors' orders, and some must have resented the fact that the family of the Finance Minister could vacation in the mountains while Germany was passing from crisis to crisis.[11]

7. Untruthfulness about Bethmann's View on Taxes

The court found Erzberger guilty of untruthfulness on five counts: in his report about his conversation with Loebell in 1906, discussed in Appendix II; his claim that he informed the government in advance about his July action, and his telling Bethmann that this action aimed at strengthening the Chancellor's position, both discussed in Chapter VIII; and two cases involving details in his testimony in the Berger and Kowastch cases respectively. The sixth count of perjury involved a statement made by Erzberger in January 1916 about the views of the Chancellor on certain taxes proposed by Helfferich. The facts are as follows:

Helfferich proposed the introduction of some new taxes in January 1916 which encountered considerable opposition in the Zentrum Party because they were felt to be regressive. Erzberger told a Zentrum caucus on January 17, 1916 that he had learned from Bethmann that the Chancellor would not insist upon the new taxes if they should provoke severe controversy. Helfferich was indignant about Erzberger's using the Chancellor's alleged statement to defeat a governmental proposal. Bethmann denied, both in 1916 and at the time of the trial in 1920, that he could possibly have made the statement which Erzberger attributed to him. The former Chancellor told the court that he had been irrevocably committed to the new taxes at the time he talked with Erzberger, and cited as proof that he had already secured *Bundesrat* approval for them. The court believed Bethmann and declared Erzberger guilty of perjury.

Bethmann was certainly a truthful man, but it turned out after the com-

---

[10] On the Swiss vacation of the Erzberger family, see *Prozess*, pp. 648–49.

[11] On Erzberger's alleged luxurious living, see *Prozess*, pp. 469–70, 474. Helfferich absurdly stated that Erzberger's *Stammtisch* (regular table) was known as the "Grave of Virtue." *ibid.*, p. 470.

pletion of the trial that he had suffered a minor lapse of memory. The records of the *Bundesrat* showed that the taxes had been approved by it only on February 15 and March 4, 1916; hence the inference that the government was already committed to them in mid-January was questionable. Bethmann had admitted on the witness stand that the fear of provoking dissension had caused some hesitation in his mind in assenting to Helfferich's proposal. Erzberger was opposed to the taxes only for fear of the political repercussions, not because he opposed new taxes *per se*. There was some question on how categorical Erzberger's statement had been at the Zentrum meeting; the main witness against him was Peter Spahn, who was morbidly suspicious of all of Erzberger's actions. The probability of a genuine misunderstanding between Erzberger and Bethmann is indicated. Erzberger had probably done most of the talking, as was his habit, emphasizing his opposition to the taxes, and he had probably gotten the impression, without Bethmann's saying so expressly, that the Chancellor agreed with his views. The fact that Bethmann continued to have close relations with Erzberger for a year and a half after the incident indicates that he did not believe the latter guilty of dishonorable conduct.[12]

Several minor cases that came up at the trial are not worth discussing in detail. They involve Erzberger's relationship with the Wolff iron firm of Cologne,[13] his intention of becoming syndic of the butchers' and meat retailers' association at a salary of 12,000 marks in October 1918,[14] his wartime interventions to secure oil and fats on behalf of manufacturers and exporters,[15] and his conferring a special favor upon a South German tailors' association whose claims were championed by a Democratic deputy named Hermann.[16] The court declared Erzberger innocent of all charges connected with these four cases.

[12] On Erzberger's alleged untruthfulness, see *Prozess,* pp. 1035–36, the court summary of the miscellaneous evidence. For a defense of Erzberger's conduct, see S. Löwenstein, *op.cit.,* pp. 45–51.

[13] *Prozess,* pp. 466–96, 670–75, 821–22, 896–98, 955–56, 1027–28.

[14] *ibid.,* pp. 589–93, 822, 868, 923, 1024–25.

[15] *ibid.,* pp. 610–29, 770–85, 823, 1025.

[16] *ibid.,* pp. 785–93, 823, 898, 1030–31.

APPENDIX VIII

Erzberger's Personal Finances and Tax Returns

A SUMMARY of Erzberger's personal financial situation is necessary in view of the widespread belief that he was both a millionaire and a notorious tax evader. Erzberger started life in very humble circumstances; all of his money, apart from his wife's dowry, was acquired through his personal efforts. Mrs. Erzberger brought 50,000 marks into the marriage, a very large sum in 1900. Erzberger considered this sum, plus the interest, untouchable. He told his friend Dr. Hammer, who urged him to abandon the controversial *Zentrums-korrespondenz* in 1907, that his family obligations made this impossible. "I stand in a free profession and can die at any time [without leaving a pension for my widow]. My professional expenses as a deputy and our family life in Berlin cost together, despite our simple tastes, about 20,000 marks a year. The pay of a *Reichstag* member is only a fraction of this amount. I must work to earn our daily bread. I can tell you that we have made some financial progress, but I must continue to work for money until we accumulate 500,000 marks, and this goal is still a long time off. Then I will be financially independent and able to devote my whole time to politics."[1] It should be noted that Mrs. Erzberger never showed any interest in the family finances and left the administration completely in the hands of her husband. She was unable to tell Dr. Hammer what the family financial situation had been in 1914.[2] Much of the money was invested in the stocks of the Berlin Zentrum newspaper *Germania,* which was Erzberger's most frequent journalistic outlet and usually took his side in political controversies.[3]

The Erzberger-Helfferich trial gave a good but unsystematic record of Erzberger's financial operations after 1914. His salary as a Thyssen director for the years 1915-1917, set at 40,000 marks per year, amounted to about 100,000 marks. He bought 40,000 marks' worth of stock in the Berger engineering firm, half in 1918 and the other half in 1919, and received 27,000 marks in total salary as a director, 1917-1918. His stock ownership in the Rechberg Leather Company amounted to 112,000 marks in 1917, and this firm paid generous dividends in the period 1916-1918. Erzberger sold his 2,000-mark investment in the Kowastch Firm for 30,000 marks in 1915 following the Marsit merger. He sold 5 of his Pnigodin shares to the *Sächsische Serumwerke* in 1915 at a slight profit. His investment in the Richter safety gadget in 1918, consisting of a 40,000 marks stock purchase and a 20,000 marks personal loan, proved a total loss. He bought 100,000 marks' worth of Hapag shipping stock slightly below par in the spring of 1919 and sold it

---

[1] Letter of Dr. Hammer to Karl Bachem, Nov. 11, 1929, dealing in detail with Erzberger's finances. Henceforth cited as *Hammer Letter. Bachem Papers,* File 89.
[2] *ibid.*
[3] *ibid.*

slightly above par in November. His total fortune probably amounted to about 250,000 marks in 1919, though this constitutes only a very rough guess in view of the fragmentary nature of the evidence available.[4]

Erzberger's personal finances aroused considerable public interest when his Conservative enemies began to denounce him as a tax evader in the spring of 1920. Their main ammunition consisted of the photostats of his tax returns printed in the *Hamburger Nachrichten* on February 22, 1920. An official investigation on how these records had been stolen from the Berlin-Charlottenburg office led nowhere. A Berlin publisher, Hermann Krüger, was identified as having the photostats and sending them on to the *Hamburger Nachrichten*. He claimed to have received them from one Dr. Ernst Bülck, editor of the ultra-Conservative *Deutsche Zeitung,* who claimed they had been sent to him through the mails by an anonymous informant. Some official or janitor at the Berlin tax office must have given the informant access to the files in January 1920, but the identity of the guilty man was never established.[5]

The returns appeared to show that Erzberger had made incorrect statements in filing his Prussian income taxes for 1916 and 1918 and on his Reich declaration on capital gains for 1916–1920. In his Prussian statement of January 1916 he had listed his Thyssen income for 1915 as 20,000 marks, since he had joined the firm at an annual salary of 40,000 marks only at mid-year. But a special law, the *Lex Schweppendieck,* required that people pay taxes at the level of their annual salary even if they received it for only a part of the year. Erzberger, as an expert on all tax matters, ought to have been familiar with this law. He made a similar mistake on his 1918 returns after leaving Thyssen in mid-summer 1917. The returns also omitted to mention any income from his writings, arbitration work, or speculative dealings. His Reich capital gains tax return for 1920 appeared to understate his holdings in the Rechberg leather firm.[6]

The head of the Charlottenburg tax office, Hering, had begun a special examination of Erzberger's returns on September 12, 1919, long before the Nationalists started their clamor. The very thorough investigation, ending on March 30, 1920, revealed some carelessness in Erzberger's returns, but nothing to indicate willful evasion or to justify prosecution. This did not satisfy Erzberger's foes. The Prussian Minister of Finance ordered a new investigation on October 6, 1920. Hering's superior, *Abteilungspräsident* Falkenhahn, asserted that the evidence warranted prosecution (November 4, 1920). His report was very hostile to Erzberger, and contemptuously dismissed Hering's investigation as a partisan defense of Erzberger. Falkenhahn's conclusions were, however, questioned in turn by his superior,

[4] Erzberger's lawyer Friedländer summarized his wartime financial gains in *Prozess,* pp. 931–33.

[5] *Reichstag Debates,* cccxlix (May 4, 1921), 3589–3622 *passim.*

[6] See Anonymous [probably K. Helfferich], *Erzberger Redivivus? Die Steuern und die Eide des Herrn Erzberger* (Berlin, 1921), Part i.

President of the *Landesfinanzamt* Heincke, in a covering letter (November 4, 1920) that defended Hering's work and asserted that Erzberger was innocent of any evasion. Such divergent views reveal the difficulty of objective judgments about Erzberger. The three officials in the case: Hering, Falkenhahn, Heincke, were all distinguished Prussian civil servants. There was some evidence that Falkenhahn was prejudiced against Erzberger, for he was known to be strongly Nationalist in his sympathies. Erzberger had refused to make him President of a *Landesfinanzamt* in his fiscal reorganization, though such a promotion was given to men with similar civil service status. Erzberger's friends claimed that Falkenhahn was vindictive, and alleged that he had bragged to a subordinate: "I will ruin Erzberger with this tax matter." [7] It was even alleged that Falkenhahn had personally handed Erzberger's returns over to his Nationalist assailants.[8]

The Nationalist press, headed by Dr. Bülck, clamored for an indictment of Erzberger, and the Prussian Minister of Finance, Lüdemann, reluctantly yielded to this clamor and sent the tax file to the public prosecutors' office (December 27, 1920). It was widely noted that this was a very unusual step, since Erzberger had been cleared both by his local office (Hering) and the President of the Berlin *Landesfinanzamt* (Heincke), with only the intermediary section chief (Falkenhahn) suspecting Erzberger of evasion. Prosecution would have been most improbable in any case that had not aroused publicity and political passions.[9]

Erzberger's parliamentary immunity had to be lifted before any prosecution could be started. The *Reichstag* sent the matter to a special committee on February 23, 1921. Erzberger addressed a letter the next day to all the members of the *Reichstag*, urging speedy action to allow his case to come to an early trial. He denounced the procrastination that had marked the entire inquiry into his finances since its commencement seventeen months ago (September 1919).[10] The special committee heard a long report on the question from Josef Wirth, the Finance Minister, which is the best survey of the entire case. It then voted 16–4 in favor of lifting the immunity, with only some Socialists being opposed on account of the obvious political motivation behind the prosecution.[11]

The question led to a long *Reichstag* debate on May 5, 1921, marked by a revival of all the passions originally stimulated by the Erzberger-Helfferich trial. Erzberger's friends, especially his fellow-Swabian André, made a sharp attack upon Helfferich's conduct of his personal finances, which led to an

[7] *Deutsches Volksblatt,* May 7, 1921.
[8] *Germania,* March 5, 1921. *Reichstag Debates,* CCCXLIX (May 4, 1921), 3593. W. Keil, *Erlebnisse,* II, 236–37. *Badischer Beobachter,* April 16, 1921. Also Wirth's Report, cited in footnote 11.
[9] Article by Erich Eyck, "Erzberger's 'Steuerhinterziehung,'" in *Vossische Zeitung,* May 4, 1921.
[10] The letter was quoted by the socialist Keil in *Reichstag Debates,* CCCXLIX (May 4, 1921), 3592.
[11] *Reichstag Debates,* Documentary Appendix 1879, CCCLXVI, 1604–12.

equally sharp rejoinder.[12] The main quarrel was about who was responsible for the undue delay in bringing the entire matter to a settlement. Erzberger's foes charged that the procrastination was due to friends shielding the fallen minister from prosecution, though Erzberger's desire for a speedy trial belied this accusation. Erzberger's friends charged, on the other hand, that the delay was calculated to prevent his return to politics by keeping his reputation under a cloud. The government pleaded as an excuse that Erzberger's tax file had gotten a run-around between the Charlottenburg tax office, the Prussian Finance Ministry, and the public prosecutors' office. The debate on this matter was inconclusive, but the *Reichstag* voted to lift the immunity.[13]

The ensuing investigation into the charges of both tax evasion and flight of capital was extremely thorough, lasting from June 1 to August 17, 1921. Erzberger was completely cleared of every charge, with the *prima facie* evidence of evasion proving deceptive in view of the complexity of wartime taxes. No official report was ever issued on the investigation, since the case was automatically closed when Erzberger was assassinated. The man in charge was *Landgerichtsrat* Amende, a Protestant and member of the Democratic Party, hence presumably not unduly favorable to Erzberger. He wrote a letter to the newspapers immediately after the assassination to tell the public about the result of his investigation.[14]

Mrs. Erzberger placed Dr. Hammer in charge of settling the financial affairs of the family after her husband's death. He describes his duties as follows:

> I negotiated with the Charlottenburg tax office in the matter of ascertaining the size of the estate and paying the inheritance taxes. These negotiations took place in a cordial atmosphere and with the greatest possible frankness and conscientiousness, as was Mrs. Erzberger's wish. The estate consisted mostly of industrial stocks, whose paper value stood high on account of the beginning of the inflation. For this reason some 40 percent of the estate went into inheritance taxes. When I groaned about this percentage the tax officials gave me the charming answer: "You are right that this sum is very severe on a widow and her children; but we are bound by the laws enacted by her husband." [15]

Hammer, like the public prosecutor's office before him, found no trace of any personal fortune deposited abroad. The existence of such a fortune was a cardinal article in the creed of Erzberger's enemies. Hammer publicly offered 50 percent of any sum that any informant might discover abroad, but found no takers. The charge of evading his own laws against the flight of

[12] *Reichstag Debates,* cccxlix (May 4, 1921), 3611–12, 3618–21.
[13] *ibid.,* pp. 3589–3622, *passim.*
[14] *Freiburger Tagespost,* Aug. 27, 1921. Bachem, *Zentrumspartei,* ix, 430. Letter of Karl Diez to Bachem, Dec. 9, 1928. *Bachem Papers,* File 90.
[15] Hammer, *Erzberger,* pp. 87–88.

capital was simply one item in the network of lies spread by the Nationalist campaign of character assassination.[16]

Mrs. Erzberger was urged by the Catholic congregation of Biberach to build a house and make it her permanent residence. She went so far as to buy a plot of land, but desisted at the last moment for fear that a house would absorb all of her resources and leave her with insufficient funds for living expenses. The government offered a small pension, but this was rejected by Mrs. Erzberger because its publication would lead to new newspaper assaults upon her dead husband. The Cuno government renewed the offer in 1923 at the height of the inflation, and it was then accepted. The interest from the investments of that part of the estate which did not go to the tax collector, when combined with the government pension, freed Mrs. Erzberger of all financial cares until the Nazi accession to power in 1933.[17] She was helped by the Catholic Church in her later years, and was living in modest comfort in a Stuttgart home run by nuns when I visited her in 1956.

[16] *ibid.,* p. 88.
[17] *Hammer Letter,* Nov. 11, 1929.

BIBLIOGRAPHICAL ESSAY

BIBLIOGRAPHICAL ESSAY

I. MANUSCRIPTS AND PRIMARY PRINTED MATTER

The *Erzberger Papers* in the German Federal Archives (*Bundesarchiv*) in Koblenz are the main source of this biography. They consist of 55 files which are substantially limited to the years 1914–1918. The papers were arranged topically by Dr. Josef Hammer, a close friend of Erzberger's, who had custody of the papers from 1921 to 1955 before they were transferred to the *Bundesarchiv*. Dr. Hammer told me that he had feared Nazi confiscation of the papers after 1933, and that he had destroyed those which he believed were unimportant, in order to facilitate hiding the remainder. Research in the papers is facilitated by the fact that they usually include both incoming (originals) and outgoing correspondence (carbons). They also contain many memoranda dictated by Erzberger about his own activities, which served as the raw materials for his book, *Erlebnisse im Weltkrieg* (Stuttgart, 1920). Dr. Hammer wrote an illuminating unpublished memoir entitled *Erzberger. Erinnerungsblätter eines persönlichen Freundes* (1947), which is filed with the *Erzberger Papers*.

A second valuable source consists of Files 89 and 90 of the *Karl Bachem Papers* in the Cologne City Archives (*Stadtarchiv*). They consist of material, especially letters and newspaper clippings, which Bachem used for his excellent study of Erzberger in his *Vorgeschichte, Geschichte, und Politik der Zentrumspartei* (9 vols., Cologne, 1926–1932), Vol. IX, pp. 400–501. Bachem knew Erzberger well, and had a reluctant admiration for him despite their frequent quarrels. He aimed at defending Erzberger against nationalist attacks which were also directed against the Zentrum Party, and his account often reads like a lawyer's brief.

The *Hertling Papers* in the Munich *Geheime Staatsarchiv* contain many letters from Erzberger to Hertling and carbon copies of Erzberger's wartime reports. The files of the *German Foreign Office,* largely available on microfilm in the National Archives, contain scattered Erzberger materials. Files 1498–1500 (Peace Moves) and 1663–66 (Cabinet protocols in 1919) are especially valuable.

The stenographic transcript of the 1920 trial, *Der Erzberger-Prozess. Stenographischer Bericht über die Verhandlungen im Beleidigungsprozess des Reichsfinanzminister Erzberger gegen den Staatsminister a. D. Dr. Karl Helfferich* (Berlin, 1920) is the most valuable source about Erzberger after the *Erzberger Papers*. It contains much detailed information about nearly all phases of Erzberger's life, while concentrating on the years 1917–1919. Siegfried Löwenstein, *Der Prozess Erzberger-Helfferich. Ein Rechtsgutachten.* (Ulm, 1921) is an excellent legal brief that seeks to refute the charges on which Erzberger was convicted.

Der Erzberger-Mord. Dokumente menschlicher und politischer Verkom-

menheit (Brühl [Baden] 1921) is a sickening collection of press voices rejoicing in the murder.

The *Stenographische Berichte der Verhandlungen des deutschen Reichstages* for the years 1904–1920 contain innumerable Erzberger speeches. The *Bericht des Ausschusses für die Geschäftsordnung über ein Schreiben des Reichsministers des Inneren, betreffend Strafverfolgung des Abgeordneten Erzberger wegen Einkommensteuerhinterziehung und Kapitalflucht.* Appendix 1879 of the *Wahlperiode 1920–1924*, Vol. cccLVI, pp. 1602–12 (Berlin, 1924) is authoritative on Erzberger's financial affairs.

The most informative newspaper sources are the two great Zentrum papers, the Berlin *Germania,* which usually supported Erzberger, and the *Kölnische Volkszeitung,* which frequently opposed him.

II. SECONDARY LITERATURE DIRECTLY ABOUT ERZBERGER

The secondary literature about Erzberger is enormous, but most of it has little scholarly value. Two exceptions are the Bachem study, cited above, and the Stanford dissertation by Bruce B. Frye, *Erzberger and German Politics, 1914–21* (Ann Arbor, University Microfilm 1954). The latter is an able analysis based upon printed sources available in this country. Ernst Bauer, *Bilder aus seinem Leben und Wirken, Kämpfen und Leiden* (2nd edition, Munich, 1925) is a brief laudatory biography written for the Catholic youth groups of Württemberg. His early life is traced by Hugo Baur in "Erzbergers Werdegang," *Allgemeine Rundschau* (April 18, 1931), pp. 244–48. Karl Widmaier, *Erzberger. Ein Kulturroman der Gegenwart* (Dillingen, 1922) is a sympathetic novel showing considerable political insight but little literary skill.

Seven hostile pamphlets contain a good bit of valuable information. Friedrich Hussong, a nationalist Berlin editor, wrote the first major indictment in his *Erzbergers Wege und Wandlungen* (2nd edition, Leipzig, n.d. [July, 1918]). His materials were largely repeated by Heinrich Frenzel, *Erzberger der Reichsverderber!* (Leipzig, 1919) and by Max Taube, *Erzberger, der Totengräber des Deutschen Reiches* (Berlin, 1919). Erzberger's conduct as Armistice Commissioner is criticized in A. Friedrich, *Die Wahrheit über die Waffenstillstandsverhandlungen. Wie Erzberger das deutsche Volk abfertigt* (Berlin, 1919). Karl Helfferich, *Fort mit Erzberger!* (Berlin, 1919), is the most eloquent of the indictments, and is important for provoking the libel suit in 1920. Helfferich was also the probable author of the anonymous pamphlet, *Erzberger Redivivus? Die Steuern und die Eide des Herrn Erzberger* (Berlin, 1921), which seeks to brand Erzberger as a tax evader and perjurer. Hans von Liebig, *Reichsverderber: Bethmann, Erzberger, Scheidemann* (Berlin, n.d. [1922]), includes a detailed attack upon Erzberger's wartime record.

Briefer attacks upon Erzberger are legion. The following will serve as samples. J. E. Freiherr von Grotthuss, "Erzberger, ein Kalauer der Weltgeschichte," in *Der Türmer,* Vol. xx, No. 9, pp. 515–20 (1918), is an early blast.

BIBLIOGRAPHICAL ESSAY

Two anonymous pamphlets denouncing his alleged untruthfulness are *Lügen des Hernn Erzberger, zur Aufklärung der deutschen Wähler* (Berlin, 1907), dealing with his colonial campaign, and *Erzberger als Enthüller. Die Wahrheit über das englische Friedensangebot* (Berlin, 1919), dealing with Erzberger's criticism of Michaelis' handling of the Papal peace mediation. The latter subject is also covered by Bruno Marwitz, *Herrn Erzbergers "Enthüllungen". Eine Kampfschrift gegen Erzberger* (Berlin, 1919). Count Paul von Hoensbroech, the well-known Jesuit renegade, seeks to prove that Erzberger's vices were all rooted in his Catholicism in "Erzberger. Eine Frucht der römisch-ultramontanen Moral," in *Das freie Wort,* Vol. xx, pp. 49–73 (May, 1920). F. C. Holtz, "Matthias Erzberger, ein Jude und Verräter," in *Fridericus,* Vol. xvii, Nr. 5 (Sept., 1934), has convinced himself that Erzberger was the illegitimate son of a Jewish father. Alfred Hugenberg, *Hugenberg gegen Erzberger. Reden aus der Nationalversammlung vom 9. Dez. 1919* (Berlin, 1919) and Wilhelm Henning, *Habt acht auf Erzberger! Das neue Steuerprogramm und der Vorschlag der Vermögensabgabe eine Täuschung des deutschen Arbeiters* (Osnabrück, n.d. [1919]) are attacks upon Erzberger's fiscal policies. Sincton Upclair, *Erzberger kommt wieder!!!* (Berlin, 1920) and Eduard Stadtler "Erzberger und kein Ende," in die *Grenzboten,* July 27, 1921, pp. 91–100, were written to prevent Erzberger's return to politics. Germanicus (pseud. for Richard Grelling), *Erzberger, ein politischer Mord?* (Berlin, 1921), assails Erzberger while denying that the anti-Erzberger agitation had any connection with the murder.

Three anonymous minor attacks upon Erzberger combine the humorous with the scurrilous: *Erzberger Monolog (Frei nach Goethe's Faust). Erzschlauberger (Der Tragödie zweiter Teil)* (Berlin, 1919); *Matthias Erzberger. Eine Lebensbeschreibung in Wort und Bild von Kristian und Peter. Wer ich bin, wie ich wurde, was ich weiss, was ich denke, was ich tat, was ich tue, was ich tun werde, und was das deutsche Volk an mir hat! Ich, Matthias Erzberger* (Munich, n.d. [late 1919]), and Senex (pseud.), *Politische Verbrecher und Narren* (Berlin, 1918).

Some light on Erzberger's secret intelligence activities is thrown by Wilhelm Patin, *Beiträge zur Geschichte der deutsch-vatikanischen Beziehungen in den letzten Jahrzehnten* (Berlin, 1942), a bibliographical rarity since it was printed for the exclusive official use of the S.S. The Nazi author worked on the basis of the confiscated papers of Erzberger's friend Stockhammern.

Erzberger's unorthodox diplomacy in 1919 is described in the important article by Fritz T. Epstein, "Zwischen Compiègne und Versailles", *Vierteljahrshefte für Zeitgeschichte,* Vol. iii (1955), pp. 412–45, which correlates American and German sources. The unpublished biography of *Brockdorff-Rantzau* by Erich Brandenburg, available on File 1083 of the *German Foreign Office Archives,* is very important for the strained relations between Erzberger and Rantzau in 1919.

Erzberger's political ideas after 1918 are popularized in Fidelis (pseud. for H. Popert), *Erzbergers Grundgedanken* (Hamburg, 1919), and Alfons Winz (Editor), *Erzberger zu den neuen Problemen der Gegenwart* (Singen, [Baden], 1921).

Three discussions of the 1920 trial favorable to Erzberger are F. Zinnecke, *Erzberger gegen Helfferich* (Berlin, 1920), pp. 1–8; Ludwig Haas, "Der Fall Erzberger," *Hilfe* (Mar. 4, 1920), pp. 147–49; and Ludwig Quessel, "Ein Rückblick auf den Prozess Helfferich-Erzberger," *Sozialistische Monatshefte* (April 12, 1920), pp. 241–48. Two hostile accounts are "A" (Adolf Stein) *Gerichtstage über Erzberger* (Berlin, 1920), and F. W. von Oertzen, *Im Namen der Geschichte! Politische Prozesse der Nachkriegszeit* (Hamburg, 1934), pp. 9–34. Erich Eyck, *Geschichte der Weimarer Republik* (2 vols., Zurich, 1954–1957), Vol. I, pp. 197–202, is a judicious summary.

The assassination produced two notable pamphlets preaching the message of Republican vigilance: Junius III (pseud. for Wilhelm Herzog), *Erzbergers Ermordung und die revolutionären Arbeiter* (Leipzig, 1921), and Philipp Scheidemann, *Zur Ermordung Erzbergers. Eine Rede gehalten am 30. Sept. 1921 im Reichstag* (Berlin, 1921).

General estimates of Erzberger can be found in the *Erzberger-Heft* of the Republican journal *Deutsche Republik,* edited by Josef Wirth, Vol. I, pp. 685–707 (Frankfurt, Aug. 26, 1927), a series of laudatory but uninformative articles; Ludwig Klages, "Charakterbild auf Grund der Handschrift Erzbergers," *Zeitschrift für Menschenkunde,* Vol. I (1925), pp. 31–37, an unflattering character portrait by a well-known graphologist; Ernst Jäckh, *Der Goldene Pflug* (Stuttgart, 1954), pp. 461–62, a reprint of a balanced letter originally written to Valentini, the former chief of William's Civil Cabinet, on November 18, 1918; and in three favorable journalistic studies: Johannes Fischart (pseud. for Erich Dombrowski), *Das Alte und das Neue System. Die politischen Köpfe Deutschlands* (Berlin, 1919), pp. 48–63; Stefan Grossmann, "Erzberger," in *Das Tage-Buch* (Sept. 3, 1921), pp. 1041–48; and Maximilian Harden, *Köpfe* (Berlin, 1924), Vol. IV, pp. 429–72. A hostile judgment by Stresemann can be found in his *Von der Revolution bis zum Frieden von Versailles* (Berlin, 1919), pp. 578–88, which should be compared with his more balanced obituary notice, reprinted in his *Reden und Schriften* (Dresden, 1926), Vol. I, pp. 378–88.

III. ERZBERGER'S OWN VOLUMINOUS WRITINGS

These are here listed in chronological order. The important ones have already been discussed in the text. Copies of many of Erzberger's newspaper articles, appearing especially in the Berlin *Germania* and the Stuttgart *Deutsches Volksblatt,* can be found in the *Erzberger* and *Bachem Papers* described above.

Christliche oder sozialdemokratische Gewerkschaften? (Stuttgart, 1898).
Sozialdemokratie und Militär. Material zur Abwehr gegen sozialdemokratische Agitation (Stuttgart, 1898).

Material zur Handwerkerfrage. Aus den Verhandlungen der Handwerkerkonferenz in Ulm am 13. April 1899 (Stuttgart, 1899).
Material zur Bekämpfung der Sozialdemokratie. Gesammelt aus den offiziellen Protokollen der sozialdemokratische Parteitage der Jahre 1890–98, Vol. I. *Sozialdemokratie und Religion* (Stuttgart, 1899).
Vol. II. *Sozialdemokratie und Frauenarbeit* (Stuttgart, 1899).
Die Säkularisation in Württemberg von 1802–10. Ihr Verlauf und ihre Nachwirkungen (Stuttgart, 1902).
Beiträge zur Parität in Württemberg (Stuttgart, 1903).
Die Sozialdemokratie in früheren Tagen. Auszüge aus den Protokollen der sozialdemokratischen Parteitage über einige wichtige Tagesfragen: Sozialreform, Schutzzoll, Bauernstand (Stuttgart, 1903).
Die Industrie-(Arbeits)-Kammern im Reichstage (Jena, 1905).
Das neue Militärpensionsgesetz für Mannschaften und Militäranwärter nebst einem Anhang über die Veteranenbeihilfe (Berlin, 1906).
Was man von dem neuen Militärpensionsgesetz wissen muss. Das Gesetz für Kapitulanten, Militäranwärter, Kriegsinvaliden, Militärrentenempfänger, sowie die Mannschaften des aktiven Heeres gemeinverständlich erleutert (Berlin, 1906).
Die Kolonialbilanz. Bilder aus der deutschen Kolonialpolitik auf Grund der Verhandlungen des Reichstags im Sessionsabschnitt 1905–06. (Berlin, 1906).
Der Toleranzantrag der Zentrumsfraktion des Reichstages (Osnabrück, 1906).
Warum ist der Reichstag aufgelöst worden? Ein offenes Wort an die Wählerschaft (Berlin, 1906).
Bilder aus dem Reichstagswahlkampf 1907. Die Agitation der Zentrumsgegner beleuchtet nach deren Wahlschriften (Berlin, 1907).
Zentrum und neuester Kurs (Berlin, 1907).
Die politischen Parteien und ihre Tätigkeit (M. Gladbach, 1907).
Sozialdemokratie und Zollpolitik. Auf Grund der Parlamentsakten und Parteitageprotokolle geschildert (M. Gladbach, 1908).
Die Wahrheit über die deutschen Kolonien. Glänzende Rechtfertigung der Kolonialpolitik des Zentrums durch Staatssekretär Bernhard Dernburg (Berlin, 1908).
Der Kampf gegen den Katholizismus in der Ostmark. Material zur Beurteilung der Polenfrage durch die deutschen Katholiken (Berlin, 1908).
Naar Ostland wollen wi ryden (Berlin, 1908).
Klerus und Gehaltsfrage. Beiträge zur Parität in den deutschen Bundesstaaten (Cologne, 1908).
"Die Bedeutung des Zentrums für das deutsche Reich," in *Zeitschrift für Politik,* Vol. II, pp. 212–35 (Berlin, 1909).
Der Humor im Reichstage. Eine systematische geordnete Sammlung von Parlaments-Scherzen (Berlin, 1910).
Millionengeschenke. Die Privilegienwirtschaft in Südwestafrika. Mit einer

Materialiensammlung über die bergrechtlichen Verhältnisse dieses Schutz-gebietes nebst Karte von Südwestafrika (Berlin, 1910).

Der Modernisteneid. Den Katholiken zur Lehr und Wehr, Andersdenkenden zur Aufklärung (Berlin, 1911).

Der Stille Kulturkampf (Hamm, 1912).

"Judentaufen," Ch. v in *Judentaufen,* edited by W. Sombart (Munich, 1912).

Das deutsche Zentrum (Amsterdam, 2nd improved edition, 1912).

Kolonial-Berufe (Berlin, 1912).

Duell und Ehre (Paderborn und Würzburg, 1913).

Der Wehrbeitrag 1913 (Stuttgart, 1913).

Politik und Völkerleben (Paderborn und Würzburg, n.d. [1914]).

Die Militäranwärterfrage. Wie helfen wir? Ein Mahnwort an alle (Berlin, 1914).

Die Rüstungsausgaben des deutschen Reichs (Stuttgart, 1914).

Die Mobilmachung (Berlin, 1914).

Der Verständigungsfriede (Stuttgart, 1917).

Der Völkerbund. Der Weg zum Weltfrieden (Berlin, 1918).

Der Völkerbund als Friedensfrage (Berlin, 1919).

"Der Waffenstillstand," in *Europäische Staats und Wirtschafts-Zeitung,* Vol. iv (n.d. [1919] nr. 12 und 13 *(Sonderheft).*

Erlebnisse im Weltkrieg (Stuttgart, 1920).

Christlicher Solidarismus als Weltprinzip (M. Gladbach, 1921).

Der Solidarismus. Europas Rettung und Zukunft (M. Gladbach, 1921).

IV. LIST OF BOOKS CITED

"A" [Adolf Stein], *Sieben Tage Buch. Kappregierung und Generalstreik* (Berlin, 1920).

Amtliche Urkunden zur Vorgeschichte des Waffenstillstandes 1918 (Berlin, 2nd enlarged edition, 1924).

Arnim, Hans and Below, Georg von, *Deutscher Aufstieg. Bilder aus der Vergangenheit und Gegenwart der Rechtsstehenden Parteien* (Berlin, 1925).

Bachem, Karl, "Adolf Gröber," in *Deutsches Biographisches Jahrbuch 1917–20* (Stuttgart, 1928), pp. 388–92.

———, "Hertling," in *ibid.* (Stuttgart, 1928), pp. 416–26.

———, "Karl Trimborn," in *Deutsches Biographisches Jahrbuch* Vol. iii, 1921 (Stuttgart, 1927), pp. 263–65.

Bane, S. L. and Lutz, R. H. (Editors), *The Blockade of Germany after the Armistice 1918–19* (Stanford, 1942).

Baudrillart, Alfred, *La Guerre allemande et le catholicisme* (Paris, 1915).

Beck, Ludwig, *Studien* (Stuttgart, 1955).

Bergsträsser, Ludwig, *Der politische Katholizismus. Dokumente seiner Ent-wicklung* (Munich, 1921–23). 2 vols.

———, *Die preussische Wahlrechtsfrage im Kriege und die Entstehung der Osterbotschaft 1917* (Tübingen, 1929).

Bernstorff, Graf Johann, *Erinnerungen und Briefe* (Zurich, 1936).

Bethmann-Hollweg, Theobald von, *Betrachtungen zum Weltkriege* (Berlin, 1919–1921). 2 vols.

———, *Kriegsreden,* edited by F. Thimme (Stuttgart, 1919).

Beusch, Paul, *Die ausserordentliche Kriegsabgabe für das Rechnungsjahr 1919 und die Kriegsabgabe vom Vermögenszuwachs. Für Steuerpflichtige dargestellt. Mit vollständigen Gesetzestexten, vielen Beispielen, und notwendigen Mustern nach Vorlagen der Ausführungsbestimmungen* (M. Gladbach, 1920).

———, *Die Neuordnung des deutschen Finanzwesens. Vier Vorträge* (M. Gladbach, 1920).

Bongard, Willy, *Die Zentrumsresolution vom 7. Oktober 1916* (Cologne, 1937).

Bonn, Moritz Julius, *Wandering Scholar* (London, 1949).

Brammer, Karl, *Fünf Tage Militärdiktatur. Dokumente zur Gegenrevolution* (Berlin, 1920).

Braun, Freiherr Magnus von, *Von Ostpreussen bis Texas* (Stollhamm, 1955).

Brinckmeyer, Hermann, *Hugo Stinnes* (Munich, 1921).

Brockdorff-Rantzau, Graf Ulrich, *Dokumente und Gedanken um Versailles* (Berlin, 3rd edition, 1925).

Bülow, Bernhard von, *Denkwürdigkeiten* (Berlin, 1930–1931), 4 vols.

Burian, Graf Stefan, *Drei Jahre aus der Zeit meiner Amtsführung im Kriege* (Berlin, 1923).

Cardauns, Hermann, *Adolf Gröber* (M. Gladbach, 1921).

———, *Karl Trimborn* (M. Gladbach, 1922).

Chamberlin, W. H., *The Russian Revolution* (New York, 1935), 2 vols.

Class, Heinrich, *Wider den Strom, vom Werden und Wachsen der nationalen Opposition im alten Reich* (Leipzig, 1932).

Craig, Gordon A., *The Politics of the Prussian Army, 1640-1945* (New York, 1956).

Croce, Benedetto, *History of Italy, 1871–1915* (Oxford, 1929).

Crothers, George, *The German Elections of 1907* (New York, 1941).

Czernin, Ottokar, *Rede über die Politik während des Weltkrieges, gehalten den 11 Dezember 1918* (Vienna, 1919).

———, *Im Weltkrieg* (Vienna, 1919).

Dal-Gal, Hieronymo, *Pius X. The Life Story of the Beatus.* Translated by Thomas F. Murray (Dublin, 1953).

Delbrück, Hans, *Regierung und Volkswille* (Berlin, 2nd edition, 1920).

Einem, Karl von, *Erinnerungen eines Soldaten* (Leipzig, 1933).

Ebers, G. J., *Italien und das Garantiegesetz* (Cologne, 1915).

Eltzbacher, Paul, *Die Presse als Werkzeug der auswärtigen Politik* (Jena, 1918).

Erdmann, August, *Die christlichen Gewerkschaften, insbesondere ihr Verhältnis zu Zentrum und Kirche* (Stuttgart, 1914).

Eschenburg, Theodor, *Das Kaiserreich am Scheideweg, Bassermann, Bülow und der Block. Nach unveröffentlichen Papieren aus dem Nachlass Ernst Bassermanns* (Berlin, 1929).

Ettighoffer, P. C., *Moskau, Compiègne, Versailles. Erlebnisse eines deutschen Nachrichtenoffiziers* (Gütersloh, 1936).

Fester, Richard, *Die Politik Kaiser Karls und der Wendepunkt des Weltkrieges* (Munich, 1925).

———, *Die politischen Kämpfe um den Frieden (1916–18) und das Deutschtum* (Munich, 1938).

Fischer, Rudolf, *Karl Helfferich* (Berlin, 1932).

Foch, Ferdinand, *Memoirs* (New York, 1931).

Foreign Relations of the United States, Paris Peace Conference (Washington, 1945), 13 vols.

Frachon, Alfred, *Les Opinions allemandes sur la Reconstruction du Droit internationale* (Paris, 1921).

Gankin, Olga and Fisher, H. H., *The Bolsheviks and the World War* (Stanford, 1940).

Gasteiger, M., *Die christliche Arbeiterbewegung in Süddeutschland. Eine geschichtliche Darstellung* (Munich, 1908).

Gatzke, Hans, *Germany's Drive to the West. A Study of Germany's War Aims during the First World War* (Baltimore, 1950).

Germany, Nationalversammlung, *Das Werk des Untersuchungsausschusses, 4. Reihe, Die Ursachen des deutschen Zusammenbruches im Jahre 1918* (Berlin, 1925–1929), 12 vols.

Geyer, Dorothea, *General Groener. Soldat und Staatsmann* (Frankfurt, 1955).

Giolitti, Giovanni, *Memoirs of My Life* (London, 1923).

Goltz, Graf Rüdiger von der, *Meine Sendung in Finnland und im Baltikum* (Leipzig, 1920).

Gordon, Harold, *The Reichswehr and the German Republic* (Princeton, 1957).

Gornik, Alfons, *Die Entwicklung der nichtsozialdemokratischen Arbeiterbewegung in Deutschland* (Halle, 1909).

Gottlieb, W. W., *Studies in Secret Diplomacy during the First World War* (London, 1957).

Graefe, Albrecht von, *Damals in Weimar 1919. Ein Blick hinter die Kulissen. Der Verrat am Deutschen Volk. Erinnerungen aus der Nationalversammlung—ein Appell an alle Deutsche* (Berlin, 1929).

Groener, Wilhelm, *Lebenserinnerungen* (Göttingen, 1957).

Gugelmeier, Erwin, *Das Schwarze Jahr (1917–1918). Erlebtes aus dem letzten Kriegsjahr im Reichstag und im Baltenland, in Hauptquartier und Heimat* (Freiburg, 1926).

Haase, Ernst, *Reichstagsreden gegen die deutsche Kriegspolitik* (Berlin, 1919).

Haenisch, Konrad, *Parvus* (Berlin, 1925).

Haferkorn, Joachim, *Bülows Kampf um das Reichskanzleramt im Jahre 1906* (Würzburg, 1939).

Hammann, Otto, *Bilder aus der letzten Kaiserzeit* (Berlin, 1922).

Hannsen, H. P., *Diary of a Dying Empire.* Translated by O. O. Winther. Edited by Ralph Lutz, Mary Schofield, and O. O. Winther (Bloomington, 1955).

Haussmann, Conrad, *Aus C. Haussmanns politischer Arbeit.* Edited by his friends (Frankfurt, 1923).

———, *Schlaglichter. Reichstagsbriefe und Aufzeichnungen* (Frankfurt, 1924).

Heffter, Heinrich, *Die deutsche Selbstverwaltung im 19. Jahrhundert* (Stuttgart, 1950).

Heinig, Kurt, *Stinnes und seine 600,000 Arbeiter* (Berlin, 1925).

Heinz, Friedrich, "Politische Attentate in Deutschland," in *Deutscher Aufstand,* edited by Curt Hötzel (Stuttgart, 1934), pp. 202–05.

Helfferich, Karl, *Reden und Aufsätze aus dem Kriege* (Berlin, 1917).

———, *Reichstagsreden 1920–1922* (Berlin, 1922).

———, *Reichstagsreden 1922–1924,* edited by J. W. Reichert, with a biographical preface by Count Westarp (Berlin, 1925).

———, *Der Weltkrieg* (Berlin, 1919), 3 vols.

Hertling, Graf Georg von, *Erinnerungen* (Munich, 1920), 2 vols.

Hertling, Graf Karl von, *Ein Jahr in der Reichskanzlei. Erinnerungen an die Kanzlerschaft meines Vaters* (Freiburg, 1919).

Hertzmann, Lewis, *The German National People's Party (DNVP) 1918–1924* (Harvard Thesis, 1954).

Herzfeld, Hans, *Die deutsche Rüstungspolitik vor dem Weltkriege* (Leipzig, 1923).

———, *Die deutsche Sozialdemokratie und die Auflösung der nationalen Einheitsfront im Weltkriege* (Leipzig, 1928).

Hess, Joseph, *Deutsche Lebensfragen? Eine Auseinandersetzung mit Martin Spahn* (Düsseldorf, 1914).

Heuss, Theodor, *Friedrich Naumann* (Stuttgart, 2nd edit., 1949).

Hilsum, J. N. I. van, *Maria Erzberger* (Bilthoven, 1956).

Hindenburg, Herbert von, *Am Rande zweier Jahrhunderte* (Berlin, 1938).

Hoelzle, Erwin, *Der Osten im ersten Weltkrieg* (Leipzig, 1944).

———, "Deutschland und die Wegscheide des ersten Weltkriegs," in *Otto Becker Festschrift,* edited by M. Göhring and A. Scharff (Wiesbaden, 1954), pp. 266–85.

Hoensbroech, Graf Paul von, *Graf Hertling, Reichskanzler und Ministerpräsident. Ein offener Brief* (Leipzig, 1918).

447

Hoffmann, Max, *Aufzeichnungen,* edited by K. F. Nowak (Berlin, 1929).

——, *Der Krieg der versäumten Gelegenheiten* (Munich, 1923).

Hohlfeld, Johannes, *Geschichte des deutschen Reichs 1871-1924* (Leipzig, 1924).

Hohn, W., *Franz Brandts* (M. Gladbach, 1914).

Holborn, Hajo, "Diplomats and Diplomacy in the Early Weimar Republic," in *The Diplomats 1919-39,* edited by G. Craig and F. Gilbert (Princeton, 1953), pp. 123-71.

Hommerich, A., *Deutschtum und Schiedsgerichtsbarkeit, ein geschichtlicher Beitrag zu einer grossen Gegenwarts und Zukunftsfrage* (Freiburg, 1918).

Hutten-Czapski, Bogdan Graf von, *Sechzig Jahre Politik und Gesellschaft* (Berlin, 1936), 2 vols.

Joos, Joseph, *Die katholischen Arbeitervereine* (M. Gladbach, 1913).

Keil, Wilhelm, *Erlebnisse eines Sozialdemokraten* (Stuttgart, 1948), 2 vols.

Keim, August, *Erlebtes und Erstrebtes. Lebenserinnerungen* (Hanover, 1925).

Keynes, John M., "Dr. Melchior; A Defeated Enemy," in *Two Memoirs* (London, 1949).

Koch, Walter, *Volk und Staatsführung vor dem Weltkriege* (Stuttgart, 1935).

Koehler, August, *Deutsches Zentrum-deutscher Rhein. Eine Untersuchung an Hand von Dokumenten und feststehenden Tatsachen* (Trier, 1932).

Kollbach, Paul, *Deutsche Handelsflotte und Versailler Vertrag* (Berlin, 1927).

Kühlmann, Richard von, *Erinnerungen* (Heidelberg, 1948).

Lama, Friedrich Ritter von, *Die Friedensvermittlung Papst Benedikt XV und ihre Vereitlung durch den deutschen Reichskanzler Michaelis. August-September 1917* (Munich, 1932).

Lasswell, H. D., *Propaganda Technique in the World War* (New York, 1927).

L'Hopital, René, *Foch, L'Armistice, et la Paix* (Paris, 1938).

Liebig, Hans Freiherr von, *Die Politik von Bethmann Hollwegs* (Munich, 1919).

Lochner, Louis P., *Tycoons and Tyrant, German Industry from Hitler to Adenauer* (Chicago, 1954).

Lotz, Walther, *Die deutsche Staatsfinanzwirtschaft im Kriege* (Stuttgart, 1927).

Luckau, Alma, *The German Delegation at the Paris Peace Conference* (New York, 1941).

Ludendorff, Erich, *Urkunden der Obersten Heeresleitung über ihre Tätigkeit 1916-18* (Berlin, 1920).

Ludendorff, Margarethe, *Als ich Ludendorff's Frau war* (Munich, 1929).

Lutz, R. H., *Fall of the German Empire 1914-18* (Stanford, 1932).

Macchio, Karl von, *Wahrheit! Fürst Bülow und ich in Rom* (Vienna, 1931).

Marhefka, Edmund (editor), *Der Waffenstillstand. Das Dokumentenmaterial der Waffenstillstandsverhandlungen* (Berlin, 1928), 3 vols.

Martin, Rudolf, *Fürst Bülow und Kaiser Wilhelm II* (Leipzig, 1909).

Max of Baden, Prince, *Erinnerungen und Dokumente* (Stuttgart, 1927).

Meinertz, M. and Sacher, H., *Deutschland und der Katholizismus* (Freiburg, 1918).

Menne, Bernhard, *Armistice and Germany's Food Supply 1918–19* (London, 1944).

Meyer, Henry C., *Mitteleuropa in German Thought and Action (1815–1945)* (The Hague, 1955).

Michaelis, Georg, *Für Volk und Staat* (Berlin, 1922).

Miller, Max, *Eugen Bolz, Staatsmann und Bekenner* (Stuttgart, 1951).

Mordacq, H., *L'Armistice du 11 Novembre* (Paris, 1937).

Müller, Hermann, *Die November Revolution. Erinnerungen* (Berlin, 1928).

Mulert, Hermann, *Antimodernisteneid, freie Forschung und theologische Fakultäten* (Halle, 1911).

Nadolny, Rudolf, *Mein Beitrag* (Wiesbaden, 1955).

Naumann, Victor, *Dokumente und Argumente* (Berlin, 1928).

——, *Profile. 30 Porträtskizzen aus den Jahren des Weltkrieges nach persönlichen Begegnungen* (Leipzig, 1925).

Nicolai, Walther, *Nachrichtendienst, Presse und Volksstimmung im Weltkrieg* (Berlin, 1920).

Noske, Gustav, *Erlebtes aus Aufstieg und Niedergang einer Demokratie* (Offenbach, 1947).

——, *Von Kiel bis Kapp* (Berlin, 1920).

Nowak, Karl Friedrich, *Versailles* (Berlin, 1927).

Obkircher, Walter, *General Erich von Gündell* (Hamburg, 1939).

Oldenburg-Januschau, Elard von, *Erinnerungen* (Leipzig, 1936).

Oppersdorff, Graf von, *Eine Gewissensfrage: Ist Martin Spahn Zentrumsmann? Material zur Begründung des Augsburger Briefes der 14 Reichstagsabgeordneten an Dr. Martin Spahn* (Berlin, 1910).

Ortner, Eugen, *Gott Stinnes. Ein Pamphlet gegen den vollkommenen Menschen* (Hannover, 1922).

Parvus [Alexander Helphand], *Die Kolonialpolitik und der Zusammenbruch* (Leipzig, 1907).

Payer, Friedrich, *Von Bethmann Hollweg bis Ebert. Erinnerungen und Bilder* (Frankfurt, 1923).

Pehl, Hans, *Die deutsche Kolonialpolitik und das Zentrum 1884–1914* (Limburg, 1934).

Pesch, Heinrich, *Liberalismus, Sozialismus, und christliche Gesellschaftsordnung* (Freiburg, 1896).

Petzold, W., *Italiens Eintritt in den Weltkrieg* (Leipzig, 1934).

Pfeilschifter, Georg, *Deutsche Kultur, Katholizismus und Weltkrieg* (Freiburg, 1915–1916).

Pfeilschifter, Georg, *Sammlung Katholischer Soldatenbriefe* (Freiburg, 1915)

Pinner, F., *Deutsche Wirtschaftsführer* (Charlottenburg, 15 edit., 1925).

Popitz, Johannes, "Die deutschen Finanzen 1918–28," in *Zehn Jahre Deutscher Geschichte* (Berlin, 1928), pp. 179–202.

Preuss, Hugo, *Das deutsche Volk und die Politik* (Jena, 1915).

Pringle, H. F., *Theodore Roosevelt: A Biography* (New York, 1931).

Prittwitz und Gaffron, Friedrich Wilhelm von, *Zwischen Petersburg und Washington. Ein Diplomatenleben* (Munich, 1952).

Rabenau, F. von, *Seeckt: Aus seinem Leben, 1918–36* (Leipzig, 1940).

Raphael, Gaston, *Hugo Stinnes: Der Mensch, sein Werk, sein Wirken* (Berlin, 1925).

Raumer, Kurt von, "Karl Helfferich," in *Deutscher Westen-Deutsches Reich. Saarpfälzische Lebensbilder,* edited by K. von Raumer and K. Baumann (Kaiserslautern, 1938).

———, "Das Ende von Helfferichs Moskauer Mission 1918," in *Srbik Festschrift. Gesamtdeutsche Vergangenheit* (Munich, 1938), pp. 392–99.

Reed, James Morgan, *Atrocity Propaganda 1914–19* (New Haven, 1941).

Reading, Marquis of, *Rufus Isaacs, First Marquess of Reading* (New York, 1940).

Rechberg, Arnold, *Reichsniedergang. Ein Beitrag zu dessen Ursachen aus meinen persönlichen Erinnerungen* (Munich, 1919).

———, *Weltfragen* (Berlin, 1918).

Respondek, Erwin, *Die Reichsfinanzen auf Grund der Reform von 1919–20* (Berlin, 1921).

Reventlow, Ernst von, *Die Neutralität der USA 1914–18* (Berlin, 1941).

Ritter, Emil, *Die katholisch-soziale Bewegung Deutschlands im 19. Jahrhundert und der Volksverein* (Cologne, 1954).

Ritter, Gerhard, *Carl Goerdeler und die deutsche Widerstandsbewegung* (Stuttgart, 1954).

Rodd, Sir James Rennell, *Social and Diplomatic Memories,* Vol. III, 1902–1919 (London, 1925).

Roeren, Hermann, *Zentrum und Kölner Richtung* (Trier, 1913).

Rosenberg, A. J., *Der deutsche Krieg und der Katholizismus; deutsche Abwehr französischer Angriffe* (Berlin, 1915).

Rosenberg, Arthur, *Entstehung der deutschen Republik* (Berlin, 1928).

Ruchti, Jacob, *Geschichte der Schweiz während des Weltkrieges, 1914–19* (Bern, 1928). 2 vols.

Rudin, Harry, *Armistice 1918* (New Haven, 1944).

Salandra, A., *Italy and the Great War* (London, 1932).

Scheffbuch, Adolf, *Helfferich: Ein Kämpfer für Deutschlands Grösse* (Stuttgart, 1934).

Scheidemann, Philipp, *Memoiren eines Sozialdemokraten* (Dresden, 1928), 2 vols.

———, *Der Zusammenbruch* (Berlin, 1920).

Schiff, Victor, *So war es in Versailles* (Berlin, 1929).

Schiffer, Eugen, *Ein Leben für den Liberalismus* (Berlin, 1951).

Schoen, Wilhelm Eduard, *Erlebtes. Beiträge zur politischen Geschichte der neuesten Zeit* (Berlin, 1921).

Schorske, Carl, *German Social Democracy 1905–17: the development of the great schism* (Cambridge, 1955).

Schreiber, Georg, *Zwischen Demokratie und Diktatur. Persönliche Erinnerungen an die Politik und Kultur des Reiches (1919–1944)*, (Münster, 1949).

Schultze, K. A., *Nationale Arbeit. Das Zentrum und sein Wirken in der Deutschen Republik* (Berlin, 1929)

Schüssler, Wilhelm, *Die Daily Telegraph Affaire. Fürst Bülow, Kaiser Wilhelm und die Krise des Zweiten Reiches 1908.* (Göttingen, 1952).

Schwedler, Wilhelm, "Das Nachrichtenwesen," in *Die deutsche Wirtschaft und ihre Führer,* edited by Emil Dovifat (Gotha, 1925), Vol. III.

Schwend, Karl, *Bayern zwischen Monarchie und Diktatur. Beiträge zur bayrischen Frage in der Zeit von 1918 bis 1933* (Munich, 1954).

Sell, Friedrich, *Die Staatspolitik des Zentrums* (Berlin, 1924).

Senger, Gerhard, *Die Politik der deutschen Zentrumspartei zur Frage Reich und Länder von 1918–28* (Hamburg, 1932).

Spahn, Martin, *Ernst Lieber als Parlamentarier* (Gotha, 1906).

———, *Deutsche Lebensfragen* (Munich, 1914).

Spellmeyer, Hans, *Die deutsche Kolonialpolitik im Reichstag* (Stuttgart, 1931).

Stegemann, Hermann, *Erinnerungen aus meinem Leben und aus meiner Zeit* (Stuttgart, 1930).

Stern-Rubarth, Edgar, *Graf Brockdorff Rantzau. Wanderer zwischen zwei Welten* (Berlin, 1929).

Thimme, Friedrich (editor), *Front wider Bülow. Staatsmänner, Diplomaten und Forscher zu seinen Denkwürdigkeiten* (Munich, 1931).

Tirpitz, Alfred von, *Erinnerungen* (Leipzig, 1929).

———, *Politische Dokumente* (Berlin, 1924–1926), 2 vols.

Tisza, Count Stefan, *Briefe 1914–18* (Berlin, 1928).

Troeltsch, Ernst, *Spectator Briefe, Aufsätze über die deutsche Revolution und die Weltpolitik 1918–22* (Tübingen, 1924).

Tschuppik, Karl, *Ludendorff. Die Tragödie des Fachmanns* (Vienna, 1931).

Valentini, Rudolf von, *Kaiser und Kabinettschef,* edited by Bernhard Schwertfeger (Oldenburg, 1931).

Vallentin, Antonina, *Stresemann* (Leipzig, 1930).

Volkmann, Erich Otto, *Die Annexionsfragen des Weltkriegs* (Berlin, 1926).

Wacker, Frida, *Die Haltung der deutschen Zentrumspartei zur Frage der Kriegsziele im Weltkrieg 1914–18* (Lohr am Main, 1937).

Waite, Robert, *Vanguard of Nazism* (Cambridge, 1952).

Wallraf, Max, *Aus einem rheinischen Leben* (Berlin, 1926).

Weber, Marianne, *Max Weber. Ein Lebensbild* (Tübingen, 1926).

Wemyss, Victoria Wester, *Life and Letters of Lord Wester Wemyss* (London, 1935).

Werkmann, K., *Deutschland als Verbündeter. Kaiser Karls Kampf um den Frieden* (Berlin, 1931).

Wermuth, Adolf, *Ein Beamtenleben* (Berlin, 1922).

Westarp, Kuno Graf von, *Konservative Politik in letzten Jahrzehnt des Kaiserreiches* (Berlin, 1935), 2 vols.

Wetterlé, Abbe E., *Behind the Scenes in the Reichstag. Sixteen years of parliamentary life in Germany.* Translated by George F. Lees (New York, 1918).

Wheeler-Bennett, John, *The Forgotten Peace: Brest-Litovsk, March 1918* (New York, 1938).

———, *Wooden Titan: Hindenburg in Twenty Years of German History 1914-34* (New York, 1936).

Wirth, Josef, *Reden während der Kanzlerzeit* (Berlin, 1925).

Wolff, T., *Through Two Decades* (London, 1936).

Wrisberg, Ernst von, *Erinnerungen an die Kriegsjahre im Königlich Preussischen Kriegsministerium* (Leipzig, 1921), 3 vols.

Zentrumspartei, *Offizieller Bericht des 1. Reichsparteitages der deutschen Zentrumspartei. Tagung zu Berlin vom 19. bis 22. Januar, 1920* (Berlin, 1920).

Ziegler, Wilhelm, *Die deutsche Nationalversammlung 1919-20 und ihr Verfassungswerk* (Berlin, 1932).

———, *Versailles. Die Geschichte eines misglückten Friedens* (Hamburg, 1933).

Ziekursch, Johannes, *Politische Geschichte des Neuen Deutschen Kaiserreiches* (Frankfurt, 1925-1930), 3 vols.

V. LIST OF ARTICLES CITED

Bergsträsser, Ludwig, "Der Riss im Zentrum," in *Akademische Blätter,* Vol. xxv (1910), pp. 241-46.

Deuerlein, Ernst, "Zur Friedenaktion Benedikts XV," in *Stimmen der Zeit,* Vol. clv (Jan. 1955), pp. 241-55.

Eisele, Hans, "Hertling," in *Hochland,* Vol. x (Sept. 1913), pp. 750-55.

Epstein, Klaus W., "The Development of German-Austrian War Aims in the Spring of 1917," in *Journal of Central European Affairs,* Vol. xvii (1957), pp. 24-47.

Ettlinger, Max, "Hertling als Gelehrter," in *Hochland,* Vol. xi (1913), pp. 227-31.

Fickentscher, F., "Die Wahrheit über den Zusammenbruch der Marine," in *Politische und Militärische Zeitfragen,* No. 29 (Berlin, 1920).

"Geheimzusätze zum Brest-Litowsker Vertrag," in *Europäische Gespräche,* Vol. iv (1926), pp. 148-53.

Grabowsky, Adolf, "Die Grundprobleme des Völkerbundes," in *Zeitschrift für Politik,* Vol. XI (1919), pp. 377–451.

Jastrow, J., "The New Tax System of Germany," in *Quarterly Journal of Economics,* Vol. XXXVII (1923), pp. 302–41.

Lassar, Gerhard, "Reichseigene Verwaltung unter der Weimarer Verfassung. Zwei Studien," in *Jahrbuch des öffentlichen Rechts,* Vol. XIV (1926), p. 1 ff.

Leiber, Robert, "Die Friedenstätigkeit Benedikts XV," in *Stimmen aus Maria Laach,* Vol. LI (1921), pp. 267–80.

Luckau, Alma, "The Unconditional Acceptance of the Treaty of Versailles by the German Government June 22–28, 1919," in *Journal of Modern History,* Vol. XVII (1945), pp. 215–20.

Mendelssohn-Bartholdy, Albrecht, "Deutsche Literatur zur Völkerbundsfrage," in *Schmollers Jahrbuch,* Vol. XLVI (1922), pp. 543–55.

Michaelis, Wilhelm, "Der Reichskanzler Michaelis und die päpstliche Friedensaktion," in *Geschichte in Wissenschaft und Unterricht,* Vol. VII (1956), pp. 14–24 and 128.

Montanus (pseud.), "Opus 117," in *Klarheit und Wahrheit,* Vol. I (1912), pp. 354–56.

Newcomer, Mabel, "Fiscal Relations of Central and Local Governments in Germany under the Weimar Constitution," in *Political Science Quarterly,* Vol. LI (1936), pp. 185–214.

Plivier, Theodor, "Im Wald von Compiègne," in *Neue Deutsche Blätter,* Vol. I (Nov.–Dec. 1933), pp. 145–56, 219–29.

Raumer, Kurt von, "Zwischen Brest Litovsk und Compiègne: die deutsche Ostpolitik vom Sommer 1918," in *Baltische Lande,* Vol. IV (1939), pp. 1–13.

Snell, John, "Benedikt XV, Wilson, Michaelis and German Socialism," in *Catholic Historical Review,* Vol. XXXVII (1951), pp. 151–78.

Spahn, Martin, "Das Jahr 1906," in *Das Deutsche Volk,* Vol. III (July 15, 1928).

Vogel, Walter, "Die Organisation der Presse und amtlichen Nachrichtenstellen von Bismarck bis 1933," in *Die Zeitungswissenschaft,* Vol. XVI, Nr. 7–8 (Berlin, 1941).

Wissell, Rudolf, "Sozialismus und christlicher Solidarismus," in *Die Glocke,* Vol. VII (1921), pp. 402–09.

Zeender, John K., "The German Center Party During World War I," in *Catholic Historical Review,* Vol. XLII (1957), pp. 441–68.

INDEX

Abdication of Emperor: E's attitude 267–68, his coresponsibility for consequences of delay 268

Abgeordnetenhaus, Lower House of Prussian parliament, its constitutional position 24–25

Admiralty: approaches E to serve as propagandist 98–99, receives E's plan for mass building of submarines 161, rejects E's plan for beginning submarine war without announcement (Jan. 1917) 162, spy network checks on E's Scandinavian activities 175, receives memorandum from E on submarine question (June 16, 1917) 186, wants treason prosecution of E after Biberach speech (Sept. 1917), 219–20

Ador, Gustav, Swiss Foreign Minister 179

African development, advocated by E 253

Agricultural machines, Foch requires their surrender 292–93

Albert, King of Belgium 113

Allied Shipping Council, German representative added 294

Alpenbote, Bavarian newspaper, prints humorous attack upon E (April 1918) 245–46

Alsace: E supports annexation to Bavaria (1914) 107–08, E's conversion to autonomous status (1917) 114ff, Majority parties press Hertling to offer autonomous status (Oct. 1917) 227–28, E calls for offer to cede to Entente (Aug. 1918) 257, 421

Alsatian constitution (1911): favored by E 87, mentioned 113. *See also* Alsace

Alsberg, Max, Helfferich's lawyer 356

Ambrogetti, German spy in Italy 163

Amende, Prussian official in charge of investigation into E's finances 434

Andlau, Austrian Jesuit 124, 129, 146

André, Josef, Zentrum politician 11, 356n, 383, 433

Angele Case 422–23

Anglo-French "Peace Offer" (Aug. 1917) 216

Annexationism, *see* War Aims

Anti-Duelling League 70

Anti-Modernist Oath, defended by E 69n

Anti-Semitism, used by E in defence of Christian trade unions 402

Arbeitervereine (Workers' Associations), founded by E 11

Arbeitsdienst (Labor Service), proposed by E (1921) 378

Arbeitskammern (Management-Labor Councils), E presses for their introduction (Oct. 1917) 223

Arbitration, international, advocated by E 252

Armenians, E unsuccessfully champions their grievances against Turks 141–42

Armistice Commission: E's appointment (Nov. 6, 1918) 269–70, Kriege makes out surrender authorization 271, E replaces Gündell as head 272–74, departure from Spa 274, at Compiègne 276–81, return to Spa 281–82, E reappointed head by Provisional Government (Nov. 14) 283, its work in winter 1918–1919 289ff, poor contact between Trier and Berlin (Jan. 16, 1919) 299–300, Simson replaces E as head (June 1919) 321n

Armistice extensions, *see* Trier negotiations

Armistice request: Ludendorff's responsibility 259, 259n, opposed by Max 260

Armistice terms (Nov. 1918): as presented by Weygand 277, modifications secured by E 280

Arms race, E believed Germany not responsible 78

Army Expansion Bill (1913), supported by E 77, 78, 82. *See also* Wehrbeitrag

Asquith, Herbert, British Prime Minister 113

Aufwandsteuer (tax on extravagance) 344

Augustinusverein (Catholic press association) 206

Austria, *see* Hapsburg Empire

Austrian alliance: supported by Erzberger 72, E criticizes Hertling government for allowing breach through Austrian Peace Note (Sept. 1918) 258

Austrian Peace Note (Sept. 14, 1918) 258, 258n

Austro-Italian negotiations (1914–15) Ch. VI *passim*

Austro-Polish Solution 116–17

"Authoritarian parties," approved by E 92

Bachem, Karl, historian of Zentrum Party: withdrew from Budget Committee 55, tells story about cruiser *Magdeburg* (1914) 100–101, memorandum on E collecting money for Vatican (1914) 102, text 408–09, receives letter from Widenmann on submarine question (March 1916) 155, report on Frankfurt Zentrum meeting 207, claims E wanted to bring down Hertling (May 1918) 242–43, his papers deposited in Cologne City Archives 439

Bad Griesbach, site of E's assassination 385

Bad Kreuznach Program (April 1917) 177

Balfour, A. J., British Foreign Secretary 215, 216

Reventlow, Ernst von, Pan German journalist 217
"Revolt of Masses": recognized by E 91. *See also* Democratization
Revolution, German: begun by naval mutiny 269, E hears rumors of revolution while negotiating at Compiègne 279, spreads to Spa General Headquarters 282, E consents to serve revolutionary government 283, E emphasizes need of restoring law and order 285, Zentrum adjusts itself to Republic 286, ended by Jan. 1919 elections 287
Richter case (railroad safety device) 427–28, 431
Richter, Max, *Staatssekretär* in Interior Ministry 413
Richthofen, Hartmann Freiherr von, National Liberal politician: asserts E did not want Hertling as Chancellor (Oct. 1917) 227, confers with Bülow and Kühlmann during Chancellor crisis 229, joins E in ultimatum to Hertling (Nov. 7, 1917) 229–30, mentioned 165, 194, 199
Riesser, National Liberal politician: figures in controversy on whether E threatened to hand his opponents over to Allies 330n, opposes E in Finance Committee 339
Risk fleet, championed by E 75
Rissio, Italian Minister of Posts 132
Ritter, Baron, Bavarian envoy to Vatican 130
Röchling, industrialist 315n
Röder, Eugen, Court Master of Ceremonies, informed Emperor of E's theory about *Daily Telegraph* Interview 84
Roedern, Siegfried Count von, Secretary of the Treasury 191n, 332
Roeren, Hermann, Zentrum politician: joins E in attack upon colonial scandals 55–56, 407, leader of Berliners in *Zentrumsstreit* 67, 88
Rohrbach, Paul, journalist 104
Roman question, E's preoccupation with 144ff
Romberg, German minister in Berne 169, 179
Roosevelt, Theodore, American President: High Command vetoes E's proposed invitation (1914) 101, Wilson defies his clamor for unconditional surrender 265
Rosenberg, A. J., Professor, replies to Baudrillart (1915) 101
Rosenberg, Arthur, historian, criticizes E's conduct during July 1917 crisis 211n
Rosenberg, Frederic Hans von, Foreign Office official 262n
Rouvier, French Premier 73
Rumania: E discusses Rumanian grievances with Tisza (June 1915) 140–01, visited by E (Feb. 1916) 142–43, Bethmann rejects proposed ultimatum towards 144
Russia: E's attitude towards Tsarism 72–73, E

demands dissolution (1914) 106, E's negotiations for a separate peace (spring 1917) 165ff, desires peace with Germany (Nov. 1917) 233, E favors policy of smashing Bolsheviks (summer 1918) 249–50, 250n, E differs with Rantzau over Russian policy 303n

Sacher, H., Catholic publicist, writes *Germany and Catholicism* sponsored by E 102
Sächsische Serumwerke 425–26, 431
Salandra, A., Italian Premier Ch. VI *passim*, conversation with E (May 4, 1915) 131, E aims at his overthrow 132, shrewd resignation (May 13, 1915) 136–37
Sangnier, Marc, French Catholic leader 73
Santini, Italian Senator 121
Savigny, Karl von, Zentrum politician 51
Scandals, colonial, *see* Colonial scandals
Scapinelli, Nuncio in Vienna 125
Scharz, Peter, Berlin Zentrum politician 424
Scheer, Reinhold, German admiral 274
Scheidemann, Philipp, Socialist politician: leaks text of Peace Resolution to *Vorwärts* 205, his inexperience in foreign affairs denounced by Max 264, joins E in patching up quarrel between Ludendorff and Government (Oct. 21, 1918) 266, proclaims Republic 279, declares Versailles Treaty "unacceptable" (May 12, 1919) 304–05, resigns when Cabinet is divided on Treaty ratification (June 19, 1919) 320, mentioned 89, 182, 205, 235, 264n, 302, 314, 318
Scheuch, Prussian War Minister 361
Schiffer, Eugen, National Liberal politician 200n, 338, 360
Schnitzer, Catholic publicist, writes *Catholic Weekly Letters* sponsored by E 102
Schönburg-Wechselburg, Count, Zentrum politician, makes attack upon E (April 1918) 247
Schofer, Josef, Zentrum politician 370, 383
Schratt, Katharina, actress 125
Schulz, Heinrich, assassin 389n
Schussen, Wilhelm, schoolmate 7
Schwäbischer Handwerkerbund, founded by E 12–13
Schwäbische Tagwart, Socialist newspaper, E charges Jewish control 402
Seeckt, Hans von, German general: resents low priority given to combatting military clauses of Versailles Treaty 314n, mentioned 157
Self-determination principle: championed by Kühlmann 233, championed by E 234–35, E suggests its manipulation in Lithuania (May 25, 1917) 238–39, E denounces its unilateral application at Versailles 379
Sell, Friedrich, Zentrum pamphleteer 286n

E's attack upon Ukrainian policy (May 8, 1918) 241, approaches E about reentry into Interparty Committee (Sept. 1918) 258–59, mentioned 90, 110, 229, 365

Stumm, Wilhelm von, Undersecretary for Foreign Affairs 168, 191n

Stumm, steel firm 110

Submarine warfare: E's early support (1914–15) 153–54, 410–12, proposes to blockade British coal ports only 154–55, supports Bethmann against Tirpitz 156–57, crucial importance of Zentrum Resolution (Oct. 7, 1916) 158–60, E tells Hammer there will be no submarine war (Dec. 1916) 160, E proposes crash building program of submarines (Dec. 1916) 160–61, E's plan for starting without prior announcement (Jan. 1917) 161–62, E's opposition gave him prestige 162–63, its failure the main cause of Peace Resolution 186

Südekum, Albert, Prussian Finance Minister (1919): opposes E in Finance Committee (July 1919) 339, mentioned 416–17

Supplementary treaties (Aug. 1918), E's opposition 248–49, Kriege's explanations 249

Supreme Command: E's main antagonist 157, favors submarine warfare 159, E long believed Supreme Command shared his point of view 160, Admiralty shared its knowledge with 175, attempt to sabotage E's Stockholm negotiations 176, Bad Kreuznach war aims 177, Bethmann's weakness toward 194, its ascendancy reduced Peace Resolution to insignificance 208–09, Hertling prevented open conflict between Supreme Command and Reichstag majority 232, its opposition to E's Lithuanian plans 237, E denies his May 8, 1918, attack was directed against Supreme Command 242, approves campaign aagainst E 246, E pushes compromise between Supreme Command and government (Oct. 21, 1918) 265–66, government fears it might sabotage peace negotiations 272, hostile to E's acceptance of Polish demarcation line (Feb. 1919) 295

Switzerland: base for E's propaganda operations 104, Helfferich accuses E of sending family to Switzerland at height of German crisis (1919) 428–29

Tägliche Rundschau, Nationalist newspaper 246

Talaat Pasha, Turkish statesman 141

Tariffs, placed upon gold basis (July 1919) 344

Tax-collecting machinery, E establishes *reichseigene Finanzämter* 335–36

Tax evasion: accusation directed against E 366, found groundless 368, 372

Temporal power, *see* Roman question

Thomas, Albert, French Socialist politician 169

Three-class voting system: description 24–25, Easter message promises its reform (1917) 183, Crown Council agrees on its abolition (July 9, 1917) 197, Hertling fails to press for its abolition 232, E calls for reform as war measure 237

Thyssen, August, industrialist: corresponds with E on war aims (June 1915) 108–09, E's wartime relations with 109ff, consulted by E before latter joined Berger firm 361, E's activities for Thyssen discussed at 1920 trial: (1) *Droit au mont* expropriation 413, (2) and operation 414, (3) ore distribution 414, (4) release of Fritz Thyssen 414, (5) taxation of private railroads 415, (6) export license 415, (7) Wendel expropriation 415–16, (8) E's change of view between May and Dec. 1917 416, (9) change of position on export taxes 416–17, (10) Longwy-Briey annexation 417–18, summary 419, friendly parting between E and Thyssen 418, financial relationship 431–32

Thyssen, Fritz, industrialist 110n, 414, 418

Tillessen, Heinrich, assassin 389n

Tippelskirch scandal 53, 55

Tirpitz, Alfred von, German admiral: pressed by E on military aviation (1912) 78n, clashed with E over dining allowances 79n, unleashes press campaign in favor of submarine war 153, E patches up compromise between Bethmann and Tirpitz (Sept. 1915) 154, interview with E (Jan. 1916) 154, dismissal (March 1916) 156, mentioned 74, 311, 411

Tisza, Count Stefan, Magyar Premier: receives copy of Bülow's Roman despatches via E 129, tussle with E about Magyar mistreatment of Rumanians (June 1915) 140–41

Tobacco tax, reorganized by E 341

Toleranzantrag (Zentrum motion for tolerance) 49–50, 69

Tontschew, Bulgar Finance Minister 142

Trier negotiations (winter 1918–1919): humiliating treatment of German negotiators 291–92, E protests against Allied conduct 293, controversies about food and shipping 293–94, Polish demarcation line 295, Vögler's attack on E's conduct 297–99

Trieste: Ch. VI *passim,* mentioned by E in talk with Sonnino 128, Salandra suggests free city status 131

Trimborn, Karl, Zentrum politician: career and personality 43, urges Hertling to accept

Trimborn, Karl (*continued*)
Chancellorship (Oct. 1917) 229n, failure as *Staatssekretär* for the Interior (Oct.–Nov. 1918) 263, mentioned 44, 51n, 62, 200n, 270, 287, 290, 365, 372, 382
Trade unions: E's approval as corrective to cartels 66, E denounces non-Christian unions as puppets of Socialist Party 401
Transportation tax 344, 345
Treason prosecution: sought by Admiralty against E (Sept. 1917) 219–20, sought by Supreme Command against E (Dec. 1917) 237
Trentino, Ch. vi *passim*
Tschirschky, Heinrich von, German ambassador to Vienna 125
Tseretelli, Russian Minister of Posts 178
Turkey, E's journey to (Feb. 1916) 141–42
Turnover tax: introduced by Helfferich 332, extended by E 344

Ukraine: E attacks German policy in (May 8, 1918) 239–41, E accused of receiving materials from Ukrainian embassy 243, his denial 243n
Ulm Speech (Sept. 23, 1917): E's first public explanation of the Peace Resolution 220–21, is prevented by military authorities from mentioning submarine fiasco 220
Unearned increment of land: E interested in 1909 tax on 82n, E proposes total confiscation (1921) 377
Urach, Duke of: supported by E for Lithuanian throne 236–39, elected King Mindaugus II (July 1918) 238

Valentini, Rudolf von, Chief of the Civil Cabinet: conversation with E (July 11, 1917) 197–98, receives delegation from Interparty Committee pressing for dismissal of Michaelis (Oct. 1917) 223
Valenzani, Italian deputy 135
Vanselow, German naval captain 154, 274, 278
Varady, Arpad, Magyar Archbishop, shows Bülow's Roman despatches to Tisza 129
Vaterländischer Unterricht (patriotic instruction) 263
Vatican, *see* Benedict XV
Vendam, Duke, brother-in-law of King Albert of Belgium 113
Versailles, Treaty of: terms presented to Germans (May 7, 1919) 303, E's memorandum on consequences of rejection (June 3, 1919) 315–17, crisis on ratification 317–23, discussion of consequences of acceptance 324–27, denounced by E as "work of devil" (1921) 379
Victor Emmanuel, King of Italy: refuses

Salandra's resignation 136–37, motivated by fear of revolution 138
Villa Malta, Bülow's residence in Rome: E took up residence (May 9, 1915) 135, mentioned 119, 130, 133–34
Vögler, Albert, steel magnate, attacks E's handling of Trier negotiations (Feb. 18, 1919) 297–99
Volksverein für das katholische Deutschland 10, 43, 111, 214
Vorwärts, Socialist newspaper: Scheidemann leaks text of Peace Resolution to it 205, alleged domination by Jews 402

Wahnschaffe, Arnold, Chancellery Chief: ridicules Bülow's story of cipher 120n, mentioned 104
Wallraff, Max, Mayor of Cologne 98
War aims: general attitude of parties 96, E's extreme annexationism (1914) 105ff, evolution of E's views (1914–1917) 108ff, Germany's Bad Kreuznach aims (April 1917) 177, E's interpretation of Peace Resolution 203–04, E's approval of Papal peace terms (July 25, 1917) 216, E admits his wartime follies (July 25, 1919) 330
War Chronicle, propaganda magazine, published by E 103
War criminals: E calls for trial by neutral tribunal 308, Foch attaches no importance to their surrender 349n, E denounces delay in bringing them to trial (1921) 380
War guilt clause, Germans inflate its importance 303, 304n
War Leather Corporation 363
War press office: accused by E of glorifying Falkenhayn 157, E placed in charge of 263
War profits tax: introduced by Helfferich (1915) 332, raised by E (July 1919) 340
Wassilko, Ukrainian nobleman, intermediary between Czernin and E 173
Weardale, Lord, British amateur diplomat, conversation with E (July 1917) 215
Weber, Max, professor, criticizes Wilson's procrastinating diplomacy 265n
Wehrbeitrag (1913): supported by E 82–83, mentioned 340, 342
Weisskirchner, Mayor of Vienna 173
Wemyss, Lord Wester, English admiral 276, 279n
Wendel Expropriation Case 415–16
Werksgenossenschaften 375–77
Wermuth, Adolf, Finance Minister, praises E's financial statesmanship 82n
Werthauer, E's lawyer 373n
Westarp, Count Kuno, Conservative politician, asks questions about E's propaganda work (June, 1918) 105n
Weygand, French general 276, 277, 279, 280

DATE DUE

DEC 1 1 1973			